Indian Air Force

Agniveer VAYU (GROUP-X)

PHYSICS

Indian Air Force

Agniveer VAYU (GROUP-X)

PHYSICS

Author
Dr. Ajay Kumar

ARIHANT PUBLICATIONS (INDIA) LIMITED

卐 **Administrative & Production Offices**

Regd. Office
'Ramchhaya' 4577/15, Agarwal Road, Darya Ganj, New Delhi -110002
Tele: 011- 47630600, 43518550

卐 **Head Office**
Kalindi, TP Nagar, Meerut (UP) - 250002
Tel: 0121-7156203, 7156204

卐 **Sales & Support Offices**
Agra, Ahmedabad, Bengaluru, Bareilly, Chennai, Delhi, Guwahati, Hyderabad, Jaipur, Jhansi, Kolkata, Lucknow, Nagpur & Pune.

卐 **PRICE** ₹235.00

Published by Arihant Publications (India) Ltd.

For further information about the books published by Arihant, log on to www.arihantbooks.com or e-mail at info@arihantbooks.com

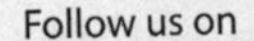    

CONTENT

Physics

1-282

1. Units and Measurement 3-8
2. Motion in a Straight Line 9-17
3. Scalar and Vectors 18-20
4. Projectile Motion 21-24
5. Laws of Motion 25-29
6. Friction 30-33
7. Work, Power and Energy 34-38
8. Collision 39-42
9. Circular Motion 43-42
10. Rotational and Moment of Inertia 48-56
11. Gravitation 57-63
12. Elasticity 64-68
13. Electric Charge and Electric Field 69-77
14. Fluid Pressure 78-81
15. Surface Tension 82-86
16. Viscosity and Fluid Flow 87-91
17. Thermometry 92-94
18. Calorimetry 95-97
19. Thermal Expansion 98-100
20. Thermodynamics 101-104
21. Kinetic Theory of Gases 105-109
22. Periodic Motion and Oscillations 110-117
23. Wave Motion 118-122
24. Superposition of Waves 123-126
25. Vibration in String 127-130
26. Speed of Sound 131-134
27. Vibration in Air Column 135-139
28. Doppler Effect 140-142
29. Musical Sound and Ultrasound 143-145
30. Gauss Theorem 146-149
31. Electrical Capacitance 150-158
32. Electric Conduction 159-161
33. Ohms Law 162-166
34. Electromotive force and Electric Cells 167-171
35. Kirchhoff's Law and Wheatstone Bridge 172-176
36. Potentiometer 177-178
37. Heating Effect of Electric Current 179-183
38. Chemical Effect of Current 184-186
39. Instruments 187-189
40. Magnetic Effects of Current 190-195
41. Electric Potential 196-199
42. Magnetic Dipole and Earths Magnetism 200-207
43. Classification of Magnetic Materials 208-211
44. Electromagnetic Induction 212-215
45. Alternating Current 216-221
46. AC Instruments 222-225
47. Electromangetic Values 226-228
48. Reflection of Light 229-236
49. Refraction of Light Through Surface 237-241
50. Interference 242-245
51. Nuclear Fission and Fusion Reaction 246-249
52. Digital Electronics 250-251
53. Diffraction 252-254
54. Semiconductor and Devices 255-259
55. Communication 260-262
56. Human Eye 263-265
57. Photometry 266-267
58. Particle Nature of Light 268-270
59. Wave Nature of Light 271-273
60. Structure of Atom 274-277
61. Nuclei and Radioactivity 278-282

All About Exam...

1. Indian Air Force invites ONLINE application from **UNMARRIED INDIAN MALE AND FEMALE CANDIDATES** for selection test from 13 October 2023 onwards to join the IAF as an AGNIVEER VAYU. The number and employability of female candidates will be decided as per service requirement.

   (THE SELECTION TEST IS NOT FOR SELECTION AS COMMISSIONED OFFICERS/ PILOTS/ NAVIGATORS).

ELIGIBILITY CRITERIA

2. Date of Birth Block

(a) Candidates born between 27 June 2003 and 27 December 2006 (both dates inclusive) are eligible to apply.

(b) In case, a candidate clears all the stages of the Selection Procedure, then the upper age limit as on date of enrolment should be 21 years.

3. Educational Qualification

(a) Science Subjects

Candidates should have passed Intermediate/10+2/ Equivalent examination with Mathematics, Physics and English from an Education Board recognised by Central, State and UT with minimum 50% marks in aggregate and 50% marks in English.

OR

Passed Three years Diploma Course in Engineering (Mechanical/ Electrical/ Electronics/ Automobile/ Computer Science/Instrumentation Technology/ Information Technology) from Central, State and UT recognised Polytechnic institute with 50% marks in aggregate and 50% marks in English in Diploma Course (or in Intermediate/Matriculation, if English is not a subject in Diploma Course).

OR

Passed Two years Vocational Course with non-vocational subjects *viz.* Physics and Maths from Education Board recognised by Central, State and UT with 50% marks in aggregate and 50% marks in English in Vocational Course (or in Intermediate/Matriculation, if English is not a subject in Vocational Course).

(b) Other Than Science Subjects

Passed Intermediate / 10+2 / Equivalent examination in any stream/subjects from Education Board recognised by Central, State and UT with minimum 50% marks in aggregate and 50% marks in English.

OR

Passed Two Years Vocational Course from Education Board recognised by Central, State and UT with minimum 50% marks in aggregate and 50% marks in English in Vocational Course or in Intermediate/Matriculation if English is not a subject in Vocational Course.

Note 1: Candidates eligible for Science Subjects examination (including Intermediate/10+2/ Three Years Diploma Course in Enginering or Two Years Vocational Course with non-vocational subjects of Physics and Maths) are also eligible for other than Science Subjects and would be given an option of appearing in both Science and Other than Science Subjects examination in one sitting while filling up the online registration form.

Note 2: Education Board recognised by Central, State and UT as on date of registration shall only be considered.

Note 3: Exact aggregate Percentage of marks before decimal as written in the marks sheet of 10+2/Intermediate/Equivalent examination/ Three Years Diploma Course/Two Years Vocational Course or calculated as per the rules of concerned Education Board/Polytechnic Institute shall only be considered (For example 49.99% should be taken as 49% and not to be rounded off to 50%).

EXAMINATION PATTERN

Phase - I

4. **Online Test :** Eligible candidates will be sent provisional admit cards for Phase - I of testing on their registered e-mail IDs 48-72 hrs prior to the examination. Candidates are required to download the admit card, take a colour printout and carry the same to the examination centre. Name of city & exam date will be intimated to candidates at an earlier date to enable them to plan their movement. This provisional admit card can also be downloaded by the candidate under candidates login on CASB web portal https://agnipathvayu.cdac.in. All candidates in possession of provisional admit card will undertake Online Test at centres designated/allotted as per their admit card. Online test will be objective type and questions will be bilingual (English & Hindi) except for English paper. Candidates are to bring one blue/black pen and original AADHAR card along with them for Phase - I testing. Details of the test are as follows:

   (a) Science Subjects : Total duration of the online test shall be **60 minutes** and shall comprise of **Physics, Mathematics and English as per 10+2 CBSE syllabus**.

   (b) Other Than Science Subjects : Total duration of the online test shall be **45 minutes** and shall comprise of **English as per 10+2 CBSE syllabus and Reasoning & General Awareness (RAGA)**.

   (c) Science Subjects & Other Than Science Subjects : Total duration of the online test shall be **85 minutes** and shall comprise of **Physics, Mathematics and English as per 10+2 CBSE syllabus and Reasoning & General Awareness (RAGA)**.

   (d) Marking pattern for online test :

   (i) One mark for every correct answer.

   (ii) Nil (0) marks for unattempted question.

   (iii) 0.25 marks shall be deducted for each wrong answer.

Note 4 : Above examination methodology has been designed to facilitate selection process based on qualifications of candidates. Irrespective of the examination methodology AGNIVEER VAYU enrolled under this entry is liable to be assigned any duty in organisational interest, at the discretion of Indian Air Force.

Physics

01

Units and Measurement

Measurement

It is the process of finding out the magnitude of a physical quantity.

Unit

It is a standard measurement in whose multiple the given magnitude of a physical quantity is expressed, *e.g.*, kg, metre, second etc.

Magnitude

Magnitude of a physical quantity is expressed in terms of a unit and how many units will express the given magnitude. Thus, magnitude is expressed as *nu*, where *n* is called the numerical value and *u* the unit used.

nu for the given magnitude remains constant whatever may be the system of units chosen.

Physical Quantity

It is that quantity or characteristic whose magnitude can be measured, directly or indirectly, *e.g.*, Mass, velocity, power etc.

Fundamental or Basic Physical Quantities

These quantities are those physical quantities which are made up of themselves only like mass, length and time.

Fundamental (or Base) Units

Units of fundamental physical quantities are called fundamental or base units, *e.g.*, metre, second etc.

Derived Units

These are units which are expressed in terms of fundamental units.

System of Units

CGS System of Units

In this system of units, the unit of length is centimetre, the unit of mass is gram and the unit of time is second.

MKS System of Units

In this system of units, the unit of length is metre, the unit of mass is kilogram and the unit of time is second.

SI Units

SI is the modernized and developed version of metric system.

System of Units

System	Length	Mass	Time	Charge	Temperature	Electric current	Luminous intensity	Quantity of matter	Plane angle	Solid angle
CGS	centimetre	gram	second	—	—	—	—	—	—	—
MKS	metre	kilogram	second	—	—	—	—	—	—	—
SI	metre	kilogram	second	Coulomb	Kelvin	Ampere	Candela	Mole	Rad	Sr

Dimensions of Physical Quantity

These are the powers to which the fundamental units of mass, length and time have to be raised to obtain its units.

e.g., Unit of velocity will be

$$\text{Velocity} = \frac{\text{Distance}}{\text{Time}} = \frac{L}{T} = LT^{-1} = [M^0LT^{-1}]$$

The velocity possesses zero dimension in mass, one in length and minus one in time.

Dimensional Formula and Equations

The dimensional formula of a physical quantity may be defined as the expression which indicates which of the fundamental units of mass, length and time enter into derived unit of that quantity and with what power.

If we represent velocity by V, then an equation such as

$$[V] = [M^0LT^{-1}]$$

is known as dimensional equation.

Uses of Dimensional Equations

(i) To test the correctness of a physical equation.

(ii) To derive the relation between different physical quantities involved in a phenomenon.

(iii) Conversion of one system of units to another.

Principle of Homogeneity

This principle states that for a physical quantity to be correct, the dimensions of both sides of the equation should be same.

e.g., Time period of a simple pendulum

$$T = 2\pi\sqrt{\frac{l}{g}}$$

where, l = length, T = time period,

g = acceleration due to gravity

LHS = T = [T]

$$\text{RHS} = 2\pi\sqrt{\frac{l}{g}} = \sqrt{\frac{L}{LT^{-2}}} = \sqrt{T^2} = [T]$$

∴ Dimension of a given relation is correct.

Dimensional Formulae and SI Units of Some Mechanical Quantities

Physical quantity	Relation with other quantities	Dimensional formula	SI unit
Area	= Length × Breadth	$L \times L = L^2 = [M^0L^2T^0]$	m^2
Volume	= Length × Breadth × Height	$L \times L \times L = L^3 = [M^0L^3T^0]$	m^3
Density	$= \frac{\text{Mass}}{\text{Volume}}$	$\frac{M}{L^3} = [M^1L^{-3}T^0]$	kg-m^{-3}
Specific gravity	$= \frac{\text{Density of body}}{\text{Density of water at 4°C}}$	$\frac{M/L^3}{M/L^3} = 1 = [M^0L^0T^0]$ → no dimensions	No units
Speed or velocity	$= \frac{\text{Distance or displacement}}{\text{Time}}$	$\frac{L}{T} = LT^{-1} = [M^0L^1T^{-1}]$	m/s
Linear momentum	= Mass × Velocity	$M \times LT^{-1} = [M^1L^1T^{-1}]$	kg-m/s
Acceleration	$= \frac{\text{Change in velocity}}{\text{Time taken}}$	$\frac{L/T}{T} = LT^{-2} = [M^0L^1T^{-2}]$	m/s^2
Acceleration due to gravity (g)	$= \frac{\text{Change in velocity}}{\text{Time taken}}$	$\frac{L/T}{T} = LT^{-2} = [M^0L^1T^{-2}]$	m/s^2
Force	= Mass × Acceleration	$M \times LT^{-2} = [M^1L^1T^{-2}]$	N (newton)
Impulse	= Force × Time	$MLT^{-2} \times T = [M^1L^1T^{-1}]$	Ns
Pressure	$= \frac{\text{Force}}{\text{Area}}$	$\frac{MLT^{-2}}{L^2} = [M^1L^{-1}T^{-2}]$	N/m^2 (Pascal)
Universal constant of gravitation (G)	From Newton's law of gravitation $F = \frac{Gm_1m_2}{r^2}$ or $G = \frac{Fr^2}{m_1m_2}$ where F is force between masses m_1, m_2 at a distance r.	$= \frac{(MLT^{-2})L^2}{MM} = [M^{-1}L^3T^{-2}]$	Nm^2/kg^2
Work	= Force × Distance	$MLT^{-2} \times L = [M^1L^2T^{-2}]$	J (Joule)
Energy (All types)	Work	$[M^1L^2T^{-2}]$	J (Joule)
Moment of force	= Force × Distance	$MLT^{-2} \times L = [M^1L^2T^{-2}]$	N-m
Power	$= \frac{\text{Work}}{\text{Time}}$	$\frac{ML^2T^{-2}}{T} = [M^1L^2T^{-3}]$	W (Watt)
Surface tension	$= \frac{\text{Force}}{\text{Length}}$	$\frac{MLT^{-2}}{L} = [M^1L^0T^{-2}]$	N/m
Surface energy	= Energy of free surface	$[M^1L^2T^{-2}]$	J
Force constant	$= \frac{\text{Force}}{\text{Displacement}}$	$\frac{MLT^{-2}}{L} = [M^1L^0T^{-2}]$	N/m

Physical quantity	Relation with other quantities	Dimensional formula	SI unit
Thrust	= Force	$[M^1L^1T^{-2}]$	N (Newton)
Tension	= Force	$[M^1L^1T^{-2}]$	N (Newton)
Stress, Pressure	$= \frac{\text{Force}}{\text{Area}}$	$\frac{MLT^{-2}}{L^2} = [M^1L^{-1}T^{-2}]$	N/m^2
Strain	$= \frac{\text{Change in dimension}}{\text{Original dimension}}$	$\frac{L}{L} = 1 = [M^0L^0T^0]$	No units
Coefficient of elasticity	$= \frac{\text{Stress}}{\text{Strain}}$	$\frac{M^1L^{-1}T^{-2}}{1} = [M^1L^{-1}T^{-2}]$	N/m^2
Radius of gyration (K)	= Distance	$L = [M^0L^1T^0]$	m
Moment of inertia (I)	= Mass (Radius of gyration)^2	$ML^2 = [M^1L^2T^0]$	kg m^2
Angle (θ) or Angular displacement (θ)	$= \frac{\text{Length } (l)}{\text{Radius } (r)}$	$\frac{L}{L} = 1 = [M^0L^0T^0]$	rad
Angular velocity (ω)	$= \frac{\text{Angle } (\theta)}{\text{Time } (t)}$	$\frac{1}{T} = T^{-1} = [M^0L^0T^{-1}]$	rad/s
Angular acceleration (α)	$= \frac{\text{Change in angular velocity}}{\text{Time taken}}$	$\frac{1/T}{T} = T^{-2} = [M^0L^0T^{-2}]$	rad/ s^2
Angular momentum	$= I\omega$	$(ML^2)(T^{-1}) = [M^1L^2T^{-1}]$	kg m^2 /s
torque	$= I\alpha$	$(ML^2)(T^{-2}) = [M^1L^2T^{-2}]$	N-m
Wavelength (λ)	= Length of one wave, *i.e.*, distance	$L = [M^0L^1T^0]$	m
Frequency (ν)	= Number of vibrations/second	$\frac{1}{T} = T^{-1} = [M^0L^0T^{-1}]$	s^{-1} or Hz (hertz)
Angular frequency (ω)	$= 2\pi \times$ Frequency	$T^{-1} = [M^0L^0T^{-1}]$	rad/s
Planck's constant (h)	$= \frac{\text{Energy } (E)}{\text{Frequency } (\nu)}$	$\frac{ML^2T^{-2}}{T^{-1}} = [M^1L^2T^{-1}]$	J-s
Linear mass density (m)	$= \frac{\text{Mass}}{\text{Length}}$	$\frac{M}{L} = [M^1L^{-1}T^0]$	kg/ m
Avogadro's number (N)	= Number of atoms/ molecules in one gram atom/mole	$[M^0L^0T^0]$	mole^{-1}
Reynold number (N_R)	$= \frac{\rho D v}{\eta}$	$[M^0L^0T^0]$	No units
Coefficient of viscosity (η)	$= \frac{F \times r}{A \times v}$	$[M^1L^{-1}T^{-1}]$	Pa-s
Refractive index (μ)	$\mu = \frac{c}{v}$	$[M^0L^0T^0]$	No units
Kinetic energy	$= \frac{1}{2}mv^2$	$M(LT^{-1})^2 = [ML^2\ T^{-2}]$	J (joule)
Potential energy	$= mgh$	$M\ (LT^{-2})\ L = [ML^2\ T^{-2}]$	J (joule)
Rotational kinetic energy	$= \frac{1}{2}I\ \omega^2$	$(ML^2)\ (T^{-1})^2 = [ML^2T^{-2}]$	J (joule)
Pressure energy	= Pressure × Volume	$(ML^{-1}\ T^{-2})\ (L^3) = [ML^2\ T^{-2}]$	J (joule)
Moment of force, Moment of couple	= Force × Distance	$(MLT^{-2}) \times L = [M^1\ L^2\ T^{-2}]$	N m
Escape velocity	$= \sqrt{2g\ R}$	$\sqrt{LT^{-2}\ L} = LT^{-1} = [M^0\ L^1\ T^{-1}]$	m/s
Critical velocity	$= \frac{N_R \eta}{\rho D}$	$\frac{(M^0L^0T^0)\ (ML^{-1}\ T^{-1})}{(ML^{-3})\ (L)}$	m/s
Centripetal acceleration	$= \frac{(\text{Velocity})^2}{\text{Radius}}$	$\frac{(LT^{-1})^2}{L} = LT^{-2} = (M^0\ L^1\ T^{-2})$	m/s^2
Wave number (k)	$= \frac{2\pi}{\lambda}$	$\frac{1}{L} = L^{-1} = [M^0\ L^{-1}\ T^0]$	m^{-1}

Dimensional Formulae and SI Units of Some Non-mechanical Quantities

Physical quantity	Relation with other quantities	Dimensional formula	SI unit
Heat (Q)	= Energy	$[M^1L^2T^{-2}]$	J (Joule)
Temperature (θ)	—	$[M^0L^0T^0K^1]$	K
Latent heat (L)	$= \frac{\text{Heat } (Q)}{\text{Mass } (m)}$	$\frac{ML^2T^{-2}}{M} = [M^0L^2T^{-2}]$	J/kg
Specific heat capacity (s)	$= \frac{Q}{m\theta}$	$\frac{ML^2T^{-2}}{MK} = [M^0L^2T^{-2}K^{-1}]$	J/kg K
Gas constant (R)	$= \frac{PV}{T}$	$\frac{(ML^{-1}T^{-2})L^3}{K} = [M^1L^2T^{-2}K^{-1}]$	J/K
Boltzmann constant (k)	$= \frac{R}{N}$, where N is Avogadro's number	$[M^1L^2T^{-2}K^{-1}]$	J/K
Coefficient of thermal conductivity (K)	From $\frac{\Delta Q}{\Delta t} = KA\left(\frac{\Delta T}{\Delta x}\right)$ $K = \frac{\Delta Q}{\Delta t}\left(\frac{\Delta x}{\Delta T}\right) \times \frac{1}{A}$	$\frac{(ML^2T^{-2})(L)}{(T)(K)L^2} = [M^1L^1T^{-3}K^{-1}]$	W/mK
Stefan's constant	$\sigma = \frac{E}{T^4}$ where E is energy/sec/ area	$\frac{ML^2T^{-2}}{TL^2K^4} = [M^1L^0T^{-3}K^{-4}]$	W/m² K⁴
Heat capacity or entropy	joule per kelvin	$ML^2T^{-2}K^{-1}$	J/K
Coefficient of thermal expansivity	$= \frac{\text{Change in dimension}}{\text{Original dimension} \times \text{Temperature}}$	$\frac{L}{L(K)} = K^{-1} = [M^0L^0T^0K^{-1}]$	K^{-1}
Electric current (I)	Ampere (A) is fundamental unit of current	$[M^0L^0T^0A^1]$	A (Ampere)
Charge (q)	= Current × Time	$[M^0L^0A^1T^1]$	C (Coulomb)
Electric potential or voltage or emf	$= \frac{\text{Work}}{\text{Charge}}$	$= \frac{ML^2T^{-2}}{AT} = [M^1L^2T^{-3}A^{-1}]$	V (Volt)
Electric intensity (E) or Electric field	$= \frac{\text{Force}}{\text{Charge}}$	$= \frac{MLT^{-2}}{AT} = [M^1L^1T^{-3}A^{-1}]$	N/C
Electric permitivity of free space (ε_0)	From $F = \frac{q_1q_2}{4\pi\varepsilon_0 r^2}$ $\varepsilon_0 = \frac{q_1q_2}{4\pi F r^2}$	$\lvert\varepsilon_0\rvert = \frac{\lvert q\rvert^2}{Fr^2} = \frac{[AT]^2}{[MLT^{-2}][L^2]}$ $= [M^{-1}L^{-3}T^4A^2]$	C² / Jm
Coefficient of self inductance (L)	From $e = \frac{LdI}{dt}$ $L = \frac{edt}{dI} = \frac{\left(\frac{W}{q}\right)dt}{dI}$	$\frac{ML^2T^{-2}}{AT} \cdot \frac{T}{A} = [M^1L^2T^{-2}A^{-2}]$	H (Henry)
Coefficient of mutual inductance (M)	From $e = M\frac{dI}{dt}$ $M = edt/dI$	$[M^1L^2T^{-2}A^{-2}]$	H (Henry)
Magnetic flux (ϕ)	From $e = \frac{d\phi}{dt}$ $d\phi = e \cdot dt = \frac{W}{q}dt$	$\frac{[ML^2T^{-2}][T]}{AT} = [ML^2T^{-2}A^{-1}]$	Wb (Weber)
Magnetic induction (B); Magnetic field; Magnetic flux density	From $F = Bqv$ $B = \frac{F}{qv}$	$\frac{[MLT^{-2}]}{[AT][LT^{-1}]} = [MT^{-2}A^{-1}]$	T (Tesla)
Magnetic dipole moment (M)	$M = IA$	$AL^2 = [M^0L^2T^0A^1]$	A m²

Physical quantity	Relation with other quantities	Dimensional formula	SI unit
Magnetic permeability of free space (μ_0)	From Coulomb's law in magnetism, $F = \frac{\mu_0}{4\pi}\frac{m_1 m_2}{r^2}$ where m_1, m_2 are strengths of two poles; $[\mu_0] = \frac{4\pi[F][r^2]}{m_1 m_2}$	$\frac{[MLT^{-2}][L^2]}{[AL]^2} = [M^1L^1T^{-2}A^{-2}]$	H/m
Resistance (R)	$= \frac{\text{Potential difference}}{\text{Current}}$	$\frac{ML^2T^{-3}A^{-1}}{A} = [M^1L^2T^{-3}A^{-2}]$	Ω (ohm)
Capacitance (C)	$= \frac{\text{Charge}}{\text{Potential difference}}$	$\frac{AT}{ML^2T^{-3}A^{-1}} = [M^{-1}L^{-2}T^4A^2]$	F (Farad)
Electric dipole moment (p)	$= q(2a)$	$AT(L) = [M^0L^1T^1A^1]$	Cm
Specific resistance or Resistivity (ρ)	$= \frac{Ra}{l}$	$\frac{(ML^2T^3A^{-2})(L^2)}{L} = [M^1L^3T^{-3}A^{-2}]$	ohm-m
Conductance (G)	$= \frac{1}{R}$	$\frac{1}{[ML^2T^{-3}A^{-2}]} = [M^{-1}L^{-2}T^3A^2]$	ohm^{-1}
Conductivity (σ)	$= \frac{1}{\rho}$	$\frac{1}{[M^1L^3T^{-3}A^{-2}]} = [M^{-1}L^{-3}T^3A^2]$	ohm^{-1}
Electric flux	= Electric field × Area	$(M^1L^1T^{-3}A^{-1})(L^2) = [M^1L^3T^{-3}A^{-1}]$	$N\ m^2/C$
Faraday constant	= Avogadro number × Elementary charge	$\frac{1}{\text{mol}} \times AT = [M^0L^0T^1A^1\text{mol}^{-1}]$	C
Decay constant (λ)	$= \frac{0.693}{\text{Half life}}$	$\frac{1}{T} = T^{-1} = [M^0L^0T^{-1}]$	s^{-1}
Inductive reactance (X_L)	= Angular frequency × Inductance	$(T^{-1})(M^1L^2T^{-2}A^{-2}) = [M^1L^2T^{-3}A^{-2}]$	ohm
Capacitative reactance (X_C)	= (Angular frequency × Capacitance)$^{-1}$	$[(T^{-1})(M^{-1}L^{-2}T^4A^2)]^{-1} = [M^1L^2T^{-3}A^{-2}]$	ohm
Resonant frequency	$= \frac{1}{2\pi\sqrt{\text{Inductance} \times \text{Capacitance}}}$	$= [(M^1L^2T^{-2}A^{-2})(M^{-1}L^{-2}T^4A^2)]^{-1/2} = [M^0L^0T^{-1}]$	hertz
Illuminance or intensity of illumination	= Luminous flux on unit area	$\frac{M^1L^2T^{-3}}{L^2} = [M^1L^0T^{-3}]$	lux or lm/m^2
Power of lens (P)	= (Focal length)$^{-1}$	$L^{-1} = [M^0L^{-1}T^0]$	dioptre
Magnification (m)	$= \frac{\text{Size of image}}{\text{Size of object}}$	$\frac{L}{L} = 1 = [M^0L^0T^0]$	No units
Radiant flux, Radiant power	$= \frac{\text{Energy emitted}}{\text{Time}}$	$\frac{M^1L^2T^{-2}}{T} = [M^1L^2T^{-3}]$	watt

Practice Questions

1. SI unit of latent heat
(a) $J\ kg^{-1}$ (b) $J^{-1}kg$ (c) J^2kg^{-1} (d) J kg

2. The physical quantity which does not have the same dimensions as the other three is
(a) spring constant (b) surface tension (c) surface energy (d) acceleration due to gravity

3. Velocity of sound in a gas is given by $v = \sqrt{\frac{\gamma p}{\rho}}$. Dimensional formula for γ is
(a) [MLT] (b) $[M^0L^0T^0]$ (c) $[M^0LT^0]$ (d) $[ML^0T^0]$

4. Which of the following quantities has units but no dimensions?
(a) Angle (b) Speed (c) Displacement (d) Couple

5. Lumen is the unit of
(a) illuminating power (b) luminous flux (c) luminous intensity (d) None of these

6. Light year is a unit of
(a) time (b) speed
(c) distance (d) None of these

7. 'Pascal-second' has the dimensions of
(a) pressure (b) coefficient of viscosity
(c) energy (d) force

8. 'Parsec' is the unit of
(a) time (b) distance
(c) angular acceleration (d) frequency

9. According to the principle of homogene in a dimensional equation.
(a) Dimension of LHS = Dimension of RHS
(b) Dimension of LHS ≠ Dimension of RHS
(c) Not related with dimensional equation
(d) Number of terms on LHS = Number of terms on RHS

10. van der Waals' equation for one mole of real gas is expressed as $\left[p+\frac{a}{V^2}\right](V-b)=RT$, where V = volume, a and b are constant, then the dimension of a and b are
(a) $a=\text{MLT}^{-2}$, $b=\text{L}^3$ (b) $a=\text{M}^2\text{L}^5\text{T}^{-2}$, $b=\text{L}^1$
(c) $a=\text{ML}^5\text{T}^{-2}$, $b=\text{L}^2$ (d) $a=\text{ML}^5\text{T}^{-2}$, $b=\text{L}^3$

11. The dimensions of $\frac{a}{b}$ in the relation $F=ax+bt$ are
(a) LT^{-1} (b) L^{-1}T
(c) LT (d) $\text{L}^{-1}\text{T}^{-1}$

12. The unit of thermal conductivity is
(a) $\text{W m}^{-1}\text{K}^{-1}$ (b) JK^{-1} (c) WmK (d) JK

13. SI unit of permittivity is
(a) $\text{C}^2\text{m}^{-2}\text{N}^{-1}$ (b) $\text{C}^2\text{m}^2\text{N}^2$
(c) $\text{C}^2\text{m}^2\text{N}^{-1}$ (d) $\text{C}^{-1}\text{m}^2\text{N}^2$

14. Dimension of magnetic induction
(a) $[\text{M}^1\text{L}^2\text{T}^{-2}\text{A}^{-2}]$ (b) $[\text{M}^1\text{L}^2\text{T}^{-3}\text{A}^{-4}]$
(c) $[\text{M}^1\text{L}^3\text{T}^{-3}\text{A}^{-2}]$ (d) $[\text{M}^1\text{L}^0\text{T}^{-2}\text{A}^{-1}]$

15. Dimension of moment of inertia
(a) $[\text{MLT}^{-1}]$ (b) $[\text{ML}^2]$ (c) $[\text{L}^2\text{T}^{-2}]$ (d) $[\text{LT}^{-1}]$

16. Dimension of latent heat
(a) $[\text{M}^0\text{L}^2\text{T}^{-2}]$ (b) $[\text{MLT}^{-2}]$
(c) $[\text{ML}^2\text{T}^{-2}]$ (d) $[\text{ML}^2\text{T}^{-1}]$

17. Dimensions of stress
(a) $[\text{ML}^{-1}\text{T}^{-2}]$ (b) $[\text{MLT}^{-2}]$
(c) $[\text{ML}^{-1}\text{T}^{-1}]$ (d) $[\text{M}^{-1}\text{L}^{-1}\text{T}^{-2}]$

18. SI unit of linear momentum
(a) kg ms^{-1} (b) kg ms^{-2}
(c) kg ms (d) $\text{kg m}^{-1}\text{s}^{-1}$

19. SI unit of power
(a) Joule (b) Power (c) N-m (d) Kelvin

20. Dimension of radius of gyration
(a) $[\text{M}^0\text{L}^1\text{T}^0]$ (b) $[\text{M}^0\text{L}^2\text{T}^0]$
(c) $[\text{M}^0\text{L}^{-1}\text{T}^0]$ (d) $[\text{M}^0\text{L}^{-2}\text{T}^0]$

Answers

1. (a)	2. (d)	3. (a)	4. (a)	5. (b)	6. (c)	7. (b)	8. (b)	9. (a)	10. (d)
11. (b)	12. (b)	13. (a)	14. (d)	15. (b)	16. (a)	17. (a)	18. (a)	19. (b)	20. (a)

Hints and Solutions

3. $v=\sqrt{\frac{\gamma p}{\rho}}$

$$\Rightarrow \gamma=\frac{v^2\rho}{p}=\frac{[\text{L}^2\text{T}^{-2}][\text{ML}^{-3}\text{T}^0]}{[\text{M}^1\text{L}^{-1}\text{T}^{-2}]}=[\text{M}^0\text{L}^0\text{T}^0]$$

7. Pascal is unit of pressure, hence its dimensional formula is $[\text{ML}^{-1}\text{T}^{-2}]$.
∴ Dimensional formula of Pascal-second is $[\text{ML}^{-1}\text{T}^{-1}]$.
From the formula of coefficient of viscosity, we have

$$\eta=\frac{F}{A\left(\frac{\Delta v}{\Delta z}\right)}$$

Where, F is force, A is area and $\frac{\Delta v}{\Delta z}$ is velocity gradient.

$$\therefore \text{Dimensions of } \eta=\frac{[\text{MLT}^{-2}]}{[\text{L}^2]\left[\frac{\text{LT}^{-1}}{\text{L}}\right]}=[\text{ML}^{-1}\text{T}^{-1}]$$

Hence, Pascal-second has dimensions of coefficient of viscosity.

10. van der Waals' constants a and b
According to gas equation, for one mole of a real gas,

$$\left[p+\frac{a}{V^2}\right](V-b)=RT \text{ or } pV+\frac{a}{V}-pb+\frac{ab}{V^2}=RT$$

As this equation is dimensionally correct, each term on either side will have same dimensions, *i.e.*,

$$\left[\frac{a}{V}\right]=[pV]$$

$$[a]=[\text{ML}^{-1}\text{T}^{-2}][\text{L}^3][\text{L}^3]=[\text{ML}^5\text{T}^{-2}]$$

and $[p\times b]=[pV]$

$$[b]=[V]=[\text{L}^3]$$

11. Here, $F=[\text{MLT}^{-2}]$ [Dimension of force]
According to principle of homogeneity

$$[\text{MLT}^{-2}]=[a\text{L}]$$
$$[a]=[\text{MT}^{-2}]$$
$$[\text{MLT}^{-2}]=[b\text{T}]$$
$$[b]=[\text{MLT}^{-3}]$$
$$\left[\frac{a}{b}\right]=\frac{[\text{MT}^{-2}]}{[\text{MLT}^{-3}]}=[\text{L}^{-1}\text{T}]$$

02

Motion in a Straight Line

Motion

An object is said to be in motion if it changes its position with time.

DEFINITIONS

Rest An object is said to be at rest if it does not change its position with time.

Distance The distance of an object in motion is given by the actual path traversed by the object in the given time.

Displacement The difference in the initial position and final position of a body in motion is known as displacement.

Speed

Speed of an object in motion is defined as the ratio of total path length (*i.e.,* actual distance covered) and the corresponding time taken by the object, *i.e.,*

$$\text{Speed} = \frac{\text{Total path length}}{\text{Time taken}} = \frac{\text{Actual distance travelled}}{\text{Time taken}}$$

Types of Speed

There are four types of speed.

1. Uniform Speed

An object is said to be moving with a uniform speed, if it covers equal distances in equal intervals of time, howsoever small these intervals may be.

2. Variable Speed

An object is said to be moving with a variable speed, if it covers equal distances in unequal intervals of time or unequal distances in equal intervals of time, howsoever small these intervals may be.

3. Average Speed

When an object is moving with a variable speed, then the average speed of the object is that constant speed with which the object covers the same distance in a given time as it does while moving with variable speed during the given time. Average speed for the given motion is defined as the ratio of the total distance travelled by the object to the total time taken *i.e.,*

$$\text{Average speed} = \frac{\text{Total distance travelled}}{\text{Total time taken}}$$

4. Instantaneous Speed

When the speed of an object is variable, then the object possesses different speeds at different instants. The speed of an object at a given instant of time is called its instantaneous speed.

$$\text{Instantaneous speed} = \lim_{\Delta t \to 0} \frac{\Delta s}{\Delta t} = \frac{ds}{dt}$$

Velocity

It is the time rate of change of displacement of an object. It is a vector quantity, thus has direction. Its units and dimensions are same as that of speed.

Average Velocity

It is that uniform velocity with which the object will cover the same displacement in same interval of time as it does with its actual variable velocity during that time interval.

Note

- Average velocity of a body, if it covers equal distances with different velocities

$$v_{av} = \frac{2v_1v_2}{v_1 + v_2}$$

- Average velocity of a body it travels with different velocities in equal interval of time

$$v_{av} = \frac{v_1 + v_2 + v_3}{3}$$

Instantaneous Velocity

The velocity of an object at a particular instant of time or at a particular point of its path is called instantaneous velocity.

$$\text{Instantaneous velocity} = \lim_{\Delta t \to 0} \frac{\Delta x}{\Delta t} = \frac{dx}{dt}$$

Acceleration

It is defined as the rate of change of velocity with respect to time.

Instantaneous Acceleration

It is acceleration at any instant and is defined as the limiting value of the average acceleration when the time interval Δt becomes very small.

$$\bar{a} = \lim_{\Delta t \to 0} \frac{\Delta v}{\Delta t} = \frac{dv}{dt}$$

Equation of Motion for a Uniformly Accelerated Motion

Here, u is initial velocity, v is final velocity, a is uniform acceleration, s is displacement in time t, S_n is the distance covered in nth second. These equations are not valid for non-uniform accelerated motion.

1. $v = u + at$
2. $s = ut + \frac{1}{2}at^2$
3. $v^2 = u^2 + 2as$

Displacement in nth second (S_n)

Case I. Directions of v and a same

Let the directions of velocity and of acceleration remain same. In such a case, displacement (*i.e.*, value of the displacement) will be equal to the distance moved.

$$S_n = u + \frac{1}{2}a(2n - 1)$$

Case II. Directions of v and a not same

If the directions of velocity and acceleration do not remain same (relatively to one another) during the time interval under consideration, then the above formula will not hold good. This is because the modulus value of the displacement will not be equal to the distance moved. Please note that S_n is displacement in the nth second. It is not equal to distance covered in nth second.

Motion Under Gravity

It is a common experience that when a body is dropped from a certain height it experiences acceleration due to gravity and its motion is in a straight path. Similarly, when a body is thrown vertically up, it goes to a certain height and then starts falling again, experiencing acceleration due to gravity throughout the motion. The value of acceleration due to gravity (g) is taken as 9.8 m / s^2 or 980 cm / s^2 or 32 ft / s^2. *Let us consider the three cases discussed below.*

Case I. Body Thrown Downward

In this case, initial motion of the body is downward so according to the sign convention, downward direction will be taken as positive and upward direction as negative. So, the kinematic equations will be

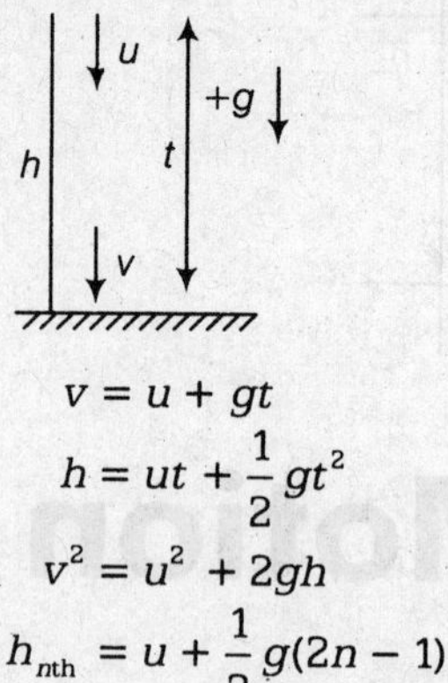

$$v = u + gt$$

$$h = ut + \frac{1}{2}gt^2$$

$$v^2 = u^2 + 2gh$$

$$h_{nth} = u + \frac{1}{2}g(2n - 1)$$

In a special case when the body is dropped/let fall/allowed to fall we will take the initial velocity (u) as zero, then equation becomes

$$v = gt; \quad h = \frac{1}{2}gt^2; \quad v^2 = 2gh; \quad h_n = \frac{1}{2}g(2n - 1)$$

Case II. Body Thrown Upward

If a body is thrown vertically up with an initial velocity (u). Hence, $a = -g$

(i) $v = u - gt$ (ii) $h = ut - \frac{1}{2}gt^2$

(iii) $v^2 - u^2 = -2gh$ (iv) $h_n = u - g\left(n - \frac{1}{2}\right)$

Maximum Height Reached by the Body

$$H = \frac{u^2}{2g}$$

Therefore, the maximum height reached by the body is directly proportional to the square of the initial velocity.

Time of Ascent

The time taken by body thrownup to reach maximum height 'h' is called its time of ascent

$$t_a = \frac{u}{g}$$

Hence, time of ascent t_a is directly proportional to the initial velocity u.

Time of Descent

The time taken by a freely falling body to reach the ground is called the time of descent.

$$t_d = \sqrt{\frac{2h}{g}}$$

and $h = \frac{v^2}{2g}$; $t_d = \sqrt{\frac{2 \times v^2}{2g \times g}} = \frac{v}{g}$

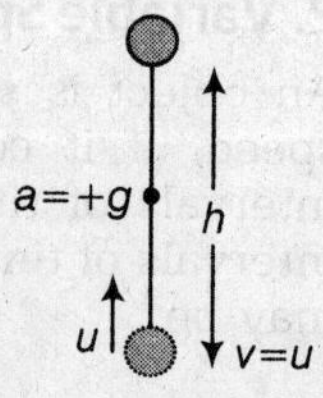

But, we know that $u = v$ *i.e.*, projected velocity of a body is equal to the velocity of the body on reaching the ground.

$$t_d = \frac{u}{g} = \text{time of ascent } (t_a)$$

$\therefore$ Time of ascent = Time of descent

Time of Flight

It is the time for which a body remains in the air and is given by sum of time of ascent and time of descent. Therefore,

$$t = t_a + t_d$$

$$t_d = \frac{u}{g} + \frac{u}{g}$$

$\therefore$ Time of flight, $t = \frac{2u}{g}$

Velocity on Reaching Ground

When a body is dropped from a height h, its initial velocity is zero. Let the final velocity on reaching the ground be v. For a freely falling body

$$v^2 - u^2 = 2gh$$

but $\quad u = 0$

$\therefore \quad v^2 - 0 = 2gh; \; v = \sqrt{2gh}$

Case III. Body Projected Vertically up from the Top of a Tower

If a body is projected vertically up from the top of a tower of height h with velocity u. Then, displacement after time t is $s = ut + \frac{1}{2}gt^2$

velocity after time t is

$$v = u - gt.$$

Its velocity on reaching the ground is $\sqrt{u^2 + 2gh}$.

Its maximum height above the ground is

$$\left\{h + \left(\frac{u^2}{2g}\right)\right\}.$$

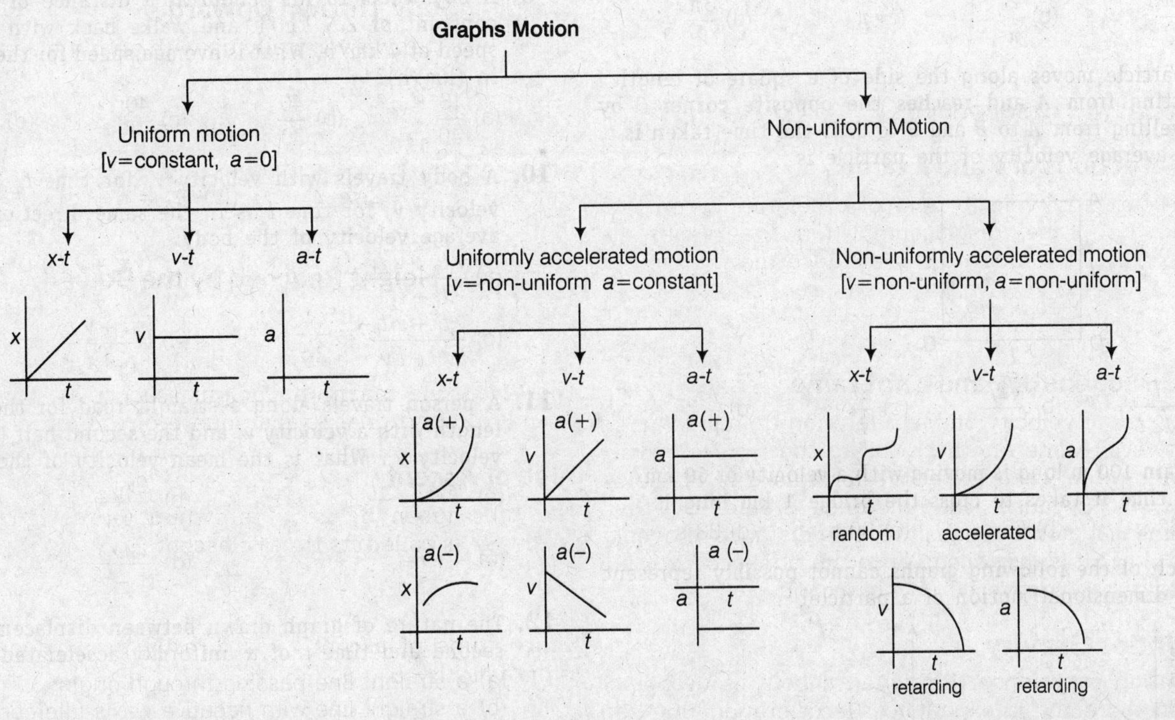

Note Slope of x-t graph gives the information of slope. Slope of v-t graph gives the information of acceleration. Area under v-t graph gives the information of displacement.

Practice Questions

Level I

1. If distance covered by a particle is zero, what can be its displacement?
(a) It may or may not be zero
(b) It cannot be zero
(c) It must be zero
(d) It is negative

2. The numerical ratio of average speed to average velocity is
(a) always equal to one
(b) always less than one
(c) always more than one
(d) equal to more than one

3. A body moves along a circular track of radius r. It starts from one end of a diameter, moves along the circular track and completes one and a half revolutions. The ratio of distance travelled by the body to its displacement is
(a) $\frac{\pi}{2}$ (b) $\frac{2}{\pi}$ (c) π (d) $\frac{3\pi}{2}$

4. A particle moves along the side of a square of length l starting from A and reaches the opposite corner C by travelling from A to B and B to C. If the time taken is t, the average velocity of the particle is

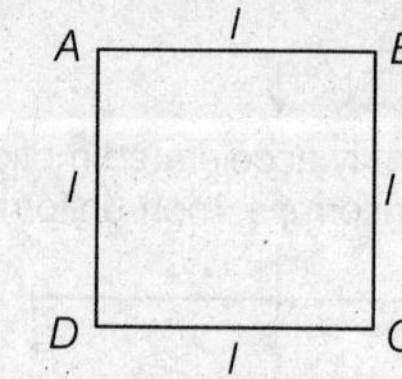

(a) $\frac{l}{\sqrt{2}\,t}$ (b) $\frac{\sqrt{2}l}{t}$ (c) $\frac{2l}{t}$ (d) $\frac{l}{t}$

5. A train 100 m long is moving with a velocity of 60 km/ . The time it takes to cross the bridge 1 km long is
(a) 60 s (b) 66 s (c) 30 s (d) 33 s

6. Which of the following graphs cannot possibly represent one dimensional motion of a particle?

Total distance covered — Time (I)

Position — Time (II)

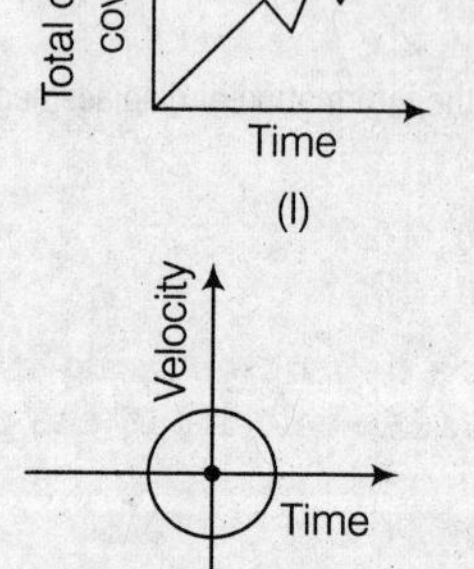

Speed — Time (IV)

(a) I and II (b) II and III
(c) II and IV (d) All of these

7. The displacement-time graph for the two particles A and B are straight lines inclined at angles of 30° and 45° with the time axis. What is ratio of the velocities $v_A : v_B$?
(a) $\sqrt{3}$ (b) $\frac{2}{\sqrt{3}}$
(c) $\frac{1}{\sqrt{3}}$ (d) $\frac{\sqrt{3}}{2}$

8. A train of 150 m length is going towards North direction at a speed of 10 m / s. A parrot flies at a speed of 5 m / s towards South direction parallel to the railway track. Time taken by the parrot to cross the train.
(a) 10 s (b) 5 s
(c) 9 s (d) 11 s

9. A boy walks to his school at a distance of 6 km with constant of 2.5 km/h and walks back with a constant speed of 4 km/h. What is average speed for the round trip in (km/h)?
(a) $\frac{13}{40}$ (b) $\frac{40}{30}$ (c) $\frac{40}{13}$ (d) $\frac{30}{40}$

10. A body travels with velocity v_1 for time t_1 s and with velocity v_2 for time t_2 s in the same direction, find the average velocity of the body.
(a) $\frac{v_1t_2 + v_2t_1}{t_1 + t_2}$ (b) $\frac{(v_1t_1 + v_2t_2)}{v_1 + v_2}$
(c) $\frac{v_1t_1 + v_2t_2}{t_1v_2 + t_2v_1}$ (d) $\frac{v_1t_1 + v_2t_2}{t_1 + t_2}$

11. A person travels along a straight road for the first half length with a velocity v_1 and the second half length with velocity v_2. What is the mean velocity of the person?
(a) $\frac{2(v_1 + v_2)}{v_1 - v_2}$ (b) $\frac{2v_1v_2}{v_1 + v_2}$
(c) $\frac{v_1v_2}{v_1 + v_2}$ (d) $\frac{2v_1v_2}{v_1 - v_2}$

12. The nature of graph drawn between displacement in tth second and time t of a uniformly accelerated motion is
(a) a straight line passing through origin
(b) a straight line with negative y-axis intercept
(c) a parabola
(d) an ellipse

13. A body can't have
(a) a constant speed and varying velocity
(b) an acceleration and a constant speed
(c) a constant velocity and varying speed
(d) non-zero speed and zero acceleration

14. A body is released from certain height. After falling for sometime, if acceleration due to gravity vanishes, then
(a) the body continues to move with uniform velocity
(b) the body continues to move with uniform acceleration
(c) the body continues to move with uniform retardation
(d) the body continues to move with variable acceleration

15. Figure shows the time-acceleration graph for a particle in rectilinear motion. Find the average acceleration in first twenty seconds.

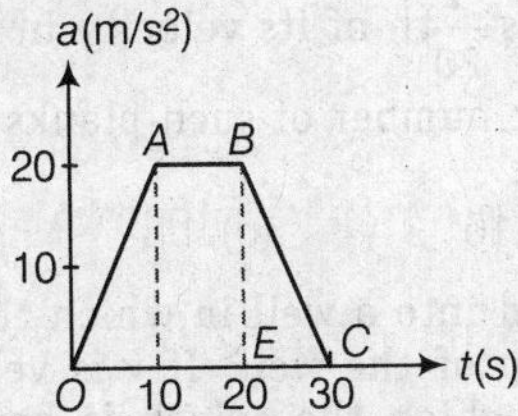

(a) 20 m/s^2
(b) 10 m/s^2
(c) 15 m/s^2
(d) 30 m/s^2

16. The ratio of the distance travelled by a body falling freely from rest in the first, second and third seconds of its fall.

(a) 1 : 3 : 6 (b) 1 : 3 : 2 (c) 1 : 3 : 4 (d) 1 : 3 : 5

17. The displacement of a particle is represented by the equation, $s = 3t^3 + 7t^2 + 5t + 8$, where s is in metres and t in seconds. The acceleration of the particle at $t = 1$ s, is

(a) 18 m/s^2
(b) 32 m/s^2
(c) zero
(d) 14 m/s^2

18. A ball thrown vertically upwards with a speed of 19.6 m/s from the top of a tower returns to the Earth in 6 s. Find the height of tower.

(a) 58.8 cm (b) 58.8 m (c) 68.8 cm (d) 68.8 m

19. A body travels a distance of 20 m in the 7th second and 24 m in 9th second. How much distance shall it travel in the 15th second?

(a) 36 m (b) 38 m (c) 40 m (d) 34 m

20. A body is allowed to fall from a height of 98 m before hitting the ground the distance travelled by it in the last second of motion ($g = 9.8 \text{ m/s}^2$) is

(a) 38.91 m (b) 40 m (c) 50 m (d) 29.91 m

21. The velocity-time graph of a body is shown in Figure. The displacement covered by the body in 8 s, is

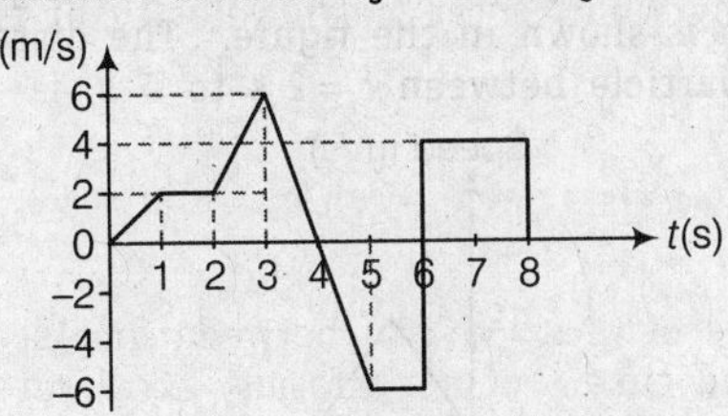

(a) 9 m (b) 12 m (c) 18 m (d) 27 m

22. For the velocity-time graph shown in the distance covered by the body in last two seconds of its motion is what fraction of the total distance covered by it in all the seven seconds?

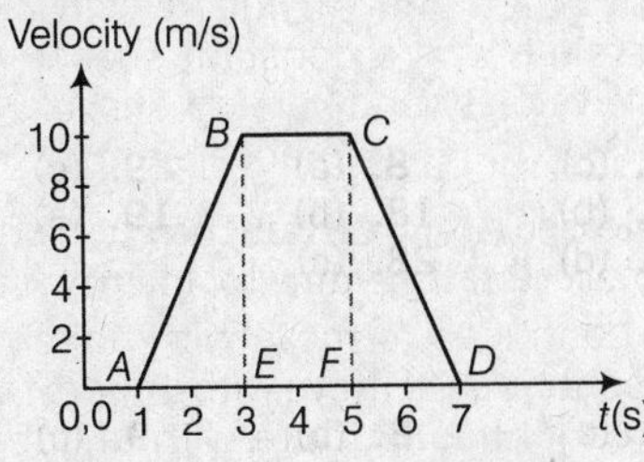

(a) $\frac{1}{2}$
(b) $\frac{1}{4}$
(c) $\frac{1}{3}$
(d) $\frac{2}{3}$

23. A particle starts from rest. Its acceleration (a) versus time (t) is as shown. The maximum speed of the particle will be

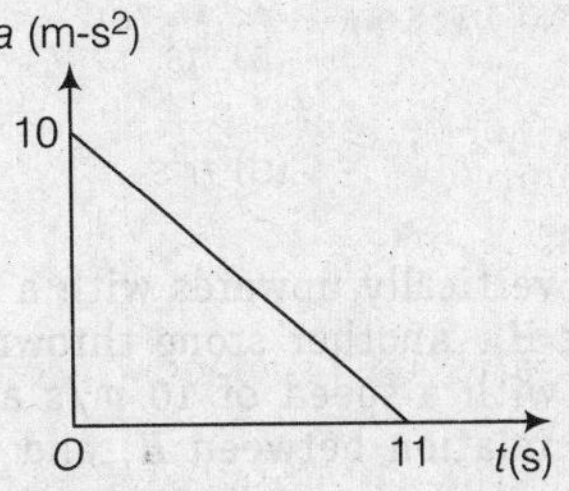

(a) 110 m/s
(b) 55 m/s
(c) 550 m/s
(d) 660 m/s

24. A body walks along an East-West street and a graph for his displacement from home is shown in the figure. The average velocity for the whole time interval is

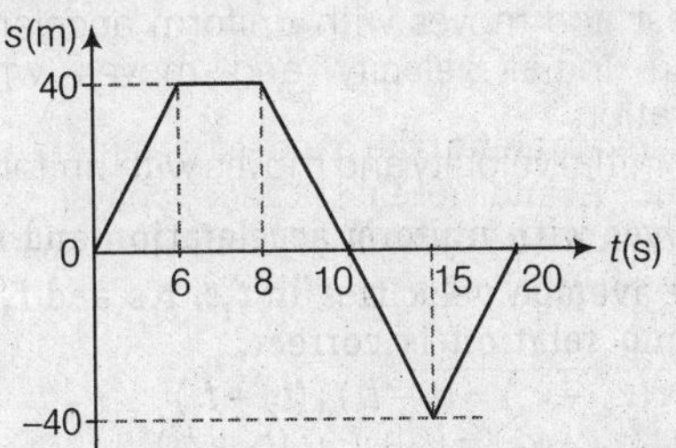

(a) 6.0 m/s
(b) 26.0 m/s
(c) 0
(d) None of these

25. The velocity of a particle at an instant is 10 m/s. After 5 s, the velocity of the particle is 20 m/s. The velocity at 3 s before from the instant when velocity of a particle is 10 m/s.

(a) 8 m/s
(b) 4 m/s
(c) 6 m/s
(d) 7 m/s

26. A rubber ball is dropped from a height of 5 m on a plane where the acceleration due to gravity is not known. On bouncing, it rises to a height of 1.8 m. On bouncing, the ball loses its velocity by a factor of

(a) $\frac{3}{5}$
(b) $\frac{9}{25}$
(c) $\frac{2}{5}$
(d) $\frac{16}{25}$

27. A ball released from a height falls 5 m in 1 s. In 4 s, it falls through

(a) 20 m
(b) 1.25 m
(c) 40 m
(d) 80 m

28. A food packet is released from a helicopter rising steadily at the speed of 2 m/s. After 2 s the velocity of the packet is ($g = 10 \text{ m/s}^2$)

(a) 22 m/s
(b) 20 m/s
(c) 18 m/s
(d) None of these

Level II

1. When the speed of a car is v, the minimum distance over which it can be stopped is s. If the speed becomes nv, what will be the minimum distance over which it can be stopped during same retardation?

(a) $\frac{s}{n}$ (b) ns

(c) $\frac{s}{n^2}$ (d) n^2s

2. A stone thrown vertically upwards with a speed of 5 m/s attains a height H_1. Another stone thrown upwards from the same point with a speed of 10 m/s attains a height H_2. The correct relation between H_1 and H_2 is

(a) $H_2 = 4H_1$ (b) $H_2 = 3H_1$

(c) $H_1 = 2H_2$ (d) $H_1 = H_2$

3. A body covers 26 m, 28 m, 30 m and 32 m in 10th, 11th, 12th and 13th seconds, respectively. The body starts

(a) from rest and moves with uniform velocity

(b) from rest and moves with uniform acceleration

(c) with an initial velocity and moves with uniform acceleration

(d) with an initial velocity and moves with uniform velocity

4. A point moves with uniform acceleration and v_1, v_2 and v_3 denote the average velocities in t_1s, t_2s and t_3s. Which of the following relation is correct?

(a) $(v_1 - v_2):(v_2 - v_3) = (t_1 - t_2):(t_2 + t_3)$

(b) $(v_1 - v_2):(v_2 - v_3) = (t_1 + t_2):(t_2 + t_3)$

(c) $(v_1 - v_2):(v_2 - v_3) = (t_1 - t_2):(t_1 - t_3)$

(d) $(v_1 - v_2):(v_2 - v_3) = (t_1 - t_2):(t_2 - t_3)$

5. The speed of the car is v, the minimum distance over which it can be stopped is x. If the speed becomes nv, then the minimum distance in which it can be stopped in same time is

(a) $\frac{x}{n}$ (b) nx

(c) $\frac{x}{n^2}$ (d) n^2x

6. A stone thrown upward with a speed u from the top of the tower reaches the ground with a velocity $3u$. The height of the tower is

(a) $\frac{3u^2}{g}$ (b) $\frac{4u^2}{g}$

(c) $\frac{6u^2}{g}$ (d) $\frac{9u^2}{g}$

7. A rifle bullet loses $\frac{1}{20}$th of its velocity in passing through a plank. The least number of such planks required just to stop the bullet is

(a) 5 (b) 10 (c) 11 (d) 20

8. A stone is dropped into a well in which the level of water is h below the top of the well. If v is velocity of sound, the time T after which the splash is heard is given by

(a) $T = \frac{2h}{v}$ (b) $T = \sqrt{\left(\frac{2h}{g}\right)} + \frac{h}{v}$

(c) $T = \sqrt{\left(\frac{2h}{v}\right)} + \frac{h}{g}$ (d) $T = \sqrt{\left(\frac{h}{2g}\right)} + \frac{2h}{v}$

9. A body dropped from a height h with an initial speed zero, strikes the ground with a velocity 3 km/h. Another body of same mass dropped from the same height h with an initial speed $u = 4$ km/h. Find the final velocity of second mass, with which it strikes the ground.

(a) 3 km/h (b) 4 km/h (c) 5 km/h (d) 6 km/h

10. The acceleration of a particle is increasing linearly with time t as bt. The particle starts from the origin with an initial velocity v_0. The distance travelled by the particle in time t will be

(a) $v_0t + \frac{1}{3}bt^2$ (b) $v_0t + \frac{1}{3}bt^3$

(c) $v_0t + \frac{1}{6}bt^3$ (d) $v_0t + \frac{1}{2}bt^3$

11. A ball is dropped downwards, after 1 s another ball is dropped downwards from the same point. What is the distance between them after 3 s?

(a) 25 m (b) 20 m (c) 50 m (d) 9.8 m

12. The speed-time graph of a particle moving along a fixed direction is shown in the figure. The distance traversed by the particle between $t = 2$ s to 6 s, is

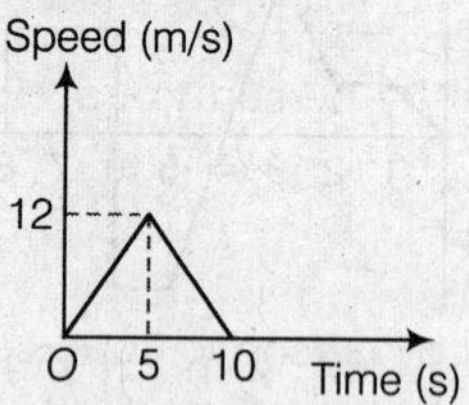

(a) 26 m (b) 36 m (c) 46 m (d) 56 m

Answers

Level I

1. (c)	**2.** (d)	**3.** (d)	**4.** (b)	**5.** (b)	**6.** (d)	**7.** (c)	**8.** (a)	**9.** (c)	**10.** (d)
11. (b)	**12.** (b)	**13.** (c)	**14.** (a)	**15.** (c)	**16.** (d)	**17.** (b)	**18.** (b)	**19.** (a)	**20.** (a)
21. (a)	**22.** (b)	**23.** (b)	**24.** (c)	**25.** (b)	**26.** (c)	**27.** (d)	**28.** (c)		

Level II

1. (d)	**2.** (a)	**3.** (c)	**4.** (b)	**5.** (b)	**6.** (b)	**7.** (c)	**8.** (b)	**9.** (c)	**10.** (c)
11. (a)	**12.** (b)								

Hints and Solutions

Level I

3. Distance travelled $= 3\pi r$ [Perimeter of semi-circle]

Displacement $= 2r$

$$\frac{\text{Distance}}{\text{Displacement}} = 3\frac{\pi r}{2r} = \frac{3\pi}{2}$$

4. Velocity $= \dfrac{\text{Displacement}}{t} = \dfrac{\sqrt{l^2 + l^2}}{t} = \dfrac{\sqrt{2}l}{t}$

5. Total distance to cross the bridge = Length of train + Length of bridge $= 100 + 1000$

$= 1100$ m

Velocity of train $v = 60 \text{ km/h} = \dfrac{100}{6}$ m/s

$$S = \frac{D}{T}$$

$$T = \frac{D}{S} = \frac{1100 \times 6}{100} = 66 \text{ s}$$

7. $\dfrac{v_A}{v_B} = \dfrac{\tan 30°}{\tan 45°} = \dfrac{(1/\sqrt{3})}{1} = 1/\sqrt{3}$

8. Relative velocity of parrot with respect to train

$= 5 + 10 = 15$ m/s

Time taken by parrot to cross the train, $t = \dfrac{150}{15} = 10$ s

9. Total time in going and coming back, $T = \dfrac{6}{2.5} + \dfrac{6}{4}$

Total distance travelled, $S = 6 + 6 = 12$ km

Average speed $= \dfrac{S}{T} = \dfrac{12}{\left(\dfrac{6}{2.5}\right) + \left(\dfrac{6}{4}\right)} = \dfrac{40}{13}$ km/h

10. Displacement travelled in time $(t_1 + t_2) = v_1t_1 + v_2t_2$

$\therefore$ Average velocity $= \dfrac{\text{Displacement}}{\text{Total time taken}} = \dfrac{v_1t_1 + v_2t_2}{(t_1 + t_2)}$

11. Time taken by person to travel first half length,

$$t_1 = \frac{\left(\dfrac{d}{2}\right)}{v_1} = \frac{d}{2v_1}$$

Time taken by person to travel second half length,

$$t_2 = \frac{\dfrac{d}{2}}{v_2} = \frac{d}{2v_2}$$

$\therefore$ Total time $= t_1 + t_2 = \dfrac{d}{2}\left[\dfrac{1}{v_1} + \dfrac{1}{v_2}\right] = \dfrac{d(v_1 + v_2)}{2v_1v_2}$

$\therefore$ Mean velocity or average velocity $= \dfrac{d}{t_1 + t_2} = \dfrac{2v_1v_2}{(v_1 + v_2)}$

15. Average acceleration $(a) = \dfrac{\text{Change in velocity}}{\text{Time taken}}$

$\therefore$ Change in velocity = Average acceleration $\times$ Time taken

= Area of acceleration − Time graph

$\therefore$ Average acceleration

$$= \frac{\text{Area of acceleration} - \text{time graph}}{\text{Time taken}}$$

$$= \frac{\text{Area } OABE}{20} = \frac{300}{20} = 15 \text{ m/s}^2$$

16. Here, $u = 0$, $a = g$;

Using the relation $S_n = u + \dfrac{a}{2}(2n - 1)$

We have $S_1 : S_2 : S_3$

$= \dfrac{g}{2}(2 \times 1 - 1) : \dfrac{g}{2}(2 \times 2 - 1) : \dfrac{g}{2}(2 \times 3 - 1) = 1 : 3 : 5$

17. $v = \dfrac{ds}{dt} = 9t^2 + 14t + 5$

$\Rightarrow \quad a = \dfrac{d^2s}{dt^2} = 18t + 14$

a at $t = 1$

$$a = \left(\frac{d^2s}{dt^2}\right)_{t=1} = 18 \times 1 + 14 = 32 \text{ m/s}^2$$

18. Taking vertical downward motion of the ball from point of projection upto ground, we have

$u = -19.6$ m/s ; $a = 9.8$ m/s^2, $t = 6$ s , $h = ?$

As, $\quad h = ut + \dfrac{1}{2}at^2$

$\therefore \quad h = -19.6 \times 6 + \dfrac{1}{2} \times 9.8 \times 6^2 = 58.8$ m

($\therefore$ neglect the minus)

19. Here $S_7 = 20$ m, $S_9 = 24$ m, $S_{15} = ?$

Let u and a be the initial velocity and uniform acceleration of the body. We known that,

$$S_n = u + \frac{a}{2}(2n - 1)$$

$\therefore \quad S_7 = u + \dfrac{a}{2}(2 \times 7 - 1)$

$\Rightarrow \quad 20 = u + \dfrac{a}{2}(2 \times 7 - 1) = u + \dfrac{13}{2}a \quad$ ...(i)

and $\quad S_9 = u + \dfrac{a}{2}(2 \times 9 - 1)$

$\Rightarrow \quad 24 = u + \dfrac{17}{2}a \quad$ ...(ii)

On subtracting Eq. (ii) from Eq. (i), we get

$4 = 2a \Rightarrow a = 2$ m/s^2

On putting this value in Eq. (i), we get

$20 = u + \dfrac{13}{2} \times 2 = u + 13$

$\Rightarrow \quad u = 20 - 13 = 7$ m/s

Hence, $\quad S_{15} = u + \dfrac{a}{2}(2 \times 15 - 1)$

$= 7 + \dfrac{2}{2} \times 29 = 36$ m

20. Given $g = 9.8$ m/s^2

$h = 98$ m

$u = 0$ (allowed to fall)

Since, the body is falling downward we will use the following equations.

$$h = ut + \frac{1}{2}gt^2$$

$$98 = 0 + \frac{1}{2} \times 9.8 \times t^2$$

$$t^2 = 20 \Rightarrow t = 4.47 \text{ s}$$

For velocity, $v = u + gt$

$$v = 0 + 9.8 \times 4.47$$

$$v = 43.81 \text{ m/s}$$

For distance travelled in the last second of motion

$$h_{nth} = u + \frac{1}{2}g(2n-1)$$

$$h_{nth} = 0 + \frac{1}{2} \times 9.8(2 \times 4.47 - 1)$$

$$h_{nth} = 38.91 \text{ m}$$

21. The displacement will be the area which velocity-time graph encloses with time axis. The area enclosed by graph above the time axis is positive and below the time axis is negative.

22. $\dfrac{\text{Area covered in last 2 s}}{\text{Area covered in 7 s}}$

$$= \frac{\text{Area of } \Delta CDF}{\text{Area of trapezium } ABCD} = \frac{\frac{(2 \times 10)}{2}}{(2+6) \times \frac{10}{2}} = \frac{10}{40} = \frac{1}{4}$$

23. Maximum velocity

$$= \text{Area under acceleration-time graph}$$

$$= \frac{1}{2} \times 10 \times 11 = 55 \text{ m/s}$$

24. Since, the body is finally returning to initial position, it means the total displacement during motion is zero. Therefore, average velocity is zero.

25. $u = 10$ m/s, $t = 5$ s, $v = 20$ m/s, $a = ?$

$$a = \frac{20-10}{5} = 2 \text{ m/s}^2$$

From the formula $v_1 = u_1 + at$, we have

$10 = u_1 + 2 \times 3 \Rightarrow u_1 = 4$ m/s

26. Downward motion

$$v^2 - 0^2 = 2 \times 9.8 \times 5 \Rightarrow v = \sqrt{98} = 9.9$$

Also for upward motion

$$0^2 - u^2 = 2 \times (-9.8) \times 1.8$$

$$\Rightarrow u = \sqrt{35.28} = 5.94$$

Fractional loss $= \dfrac{9.9 - 5.94}{9.9} = 0.4$

27. Since, $s = ut + \frac{1}{2}gt^2$

where u is initial velocity and a is acceleration.

In this case $u = 0$ and $a = g$

So, distance travelled in 4 s is

$$s = \frac{1}{2} \times 10 \times 16 = 80 \text{ m}$$

28. The food packet has an initial velocity of 2 m/s in upward direction, therefore

$$v = -u + gt$$

$$\Rightarrow v = -2 + 10 \times 2 = 18 \text{ m/s}$$

Level II

1. $v^2 = u^2 + 2as \Rightarrow v^2 - u^2 = 2as$

Maximum retardation, $a = \dfrac{v^2}{2s}$

When the initial velocity is nv, then the distance over which it can be stopped is given by

$$S_n = \frac{u_0^2}{2a} = \frac{(nv)^2}{2\left(\frac{v^2}{2s}\right)} = n^2 s$$

2. From third equation of motion $v^2 = u^2 + 2ah$

In first case initial velocity $u_1 = 5$ m/s

final velocity $v_1 = 0$, $a = -g$

and maximum height obtained is H_1, then,

$$H_1 = \frac{25}{2g} \quad \text{... (i)}$$

In second case $u_2 = 10$ m/s, $v_2 = 0$, $a = -g$

and maximum height is H_2, then $H_2 = \dfrac{100}{2g}$.

From Eqs. (i) and (ii), $H_2 = 4H_1$

3. The distance covered in nth second is

$$S_n = u + \frac{1}{2}(2n-1)a$$

Where, u is initial velocity and a is acceleration, then

$$26 = u + \frac{19a}{2} \quad \text{...(i)}$$

$$28 = u + \frac{21a}{2} \quad \text{...(ii)}$$

$$30 = u + \frac{23a}{2} \quad \text{...(iii)}$$

$$32 = u + \frac{25a}{2} \quad \text{...(iv)}$$

From Eqs. (i) and (ii), we get $u = 7$ m/s, $a = 2$ m/s^2

$\therefore$ The body starts with initial velocity $u = 7$ m/s and moves with uniform acceleration $a = 2$ m/s^2

4. Let u be the initial velocity.

$\therefore v_1' = u + at_1$, $v_2' = u + a(t_1 + t_2)$

$v_3' = u + a(t_1 + t_2 + t_3)$

Now,

$$v_1 = \frac{u + v_1'}{2} = \frac{u + (u + at_1)}{2} = u + \frac{1}{2}at_1$$

$$v_2 = \frac{v_1' + v_2'}{2} = u + at_1 + \frac{1}{2}at_2$$

$$v_3 = \frac{v_2' + v_3'}{2} = u + at_1 + at_2 + \frac{1}{2}at_3$$

So, $v_1 - v_2 = -\frac{1}{2}a(t_1 + t_2)$

and $v_2 - v_3 = -\frac{1}{2}a(t_2 + t_3)$

$$\therefore (v_1 - v_2) : (v_2 - v_3) = (t_1 + t_2) : (t_2 + t_3)$$

5. In first case, retardation is

$$a = \frac{0 - v}{t} = -\frac{v}{t}$$

$$\therefore x = vt + \frac{1}{2}at^2 = vt - \frac{vt}{2} = \frac{vt}{2}$$

In second case, retardation is

$$a' = \frac{0 - nv}{t} = -\frac{nv}{t}$$

$\therefore$ $$s = nvt - \frac{1}{2}\frac{nv}{t}\cdot t^2 = \frac{nvt}{2}$$

but $\frac{vt}{2} = x$

$\therefore$ $s = nx$

6. The stone rises up till its vertical velocity is zero and again reached the top of the tower with a speed u (downward). The speed of the stone at the base is $3u$.

u ↑ + ↓ v, g, h

Hence, $(3u)^2 = (-u)^2 + 2gh$

$\Rightarrow$ $$h = \frac{4u^2}{g}$$

7. Let x be the thickness of each plank and v be the initial velocity. Let F be the resistance of the plank

$\therefore$ $$\frac{1}{2}mv^2 - \frac{1}{2}m\left(\frac{19v}{20}\right)^2 = F.x$$

Suppose the velocity becomes zero after passing through n such planks. Then,

$$\frac{1}{2}m\left(\frac{19v}{20}\right)^2 - 0 = nF\cdot x$$

$\Rightarrow$ $$\frac{1}{2}m\left(\frac{19v}{20}\right)^2 = n\left[\frac{1}{2}mv^2 - \frac{1}{2}\frac{mv^2 \times 361}{400}\right]$$

$\therefore$ $$n = \frac{\frac{1}{2}(361mv^2 / 400)\times.400}{\frac{1}{2}mv^2[400 - 361]} = \frac{361}{39} = 9.2$$

$\therefore$ A total number of planks that the bullet will have to pass through before coming to rest $= (1 + 9.2) = (10.2) \simeq 11$.

8. Time taken by the stone to reach the water level

$$t_1 = \sqrt{\frac{2h}{g}}$$

Time taken by sound to come to the mouth of the well,

$$t_2 = \frac{h}{v}$$

$\therefore$ Total time $T = t_1 + t_2 = \sqrt{\frac{2h}{g}} + \frac{h}{v}$

9. From third equation of motion, $v^2 = u^2 + 2as$

where, v and u are final and initial velocity, a is acceleration, s is distance.

For first case $v_1 = 3$ km/h

$u_1 = 0$, $a_1 = g$ and $s_1 = ?$

$$s_1 = \frac{9 \times 100}{36 \times 36 \times 20} \text{ m}$$

For second case $v_2 = ?$, $u_2 = 4$ km/h

$a_2 = g = 10$ m/s

and $s_1 = s_2 = \frac{9 \times 100}{36 \times 36 \times 20}$

so, $$v_2^2 = \frac{16 \times 1000 \times 1000}{3600 \times 3600} + \frac{2 \times 10 \times 9 \times 100}{20 \times 36 \times 36}$$

$\Rightarrow$ $v_2 = 5$ km/h

10. $a = bt$ or $\frac{dv}{dt} = bt$

Integrating, we get

$$v = \frac{bt^2}{2} + c, \text{ where } c \text{ is a constant of integration.}$$

At $t = 0$, $v = v_0$

Thus, $v_0 = c$

Now, $$v = \frac{ds}{dt} = \frac{bt^2}{2} + v_0$$

$\therefore$ $$ds = \left(\frac{bt^2}{2} + v_0\right)dt$$

Integrating we get, $S = \frac{bt^3}{6} + v_0 t$

11. $s = ut + \frac{1}{2}at^2$, here $a = g$

For first body $u_1 = 0$ $\Rightarrow$ $s_1 = \frac{1}{2}g \times 9$

For second body $u_2 = 0$

$\Rightarrow$ $$s_2 = \frac{1}{2}g \times 4$$

So, difference between them after 3 s.

$$= s_1 - s_2 = \frac{1}{2}g \times 5$$

If $g = 10\text{ m/s}^2$ then $s_1 - s_2 = 25$ m

12. Let s_1 be the distance travelled by particle in time 2 to 5 s and s_2 be the distance travelled by particle in time 5 to 6 s.

$\therefore$ Total distance travelled, $s = s_1 + s_2$

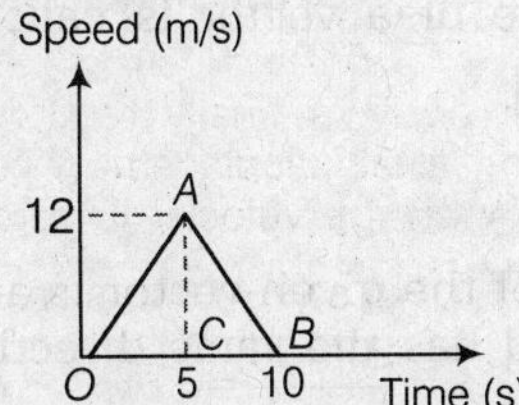

During the time interval 0 to 5 s, the acceleration of particle is equal to the slope of OA *i.e.*,

$$a = \frac{12}{5} = 2.4\text{ m/s}^2$$

Velocity at the end of 2 s will be,

$$v = 0 + 2.4 \times 2 = 4.8\text{ m/s}$$

Taking motion of particle for time interval 2 s to 5 s, we have

$u = 4.8$ m/s, $a = 2.4$ m/s^2, $s = s_1$, $t = 5 - 2 = 3$ s

$\therefore$ $s_1 = 4.8 \times 3 + \frac{1}{2} \times (2.4) \times 3^2 = 14.4 + 10.8 = 25.2$ m

Acceleration of the particle during the motion $t = 5$ s to $t = 10$ s is

$a =$ slope of line $AB = -\frac{12}{5} = -2.4\text{ m/s}^2$

Taking motion of the particle for the time 1 s (*i.e.*, 5 s to 6 s), we have

$u = 12$ m/s, $a = -2.4$ m/s^2, $t = 1$ s, $s = s_2$

$\therefore$ $s_2 = 12 \times 1 + \frac{1}{2}(-2.4) \times 1^2 = 10.8$ m

$\therefore$ $s = s_1 + s_2 = 25.2 + 10.8 = 36$ m

03

Scalar and Vectors

Scalar Quantities

Those physical quantities which have magnitude only but no direction. *e.g.*, Mass, length, time and work.

Vector Quantities

Those physical quantities which have both magnitude and direction.

e.g., Velocity, acceleration, force, momentum.

Modulus of a Vector

The magnitude of a vector is called modulus of that vector $|\vec{A}|$.

Unit Vector

A unit vector of the given vector is a vector of unit magnitude and has the same direction.

X, Y and Z axis have unit vectors, $\hat{i}$, $\hat{j}$ and $\hat{k}$, respectively.

$$|\hat{i}| = |\hat{j}| = |\hat{k}| = 1$$

$$\vec{A} = \hat{A}|A|$$

Types of Vector

Equal Vectors

Two vectors are said to be equal, if they have same magnitude and direction.

Opposite or Negative Vectors

A negative or opposite vector is a vector of same magnitude but in a direction opposite to that of the given vector.

Null Vector

A vector whose magnitude is zero, is known as a null vector.

Resultant Vector

The resultant vector of two or more vectors is defined as that single vector which produces the same effect as is produced by individual vectors together.

$$\vec{R} = \vec{A} + \vec{B}$$

Magnitude of the resultant vector is given

$$|R| = \sqrt{|A^2| + |B^2| + 2AB\cos\theta}$$

R is maximum, when

$$\theta = 0^\circ$$

$$\Rightarrow \quad \cos\theta = +1$$

$$R_{max} = \sqrt{A^2 + B^2 + 2AB} = A + B$$

R is minimum, when

$$\theta = 180^\circ$$

$$\Rightarrow \quad \cos\theta = -1$$

$$R = \sqrt{A^2 + B^2 - 2AB} = A - B$$

Rectangular Components of a Vector

$$A_x = A\cos\theta$$

$$A_y = A\sin\theta$$

$$A = \sqrt{A_x^2 + A_y^2}$$

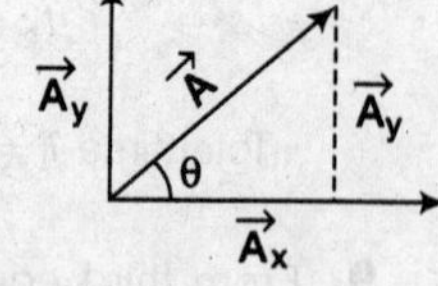

Scalar Product of Two Vectors

$$\vec{A}\cdot\vec{B} = |\vec{A}||\vec{B}|\cos\theta = AB\cos\theta$$

When, $\theta = 0^\circ \Rightarrow \cos\theta = 1$

$$\vec{A}\cdot\vec{B} = AB$$

When, $\theta = 90^\circ \Rightarrow \cos\theta = 0$

$$\vec{A}\cdot\vec{B} = AB\cos 90^\circ = 0$$

When, $\theta = 180^\circ \Rightarrow \cos\theta = -1$

$$\vec{A}\cdot\vec{B} = -AB$$

IMPORTANT FORMULAE

- $\hat{i}\cdot\hat{i} = i^2 = 1, \hat{j}\cdot\hat{j} = j^2 = 1, \hat{k}\cdot\hat{k} = k^2 = 1$
- $\hat{i}\cdot\hat{j} = \hat{j}\cdot\hat{k} = \hat{k}\cdot\hat{i} = 0$
- $\vec{A}\cdot\vec{A} = A^2$

Vector Product of Two Vectors

$$\vec{A}\cdot\vec{B} = |A||B|\sin\theta\hat{n} = AB\sin\theta\hat{n}$$

Here, the resultant vector is perpendicular to the $\vec{A}, \vec{B}$ vector plane, therefore the direction is normal to the plane having unit vector $\hat{n}$.

If $\theta = 0°$ or $\theta = 180°$, then $\sin\theta = 0$

$$\therefore \quad \vec{A}\times\vec{B} = 0$$

If $\theta = 90°$, then $\sin\theta = 1$

$$\therefore \quad \vec{A}\times\vec{B} = AB$$

IMPORTANT FORMULAE

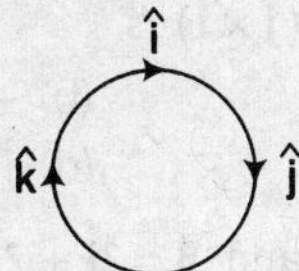

- $\hat{i}\times\hat{i} = \hat{j}\times\hat{j} = \hat{k}\times\hat{k} = 0$
- $\hat{i}\times\hat{j} = \hat{k}, \hat{j}\times\hat{k} = \hat{i}, \hat{k}\times\hat{i} = \hat{j}$
- $\hat{j}\times\hat{i} = -\hat{k}, \hat{k}\times\hat{j} = -\hat{i}, \hat{i}\times\hat{k} = -\hat{j}$

Note

- If vector $\vec{A}$ and $\vec{B}$ are parallel to each other $\theta = 0$, then $\vec{A}\times\vec{B} = 0, \vec{A}\cdot\vec{B} = |A||B|$
- If vectors $\vec{A}$ and $\vec{B}$ are perpendicular to each other $\theta = 90°$, then $\vec{A}\times\vec{B} = AB\sin\theta\hat{n}$ and $\vec{A}\cdot\vec{B} = 0$.

Practice Questions

1. Which of the following is a scalar quantity?
(a) Force (b) Velocity
(c) Speed (d) Momentum

2. Which of the following is a vector quantity?
(a) Time (b) Distance
(c) Displacement (d) Speed

3. If $\vec{A}\times\vec{B} = 0$, then
(a) A and B are parallel to each other
(b) A and B are perpendicular to each other
(c) the magnitude of A and B is zero
(d) None of the above

4. If $\vec{A}$ is a vector and $\hat{A}$ is its unit vector, then
(a) $\hat{A} = \frac{\vec{A}}{|\vec{A}|}$ (b) $\hat{A} = \vec{A}|A|$
(c) $\hat{A} = \frac{|\vec{A}|}{\vec{A}}$ (d) $\hat{A} = \vec{A}\times\hat{A}$

5. The angle between the vector $\vec{A} = 2\hat{i} + 3\hat{j}$ and $\vec{B} = 3\hat{i} - 2\hat{j}$ is
(a) π (b) $0°$ (c) $\frac{\pi}{2}$ (d) $\frac{\pi}{4}$

6. Two equal forces have their resultant equal to either. At what angle are they inclined?
(a) 100° (b) 12° (c) 120° (d) 10°

7. The direction of $\vec{A}\times\vec{B}$ is
(a) in the direction of $\vec{A}$
(b) in the direction of $\vec{B}$
(c) in the direction of both $\vec{A}$ and $\vec{B}$
(d) perpendicular to both of $\vec{A}$ and $\vec{B}$

8. If unit vector $\hat{A}$ and $\hat{B}$ are inclined at angle θ, then
(a) $|\hat{A}+\hat{B}| = 2\sin\frac{\theta}{2}$ (b) $|\hat{A}\times\hat{B}| = 2\sin\frac{\theta}{2}$
(c) $|\hat{A}\cdot\hat{B}| = 2\sin\frac{\theta}{2}$ (d) $|\hat{A}-\hat{B}| = 2\sin\frac{\theta}{2}$

9. If $\vec{A} = (\hat{i} + 2\hat{j} - \hat{k})$ and $\vec{B} = (-\hat{i} - 2\hat{j} - 2\hat{k})$, find the value of $|\vec{A}\times\vec{B}|$.
(a) 45 (b) $\sqrt{45}$
(c) 40 (d) $\sqrt{40}$

10. If $|\vec{A}\times\vec{B}| = \vec{A}\cdot\vec{B}$, then the angle between the vectors is
(a) π (b) $\frac{\pi}{2}$
(c) $\frac{\pi}{4}$ (d) 0

11. If a vector $\vec{A} = 2\hat{i} + 3\hat{j}$, then the magnitude of a vector is
(a) $\sqrt{10}$ (b) $\sqrt{8}$ (c) $\sqrt{3}$ (d) $\sqrt{13}$

12. For two vectors $\vec{A}$ and $\vec{B}$, if $|\vec{A}+\vec{B}| = |\vec{A}-\vec{B}|$ is always true, when
(a) $|\vec{A}| = |\vec{B}| \neq 0$
(b) $\vec{A} \perp \vec{B}$
(c) $\vec{A}$ and $\vec{B}$ are parallel to each other
(d) when either $|\vec{A}|$ or $|\vec{B}|$ is zero

13. The unit vector of a vector $\vec{A} = \hat{i} + 2\hat{j} + 3\hat{k}$ is
(a) $\frac{\hat{i}+2\hat{j}+3\hat{k}}{\sqrt{14}}$ (b) $\frac{\hat{i}+2\hat{j}+3\hat{k}}{6}$
(c) $\frac{\hat{i}+2\hat{j}+3\hat{k}}{14}$ (d) $\frac{\hat{i}+2\hat{j}+3\hat{k}}{\sqrt{6}}$

14. If $\hat{\mathbf{i}}$, $\hat{\mathbf{j}}$ and $\hat{\mathbf{k}}$ are the unit vectors of X, Y and Z-axis respectively, then $(\hat{\mathbf{j}} \times \hat{\mathbf{i}})$ is

(a) 0 (b) $-\hat{\mathbf{k}}$
(c) $\hat{\mathbf{k}}$ (d) $\hat{\mathbf{j}}$

15. If $\vec{\mathbf{A}} = 3\hat{\mathbf{i}} + 4\hat{\mathbf{j}} + 2\hat{\mathbf{k}}$ and $\vec{\mathbf{B}} = 2\hat{\mathbf{i}} + 2\hat{\mathbf{j}} + \hat{\mathbf{k}}$, then $\vec{\mathbf{A}} \cdot \vec{\mathbf{B}}$ is

(a) 16 (b) 20 (c) 10 (d) 11

16. If the sum of A and B vector is equal to their difference, then

(a) $A = B$ (b) $A = 2B$
(c) $B = 2A$ (d) None of these

17. The angle between the vectors $\vec{\mathbf{A}} = \hat{\mathbf{i}} + \hat{\mathbf{j}}$ and $\vec{\mathbf{B}} = \hat{\mathbf{i}} - \hat{\mathbf{j}}$ is

(a) 45° (b) 90°
(c) −45° (d) 180°

18. The result of $(\vec{\mathbf{A}} + \vec{\mathbf{B}}) \times (\vec{\mathbf{A}} - \vec{\mathbf{B}})$ is

(a) $2(A \times B)$ (b) $(A \times B)$
(c) $2(\vec{\mathbf{A}} \cdot \vec{\mathbf{B}})$ (d) $2(\vec{\mathbf{B}} \times \vec{\mathbf{A}})$

19. If $(3\hat{\mathbf{i}} - 2\hat{\mathbf{j}} + 2\hat{\mathbf{k}}) \cdot (2\hat{\mathbf{i}} - x\hat{\mathbf{j}} + 3\hat{\mathbf{k}}) = -12$, then the value of x is

(a) 6 (b) −6
(c) 12 (d) −12

20. If $A + B + C = 0$, then

(a) $|\vec{\mathbf{A}}| + |\vec{\mathbf{B}}| = |\vec{\mathbf{C}}|$
(b) $|\vec{\mathbf{A}} + \vec{\mathbf{B}}| = |\vec{\mathbf{C}}|$
(c) $|\vec{\mathbf{A}}| - |\vec{\mathbf{B}}| = |\vec{\mathbf{C}}|$
(d) $|\vec{\mathbf{A}} - \vec{\mathbf{B}}| = |\vec{\mathbf{C}}|$

Answers

1. (c)	**2.** (c)	**3.** (a)	**4.** (a)	**5.** (c)	**6.** (c)	**7.** (d)	**8.** (d)	**9.** (b)	**10.** (c)
11. (d)	**12.** (b)	**13.** (a)	**14.** (b)	**15.** (a)	**16.** (a)	**17.** (b)	**18.** (d)	**19.** (d)	**20.** (b)

Hints and Solutions

5. $\cos\theta = \dfrac{\vec{\mathbf{A}} \cdot \vec{\mathbf{B}}}{|\vec{\mathbf{A}}||\vec{\mathbf{B}}|} = \dfrac{(2\hat{\mathbf{i}} + 3\hat{\mathbf{j}}) \cdot (3\hat{\mathbf{i}} - 2\hat{\mathbf{j}})}{|2\hat{\mathbf{i}} + 3\hat{\mathbf{j}}||3\hat{\mathbf{i}} - 2\hat{\mathbf{j}}|} = \dfrac{6-6}{6 \times 6}$

$\Rightarrow \cos\theta = 0$

$\theta = \dfrac{\pi}{2}$

6. Here, $A = F$; $B = F$; $R = F$; $\theta = ?$

Now, $R = \sqrt{A^2 + B^2 + 2AB\cos\theta}$

$\therefore \quad F = \sqrt{F^2 + F^2 + 2F \cdot F \cdot \cos\theta} = F\sqrt{2(1 + \cos\theta)}$

$\Rightarrow \quad 1 = 2(1 + \cos\theta)$

$\Rightarrow \cos\theta = -\dfrac{1}{2} = \cos 120°$

$\therefore \quad \theta = 120°$

8. We know that, $|\hat{\mathbf{A}} - \hat{\mathbf{B}}|^2 = (\hat{\mathbf{A}} - \hat{\mathbf{B}}) \cdot (\hat{\mathbf{A}} - \hat{\mathbf{B}})$

$\Rightarrow \quad |\hat{\mathbf{A}} - \hat{\mathbf{B}}|^2 = \hat{\mathbf{A}} \cdot \hat{\mathbf{A}} + \hat{\mathbf{B}} \cdot \hat{\mathbf{B}} - 2\hat{\mathbf{A}} \cdot \hat{\mathbf{B}}$

$= 1 + 1 - 2(1)(1)\cos\theta = 2(1 - \cos\theta)$

$= 2\left[1 - \left(1 - 2\sin^2\dfrac{\theta}{2}\right)\right] = 4\sin^2\dfrac{\theta}{2}$

$[\because \cos 2\theta = 1 - 2\sin^2\theta]$

$\therefore \quad |\hat{\mathbf{A}} - \hat{\mathbf{B}}| = 2\sin\dfrac{\theta}{2}$

9. $\vec{\mathbf{A}} \times \vec{\mathbf{B}} = (\hat{\mathbf{i}} + 2\hat{\mathbf{j}} - \hat{\mathbf{k}}) \times (-\hat{\mathbf{i}} - 2\hat{\mathbf{j}} - 2\hat{\mathbf{k}})$

$= \begin{vmatrix} \hat{\mathbf{i}} & \hat{\mathbf{j}} & \hat{\mathbf{k}} \\ 1 & 2 & -1 \\ -1 & -2 & -2 \end{vmatrix}$

$= \hat{\mathbf{i}}[2 \times (-2) - (-1)(-2)]$
$+ \hat{\mathbf{j}}[(-1)(-1) - 1 \times (-2)] + \hat{\mathbf{k}}[1 \times (-2) - 2 \times (-1)]$

$= \hat{\mathbf{i}}[-4 - 2] + \hat{\mathbf{j}}[1 + 2] + \hat{\mathbf{k}}[-2 + 2] = -6\hat{\mathbf{i}} + 3\hat{\mathbf{j}}$

$|\vec{\mathbf{A}} \times \vec{\mathbf{B}}| = \sqrt{(-6)^2 + (3)^2} = \sqrt{45}$

11. $|A| = \sqrt{(2)^2 + (3)^2} = \sqrt{4 + 9} = \sqrt{13}$

13. $\hat{\mathbf{A}} = \dfrac{\vec{\mathbf{A}}}{|A|} = \dfrac{\hat{\mathbf{i}} + 2\hat{\mathbf{j}} + 3\hat{\mathbf{k}}}{\sqrt{(1)^2 + (2)^2 + (3)^2}} = \dfrac{\hat{\mathbf{i}} + 2\hat{\mathbf{j}} + 3\hat{\mathbf{k}}}{\sqrt{14}}$

15. $\vec{\mathbf{A}} \cdot \vec{\mathbf{B}} = (3\hat{\mathbf{i}} + 4\hat{\mathbf{j}} + 2\hat{\mathbf{k}}) \cdot (2\hat{\mathbf{i}} + 2\hat{\mathbf{j}} + \hat{\mathbf{k}})$

$= 3 \times 2 + 4 \times 2 + 2 \times 1$

$= 16$

19. $(3\hat{\mathbf{i}} - 2\hat{\mathbf{j}} + 2\hat{\mathbf{k}}) \cdot (2\hat{\mathbf{i}} - x\hat{\mathbf{j}} + 3\hat{\mathbf{k}}) = -12$

$\Rightarrow \quad 6 + 2x + 6 = -12$

$\Rightarrow \quad 2x = -24$

$\therefore \quad x = -12$

Projectile Motion

Projectile

It is the name given to a body thrown with some initial velocity with the horizontal direction and then allowed to move in two dimensions under the action of gravity alone, without being propelled by any engine or fuel.

The path followed by a projectile is called its trajectory.

Examples of projectile are

- A body dropped from the window of a moving train.
- A bomb released from an aeroplane in flight.
- A bullet fired from a rifle.
- A piece of stone thrown in any direction.
- A javelion or hammer thrown by an athlete.
- A jet of water issuing from a hole near the bottom of water tank.

In the above examples, we find that a projectile moves under the combined effect of two velocities.

1. A uniform velocity in the horizontal direction, which would not change provided there is no air resistance.
2. A uniformly changing velocity (*i.e.*, increasing or decreasing) in the vertical direction due to gravity.

These two perpendicular velocities have no effect on each other.

Motion of a Projectile

Let us consider

(i) There is no frictional resistance of air.

(ii) The effect due to rotation of Earth and curvature of the Earth is negligible.

(iii) The acceleration due to gravity is constant in magnitude and direction at all points of the motion of projectile.

Projectile Fired at an Angle with Horizontal

Consider an object is thrown with an initial velocity u making an angle θ with the horizontal. The object reaches the highest point A and then passes to Q the lowest point taking total time of fight T.

Components of u

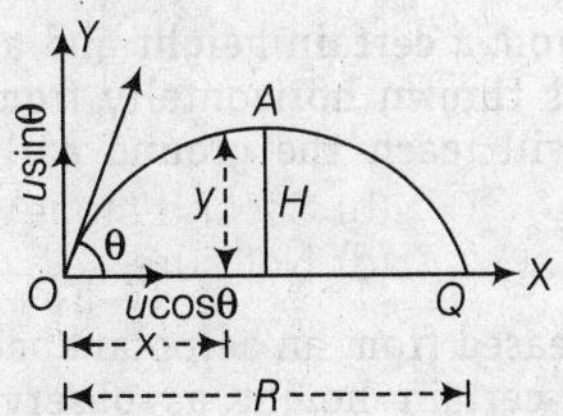

On resoluting the components of u, we get $u \sin\theta$ and $u\cos\theta$.

During the projectile motion $u\cos\theta$ component will be same but $u\sin\theta$ component will keep on changing due to g acceleration due to gravity.

Note At the highest point $u \sin\theta = 0$.

Path of Projectile

Consider at time t at a point $P(x, y)$, the particle has covered x distance from x-axis and y distance from y-axis. Then, equation of projectile will be

$$x = u\cos\theta \times t$$

$$\Rightarrow \quad t = \frac{x}{u\cos\theta}$$

$$\Rightarrow \quad y = u\sin\theta \times t - \frac{1}{2}gt^2 \quad [\because a_y = -g]$$

$$= u\sin\theta \times \frac{x}{u\cos\theta} - \frac{1}{2}g\left(\frac{x}{u\cos\theta}\right)^2$$

$$\therefore \quad y = x\tan\theta - \left(\frac{g}{2u^2\cos^2\theta}\right)x^2$$

This is known as equation of projectile.

IMPORTANT FORMULAE

u = Velocity of projection
θ = Angle of projection
R = Horizontal range
T = Total time of flight
H = Maximum height
T_a = Time of ascent
T_d = Time of decent

$$T = \frac{2u\sin\theta}{g}; T_a = \frac{u\sin\theta}{g}; T_d = \frac{u\sin\theta}{g}$$

$\therefore \quad T = T_a + T_d$

Acceleration in x-axis $(a_x) = 0$

$$R = u\cos\theta \times T = u\cos\theta \times \frac{2u\sin\theta}{g}$$

$$\therefore \quad R = \frac{u^2 \sin 2\theta}{g} \quad [\because 2\sin\theta\cdot\cos\theta = \sin 2\theta]$$

$$R_{max} = \sin 2\theta = 1$$

$$\sin 2\theta = 1 = \sin 90°$$

$$\therefore \quad \theta = 45°$$

$$\therefore \quad R_{max} = \frac{u^2}{g}$$

$\therefore$ Range is maximum when the angle with the horizontal is 45°.

Height, $H = \dfrac{u^2 \sin^2\theta}{2g}$, Maximum height, $H_{max} = \dfrac{u^2}{2g}$

Note Range of an object thrown at complementary angles is same. *e.g.*, [30°, 60°], [50°, 40°], [80°, 10°]

Practice Questions

Level I

1. A stone is dropped from a certain height and at the same time another stone is thrown horizontally from the same height. Which one will reach the ground earlier?
(a) First stone (b) Second stone
(c) Simultaneously (d) Not sure

2. Path of the bomb released from an aeroplane moving with uniform velocity at certain height as observed by the pilot is
(a) a straight line (b) a parabola
(c) a circle (d) None of these

3. A ball is projected horizontally with a velocity of 5 m/s from the top of a building 19.6 m high. How long will the ball take to hit the ground?
(a) $\sqrt{2}$ s (b) 2 s (c) $\sqrt{3}$ s (d) 3 s

4. The speed of a projectile at its maximum height is half of its initial speed. The angle of projection is
(a) 60° (b) 15° (c) 30° (d) 45°

5. The angle of projection at which the horizontal range and maximum height of projectile are equal is
(a) 45° (b) 60°
(c) $\theta = \tan^{-1}(4)$ (d) $\theta = \tan^{-1}(0.25)$

6. A ball thrown by one player reaches the other in 2 s. The maximum height attained by the ball above the point of projection will be
(a) 2.5 m (b) 5.0 m (c) 7.5 m (d) 10 m

7. Two bodies are projected at angles of 45° and 60° with the horizontal with same velocity simultaneously. Ratio of their horizontal range is
(a) 1 : 2 (b) 2 : 1 (c) $\sqrt{3}:2$ (d) $2:\sqrt{3}$

8. The height attained by the object above the point of projection during its flight is given by
(a) $h = \dfrac{u\sin^2\theta}{2g}$ (b) $h = \dfrac{u\sin\theta}{2g}$
(c) $h = \dfrac{u^2\sin^2\theta}{2g}$ (d) $h = \dfrac{u^2\sin^2\theta}{g}$

9. A cricket ball is thrown at a speed of 28 m/s in a direction 30° above the horizontal, the maximum height
(a) 10 m (b) 12 m
(c) 8 m (d) 5 m

10. In the motion of a projectile falling freely under gravity, its
(a) total energy is conserved
(b) momentum is conserved
(c) energy and momentum both are conserved
(d) None is conserved

11. A projectile is fired at 30° with momentum p. Neglecting friction, the change in kinetic energy when it returns to the ground will be
(a) No change (b) 30%
(c) 60% (d) 100%

12. In the above question, the change in momentum on return to the ground will be
(a) zero (b) 30%
(c) 60% (d) 100%

13. A projectile is fired with initial velocity u at some angle θ has a range R. If the initial velocity is doubled at the same angle of projection, then the range will be
(a) $\dfrac{R}{2}$ (b) R
(c) $2R$ (d) $4R$

14. If the initial velocity of a projection be doubled, keeping the angle of projection same, the maximum height reached by it will
(a) remains the same (b) be halved
(c) be doubled (d) become four times

15. Which one is the largest when the height attained by the projectile is the greatest?
(a) Range
(b) Time of flight
(c) Angle of projectile with the vertical
(d) None of the above

Level II

1. A particle moves in a plane with a constant acceleration in a direction different from the initial velocity. The path of the particle is
(a) staright line (b) arc of a circle
(c) parabola (d) ellipse

2. Two projectiles A and B are thrown with the same speed but angles of 40° and 50° with the horizontal. Which projectile will fall earlier?
(a) A
(b) B
(c) Both will fall at the same time
(d) None of the above

3. A cricket ball is hit at 45° to the horizontal with a kinetic energy K. The kinetic energy at the highest point is
(a) K (b) $\frac{K}{2}$ (c) $K \sin 45°$ (d) zero

4. A projectile is projected with a kinetic energy E. Its range is R. It will have the minimum kinetic energy, after covering a horizontal distance equal to
(a) 0.25 R (b) 0.5 R
(c) 0.75 R (d) R

5. A projectile is projected with kinetic energy E. If it has the maximum possible horizontal range, then its kinetic energy at the highest point will be
(a) 0.25 E (b) 0.5 E
(c) 0.75 E (d) E

6. A particle is projected at an angle of 45° with a velocity of $9.8 \frac{\text{m}}{\text{s}}$. The horizontal range will be (take $g = 9.8 \text{ m/s}^2$)
(a) 9.8 m (b) 4.9 m
(c) $\frac{9.8}{\sqrt{2}}$ m (d) $9.8\sqrt{2}$ m

7. A football player throws a ball with a velocity of 50 m/s at an angle of 30° from the horizontal. The ball remains in the air for ($g = 10 \text{ m/s}^2$)
(a) 2.5 s (b) 1.25 s
(c) 5 s (d) 0.625 s

8. A body is projected at an angle θ with respect to horizontal direction with velocity u. The maximum range of the body is
(a) $R = \frac{u^2 \sin 2\theta}{g}$ (b) $R = \frac{u^2 \sin^2 \theta}{2g}$
(c) $R = \frac{u^2}{g}$ (d) $R = u^2 \sin\theta$

9. An object is projected so that its horizontal range R is maximum. If the maximum height attained by the object is H, then the ratio of $\frac{R}{H}$ is
(a) 4 : 1 (b) $\frac{1}{4}$
(c) 2 : 1 (d) $\frac{1}{2}$

10. Two stones having different masses m_1 and m_2 are projected at an angle θ and $(90° - \theta)$ with same speed from same point. The ratio of their maximum heights is
(a) 1 : 1 (b) $1 : \tan\theta$
(c) $\tan\theta : 1$ (d) $\tan^2\theta : 1$

Answers

Level I

1. (c)	2. (a)	3. (b)	4. (a)	5. (c)	6. (b)	7. (d)	8. (c)	9. (a)	10. (a)
11. (a)	12. (d)	13. (d)	14. (d)	15. (b)					

Level II

1. (b)	2. (a)	3. (b)	4. (b)	5. (b)	6. (a)	7. (c)	8. (c)	9. (a)	10. (d)

Hints and Solutions

Level I

3. Here, $h = ut + \frac{1}{2}gt^2$

But vertical component of u that $u\sin\theta = 0$.

$$-19.6 = -\frac{1}{2} \times 9.8 \times t^2$$

$\therefore$ $t = 2$ s

5. We know that,

$$R = \frac{u^2 \sin 2\theta}{g} \text{ and } h_{max} = \frac{u^2 \sin^2\theta}{2g}$$

Given, $R = h_{max}$

$$\frac{u^2 \sin 2\theta}{g} = \frac{u^2 \sin^2\theta}{2g} \Rightarrow 2\sin\theta\cos\theta = \frac{\sin^2\theta}{2}$$

$$\Rightarrow \tan\theta = 4 \Rightarrow \theta = \tan^{-1}(4)$$

6. Here, total time of flight = 2 s

$$2 = \frac{2u\sin\theta}{g} \Rightarrow u\sin\theta = g$$

Height, $H = \frac{u^2 \sin^2\theta}{2g}$

$$\therefore H = \frac{g^2}{2g} = \frac{g}{2} = \frac{10}{2} = 5 \text{ m}$$

7. $R = \frac{u^2 \sin 2\theta}{g}$

$$\frac{R_1}{R_2} = \frac{u^2 \sin 2 \times 45°}{g} \times \frac{g}{u^2 \sin 2 \times 60°}$$

$$\therefore \frac{R_1}{R_2} = \frac{\sin 90°}{\sin 120°} = 2 : \sqrt{3}$$

9. Here, $u = 28 \text{ ms}^{-1}$, $\theta = 30°$

Maximum height,

$$h = \frac{u^2 \sin^2\theta}{2g} = \frac{(28)^2(\sin 30°)^2}{2 \times 9.8} = 10 \text{ m}$$

10. As external force by gravity is present throughout the motion, so momentum will not be conserved.

11. On return to the ground, the speed is the same as on firing. So, there is no change in kinetic energy.

12. $\Delta p = 2\,p\sin\theta = 2p\sin 30° = p$

$$\therefore \frac{\Delta p}{p} = 1 \text{ or } 100\%$$

13. We know that, $R = \frac{u^2 \sin 2\theta}{g} \Rightarrow R \propto u^2$

When the velocity is doubled, the range becomes four times.

14. $h = \frac{u^2 \sin^2\theta}{2g} \Rightarrow h \propto u^2$

If the initial velocity is doubled, then the maximum height reached will become four times.

15. y_m is largest when $\theta = 90°$ from the horizontal. So, time of flight is greatest.

Level II

1. Only in case of parabolic motion, the direction and magnitude of the acceleration remains same. Moreover, in case of uniform circular motion, the direction changes.

2. $T = \frac{2u\sin\theta}{g}$, lesser is the value of θ, lesser is $\sin\theta$ and hence lesser will be the time taken. Hence, A will fall earlier.

3. We know that, horizontal motion is uniform motion.

Horizontal velocity $= v\cos 45° = \frac{v}{\sqrt{2}}$

At the top, the vertical velocity is zero. Hence, at the top

$$\text{KE} = \frac{1}{2}m\left(\frac{v}{\sqrt{2}}\right)^2$$

$$= \frac{1}{2}\left(\frac{1}{2}mv^2\right) = \frac{K}{2}$$

4. KE is minimum at the highest point. So, the horizontal distance is half of the range R *i.e.*, 0.5 R.

5. Here, $\theta = 45°$ because range is maximum.

So, $v_x = v\cos 45° = \frac{v}{\sqrt{2}}$

KE at highest point

$$= \frac{1}{2}m\left(\frac{v}{\sqrt{2}}\right)^2 = \frac{1}{4}mv^2 = \frac{E}{2} = 0.5\,E$$

6. $R = \frac{u^2 \sin 2\theta}{g} = \frac{(9.8)^2 \sin 90°}{9.8} = 9.8 \text{ m}$

7. $T = \frac{2u\sin\theta}{g} = \frac{2 \times 50 \times \sin 30°}{10} = 5 \text{ s}$

8. $R = \frac{u^2 \sin 2\theta}{g}$, At $\theta = 45°$, $R = \max$

$$\therefore R_{max} = \frac{u^2}{g}$$

9. Horizontal range, $R = \frac{u^2 \sin 2\theta}{g}$

R is maximum, when $\theta = 45°$

$$R_{max} = \frac{u^2}{g}$$

H for $\theta = 45°$

$$H = \frac{u^2 \sin^2\theta}{2g} = \frac{u^2}{4g}$$

$$\therefore \frac{R}{H} = \frac{\frac{u^2}{g}}{\frac{u^2}{4g}} = 4 : 1$$

10. We know that, $h \propto \sin^2\theta$

$$\frac{h_1}{h_2} = \frac{\sin^2\theta}{\sin^2(90° - \theta)} = \tan^2\theta$$

$$\therefore h_1 : h_2 = \tan^2\theta : 1$$

05

Laws of Motion

Force

Force is push or pull which can change the position of a body as required.

Forces are two types

1. Balanced Forces

If there are many forces acting on a body, but resultant of all forces is zero, then the forces are called balanced forces.

2. Unbalanced Forces

If the resultant of all forces is not zero, then the forces are called unbalanced forces.

Newton's Law of Motion

There are three laws of motion

1. First Law of Motion

Every body remains in its state of rest of state of motion, untill on external force is applied on it. This law is also known as law of inertia.

Law of Inertia

Inertia is the virtue of body due to which it tries to retain its state. Inertia is two types

1. **Inertia of Rest** If a body is in rest, then it will remain in rest untill an external force is applied on it.
2. **Inertia of Motion** If a body is in motion,then it will remain in motion, untill an external force is applied on it.

There are some examples of inertia in everyday life.

- A glass is broken into pieces when a stone strike on it, but when a high speed bullet hits the glass it makes a clean hole.
- A man getting down of a moving bus falls forward.

2. Second Law of Motion

The force applied on a body is equal to the product of mass of the body and the acceleration produced in it.

$$\vec{F} = m\vec{a}$$

and also the rate of change of linear momentum. $\vec{P} = m\vec{v}$ of the body is proportional to force applied in direction of force.

$$\vec{F} = \frac{d\vec{p}}{dt}$$

3. Third Law of Motion

Newton's third law of motion states that to every action there is always an equal and opposite reaction. The force of reaction is equal in magnitude but opposite in direction to the action force. Action and reaction forces act simultaneously.

Linear Momentum

The product of mass and velocity of a body is called linear momentum. It is represented by p, its unit is kg-m/s. It is a vector quantity.

$$\vec{p} = m\vec{v}$$

If two particles of masses m_1 and m_2 move with velocities u_1 and u_2 before collision and after collision with velocities v_1 and v_2, then from law of conservation of momentum.

$m_1u_1 + m_2u_2 = m_1v_1 + m_2v_2$

Impulse

Impulse received during an impact is defined as the product of the average force and the time for which the force acts.

Impulse, $(I) = F_{av}t$

$F_{av}t = m\Delta v$

$F_{av}t = \Delta p$ $\quad [\because \Delta p = m\Delta v]$

So, the impulse to a body is equal to the change in the momentum of the body.

Apparent Weight in a Lift

- Apparent weight in moving lift is more than its actual weight, when the lift is moving vertically upward with an acceleration a.

  Apparent weight $= m(g + a)$.
- When lift is moving down with acceleration a.

  Apparent weight $= m(g - a)$.
- Freely falling body is always weightless.

Law of Conservation of Linear Momentum and its Applications

- If there is no net external force, then the total linear momentum of the system must remain conserved.
- Mathematically, $F_{ext} = 0$, then

$$p = p_1 + p_2 + p_3 + \ldots = \sum_{i=1}^{n} p_i = \text{Constant}$$

- For an isolated system, the linear momentum of individual particles may change but their vector sum remains conserved.
- The law is independent of the frame of reference.

Motion of a Block on a Horizontal Smooth Surface

(a) (i) $R = mg$

(ii) $a = \dfrac{F}{m}$

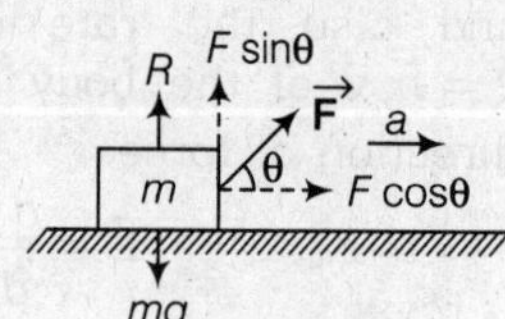

(b) (i) $R = mg - F\sin\theta$

(ii) $a = \dfrac{F\cos\theta}{m}$

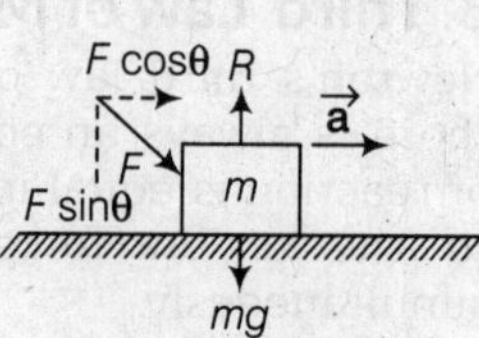

(c) (i) $R = mg + F\sin\theta$

(ii) $a = \dfrac{F\cos\theta}{m}$

Motion of Bodies in Contact

(a) (i) $a = \dfrac{F}{m_1 + m_2}$

(ii) $f = \dfrac{m_1 F}{m_1 + m_2}$

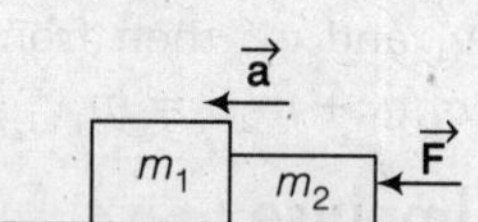

(b) (i) $a = \dfrac{F}{m_1 + m_2}$

(ii) $f = \dfrac{m_2 F}{m_1 + m_2}$

(c) (i) $a = \dfrac{F}{m_1 + m_2 + m_3}$

(ii) $T_1 = \dfrac{(m_2 + m_3) F}{m_1 + m_2 + m_3}$

(iii) $T_2 = \dfrac{m_3 F}{m_1 + m_2 + m_3}$

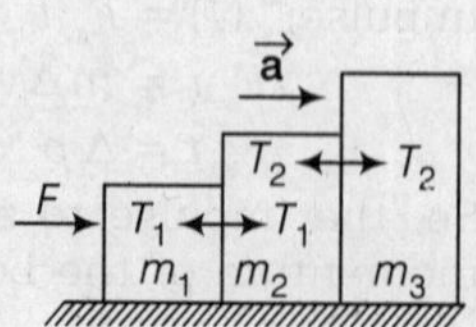

(d) (i) $a = \dfrac{F}{(m_1 + m_2 + m_3)}$

(ii) $T_1 = \dfrac{m_1 F}{(m_1 + m_2 + m_3)}$

(iii) $T_2 = \dfrac{(m_1 + m_2) F}{(m_1 + m_2 + m_3)}$

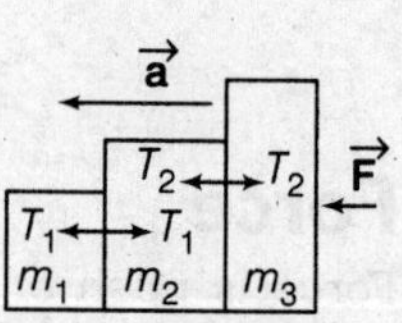

Motion of Connected Bodies

(a) (i) $a = \dfrac{F}{m_1 + m_2}$

(ii) $T = \dfrac{m_1 F}{m_1 + m_2}$

(b) (i) $a = \dfrac{F}{(m_1 + m_2 + m_3)}$

(ii) $T_1 = \dfrac{m_1 F}{(m_1 + m_2 + m_3)}$

(iii) $T_2 = \dfrac{(m_1 + m_2) F}{(m_1 + m_2 + m_3)}$

(c) (i) $a = \left(\dfrac{m_1 - m_2}{m_1 + m_2}\right) g$

(ii) $T = \left(\dfrac{2m_1 m_2}{m_1 + m_2}\right) g$

(iii) $T' = 2T = \left(\dfrac{4m_1 m_2}{m_1 + m_2}\right) g$

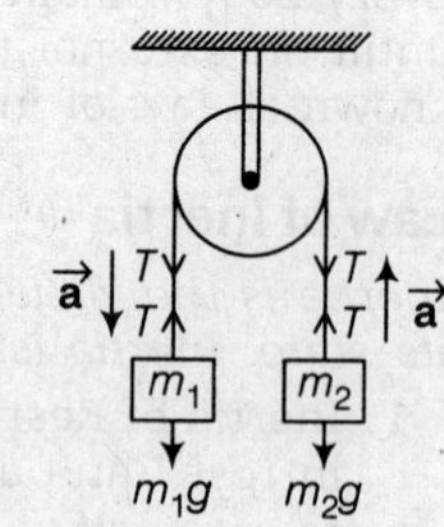

(d) (i) $a = \dfrac{m_2 g}{m_1 + m_2}$

(ii) $T = \dfrac{m_1 m_2 g}{m_1 + m_2}$

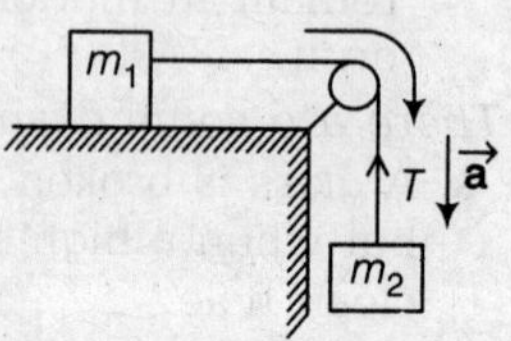

Practice Questions

Level I

1. **A constant force acting on a body of mass 3 kg changes its speed from 2 m/s to 3.5 m/s in 25 s. The magnitude of force, if the direction of force remains unchanged**
(a) 0.80 N (b) 0.18 N (c) 1.8 N (d) 18 N

2. **A 40 kg shell is flying at a speed of 72 km/h. It explodes into two pieces, one piece of mass 15 kg stops. The velocity of the other piece**
(a) 32 m/s (b) 40 m/s (c) 20 m/s (d) 25 m/s

3. **A block of metal weighing 2 kg is resting on a frictionless plane. It is struck by a jet releasing water at a rate of 1 kg/s and at a speed of 5 m/s. The initial acceleration of the block is**
(a) 2 m/s^2 (b) 2.5 m/s^2
(c) 3 m/s^2 (d) 4 m/s^2

4. **A bullet of mass 0.04 kg moving with a speed of 90 m/s enters a heavy wooden block and is stopped after a distance of 60 cm. The average resistive force exerted by the block on the bullet is**
(a) 200 N (b) 250 N (c) 180 N (d) 270 N

5. **An external force is required to keep a body in uniform motion. This statement was given by**
(a) Aristotle (b) Newton
(c) Archimedes (d) Einstein

6. **For a body of given mass, graph between velocity of the body and its linear momentum is**
(a) a straight line with slope = 0
(b) a straight line with positive slope
(c) a straight line with negative slope
(d) a parabola

7. **Newton's first law defines**
(a) force only (b) inertia only
(c) Both (a) and (b) (d) Neither (a) nor (b)

8. **The mud guards over the wheels of a car work on the basis of**
(a) inertia of rest (b) inertia of direction
(c) inertia of motion (d) None of these

9. **The linear momentum of a body changes at the rate of 10 kg-m/s. Force acting on the body is**
(a) 1 N (b) 10 N
(c) 1 kgf (d) 10 kgf

10. **The correct relation between absolute units of force on MKS system and CGS system is**
(a) 1 kgf = 9.8 N (b) 1 kgf = 1000 gf
(c) 1 gf = 980 dyne (d) 1 N = 10^5 dyne

11. **Accelerated motion is always due to**
(a) internal force (b) friction
(c) external force (d) None of these

12. **For a given change in linear momentum, when time of impact increases, force**
(a) decreases (b) increases
(c) remains same (d) None of these

13. **Forces of action and reaction never cancel each other as they are**
(a) always equal (b) always opposite
(c) acting on same body (d) acting on different bodies

14. **A lift is moving down with an acceleration a. A man in the lift drops a ball inside the lift. The acceleration of the ball as observed by the man in the lift and a man standing stationary on the ground are respectively**
(a) g, g (b) a, a (c) $(g-a), g$ (d) a, g

15. **Two bodies have same mass and speed, then**
(a) their momentums are same
(b) the ratio of momentums is not determined
(c) the ratio their magnitudes of momentum is one
(d) (a) and (b) are correct

16. **A parrot is sitting on the floor of a closed glass cage which is in a boy's hand. If the parrot starts flying with a constant speed, the boy will feel the weight of cage as**
(a) unchanged
(b) reduced
(c) increased
(d) Nothing can be said

17. **A man is pulling a rope attached to a block on a smooth horizontal table. The tension in the rope will be the same at all points**
(a) if and only if the rope is not accelerated
(b) if and only if the rope is massless
(c) if either the rope is not accelerated or is massless
(d) always

18. **The mass m is placed on a body of mass M. There is no friction. The force F is applied on M and it moves with acceleration a. Then, the net force on the top body is**
(a) F (b) ma
(c) $F - ma$ (d) None of these

19. **The weight of a person will be greater when the lift**
(a) accelerates downwords (b) fall with uniform velocity
(c) accelerates upwards (d) ratards upwards

20. **Two masses M and $M/2$ are joined together by means of light inextensible string passed over a frictionless pulley as shown in figure.**

When the bigger mass is released, the small one will ascend with an acceleration of

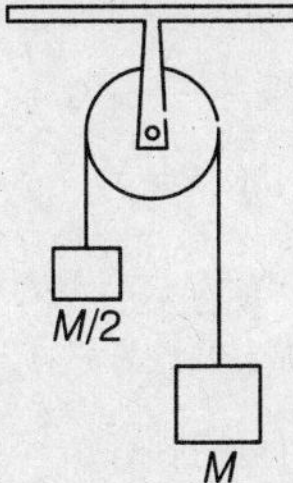

(a) $\frac{g}{3}$ (b) $\frac{3g}{2}$ (c) g (d) $\frac{g}{2}$

Level II

1. A ball of mass 0.2 kg is thrown vertically upwards by applying a force by hand. If the hand moves 0.2 m while applying the force and the ball goes upto 2 m height further, find the magnitude of the force. Consider $g = 10\ m/s^2$

(a) 16 N (b) 20 N
(c) 22 N (d) 4 N

2. A player caught a cricket ball of mass 150 g moving at a rate of 20 m/s. If the catching process is completed in 0.1 s, the force of the blow exerted by the ball on the hands of the player is equal to

(a) 3 N (b) 30 N
(c) 300 N (d) 150 N

3. The tension in the string in the pulley system shown in figure is

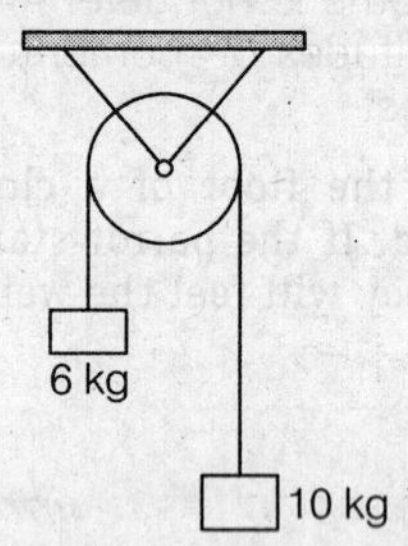

(a) 5.7 N
(b) 7 N
(c) 7.5 N
(d) 74 N

4. A block of mass m is connected to another block of mass M by a spring (massless) of spring constant k. The blocks are kept on a smooth horizontal plane. Initially, the blocks are at rest and the spring is unstretched. Then, a constant force F starts acting on the block of mass M to pull it. Find the force on the block of mass m.

(a) $\frac{mF}{m+M}$ (b) $\frac{MF}{m+M}$
(c) $\frac{(M+m)F}{m}$ (d) $\frac{mF}{M}$

5. In a given figure, if $m_1 = 5$ kg, $m_2 = 10$ kg and $F = 80$ N. The tension in the string will be

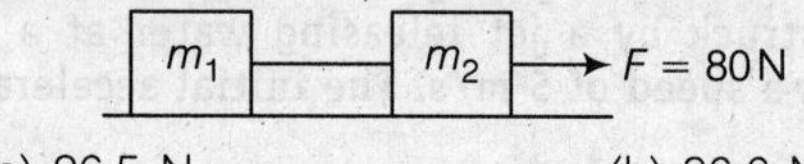

(a) 26.5 N (b) 26.6 N
(c) 26.4 N (d) 26.3 N

6. The tension in the string is ($g = 10\ m/s^2$)

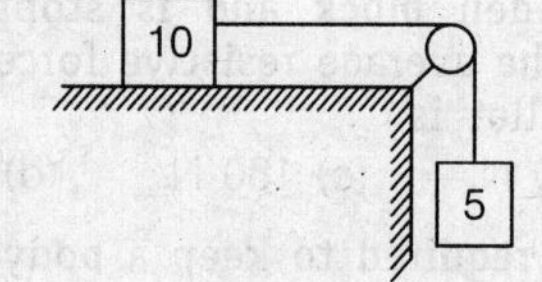

(a) $\frac{100}{3}$ N (b) $\frac{10}{3}$ N
(c) $\frac{3}{100}$ N (d) $\frac{3}{10}$ N

Answers

Level I

1. (b)	**2.** (a)	**3.** (b)	**4.** (d)	**5.** (a)	**6.** (b)	**7.** (c)	**8.** (b)	**9.** (b)	**10.** (d)
11. (c)	**12.** (a)	**13.** (d)	**14.** (c)	**15.** (d)	**16.** (a)	**17.** (c)	**18.** (d)	**19.** (c)	**20.** (a)

Level II

1. (b)	**2.** (b)	**3.** (d)	**4.** (a)	**5.** (d)	**6.** (a)

Hints and Solutions

Level I

1. Here, $m = 3\,\text{kg}, u = 2$ m/s $v = 3.5$ m/s, $t = 25$ s, $F = ?$

$$F = ma = m\frac{(v-u)}{t} \Rightarrow F = \frac{3\,(3.5-2)}{25} = 0.18\text{ N}$$

2. Here, $m = 40\,\text{kg}, v = 72$ km/h

$$= \frac{72 \times 1000}{60 \times 60} = 20\text{ m/s}$$

$m_1 = 15\,\text{kg}, v_1 = 0, m_2 = 40 - 15 = 25\,\text{kg}, v_2 = ?$

Applying the principle of conservation of linear momentum

$$m_1v_1 + m_2v_2 = mv$$

$$\Rightarrow \quad 15 \times 0 + 25 \times v_2 = 40 \times 20$$

$$\therefore \quad v_2 = \frac{800}{25} = 32\text{ m/s}$$

3. Force exerted by the jet of water

$$F = \frac{d}{dt}(p) = \frac{d}{dt}(mv) = v\frac{dm}{dt}$$

$$F = 5 \times 1 = 5\text{ N}$$

$m = 2$ kg, $a = ?$

$$F = ma \Rightarrow a = F/m = \frac{5}{2} = 2.5\text{ m/s}^2$$

4. Here, $m = 0.04\,\text{kg}, u = 90$ m/s, $v = 0$,

$s = 60$ cm $= 0.6$ m, $F = ?$

From $v^2 - u^2 = 2as$

$$\Rightarrow \quad 0 - 90^2 = 2a \times 0.6$$

$$\therefore \quad a = \frac{-90 \times 90}{2 \times 0.6}$$

$$= -6750\text{ m/s}^2$$

From $F = ma = 0.04 \times (-6750) = -270$ N

Negative sign is for resistive force, which is opposing.

9. As, $F = \frac{dP}{dt}$, here $\frac{dP}{dt} = 10$

$\therefore \quad F = 10$ N

14. When dropped, acceleration of the ball is g, as will be observed by a man standing stationary on the ground. The man inside the lift is having its own downward acceleration $= a$. Therefore, relative acceleration of the ball as observed by the man in the lift $(g - a)$.

20. Here, $m_1 = M, m_2 = M/2$

$$a = \frac{(m_1 - m_2)\,g}{m_1 + m_2} = \frac{(M - M/2)\,g}{M + M/2} = \frac{g}{3}$$

Level II

1. Let v be the velocity given by hand when the ball reaches a height h.

$$\therefore \quad \frac{1}{2}mv^2 = mgh \qquad \text{...(i)}$$

If F is the force applied by the hand, then as per question,

$$\frac{1}{2}mv^2 + F \times 0.2 = mg\,(h + 2)$$

Using Eq. (i) $mgh + F \times 0.2 = mgh + mg \times 2$

$$F = \frac{mg \times 2}{0.2} = 10\,mg$$

$$\therefore \quad F = 10 \times 0.2 \times 10 = 20\text{ N}$$

2. Impulse = Change in linear momentum

$$F \times t = m\,(v - u)$$

$$\therefore \quad F = \frac{m\,(v-u)}{t} = \frac{150 \times 10^{-3}\,(0 - 20)}{0.1}$$

$= -30$ N (Negative sign for opposing force)

3. Use formula,

$$T = \left(\frac{2\,m_1m_2}{m_1 + m_2}\right)g$$

Given, $m_1 = 6$ kg, $m_2 = 10$ kg

$$T = \frac{2 \times 6 \times 10}{(6 + 10)}\,g = \frac{12 \times 10}{16} \times (9.8)$$

$$= 73.5$$

$$\therefore \quad T = 74\text{ N}$$

6. Use formula,

$$T = \left(\frac{m_1\,m_2\,g}{m_1 + m_2}\right)$$

Given, $m_1 = 10$ kg, $m_2 = 5$ kg

$$\therefore \quad T = \frac{10 \times 5 \times 10}{10 + 5}$$

$$= \frac{10 \times 50}{15} = \frac{100}{3}\text{ N}$$

06

Friction

Friction

Whenever, an object actually slides or moves over the surface of another body or tends to do, then a force opposing the relative motion acts between these two surfaces in contact. It is known as friction or force due to friction.

Force of friction acts tangential to the surfaces in contact in a direction opposite to the direction of relative motion.

Types of Friction

There are many types of friction

Static Friction

It is the opposing force that comes into play when one body is at rest and tends to move over the surface of another body.

If applied force F is such that the body remains at rest inspite of action of force, frictional force $f_s = F$.

Static friction is thus, a self adjusting force and is always equal and opposite to the applied force.

Limiting Friction

It is the limiting (maximum) value of static friction when a body is just on the verge of starting motion over the surface of another body.

Kinetic (Sliding) Friction

It is the opposing force that comes into play when one body is actually sliding over the surface of another body. Force of kinetic friction f_k is directly proportional to normal reaction N and the ratio $\frac{f_k}{N}$ is called coefficient of kinetic friction μ_k.

Value of μ_k is slightly less than μ_l ($\mu_k < \mu_l$).

Rolling Friction

It is the opposing force that comes into play when one body of symmetric shape (wheel or cylinder or disc etc.) rolls over the surface of another body. Force of rolling friction f_r is directly proportional to normal reaction N and inversely proportional to radius (r) of wheel.

Thus, $f_r \propto \frac{N}{r}$ or $f_r = \mu_r \frac{N}{r}$

The constant μ_r is known as the coefficient of rolling friction, μ_r has the unit and dimensions of length.

Magnitudewise $\mu_r << \mu_k$ or μ_l

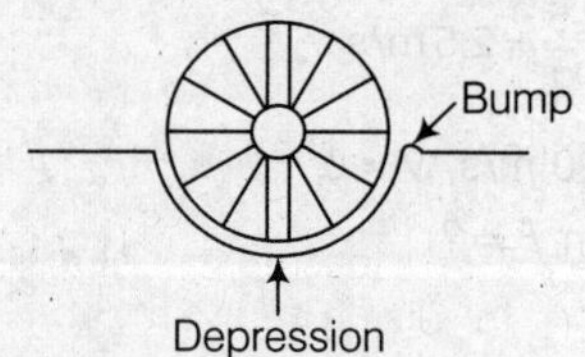

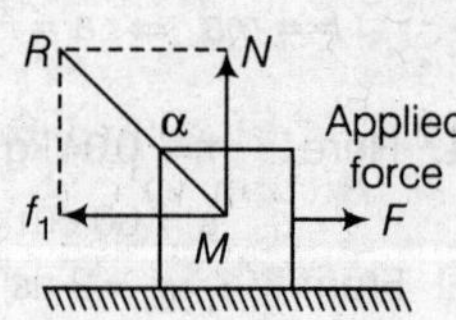

Angle of Friction

It may be defined as the angle which the resultant of the limiting friction and normal reaction makes with the normal reaction. It is denoted by α. Mathematically, $\tan \alpha = \mu_1$.

Angle of Repose It may be defined as the angle of the inclined plane at which a body placed on it just begins to slide. It is denoted by θ. Mathematically, $\tan \theta = \mu_1$.

Minimum Force Required to Move up and down a Rough Inclined Plane

(i) Down

Consider a rough inclined plane at an angle θ with the horizontal. If a body of mass m is placed over inclined plane and the coefficient of limiting friction for given body is μ, then the downward force to be applied to just move the body is $mg\,(\mu \cos\theta - \sin\theta)$. The relation is true only where θ is less than angle of friction α. If $\theta \geq \alpha$ body will begin to slide down on its own.

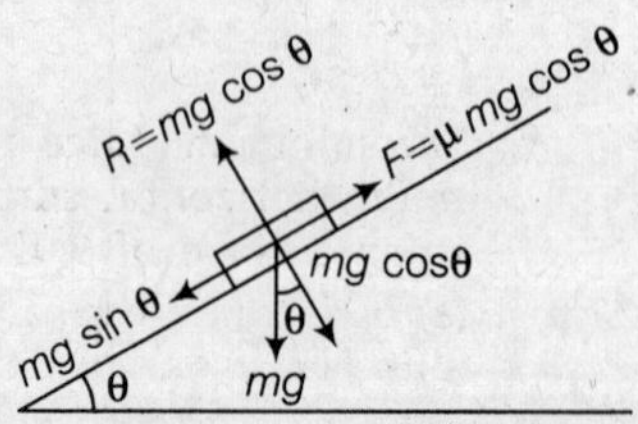

(ii) Motion up the Inclined Plane

Net force to be applied upward to just move the body up the inclined plane is
$mg\ (\mu \cos\theta + \sin\theta)$

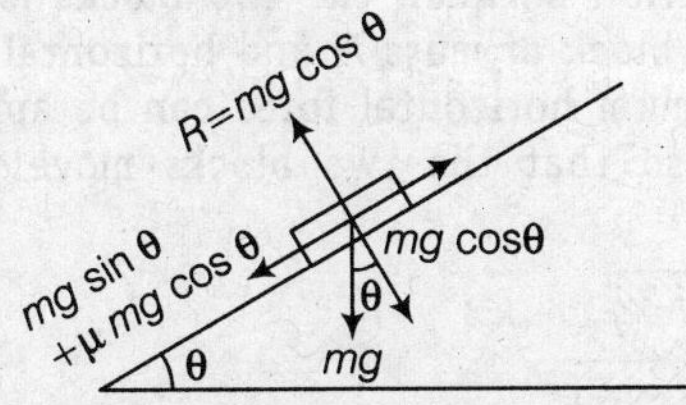

Friction is a Necessary Evil

(a) Friction is Necessary

1. For walking on the ground
2. For rolling
3. For braking
4. For writing on a paper.
5. For lightening a match stick, sewing of cloths and making a knot.
6. For nails and screws to hold things together.

(b) Friction is Evil

(i) Some force is wasted in overcoming friction and so the efficiency of a machine decreases due to friction.
(ii) The heat produced due to friction has adverse effects.
(iii) Friction wears out the rubbing surfaces.

Methods of Reducing Friction

1. Polishing 2. Lubricating 3. Using ball bearings

Note Frictional force is a conservative force.
[That force whose work done depend upon the path.]

Practice Questions

Level I

1. If the applied force is doubled, then the coefficient of friction will
(a) be doubled (b) be remain same
(c) be half (d) be four times

2. The ration of $\frac{\mu_k}{\mu_l}$ is
(a) less than 1 (b) greater than1
(c) equal to 1 (d) 0

3. The normal reaction of a body of weight w placed on an inclined plane is having an angle θ
(a) w cosec θ (b) $w \cos\theta$ (c) $w \tan\theta$ (d) $w \cot\theta$

4. Frictional force always acts
(a) in the direction of motion
(b) against the direction of motion
(c) perpendicular to the direction of motion
(d) making an angle with the velocity vector

5. In rolling friction, the relation between frictional force f and the radius of the body is R.
(a) $f \propto \frac{1}{R^2}$ (b) $f \propto \frac{1}{R}$
(c) $f \propto R$ (d) $f \propto R^2$

6. The minimum force required just to move a block on a rough horizontal surface is 5 N. The block fails to move when a force of 3 N is applied on it. Static frction is
(a) 5 N (b) 3N
(c) 4 N (d) zero

7. When the surfaces in contact are made too smooth by polishing, force of friction
(a) decreases (b) increases
(c) becomes zero (d) becomes infinite

8. Angle of repose for a rough inclined plane is 60°. The coefficient of friction is
(a) $\sqrt{3}$ (b) $1/\sqrt{3}$ (c) 1 (d) zero

9. In moving a body of mass m once up and down a smooth incline of inclination θ, total work done is (S is length of the plane.)
(a) $mg \sin\theta \times S$ (b) $mg \cos\theta \times S$
(c) $mg\ (\sin\theta - \cos\theta)\ S$ (d) zero

10. A ball rolling on ice with a velocity of 5.6 m/s stops after travelling 8 m. If $g = 9.8\ \text{m/s}^2$, coefficient of friction is
(a) 0.1 (b) 0.2 (c) 0.3 (d) 0.4

11. A block of mass 2 kg is placed on the floor. The coefficient of static friction is 0.4. A force F of 2.5 N is applied on the block the force of friction between the block and the floor.
(a) 3 N (b) 2 N (c) 2.5 N (d) 1 N

12. A bend in a level road has a radius of 80 m the maximum speed which a car turning this bend may have without skidding, if the coefficient of friction between the car tyres and the road is 0.25 is
(a) 14 m/s (b) 10 m/s (c) 28 m/s (d) 12 m/s

13. It is easier to pull a lawn roller than to because pulling
(a) involves sliding friction
(b) involves dry friction
(c) increases the effective weight
(d) decreases normal reaction

14. A box is placed on an inclined plane and has to be pushed down. The angle of inclination is
(a) equal to angle of friction
(b) more than angle of friction
(c) equal to angle of repose
(d) less than angle of repose

Level II

1. Which is true for rolling friction (μ_r), static friction (μ_s) and kinetic friction (μ_k)?

(a) $\mu_s > \mu_k > \mu_r$ (b) $\mu_s < \mu_k < \mu_r$
(c) $\mu_s < \mu_k > \mu_r$ (d) $\mu_s > \mu_r > \mu_k$

2. A block is gently placed on a conveyor belt moving horizontally with constant speed. After $t = 4$ s, the velocity of the block becomes equal to velocity of the belt. If the coefficient of friction between the block and the belt is $\mu = 0.2$, then the velocity of the conveyor belt is

(a) 8 m/s (b) 6 m/s (c) 4 m/s (d) 2 m/s

3. A car having a mass of 1000 kg is moving at a speed of 30 m/s. Brakes are applied to bring the car to rest. If the frictional force between the tyres and the road surface is 5000 N, the car will come to rest in

(a) 5 s (b) 8 s (c) 12 s (d) 6 s

4. A body is projected along a rough horizontal surface with a velocity 6 m/s. If the body comes to rest after travelling 9 m, then coefficient of sliding friction is ($g = 10\ \text{m/s}^2$).

(a) 0.2 (b) 0.4 (c) 0.5 (d) 0.6

5. If μ is the coefficient of friction between the tyres and road, then the minimum stopping distance for a car of mass m moving with velocity v is

(a) $\dfrac{v^2}{2\mu g}$ (b) $2\mu g v^2$ (c) μg (d) $\mu g + v^2$

6. A body having kinetic energy K, moving on a rough horizontal surface is stopped in a distance x. The force of friction exerted on the body is

(a) $\sqrt{K}/x$ (b) K/x (c) $K/\sqrt{x}$ (d) Kx

7. A block of weight 5 N is pushed against a vertical wall by a force 12 N. The coefficient of friction between the wall and block is 0.6. The magnitude of the force exerted by the wall on the block is

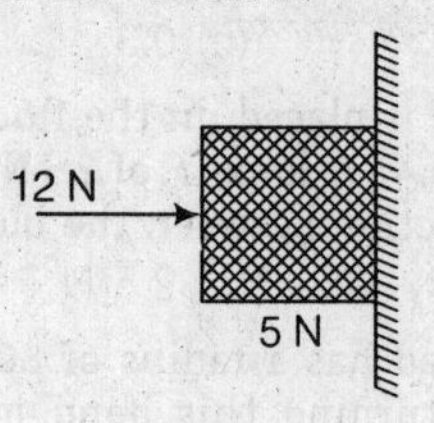

(a) 12 N (b) 5 N (c) 7.2 N (d) 13 N

8. A block of mass m is placed on another block of mass M which itself is lying on a horizontal surface. The coefficient of friction between the two blocks is μ_1 and that between the block of mass M and horizontal surface is μ_2. What maximum horizontal force can be applied to the lower block so that the two blocks move without separation?

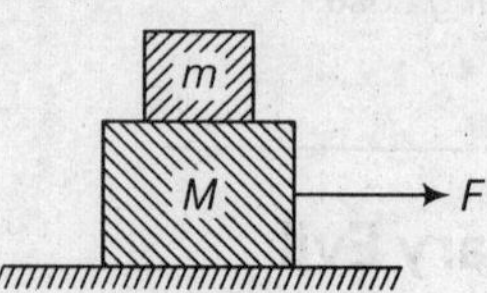

(a) $(M + m)(\mu_2 - 1) g$
(b) $(M - m)(\mu_2 - \mu_1) g$
(c) $(M - m)(\mu_2 + \mu_1) g$
(d) $(M + m)(\mu_2 + \mu_1) g$

9. A block of mass m is placed on the top of another block of mass M as shown in figure. The coefficient of friction between them is μ. What is the maximum acceleration with which the block M may move so that m also moves along it?

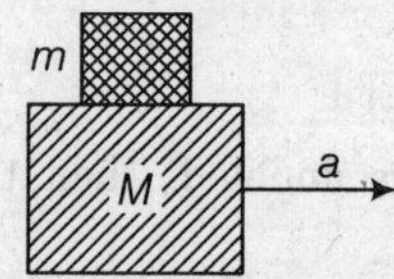

(a) μg (b) g/μ
(c) μ^2/g (d) g/μ^2

10. A body of mass m, having momentum p is moving on a rough horizontal surface. If it is stopped in a distance x, the coefficient of friction between the body and the surface is given by

(a) $\mu = \dfrac{p}{2mgx}$

(b) $\mu = \dfrac{p^2}{2mgx}$

(c) $\mu = \dfrac{p^2}{2gm^2x}$

(d) $\mu = \dfrac{p^2}{2gm^2x^2}$

Answers

Level I

1. (b)	**2.** (a)	**3.** (b)	**4.** (b)	**5.** (a)	**6.** (b)	**7.** (b)	**8.** (a)	**9.** (d)	**10.** (b)
11. (c)	**12.** (a)	**13.** (d)	**14.** (d)						

Level II

1. (a)	**2.** (a)	**3.** (d)	**4.** (a)	**5.** (a)	**6.** (b)	**7.** (d)	**8.** (d)	**9.** (a)	**10.** (c)

Hints and Solutions

Level I

8. Angle of repose

$\tan\theta = \mu,$

$\Rightarrow \tan 60° = \mu, \ \mu = \sqrt{3}$

9. $W = F \cdot S = FS\cos\theta$

Here, the angle between F and S is 90°.

$\therefore W \ \ FS\cos 90° = 0$

10. Here, $v = 5.6$ m/s, $u = 0$, $s = 8$ m

$\therefore v^2 - u^2 = 2as$

$$a = \frac{0 - (5.6)^2}{2 \times 8} = -19.6 \text{ m/s}^2$$

$\therefore \ m \times a = \mu R \ \Rightarrow \ ma = \mu mg$

$$\mu = \frac{a}{g} = \frac{1.96}{9.8} = 0.2$$

11. Here, $m = 2$ kg, $\mu_s = 0.4$, $F = 2.5$ N

The limiting force of friction

$f_s = \mu_s R = \mu_s \ mg = 0.4 \times 2 \times 9.8 = 7.84$ N

As $F < f_2$

It must be equal to 2.5 N only.

12. Here, $r = 80$ m, Maximum speed, $v = ?$, $\mu = 0.25$

On a level road, there will be no skidding, when force of friction is enough to provide the necessary centripetal force

i.e., $\dfrac{mv^2}{r} = F = \mu R = \mu \ mg$

$v = \sqrt{\mu r g} = \sqrt{0.25 \times 80 \times 9.8}$

$v = \sqrt{196} = 14$ m/s

Level II

2. On account of friction ($a = \mu g$), velocity of block will become equal to velocity of conveyor belt and the relative motion between the two will stop.

$v = at = \mu \ gt = 0.2 \times 10 \times 4 = 8$ m/s

3. Retardation produced,

$$a = \frac{F}{m} = \frac{-5000}{1000} = -5 \text{ m/s}^2$$

From $\quad v = u + at$

$0 = 30 - 5 \times t, t = 6$ s

4. Given $v = 6$ m/s, $u = 0$, $s = 9$ m, $\mu = ?$

From the equation,

$v^2 = u^2 + 2\,as$

$6^2 = 0^2 + 2 \times a \times 9$

$36 = 189 \Rightarrow a = 2$ m/s²

$$\mu = \frac{a}{g}$$

$$\mu = \frac{2}{10} \ \Rightarrow \mu = 02$$

5. From $v^2 - u^2 = 2\,as$

$$(\mu mg)\,s = \frac{1}{2}mv^2 \ \Rightarrow s = \frac{v^2}{2\,\mu g}$$

6. Let f be the force of friction and m, the mass of the body.

$\therefore$ Retardation $a = f/m$

Let v be the initial velocity of the body, then

$$v^2 = 2ax \ \Rightarrow \frac{1}{2}mv^2 = m\,a\,x$$

$\Rightarrow \quad K = f\,x \quad (\because ma = f)$

$\therefore \quad f = K/x$

7. Force applied = 12 N

$\therefore \ f_{max} = \mu\,R = 0.6 \times 12 = 7.2$ N

This shows that $f_{max} > W$

The net contact force is given by

$$F = \sqrt{(R^2 + f^2)} = \sqrt{(12)^2 + (5)^2} \ \Rightarrow \ F = 13 \text{ N}$$

8. Here, the force applied should be such that the force on block of mass m should not exceed the force of friction ($\mu_1\,mg$). Let the system move with acceleration a. Then,

$$F - \mu_2\,(M + m)\,g = (M + m)\,a \qquad \text{...(i)}$$

For block of mass m,

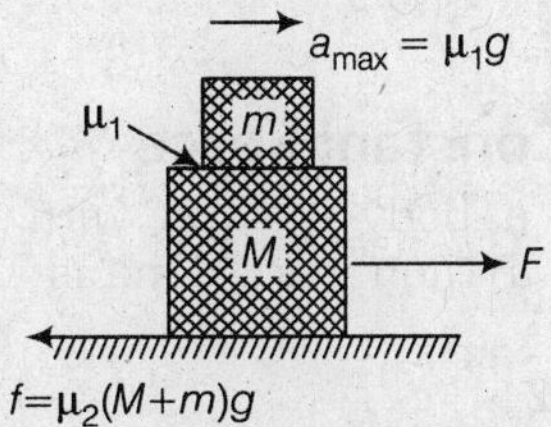

$$F_1 = ma = \mu_1\,mg \ \Rightarrow \ a = \mu_1\,g \qquad \text{...(ii)}$$

From Eqs. (i) and (ii), we get

$F = \mu_2\,(M + m)\,g + (M + m)\mu_1\,g$

$= (M + m)\,g\,(\mu_1 + \mu_2)$

9. The block m will move alongwith M, when

$ma = \mu\,m\,g \ \Rightarrow \ a = \mu\,g$

10. The force of friction $= \mu\,m\,g$

$\therefore$ Retardation $a = \dfrac{\mu\,mg}{m} = \mu g$

Now, $\quad v^2 = 2\,a\,x = 2\,\mu\,g\,x$

$\Rightarrow \quad m^2\,v^2 = 2\,m^2\,\mu\,g\,x \Rightarrow p^2 = 2\,m^2\,\mu\,g\,x$

$$\therefore \quad \mu = \frac{p^2}{2\,g\,m^2\,x}$$

07

Work, Power and **Energy**

Work

It is said to be done when a force (F) applied on the body displaces the body through a certain distance (s) in the direction of force.

$$W = \vec{F} \cdot \vec{s} = Fs\cos\theta$$

It is a scalar quantity, its units in SI system is joule and in CGS system is erg.

$$1 \text{ J} = 1 \text{N-m} = 10^7 \text{ erg}$$

Work Done by Variable Force

Work done by variable force which displaces a body from s_1 to s_2 is

$$W = \int_{s_1}^{s_2} \vec{F} \cdot d\vec{s}$$

Work Done by a Constant Force

When force acts on a body moving with constant acceleration a, then work done is

$$W = \frac{1}{2} ax^2$$

Where, x is the displacement.

Types of Work

Work can be positive (+ve), negative (–ve) and zero.

Positive Work

If $0° \leq \theta < 90°$, then $W > 0$, that is work done is positive.

Negative Work

If $90° < \theta \leq 180°$, then $W < 0$ that is work done is negative.

Zero Work

If $\theta = 90°$, $s = 0$
or $F = 0$, then $W = 0$

Conservative and Non-conservative Forces

Conservative Forces

A force is said to be conservative, if the work done by the force (or against the force) in moving a body depends only upon the initial and final positions of the body and is independent of the path followed between the initial and final positions. *e.g.*, Electrostatic force, gravitational force etc.

Non-conservative Forces

A force is said to be non-conservative, if work done by the force (or against the force) in moving a body from the position to another, depends upon the path followed between the two positions. *e.g.*, friction, viscous force, damping force etc.

Energy

It is defined as the capacity or ability of a body to do work. Energy is scalar quantity and its units and dimensions are the same as that of work. Thus, SI unit of energy is Joule. Some other commonly used units of energy are

$$1 \text{ erg} = 10^{-7} \text{ J},$$
$$1 \text{ cal} = 4.186 \text{ J} = 4.2 \text{ J}$$
$$1 \text{ kcal} = 4186 \text{ J},$$
$$1 \text{ kWh} = 3.6 \times 10^6 \text{ J},$$

and 1 electron volt $= 1 \text{ eV} = 1.60 \times 10^{-19} \text{ J}$

Kinetic Energy

Kinetic energy of a body is the energy possessed by it due

$$K = \frac{1}{2} mv^2,$$

$$K = \frac{p^2}{2m} \quad \text{or} \quad p = \sqrt{2mK}$$

Here, p is momentum.

Potential Energy

It is the energy stored in a body or a system by virtue of its position in a field of force or due to its configuration. It is measured by the amount of work that a body can do in passing from its present position or configuration to some standard position or configuration, called zero position or the zero configuration.

Generally, potential energy is of two types are given below

1. Gravitational Potential Energy

It is the energy associated with the state of separation between two bodies which interact *via* the gravitational force. Generally, one of the two bodies is our Earth of mass M and radius R. If m is the mass of the other body, situated at a distance r $(r \geq R)$ from the centre of Earth, the potential energy of the body is

$$U(r) = -\frac{GMm}{r}$$

2. Elastic Potential Energy

It is the energy stored in a spring when the spring of force constant k is elongated by Δx.

$$U = \frac{1}{2} k\Delta x^2$$

Where, k is the spring constant.

Elastic potential energy is always positive.

Work-Energy Theorem

According to this theorem, work done by a force (or forces) on a body equals a change in the kinetic energy of the body.

$$W_{\text{total}} = \Delta K = K_f - K_i$$

If work is being done by the force on the body, then its kinetic energy increases, *i.e.*, $\Delta K =$ positive. On the other hand, if work is being done by the body on the force, then its kinetic energy decreases *i.e.*, $\Delta K =$ negative. The theorem is true for all type of forces.

Mass-Energy Equivalence

The mass and energy are two different forms of the same entity and they are inter convertible. Mass-energy equivalence relation, $E = mc^2$.

Where, E is the energy obtained when a mass m is completely converted into energy and c is the velocity of light in free space.

$(c = 3 \times 10^8 \text{m/s})$

Conservation Law of Energy

Energy can neither be created nor destroyed and total energy of an isolated system should remain conserved. Of course energy may be transformed from one form to another form, such that energy lost in one form exactly reappears in the other form.

Power

The rate of doing work by an agent or a machine, is called power of the agent or the machine.

$$\text{Power} = \frac{\text{Work}}{\text{Time}} = \frac{F \cdot s \cos\theta}{t} = Fv\cos\theta = mav\cos\theta$$

Unit of power is watt (W).

Some other units of power are below

1 kW = 10^3 W

1 MW = 10^6 W

1 HP = 746 W

Practice Questions

Level I

1. The correct relation between joule and erg is

(a) 1 J = 10^{-7}erg (b) 1 J = 10^7 erg
(c) 1 J = 10^{-5}erg (d) 1 J = 10^5erg

2. When a body is thrown up, work done by gravity on the body is

(a) positive (b) zero
(c) negative (d) Can't say

3. A person holds on a weight of 10 kg at a height of 5 m above the ground for 5 min. Work done by him is

(a) zero (b) 50 J
(c) 250 J (d) 300 J

4. A body is undergoing non-uniform circular motion. Work done by radial force on the body is

(a) zero (b) positive
(c) negative (d) None of these

5. In above question, work done by tangential force on the body is

(a) zero
(b) non-zero
(c) sometimes zero and other times not
(d) Can't say

6. Which one of the following is a non-conservative force?

(a) Gravitational force
(b) Electrostatic force
(c) Magnetic force
(d) Force of friction

7. The linear momentum of a body is increased by 10%. What is the percentage increase in its KE?

(a) 10 (b) 20
(c) 21 (d) None of these

8. A bullet fired in a horizontal direction which immersed in a wooden block. If the block placed on frictionless horizontal plane, then
(a) only kinetic energy is conserved
(b) only momentum is conserved
(c) only potential energy is conserved
(d) (b) and (c)

9. If the momentum are similar for a light body and a heavy body, then
(a) kinetic energy of heavy body will be more
(b) kinetic energy of heavy body will be less
(c) kinetic energy of both bodies will be same
(d) None of the above

10. Slope of kinetic-energy-displacement curve for a dynamic particle is
(a) equal to acceleration of particle
(b) Inversally proportional to the acceleration
(c) directly proportional to the acceleration
(d) None of the above

11. On collision of two ball at same temperature, the conserved physical quantity is
(a) temperature (b) velocity
(c) kinetic energy (d) momentum

12. 1 HP equal to
(a) 246 W (b) 746 W
(c) 146 W (d) 481 W

13. If velocity of a moving body become halves, then its kinetic energy will be
(a) halves (b) double
(c) four times (d) one-fourth

14. If W = work done, F = applied force, x = displacement and θ = angle between force and displacement.
(a) $W = Fx\tan\theta$ (b) $W = Fx\cos\theta$
(c) $W = Fx\sin\theta$ (d) $W = Fx$

15. If force F is applied on a body and v is the velocity achieved by the body, then the power of the body is given by
(a) $F \times v$ (b) $\frac{F}{v^2}$ (c) F/v (d) $F \times v^2$

16. Work is always done on a body when
(a) a force acts on it
(b) it moves through a certain distance
(c) it experiences an increase in energy through a mechanical influence
(d) None of the above

17. A man pushes a wall and fails to displace it. He does
(a) negative work
(b) positive but not maximum work
(c) no work at all
(d) maximum work

18. A light and a heavy body have equal momentum. Which one has greater KE?
(a) The light body
(b) Both have equal KE
(c) The heavy body
(d) Data given is incomplete

19. A light and a heavy body have equal KE. Which has greater momentum?
(a) The heavy body
(b) The light body
(c) Both have equal momentum
(d) Data given is incomplete

20. The principle of conservation of linear momentum can be strictly applied during a collision between two particles provided the time of impact is
(a) extremely small
(b) moderately small
(c) extremely large
(d) depends on a particular case

Level II

1. Force of 4 N is applied on a body of mass 20 kg. The work done in 3rd second is
(a) 2 J (b) 4 J (c) 16 J (d) 1.2 J

2. A gun fires bullets each of mass 1 g with velocity of 10 m/s by exerting a constant force of 5 g weight. Then, the number of bullets fired per second is (Then $g = 10 \text{ m/s}^2$)
(a) 50 (b) 5 (c) 10 (d) 25

3. A rod of mass m and length l is lying on a horizontal table. Work done in making it stand on one end will be
(a) mgl (b) $\frac{mgl}{2}$ (c) $\frac{mgl}{4}$ (d) $2mgl$

4. A body of mass 2 kg is initially at rest. A constant force of 5 N acts on it for 10 s. Then, the average power of the force is
(a) 62.5 W (b) 125 W
(c) 50 W (d) 25 W

5. When the KE of a body is increased by 300%, the momentum of the body is increased by
(a) 20% (b) 50% (c) 100% (d) 200%

6. A particle moves along the x-axis from $x = 0$ to $x = 5$ m under the influence of a force given by $F = (7 - 2x + 3x^2)$ N. Work done (in J) is
(a) 70 (b) 270 (c) 35 (d) 135

7. In which case does the potential energy decrease?
(a) On compressing the spring
(b) On stretching a spring
(c) On moving a body against gravitational pull
(d) On the raising of an air bubble in water

8. Certain distance d, starting from rest, under the action of a constant force is directly proportional to
(a) m (b) $\sqrt{m}$
(c) $\frac{1}{\sqrt{m}}$ (d) None of these

9. A body is initially at rest. It undergoes one dimensional motion with constant acceleration. The power delivered to it at time t is proportional to

(a) $t^{1/2}$ (b) t (c) $t^{3/2}$ (d) t^2

10. In a gravitational force field a particle is taken from A to B along different paths as shown in figure. Then,

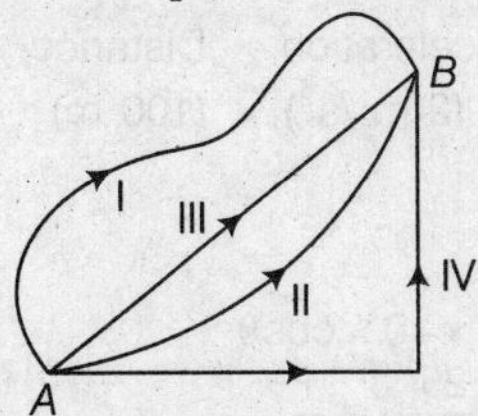

(a) work done along path I will be maximum
(b) work done along path III will be minimum
(c) work done along path IV will be maximum
(d) work done along all the paths will be the same

11. How much work must be done by a force on 100 kg body in order to accelerate it from 0 to 20 m/s in 10 s?

(a) 2×10^3 J (b) 4×10^3 J
(c) 2×10^4 J (d) 4×10^4 J

12. A body moves a distance of 10 m along a straight line under the action of a 5 N force. If the work done is 25 J, then angle between the force and direction of motion of the body is

(a) 30° (b) 45° (c) 60° (d) 75°

13. If g is acceleration due to gravity on the Earth's surface, the gain in the potential energy of an object of mass m raised from surface of Earth to a height equal to radius R of the Earth is

(a) $\frac{1}{2}mgR$ (b) $2\,mgR$ (c) mgR (d) $\frac{1}{4}\,mgR$

14. A force F acting on an object varies with distance x as shown in figure. The work done by the force in moving the object from $x = 0$ to $x = 6$ m is

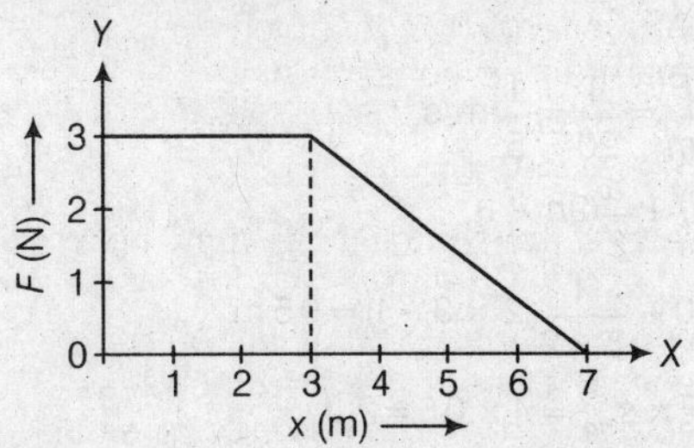

(a) 4.5 J (b) 13.5 J
(c) 9.0 J (d) 18.0 J

15. A body is moved along a straight line by a machine delivering constant power. The distance moved by the body in time t is proportional to

(a) $t^{1/2}$ (b) $t^{3/4}$
(c) $t^{3/2}$ (d) t^2

16. A body of mass 5 kg is moving with a momentum of 10 kg m/s. A force of 0.2 N acts on it in the direction of motion of the body for 10 s. The increase in its kinetic energy is

(a) 2.8 J (b) 3.2 J
(c) 3.8 J (d) 4.4 J

17. A ball of mass 1 kg moving with velocity 3 m/s collides with spring of natural length 2 m and force constant 144 N/m. What will be length of compressed spring?

(a) 2 m
(b) 1.5 m
(c) 1 m
(d) 0.5 m

Answers

Level I

1. (b)	**2.** (c)	**3.** (a)	**4.** (a)	**5.** (b)	**6.** (d)	**7.** (c)	**8.** (d)	**9.** (b)	**10.** (c)
11. (d)	**12.** (b)	**13.** (d)	**14.** (b)	**15.** (a)	**16.** (c)	**17.** (c)	**18.** (a)	**19.** (a)	**20.** (a)

Level II

1. (a)	**2.** (b)	**3.** (b)	**4.** (a)	**5.** (c)	**6.** (d)	**7.** (d)	**8.** (d)	**9.** (b)	**10.** (d)
11. (c)	**12.** (c)	**13.** (a)	**14.** (b)	**15.** (c)	**16.** (d)	**17.** (b)			

Hints and Solutions

Level II

1. Here, $a = \frac{F}{m} = \frac{4}{20} = \frac{1}{5}$ m/s^2

$$s_{nth} = u + \frac{a}{2}(2n-1)$$

$$s_{3rd} = 0 + \frac{1}{5 \times 2}(2 \times 3 - 1) = 0.5 \text{ m}$$

$$W = F \times s_{3rd} = 4 \times 0.5 = 2 \text{ J}$$

2. From $F = n m v$

$$n = \frac{F}{mv} = \frac{5 \times 10^{-3} \times 10}{10^{-3} \times 10} = 5$$

3. Work done = Final PE − Initial PE

$$= m g(l/2) - m g(0) = m g \frac{l}{2}$$

4. $a = F/m = \frac{5}{2}$ m/s^2

From $v = u + at$

$$v = 0 + 5/2\,(10) = 25 \text{ m/s}$$

$$v_{av} = \frac{0 + 25}{2} = 12.5 \text{ m/s}$$

$$P_{av} = F \times v_{av} = 5 \times 12.5 = 62.5 \text{ W}$$

5. Final KE = 100 + 300 = 400%

$\therefore$ $E_2 = 4E_1$

$$\frac{1}{2}mv_2^2 = 4 \times \frac{1}{2}mv_1^2 \text{ or } v_2^2 = 4v_1^2,$$

$$v_2 = 2v_1$$

$\therefore$ $p_2 = 2p_1$ *i.e.*, momentum becomes twice. Increase in momentum = 100%

6. $W = \int_0^5 F\,dx = \int_0^5 (7 - 2x + 3x^2)\,dx$

$$= [7x - x^2 + x^3]_0^5 = [35 - 25 + 125] = 135 \text{ J}$$

7. Potential energy decrease on the raising of an air bubble in water.

8. KE $= \frac{1}{2} m v^2 = \frac{1}{2}m(u^2 + 2as)$

KE $= \frac{1}{2}m\,[0 + 2\,F/m \times d] = F \times d$

KE does not depend on mass.

9. $v = u + at = 0 + at = at$

$P = F \times v = (ma) \times at = ma^2t$

$\therefore$ $P \propto t$

10. The gravitational force conservative force and hence the work done is independent of path. So, work done along all the paths will be same.

11. $u = 0$, $v = 20$ m/s and $t = 10$ s

$\therefore$ $v = u + at$

$\Rightarrow$ $20 = a \times 10$

$\therefore$ $a = 2$ m/s^2

Further $s = ut + \frac{1}{2}at^2 = 0 + \frac{1}{2} \times 2 \times (10)^2 \Rightarrow s = 100$ m

Work = Force × Distance

= Mass × Acceleration × Distance

= (100 kg) × (2 m/s^2) × (100 m)

$= 2 \times 10^4$ J

12. $W = F s \cos\theta$

$\Rightarrow$ $25 = 5 \times 10 \times \cos\theta$

$$\cos\theta = \frac{25}{5 \times 10} = \frac{1}{2}$$

$\Rightarrow$ $\theta = \cos^{-1}\left(\frac{1}{2}\right) = 60°$

13. $W = \int_R^{2R} \frac{G\,m\,M}{x^2}\,dx = G\,m\,M \int_R^{2R} x^{-2}dx = G\,m\,M\left[\frac{x^{-1}}{-1}\right]_R^{2R}$

$$= G\,m\,M\left[\frac{1}{R} - \frac{1}{2R}\right]$$

$$= \frac{G\,m\,M}{2R} = \frac{1}{2}m\,R\left[\frac{G\,M}{R^2}\right]$$

$$= \frac{1}{2}m\,R\,g = \frac{1}{2}\,m\,g\,R$$

14. W = Area of F-x graph

$$= 3 \times 3 + \frac{1}{2}(3 \times 3) = 9 + 4.5 = 13.5 \text{ J}$$

15. $P = \frac{F \times s}{t}$ = Constant (given)

$\therefore$ $F \times s \propto t$ ...(i)

We know that $F = \frac{m\,(v-u)}{t}$

or $F \propto \frac{s}{t^2}$ ($\because$ m = constant)

Now from Eq. (i), we have

$$\frac{s}{t^2} \times s \propto t$$

$\Rightarrow$ $s^2 \propto t^3$

$\therefore$ $s \propto t^{3/2}$

16. Initial KE $= \frac{p_1^2}{2m} = \frac{10 \times 10}{2 \times 5} = 10$ J

Impulse $= p_2 - p_1 = F \times t$

$p_2 - 10 = 0.2 \times 10 \Rightarrow p_2 = 12$ kg m/s

Final KE $= \frac{p_2^2}{2m} = \frac{12 \times 12}{2 \times 5} = 14.4$ J

Increase in KE = 14.4 − 10 = 4.4 J

17. Elastic PE of spring = KE of ball

$$\frac{1}{2}Kx^2 = \frac{1}{2}mv^2$$

$$x = \sqrt{\frac{mv^2}{K}} = \sqrt{\frac{4 \times 3^2}{144}} = \frac{1}{2} = 0.5 \text{ m}$$

$\therefore$ Length of compressed spring $= l - x = 2 - 0.5 = 1.5$ m

08

Collision

Collision

Collision between two bodies (or particles) is said to occur when they either physically strike against each other or if the path of the motion of one is influenced by the other.

There are two types of collision as below

1. Elastic collision
2. Inelastic collision

Elastic Collision : Perfectly Elastic Collision in One Dimension

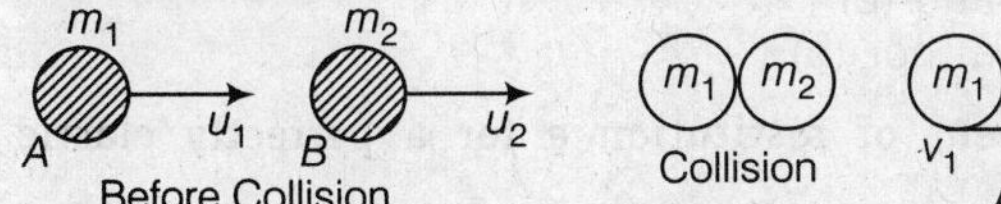

In a perfectly elastic collision, total energy and total linear momentum of colliding particles remain conserved. Moreover, the forces involved in interaction are conservative in nature and the total kinetic energy before and after the collision, remains unchanged. If two bodies A and B of masses m_1 and m_2 and having initial velocities u_1 and u_2 in one dimension, collide elastically and after collision move with velocities v_1 and v_2, then we find that

(a) Relative velocity of approach = Relative velocity of separation *i.e.*, $u_1 - u_2 = v_2 - v_1$

(b) $v_1 = \left(\dfrac{m_1 - m_2}{m_1 + m_2}\right) u_1 + \left(\dfrac{2m_2}{m_1 + m_2}\right) u_2$

and $v_2 = \left(\dfrac{2m_1}{m_1 + m_2}\right) u_1 + \left(\dfrac{m_2 - m_1}{m_1 + m_2}\right) u_2$

Special Cases

Case I When $m_1 = m_2$, then $v_1 = u_2$ and $v_2 = u_1$ *i.e.*, velocities of two colliding bodies are interchanged.

Case II $m_1 >> m_2$ and $u_2 = 0$ (Ball A is very heavy and lighter ball B is at rest.)
$v_1 = u_1$ and $v_2 = 2u_1$ *i.e.*, heavier ball A keeps moving with the same speed and lighter ball B moves with double the speed of A.

Case III $m_2 >> m_1$ and $u_2 = 0$ (Ball B is very heavy and it is at rest.)
$v_1 = -u_1, v_2 = 0$ *i.e.*, (lighter ball A rebounds with the same speed whereas heavy ball B remains at rest).

Elastic Collision in Two Dimensions

Suppose two balls A and B moving with velocities u_1 and u_2 initially in a straight line collide and after collision move at angles θ and ϕ from the line of action (x-axis) with velocities v_1 and v_2, respectively.

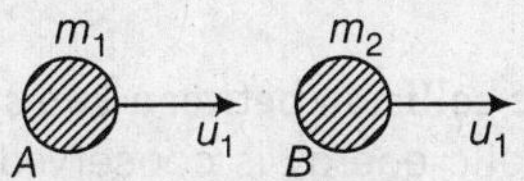

Before Collision

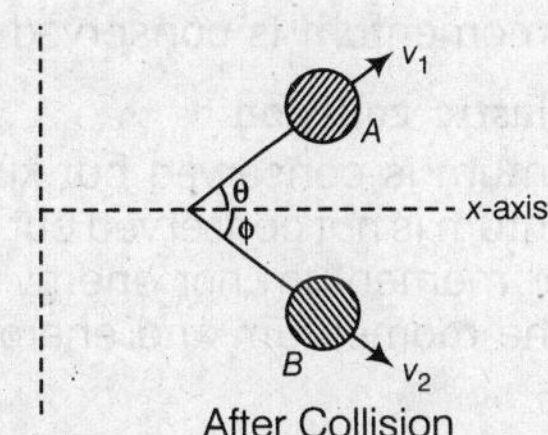

After Collision

Conserving kinetic energy,

$$\frac{1}{2} m_1 u_1^2 + \frac{1}{2} m_2 u_2^2 = \frac{1}{2} m_1 v_1^2 + \frac{1}{2} m_2 v_2^2 \quad \text{...(i)}$$

Conserving linear momentum along x-axis,

$$m_1 u_1 + m_2 u_2 = m_1 v_1 \cos\theta + m_2 v_2 \cos\phi \quad \text{...(ii)}$$

Conserving linear momentum along y-axis,

$$0 = m_1 v_1 \sin\theta - m_2 v_2 \sin\phi \quad \text{...(iii)}$$

Inelastic Collision : Inelastic Collision in One Dimension

In an inelastic collision, the total linear momentum as well as total energy remain conserved but total kinetic energy after collision is not equal to kinetic energy before collision.

(a) $v_1 = \left(\dfrac{m_1 - em_2}{m_1 + m_2}\right) u_1 + \left(\dfrac{(1+e)m_2}{m_1 + m_2}\right) u_2$

$v_2 = \left(\dfrac{(1+e)m_1}{m_1 + m_2}\right) u_1 + \left(\dfrac{m_2 - em_1}{m_1 + m_2}\right) u_2$

(b) Coefficient of Restitution,

$$e = \frac{v_2 - v_1}{u_1 - u_2}$$

Note For a perfectly elastic collision, $e = 1$.

- If $0 < e < 1$, the collision is said to be partially elastic.
- But if $e = 0$, the collision is said to be perfectly inelastic.

In case of rebounding, $e = \sqrt{\frac{h}{H}}$

Where,

h = Height of rebound, H = Height of fall

If $e = 1$, then $h = H$

If $e = 0$, $h = 0$

If $e < 1$, $h < H$

Rebounding of a Ball on Collision with the Floor

- Speed of the ball after the nth rebound, $v_n = e^n v_0 = e^n \sqrt{2gh_0}$
- Height covered by the ball after the nth rebound, $h_n = e^{2n} h_0$
- Total distance (vertical) covered by the ball before it stops bouncing, $H = h_0 + 2h_1 + 2h_2 + 2h_3 + \dots$

$$= h_0 \left(\frac{1+e^2}{1-e^2}\right)$$

- Total time taken by the ball before it stops bouncing, $T = t_0 + t_1 + t_2 + t_3 + \dots$

$$= \sqrt{\frac{2h_0}{g}} + 2\sqrt{\frac{2h_1}{g}} + 2\sqrt{\frac{2h_2}{g}} + \dots = \sqrt{\frac{2h_0}{g}}\left(\frac{1+e}{1-e}\right)$$

Practice Questions

Level I

1. For inelastic collision between two spherical rigid bodies
(a) total kinetic energy is conserved
(b) linear momentum is not conserved
(c) total mechanical energy is conserved
(d) linear momentum is conserved

2. In an inelastic collision
(a) momentum is conserved but kinetic energy is not
(b) momentum is not conserved but energy is conserved
(c) Neither momentum nor energy is conserved
(d) Both the momentum and energy are conserved

3. In any kind of collision
(a) linear momentum is always conserved
(b) kinetic energy is always conserved
(c) Both (a) and (b)
(d) Neither (a) nor (b)

4. The coefficient of restitution e for a perfectly elastic collision is
(a) 1 (b) 0 (c) ∞ (d) -1

5. The coefficient of restitution e for a perfectly inelastic collision is
(a) 1 (b) 0 (c) ∞ (d) -1

Level II

1. The first ball of mass m moving with the velocity v collides head on with the second ball of mass m at rest. If the coefficient of restitution is e, then the ratio of the velocities of the first and the second ball after the collision is
(a) $\frac{1-e}{1+e}$ (b) $\frac{1+e}{1-e}$ (c) $\frac{1+e}{2}$ (d) $\frac{1-e}{2}$

2. A ball is dropped on the ground from a height of 1 m. The coefficient of restitution is 0.6. The height to which the ball will rebound is
(a) 0.6 m (b) 0.4 m (c) 0.36 m (d) 0.16 m

3. If two masses m_1 and m_2 collide, the ratio of change in their respective velocities is proportional to
(a) $\frac{m_1}{m_2}$ (b) $\sqrt{\frac{m_1}{m_2}}$ (c) $\frac{m_2}{m_1}$ (d) $\sqrt{\frac{m_2}{m_1}}$

4. An object of mass 40 kg and having velocity 4 m/s collides with another object of mass 60 kg having velocity 2 m/s. The loss of energy when the collision is perfectly inelastic is
(a) 392 J (b) 440 J (c) 48 J (d) 110 J

5. A ball hits the floor and rebounds after inelastic collision. In this case
(a) the momentum of the ball just after the collision is the same as that just before the collision
(b) the mechanical energy of the ball remains the same in the collision
(c) the total momentum of the ball and the Earth is conserved
(d) the total energy of the ball and the Earth is conserved

6. A mass is released from a height H and after hitting the ground it rebounds to a height h. The coefficient of restitution between the ground and mass.
(a) $e = \sqrt{\frac{H}{h}}$ (b) $e = \frac{\sqrt{H}}{h}$
(c) $e = \sqrt{\frac{h}{H}}$ (d) $e = \frac{\sqrt{h}}{H}$

7. If the coefficient of restitution be 0.5, what is the percentage loss of energy on each rebounding of a ball dropped from a height?
(a) 12.5 (b) 25
(c) 50 (d) 75

8. A body of mass m collides against a wall with the velocity v and rebounds with the same speed. Its change of momentum is

(a) $2\,mv$ (b) mv (c) $-mv$ (d) 0

9. A ball is dropped from a height h on the ground. If the coefficient of restitution is e, the height to which the ball goes up after it rebounds for the nth time is

(a) he^{2n} (b) he^{n} (c) $\frac{e^{2n}}{h}$ (d) $\frac{h}{e^{2n}}$

10. A ball is dropped from a height h. If the coefficient of restitution be e, then to what height will it rise after jumping twice from the ground?

(a) $eh/2$ (b) $2eh$ (c) eh (d) e^4h

11. A particle of mass m moving with velocity v collides with another heavy particle (at rest) of mass $2m$ and sticks together. The velocity of this system will be

(a) $\frac{v}{2}$ (b) $2v$

(c) $\frac{v}{3}$ (d) $3v$

12. A particle of mass m is moving with velocity $\vec{\mathbf{v}}$. This particle directly collides with another particle (at rest) of the same mass elastically. After collision, the velocity of first particle will be

(a) $\vec{\mathbf{v}}$ (b) $-\vec{\mathbf{v}}$ (c) $-\vec{\mathbf{v}}/2$ (d) zero

13. A particle of mass m moving from the East with speed of v collides with another particle of coming from the North of same speed (v) and mass (m) and stuck together. The speed of new particle of mass $2m$ will be

(a) v (b) $\frac{v}{2}$

(c) $\frac{v}{2v_2}$ (d) $\frac{v_2}{v}$

14. If t_1 be the time of falling and t_2 be the time of rising, then coefficient of elasticity is

(a) $t_1 + t_2$ (b) $\frac{t_2}{t_1}$

(c) $\sqrt{t_1 t_2}$ (d) $\frac{t_1}{t_2}$

Answers

Level I

1. (d) **2.** (a) **3.** (a) **4.** (a) **5.** (b)

Level II

1. (a) **2.** (c) **3.** (c) **4.** (c) **5.** (c) **6.** (c) **7.** (d) **8.** (a) **9.** (a) **10.** (d)
11. (d) **12.** (d) **13.** (b) **14.** (d)

Hints and Solutions

Level II

1. Here, $m_1 = m_2 = m, u_1 = u, u_2 = 0$. Let v_1, v_2 be their velocities after collision.

According to principle of conservation of linear momentum.

$$mu + 0 = m(v_1 + v_2) \Rightarrow v_1 + v_2 = u \quad \text{...(i)}$$

By definition, $e = \frac{v_2 - v_1}{u - 0}$

$$\Rightarrow \quad v_2 - v_1 = eu \quad \text{...(ii)}$$

On adding Eqs. (i) and (ii), we get

$$v_2 = \frac{u(1+e)}{2}$$

On subtracting Eqs. (ii) from (i), we get

$$v_1 = \frac{(1-e)u}{2}$$

$$\therefore \quad \frac{v_1}{v_2} = \frac{1-e}{1+e}$$

2. Here, $h_1 = 1$ m, $h_2 = ?$

From $e = \frac{v_2}{v_1} = 0.6$, $v_2 = 0.6\,v_1$

As, $\frac{h_2}{h_1} = \frac{v_2^2}{v_1^2} = (0.6)^2 = 0.36$

$\therefore \quad h_2 = 0.36\,h_1 = 0.36$ m

4. Here,

$m_1 = 40$ kg, $u_1 = 4$ m/s

$m_2 = 60$ kg, $u_2 = 2$ m/s

Final velocity after collision,

$$v = \frac{m_1u_1 + m_2u_2}{(m_1 + m_2)}$$

$$v = \frac{40 \times 4 + 60 \times 2}{(40 + 60)}$$

$$= 2.8 \text{ m/s}$$

Loss of energy

$$= \frac{1}{2}m_1u_1^2 + \frac{1}{2}m_2u_2^2 - \frac{1}{2}(m_1 + m_2)v^2$$

$$= \frac{1}{2} \times 40 \times 4^2 + \frac{1}{2} \times 60 \times 2^2 - \frac{1}{2}(40 + 60) \times (2.8)^2$$

$$= 320 + 120 - 392$$

$$= 48 \text{ J}$$

6. Take the mass as body 1 and the Earth as body 2. So,

$$u_1 = \sqrt{2gH},$$

$$v_1 = -\sqrt{2gh}$$

and $u_1 = v_2 = 0$

Using, $e = \frac{v_2 - v_1}{u_1 - u_2}$

$\therefore$ $e = \sqrt{\frac{h}{H}}$

7. Given that, $e = \frac{v}{u} \Rightarrow v = e\,u = 0.5\,u$

Now, percentage loss of energy

$$= \frac{\frac{1}{2}mu^2 - \frac{1}{2}mv^2}{\frac{1}{2}mu^2} \times 100$$

$$= \frac{\frac{1}{2}mu^2 - \frac{1}{2}m\frac{u^2}{4}}{\frac{1}{2}mu^2} \times 100$$

$$= \frac{3}{4} \times 100 = 75\%$$

8. Change in momentum $= mv - (-mv) = 2mv$

9. Let v_0 be the velocity with which the ball strikes the Earth first time and v_n be the velocity after nth rebound. According to the definition of coefficient of restitution, we have

$$e = \frac{v_1}{v_0} = \frac{v_2}{v_1} = \frac{v_3}{v_2} = \dots = \frac{v_n}{v_{n-1}}$$

Further $e^n = \frac{v_1}{v_0} \times \frac{v_2}{v_1} \times \frac{v_3}{v_2} \times \dots \times \frac{v_n}{v_{n-1}} = \frac{v_n}{v_0}$

Here, $v_0 = \sqrt{2gh}$

and $v_n = \sqrt{2gH}$

$\therefore$ $e^n = \frac{\sqrt{2gH}}{\sqrt{2gh}} = \frac{\sqrt{H}}{\sqrt{h}}$

$\Rightarrow$ $e^{2n} = \frac{H}{h}$

$\therefore$ $H = he^{2n}$

10. $H = he^{2n}$

$\therefore H = he^{2\times 2} = he^4$

14. On falling,

$$v = u + gt_1$$

$$v = 0 + gt_1$$

$$v = gt_1 \qquad \text{...(i)}$$

On rising,

$$v = u - gt_2$$

$$0 = u - gt_2$$

$\therefore$ $u = gt_2 \qquad$ ...(ii)

$$e = \frac{v}{u} = \frac{gt_1}{gt_2} = \frac{t_1}{t_2}$$

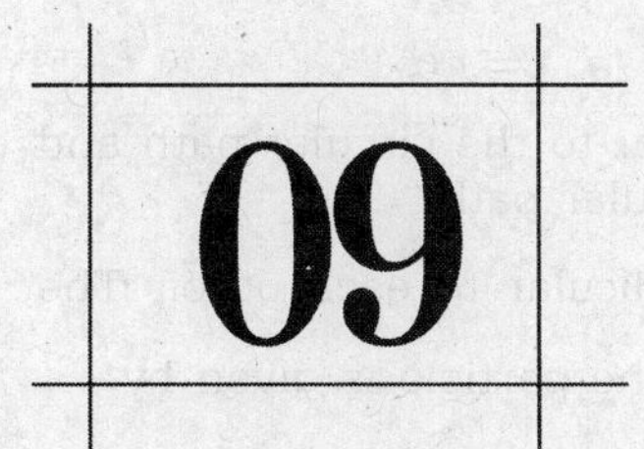

Circular Motion

Uniform Circular Motion

When a point object is moving on a circular path with a constant speed (*i.e.*, it covers equal distances on the circumference of the circle in equal intervals of time), then the motion of the object is said to be a uniform circular motion.

Time Period

In circular motion, the time period is defined as the time taken by the object to complete one revolution on its circular path.

It is generally denoted by T and is expressed in second.

Frequency

In circular motion, the frequency is defined as the number of revolutions completed by the object on its circular path in a unit time.

It is generally denoted by ν. Its unit is s^{-1} or hertz (Hz).

Relation between Time Period and Frequency

If ν is the frequency of revolution of an object in circular motion, then the object completes ν revolutions in 1 s. Therefore, the object will complete one revolution (called time period of revolution T say) in $\frac{1}{\nu}$ s.

$$\therefore \quad T = \frac{1}{\nu} \quad \text{or} \quad \nu = \frac{1}{T} \quad \text{or} \quad \nu T = 1$$

Angular Displacement

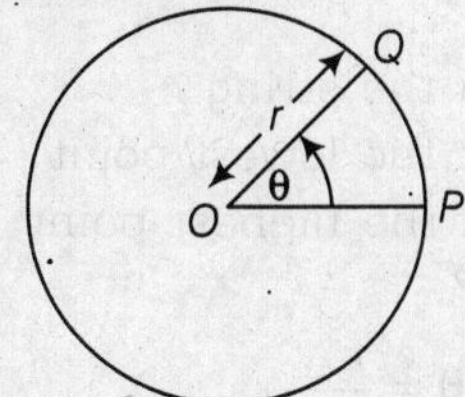

Here, θ is known as angular displacement of the object in time t.

Thus, angular displacement of the object in a given time, moving around a circular path is defined as the angle traced out by the radius vector at the centre of the circular path in the given time.

Since, $\quad \text{angle} = \frac{\text{Arc}}{\text{Radius}} \Rightarrow \theta = \frac{PQ}{r}$

The angle θ represents the magnitude of angular displacement and is expressed in radians (denoted by rad).

Angular Velocity

Angular velocity of an object in circular motion is defined as the time rate of change of its angular displacement.

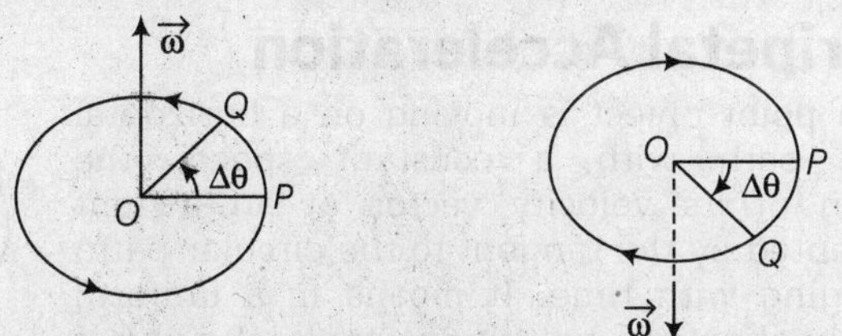

Angular velocity

$$\omega = \frac{\text{Angle traced}}{\text{Time taken}} = \lim_{\Delta t \to 0} \frac{\Delta\theta}{\Delta t} = \frac{d\theta}{dt}$$

Angular velocity is a vector quantity. Its direction is the same as that of $\Delta\vec{\theta}$.

Relation between Angular Velocity, Frequency and Time Period

Consider a point object describing a uniform circular motion with frequency ν and time period T. When the object completes one revolution, the angle traced at its axis of circular motion is 2π radians. It means, when time $t = T$, $\theta = 2\pi$ radians. Hence, angular velocity

$$\omega = \frac{\theta}{t} = \frac{2\pi}{T} = 2\pi\nu \qquad \left[\because T = \frac{1}{\nu}\right]$$

Relation between Angular Velocity and Linear Velocity

$$v = \omega r$$

Angular Acceleration

Angular acceleration of an object in circular motion is defined as the time rate of change of its angular velocity.

It is generally denoted by α. Let $\Delta\omega$ be the change in angular velocity of the object in time interval t and $t + \Delta t$, while moving on a circular path, then angular acceleration of the object will be

$$\alpha = \lim_{\Delta t \to 0} \frac{\Delta\omega}{\Delta t} = \frac{d\omega}{dt}$$

SI unit of angular acceleration is rad/s^2 and its dimensional formula is $[M^0L^0T^{-2}]$.

Relation between Linear Acceleration and Angular Acceleration

We know that, linear velocity v is related with angular velocity ω by the relation, $v = \omega r$.

On differentiating it with respect to time, we have

$$\frac{dv}{dt} = \frac{d}{dt}(\omega r) = \left(\frac{d\omega}{dt}\right) r$$

[$\because$ r is constant in circular motion.]

$$\Rightarrow \quad a = \alpha r$$

Where, a is the linear acceleration and α is the angular acceleration.

$$\therefore \quad a = \omega^2 r = \frac{v^2}{r}$$

Centripetal Acceleration

When a point object is moving on a horizontal circular path with a constant speed, the direction of its velocity vector at an instant (represented by the tangent to the circular path) is changing with time. It means in a uniform circular motion, the velocity vector of the object is changing with time. This indicates that the uniform circular motion is an example of accelerated motion.

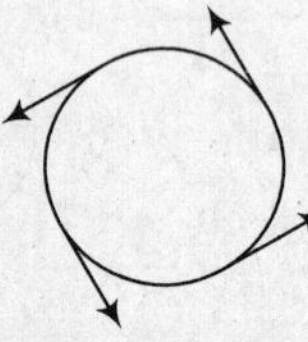

Acceleration acting on the object undergoing a uniform circular motion is called centripetal acceleration.

It always acts on the object along the radius towards the centre of the circular path.

Expression for centripetal acceleration,

$$|\vec{a}| = \frac{\Delta v}{\Delta t} = \omega^2 r = \left[\frac{v}{r}\right]^2 r = \frac{v^2}{r} = v\omega$$

Tangential Acceleration and Centripetal Acceleration

Consider a particle describing a circular path of radius r with centre at O. Let the linear speed of the particle be changing with time. Let at an instant, v be the linear speed, ω be the angular velocity and α be the angular acceleration of the particle.

The particle has two types of accelerations.

1. Centripetal Acceleration $(a_c) = \dfrac{v^2}{r} = v\omega$

   It acts along the radius and is directed towards the centre of the circular path.

2. Tangential Acceleration $(a_T) = r\alpha$

   It acts along the tangent to the circular path and in the plane of the circular path.

   $\vec{a}_c$ and $\vec{a}_T$ are perpendicular to each other. The total acceleration $\vec{a}$ of the particle is given by

   $$\vec{a} = \vec{a}_c + \vec{a}_T$$

   $$\therefore \quad |\vec{a}| = \sqrt{a_c^2 + a_T^2} = \sqrt{(v\omega)^2 + (r\alpha)^2}$$

SPECIAL CASES

Case I. If $a_T = 0$, the particle will have only centripetal acceleration. The particle will move on a circular path with constant angular velocity. The magnitude of centripetal acceleration, is $a_c = \dfrac{v^2}{r}$.

Case II. If $a_c = 0$, the particle will have only tangential acceleration. Now, the particle will accelerate along the tangent of the circular path.

Centripetal Force

A force that pulls an object moving in a circular path towards the centre of its path is known as centripetal force.

$$F = \frac{mv^2}{r} = mr\omega^2 = \frac{4\pi^2 mr}{T^2} = 4\pi^2 mrn^2$$

Centrifugal Force

A force that causes an object moving in a circular path to move out and away from the centre of its path is known as centrifugal force.

Minimum condition for a body to remain in a circular motion is centripetal force = centrifugal force.

Motion in a Vertical Circle

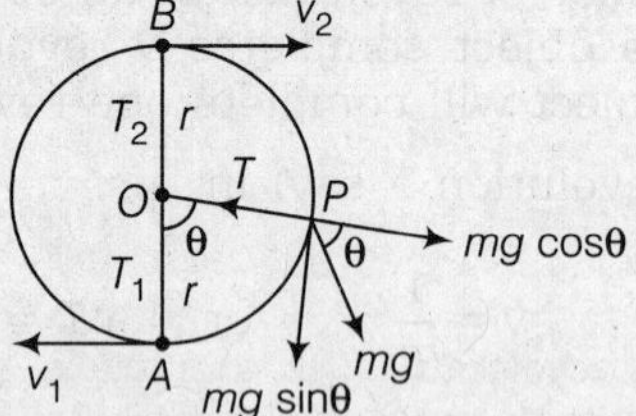

If m = Mass of an object

r = Radius

T = Tension in the string

v_1 = Velocity at the lowest point

v_2 = Velocity at the highest point

Equation at point P

$$T - mg\cos\theta = \frac{mv^2}{r}$$

At point A,

$$\theta = 0° \Rightarrow \cos 0° = 1$$

$$T_1 - mg = \frac{mv_1^2}{r}$$

At point B,

$$T_2 + mg = \frac{mv_2^2}{r} \quad [\because \cos 180° = -1]$$

v_2 will be minimum, if $T_2 = 0$

$$mg = \frac{mv_2^2}{r}$$

$$\therefore \quad v_2 = \sqrt{rg}$$

This is also known as critical velocity.

Note The minimum velocity at the highest point for a body to remain in a vertical circular motion.

Now, $\quad v_1^2 = v_2^2 + 2gh$

Here, $\quad v_2 = \sqrt{rg},\ h = 2r$

$$v_1^2 = rg + 2g \times 2r = 5rg$$

$$v_1 = \sqrt{5rg}$$

The minimum velocity at the lowest point for a body to remain in a vertical circular motion.

Note The difference in the tension of the string at the lowest and the highest point.

$$T_L - T_H = 6\,mg$$

Motion of a Car on a Level Road

Three forces act on the car

(i) It's weight, $= mg$

(ii) Normal reaction, $N = mg$

(iii) Frictional force, $F \le \mu N \le \mu\, mg$

Frictional force supplies the necessary centripetal force, so

$$F \le \mu\, mg = \frac{mv^2}{r}$$

$$v^2 \le \mu\, rg$$

$$\therefore \quad v_{max} = \sqrt{\mu rg}$$

Motion of a Car on a Banked Road

Banking is done

1. to reduce frictional wear and tear of tyres.
2. to avoid skidding.
3. to avoid overturning of vehicles.

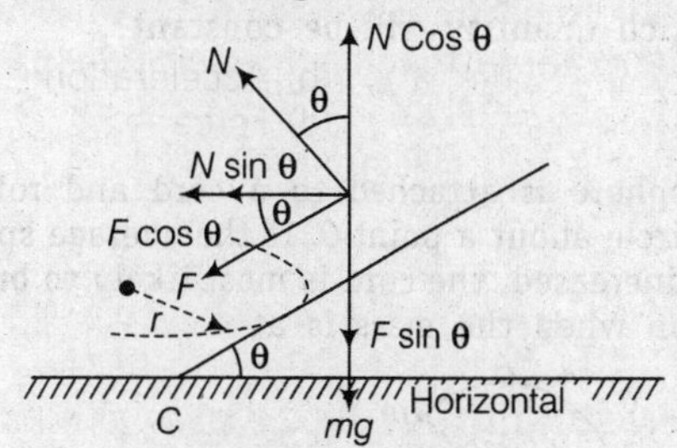

$$\tan\theta = \frac{v^2 - \mu\, rg}{rg + \mu v^2} \quad \ldots\text{(i)}$$

$$v^2 = rg\,\frac{\mu + \tan\theta}{1 - \mu\tan\theta} \quad \ldots\text{(ii)}$$

Eq. (i) gives the angle of banking for the maximum velocity v and Eq. (ii) gives the value of the maximum velocity which the vehicles should be allowed on a road banked at an angle θ.

Notes

- The value of μ is the minimum value of μ required. The value of v is the maximum allowable velocity.
- The best angle of banking θ, so that there is absolutely nil wear and tear due to frictional forces for the given values of v and r can be determined by putting $\mu = 0$ in this formula.

  If we put $\mu = 0$ in Eq. (i), we get

  $$\tan\theta = \frac{v^2}{rg}$$

  Further, for zero frictional wear and tear, the velocity for the given values of θ and r will be

  $$v = \sqrt{rg\tan\theta}$$

Practice Questions

Level I

1. The angular acceleration of a particle moving along a circular path with uniform speed is

(a) uniform but non-zero
(b) zero
(c) variable
(d) such as cannot be predicted from the given information

2. A particle moves in a circle of radius 0.5 m with a speed that uniformly increases. Find the angular acceleration of the particle, if it speed changes from 2.0 m/s to 4.0 m/s in 4.05.

(a) 1 rad/s (b) 2 rad/s
(c) 3 rad/s (d) 4 rad/s

3. A particle covers equal distances around a circular path, in equal intervals of time. Which of the following quantities connected with the motion of particle remains constant with time?

(a) Displacement (b) Velocity
(c) Speed (d) Acceleration

4. The speed of revolution of particle going around a circle is doubled and its angular speed is halved. What happens to the centripetal acceleration?

(a) Remains unchanged
(b) Halved
(c) Doubled
(d) Becomes four times

5. A body moving in circular motion, with constant speed, has constant

(a) velocity (b) acceleration
(c) kinetic energy (d) displacement

6. For a body rotating with constant speed in a horizontal circle, which quantity will be constant?

(a) Velocity (b) Acceleration
(c) KE (d) Force

7. A small sphere is attached to a cord and rotated in a vertical circle about a point *O*. If the average speed of the sphere is increased, the cord is most likely to break at the orientation when the mass is at

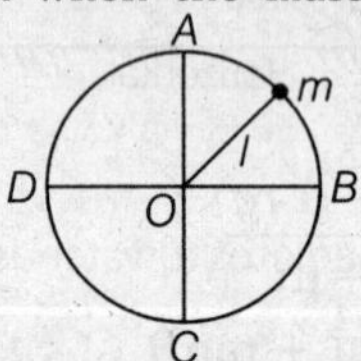

(a) bottom point *C* (b) at point *B*
(c) at point *D* (d) at point *A*

8. Which of the following is the relation of centripetal force?

(a) $\frac{mv}{r}$ (b) $\frac{mv^2}{r}$ (c) $\frac{mv^3}{r}$ (d) $\frac{mv^2}{r^2}$

9. A motor car travelling at 30 m/s on a circular road of radius 500 m. It is increasing its speed at the rate of 2 m / s^2. What is the acceleration?

(a) 2.7 m/s^2 (b) 3 m/s^2
(c) 2.5 m/s^2 (d) 2 m/s^2

10. The angular speed of the flywheel making 240 revolutions/min is

(a) 100π rad/s (b) 8π rad/s
(c) 180π rad/s (d) 200π rad/s

11. A ball of mass 0.25 kg attached to the end of a string of length 1.96 m is moving in a horizontal circle. The string will break if the tension is more than 25 N. What is the maximum speed with which the ball can be moved?

(a) 14 m/s (b) 3 m/s
(c) 4 m/s (d) 5 m/s

12. The angular velocity of the second needle of a watch λ will be

(a) $\frac{60}{\pi}$ (b) 2π (c) π (d) $\frac{\pi}{30}$

13. The minimum velocity at the lowest point in a vertical circular motion, to reach at the highest point is

(a) $\sqrt{rg}$ (b) $\sqrt{2rg}$
(c) $\sqrt{5rg}$ (d) $\sqrt{6rg}$

14. A bend in a level road has a radius of 100 m, the maximum speed which a car turning this bend may have without skidding, if coefficient of friction between the tyres and the road is 0.8.

(a) 28 m/s (b) 20 m/s
(c) 30 m/s (d) 40 m/s

15. Cause of separating butter from milk

(a) due to gravitational force
(b) due to centripetal force
(c) due to centrifugal force
(d) due to frictional force

Level II

1. A circular disc rotates at 60 rpm. A coin of 18 g is placed at a distance of 8 cm from the centre. Calculate the centrifugal force on the coin.

(a) 5.689×10^{-2} N (b) 7.689×10^{-2} N
(c) 4×10^{-2} N (d) 4.689×10^{-2} N

2. Maximum safe speed of a car on a circular track is 10 m/s, if the road is dry. When the road is wet, frictional coefficient becomes half, then the maximum safe speed will be

(a) 10 m/s (b) $5\sqrt{2}$ m/s
(c) $10\sqrt{2}$ m/s (d) 6 m/s

3. A particle hold on the top of a hemisphere of radius *R*. How much minimum horizontal velocity applied on that particle so that particle left the hemisphere without sliding?

(a) $\sqrt{gR}$ (b) $\sqrt{2gR}$ (c) $\sqrt{5gR}$ (d) gR

4. In a vertical circular motion, the difference between the tension at the lowest point and the highest point is

(a) $T_H - T_L = 6\,mg$ (b) $T_H - T_L = 5\,mg$
(c) $T_L - T_H = mg$ (d) $T_L - T_H = 6\,mg$

5. A car when passes through a convex bridge exerts force on it which is equal to

(a) $mg + \frac{mv^2}{r}$ (b) $\frac{mv^2}{r}$
(c) $mg - \frac{mv^2}{r}$ (d) None of these

Answers

Level I

1. (b)	**2.** (a)	**3.** (c)	**4.** (a)	**5.** (c)	**6.** (c)	**7.** (a)	**8.** (b)	**9.** (a)	**10.** (b)
11. (a)	**12.** (d)	**13.** (c)	**14.** (a)	**15.** (c)					

Level II

1. (a)	**2.** (b)	**3.** (a)	**4.** (d)	**5.** (c)

Hints and Solutions

Level I

1. As angular velocity of the particle is constant and hence angular acceleration is zero.

2. Tangential acceleration of the particle is

$$a_t = \frac{dv}{dt} = \frac{4.0 - 2.0}{4.0}$$
$$= 5.0$$

The angular acceleration is

$$\alpha = \frac{a_t}{r}$$
$$= \frac{0.5}{0.5} = 1 \text{ rad/s}$$

3. The direction of displacement, velocity and acceleration continuously changes.

4. $a = \frac{v^2}{r} = \frac{v \times v}{r}$

$$= \frac{v \times r\omega}{r} = v\omega$$

When, v is doubled and ω is halved, a remains unchanged.

5. When a body moves in circular motion with constant speed, its kinetic energy is constant.

6. Kinetic energy will be constant.

7. The largest tension T in the string is given by

$$T_{max} = \frac{mv^2}{r} + mg$$

8. $F_c = \frac{mv^2}{r}$

9. Here, $v = 30 \text{ m/s}$, $r = 500$ m, $a_T = 2 \text{ m/s}^2$

Centripetal acceleration,

$$a_c = \frac{v^2}{r} = \frac{30 \times 30}{500} = 1.8 \text{ m/s}^2$$

Here, a_T is acting tangential to the circular path and a_c is acting along the radius towards the centre of the circular path.

The effective acceleration,

$$a = \sqrt{a_c^2 + a_T^2}$$
$$= \sqrt{(1.8)^2 + (2)^2}$$
$$= 2.7 \text{ m/s}^2$$

10. Here, $\theta = 240 \times 2\pi$ rad and $t = 60$ s

$\therefore$ Angular speed, $\omega = \frac{\theta}{t} = \frac{240 \times 2\pi}{60} = 8\pi$ rad/s

11. We know that, $T = \frac{mv^2}{r}$

$$v = \sqrt{\left(\frac{Tr}{m}\right)}$$

$$\therefore \quad v = \sqrt{\left[\frac{(25 \times 1.96)}{0.25}\right]} = 14 \text{ m/s}$$

12. $\omega = \frac{2\pi}{T} = \frac{2\pi}{60} = \frac{\pi}{30}$

[$\because$ Period of the second needle of a watch is 60 s.]

14. Here, $r = 100$ m, $v = ?$, $\mu_s = 0.8$

As, $\quad v = \sqrt{\mu_s rg}$

$\therefore \quad v = \sqrt{0.8 \times 100 \times 9.8} = 28 \text{ m/s}$

Level II

1. Here, $n = 60 \text{ rpm} = \frac{60}{60} = 1 \text{ rps}$

$m = 18 \text{ g} = 18 \times 10^{-3}$ kg, $r = 8 \text{ cm} = 8 \times 10^{-2}$ m

Centrifugal force,

$$F = mr\omega^2 = mr(2\pi n)^2 = 4\pi^2 mrn^2$$
$$= 4 \times \frac{22}{7} \times \frac{22}{7} \times (18 \times 10^{-3}) \times (8 \times 10^{-2}) \times 1^2$$
$$= 5.689 \times 10^{-2} \text{ N}$$

2. $\quad v_{max} = \sqrt{\mu gr}$

$\therefore \quad v_{max} \propto \sqrt{\mu}$

$$\frac{v'_{max}}{v_{max}} = \sqrt{\frac{\mu'}{\mu}} = \sqrt{\frac{\frac{\mu}{2}}{\mu}} = \frac{1}{\sqrt{2}}$$

$$v'_{max} = \frac{v_{max}}{\sqrt{2}} = \frac{10}{\sqrt{2}} = 5\sqrt{2} \text{ m/s}$$

3. $mg - N = \frac{mv^2}{R}$

At $\quad N = 0$

$$\therefore \quad mg = \frac{mv^2}{R}$$
$$v = \sqrt{gR}$$

10

Rotational and Moment of Inertia

Centre of Mass of a System of Particles

The centre of mass of the system is defined as that point at which the mass of whole system is thought to be concentrated and its motion would be same as that of the system if the external forces acting on it are directly applied to that point.

Centre of Mass of a Rigid Body

The centre of mass of a rigid body is a fixed point and it does not change when external forces are applied on the rigid body.

The centre of mass of a rigid body depends upon the shape of the body and the way the mass of a body is distributed throughout its volume.

Centre of mass can lie outside the rigid body. *e.g.,* The centre of mass of a circular ring is at its geometrical centre.

Determination of Centre of Mass (CM)

***Case* 1.** Centre of mass of such objects whose mass is uniformly distributed about a point will be that point itself. *e.g.,* CM of circular ring, disc, rod and sphere of uniform density will be their centres of symmetry.

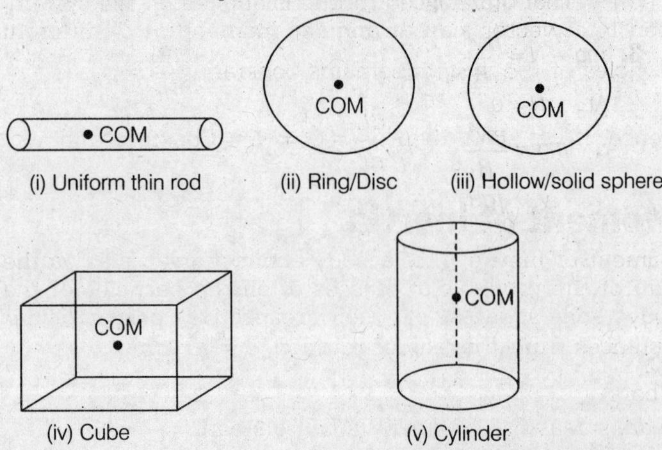

(i) Uniform thin rod (ii) Ring/Disc (iii) Hollow/solid sphere

(iv) Cube (v) Cylinder

Centre of mass is at centroid which is the point of intersection of medians.

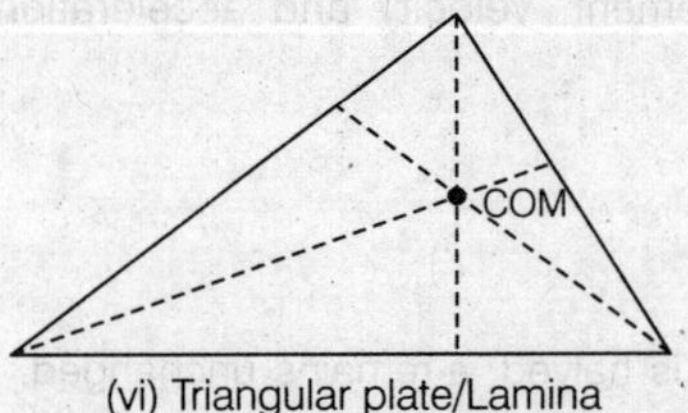

(vi) Triangular plate/Lamina

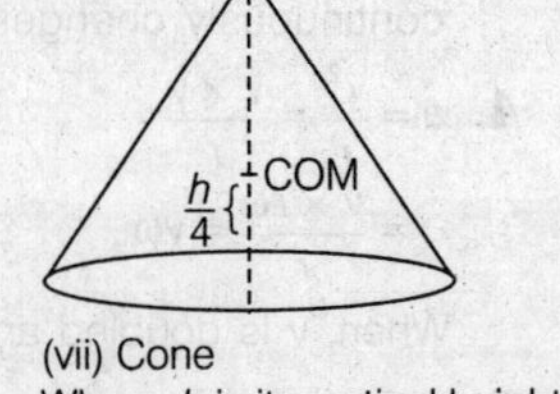

(vii) Cone
Where, h is its vertical height.

***Case* 2. CM of Discrete Point Masses**

y
• $M_4:(x_4, y_4)$
• $M_3:(x_3, y_3)$
• CM:(x, y)
• $M_2:(x_2, y_2)$
• $M_1:(x_1, y_1)$
O x

The coordinates of CM : $(\bar{x}, \bar{y})$ will be given by

$$\bar{x} = \frac{m_1x_1 + m_2x_2 + m_3x_3 + \ldots}{m_1 + m_2 + m_3 + \ldots}$$

$$\bar{y} = \frac{m_1y_1 + m_2y_2 + m_3y_3 + \ldots}{m_1 + m_2 + m_3 + \ldots}$$

In terms of vector notations we can write

$$\vec{r}_{CM} = \frac{m_1\vec{r}_1 + m_2\vec{r}_2 + \ldots}{m_1 + m_2 + \ldots}$$

Note In case of two bodies of mass m_1 and m_2, kept at a distance r apart,

$$r_1 = \frac{m_2}{m_1 + m_2} r$$

and

$$r_2 = \frac{m_1}{m_1 + m_2} r$$

Where, r_1 and r_2 are the distances of m_1 and m_2 from their centre of mass.

Case 3. CM of Continuous Figures or Bodies is Determined by Integration Method

The bodies which are not made of discrete particles but have continuous distribution of matter, then the coordinates for the centre of mass can be located by following formulae

$$X_{COM} = \frac{\int x\,dm}{\int dm} \Rightarrow X_{COM} = \frac{\int x\,dm}{M};$$

$$Y_{COM} = \frac{\int y\,dm}{\int dm} \Rightarrow Y_{COM} = \frac{\int y\,dm}{M}$$

$$Z_{COM} = \frac{\int z\,dm}{\int dm} \Rightarrow Z_{COM} = \frac{\int z\,dm}{M}$$

Where, dm is small element having mass dm and x, y and z are distance of this element from X, Y and Z axes, respectively.

Motion of Centre of Mass

The centre of mass of a system of particles moves as if all the mass of the system was concentrated at the centre of mass and all the external forces were applied at that point.

$$MA = F_{ext}$$

For an isolated system

$$F_{ext} = 0$$

$$\therefore \quad MA = 0$$

$$\Rightarrow \quad M\frac{d}{dt}(V_{CM}) = 0$$

$$\Rightarrow \quad V_{CM} = \text{Constant}$$

Centre of mass of an isolated system has a constant velocity.

Difference between Circular and Rotational Motion

If a particle moves along a circle, it is called circular motion. However, if a rigid body moves along a circle, it is called rotational motion.

Couple

Two equal and opposite forces with some finite perpendicular distance between them constitute a couple of forces.

Moment of a Couple of Forces

Torque ($\vec{\tau}$) is defined as the product of the magnitude of any of the two forces and the perpendicular distance between the two forces. It is taken as positive in case it has anti-clockwise turning effect and negative, if it has clockwise turning effect.

Vectorially, $\quad \vec{\tau} = \vec{r} \times \vec{F}$

Where, $\vec{r}$ is the position vector of any point in the direction of one of the two forces with respect to any point in the direction of the other force taken as origin.

The perpendicular distance is called moment arm. The net resultant force in case of a couple of forces is always zero. Torque produces turning effect without causing any translation/linear effect.

Torque

It is the moment of a force about a point. It is the product of the force and the perpendicular distance of the point from the direction of the force.

Vectorially,

$$\vec{\tau} = \vec{r} \times \vec{F}$$

Where,

$\vec{\tau}$ = Torque

$\vec{r}$ = position vector of any point in the direction of the force

$\vec{F}$ = assuming the point about which moment is required, as origin.

Importance of Torque

Force causes linear acceleration while torque causes angular acceleration.

Angular Momentum ($\vec{L}$) of a Particle

Angular momentum ($\vec{L}$) of a particle about a point is defined as the moment of momentum of the particle about that point.

Vectorially, $\quad \vec{L} = \vec{r} \times \vec{p}$

Relation between $\vec{\tau}$ and $\vec{L}$ in Case of One Particle

$$\frac{d\vec{L}}{dt} = \vec{\tau}$$

The net external torque applied on a system is equal to the rate of change of angular momentum of the system.

Law of Conservation of Angular Momentum

If no external unbalanced torque is applied on the system, then total vector sum of angular momentum of different particles of the system remains constant. $\frac{dL}{dt} = \tau_{ext}$

Hence, if $\tau_{ext} = 0$, then $\frac{dL}{dt} = 0 \Rightarrow L = \text{Constant}$

Moment of Inertia

Moment of Inertia (I) of a body about a given axis as the sum of the products of masses of all the particles of the body and squares of their respective perpendicular distances from the axis of rotation. $I = \int r^2\,dm$

Where,

dm = Mass of extremely small element.

r = Perpendicular distance r from the axis of rotation.

Relation between Angular Momentum and Moment of Inertia

$$\vec{L} = \vec{I}\omega$$

Angular momentum = Inertia × Angular velocity

Relation between Torque (τ) and Moment of Inertia (I)

$$\vec{\tau} = I\vec{\alpha}$$

Torque = Moment of Inertia × Angular acceleration.

Comparison of Linear and Rotation Motion

S.No.	Linear Motion	Rotational Motion
1.	Distance/Displacement (s)	Angle or angular displacement (θ)
2.	Linear velocity $v = \dfrac{ds}{dt}$	Angular velocity $\omega = \dfrac{d\theta}{dt}$
3.	Linear acceleration $a = \dfrac{dv}{dt} = \dfrac{d^2s}{dt^2} = v \cdot \dfrac{dv}{ds}$	Angular acceleration $\alpha = \dfrac{d\omega}{dt} = \dfrac{d^2\theta}{dt^2} = \omega \cdot \dfrac{d\omega}{d\theta}$
4.	Mass (m)	Moment of inertia (I)
5.	Linear momentum $p = mv$	Angular momentum $L = I\omega$
6.	Force $F = ma$	Torque $\tau = I\alpha$
7.	Also, force $F = \dfrac{dp}{dt}$	Also, torque $\tau = \dfrac{dL}{dt}$
8.	Translational KE $= \dfrac{1}{2}mv^2 = \dfrac{p^2}{2m}$	Rotational KE $= \dfrac{1}{2}I\omega^2 = \dfrac{L^2}{2I}$
9.	Work done, $W = \int \vec{F} \cdot d\vec{s} = Fs$	Work done, $W = \int \vec{\tau} \cdot d\vec{\theta} = \tau\theta$
10.	Power $P = Fv$	Power $P = \tau\omega$
11.	Linear momentum of a system is conserved when no external force acts on the system. (Principle of conservation of linear momentum)	Angular momentum of a system is conserved when no external torque acts on the system. (Principle of conservation of angular momentum)
12.	Equations of translational motion (i) $v = u + at$ (ii) $s = ut + \dfrac{1}{2}at^2$ (iii) $v^2 - u^2 = 2as$ Where, the symbols have their usual meaning.	Equations of rotational motion (i) $\omega_f = \omega_i + \alpha t$ (ii) $\theta = \omega_i t + \dfrac{1}{2}\alpha t^2$ (iii) $\omega_f^2 - \omega_i^2 = 2\alpha\theta$ Where, the symbols have their usual meaning.
13.	Distance travelled or displacement in nth second $S_{nth} = u + \dfrac{a}{2}(2n-1)$	Angle traced out or angular displacement in nth second $\theta_{nth} = \omega_i + \dfrac{\alpha}{2}(2n-1)$

Theorem of Perpendicular Axes

It states that the moment of inertia of a plane lamina about an axis perpendicular to its plane is equal to the sum of the moments of inertia of the lamina about any two mutually perpendicular axes in its plane and intersecting each other at the point, where the perpen- dicular axis passes through it.

Mathematically, $I = I_x + I_y$, where X and Y-axes lie in the plane of the lamina and z-axis is perpendicular to its plane and passes through the point of intersection of X and Y-axes.

Theorem of Parallel Axes

It states that the moment of inertia of a rigid body about any axis is equal to its moment of inertia about a parallel axis through its centre of mass plus the product of the mass of the body and the square of the perpendicular distance between the axes.

Mathematically, $I = I_G + Mh^2$, where I_G is moment of inertia of the body about an axis through its centre of mass and h, the distance between the two axes.

Table of Moments of Inertia

Body		Axis of Rotation	Sketch	Moment of Inertia (I)
Thin rod of length l and mass M	(i)	passing through centre and perpendicular to the rod		$\frac{Ml^2}{12}$
	(ii)	about one of its ends		$\frac{Ml^2}{3}$
Uniform circular ring of radius R and mass M	(i)	about an axis passing through centre and perpendicular to its plane.		MR^2
	(ii)	about a diameter		$\frac{1}{2}MR^2$
	(iii)	about a tangent in its own plane		$\frac{3}{2}MR^2$
	(iv)	about a tangent perpendicular to its plane		$2MR^2$
Uniform circular disc of radius R and mass M	(i)	about an axis passing through centre and perpendicular to its plane		$\frac{1}{2}MR^2$
	(ii)	about a diameter		$\frac{1}{4}MR^2$
	(iii)	about a tangent in its own plane		$\frac{5}{4}MR^2$
	(iv)	about a tangent perpendicular to its plane		$\frac{3}{2}MR^2$
Solid sphere of radius R and mass M	(i)	about its diameter		$\frac{2}{5}MR^2$

Body	Axis of Rotation	Sketch	Moment of Inertia (I)
	(ii) about a tangential axis		$\frac{7}{5}MR^2$
Solid cylinder of length l, radius R and mass M	(i) about its own axis		$\frac{1}{2}MR^2$
	(ii) about an axis passing through centre of gravity and perpendicular to its own axis		$M\left[\frac{l^2}{12}+\frac{R^2}{4}\right]$
	(iii) about the diameter of one of the faces of cylinder		$M\left[\frac{l^2}{3}+\frac{R^2}{4}\right]$

Kinetic Energy of Rolling Body

Let mass $= m$

Linear velocity $= v$,

Angular velocity $= \omega$, then

$$E_k = \frac{1}{2}mv^2 + \frac{1}{2}I\omega^2$$

Now, $\omega = \frac{v}{r}$

$\because$ $E_k = \frac{1}{2}mv^2 + \frac{1}{2}I\left(\frac{v^2}{r^2}\right)$

Special Cases

Case I. If rolling body of radius r and mass m be a solid sphere, then

$$I = \frac{2}{5}mr^2$$

Now, putting the value of I in the Eq.

$$E_k = \frac{1}{2}mv^2 + \frac{1}{2}I\left(\frac{v^2}{r^2}\right)$$

$$E_k = \frac{1}{2}mv^2 + \frac{1}{2}\times\frac{2}{5}mr^2\times\frac{v^2}{r^2}$$

$$= \frac{1}{2}mv^2 + \frac{2}{10}mv^2$$

$$= \frac{1}{2}mv^2 + \frac{1}{5}mv^2 = \frac{7}{10}mv^2$$

Case II. If rolling body of radius r and mass m be a hollow sphere, then

$$I = \frac{2}{3}mr^2$$

$\therefore$ $E_k = \frac{1}{2}mv^2 + \frac{1}{2}\times\frac{2}{3}mr^2\times\frac{v^2}{r^2}$

$$= \frac{1}{2}mv^2 + \frac{1}{3}mv^2$$

$$= \frac{5}{6}mv^2$$

Case III. If rolling body of radius r and mass m be a solid cylinder, then

$$I = \frac{1}{2}mr^2$$

$\therefore$ $E_k = \frac{1}{2}mv^2 + \frac{1}{2}\times\frac{1}{2}mr^2\times\frac{v^2}{r^2}$

$$= \frac{1}{2}mv^2 + \frac{1}{4}mv^2 = \frac{3}{4}mv^2$$

IMPORTANT FACTS

- Both the velocity and acceleration of the centre of the mass of the solid cylinder rolling down an inclined plane without slipping are independent of the mass and radius of the solid cylinder. This means all homogeneous solid cylinders would experience the same velocity and acceleration on a given incline. Similarly, it applies to all solid spheres too.
- In all these cases, mass does not play any role.
- In case of a solid sphere, a solid cylinder a disc, a spherical shell and cylindrical shell a ring, at any point on the incline or when they reach ground $v_{ring} > v_{sph\ shell} > v_{disc} > v_{sphere}$ and $t_{ring} < t_{sph\ shell} < t_{disc} < t_{sphere}$

Practice Questions

Level I

1. The centre of mass of a body is moving with a uniform velocity of 10 cm/s. Three forces are applied on the body, which are in equilibrium. The velocity of centre of mass would become

(a) zero (b) > 10 cm/s
(c) < 10 cm/s (d) 10 cm/s

2. A fire cracker following parabolic path explodes in mid air. The centre of mass of all the fragments will follow a path

(a) along horizontal (b) along vertical
(c) along same parabola (d) along circle

3. The correct relation between linear velocity $\vec{\mathbf{v}}$ and angular velocity $\vec{\omega}$ of a particle is

(a) $\vec{\mathbf{v}} = \vec{\omega} \times \vec{\mathbf{r}}$ (b) $\vec{\omega} = \vec{\mathbf{v}} \times \vec{\mathbf{r}}$
(c) $\vec{\omega} = \vec{\mathbf{r}} \times \vec{\mathbf{v}}$ (d) $\vec{\mathbf{v}} = \vec{\mathbf{r}} \times \vec{\omega}$

4. The expression for torque in polar coordinates is

(a) $\tau = rF \sin\phi$ (b) $\tau = rF \cos\phi$
(c) $\tau = rF \tan\phi$ (d) $\tau = \frac{F \sin\phi}{r}$

5. The moment of linear momentum is called

(a) torque (b) couple
(c) angular momentum (d) None of these

6. To maintain a rotor at a uniform angular speed of 100 s^{-1}, an engine needs to transmit a torque of 90 N-m. The power of engine must be

(a) 9 kW (b) 90 kW (c) 9 MW (d) 90 MW

7. The correct relation between torque τ and angular momentum L is

(a) $\tau = \frac{dL}{dt}$ (b) $L = \frac{d\tau}{dt}$
(c) $\tau = L \times t$ (d) $L = \tau \times t$

8. A rigid body is said to be in translational equilibrium, when its velocity $\vec{\mathbf{v}}$ is

(a) zero (b) constant
(c) constant or zero (d) Neither constant nor zero

9. A rigid body is said to be in partial equilibrium, when it is in

(a) translational equilibrium only
(b) rotational equilibrium only
(c) Either (a) or (b)
(d) Neither (a) nor (b)

10. Moment of inertia of a body depends upon

(a) mass of body
(b) shape and size of body
(c) position and orientation of axis of rotation
(d) All of the above

11. Formation of a neutron star is explained on the basis of

(a) conservation of linear momentum
(b) conservation of energy
(c) conservation of angular momentum
(d) None of the above

12. Moment of inertia of a uniform circular ring of mass 2 kg and diameter 1 m about its diameter is

(a) 0.25 kg m^2 (b) 0.5 kg m^2
(c) 1 kg m^2 (d) 2 kg m^2

13. The radius of gyration of a uniform circular disc of radius R, about any diameter of the disc is

(a) $K = R$ (b) $K = \frac{R}{2}$
(c) $K = 2R$ (d) None of these

14. Moment of inertia of a hollow cylinder of mass M and radius R, about the axis of cylinder is

(a) $\frac{1}{2}MR^2$ (b) MR^2 (c) $\frac{2}{3}MR^2$ (d) $\frac{2}{5}MR^2$

15. Kinetic energy of a body rolling without slipping is

(a) $K = \frac{1}{2}mv^2$ (b) $K = \frac{1}{2}I\omega^2$
(c) $K = \frac{1}{2}mv^2 + \frac{1}{2}I\omega^2$ (d) $K = \frac{1}{2}mv^2 - \frac{1}{2}I\omega^2$

16. Acceleration of a solid cylinder rolling without slipping down an incline of inclination θ is

(a) $\frac{2}{3}g\sin\theta$ (b) $\frac{2}{3}g\cos\theta$ (c) $\frac{2}{3}g$ (d) $\frac{2}{3}g\tan\theta$

17. The rotational angular of force is

(a) momentum (b) angular momentum
(c) torque (d) None of these

18. A grindstone of moment of inertia 6 kg m^2 is found to have a speed of 150 rpm, 10 sec after starting from rest. Torque applied is

(a) 6π Ns (b) 3π Ns
(c) 9π Ns (d) 12π Ns

19. What would be the length of the day, if Earth were to shrink suddenly to $\frac{1}{64}$th of its original volume?

(a) 24 h (b) 12 h (c) 6 h (d) 1.5 h

20. If the moment of inertia of two rotating bodies A and B is such that $I_A > I_B$ and have equal angular moments, then the relation between their kinetic energy K_A and K_B is

(a) $K_A > K_B$ (b) $K_A = K_B$
(c) $K_B > K_A$ (d) $K_A = K_B^2$

21. A point of a system on which whole mass centred called

(a) centre of gravity of that body
(b) centre of mass of that body
(c) mean centre of that body
(d) geometrical centre of that body

22. Two particle of same masses, one is rest and the other is accelerated with $\bar{\mathbf{a}}$. The acceleration of the centre of mass of this system will be

(a) zero (b) $\bar{\mathbf{a}}$ (c) $\frac{\bar{\mathbf{a}}}{2}$ (d) $2\bar{\mathbf{a}}$

23. The distance between two particles of masses m and $2m$ is r. If place of these masses are exchange then the displacement of the centre of mass will become

(a) $\frac{r}{3}$ (b) $\frac{r}{6}$

(d) $\frac{r}{2}$ (d) unchanged

24. If mass of a body be M and moment of inertia around an axis be I, then rotational radius around that axis be

(a) $\frac{I}{M}$ (b) $\sqrt{\frac{M}{I}}$

(c) $\frac{I^2}{M}$ (d) $\sqrt{\frac{I}{M}}$

25. When a disc rotates with uniform angular velocity, which of the following is not true?

(a) The sense of rotation remains same
(b) The orientation of the axis of rotation remain same
(c) The speed of rotation is non-zero and remain same
(d) The angular acceleration is non-zero and remain same

26. Two cars of masses m_1 and m_2 are moving in a circles of radius r_1 and r_2, respectively. The speed of these two cars are such that each car complete one rotation in time t. The ratio of angular momentum of first and second car is

(a) $m_1 : m_2$ (b) $m_1r_1^2 : m_2r_2^2$
(c) $r_1 : r_2$ (d) $m_1r_1 : m_2r_2$

27. Two particles of same masses are located on x-axis at the distance of 2 unit and 4 unit respectively from the origin. The distance of resultant centre of mass from origin will be

(a) 6 unit (b) 2 unit (c) 3 unit (d) zero

28. A circular plate have unit mass and unit diameter. What will be the moment of inertia around a diameter?

(a) $\frac{1}{2}$ unit (b) $\frac{1}{8}$ unit

(c) $\frac{1}{4}$ unit (d) $\frac{1}{16}$ unit

29. The SI unit of angular momentum is

(a) kg-ms (b) kg m/s
(c) kg m^2/s (d) None of these

30. Which of the following relation is correct?

(a) $\theta = \omega t$ (b) $\theta = \frac{\omega}{t}$

(c) $\theta = \frac{t}{\omega}$ (d) None of these

31. A particle of mass M is moving with constant velocity parallel to x-axis. Its angular momentum with respect to origin will be

(a) zero (b) decrease (c) constant (d) increase

32. Moment of linear momentum known as

(a) torque (b) angular momentum
(c) impulse of force (d) pair of forces

Level II

1. What is the moment of inertia of a solid sphere of density ρ and radius R about its diameter?

(a) $\frac{105}{176}R^5\rho$ (b) $\frac{105}{176}R^2\rho$

(c) $\frac{176}{105}R^5\rho$ (d) $\frac{176}{105}R^2\rho$

2. A particle moves in a circle of radius 0.25 m at 2 rps. The acceleration of the particle (in m/s^2) is

(a) π^2 (b) $8\pi^2$
(c) $4\pi^2$ (d) $2\pi^2$

3. Angular momentum is

(a) a polar vector (b) an axial vector
(c) a scalar (d) None of these

4. If a running boy jumps on a rotating table, which of the following is conserved?

(a) Linear momentum (b) Kinetic energy
(c) Angular momentum (d) None of these

5. A gymnast takes turns with her arms and legs stretched. When she pulls her arms and legs

(a) the angular velocity decreases
(b) the moment of inertia decreases
(c) the angular velocity stays constant
(d) the angular momentum increases

6. two identical particles move towards each other with velocity $2v$ and v, respectively. The velocity of centre of mass is

(a) v (b) $\frac{v}{3}$ (c) $\frac{v}{2}$ (d) zero

7. Moment of inertia of a circular wire of mass M and radius R about its diameter is

(a) $\frac{MR^2}{2}$ (b) MR^2 (c) $2MR^2$ (d) $\frac{MR^2}{4}$

8. A particles performing uniform circular motion. Its angular frequency is doubled and its kinetic energy halved, then the new angular momentum is

(a) $\frac{L}{4}$ (b) $2L$ (c) $4L$ (d) $\frac{L}{2}$

9. A solid sphere is rotating in free space. If the radius of the sphere is increased keeping mass same which one of the following will not be affected?

(a) Angular velocity
(b) Angular momentum
(c) Moment of inertia
(d) Rotational kinetic energy

10. Consider a system of two particles having masses m_1 and m_2. If the particle of mass m_1 is pushed towards the mass centre of particles through a distance d, by what distance would the particle of mass m_2 move so as to keep the mass centre of particles at the original position?

(a) $\frac{m_2}{m_1}d$ (b) $\frac{m_1}{m_1 + m_2}d$ (c) $\frac{m_1}{m_2}d$ (d) d

11. The moment of inertia of a uniform circular disc of radius R and mass M about an axis passing from the edge of the disc and normal to the disc is

(a) MR^2 (b) $\frac{1}{2}MR^2$ (c) $\frac{3}{2}MR^2$ (d) $\frac{7}{2}MR^2$

12. A mass is tied to a string and rotated in a vertical circle, the minimum velocity of the body at the top is

(a) $\sqrt{gr}$ (b) $\frac{g}{r}$ (c) $\left(\frac{g}{r}\right)^{\frac{3}{2}}$ (d) gr

13. The moment of inertia of a disc of mass M and radius R about an axis, which is tangential to the circumference of the disc and parallel to its diameter, is

(a) $\frac{3}{2}MR^2$ (b) $\frac{2}{3}MR^2$ (c) $\frac{5}{4}MR^2$ (d) $\frac{4}{5}MR^2$

14. Two bodies have their moments of inertia l and $2l$ respectively about their axis of rotation. If their kinetic energies of rotation are equal, their angular momenta will be in the ratio

(a) 2 : 1 (b) 1 : 2 (c) $\sqrt{2}$: 1 (d) 1: $\sqrt{2}$

15. A ball rolls without slipping. The radius of gyration of the ball about an axis passing through its centre of mass is K. If radius of the ball be R, then the fraction of total energy associated with its rotational energy will be

(a) $\frac{R^2}{K^2+R^2}$ (b) $\frac{K^2+R^2}{R^2}$ (c) $\frac{K^2}{R^2}$ (d) $\frac{K^2}{K^2+R^2}$

16. Moment of inertia does not depend upon

(a) angular velocity of body
(b) shape and size
(c) mass
(d) position of axis of rotation

17. A sphere of mass 2000 g and radius 5 cm is rotating at the rate of 300 rpm. Then, the torque required to stop it in 2π revolutions, is

(a) 1.6×10^2 dyne cm (b) 1.6×10^3 dyne cm
(c) 2.5×10^4 dyne cm (d) 2.5×10^5 dyne cm

18. Five masses are placed in a plane as shown in figure. The coordinates of the centre of mass are nearest to

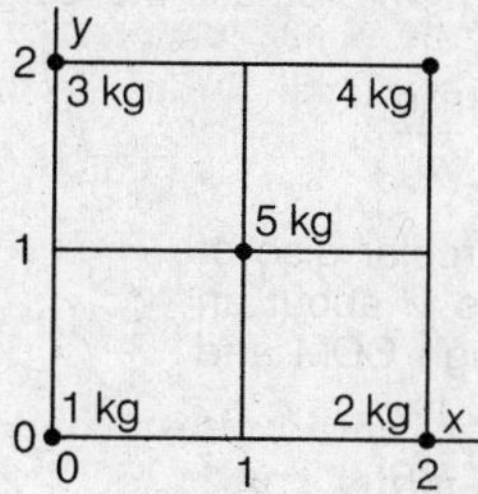

(a) 1.2, 1.4 (b) 1.3, 1.1
(c) 1.1, 1.3 (d) 1.0, 1.0

19. A sphere rolls down on a inclined plane of inclination θ. What is the acceleration as the sphere reaches bottom?

(a) $\frac{5}{7}g\sin\theta$ (b) $\frac{3}{5}g\sin\theta$ (c) $\frac{2}{7}g\sin\theta$ (d) $\frac{2}{5}g\sin\theta$

20. Two particles A and B, initially at rest, moves towards each other under a mutual force of attraction. At the instant when the speed of A is v and the speed of B is $2v$, the speed of centre of mass is

(a) zero (b) v (c) $1.5v$ (d) $3v$

Answers

Level I

1. (d)	**2.** (c)	**3.** (a)	**4.** (a)	**5.** (c)	**6.** (a)	**7.** (a)	**8.** (c)	**9.** (c)	**10.** (d)
11. (c)	**12.** (a)	**13.** (b)	**14.** (b)	**15.** (c)	**16.** (a)	**17.** (c)	**18.** (b)	**19.** (d)	**20.** (c)
21. (b)	**22.** (b)	**23.** (a)	**24.** (b)	**25.** (d)	**26.** (d)	**27.** (c)	**28.** (d)	**29.** (b)	**30.** (a)
31. (b)	**32.** (d)								

Level II

1. (c)	**2.** (c)	**3.** (b)	**4.** (c)	**5.** (b)	**6.** (c)	**7.** (a)	**8.** (a)	**9.** (b)	**10.** (c)
11. (c)	**12.** (a)	**13.** (c)	**14.** (d)	**15.** (d)	**16.** (a)	**17.** (d)	**18.** (c)	**19.** (a)	**20.** (a)

Hints and Solutions

Level II

1. For solid sphere

$$I = \frac{2}{5}MR^2 = \frac{2}{5}\left(\frac{4}{3}\pi R^3\rho\right)R^2 = \frac{8}{15} \times \frac{22}{7}R^5\rho = \frac{176}{105}R^5\rho$$

2. Centripetal acceleration

$$a_c = 4\pi^2 v^2 r = 4\pi^2 \times 2 \times 2 \times 025 = 4\pi^2 \text{ m/s}^2$$

3. Angular momentum $\vec{L}$ is defined as $\vec{L} = \vec{r} \times m(\vec{v})$, so $\vec{L}$ is an axial vector.

4. The boy does not exert a torque to rotating table by jumping, so angular momentum is

conserved *i.e.*, $\frac{d\vec{L}}{dt} = 0 \Rightarrow \vec{L} = \text{Constant}$

5. Since, no external torque act on gymnast, so angular momentum ($L = I\omega$) is conserved. After pulling her arms and legs, the angular velocity increases but moment of inertia of gymnast, decreases in, such a way that angular momentum remains constant.

6. Conserving linear momentum

$$2Mv_c = 2Mv - Mv \Rightarrow v_c = v/2$$

8. Angular momentum $\propto \dfrac{1}{\text{Angular frequency}} \propto$ Kinetic energy

$$\Rightarrow \quad \vec{L} = \frac{KE}{\omega}$$

$$\frac{L_1}{L_2} = \left(\frac{KE_1}{\omega_1}\right) \times \frac{\omega_2}{KE_2} = 4 \Rightarrow L_2 = \frac{L}{4}$$

9. Angular momentum will remain the same, since external torque is zero.

10. $m_1 d = m_2 d_2 \Rightarrow d_2 = \dfrac{m_1 d}{m_2}.$

11. MI of a uniform circular disc of radius R and mass M about an axis passing through COM and normal to the disc is

$$I_{com} = \frac{1}{2} MR^2$$

From parallel axis theorem

$$I_T = I_{COM} + MR^2 = \frac{1}{2} MR^2 + MR^2$$

$$= \frac{3}{2} MR^2$$

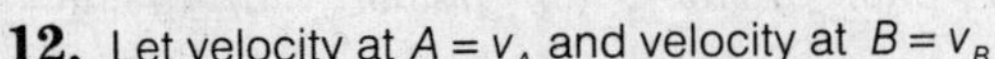

12. Let velocity at $A = v_A$ and velocity at $B = v_B$

Applying conservation of energy at A and B

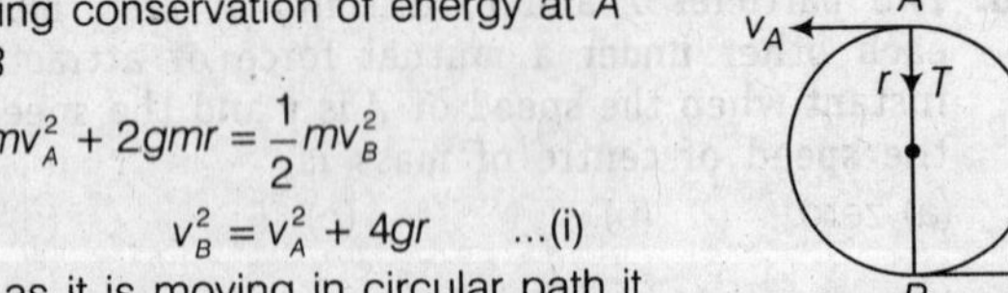

$$\frac{1}{2} mv_A^2 + 2gmr = \frac{1}{2} mv_B^2$$

$$v_B^2 = v_A^2 + 4gr \quad \text{...(i)}$$

Now, as it is moving in circular path it has centripetal force.

At point $A \Rightarrow T + mg = \dfrac{mv_A^2}{r}$

For minimum velocity $T \geq 0$

$$\Rightarrow \quad \frac{mv_A^2}{r} \geq mg \quad \Rightarrow \quad v_A^2 \geq gr \quad \Rightarrow v_A \geq \sqrt{gr}$$

13. Moment of inertia of disc about its diameter is $I_d = \dfrac{1}{4} MR^2$

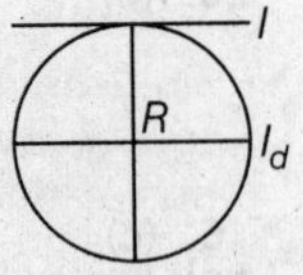

MI of disc about a tangent passing through rim and in the plane of disc is

$$I = I_G + MR^2 = \frac{1}{4} MR^2 + MR^2 = \frac{5}{4} MR^2$$

14. $K = \dfrac{L^2}{2I} \quad \Rightarrow \quad L^2 = 2KI \quad \Rightarrow \quad L = \sqrt{2KI}$

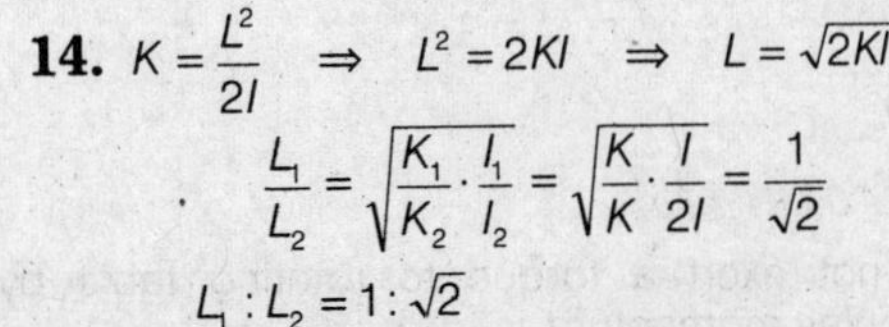

$$\frac{L_1}{L_2} = \sqrt{\frac{K_1}{K_2} \cdot \frac{I_1}{I_2}} = \sqrt{\frac{K}{K} \cdot \frac{I}{2I}} = \frac{1}{\sqrt{2}}$$

$$L_1 : L_2 = 1 : \sqrt{2}$$

15. Rotational energy $= \dfrac{1}{2} I(\omega)^2 = \dfrac{1}{2}(mK^2)\,\omega^2$

Linear kinetic energy $= \dfrac{1}{2} m\omega^2 R^2$

$$\therefore \text{ Required fraction} = \frac{\frac{1}{2}(mK^2)\,\omega^2}{\frac{1}{2}(mK^2)\,\omega^2 + \frac{1}{2} m\omega^2 R^2} = \frac{K^2}{K^2 + R^2}$$

17. Use $\tau = I\alpha$

and $\omega^2 - \omega_0^2 = 2\alpha\theta$ Here $I = \dfrac{2}{5} MR^2$

Given, $\quad M = 2000\text{ g} = 2\text{ kg}$

$$R = 5\text{ cm} = 5 \times 10^{-2}\text{ m}$$

$$\theta = 2\pi \times 2\pi \text{ radians}$$

$$n = 300\text{ rpm} = 5\text{ rps}$$

$$\therefore \quad \tau = I\alpha = \left(\frac{2}{5} MR^2\right)\left(\frac{\omega^2 - \omega_0^2}{2\theta}\right)$$

$$= \frac{2}{5} \times 2 \times (5 \times 10^{-2})^2 \, \frac{4\pi^2(5^2 - 0^2)}{2 \times 4\pi^2}$$

$$= 0.025\text{ N-m} = 2.5 \times 10^5 \text{ dyne cm}$$

18. $X_{COM} = \dfrac{1 \times 0 + 2 \times 2 + 3 \times 0 + 4 \times 2 + 5 \times 1}{1 + 2 + 3 + 4 + 5}$

$$= \frac{4 + 8 + 5}{15} = \frac{17}{15} = 1.1$$

$$Y_{COM} = \frac{1 \times 0 + 2 \times 0 + 3 \times 2 + 4 \times 2 + 5 \times 1}{1 + 2 + 3 + 4 + 5} = \frac{6 + 8 + 5}{15} = 1.3$$

19. Acceleration of a body rolling down an inclined plane is given by,

$$a = \frac{g \sin\theta}{1 + \dfrac{K^2}{R^2}} \quad \text{...(i)}$$

In case of a solid sphere, we have

$$\frac{K^2}{R^2} = \frac{[(I/M)]}{R^2} = \frac{I}{MR^2} = \frac{(2/5)\,MR^2}{MR^2} = \frac{2}{5}$$

On substituting $\dfrac{K^2}{R^2} = \dfrac{2}{5}$ in Eq. (i), we get

$$a = \frac{5}{7} g \sin\theta$$

20. Force F_A on particle A is given by

$$F_A = m_A a_A = \frac{m_A v}{t} \quad \text{...(i)}$$

Similarly,

$$F_B = m_B a_B = \frac{m_B \times 2v}{t} \quad \text{...(ii)}$$

Now, $\quad \dfrac{m_A v}{t} = \dfrac{m_B \times 2v}{t} \quad (\because F_A = F_B)$

So, $\quad m_A = 2\, m_B$

For the centre of mass of the system

$$v = \frac{m_A v_A + m_B v_B}{m_A + m_B}$$

$$\Rightarrow \quad v = \frac{2m_B v - m_B \times 2v}{2m_B + m_B} = 0$$

Negative sign is used because the particles are travelling in opposite directions.

Shortcut Method

If we consider the two masses in a system, then no external force is acting on the system. Mutual forces are internal forces. Since, the centre of mass is initially at rest, it well remain at rest.

Gravitation

Universal Law of Gravitation

Every object in the universe attracts every other object with a force, which is proportional to the product of their masses and inversely proportional to the square of the distance between them. The force is along the line joining the centres of two object. This whole phenomenon is called gravitation. This is also known as Newton's law of gravitation.

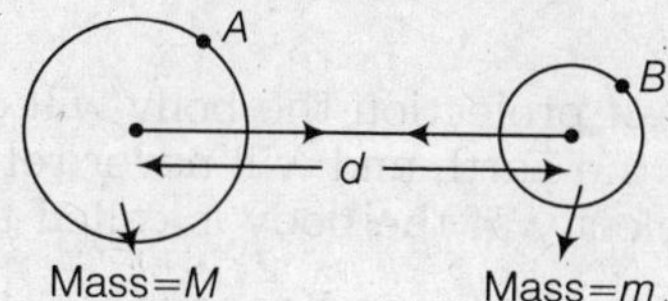

Thus, $F \propto \frac{1}{d^2}$ and $F \propto M \times m$

$$\Rightarrow \quad F = G\frac{M \times m}{d^2}$$

Here, G is the constant of proportionality and is called the universal gravitational constant. Its SI unit is $\text{Nm}^2\text{kg}^{-2}$ and value is

$$6.673 \times 10^{-11} \text{Nm}^2 \text{ kg}^{-2}.$$

The value of G was found out by Henry Cavendish.

Acceleration Due to Gravity

When a body is falling freely, then the increase in its velocity per second is called acceleration due to gravity. It is represented by g.

$$g = \frac{GM_e}{R_e^2}$$

Where, M_e = Mass of Earth,

R_e = Radius of Earth.

Variation in Value of (g)

- The value of g is minimum at equator and maximum at poles (it happens due to non-spherical shape of the Earth).
- The observed value of g at the lattitude λ is

$$g_\lambda = g - R_e\omega^2 \cos^2 \lambda$$

At equator, $g_\lambda = g - R_e\omega^2$ $\quad (\because \lambda = 0)$

At pole, $g_\gamma = g$ $\quad (\because \lambda = 90°)$

- Value of g at height h above Earth surface decreases.

$$g' = \frac{g}{\left(1 + \frac{h}{R_e}\right)^2} \approx g\left(1 - \frac{2h}{R_e}\right)$$

- Value of g at height h below the Earth's surface decreases.

$$g' = g\left(1 - \frac{h}{R_e}\right)$$

Gravitational Field

Every particle in the universe attracts every other particle with a force called the gravitational force. The space around the attracting particle in which the gravitational force of that particle can be experienced is called gravitational field of that particle.

Gravitational Field Strength

The force experienced by a unit mass placed at a point in a gravitational field is called the gravitational field strength or intensity of gravitational field at that point.

If a force F N acts on a mass of m kg placed in a gravitational field, then gravitational field strength will be $\left(\frac{F}{m}\right)\left(\frac{\text{J}^{-1}}{\text{kg}}\right)$. Its dimensions are $[\text{LT}^{-1}]$.

Gravitational Potential

The work done is bringing a unit mass from infinity to a point in the gravitational field is called the gravitational potential at that point.

If W J is the work obtained in bringing a body of mass m kg from infinity to a point in the gravitational field, then the gravitational potential at the point is given by

$$V = \frac{W}{m} \text{J / kg}$$

The gravitational potential is always negative. Gravitational potential is a scalar quantity. Its dimensions are $[\text{L}^2\text{T}^{-2}]$.

Gravitational Potential Energy

The energy is used in bringing a body from infinity to a point in a gravitational field is called gravitational potential energy of the body at that point.

The gravitational potential energy is always negative.

Gravitational potential energy

$$(U) = -\frac{GM_e m}{R_e}$$

If the body is at a height h above the Earth's surface, then its gravitational potential energy

$$U = -\frac{GM_e m}{R_e + h}$$

Satellites

Just as various planets revolve around the Sun, in the same way few celestial bodies revolve around these planets. These bodies are called satellites. *e.g.*, Earth is a planet and Moon is a satellite of the Earth.

Orbital Speed of Satellite

A satellite of mass m is revolving around the Earth with a speed v_0 in a circular orbital of radius r. The centripetal force on the satellite is $\frac{mv_0^2}{r}$.

For revolution of satellite around the Earth, the gravitational force provides the required centripetal force.

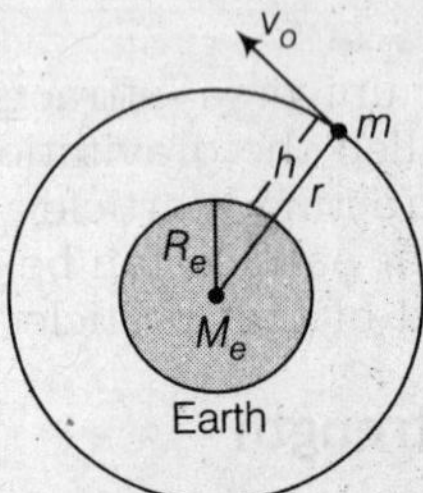

Hence, $$G\frac{M_e m}{r^2} = \frac{mv_0^2}{r}$$

$$\Rightarrow \quad v_0 = \sqrt{\frac{GM_e}{r}}$$

Period of Revolution

$$T = 2\pi\sqrt{\frac{r^3}{GM_e}}$$

$$T = 2\pi\sqrt{\frac{r^3}{gR_e}}$$

Height of a Satellite above the Earth's Surface

$$h = \left[\frac{T^2 gR_e^2}{4\pi^2}\right]^{1/3} - R_e$$

Energy of a Satellite

The total energy of the satellite is $E = \frac{-1}{2}\frac{GM_e m}{R_e}$.

Binding Energy

The energy required for a satellite to leave its orbit around the Earth and escape to infinity is called the binding energy.

Binding energy of the satellite $(B) = +\frac{1}{2}\frac{GM_e m}{R_e}$.

Geostationary Satellites

If the height of an artificial satellite above the Earth's surface be such that its period of revolution is exactly equal to the period of revolution (24 h) of the axial motion of the Earth, then the satellite would appear stationary over a point on Earth's equator. It would be synchronous with Earth's spin. Such a satellite is known as geostationary satellite.

It is used to reflect TV signals and telecast TV programs from one part of the world to another.

Escape Velocity

At a certain velocity of projection the body will go out the gravitational field of the Earth and will never return to the Earth. This initial velocity of the body is called the escape velocity.

$$v_e = \sqrt{\frac{2GM_e}{R_e}}$$

$$v_e = \sqrt{2gR_e}$$

We throw a body upward with a velocity of 11.2 km/s, then it will never return to the Earth.

Kepler's Law

1. Planet moves on elliptical path with the Sun is at one of its focus.
2. The radius vector sweep by equal area in equal time interval.
3. The squared time period of planet is equal to cube of length of semi-major axis.

$$T^2 \propto r^3$$

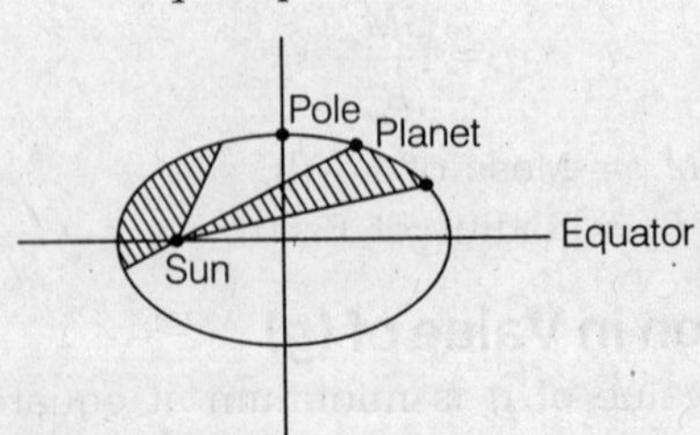

Practice Questions

Level I

1. The weight of a body at the centre of the Earth is
(a) zero
(b) infinite
(c) same as on the surface of Earth
(d) None of the above

2. If the speed of rotation of Earth about its axis increases, then the weight of the body at the equator will
(a) increase
(b) decrease
(c) remain unchanged
(d) sometimes decrease and sometimes increase

3. The weight of a body at Earth's surface is W. At a depth half way to the centre of the Earth, it will be (assuming uniform density in Earth)
(a) W (b) $W/2$ (c) $W/4$ (d) $W/8$

4. The value of g on poles is
(a) maximum (b) minimum
(c) zero (d) None of these

5. The value of the universal gravitational constant
(a) changes with change of place
(b) does not change from place to place
(c) becomes more at night
(d) becomes more during day

6. Two iron and wooden balls identical in size are released from the same height in vacuum. The time taken by them to reach the ground are
(a) zero (b) not equal
(c) roughly equal (d) exactly equal

7. Two stars of masses m and $5m$ are 3000 parsec apart. If the force on the large one is F, the force on the small star is
(a) $F/25$ (b) $F/5$
(c) F (d) $5F$

8. What is the acceleration of a meteor passing by the Earth at an altitude of 55000 km?
(a) $0.11\,m/s^2$ (b) $11\,m/s^2$
(c) $1.11\,m\ s^2$ (d) $5.18\,m/s^2$

9. Determine the gravitational attraction between two asteroids separated by 22000 m, if their masses are 450000 kg and 700000 kg, respectively
(a) 1.2×10^{-6} N (b) 1.2×10^{-8} N
(c) 4.3×10^{-8} N (d) 2.1×10^{-6} N

10. The radius of the Earth is 6400 km. What is its mass?
(a) 6.0×10^{24} kg (b) 5.0×10^{24} kg
(c) 1.0×10^{22} kg (d) 6.5×10^{14} kg

11. How much is the gravitational force that keeps an artificial satellite of mass 3500 kg in orbit around the Earth at an altitude of 4200 km
(a) 12000 N (b) 12500 N
(c) 13000 N (d) 10000 N

12. If G is gravitational constant and R is the radius of the Earth, then acceleration due to gravity g and the mean density of Earth D are related by the equation
(a) $D=\dfrac{g}{G}\left(\dfrac{4\pi R^3}{3}\right)$ (b) $D=\dfrac{g/G}{\left(\dfrac{4}{3}\pi R\right)}$
(c) $D=\left(\dfrac{g}{G}\right)\left(\dfrac{4}{3}\pi R^2\right)$ (d) $D=\dfrac{g/G}{\dfrac{4}{3}\pi R^3}$

13. A balloon filled with CO_2 released on Earth would (neglect viscosity of air)
(a) climb with an acceleration $9.8\ m/s^2$
(b) fall with an acceleration $9.8\ m/s^2$
(c) fall with a constant acceleration $3.4\ m/s^2$
(d) fall with acceleration and then would attain a constant velocity

14. Let us say F_1 is the magnitude of the force exerted on Sun by Earth and F_2 is the magnitude of force exerted on Earth by Sun, then
(a) $F_1>F_2$ (b) $F_1=F_2$
(c) $F_1<F_2$ (d) None of these

15. The gravitational force of attraction between two bodies is F N. If the mass of each body and the distance between them are doubled, then the gravitational force between them in Newton is
(a) $16F$ (b) $F/16$
(c) $F/4$ (d) F

16. If the density of the Earth is doubled keeping its radius constant, then acceleration due to gravity (present value $9.8\ m/s^2$) will be
(a) $2.45\ m/s^2$ (b) $4.9\ m/s^2$
(c) $9.8\ m/s^2$ (d) $19.6\ m/s^2$

17. If the Earth stops rotating about its axis, the acceleration due to gravity will remain unchanged at
(a) equator (b) latitude 45°
(c) latitude 60° (d) poles

18. If a man weighs 60 kg on the surface of the Earth, the height above the surface of the Earth where his weight is 30 kg is
(a) $0.41R$ (b) $\sqrt{2}R$ (c) $R/\sqrt{2}$ (d) $R/2$

19. The escape velocity of a body depends upon mass as
(a) m^0 (b) m^1 (c) m^2 (d) m^3

20. A hypothetical planet has a mass of half that of the Earth and a radius of twice that of the Earth. What is the acceleration due to gravity on the planet in terms of g?
(a) g (b) $g/2$ (c) $g/4$ (d) $g/8$

21. The force of gravitation between objects of ordinary size kept at a distance of 1m from each other is of the order of
(a) 10 N (b) 100 N
(c) 10^{-8} N (d) 10^{-11}N

22. A ball is thrown vertically upwards and attains a maximum height of 100 m. It was thrown with a speed
(a) 9.8 m/s (b) 44.3 m/s
(c) 19.6 m/s (d) 98 m/s

23. A stone is thrown vertically upwards and caught at the point of projection after 10 s. The time taken by the stone to reach the highest point is
(a) 5 s (b) 10 s
(c) 9.8 s (d) 4.9 s

24. A stone is dropped from the roof of a house and is found to reach the ground in 1 s. The height of the house is
(a) 4.9 m (b) 9.8 m
(c) 12 m (d) 19.6 m

25. A wooden cube floating in water supports a mass $m = 0.2$ kg on its stop. When the mass is removed the cube rises by 2cm. The side of the cube is (density of water 10^3 kg/m^3)
(a) 6 cm (b) 12 cm (c) 8 cm (d) 10 cm

26. A ball of relative density 0.8 fall into water from a height of 2 m. The depth to which the ball will sink is
(a) 8 m (b) 2 m (c) 6 m (d) 4 m

27. The mass of the moon is 1/81 of Earth's mass and its radius 1/4 that of the Earth. If the escape velocity from the Earth's surface is 11.2 km/s, its value for the moon will be
(a) 0.14 km/s (b) 0.5 km/s
(c) 2.5 km/s (d) 5.0 km/s

28. Time period of a simple pendulum inside a satellite orbiting Earth is
(a) zero (b) ∞ (c) T (d) $2T$

29. The potential energy of a satellite of mass m and revolving at a height R above the surface of Earth, where R_e = radius of Earth, is
(a) $-mg R_e$ (b) $\frac{-mg R_e}{2}$
(c) $\frac{-mg R_e}{3}$ (d) $\frac{-mg R_e}{4}$

30. Energy required to move a body of mass m from an orbit of radius $2R$ to $3R$ is
(a) $GMm/12R^2$ (b) $GMm/3R^2$
(c) $GMm/8R$ (d) $GMm/6R$

Level II

1. In planetary motion
(a) the angular speed remains constant
(b) the total angular momentum remains constant
(c) the linear speed remains constant
(d) neither the angular momentum nor angular speed remains constant

2. A satellite of mass M is orbiting in an orbit of radius R. Work done by gravity per revolution on the satellite is given by
(a) $M g R/2$ (b) $M g R$
(c) $M g \times 2\pi R$ (d) None of these

3. Kepler's second law regarding constancy of aerial velocity of a planet is a consequence of the law of conservation of
(a) energy (b) angular momentum
(c) linear momentum (d) None of these

4. The planet mercury is revolving in an elliptical orbit around the Sun as shown in figure. The kinetic energy of mercury will be greatest at

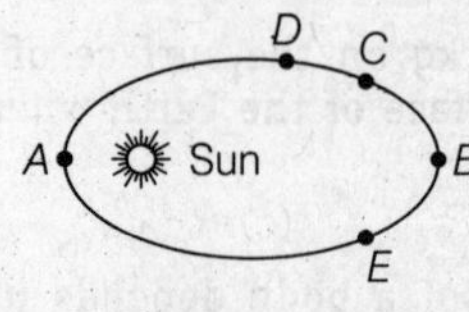

(a) A (b) B (c) C (d) D

5. Two satellites are orbiting around the Earth in circular orbits of same radius. One of them is 10 times greater in mass than the other. Their period of revolutions are in the ratio
(a) 100 : 1 (b) 1 : 100
(c) 10 : 1 (d) 1 : 1

6. A double star system consists of two stars A and B, which have time period T_A and T_B, radius R_A and R_B and mass M_A and M_B. Then,
(a) if $T_A > T_B$, then $R_A > R_B$
(b) if $T_A > T_B$, then $M_A > M_B$
(c) $(T_A/T_B) = (R_A/R_B)^3$
(d) $T_A = T_B$

7. The acceleration due to gravity on the Earth of radius R_e is g_e and that on moon of radius R_m is g_m. The ratio of the masses of the Earth and moon is given by
(a) $\frac{g_e}{g_m}\sqrt{\left(\frac{R_e}{R_m}\right)}$ (b) $\frac{g_e}{g_m}\cdot\frac{R_e}{R_m}$
(c) $\frac{g_e^2}{g_m^2}\times\frac{R_e}{R_m}$ (d) $\frac{g_e}{g_m}\times\frac{R_e^2}{R_m^2}$

8. The escape velocity from the Earth is 11 km/s. The escape velocity from a planet having twice the radius and the same mean density as the Earth would be
(a) 5.5 km/s (b) 11 km/s
(c) 15.5 km/s (d) 22 km/s

9. If the length of a simple pendulum is increased by 2%, then the time period
(a) increases by 2% (b) decreases by 2%
(c) increases by 1% (d) decreases by 1%

10. The escape velocity on the surface of the Earth is 11.2 km/s. If mass and radius of a planet is 4 and 2 times respectively than that of Earth, what is the escape velocity from the planet?
(a) 11.2 km/s (b) 1.112 km/s
(c) 15.8 km/s (d) 22.4 km/s

11. If g is the acceleration due to gravity on the surface of Earth, its value at a height equal to double the radius of Earth is

(a) g (b) $\frac{g}{2}$ (c) $\frac{g}{3}$ (d) $\frac{g}{9}$

12. The distance between the Sun and the Earth is r and the Earth takes time T to make one complete revolution around the Sun. Assuming the orbit of the Earth around the Sun to be circular, the mass of the Sun will be proportional to

(a) $\frac{r}{T}$ (b) $\frac{r^2}{T^2}$ (c) $\frac{r^3}{T^2}$ (d) $\frac{r^2}{T^3}$

13. The kinetic energy of a satellite in its orbit around the Earth is E. What should be the kinetic energy of the satellite so as to enable it escape from the gravitational pull of the Earth?

(a) $4E$ (b) $2E$ (c) $\sqrt{2}E$ (d) E

14. An Earth satellite of mass m revolves in a circular orbit at a height h from the surface of the Earth. R is the radius of the Earth and g is acceleration due to gravity at the surface of the Earth. The velocity of the satellite in the orbit is given by

(a) $\frac{gR^2}{R+h}$ (b) gR

(c) $\frac{gR}{R+h}$ (d) $\sqrt{\left(\frac{gR^2}{R+h}\right)}$

15. A satellite in a circular orbit of radius R has a period of 4 h. Another satellite with orbital radius 3 R around the same planet will have a period (in hours)

(a) 16 (b) 4 (c) $4\sqrt{27}$ (d) $4\sqrt{8}$

16. For a satellite moving in an orbit around the Earth, the ratio of kinetic energy to potential energy is

(a) $1/\sqrt{2}$ (b) $1/2$ (c) $\sqrt{2}$ (d) 2

17. An artificial satellite is moving in a circular orbit around the Earth at a height R from the surface of the Earth. If the satellite is stopped suddenly in its orbit and allowed to fall freely on the Earth, the speed with which it will hit the surface of the Earth will be

(a) $\sqrt{gR}$ (b) $\sqrt{(2gR)}$

(c) $\sqrt{(3gR)}$ (d) $2\sqrt{gR}$

18. A satellite of mass m is orbiting the Earth at a height h from its surface. If M be the mass of Earth and R, its radius, then the energy required to pull the satellite from Earth's gravitational field will be

(a) $\frac{GmM}{2(R+h)}$ (b) $\frac{2GmM}{(R+h)}$ (c) $\frac{GmM}{2(R+h)^2}$ (d) $\frac{4GmM}{(R+h)^2}$

19. The variation of acceleration due to gravity as one moves away from Earth's centre is given by the graph

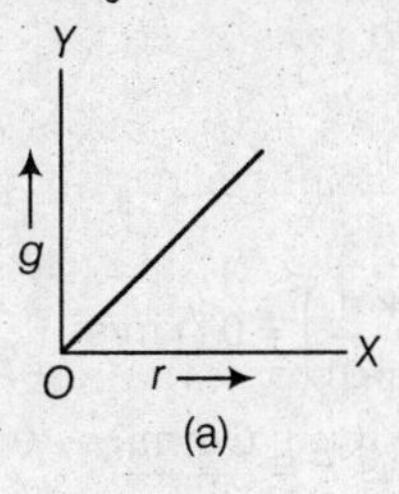

(a)

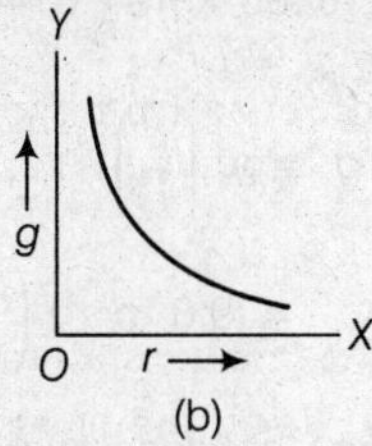

(b)

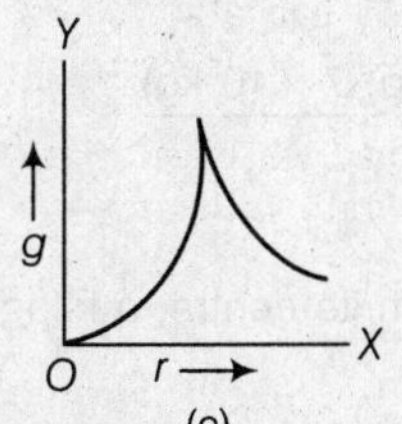

(c)

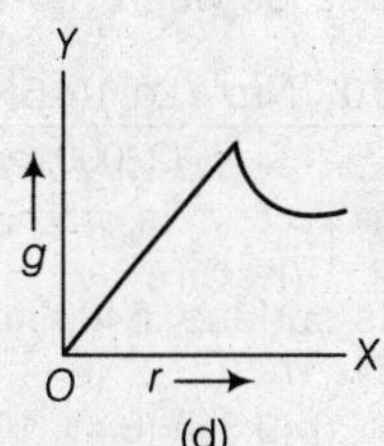

(d)

20. Which of the following graphs represents the motion of a planet moving about the Sun?

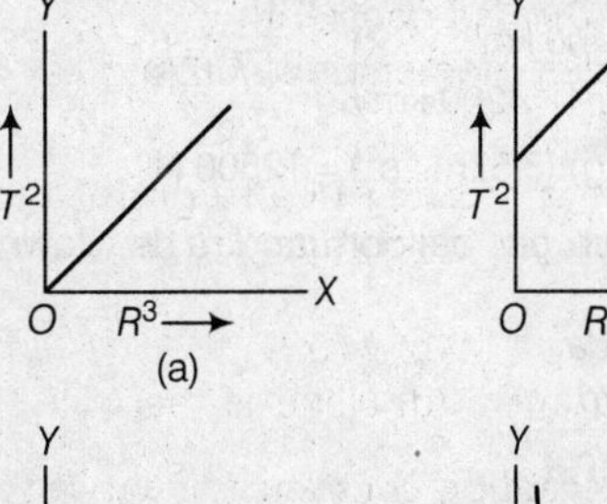

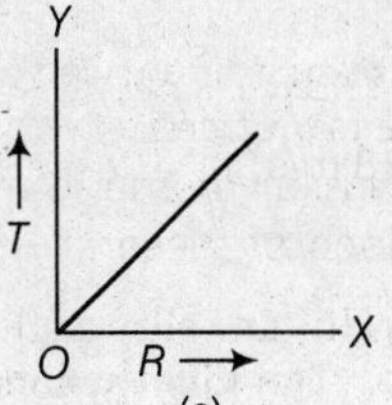

(c)

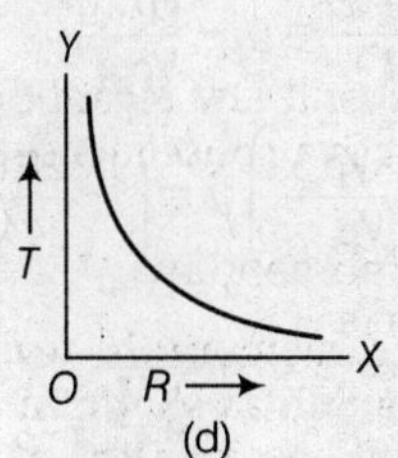

(d)

Answers

Level I

1. (a) **2.** (b) **3.** (b) **4.** (a) **5.** (b) **6.** (a) **7.** (c) **8.** (a) **9.** (c) **10.** (a)
11. (b) **12.** (b) **13.** (c) **14.** (b) **15.** (d) **16.** (d) **17.** (d) **18.** (a) **19.** (a) **20.** (d)
21. (c) **22.** (b) **23.** (a) **24.** (a) **25.** (d) **26.** (a) **27.** (c) **28.** (b) **29.** (b) **30.** (d)

Level II

1. (b) **2.** (d) **3.** (b) **4.** (a) **5.** (d) **6.** (d) **7.** (d) **8.** (d) **9.** (c) **10.** (c)
11. (d) **12.** (c) **13.** (b) **14.** (d) **15.** (c) **16.** (b) **17.** (a) **18.** (a) **19.** (c) **20.** (a)

Hints and Solutions

Level I

8. The acceleration is due to gravity along, so $g \propto 1/r^2$ and gr^2 is a constant. We know g and r at the surface of the Earth. For the meteor r is its altitude plus the radius of the Earth : 55000 km + 6400 km = 61400 km.

Then, $$g_1 r_1^2 = g_2 r_2^2$$

$$\Rightarrow \quad g_2 = g_1\left(\frac{r_1}{r_2}\right)^2$$

$$= (9.8\text{ m/s}^2)\left(\frac{6400\text{ km}}{61400\text{ km}}\right)^2 = 0.11\text{ m/s}^2$$

9. Attraction force between two masses $F = \dfrac{Gm_1m_2}{r^2}$

$$= \frac{(6.67\times 10^{-11}\text{Nm}^2/\text{kg}^2)(4.5\times 10^5\text{kg})(7\times 10^5\text{kg})}{(22000\text{ m})^2}$$

$$= 4.3\times 10^{-8}\text{ N}$$

10. At the Earth's surface, 6400 km from its centre, a kilogram weighs 9.8 N. Then,

$$m_1 = \frac{F_{grav}r^2}{Gm_2} = \frac{(9.8\text{N})\,(6.4\times 10^6\text{m})^2}{(6.67\times 10^{-11}\text{Nm}^2/\text{kg}^2)\,(1\text{kg})}$$

$$m_1 = 6.0\times 10^{24}\text{ kg}$$

11. First find the acceleration due to gravity

$$g = (9.8\text{m}\ \ \text{s}^2)\left(\frac{6400\text{ km}}{6400\text{ km} + 4200\text{ km}}\right) = 3.57\text{ m/s}^2$$

Then, $w = mg = (3500\text{ kg})\,(3.57\text{m}\ \ \text{s}^2) = 12500\text{ N}$

13. If B is upthrust of air on balloon and a is downward acceleration, then

$$Mg - B = Ma$$

$$\Rightarrow \ a = \frac{Mg - B}{M} = g - \frac{V\rho\ \ g}{V\rho_{CO_2}}$$

$$= \left(1 - \frac{V\rho_{air}}{V\rho_{CO_2}}\right)g = \left(1 - \frac{28.8}{44}\right)\times 9.8\text{ m/s}^2$$

$$= 3.4\text{ m/s}^2$$

27. $$v_e = \sqrt{\frac{2GM_e}{R_e}};\ v_m = \sqrt{\frac{2G\dfrac{M_e}{81}}{\dfrac{R_e}{4}}} = \frac{2}{9}v_e$$

$$= \frac{2\times 11.2}{9} = \frac{22.4}{9} = 2.48 \simeq 2.5\text{ km/s}$$

29. At a height h above the surface of Earth the gravitational potential energy of the particle of mass m is

$$U_h = -\frac{GM_em}{R_e + h}$$

Where, M_e and R_e are the mass and radius of Earth respectively.

In this question, since $h = R_e$

So, $$U_h = R_e = -\frac{GM_em}{2R_e} = \frac{-mgR_e}{2}$$

30. Energy required to move a body of mass m from an orbit of radius $2R$ to $3R$ is

$$\Delta U = -\frac{GMm}{3R} - \frac{-GMm}{2R}$$

$$= \frac{GMm}{2R} - \frac{GMm}{3R} = \frac{GMm}{6R}$$

Level II

2. Centripetal force acts perpendicular to the displacement. So, the work done is zero.

6. In case of binary system, angular velocity and hence time period of both the stars are equal. Therefore, $T_A = T_B$.

7. For Earth, $G = g_eR_e^2/M_e$

For Moon, $G = g_mR_m^2/M_m$

$$\therefore \quad \frac{g_eR_e^2}{M_e} = \frac{g_mR_m^2}{M_m}$$

$$\Rightarrow \quad \frac{M_e}{M_m} = \frac{g_e}{g_m}\times\frac{R_e^2}{R_m^2}$$

8. Escape velocity $v_e = \sqrt{\dfrac{2\,GM}{R}}$

$$v_e = \sqrt{\frac{2G\times\frac{4}{3}\pi R^2\times d}{R}}$$

$$= \sqrt{2G\times\frac{4}{3}\pi R^2\times d}$$

$$= R\sqrt{\frac{8}{3}\pi Gd}$$

$$v_e \propto R\sqrt{d}$$

$$\frac{v_e}{v_p} = \frac{R_e}{R_P}\sqrt{\frac{d_e}{d_p}}$$

$$= \frac{R_e}{2R_e}\sqrt{\frac{d_e}{d_p}}$$

$$v_p = 2v_e = 2\times 11 = 22\text{ km/s}$$

9. Given that $l_2 = 1.02l_1$

We know that $T = 2\pi\sqrt{\left(\dfrac{l}{g}\right)}$

$$\Rightarrow \quad T \propto \sqrt{l}$$

$$\therefore \quad \frac{T_2}{T_1} = \sqrt{\left(\frac{l_2}{l_1}\right)} = \sqrt{\frac{(1.02l_1)}{l_1}} = 1.01$$

Thus, time period increases by 1%.

10. Escape velocity

$$= \sqrt{2g/R} = \sqrt{2(GM/R)}$$

$$= \sqrt{\frac{2\times G\times 4M}{2R}} = \sqrt{2}\ \sqrt{\left(\frac{2\,GM}{R}\right)}$$

$$= \sqrt{2}\times 11.2 = 15.8\text{ km/s}$$

11. Acceleration due to gravity at a height h from the surface of the Earth.

$$g' = g\frac{1}{\left[1+\frac{h}{R}\right]^2} = g\left[\frac{1}{(1+2)^2}\right] \qquad [\because h = 2R]$$

$$g' = g/9$$

12. We know that $\frac{G\,m\,M}{r^2} = \frac{m\,v^2}{r}$

$$M = (v^2 r / G)$$

Further, $v = (2\pi r / T)$

$\therefore \quad M = \frac{4\pi^2 r^3}{T^2 G}$

$\Rightarrow \quad M \propto \frac{r^3}{T^2}$

13. We know that $v_{es} = \sqrt{2} v_0$

KE in the orbit, $E = \frac{1}{2} M\,v_0^2$

KE to escape $= \frac{1}{2} M\,v_{es}^2 = \frac{1}{2} M(2v_0^2)$

$$= \frac{1}{2} M\,v_0^2 \times 2 = 2E$$

14. For a body to be a satellite, the gravitational force between planet and the satellite must supply centripetal force

$\therefore \quad \frac{G\,M\,m}{r^2} = \frac{m\,v_0^2}{r}$

Where, $r = (R + h)$

$\Rightarrow \quad v_0 = \sqrt{\left(\frac{G\,M}{r}\right)} = \sqrt{\left(\frac{G\,M}{R+h}\right)} = \sqrt{\left(\frac{g\,R^2}{R+h}\right)} \quad \left(\because g = \frac{G\,M}{R^2}\right)$

15. Let T' be the new time period. Then,

$$\left(\frac{T'}{T}\right)^2 = \left(\frac{3\,R}{R}\right)^3 \Rightarrow \frac{(T')^2}{(4)^2} = 27$$

$\therefore \quad T' = 4\sqrt{27}$

16. The kinetic energy of a satellite moving in an orbit around the Earth is given by

$$K = \frac{1}{2} m\,v^2$$

$$= \frac{1}{2} m\left(\frac{G\,M}{r}\right) = \frac{G\,M\,m}{2\,r} \qquad \text{...(i)}$$

The potential energy of satellite and Earth system is given by

$$U = \frac{G\,M\,m}{r} \qquad \text{...(ii)}$$

Where, r is the distance of the satellite from the centre of the Earth.

$\therefore \quad \frac{K}{U} = \frac{G\,M\,m/2\,r}{G\,M\,m/r} = \frac{1}{2}$

17. When the satellite is stopped, its kinetic energy is zero and total energy is only potential energy. This is given by

$$E_1 = -\frac{G\,M\,m}{r} = -\frac{G\,m\,M}{2\,R} \quad (r = R + R)$$

Potential energy of the satellite on the Earth

$$E_2 = -\frac{G\,m\,M}{R}$$

Loss of potential energy

$$= E_1 - E_2 = -\frac{G\,m\,M}{2\,R} - \left(-\frac{G\,m\,M}{R}\right)$$

$$= \frac{G\,m\,M}{2\,R}$$

This is converted into kinetic energy. Hence,

$$\frac{1}{2} m\,v^2 = \frac{G\,M\,m}{2\,R}$$

$\Rightarrow \quad v^2 = \frac{G\,M}{R} = g\,R$

$\Rightarrow \quad v = \sqrt{(g\,R)}$

18. Distance of the satellite from the centre of Earth $r = (R + h)$.

$\therefore \quad \frac{m\,v^2}{(R+h)} = \frac{G\,m\,M}{(R+h)^2}$

$\Rightarrow \quad \frac{1}{2} m\,v^2 = \frac{G\,M\,m}{2\,(R+h)}$

$\Rightarrow \quad \text{KE} = \frac{G\,M\,m}{2\,(R+h)}$

$$\text{PE} = -\frac{G\,m\,M}{r} = -\frac{G\,m\,M}{(R+h)}$$

Total energy = KE + PE

$$= \frac{G\,m\,M}{2\,(R+h)} - \frac{G\,m\,M}{(R+h)} = -\frac{G\,m\,M}{2\,(R+h)}$$

So, energy needed $= [G\,m\,M/2(R+h)]$.

12

Elasticity

Elasticity

The property of the body by virtue of which it tends to regain its original shape and size after removing the deforming force is called elasticity. If the body regains its original shape and size completely, after the removal of deforming forces, then the body is said to be perfectly elastic.

Plasticity

The property of the body by virtue of which it tends to retain its deformed state after removing the deforming force is called plasticity. If the body does not have any tendency to recover its original shape and size, it is called perfectly plastic.

Stress

When a deforming force is applied on a body, it changes the configuration of the body by changing the normal positions of the molecules or atoms of the body. As a result, an internal restoring force comes into play, which tends to bring the body back to its initial configuration. This internal restoring force acting per unit area of a deformed body is called stress. *i.e.,*

$$\text{Stress} = \frac{\text{Restoring force}}{\text{Area}}$$

Strain

When a deforming force is applied on a body, there is a change in the configuration of the body. The body is said to be strained or deformed. The ratio of change in configuration to the original configuration is called strain. *i.e.,*

$$\text{Strain} = \frac{\text{Change in configuration}}{\text{Original in configuration}}$$

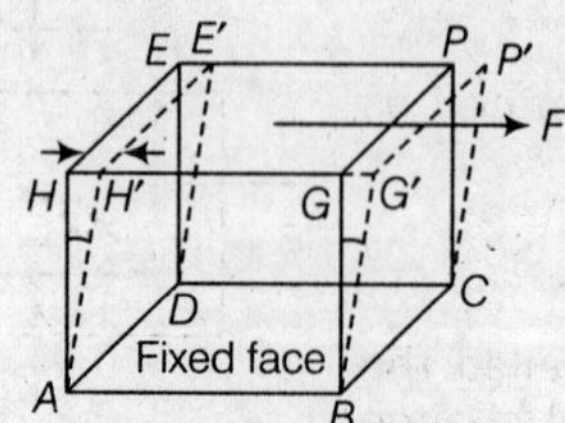

Strain being the ratio of two like quantities has no units and dimensions.

The change in the length ΔL to the original length L of the body is known as longitudinal strain.

$$\text{Longitudinal strain} \quad \frac{\Delta L}{L}$$

If a relative displacement Δx between opposite faces of the body due to tangential force occurs, then the strain so produced is known as shearing strain.

$$\text{Shearing strain} \quad \frac{\Delta x}{L} = \tan \theta$$

Where, θ is the angular displacement of the body from the vertical (original position of the body). Usually θ is very small, $\tan \theta$ is nearly equal to angle θ, (if $\theta = 10°$, *e.g.,* There is only 1% difference between θ and $\tan \theta$).

The strain produced by a hydraulic pressure is called volume strain and is defined as the ratio of change in volume (ΔV) to the original volume (V).

$$\text{Volume strain} = \frac{\Delta V}{V}$$

HOOKE'S LAW

Elastic limit is the upper limit of deforming force upto which, if deforming force is removed, the body regains its original form completely and beyond which if deforming force is increased, the body loses its property of elasticity and gets permanently deformed.

Within elastic limit, the extension of an elastic body is directly proportional to the force. Stress is proportional to strain, within the elastic limit.

$$\frac{\text{Stress}}{\text{Strain}} = \text{Constant}$$

This constant is known as modulus of elasticity or coefficient of elasticity. It depends upon the nature of materials.

Stress-strain Curve

The stress-strain graph of a ductile metal is shown in figure. Initially, the stress-strain graph is linear and it obeys the Hooke's law upto the point P called the proportional limit. After the proportional limit the graph is non-linear but it still remains elastic upto the yield point Y where the slope of the curve is zero. At the yield point the material starts deforming under constant stress and it behaves like a viscous liquid.

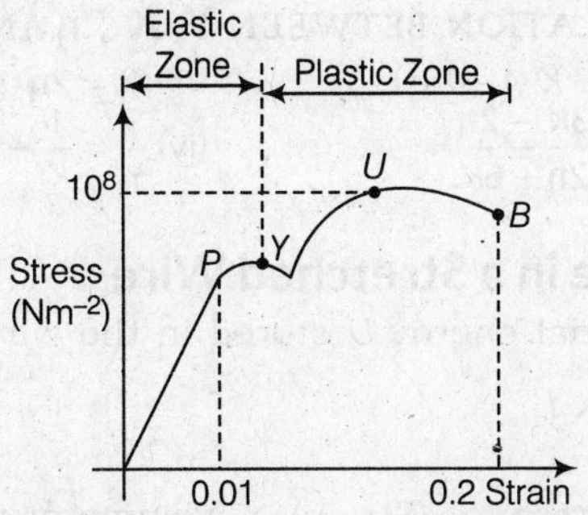

The yield point is the beginning of the plastic zone. After the yield point, the material starts gaining strength due to excessive deformation and this phenomenon is called strain hardening. The point shows the ultimate strength of the material. It is the maximum stress that the material can sustain without failure. After the point the curve goes down towards the breaking point because the calculation of the stress is based on the original cross-sectional area whereas the cross-sectional areas of the sample actually decrease.

Brittle, Ductile and Malleable Solids

There are some materials which break as soon as the stress is increased beyond the elastic limit. They are called brittle. *e.g.,* Glass, ceramics etc.

Materials which have large plastic range of extension are called ductile. Using this property, materials can be drawn into thin wires.

e.g., Copper, aluminium etc.

Materials which can be hammered into thin sheets are called malleable. *e.g.,* Gold, silver, lead etc.

Elastomers

Rubber has a large elastic region. It can be stretched several times its original length. On the removal of stress it returns to its original state. But the stress-strain graph is not a straight line. This means, it does not obey Hooke's law.

Elastic Moduli

According to Hooke's law, within elastic limit,

$$\text{Stress} \propto \text{Strain}$$

$$\Rightarrow \quad \text{Stress} = E \times \text{Strain}$$

$$\Rightarrow \quad \frac{\text{Stress}}{\text{Strain}} = E = \text{Constant}$$

Thus, modulus of elasticity or coefficient of elasticity of a body is defined as the ratio of the stress to the corresponding strain produced, within the elastic limit.

Types of Modulus of Elasticity

Corresponding to three types of strain, there are three types of modulus of elasticity as described below

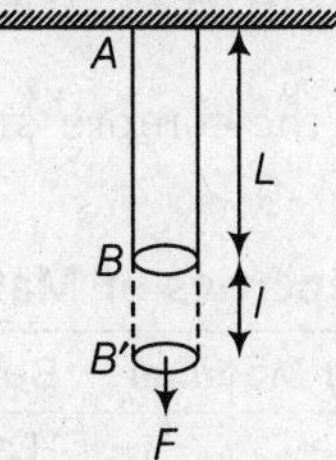

1. Young's Modulus of Elasticity (Y)

It is defined as the ratio of normal stress to the longitudinal strain within the elastic limit.

Thus, $$Y = \frac{\text{Normal stress}}{\text{Longitudinal strain}}$$

$$\therefore \quad Y = \frac{F / \pi r^2}{l / L} = \frac{mgL}{\pi r^2 l}$$

2. Shear Modulus (Modulus of Rigidity)

The shear modulus of a solid measures its resistance to a shearing force, which is a force applied tangentially to a surface, as shown in the figure. (Since, the bottom of the solid is assumed to be at rest, there is an equal and opposite force on the lower surface). The top surface is displaced by x relative to the bottom surface.

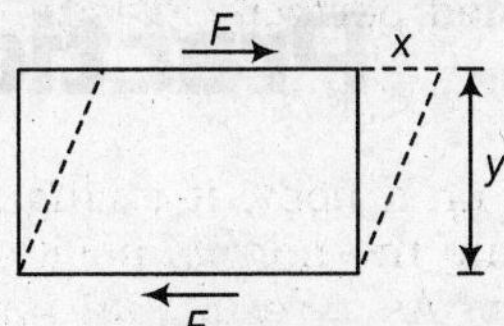

The shear modulus G is defined as

$$G = \frac{\text{Shear stress}}{\text{Shear strain}}, \; G = \frac{F / A}{x / y} = \frac{F}{A}\frac{y}{x}$$

Shear modulus (or modulus of rigidity) is generally less than Young's modulus. For most materials $G \approx Y / 3$.

3. Bulk Modulus

The bulk modulus of a solid or a fluid indicates its resistance to a change in volume. Consider a cube of some material, solid or fluid, as shown in the figure. We assume that all faces experience the same force F_n normal to each face. (One way to accomplish this is to immerse the body in a fluid as long as the change in pressure over the vertical height of the cube is negligible).

The pressure on the cube is defined as the normal force per unit area.

$$p = \frac{F_n}{A}$$

The change in pressure Δp is called the volume stress and the fractional change in volume $\Delta V / V$ is called the volume strain. The bulk modulus of the material is defined as

$$\text{Bulk modulus} = \frac{\text{Volume stress}}{\text{Volume strain}}$$

$$\Rightarrow \qquad B = \frac{-\Delta p}{\Delta V / V}$$

The negative sign is included to make a positive number, since an increase in pressure ($\Delta p > 0$) leads to decrease in volume ($\Delta V < 0$).

The inverse of B is called the compressibility factor k. *i.e.*, $k = 1/B$.

Elastic Properties of Matter

State	Shear Modulus	Bulk Modulus
Solid	Large	Large
Liquid	Zero	Large
Gas	Zero	Small

Poisson's Ratio

It is defined as the ratio of lateral strain to the longitudinal strain. It is denoted by σ. *i.e.*,

$$\sigma = \frac{\text{Lateral strain}}{\text{Longitudinal strain}}$$

Where, lateral strain is the strain in the direction perpendicular to the force, longitudinal strain is the strain in the direction of the force.

Poisson's ratio is a dimensionless and unitless quantity.

Theoretical value of Poisson's ratio $-1 < \sigma < 1/2$

Practical value of Poisson's ratio $0 < \sigma < 1/2$

Relation between Y, K, η and σ

(i) $Y = 3K(1 - 2\sigma)$ (ii) $Y = 2\eta(1 + \sigma)$

(iii) $\sigma = \dfrac{3K - 2\eta}{2\eta + 6K}$ (iv) $\dfrac{9}{Y} = \dfrac{1}{K} + \dfrac{3}{\eta}$

Work Done in a Stretched Wire

Elastic potential energy U stored in the wire is given by

$$U = \frac{1}{2} F \times l$$

$$= \frac{1}{2} (\text{Stress}) \times (\text{Strain}) \times \text{Volume of the wire}$$

$\therefore$ Elastic potential energy per unit volume of the wire (energy density).

$$U = \frac{1}{2} (\text{Stress} \times \text{Strain}$$

$$= \frac{1}{2} (\text{Young's modulus} \times \text{Strain}) \times \text{Strain}$$

($\because$ Young's modulus = Stress/Strain)

$$\therefore \quad U = \frac{1}{2} (\text{Young's modulus}) \times (\text{Strain})^2$$

Practice Questions

Level I

1. Young's modulus is defined as
(a) the ratio of linear strain to the normal stress
(b) the ratio of normal stress to strain
(c) product of linear strain and normal stress
(d) square of the ratio of normal stress to linear strain

2. Shearing strain is expressed by
(a) angle of shear (b) angle of twist
(c) decrease in volume (d) increase in volume

3. The effect of temperature on the value of Young's modulus of elasticity for various substances in general is
(a) it increases with increase in temperature
(b) it remains constant
(c) it decreases with rise in temperature
(d) it sometimes increases and sometimes decreases with temperature

4. The breaking stress for a wire of unit cross-section is called its
(a) yield point (b) tensile strength
(c) elastic fatigue (d) Young's modulus

5. When a body undergoes a linear tensile strain it experiences a lateral contraction also. The ratio of lateral constraction to longitudinal strain is known as
(a) Young's modulus (b) Bulk modulus
(c) Poisson's ratio (d) Hooke's law

6. Energy in a stretched wire is
(a) (1/2) load $\times$ strain
(b) load $\times$ strain
(c) stress $\times$ strain
(d) (1/2) stress $\times$ strain

7. Theoretical value of Poisson's ratio lies between
(a) -1 and $+0.5$ (b) -1 and -2
(c) -0.5 and $+1$ (d) -1 and 0

8. The Young's modulus of a wire of length L and radius r is Y N/m^2. If the length is reduced to $L/2$ and radius $r/2$, its Young's modulus will be
(a) $Y/2$ (b) Y
(c) $2Y$ (d) $4Y$

9. For steel $Y = 2 \times 10^{11}$ N/m^2. The force required to double the length of a steel wire of area 1 cm^2 is
(a) 2×10^7 N
(b) 2×10^6 N
(c) 2×10^8 N
(d) 2×10^5 N

10. Two wires of copper having the length in the ratio 4 : 1 and their radii as 1 : 4 are stretched by the same force. The ratio of longitudinal strain in the two will be
(a) 1 : 16 (b) 16 : 1
(c) 1 : 64 (d) 64 : 1

Level II

1. If the work done in stretching a wire by 1 mm is 2 , the work necessary for stretching another wire of the same material but with double radius of cross-section and half the length by 1 mm is (in J)
(a) 16 (b) 8 (c) 4 (d) 1/4

2. A body subjected to strain several times will not obey Hooke's law due to
(a) yield point (b) permanent state
(c) elastic fatigue (d) breaking stress

3. For most materials the Young's modulus is n times the rigidity modulus, where n is
(a) 2 (b) 3 (c) 4 (d) 5

4. Two bars A and B of circular cross-section and of same volume made of the same material are subjected to tension. If the diameter of A is half that of B and if the force applied to both the rods is the same, the ratio of extension of A to that of B will be
(a) 16 (b) 15 (c) 8 (d) 24

5. Two wires A and B are of the same material. Their lengths are in the ratio 1 : 2 and the diameters are in the ratio 2 : 1. If they are pulled by the same force, their increase in length will be in the ratio
(a) 2 : 1 (b) 1 : 4 (c) 1 : 8 (d) 8 : 1

6. The bulk modulus of rubber is 9.1×10^8 N m^2. To what depth a rubber ball be taken in a lake, so that its volume is decreased by 0.1%?
(a) 1 km (b) 25 m
(c) 100 m (d) 200 m

7. Two springs of equal lengths and equal cross-sectional area are made of material whose Young's moduli are in the ratio of 2 : 3. They are suspended and loaded with the same mass. When stretched and released, they will oscillate with time periods in the ratio of
(a) $\sqrt{3} : \sqrt{2}$ (b) 3 : 2
(c) $3\sqrt{3} : 2\sqrt{2}$ (d) 9 : 4

8. A wire of length L and radius r is fixed at one end and a force F applied to the other end produced an extension l. The extension produced in another wire of the same material of length $2L$ and radius $2r$ by a force $2F$ is
(a) l (b) $2l$ (c) $l/2$ (d) $4l$

9. A metal bar of length L, area of cross-section A, Young's modulus Y and coefficient of linear expansion α, is clamped between two stout pillars. Now, it is heated through t°C. The force exerted by the bar is
(a) $YA\alpha t$ (b) $YALt$
(c) $YA\alpha Lt$ (d) $Y\alpha Lt/A$

10. The stress required to double the length of wire of Young's modulus Y is
(a) $\frac{Y}{2}$ (b) $2Y$
(c) Y (d) $4Y$

11. The relationship between Young's modulus Y, bulk modulus K and modulus of rigidity η is
(a) $Y = \frac{9\eta K}{\eta + 3K}$ (b) $\eta = \frac{9YK}{Y + 3K}$
(c) $Y = \frac{9\eta K}{3\eta + K}$ (d) $Y = \frac{3\eta K}{9\eta + K}$

12. A wire of length l and cross-sectional area A is made of a material of Young's modulus Y. If the wire is stretched by an amount x, the work done is
(a) $\frac{YAx^2}{2L}$ (b) $\frac{YAx}{2L^2}$
(c) $\frac{YAx}{2L}$ (d) $\frac{YAx^2}{L}$

13. In a wire stretched by hanging a weight from its end, the elastic potential energy per unit volume in terms of the longitudinal strain σ and modulus of elasticity Y is
(a) $Y\sigma^2/2$ (b) $Y\sigma/2$
(c) $2Y\sigma^2/2$ (d) $Y^2\sigma/2$

14. When an elastic material with Young's modulus Y is subjected to a stretching stress s, the elastic energy stored per unit volume of the material is
(a) $Ys/2$ (b) $s^2Y/2$
(c) $s^2/2Y$ (d) $s/2Y$

15. A long string is stretched by 2 cm and the potential energy is V. If the spring is stretched by 10 cm, its potential energy will be
(a) $V/25$ (b) $V/5$
(c) $5V$ (d) $25V$

Answers

Level I

1. (b)	**2.** (a)	**3.** (b)	**4.** (b)	**5.** (c)	**6.** (d)	**7.** (a)	**8.** (b)	**9.** (a)	**10.** (b)

Level II

1. (a)	**2.** (a)	**3.** (b)	**4.** (a)	**5.** (c)	**6.** (c)	**7.** (a)	**8.** (a)	**9.** (a)	**10.** (a)
11. (a)	**12.** (a)	**13.** (a)	**14.** (c)	**15.** (d)					

Hints and Solutions

Level I

3. Always constant for practical use.

9. The stress required to double the length is called Young's modulus.

$Y = \dfrac{F}{A} \Rightarrow F = Y \times A$

$\therefore F = (2 \times 10^{11}) \times (10^{-4}) = 2 \times 10^7$ N

10. Strain $\propto$ Stress $\propto F/A$

$\therefore$ Ratio of strain $= \dfrac{A_2}{A_1} = \left(\dfrac{r_2}{r_1}\right)^2 = \left(\dfrac{4}{1}\right)^2 = \dfrac{16}{1}$

Level II

1. $Y = FL/Al$

In both the cases Y and l are the same.

$\therefore \dfrac{F_1 L}{\pi r^2} = \dfrac{F_2 (L/2)}{\pi (2r)^2} \Rightarrow F_2 = 8F_1 = 16$ J

3. $G = 1/3\,Y$

$Y = 3G \quad \therefore \quad n = 3$

4. $Y = \dfrac{mgL}{\pi r^2 l} = \dfrac{mgL \times \pi r^2}{\pi^2 r^4 R} = \dfrac{mgV}{\pi r^4 l}$

Here, Y, volume V and mg are constants. Hence,

$r^4 l =$ Constant

$\therefore r_1^4 l_1 = r_2^4 l_2 \Rightarrow (l_1/l_2) = (r_2/r_1)^4$

$\Rightarrow l_1/l_2 = (2r/r)^4 = 16$

5. We know that, $Y = \dfrac{F}{\pi r^2} \times \dfrac{L}{l}$

Since, Y, F are same for both the wires, we have

$\dfrac{1}{r_1^2}\dfrac{L_1}{l_1} = \dfrac{1}{r_2^2}\dfrac{L_2}{l_2} \Rightarrow \dfrac{l_1}{l_2} = \dfrac{r_2^2 \times L_1}{r_1^2 \times L_2} = \dfrac{(D_2/2)^2 \times L_1}{(D_1/2)^2 \times L_2}$

$\Rightarrow \dfrac{l_1}{l_2} = \dfrac{D_2^2 \times L_1}{D_1^2 \times L_2} = \dfrac{D_2^2}{(2D_2)^2} \times \dfrac{L_1}{2L_1} = \dfrac{1}{8}$

So, $l_1 : l_2 = 1 : 8$

6. We know that,

$B = \dfrac{pV}{\Delta V}$, where $p = h\rho g = h \times 10^3 \times 9.8$

$$\frac{\Delta V}{V} = 0.1\% = \frac{0.1}{100} = 0.1 \times 10^{-2}$$

$$B = 9.1 \times 10^8 \text{ N/m}^2$$

$\therefore \quad 9.1 \times 10^8 = \dfrac{h \times 10^3 \times 9.8}{0.1 \times 10^{-2}} \quad h \approx 100$ m

7. We know that, $Y = FL/Al$

Force constant $k = F/l = YA/L$

So, time period T is given by

$$T = 2\pi\sqrt{\left(\frac{M}{k}\right)} = 2\pi\sqrt{\left(\frac{ML}{YA}\right)}$$

$\therefore \dfrac{T_1}{T_2} = \sqrt{\left(\dfrac{Y_2}{Y_1}\right)} = \sqrt{\left(\dfrac{3}{2}\right)}$

8. $Y = \dfrac{F/\pi r^2}{l/L} = \dfrac{FL}{\pi r^2 l}$

$\Rightarrow \quad l = \dfrac{FL}{\pi r^2 Y}$

Let l' be the extension produced when a force $2F$ is applied. Then,

$$l' = \frac{(2F)(2L)}{\pi (2r)^2 Y} = \frac{FL}{\pi r^2 Y} = l$$

9. $Y = \dfrac{(F/A)}{(l/L)} \Rightarrow F = \dfrac{YAl}{L}$

Further, $\quad l = L\alpha t$

$\therefore \quad F = \dfrac{YAL\alpha t}{L} = YA\alpha t$

10. We know that,

Young's modulus, $Y = \dfrac{\text{Stress}}{\text{Strain}}$

$\Rightarrow \quad Y = \dfrac{FL}{Al} \Rightarrow Y \propto \dfrac{1}{l}$

$\therefore \quad \dfrac{Y_1}{Y_2} = \dfrac{l_2}{l_1} \Rightarrow \dfrac{Y}{Y_2} = \dfrac{2l}{l}$

$\Rightarrow \quad Y_2 = \dfrac{Y}{2}$

11. $\dfrac{9}{Y} = \dfrac{3}{\eta} + \dfrac{1}{K}$

$\dfrac{9}{Y} = \dfrac{3K + \eta}{K\eta} \Rightarrow Y = \dfrac{9K\eta}{3K + \eta}$

12. $Y = \dfrac{FL}{Al} \Rightarrow F = \dfrac{YAl}{L}$

$dW = F\,dl = \dfrac{YA}{L}\,l\,dl$

$\therefore \quad W = \displaystyle\int_0^x \frac{YA}{L}\,l\,dl = \frac{YA}{L}\left[\frac{l^2}{2}\right]_0^x = \frac{YAx^2}{2L}$

13. Elastic potential energy per unit volume

$= \dfrac{1}{2} \times$ Stress $\times$ Strain

$= \dfrac{1}{2} \times$ [Young's modulus $\times$ Strain] $\times$ Strain

$= \dfrac{1}{2} \times Y \times \sigma^2 = \dfrac{Y\sigma^2}{2}$

14. $E =$ Energy stored per unit volume

$= \dfrac{1}{2} \times$ Stress $\times$ Strain $= \dfrac{1}{2} \times s \times$ Strain

Further, Strain $= \dfrac{\text{Stress}}{Y} = \dfrac{s}{Y}$

$\therefore \quad E = \dfrac{1}{2} \times s \times \dfrac{s}{Y} = \dfrac{s^2}{2Y}$

15. $V = \dfrac{1}{2}k(x)^2 = \dfrac{1}{2}k(2)^2 \Rightarrow k = \dfrac{2V}{4} = \dfrac{V}{2}$

$V' = \dfrac{1}{2}k(10)^2 = \dfrac{1}{2} \times \left(\dfrac{V}{2}\right)(10)^2 = 25V$

13

Electric Charge and Electric Field

Electrostatics

It is a branch of Physics by which study electric charge at rest, called electrostatics.

Electric Charge

It change is a fundamental property of matter like mass. Electric charge is a scalar quantity and its SI unit is Coulomb (C).

Kinds of Electric Charges

There are only two kinds of electric charge

(i) Positive (ii) Negative

Like (*i.e.*, similar) charges repel and unlike (*i.e.*, opposite) charge attract each other. This is also known as fundamental law of electrostatics.

A Body Can be Charged by Three Way

(i) Charging by friction
(ii) Charging by induction
(iii) Charging by conduction

Different substances can be arranged in a series in such a way that if any two of them are rubbed together, then the one occurring earlier in the series acquires a positive charge while the other occurring later acquires a negative charge

- Fur
- Sealing wax
- Cotton
- Silk
- Wood
- Rubber
- Amber
- Ebonite
- Flannel
- Glass
- Paper
- Human body
- Metals
- Resin
- Sulphur
- Guta parcha

Thus, glass acquires a positive charge when rubbed with silk but it acquires negative charge when rubbed with flannel.

Quantization of Electric Charge

The total charge (q) of a body is always an integral multiple of a basic quantum of charge (*i.e.*, charge on an electron) denoted by e. *i.e.*,

$$q = ne$$

Where, $n = 0, \pm 1, \pm 2, \pm 3, \ldots$

$e = 1.6 \times 10^{-19}$C

q = Total charge of a body

One Coulomb of Charge and Charge on an Electron

One coulomb of charge is bigger than the charge on an electron. As we know,

Charge on one electron, $e = 1.6 \times 10^{-19}$C

$\therefore$ Number of electronic charges in one coulomb,

$$n = \frac{q}{e} = \frac{1\text{C}}{1.6 \times 10^{-19}\text{C}} = 6.25 \times 10^{18}$$

Coulomb's Law

It states that the force of attraction or repulsion between two stationary point charges is

(i) directly proportional to the product of the magnitudes of the two charges.
(ii) inversely proportional to the square of the distance between them. This force acts along the line joining the two charges.

q_1 ——— r ——— q_2

If two point charges q_1 and q_2 are separated by distance r, then the force F of attraction or repulsion between them is such that

$$F \propto q_1 q_2 \quad \text{and} \quad F \propto \frac{1}{r^2}$$

$$\therefore \quad F \propto \frac{q_1 q_2}{r^2} \quad \Rightarrow \quad F = k\frac{q_1 q_2}{r^2}$$

where, k is a constant of proportionality, called electrostatic force constant. The value of k depends on the nature of the medium between the two charges and the system of units chosen to measure F, q_1, q_2 and r.

For the two charges located in free space and in SI units, we have

$$k = \frac{1}{4\pi\varepsilon_0} = 9 \times 10^9 \text{Nm}^2\text{C}^{-2}.$$

where, ε_0 is called permittivity of free space. So, we can express Coulomb's law in SI units as

$$F = \frac{1}{4\pi\varepsilon_0} \cdot \frac{q_1 q_2}{r^2}$$

Relative Permittivity

Relative electrical permittivity of a medium in also called dielectric constant of the medium and is denoted by K. *i.e.*,

$$K = \frac{\varepsilon}{\varepsilon_0} = \frac{F_0}{F_m}$$

where, F_0= Force between same two charges held the same distance apart in vacuum.

F_m = Force between two charges in medium other than free space (vacuum, air).

The force between the same two charges held the distances r_1 and r_2 are F_1 and F_2 respectively, then

$$\frac{F_2}{F_1} = \left(\frac{r_1}{r_2}\right)^2 \text{ at constant charge}$$

If $r_2 = nr_1$, then

$F_2 = F_1 / n^2$

$\Rightarrow$ $F_1 = n^2 F_2$

Where, $n = 1, 2, 3, \ldots$

Unit of Charge

In SI system, unit of charge is coulomb (C) and one coulomb is that much charge which when placed in vacuum at a distance of 1 m from an equal and similar charge would repel it with a force of 9×10^9 N. In CGS system, unit of charge is esu (electrostatic unit of charge) or stat. coulomb.

1 coulomb = 3×10^9 esu or stat coulomb.

Electromagnetic Unit of Charge

emu is electromagnetic unit of charge

1 emu = 3×10^{10} esu = 10 C

Continuous Distribution of Charge

Continuous Charge Distribution

In practice, we deal with charges much greater in magnitude than the charge on an electron, so we can ignore the quantum nature of charges and imagine that the charge is spread in a region in a continuous manner. Such a charge distribution is known as a continuous charge distribution.

Different Types of Continuous Charge Distributions

(a) **Volume Charge Distribution** It is a charge distribution spread over a three dimensional volume or region V of space. We define the volume charge density at any point in this volume as the charge contained per unit volume at that point, *i.e.*, $\rho = \frac{dq}{dV}$

The SI unit for ρ is coulomb per cubic metre (Cm^{-3}).

e.g., If a charge q is distributed over the entire volume of a sphere of radius R, then its volume charge density is

$$\rho = \frac{q}{\frac{4}{3}\pi R^3} \text{ Cm}^{-3}$$

The charge contained in small volume dV is

$$dq = \rho\, dV$$

(b) **Surface Charge Distribution** It is a charge distribution spread over a two-dimensional surface S in space. We define the surface charge density at any point on this surface as the charge per unit area at that point, *i.e.*,

$$\sigma = \frac{dq}{dS}$$

The SI unit for σ is Cm^{-2}.

e.g., If a charge q is uniformly distributed over the surface of a spherical conductor of radius R, then its surface charge density is $\sigma = \frac{q}{4\pi R^2} \text{ Cm}^{-2}$

The charge contained in small area dS is

$$dq = \sigma dS$$

(c) **Line Charge Distribution** It is a charge distribution along a one-dimensional curve or line L in space. We define the line charge density at any point on this line as the charge per unit length of the line at that point,

i.e., $\lambda = \frac{dq}{dL}$.

The SI unit for λ is Cm^{-1}.

e.g., If a charge q is uniformly distributed over a ring of radius R, then its linear charge density is

$$\lambda = \frac{q}{2\pi R} \text{ Cm}^{-1}$$

The charge contained in small length dL is

$$dq = \lambda\, dL$$

Electric Field

When an electric charge q_0 is held in the vicinity of another charge Q, then the charge q_0 experiences a force of attraction or repulsion. We say that this force is due to interaction of electric fields of two charges Q and q_0. Thus, we may define.

Electric field due to a given charge as the space around the charge in which electrostatic force of attraction or repulsion due to the charge can be experienced by any other charge.

Electric Field Intensity or Electric Field Strength

The electric field intensity at any point is the strength of electric field at that point. It is defined as the force experienced by unit positive charge placed at that point. If $\vec{F}$ is the force acting on a small test charge $+q_0$ at any point $\vec{r}$, then electric field intensity at this point is given by

$$\vec{E}(\vec{r}) = \frac{\vec{F}(\vec{r})}{q_0}$$

The SI unit of electric field intensity is newton per coulomb (N/C).

Electric field intensity is obviously a vector. The direction of $\vec{E}$ is the same as the direction of $\vec{F}$.

Dimensional formula of the electric field intensity is $[MLT^{-3}A^{-1}]$.

Electric Field Intensity Due to a Point Charge

Suppose, we have to calculate electric field intensity at any point P due to a point charge Q at O, where $OP = r_0$. Imagine a small positive test charge q_0 at P. According to Coulomb's law, force on charge q_0 at P is

$$\vec{F} = \frac{1}{4\pi \epsilon_0} \frac{Qq_0}{r_0^2} \hat{r}_0$$

Where, $\hat{r}_0$ is unit vector directed from Q towards q_0.

As, $\vec{E} = \frac{\vec{F}}{q_0}$

$\therefore$ $$\vec{E} = \frac{1}{4\pi \epsilon_0} \frac{Q}{r_0^2} \hat{r}_0$$

O Q —— P q_0 → $\vec{F}$

← r_0 →

Electric Field Intensity Due to a Group of Charge

The electric field intensity at any point due to a group of point charges in equal to the vector sum of the electric field intensities due to individual charges at the same point. For this, we first calculate the electric field intensity at the given point P due to individual charges, as if other charges were not there and then add them vectorially *i.e.*,

$$\vec{E} = \vec{E}_1 + \vec{E}_2 + \vec{E}_3 + \ldots + \vec{E}_n$$

$$\vec{E} = \frac{1}{4\pi \epsilon_0} \sum_{i=1}^{i=n} \frac{Q_i}{r_i^2} \hat{r}_i$$

Here, r_i is the distance of the point P from the ith charge Q_i and $\hat{r}_i$ is unit vector directed from Q_i to the point P.

Now, suppose the point charges $Q_1, Q_2, Q_3, \ldots, Q_n$ are located in vacuum at position $\vec{r}_1, \vec{r}_2, \vec{r}_3 \ldots \vec{r}_n$, respectively. We have to calculate electric field intensity $\vec{E}$ at any point P whose position vector is $\vec{r}_0$. As net force at P is vector sum of the forces due to individual charges, therefore we can write

$$\vec{F} = \frac{q_0}{4\pi \epsilon_0} \sum_{i=1}^{i=n} \frac{Q_i}{|\vec{r}_0 - \vec{r}_i|^3} (\vec{r}_0 - \vec{r}_i)$$

$$\vec{E} = \frac{\vec{F}}{q_0} = \frac{1}{4\pi \epsilon_0} \sum_{i=1}^{i=n} \frac{Q_i}{|\vec{r}_0 - \vec{r}_i|^3} (\vec{r}_0 - \vec{r}_i)$$

Note $\vec{E}$ is a vector quantity that varies from one point to another point in space. Its value depends on the positions of the source charges. The direction of $\vec{E}$ due to a group of discrete charges is determined using polygon law of vectors.

Force on Electric Charge in Electric Field

The electric force $(\vec{F})$ on a charge q_0 in an electric field of intensity $\vec{E}$ is

$$\vec{F} = q_0 \cdot \vec{E}$$

$$\Rightarrow \quad |\vec{F}| = F = q_0 \cdot E$$

Direction of $\vec{F}$ on (+)ve is in the direction of field while on (–)ve, direction of $\vec{F}$ is opposite direction of field.

Electric Field at an Axial Point of a Circular Charged Ring

$$E = \frac{1}{4\pi \epsilon_0} \left[\frac{q.x}{(r^2 + x^2)^{3/2}} \right]$$

Where, r = Radius of the ring

q = Charge on ring

x = Distance of axial point from its centre

Lines of Electric Force

Electric Lines of Force or Electric Field Lines

- The concept of electric field was introduced by Michael Faraday. The magnitude of electric field strength at any point is measured by the number of electric lines of force passing per unit small area around that point normally and the direction of field at any point is given by the tangent to the line of force at the point.
- An electric line of force is that imaginary smooth curve drawn in an electric field along which a free isolated unit positive (initially at rest) charge moves.

Properties

- The lines of force diverge out radially from a (+ve) charge and converge at a (–ve) charge. More correctly the lines of force are always directed from higher to lower potential.

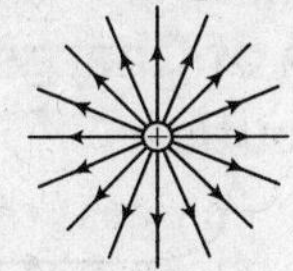

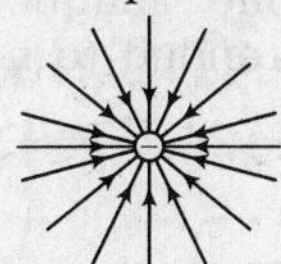

- The tangent drawn at any point on line of force gives the direction of force acting on a positive charge placed at that point.
- Two lines of force never intersect. If they are assumed to intersect, there will be two directions of electric field at the point of intersection, which is impossible.
- These lines have a tendency to contract in tension like a stretched elastic string. This actually explains attraction between opposite charges.

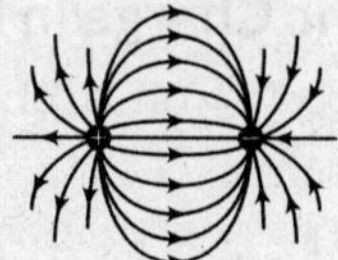

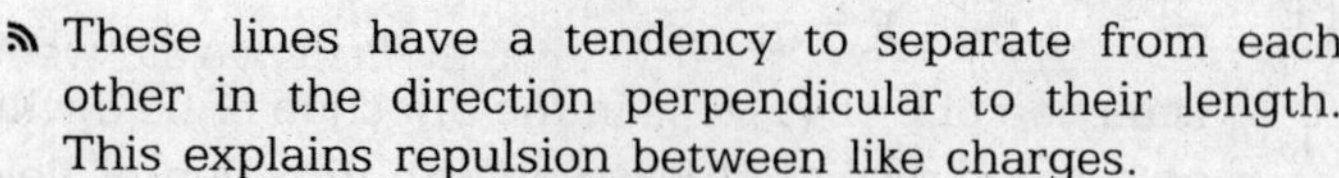

- These lines have a tendency to separate from each other in the direction perpendicular to their length. This explains repulsion between like charges.

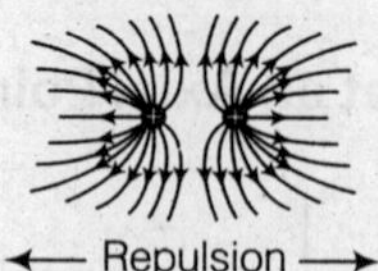

- The number of lines originating or terminating on a charge is proportional to the magnitude of charge. In rationalized MKS system ($1/\varepsilon_0$) electric lines are associated with unit charge. So, if a body encloses a charge q. Total line of force associated with it (called flux) will be $\dfrac{q}{\varepsilon_0}$

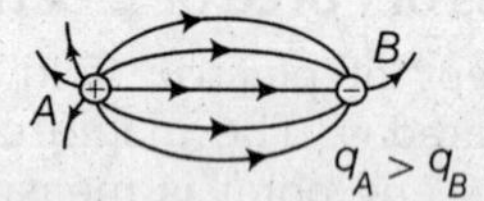

- Total lines of force may be fractional as lines of force are imaginary.
- Lines of force ends or starts normally on the surface of a conductor.
- If there in no electric field there will be no lines of force.
- Lines of force per unit area normal to the area at a point represents magnitude of intensity, crouded lines represent strong field while distant lines represent weak field.
- Electric lines of force differ from magnetic lines of force.
  (a) Electric lines of force never form closed loop while magnetic lines are always closed or extended to infinity.

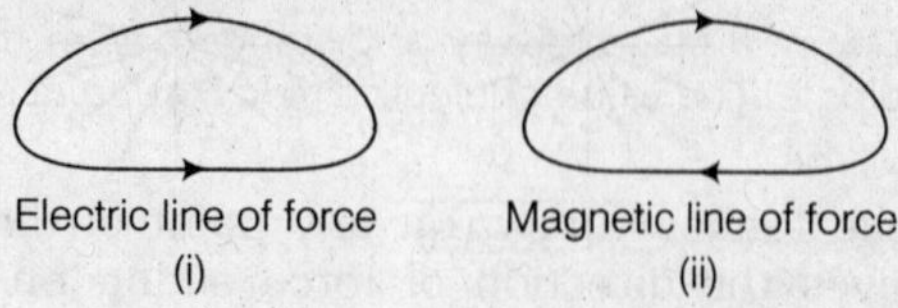

  (b) Electric lines of force always emerge or terminate normally on the surface of charged conductor, while magnetic lines emerge or terminate on the surface of a magnetic material at any angle.
  (c) Electric lines of force do not exist inside a conductor but magnetic lines of force may exist inside magnetic material.

Lines of force do not exist inside a conductor (as field inside a conductor is zero) as shown. (Electrostatic shielding)

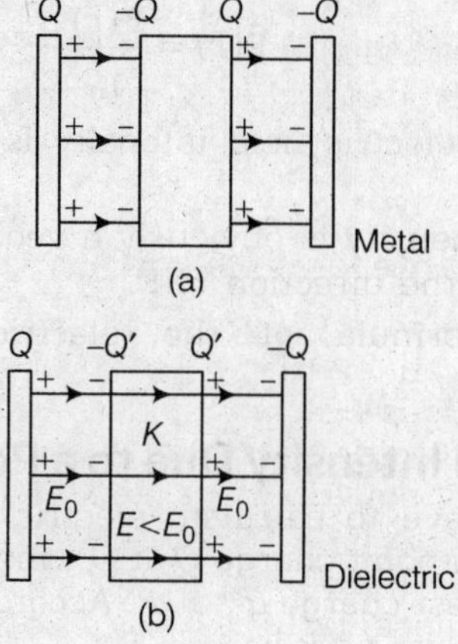

Electric Dipole

A pair of equal and opposite charges separated by a small distance is called an electric dipole.

Examples of Electric Dipoles

Dipoles are common in nature. In molecules like H_2O, HCl, C_2H_5OH, CH_3COOH, etc., the centre of positive charges does not fall exactly over the centre of negative charges. Such molecules are electric dipoles. They have a permanent dipole moment.

Dipole Moment

It measures the strength of an electric dipole. The dipole moment of an electric dipole is a vector whose magnitude is either charge times the separation between the two opposite charges and the direction is along the dipole axis from the negative to the positive charge.

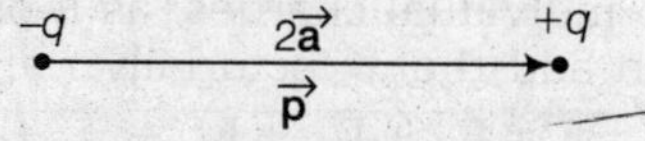

As shown in figure above consider an electric dipole consisting of charges $+q$ and $-q$ and separated by distance $2a$. The line joining the charges is called dipole axis.

Dipole moment = Either charge × a vector drawn from negative to positive charge.

or $\vec{p} = q \times 2\vec{a}$

Thus, the dipole moment $\vec{p}$ is a vector quantity. Its direction is along the dipole axis from $-q$ to $+q$ and its magnitude is

$$p = q \times 2a$$

The SI unit of dipole moment is coulomb metre (Cm). When both the charge q and separation $2a$ are finite, the dipole has a finite size (equal to $2a$), a location (midpoint between $+q$ and $-q$), a direction and strength.

Dimensional formula of dipole moment is $[M^{\circ} LTA]$.

Note

- Debye (D) is also a unit of Dipole moment $1D = \frac{1}{3} \times 10^{-29}$ Cm
- Dipole placed in an external electric field experiences a pair of forces which causes rotational motion.

Dipole Field

The electric field produced by an electric dipole is called a dipole field. This can be determined by using (*a*) the formula for the field of a point charge and (b) the principle of superposition.

Variation of Dipole Field with Distance

The total charge of an electric dipole is zero. But the electric field of an electric dipole is not zero. This is because the charges + *q* and −*q* are separated by some distance, so the electric fields due to them when added do not exactly cancel out. However, at distances much larger than the dipole size ($r >> 2a$), the fields of + *q* and − *q* nearly cancel out. Hence, we expect a dipole field to fall off, at larger distance, faster than $1/r^2$, typical of the field due to a single charge. In fact a dipole field at larger distances falls off as $1/r^3$.

Torque on a Dipole in a Uniform Electric Field

As shown in figure (a), consider an electric dipole consisting of charges +*q* and −*q* and of length 2*a* placed in a uniform electric field $\vec{E}$ making an angle θ with it. It has a dipole moment of magnitude,

$$p = q \times 2a$$

Force exerted on charge + *q* by field $\vec{E} = q\vec{E}$. (along $\vec{E}$)

Force exerted on charge −*q* by field $\vec{E} = -q\vec{E}$. (opposite to $\vec{E}$)

$$\vec{E}_{\text{Total}} = +q\vec{E} - q\vec{E} = 0$$

(a)

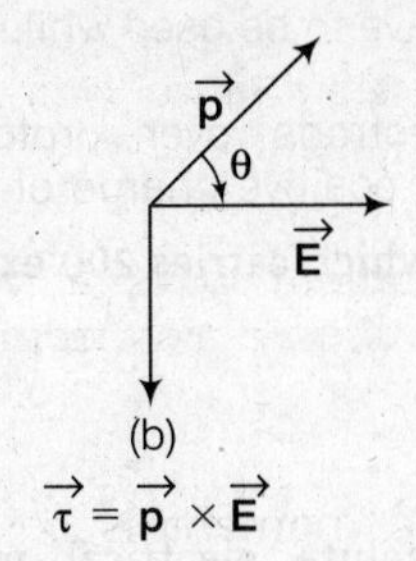

(b)

$$\vec{\tau} = \vec{p} \times \vec{E}$$

(a) Torque on a dipole in a uniform electric field.

(b) Direction of torque as given by right hand screw rule.

Hence, the net translating force on a dipole in a uniform electric field is zero. But the two equal and opposite forces act at different points of the dipole. They form a couple which exerts a torque.

Torque = Either force × Perpendicular distance between the two forces

$$\tau = qE \times 2a\sin\theta = (q \times 2a)\, E\sin\theta$$

$$\Rightarrow \tau = pE\sin\theta \quad (p = q \times 2a)$$

As the direction of torque $\vec{\tau}$ is perpendicular to both $\vec{p}$ and $\vec{E}$, so we can write

$$\vec{\tau} = \vec{p} \times \vec{E}$$

The direction of vector $\vec{\tau}$ is that in which a right handed screw would advance when rotated from $\vec{p}$ to $\vec{E}$. As shown in Figure (b), the direction of vector $\vec{\tau}$ is perpendicular to and points into the plane of paper.

When the dipole is released, the torque $\vec{\tau}$ tends to align the dipole with the field $\vec{E}$ *i.e.,* tends to reduce angle θ to 0. When the dipole gets aligned with $\vec{E}$, the torque $\vec{\tau}$ becomes zero.

Clearly, the torque on the dipole will be maximum when the dipole is held perpendicular to $\vec{E}$. Thus,

$$\tau_{\max} = pE\sin 90° = pE$$

WORK DONE BY ELECTRIC DIPOLE

$W = PE(1 - \cos\theta)$

Work done is stored in the form of potential energy in dipole. i.e., Stored potential energy in electric dipole is

$E_p = W = PE(1 - \cos\theta)$

Explanation of $W = E_p = PE(1 - \cos\theta)$

- If $\theta = 0°$, then $\cos\theta = 1$,
  $W = E_p = PE(1 - 1) = 0$
- If $\theta = 90°$, then $\cos\theta = 0$
  $w = E_p = PE$
- If $\theta = 180°$, then $\cos 180° = -1$
  $\therefore W = EP = 2PE$

Electric Field and Potential Due to Electric Dipole

Suppose a point *P* placed away at distance *r* from the middle point of a dipole. The value of electric field *E* at point $P(r, \theta)$ due to dipole will be

$$E = \frac{1}{4\pi\varepsilon_0} \frac{P}{r^3} \sqrt{1 + 3\cos^2\theta}$$

(In air or vacuum)

Practice Questions

Level I

1. Number of electronic charge in 1 C is

(a) 6.50×10^{18} (b) 6.00×10^{19}
(c) 6.25×10^{18} (d) None of these

2. The charge developed on a glass rod when rubbed with silk is called

(a) negative (b) positive
(c) neutral (d) None of these

3. Coulomb's law is valid only

(a) for like charges (b) for unlike charges
(c) for point charge (d) None of these

4. SI unit of permittivity is

(a) $C^2N^{-1}m^{-2}$ (b) Fm
(c) Fm^{-1} (d) None of these

5. Two protons in a molecule is separated by 3×10^{-10}m. The electrostatic force exerted by one proton on the other is

(a) 2×10^{-9}C (b) 2.56×10^{-9}C
(c) 1.9×10^{-9}C (d) 2.22×10^{-10}C

6. Electric force between two point charges q and Q at rest is F. Now if a charge $-q$ is placed next to q what will be the total force on Q?

(a) $\left(\frac{q'}{q}\right)F$ (b) zero
(c) qF (d) None of these

7. Electric lines of force about a negative point charge are

(a) circular anti-clockwise
(b) circular clockwise
(c) radial, inwards
(d) radial, outwards

8. Electric lines of force

(a) exist everywhere
(b) exist only in the immediate vicinity of electric charges
(c) exist only when both positive and negative charges are near one another
(d) are imaginary

9. Debye is the unit of

(a) electric flux
(b) electric dipole moment
(c) electric potential
(d) electric field intensity

10. What is the mass of an electron?

(a) 9.1×10^{-31} kg
(b) 9.1×10^{-31} g
(c) 1.6×10^{-19} kg
(d) 1.6×10^{-19} g

11. Which of the following is not an insulator?

(a) glass
(b) rubber
(c) ebonite
(d) human body

12. An object is charged when it has a charge imbalance, which means the

(a) object contains no electrons
(b) objeet contains no protons
(c) object contains equal number of electrons and protons
(d) object contains unequal number of electrons and protons

13. The cause of charging is

(a) actual transfer of protons
(b) actual transfer of electrons
(c) actual transfer of neutrons
(d) None of the above

14. When a plastic comb is passed through dry hair, the charge acquired by the comb is

(a) always negative
(b) always positive
(c) sometimes negative
(d) None of the above

15. Out of glass (rod) and silk (cloth), work function of glass is

(a) smaller
(b) larger
(c) equal
(d) None of the above

16. The cause of quantization of electric charge is

(a) transfer of electrons
(b) transfer of protons
(c) transfer of integral number of electrons
(d) None of the above

17. What is not true?

(a) It is not possible to create or destroy net charge carried by any isolated system
(b) Charges can be created or destroyed in equal and unlike pairs only
(c) Proper signs have to be used while adding the charges in a system
(d) Excess of electrons over protons in a body is responsible for positive charge of the body

18. Charge on a body which carries 200 excess electrons is

(a) -3.2×10^{-18} C
(b) 3.2×10^{-18} C
(b) -3.2×10^{-17} C
(c) 3.2×10^{-17} C

19. The value of absolute electrical permittivity of free space is

(a) 9×10^{9} Nm^2C^{-2}
(b) 9×10^{-9} Nm^2C^{-2}
(b) 8.85×10^{-12} $C^2N^{-1}m^{-2}$
(c) $8.85 \times 10^{-12} C^2Nm^{-2}$

20. SI unit of electric field in tarsity is

(a) $C \times m$ (b) NC
(c) NC^{-1} (d) $A \times m$

Level II

1. Two charges are placed a certain distance apart in air. If a glass slab is introduced between them, the force between them will
(a) increase (b) decrease
(c) remains the same (d) be zero

2. The ratio of electric force between two electrons to two protons separated by the same distance in air is
(a) 10^0 (b) 10^6 (c) 10^4 (d) None

3. Two charges are placed a certain distance apart. A metallic sheet is placed them. What will happen to the force between the charges?
(a) increase (b) decrease
(c) remains unchanged (d) Either (a) or (b)

4. The electric field created by a point charge falls with distance r from the point charge as
(a) $\frac{1}{r}$ (b) $\frac{1}{r^2}$
(c) $\frac{1}{r^3}$ (d) $\frac{1}{r^4}$

5. A soap bubble is given a negative charge, then its radius
(a) decreases
(b) increases
(c) remain unchanged
(d) nothing can be predicted as information is insufficient

6. If a unit positive charge is taken from one point to another over an equipotential surface, then
(a) work is done on the charge
(b) work is done by the charge
(c) work done is constant
(d) no work is done

7. An electric dipole is placed in an electric field generated by a point charge
(a) the net electric force on the dipole must be zero
(b) the net electric force on the dipole may be zero
(c) the torque on the dipole due to the field must be zero
(d) the torque on the dipole due to the field may be zero

8. An electric dipole of moment $\vec{\mathbf{P}}$ is placed in the position of stable equilibrium in uniform electric field of intensity $\vec{\mathbf{E}}$. The couple required to rotate it through an angle θ from the initial position is
(a) $pE\cos\theta$ (b) $pE\sin\theta$
(c) $pE\tan\theta$ (d) $-pE\cos\theta$

9. An electric dipole of moment $\vec{\mathbf{P}}$ is placed in the position of stable equilibrium in uniform electric field of intensity $\vec{\mathbf{E}}$. This is rotated through an angle θ from the initial position. The potential energy of the electric dipole in the final position is
(a) $pE\cos\theta$ (b) $pE\sin\theta$
(c) $pE(1-\cos\theta)$ (d) $-pE\cos\theta$

10. In the above question, the work done in deflecting the electric dipole through an angle θ from initial position of stable equilibrium is
(a) $pE\sin\theta$ (b) $-pE\cos\theta$
(c) $pE(1-\cos\theta)$ (d) $pE\cos\theta$

11. An electric dipole when placed in a uniform electric field $\vec{\mathbf{E}}$ will have minimum potential energy if the dipole moment makes the following angle with $\vec{\mathbf{E}}$.
(a) π (b) $\pi/2$
(c) zero (d) $3\pi/2$

12. F_G and F_e represent gravitational and electrostatic force respectively between electrons situated at a distance of 10 cm. The ratio of F_G/F_e is of the order
(a) 10^{42} (b) 10 (c) 1 (d) 10^{-42}

13. Three particles have charges + 20 μC each and they are fixed at the corners of an equilateral triangle of side 0.5 m. The force on each of the particles has magnitude
(a) zero (b) 14.4 N
(c) 28.8 N (d) $14.4\sqrt{3}$ N

14. How far would the electron of hydrogen atom have to be removed from the nucleus for the force of electrostatic attraction to equal the weight of the atom? (Avogadro's number $= 6.02 \times 10^{23}$ gm-atom)
(a) 0.25 m (b) 1.19 m
(c) 1.5 m (d) 12 m

15. Two point charges are placed at separation of 3 m. The minimum possible force between them will be
(a) 2.56×10^{-29} N (b) 9×10^9 N
(c) 1.6×10^{-19} N (d) 3×10^9 N

16. Two identical metal balls with charges $+2Q$ and $-Q$ are separated by some distance and exert a force F on each other. They are joined by a conducting wire, which is then removed. The force between them will now be
(a) F (b) $F/2$
(c) $F/4$ (d) $F/8$

17. Two point charges q_1 and q_2 are placed at separation d in vacuum. the force acting between them is decreased by 75% when a dielectric slab of dielectric constant k and thickness $d/2$ is placed between them. The value of k is
(a) 4 (b) 9
(c) 16 (d) 25

18. An electron is sent in electric field of intensity 9.1×10^6 NC^{-1} The acceleration produced is (mass of electron $= 9.1 \times 10^{-31}$ kg)
(a) 1.6 ms^{-2} (b) 1.6×10^{18} ms^{-2}
(c) 3.2×10^{18} ms^{-2} (d) 0.8×10^{18} ms^{-2}

19. A charge q is placed at the centre of the line joining the equal charges Q. The system of three charges will be in equilibrium if q is equal to
(a) $-Q/2$ (b) $-Q/4$
(c) $-4Q$ (d) $+Q/2$

20. Three charges $+4q$, Q and q are placed in a straight line of length l at points distance 0, $(l/2)$ and l respectively. What should be Q in order to make the net force on q to be zero?
(a) $-q$ (b) $-2q$
(c) $-q/2$ (d) $4q$

21. A point positive charge is brought near an isolated conducting sphere, figure. The electric field is best given by

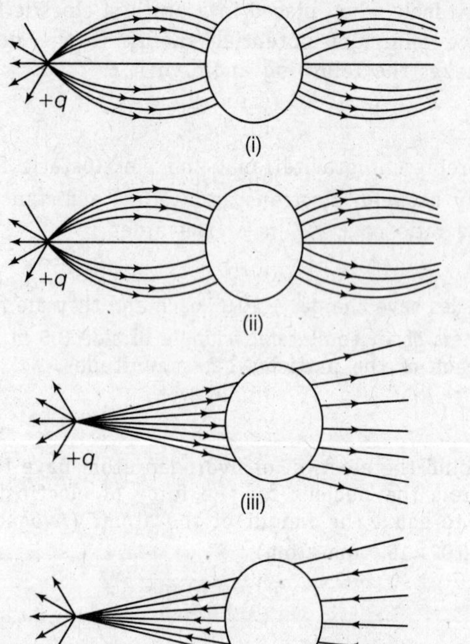

(a) figure (i) (b) figure (ii)
(c) figure (iii) (d) figure (iv)

22. Two plates are 1 cm apart and the potential difference between them is 10 volt. The electric field between the plates is
(a) 10 N/C
(b) 500 N/C
(c) 1000 N/C
(d) 250 N/C

23. A semi-circular arc of radius a is charged uniformly and the charge per unit length is λ. The electric field at its centre is
(a) $\lambda/(2\pi\varepsilon_0 a^2)$
(b) $\lambda/(4\varepsilon_0 a)$
(c) $\lambda^2/(2\pi\varepsilon_0 a)$
(d) $\lambda/(2\pi\varepsilon_0 a)$

24. The electric strength of air is 2.0×10^6 N/C. The largest charge that a metallic sphere of 3 mm radius can hold is
(a) 2 nC
(b) 3 nC
(c) 1.5 nC
(d) 6 nC

25. Two point charges of 20 μC and 80 μC are 10 cm apart. Where will the electric field strength be zero on the line joining the charges?
(a) –0.1 m
(b) –0.04 m
(c) 0.033 m
(d) –0.33 m

Answers

Level I

1. (c)	**2.** (b)	**3.** (c)	**4.** (a)	**5.** (b)	**6.** (b)	**7.** (c)	**8.** (d)	**9.** (b)	**10.** (a)
11. (d)	**12.** (d)	**13.** (b)	**14.** (a)	**15.** (a)	**16.** (c)	**17.** (d)	**18.** (c)	**19.** (c)	**20.** (c)

Level II

1. (b)	**2.** (a)	**3.** (b)	**4.** (b)	**5.** (b)	**6.** (d)	**7.** (d)	**8.** (b)	**9.** (d)	**10.** (c)
11. (b)	**12.** (d)	**13.** (d)	**14.** (a)	**15.** (a)	**16.** (d)	**17.** (b)	**18.** (b)	**19.** (b)	**20.** (a)
21. (a)	**22.** (c)	**23.** (b)	**24.** (a)	**25.** (c)					

Hints and Solutions

Level II

1. $F_g = \dfrac{1 q_1 q_2}{4\pi\varepsilon_0 r^2} = \dfrac{F_v}{K}$

As K (for glass) > 1. $\therefore F_g < F_v$

2. $\dfrac{F_{e.e}}{F_{p.p}} = 10^0 = 1$, because force depends only on charges distance and nature of medium.

3. $F_m = \dfrac{F_0}{K}$. For metals $K = \infty$, therefore, $F_m \to 0$, in the thickness of sheet. Hence, force between the charges will decrease.

4. $E = \dfrac{1}{4\pi\varepsilon_0}\cdot\dfrac{q}{r^2}$

5. For brass, $k = \infty$

$$F = \frac{1}{4\pi\varepsilon_0}\times\frac{1}{k}\times\frac{q_1 q_2}{r^2} = 0$$

6. The Coulomb's force obeys the Newton's third law of motion. Hence, the ratio of the forces acting on them will be 1 : 1.

7. $F_a = \dfrac{1}{4\pi\varepsilon_0}\times\dfrac{q_1 q_2}{r^2}$ and $F_m = \dfrac{1}{4\pi\varepsilon_0}\times\dfrac{1}{k}\times\dfrac{q_1 q_2}{r^2}$

$\therefore \dfrac{F_a}{F_m} = \dfrac{k}{1}$

11. $U_p = \vec{p}\cdot\vec{E} = pE\cos\theta$

$(U_p) = \text{minimum} = 0$

$\therefore\ p = pE\cos\theta$ or $\cos\theta = 0$ or $\theta = 90°$

12. $F_e = (9\times10^9)\left[\frac{e\times e}{r^2}\right]$ and $F_G = (6.6\times10^{-11})\left[\frac{m_e\times m_e}{r^2}\right]$

$$\therefore \frac{F_G}{F_e} = \frac{6.6\times10^{-11}}{9\times10^9}\times\frac{(m_e)^2}{(e)^2}$$

$$= \frac{6.6\times10^{-11}}{9\times10^9}\times\frac{(9.1\times10^{-31})^2}{(1.6\times10^{-19})^2} = 10^{-42}$$

13. On every particle, there will be two forces of equal magnitude F and inclined at 60°. Here

$$F = \frac{1}{4\pi\varepsilon_0}\times\frac{q_1q_2}{r^2}$$

$$= (9\times10^9)\times\frac{(20\times10^{-6})(20\times10^{-6})}{(0.5)^2} \approx 14.4\text{ N}$$

Hence, resultant force is given by

$$= [F^2 + F^2 + 2FF\cos60°]^{1/2} = \sqrt{3}F = 14.4\sqrt{3}\text{ N}$$

14. $\frac{1}{4\pi\varepsilon_0}\times\frac{e^2}{r^2} = mg$ or $r^2 = \frac{e^2}{4\pi\varepsilon_0\times mg}$

$$\therefore\ r^2 = \frac{(9\times10^9)(1.6\times10^{-19})^2}{\left\{\frac{1\times10^{-3}}{(6.02\times10^{23})}\right\}\times9.8}$$

Solving, we get $r = 0.25$ m

15. We know that, $F = \frac{1}{4\pi\varepsilon_0}\times\frac{q_1q_2}{r^2}$

The force between the two charges separated at a distance r will be minimum when $q_1 = q_2 = e$

$$\therefore\ F_{\min} = \frac{1}{4\pi\varepsilon_0}\times\frac{e^2}{r^2} = (9\times10^9)\frac{(1.6\times10^{-19})^2}{(3)^2}$$

$$= 2.56\times10^{-29}\text{ N}$$

16. $F = \frac{1}{4\pi\varepsilon_0}\times\frac{2Q\times Q}{r^2} = \frac{1}{4\pi\varepsilon_0}\times\frac{2Q^2}{r^2}$

After joining by a conducting wire, the charge on each metal ball will be

$(2Q - Q)/2 = Q/2$

$$\therefore\ F' = \frac{1}{4\pi\varepsilon_0}\times\frac{(Q/2)(Q/2)}{r^2} = \frac{1}{4\pi\varepsilon_0}\left(\frac{Q^2}{4r^2}\right) = \frac{F}{8}$$

17. We know that, $F \propto \frac{1}{d^2}$ ...(i)

When dielectric is introduced, then

$$\frac{F}{4} \propto \frac{1}{\left(\frac{d}{2}+\frac{d}{2}\sqrt{k}\right)^2} \quad ...(ii)$$

Dividing Eq. (ii) by Eq. (i), we get

$$\frac{1}{4} = \frac{4}{(1+\sqrt{k})^2}$$

$\Rightarrow\ 1+\sqrt{k} = 4 \Rightarrow \sqrt{k} = 3 \Rightarrow k = 9$

18. Electric field intensity is given by

$$E = \frac{F}{q} = \frac{F}{e} \text{ (Here, } q = e)$$

$\Rightarrow\ F = eE$

$\Rightarrow\ ma = eE$ (Because $F = ma$)

$\Rightarrow\ a = \frac{eE}{m}$

Substituting

$e = 1.6\times10^{-19}$ C; $E = 9.1\times10^6$ NC^{-1}

$m = 9.1\times10^{-31}$ kg,

We get $a = 1.6\times10^{18}$ ms^{-2}.

19. Let the distance between the two charges Q and Q be r.

Force on Q due to charge q at a distance $(r/2)$

$$= \frac{1}{4\pi\varepsilon_0}\times\frac{qQ}{(r/2)^2}$$

Force on Q due to other charge Q at a distance r

$$= \frac{1}{4\pi\varepsilon_0}\times\frac{Q\times Q}{(r)^2}$$

$$\therefore\ \frac{1}{4\pi\varepsilon_0}\times\frac{qQ}{(r/2)^2} + \frac{1}{4\pi\varepsilon_0}\times\frac{Q\times Q}{r^2} = 0$$

$$4q = -Q \Rightarrow q = -Q/4$$

20. Force on q due to charge $+4q$ which is at a distance l

$$= \frac{1}{4\pi\varepsilon_0}\times\frac{4q\times q}{(l)^2}$$

Force on q due to charge Q at a distance $l/2$

$$= \frac{1}{4\pi\varepsilon_0}\times\frac{qQ}{(l/2)^2}$$

Hence $\frac{1}{4\pi\varepsilon_0}\times\frac{4q\times q}{l^2} + \frac{1}{4\pi\varepsilon_0}\frac{qQ}{(l/2)^2} = 0$

$\therefore\ Q = -q$

21. When a point positive charge is brought near an isolated conducting sphere, there developes some negative charge on left side of the sphere and an equal positive charge on the right side of the sphere. Electric lines of force emitting from the point positive charge and normally on the left side of the sphere. And due to positive charge on the right side of the sphere, the electric lines of force emanate normally from the right side. The electric field is best given by figure (i).

22. $E = \frac{V}{d} = \frac{10\text{ volt}}{0.01\text{ m}} = 1000$ N/C

23. $E = \Sigma\frac{dQ}{4\pi\varepsilon_0a^2} = \Sigma\frac{\lambda dl}{4\pi\varepsilon_0a^2} = \frac{\lambda(\pi a)}{4\pi\varepsilon_0a^2} = \frac{\lambda}{4\varepsilon_0a}$

24. Electric field on the surface of the sphere should not exceed 2.0×10^6 N/C. The electric field on metallic sphere

$$= \frac{1}{4\pi\varepsilon_0}\times\frac{q}{r^2} = (9\times10^9)\frac{q}{(3\times10^{-3})^2}$$

Hence $(9\times10^9)\frac{q}{(3\times10^{-3})^2} = 2.0\times10^6$

$\Rightarrow\ q = 2\times10^{-9}\text{C} = 2$ nC.

25. Let the electric field strength be zero at a distance x. Then

$$\frac{1}{4\pi\varepsilon_0}\times\frac{(20\times10^{-6})}{x^2} = \frac{1}{4\pi\varepsilon_0}\times\frac{(80\times10^{-6})}{(10-x)^2}$$

$$\Rightarrow\ \frac{(10-x)^2}{x^2} = 4 \Rightarrow \frac{10-x}{x} = \pm2$$

This gives $x = -10$ cm $\Rightarrow$ 3.33 cm *i.e.,* 0.033 m.

14

Fluid Pressure

Pressure

It is defined as the force per unit area acting normally on an infinitesimally *i.e.*, very small element of area.

Pressure is a scalar physical quantity having no directional properties. This is so because if we immerse a pressure sensor in a fluid, whatever be the orientation of the pressure sensor, the reading comes out to be the same.

$$p_{av} = \frac{F}{A}$$

$$p = \lim_{\Delta A \to 0} \frac{\Delta F}{\Delta A} = \frac{dF}{dA}$$

Where, p = pressure, F = force, A = area

Pressure Due to Fluid Column

The liquid pressure at a depth h is given by $p = \rho g h$, where ρ is the density of the liquid.

$\therefore \quad p \propto h$

Units of Pressure

SI unit is Pa or pascal.

$$1 \text{ Pa} = 1 \text{ N/m}^2$$

Other related units are

$$1 \text{ atm} = 1.01 \times 10^5 \text{ Pa} = 760 \text{ torr}$$
$$= 14.7 \text{ lb/in}^2$$

1 torr = Pressure exerted by 1 mm of mercury column = 133 Pa

$$1 \text{ bar} = 10^5 \text{ Pa}$$
$$1 \text{ millibar} = 10^2 \text{ Pa}$$

Density

Density ρ of a substance is defined as its mass per unit volume. Density is scalar. Its SI unit is kg/m^3.

Density of Mixtures

If m_1 and m_2 are the masses whose densities are ρ_1 and ρ_2. Then, the density of the mixture will be

$$\rho = \frac{m}{V} = \frac{m_1 + m_2}{\frac{m_1}{\rho_1} + \frac{m_2}{\rho_2}} = \frac{\Sigma m_i}{\Sigma \frac{m_i}{\rho_i}}$$

If $\quad m_1 = m_2, \; \rho = \frac{2\rho_1\rho_2}{\rho_1 + \rho_2}$

If V_1 and V_2 are the two volumes of mass densities ρ_1 and ρ_2, then the density of mixture will be

$$\rho = \frac{m}{V} = \frac{\rho_1 V_1 + \rho_2 V_2}{V_1 + V_2} = \frac{\Sigma \rho_i V_i}{\Sigma V_i}$$

If $\quad V_1 = V_2 = V$, then $\rho = \frac{\rho_1 + \rho_2}{2}$

Pascal's Law

It can be stated in any of the following ways.

Pressure applied to an enclosed fluid is transmitted undiminished to all parts of the fluid and to the walls of the container.

Or

A liquid exerts equal pressure in all directions.

Applications of Pascal's Law

1. Hydraulic lifts, presses etc.
2. Hydraulic brakes

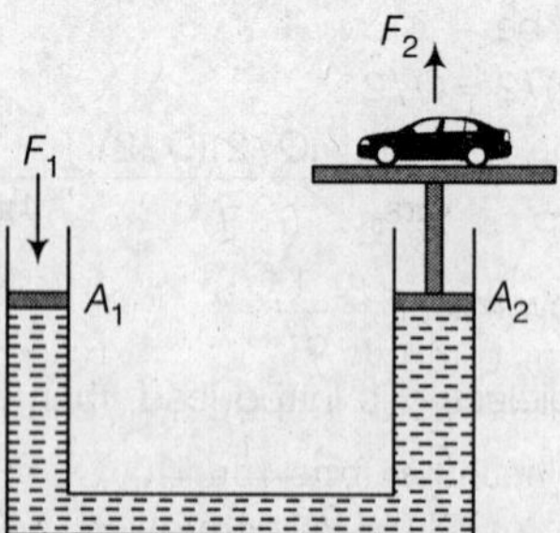

The pressure due to a small force F_1 applied to a piston of area A_1 is transmitted to the larger piston of area A_2. The pressure at the two pistons is the same because they are at the same level.

$$p = \frac{F_1}{A_1} = \frac{F_2}{A_2} \quad \Rightarrow \quad F_2 = \left(\frac{A_2}{A_1}\right) F_1$$

Consequently, the force on the larger piston is large. Thus, a small force F_1 acting on a small area A_1 results in a larger force F_2 acting on a larger area A_2.

Specific Gravity (Sp. Gr.)

It is the modern name of Relative Density (RD). It is the density of a substance as compared to the density of water.

$$\text{Sp.Gr.} = \text{RD} = \frac{\text{Density of the substance}}{\text{Density of water}}$$

$$\text{RD} = \frac{\text{Weight of object in air}}{\text{Loss of weight of object in water}}$$

$$\text{RD} = \frac{\text{Weight in air}}{(\text{Weight in air}) - (\text{Weight in water})}$$

$$\text{RD} = \frac{\text{Volume of object immersed in water}}{\text{Total volume of object}}$$

Buoyant Force

Whenever an object is placed in a fluid, the fluid exerts an upward force on it. This is called buoyant force.

Factors Affecting the Buoyant Force

(i) The buoyant force increases with increase of volume submerged.

(ii) The buoyant force increases with increase of density of liquid.

(iii) The buoyant force increases with increase of value of acceleration due to gravity.

Archimedes' Principle

When a body is immersed partially or wholly in a liquid, its weight appears to be reduced and the apparent loss in weight of the body is equal to the weight of liquid displaced by the body.

Let a body of mass M, volume V and density σ be immersed in liquid of density ρ, then according to Archimedes' principle, the loss in weight of body

= Force of buoyancy (F) acting upward

= Weight of liquid displaced by body = $V\rho g$

Apparent weight of body in liquid

$= V\sigma g - V\rho g = V(\sigma - \rho)g$

Upthrust

When a body is partly or wholly dipped in a fluid, the fluid exerts force on the body. The exerts force is called upthrust or buoyancy.

Laws of Floatation

When a body is immersed in a liquid ,then two forces act on it.

1. Weight of the body (w, vertically downwards).
2. Upthrust (F, upwards)

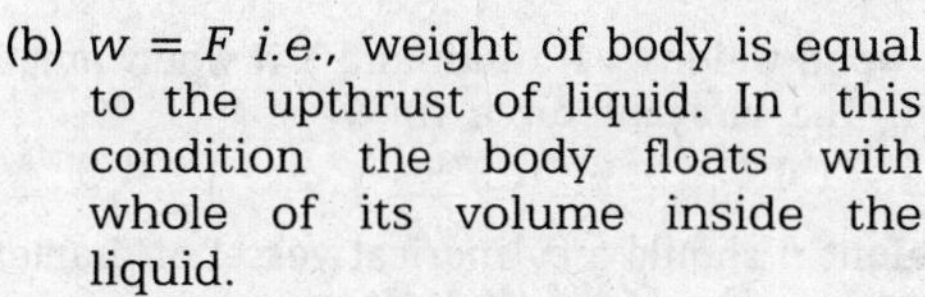

(a) $w > F$ *i.e.*, weight of body is greater than upthrust of liquid. In this condition body will sink.

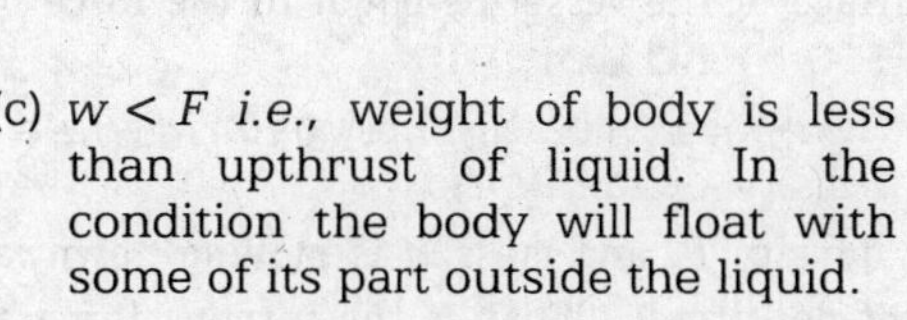

(b) $w = F$ *i.e.*, weight of body is equal to the upthrust of liquid. In this condition the body floats with whole of its volume inside the liquid.

(c) $w < F$ *i.e.*, weight of body is less than upthrust of liquid. In the condition the body will float with some of its part outside the liquid.

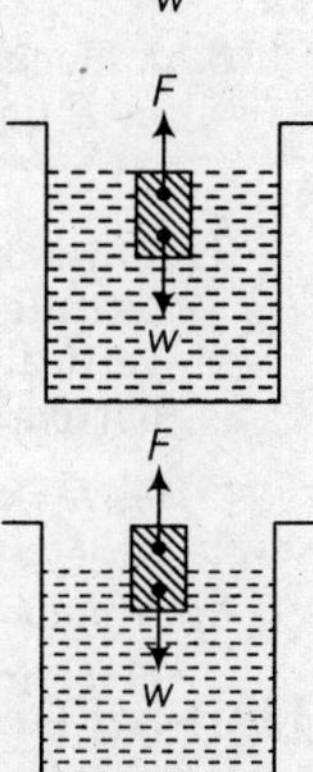

Practice Questions

Level I

1. Pressure is a
(a) vector quantity (b) scalar quantity
(c) Neither vector nor scalar (d) Either vector or scalar

2. If area becomes one-fourth, then pressure will become
(a) double (b) four times (c) one-fourth (d) same

3. The pressure exerted at any point on an enclosed liquid is transmitted equally in all directions. This statements known as
(a) Boyle's law (b) Archimedes' principle
(c) Pascal's law (d) Hook's law

4. The hydraulic brakes concept works on
(a) Charle's law (b) Pascal's law
(c) Boyle's law (d) None of these

5. If atmospheric pressure is suddenly down. It shows
(a) storm (b) raining
(c) extremely cold (d) clean sky

6. A piece of ice put inside a glass of full water in such a way that a part of floating ice outside the water. The level of water in the gllas if piece of ice completely melt will become
(a) high (b) same as earlier
(c) down (d) some rose then down

7. A pigion inside a parrot hanging with spring balance. If the parrot starts to fly, then reaching of spring balance will become
(a) raised (b) less
(c) zero (d) no change

8. Specific gravity of a material is 1.8 and its mass be 108 g. Volume of the material will becomes
(a) 108 cm^3 (b) 54 cm^3
(c) 60 cm^3 (d) 62 cm^3

Level II

1. Which will be affected in a gravity free space?
(a) Motion of charge (b) Viscosity
(c) Archimedes' uplift (d) None of these

2. A man is sitting in a boat which is floating in pond. If the man drinks some water from the pond, the level of water in the pond will
(a) rise a little (b) fall a little
(c) remain stationary (d) None of these

3. The pressure energy per unit volume of a liquid is
(a) $\frac{p}{\rho}$ (b) p (c) $p \times \rho$ (d) $\frac{\rho}{p}$

4. A body of mass 2 kg is floating in water with half its volume submerged. What would be the force required to wholly submerge it into water?
(a) 2 N (b) 9.8 N (c) 19.6 N (d) 4.9 N

5. A body weighs 50 *g* in air and 40 *g* in water. How much would it weigh in a liquid of specific gravity 1.5?
(a) 65 *g* (b) 45 *g*
(c) 30 *g* (d) 35 *g*

6. A block of wood weighs 4 N in air and 3 N when immersed in a liquid. The buoyant force (in N) is
(a) zero (b) 1 (c) 3/4 (d) 4/3

7. To what height h should a cylindrical vessel of diameter d be filled with a liquid so that the total force on the vertical surface of the vessel be equal to the force on the bottom?
(a) $h = d$ (b) $h = 2d$ (c) $h = 3d$ (d) $h = \frac{d}{2}$

8. A body of density D_1 and mass M is moving downward in glycerine of density D_2. What is the viscous force acting on it?
(a) $Mg\left(1 - \frac{D_2}{D_1}\right)$ (b) $Mg\left(1 - \frac{D_1}{D_2}\right)$
(c) MgD_1 (d) MgD_2

9. A large tank filled with water to a height h is to be emptied through a small hole at the bottom. The ratio of times taken for the level of water to fall from h to $\frac{h}{2}$ and from $\frac{h}{2}$ to zero is
(a) $\sqrt{2}$ (b) $\frac{1}{\sqrt{2}}$ (c) $\sqrt{2} - 1$ (d) $\frac{1}{\sqrt{2} - 1}$

10. From the figure, the correct observation is

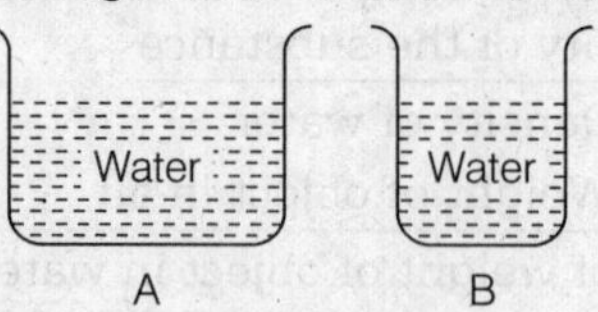

(a) the pressure on the bottom of tank (A) is greater than at the bottom of (B)
(b) the pressure on the bottom of the tank (A) is smaller than at the bottom of (B)
(c) the pressure depends on the shape of the container
(d) the pressure on the bottom of (A) and (B) is the same

11. At what speed, the velocity head of water is equal to pressure head of 40 cm of Hg?
(a) 10.3 m/s (b) 2.8 m/s
(c) 5.6 m/s (d) 8.4 m/s

12. An incompressible fluid flows steadily through a cylindrical pipe which has radius $2r$ at point A and radius r at B further along the flow direction. If the velocity at point A is v, its velocity at point B is
(a) $2v$ (b) v
(c) $\frac{v}{2}$ (d) $4v$

13. The cylindrical tube of a spray pump has a cross-section of 8 cm^2, one end of which has 40 fine holes each of area $10^{-8} m^2$. If the liquid flows inside the tube with a speed of 0.15 m/min, the speed with which the liquid is ejected through the holes is
(a) 50 m/s (b) 5 m/s
(c) 0.05 m/s (d) 0.5 m/s

14. A cylinder containing water stands on a table of height H. A small hole is punched in the side of cylinder at its base. The stream of water strikes the ground at a horizontal distance R from the table. Then, the depth of water in the cylinder is
(a) H (b) R
(c) $\sqrt{(RH)}$ (d) $R^2/4H$

15. A raft of wood of mass 120 kg floats in water. The weight that can be put on the raft to make it just sink, should be ($d = 600 \text{ kg/m}^3$)
(a) 80 kg (b) 50 kg
(c) 60 kg (d) 30 kg

Answers

Level I

1. (b)	2. (b)	3. (c)	4. (b)	5. (a)	6. (b)	7. (b)	8. (c)

Level II

1. (c)	2. (c)	3. (b)	4. (c)	5. (d)	6. (b)	7. (d)	8. (a)	9. (c)	10. (d)
11. (a)	12. (d)	13. (b)	14. (d)	15. (a)					

Hints and Solutions

Level II

4. Upthrust $= \left(\frac{V}{2} \times 1000\,g\right)$ N

For equilibrium, $2g = \frac{V}{2} \times 1000 \times g \Rightarrow V = \frac{4}{1000}\text{m}^3$

$\therefore$ Upthrust $= \frac{4 \times 1000 \times g}{1000 \times 2} = 2 \times 9.8 = 19.6$ N

5. Density of water, $\rho_w = 1\,\text{g/cm}^3$.

Density of liquid, ρ_l = Specfic gravity of liquid × Density of water $= 1.5 \times 1 = 1.5\,\text{g/cm}^3$

If V is the volume of the body, then weight of body in water = Weight of body in air − Upthrust of liquid

$\because \quad 40\,g = 50\,g - V \times \rho_w \times g$

$\Rightarrow \quad V = 50 - 40 = 10\,\text{cm}^3$

Weight of body in liquid

= Weight of body in air − Upthrust of liquid

$= 50\,g - V\rho_l\,g$

$= (50 - 10 \times 1.5)g = 35\,g$

6. Buoyant force F_B = Loss of weight of body in liquid $= 4 - 3 = 1$N

7. Let r be the radius of the vessel.

Force on the bottom $= \pi r^2 \times h\rho g$

Mean pressure on wall $= \frac{1}{2}\rho gh$

$\therefore$ Total force on the wall $= 2\pi rh \times \frac{1}{2}\rho gh$

Now, $\pi r^2 \times h\rho g = 2\pi rh \times (1/2)\,\rho gh$

This gives $h = r = (d/2)$

8. Volume of the body $V = M/D_1$

Mass of the liquid displaced by body,

$$M' = V\,D_2 = \frac{MD_2}{D_1}$$

Viscous force = Effective weight of the body

$$= Mg - M'g = Mg - \frac{MD_2}{D_1}g = Mg\left(1 - \frac{D_2}{D_1}\right)$$

9. The velocity of efflux when the tank is full is given by

$$v_1 = \sqrt{(2gh)}$$

The velocity of efflux when the tank is half

$$v_2 = \sqrt{\{2g(h/2)\}} = \sqrt{(gh)}$$

Similarly, the velocity of efflux when the tank is empty

$$v_3 = \sqrt{2g \times 0} = 0$$

Therefore, velocities for emptying from h to $h/2$ and from $h/2$ to 0 are given as

$$v' = \frac{\sqrt{(2gh)} + \sqrt{(gh)}}{2} \quad \text{and} \quad v'' = \frac{(gh) - 0}{2}$$

If area of the hole be a and time taken to empty the tank from h to $h/2$ is given by

$$v' \times a \times t_1 = A \times \left(h - \frac{h}{2}\right) \quad \text{... (i)}$$

Where, A is area of cross-section of the tank. Similarly,

$$v'' \times a \times t_2 = A\left(\frac{h}{2} - 0\right) \quad \text{... (ii)}$$

On solving Eqs. (i) and (ii), we get

$$\frac{t_1}{t_2} = \sqrt{2} - 1.$$

10. We know that, $p = h\rho g$. The pressure at the bottom is independent of the area of the bottom of the tank. The pressure for the same liquid (ρ = same) depends only on the height of water upto which the tank is filled with water. So, the pressure on the bottom of (A) and (B) is the same.

11. We know that

$$p + \frac{1}{2}\rho v^2 + mgh = \text{Constant}$$

On dividing this equation by ρg, we get

$$\frac{p}{\rho g} + \frac{v^2}{2g} + h = \text{Constant}$$

Here, $\frac{p}{\rho g}$ = Pressure head

and $\frac{v^2}{2g}$ = Velocity head

Given that, velocity head = pressure head

$$\therefore \quad \frac{v^2}{2g} = \frac{p}{\rho g} \Rightarrow v^2 = \frac{2p}{\rho}$$

$$\Rightarrow \quad v^2 = \frac{2 \times 13.6 \times 10^3 \times 40 \times 10^{-2} \times 9.8}{10^3}$$

On solving, we get $v = 10.3$ m/s

12. Using equation of continuity, we have

$$\pi(2r)^2 v = \pi r^2 v' \Rightarrow v' = 4v.$$

13. Using equation of continuity

$$A_1 v_1 = A_2 v_2$$

$$(40 \times 10^{-8})v_1 = (8 \times 10^{-4}) \times \left(\frac{0.15}{60}\right)$$

On solving, we get $v_1 = 5$ m/s

14. Let h be the height of liquid surface in the vessel. The velocity of efflux is given by

$$v_{\text{eff}} = \sqrt{(2gh)}$$

If H be the height of table, then

$$H = \frac{1}{2}gt^2$$

$$\Rightarrow \quad t = \sqrt{(2H/g)}$$

$$\therefore \quad R = v_{\text{eff}} \times t = \sqrt{(2gh)} \times \sqrt{(2H/g)}$$

$$\Rightarrow \quad R^2 = 4hH \Rightarrow h = R^2/4H$$

15. Volume of the raft

$$V = \frac{m}{d} = \frac{120}{600} = 0.2\,\text{m}^3$$

If the raft is immersed fully in water, then weight of water displaced

$$= Vd_{\text{water}} = 0.2 \times 10^3 = 200\text{ kg}$$

Therefore, the additional weight which can be put on the raft

$$= 200\text{ kg} - 120\text{ kg} = 80\text{ kg}$$

15

Surface Tension

Surface Tension

In the absence of gravity or in an effectively weightless environment, a drop of water would draw itself into a sphere. Free-falling raindrops are roughly spherical-though only roughly because of the air friction. If we shake some mercury in a jar, thousands of tiny, almost spherical beads will be forced on the glass, beads quite unwilling to conform to the shape of the container's walls. These familiar liquid 'tricks' are the outward manifestations of internal interactions that give rise to what is called surface tension.

Definition of Surface Tension

The surface tension of a liquid is defined as the force per unit length in the plane of the liquid surface at right angles to either side of an imaginary line drawn on that surface.

So, $T = \frac{F}{l}$, where T = surface tension of liquid.

Unit of surface tension in MKS system → N/m, J/m^2

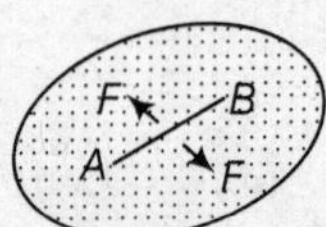

CGS system → Dyne/cm, erg/cm^2

Dimension of surface tension = $M^1L^0T^{-2}$

Effects on Surface Tension

Effect of Impurity The surface tension of a liquid increases due to solvent impurity in the liquid. By solving salt in water the surface tension of water increases. If the solvent impurity is less soluble then surface tension decreases, for example, after solving soap in water the surface tension of water decreases.

Effect of Temperature Due to increase in temperature the cohesive forces between the molecules of the liquid decreases so the surface tension decreases and on critical temperature it becomes zero.

Effect of Floating Impurity If there is dust, oil or grease then also surface tension of liquid decreases.

Flowing of Electricity in the Liquid Flowing of electricity in the liquid a force acts normally on the free surface of the liquid. Therefore, the surface tension of the liquid decreases.

Surface Energy

In order to increase the surface area, the work has to be done over the surface of the liquid. This work done is stored in the liquid surface as its potential energy. Hence, the surface energy of a liquid can be defined as the excess potential energy per unit area of the liquid surface.

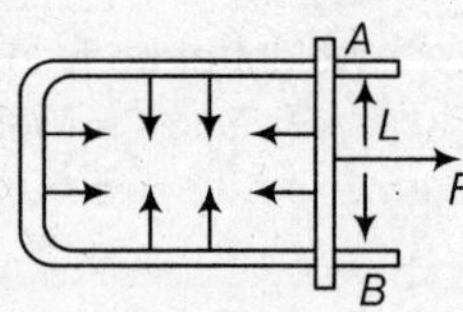

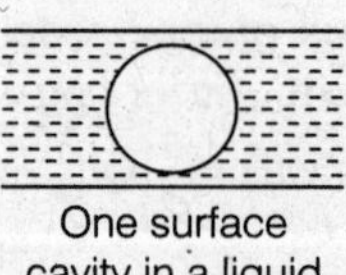

One surface cavity in a liquid

$$W = T\Delta A$$

Where, ΔA = Increase in surface area,

T = Surface tension of the liquid.

Some problems related to surface energy.

1. **For a Liquid Drop** (Only one free surface)

   For increasing radius 0 to R

   Initial surface area = 0

One surface (drop)

   Final surface area = $4\pi R^2$

   So, surface energy = $T\Delta A = 4\pi T(R^2 - 0)$

   $= 4\pi R^2 T$

2. **For a Soap Bubble** (For two free surfaces)

   For increasing radius, R_1 to R_2 where $R_2 > R_1$

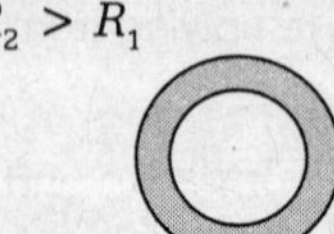

Bubble in air two surfaces

   So, surface energy

   $= T\Delta A = T \times 2\,(4\pi R_2^2 - 4\pi R_1^2)$

   $= 8\pi T\,(R_2^2 - R_1^2)$

Excess Pressure in Liquid Drop

$$P = \frac{2T}{R}$$

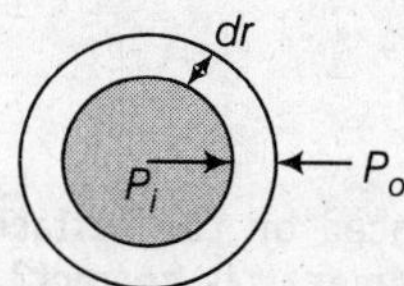

Excess Pressure in the Bubble Formed in a Liquid

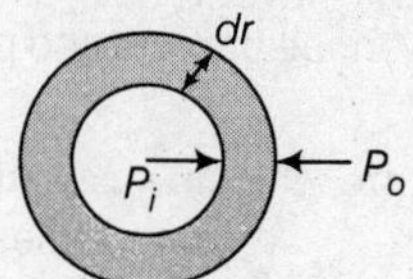

$$P = \frac{2T}{R}$$

Excess Pressure in Soap Bubble

There is two free surfaces in a soap bubble so

$$P = \frac{4T}{R}$$

Cohesives Force

The force of attraction between the molecules of the same substance is called cohesive force.

Adhesive Force

The force of attraction between the molecules of different substances is called adhesive forces.

Angle of Contact

At the point of contact of a liquid and a solid, if we draw a tangent to the surface of the liquid, it makes an angle with the side of the container, inside the liquid. This is called the angle of contact.

(i) Those liquids which wets solids and rises in capillary tubes have the angle of contact acute and the liquid surface is concave. $\theta < 90°$

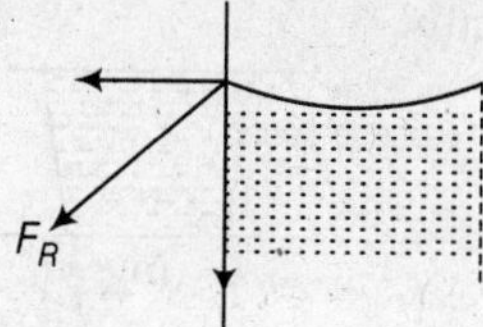

(ii) Those liquids which does not wet solids and their level falls in capillary tube have angle of contact obtuse and their surface is convex. $\theta > 90°$

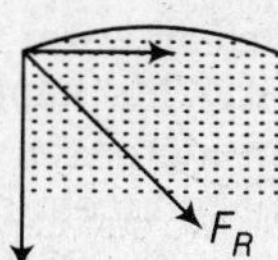

(iii) Those liquids which neither rises nor falls in a capillary tube have angle of contact right angle. Their liquid surface is plane. $\theta = 90°$

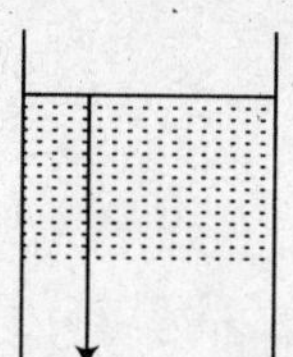

If θ	Meniscus	Wetting or not the container walls	Rise or depression in capillary
< 90° (*e.g.*, water and glass	Concave upwards	Wets	Rise, Adhesive force > Cohesive force
> 90° (*e.g.*, mercury and glass)	Convex upwards	Does not wet	Fall/ Depression, Cohesive force > Adhesive force

Capillary Rise

Consider two points A and B at the same horizontal level as shown. As per Pascal's law,

$$p_A = p_B$$

$$p_A = p_C + \rho gh = p_0 + \rho gh$$

Or $$p_A - P_0 = \rho gh \quad \text{...(i)}$$

The point C is on the curved meniscus which has p_A and p_0 as the two pressures on its concave and convex sides respectively.

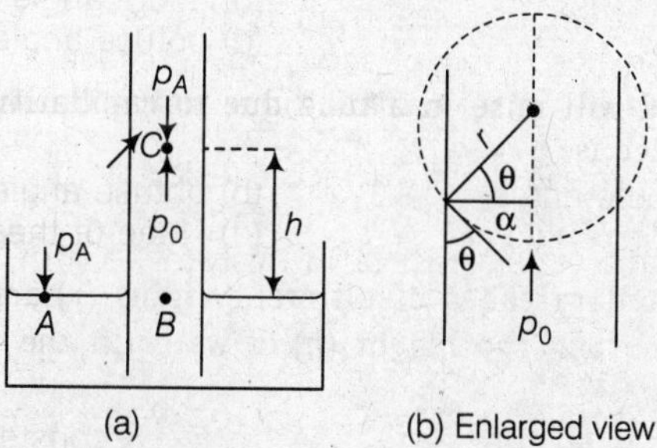

(a) (b) Enlarged view

r = radius of the meniscus

a = radius of the capillary tube

$$\therefore \quad r = \frac{a}{\cos\theta}$$

θ = angle of contact

$$\therefore \quad p_A - p_0 = \frac{2\sigma}{r} = \frac{2\sigma}{a/\cos\theta} \quad \text{...(ii)}$$

Putting (ii) in (i), we get

$$\frac{2\sigma}{a/\cos\theta} = \rho gh \Rightarrow 2\sigma\cos\theta = a\rho gh$$

$$h = \frac{2\sigma\cos\theta}{a\rho g} \Rightarrow h \propto \frac{1}{a} \Rightarrow h_1a_1 = h_2a_2$$

Practice Questions

Level I

1. Surface tension of liquid
(a) increases with increase in area
(b) increases with increase is temperature
(c) decreases with decrease in area
(d) decreases with increase in temperature

2. Cause of origin of surface tension
(a) cohesive force (b) adhesive force
(c) shape of liqui (d) frictional force

3. Dimensional formula of surface tension is
(a) MLT^{-1} (b) ML^2T^0
(c) ML^0T^{-2} (d) $ML^{-1}T^{-1}$

4. SI unit of surface tension is
(a) $N\ m^{-1}$ (b) $J\ m^{-2}$
(c) Both of (a) and (b) (d) $J\ m^{-1}$

5. Cause of spherical shape of rain droplet is
(a) Viscosity (b) Surface tension
(c) Gravity (d) Atmospheric pressure

6. If a liquid does not wet the surface of a solid in contact, then angle of contact between them will be
(a) 0° (b) acute angle
(c) 45° (d) obtuse angle

7. Liquid will raise in a tube due to capillarity, if angle of contact is
(a) acute angle (b) obtuse angle
(c) right angle (d) None of these

8. If capillary tubes of different radius (r) are immerse in water, then the height (h) of water in the tubes will in such that
(a) $\frac{h}{r}$ = constant (b) hr^2 = constant
(c) hr = constant (d) $\frac{h}{r^2}$ = constant

9. A vessel is full of liquid. Adhesive force between the molecules of liquid and solid is very less than cohesive force between the molecules of liquid. Shape of liquid level in contact of solid will be
(a) horizontal (b) concave
(c) convex (d) approx vertical

10. Shape of the surface of mercury in a capillary tube will be
(a) concave (b) plane
(c) convex (d) not defined

11. Surface tension may be defined as
(a) the work done per unit area in increasing the surface area of a liquid under isothermal condition
(b) the work done per unit area in increasing the surface area of a liquid under adiabatic condition
(c) the work done per unit area in increasing the surface area of a liquid under both isothermal and adiabatic conditions
(d) free surface energy per unit volume

12. A drop of oil is placed on the surface of water. Which of the following statements is correct?
(a) It will remain on it as a sphere
(b) It will spread as a thin layer
(c) It will partly be as spherical droplets and partly as thin film
(d) None of the above

13. With a rise in temperature, the surface tension of a liquid
(a) increases (b) decreases
(c) does not change (d) changes erratically

14. Soap helps in cleaning the clothes because
(a) it reduces the surface tension of solution
(b) it gives strength to solution
(c) it absorbs the dirt
(d) chemical of soaps change

15. Meniscus of mercury in capillary is
(a) concave (b) convex
(c) plane (d) cylindrical

16. When two capillary tubes of different diameters are dipped vertically, the rise of the liquids is
(a) same in both the tubes
(b) more in tube of larger diameter
(c) less in tube of smaller diameter
(d) more in tube of smaller diameter

17. When two small bubbles join to form a bigger one, energy is
(a) released (b) absorbed
(c) both (a) and (b) (d) None of these

18. A soap bubble formed in soap solution has an excess pressure p in it. A soap bubble of same radius formed in air has excess pressure of
(a) p (b) $2p$ (c) $p/2$ (d) $4p$

19. When a drop of water is placed between two glass plates, the drop squeezes into

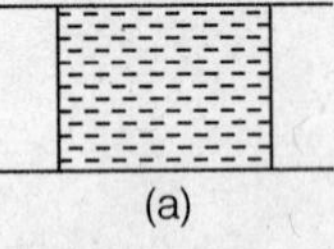
(a)

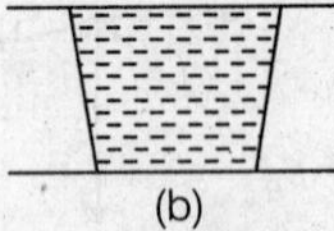
(b)

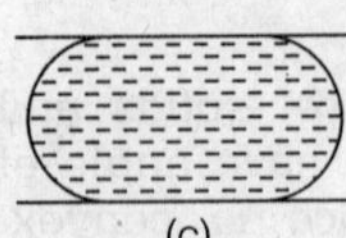
(c)

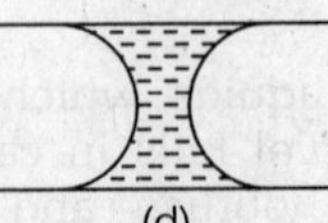
(d)

20. A needle can float on clear water but sinks when some detergent is added to it. This happens because
(a) addition of detergent increases the density of water
(b) addition of detergent reduces the density of water
(c) addition of detergent reduces the surface tension of water
(d) addition of detergent increases the surface tension of water

Level II

1. A capillary tube is dipped vertically in a liquid. If the liquid surface is hemispherical, then the angle of contact is given by
(a) $\theta = 90°$ (b) $\theta = 0°$
(c) $\theta > 90°$ (d) $\theta < 90°$ but not $0°$

2. Excess of pressure inside a soap bubble is
(a) inversely proportional to its radius
(b) directly proportional to its radius
(c) directly proportional to square root of its radius
(d) independent of its radius

3. Two spherical soap bubbles of radii r_1 and r_2 in vacuum coalesce under isothermal conditions. The resulting bubble has a radius R such that
(a) $R = (r_1 + r_2)/2$ (b) $R = [r_1 r_2 / (r_1 + r_2)]$
(c) $R = \sqrt{(r_1^2 + r_2^2)}$ (d) $R = r_1 + r_2$

4. A spherical liquid drop of radius R is divided into eight equal droplets. If surface tension is T, then the work done in this process will be
(a) $2\pi R^2 T$ (b) $3\pi R^2 T$
(c) $4\pi R^2 T$ (d) $2\pi R T^2$

5. The work done to get n smaller equal size spherical drops from a bigger size spherical drop of water is proportional to
(a) $1/n^{2/3} - 1$ (b) $1/n^{1/3} - 1$
(c) $n^{1/3} - 1$ (d) $n^{4/3} - 1$

6. A vessel, whose bottom has round holes with diameter of 0.1 mm, is filled with water. The maximum height to which the water can be filled without leakage is (ST of water $= 75$ dynes/cm, $g = 1000$ cm/s^2)
(a) 100 cm (b) 75 cm
(c) 50 cm (d) 30 cm

7. Two soap bubbles have radii in the ratio 2 : 1. What is the ratio of excesses of pressure inside them?
(a) 1 : 2 (b) 2 : 1
(c) 1 : 4 (d) 4 : 1

8. Water rises in a capillary tube through a height h. If the tube is inclined to the liquid surface at 45°, the liquid will rise in the tube upto its length equal to
(a) $h/\sqrt{2}$ (b) h
(c) $\sqrt{2}\,h$ (d) $2h$

9. A liquid drop of radius R breaks into 64 tiny drops each of radius r. If the surface tension of the liquid is T, then the gain in energy is
(a) $48\pi R^2 T$
(b) $12\pi r^2 T$
(c) $96\pi R^2 T$
(d) $192\pi r^2 T$

10. The excess pressure inside a cylindrical drop of liquid or a cylindrical bubble of radius R in a liquid of surface tension T is
(a) $\frac{T}{4R}$ (b) $\frac{T}{R}$
(c) $\frac{2T}{R}$ (d) $\frac{4T}{R}$

11. A frame made of metallic wire enclosing a surface area A is covered with a soap film. If the area of the frame of metallic wire is reduced by 50%, the energy of the soap film will be changed by
(a) 100% (b) 75%
(c) 50% (d) 25%

12. The excess pressure inside a spherical drop of water is four times that of another drop. Then, their respective mass ratio is
(a) 1 : 16 (b) 8 : 1
(c) 1 : 4 (d) 1 : 64

13. Water rises to a height of 10 cm in a capillary tube and mercury falls to a depth of 3·42 cm in the same capillary tube. If the density of mercury is 13.6 and the angle of contact is 135°, the ratio of surface tension for water and mercury is
(a) 1 : 0.5 (b) 1 : 3
(c) 1 : 6.5 (d) 1.5 : 1

14. Water rises to a height of 5 cm in a glass capillary tube. If the area of cross-section of the tube is reduced to (1/16)th of the former value, the water rises to a height of
(a) 10 cm (b) 20 cm
(c) 30 cm (d) 40 cm

15. Excess of pressure in a soap bubble of diameter 10 mm when the surface tension is 0·04 N/m is
(a) 16 Pa (b) 32 Pa
(c) 4 Pa (d) 64 Pa

Answers

Level I

1. (d)	**2.** (a)	**3.** (c)	**4.** (c)	**5.** (b)	**6.** (d)	**7.** (a)	**8.** (c)	**9.** (c)	**10.** (c)
11. (a)	**12.** (b)	**13.** (b)	**14.** (a)	**15.** (b)	**16.** (d)	**17.** (a)	**18.** (b)	**19.** (d)	**20.** (c)

Level II

1. (b)	**2.** (a)	**3.** (c)	**4.** (c)	**5.** (c)	**6.** (d)	**7.** (a)	**8.** (c)	**9.** (d)	**10.** (b)
11. (c)	**12.** (d)	**13.** (c)	**14.** (b)	**15.** (b)					

Hints and Solutions

Level II

3. The bubbles coalesce in vacuum and hence there is no change in temperature. So, the surface energy does not change. This means that surface area remaining unchanged. Hence

$4\pi r_1^2 + 4\pi r_2^2 = 4\pi R^2 \Rightarrow R = (r_1^2 + r_2^2)^{1/2}$

4. Work done = (Change in area) × Surface tension

$$= (4\pi r^2 n - 4\pi R^2)\,T$$
$$= \{4\pi(R^2/(8)^{2/3}) \times 8 - 4\pi R^2\}\,T$$
$$= 4\pi R^2 T\left[\frac{8}{4} - 1\right] = 4\pi R^2 T\,[2-1]$$
$$= 4\pi R^2 T$$

5. $\frac{4}{3}\pi R^3 = n \times \frac{4}{3}\pi r^3$ or $r = \frac{R}{n^{1/3}}$

Now, Work done = Increase in area × Surface tension

$$= (4\pi r^2 n - 4\pi R^2) \times T$$
$$= 4\pi\left(\frac{R^2}{n^{2/3}}n - R^2\right) \times T \propto (n^{1/3} - 1)$$

6. $h = \frac{2T\cos\theta}{\rho r g} = \frac{2 \times 75 \times 1}{1 \times 0.005 \times 1000} = 30$ cm

7. Excess of pressure $= \frac{4T}{r} \propto \frac{1}{r}$

$p_1 \propto 1/2r$ and $p_2 \propto 1/r$

$p_1/p_2 = \frac{1}{2} \Rightarrow p_1 : p_2 = 1:2$

8. If H be the height to which a liquid rises in the inclined tube, then

$H = h/\sin\theta$

$\therefore \; H = h/\sin 45° = h/(1/\sqrt{2}) = \sqrt{2}\,h$

9. Volume of big drop = 64 × Volume of a tiny drop

$$\Rightarrow \quad \frac{4}{3}\pi R^3 = 64 \times \frac{4}{3}\pi r^3$$
$$\Rightarrow \quad R = 4r$$

So, the gain in surface energy

= Work done in splitting a liquid drop of radius R into n identical drops

$$= 4\pi T R^2 (n^{1/3} - 1)$$
$$= 4\pi T (4r)^2 (64^{1/3} - 1) = 192\,\pi r^2 T$$

10. The excess pressure inside a cylindrical drop of liquid or cylindrical bubble of radius R in a liquid of surface tension T is

$$\Delta p = \frac{T}{R}$$

11. Surface energy = Surface tension × Surface area

$$E = T \times 2A$$

New surface energy,

$$E_1 = T \times 2\left(\frac{A}{2}\right) = T \times A$$

Percentage of decrease in surface energy

$$= \frac{E - E_1}{E} \times 100 = \frac{2TA - TA}{2TA} \times 100 = 50\%$$

12. The excess of pressure inside a spherical drop of water is given by

$$p = \frac{2T}{R}$$

For two drops,

$$p_1 = \frac{2T}{R_1} \text{ and } p_2 = \frac{2T}{R_2}$$

$$\therefore \quad \frac{p_1}{p_2} = \frac{R_2}{R_1}$$

Given that $\quad p_1 = 4p_2$

$\therefore \quad R_2 = 4R_1$

The ratio of their masses is given by

$$\frac{m_1}{m_2} = \frac{\frac{4}{3}\pi R_1^3 \rho}{\frac{4}{3}\pi R_2^3 \rho} = \left(\frac{R_1}{R_2}\right)^3 = \left(\frac{R_1}{4R_1}\right)^3 = \frac{1}{(4)^3}$$

$$\therefore \quad \frac{m_1}{m_2} = 1:64$$

13. $T = \frac{\rho r g h}{2\cos\theta}$

For water, $T_1 = \frac{rg \times 10}{2\cos\theta} = 5\,rg$

For mercury,

$$T_2 = \frac{rg \times 3.42 \times 13.6}{2\cos 135°} = 6.5 \times 5\,rg$$

$$\frac{T_1}{T_2} = \frac{1}{6.5} \Rightarrow T_1 : T_2 = 1:6.5$$

14. $h_1 r_1 = h_2 r_2 \Rightarrow h_2 = (h_1 r_1)/r_2$

Here $\quad \frac{A_1}{A_2} = \frac{r_1^2}{r_2^2}$, where $A_1 = A$ and $A_2 = (A/16)$

$$\frac{r_1^2}{r_2^2} = \frac{16}{1} \Rightarrow \frac{r_1}{r_2} = \frac{4}{1}$$

Hence, $\quad h_2 = \left[\frac{4}{1}\right] \times 5 = 20$ cm

16

Viscosity and Fluid Flow

Viscosity

It is the property of fluids due to which a backward dragging force acts tangentially on the layers of the liquid in motion and opposes the relative motion between them. Thus, viscosity is internal friction offered by a fluid itself against its own flow.

Related Terms

Streamline

The path taken by a fluid particle under steady flow is called a streamline. The direction of velocity of the fluid particle at a point is always a tangent to the streamline at that point.

Critical Velocity

It is the velocity of the fluid beyond which steadiness of flow changes to turbulent flow.

Laminar (Fluid) Flow

It is steady flow in which the fluid moves in parallel layers or laminae, the velocities of the fluid particles within each lamina not being necessarily equal.

Coefficient of Viscosity (η)

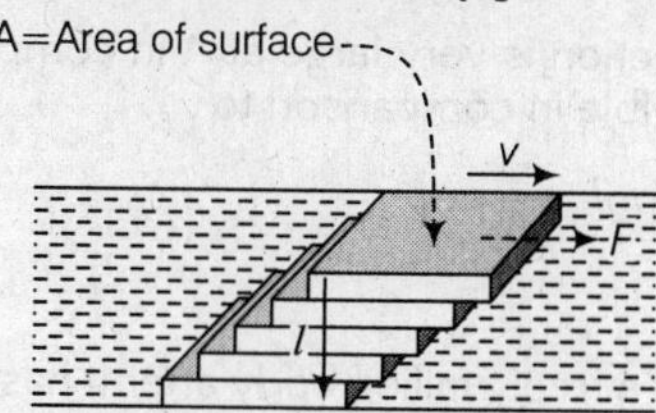

It is defined as the tangential force F required per unit area A to maintain unit velocity gradient perpendicular to the direction of flow.

$$\therefore \quad \eta = \frac{\text{Tangential stress}}{\text{Velocity gradient}}$$

$$\eta = \frac{\frac{F}{A}}{\frac{v}{l}} \Rightarrow \eta = \frac{\frac{F}{A}}{\frac{dv}{dl}}$$

Effect of Temperature on Viscosity η of a liquid decreases sharply with increase in its temperature and becomes zero at its boiling temperature. On the other hand, η of gases increases with temperature.

Reynold's Number (N_R or k)

Reynold's number N_R or k is a dimensionless number whose value gives an approximate idea whether the flow would be turbulent. It is defined by the equation

$$N_R \text{ or } k = \frac{v\, l\, \rho}{\eta}$$

When η and ρ are the viscosity and density respectively of the fluid, v is the speed of the bulk of the fluid and l is a characterstic dimension of the solid body concerned.

In case of a pipe,

$$N_R = \frac{\rho\, v\, d}{\eta}$$

where ρ is the density of the fluid flowing with a speed v, d stands for the dimension of the pipe and η is the viscosity of the fluid.

For cylindrical pipes, when

$N_R < 2200$ flow is steady.

$N_R \approx 2200$ flow is unstable (critical velocity v_c).

$N_R > 2200$ flow is usually turbulent.

Stoke's Law

The backward dragging force acting on a small sphere falling with uniform velocity through a viscous fluid is found to depend upon

(i) the viscosity η of the fluid,

(ii) the velocity v and radius r of the sphere

$$F = 6\pi\eta v r$$

Stoke's law only holds for steady motion in a fluid of infinite extent.

Terminal Velocity

When a sphere falls vertically under gravity in a viscous fluid, *three forces act on it*

(i) its weight W, acting downwards;

(ii) the upthrust U due to the weight of fluid displaced, acting upwards and

(iii) the viscous drag F, acting upwards.

The resultant downward force is $W - U - F$ and causes the sphere to accelerate until its velocity and so the viscous drag, reach values such that $W - U - F = 0$

The sphere then continues to fall with a constant velocity, known as its terminal velocity, of say v_t.

$$W = \frac{4}{3}\pi r^3 \rho g$$

Where, ρ is the density of the sphere

and $$U = \frac{4}{3}\pi r^3 \sigma g$$

Where, σ is the density of the fluid. Also, if steady conditions still hold when velocity v_t is reached, then by Stoke's law

$$F = 6\,\pi\eta r v_t$$

Hence,

$$\frac{4}{3}\pi r^3 \rho g - \frac{4}{3}\pi r^3 \sigma g - 6\pi\eta\, r v_t = 0$$

$$\therefore \quad v_t = \frac{2r^2(\rho - \sigma)g}{9\eta}$$

Continuity Equation

When a fluid is in motion, in such a way that the mass is conserved if the inflow and outflow are in one dimension.

$$\rho A_1 v_1 = \rho A_2 v_2$$

This equation is called equation of continuity if the liquid is incompressible, then

$$A_1 v_1 = A_2 v_2$$

Where, A_1 and A_2 are area of cross-section and v_1 and v_2 are the velocities respectively.

Bernoulli's Theorem

Bernoulli's theorem is an expression of the conservation of energy in the steady flow of an incompressible, inviscid (frictionless, without any viscosity) fluid.

Assumptions are as follows

(i) The fluid flow is steady, *i.e.*, its velocity at each point is constant with time.

(ii) The fluid is incompressible.

(iii) The fluid is non-viscous.

(iv) The fluid flow is irrotational.

It states that total energy of the fluid per unit volume is constant *i.e.*, the quantity

$$p + \rho g h + \frac{1}{2}\rho v^2 = \text{Constant}$$

along any streamline, is conserved, where p is the fluid pressure, ρ is mass density of fluid, g is acceleration due to gravity, h is the vertical height and v is the fluid velocity.

In this form, we call

$\frac{p}{\rho g}$ as pressure head

h as gravitational head

$\frac{1}{2}\frac{v^2}{g}$ as velocity head

Applications of Bernoulli's Theorem

- Venturimeter (flow meter)
- Pitot tube (flow meter)
- Sprayer or Atomiser
- Jet and nozzles
- Spinning ball (Magnus effect)
- Aerofoil
- Blowing off of the roof-tops during cyclones
- Pull-in force by fast moving trains
- Attraction between sailing ships
- **Torricelli's Theorem** (Velocity of Efflux)

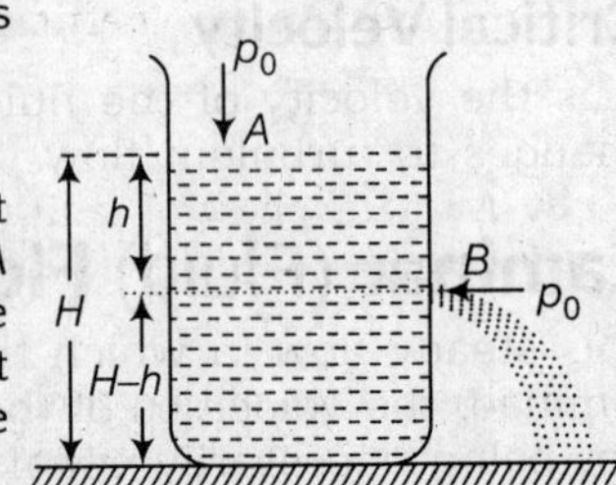

Applying Bernoulli's theorem at two fluid particles at position A and B. B is just outside the orifice (narrow hole), hence pressure at A and B is same p_0, the atmospheric pressure.

$$\therefore p_0 + \rho g H + \frac{1}{2}\rho v_A^2 = p_0 + \rho g(H - h) + \frac{1}{2}\rho v_B^2$$

Since, area of cross-section is very large at A in comparison to that at B, so v_A is negligible in comparison to v_B.

$$\therefore \quad \rho g H = \rho g H - \rho g h + \frac{1}{2}\rho v_B^2$$

$$v_B = \sqrt{2gh}$$

It is the same as that of a freely falling body after it has dropped through a height h.

Practice Questions

Level I

1. An ideal lubricant have the property of
(a) high viscosity (b) high density
(c) high surface tension (d) None of these

2. There is a hole near the base of a tank.The volume of water per second does not depend on
(a) area of the hole
(b) density of liquid
(c) acceleration due to gravity
(d) height of liquid from base above the hole

3. An aeroplane works on
(a) Archemedes's principle (b) Pascal's law
(c) Bernoulli's principle (d) Stoke's law

4. Paint gun are based on
(a) Bernoulli's principle (b) Faradey's law
(c) Archemedes' principle (d) Boyle's law

5. When velocity of flowing liquid from a tube is increase, then its pressure
(a) increase (b) remains halves
(c) decreases (d) None of these

6. Viscous force acts on a moving sphere of radius r inside a viscous liquid is directly proportional to
(a) r (b) r^{-1} (c) r^2 (d) r^3

7. SI unit of the coefficient of viscosity is
(a) kgms (b) $kgm^{-2}s^{-2}$
(c) $kgm^{-1}s^{-1}$ (d) $kgms^{-3}$

8. A small sphere of radius r is falling into viscous liquid. Its terminal velocity is directly proportional to
(a) r (b) r^{-1} (c) r^2 (d) r^3

9. The value of Reynold's number for flow of liquid in a narrow tube be approximate
(a) 10 (b) 1
(c) 1000 (d) 10^{-6}

10. With increase in temperature, viscosity of the most of the liquids are
(a) decreases
(b) unchanged
(c) increases
(d) first increases then decreases

11. A sphere of steel of radius r attain terminal velocity v when falling it into viscous liquid. Then, viscous force acted upon it directly proportional to
(a) rv (b) r^2v
(c) r^2v^2 (d) rv^2

12. Terminal velocity by a falling oil-droplet in air is
(a) directly proportional to the radius of droplet
(b) inversely proportional to the radius of droplet
(c) directly proportional to the square of radius of droplet
(d) None of the above

13. Water is flowing inside a pipe of dissimilar radius. The ratio of the radii of enter end and exit end inside pipe is 3 : 2. The ratio of the velocities of entering water and outgoing water in the pipe will be
(a) 8 : 27 (b) 1 : 1
(c) 4 : 9 (d) 9 : 4

14. A liquid is flowing inside a pipe of dissimilar area of cross-section. If A_1 and A_2 be the area of cross-section at two points of the pipe, then the ratio of velocities of flowing liquid at these two points will become
(a) $\frac{A_1}{A_2}$ (b) $\frac{A_1^2}{A_2^2}$
(c) $\frac{A_2}{A_1}$ (d) $\frac{1}{A_1A_2}$

15. On increase in temperature, the viscosity of gases are
(a) decreases (b) unchanged
(c) increases (d) None of these

Level II

1. Streamline motion is that motion in which there is
(a) only longitudinal velocity gradient
(b) only radial velocity gradient
(c) longitudinal as well as radial velocity gradient
(d) Neither (a) nor (b)

2. With the rise in temperature, the coefficient of viscosity of a gas
(a) increases
(b) decreases
(c) does not change
(d) may increase or decrease depending upon the range of temperature

3. Two small spheres of radii r and $4r$ fall through a viscous liquid with the same terminal velocity. The ratio between the viscous forces acting on them is
(a) 1 : 2 (b) 4 : 1
(c) 1 : 16 (d) 1 : 4

4. A sphere of radius R is gently dropped into liquid on viscosity η in a vertical uniform tube. It attains a terminal velocity v. Another sphere of radius $2R$, when dropped into the same liquid, will attain its terminal velocity
(a) v (b) $2v$
(c) $4v$ (d) $9v$

5. Two solid spheres of same metal but of mass M and $8M$ fall simultaneously on a viscous liquid and their terminal velocities are v and $n\,v$, then value of n is
(a) 16 (b) 8
(c) 4 (d) 2

6. A lead sphere of mass m falls in a viscous liquid with a terminal velocity v_0. Another lead sphere of mass 8 m will fall through the same liquid with a terminal velocity

(a) v_0 (b) $4v_0$ (c) $8v_0$ (d) $64v_0$

7. Liquid flows through a horizontal tube of variable diameter. The pressure is lower where

(a) velocity is lowest
(b) velocity is highest
(c) diameter is largest
(d) both velocity and diameter are largest

8. The rate of outflow of liquid through an orifice does not depend upon

(a) radius of the orifice
(b) height of liquid column
(c) acceleration due to gravity
(d) density of the liquid

9. Bernoulli's principle is based on the law of conservation of

(a) mass (b) momentum
(c) energy (d) None of these

10. A cylinder of radius R is filled with water upto a height H, so that the thrust on the walls is equal to that on bottom. The relation between H and R is

(a) $H = \frac{R}{2}$ (b) $H = R$ (c) $\frac{H}{2} = R$ (d) $H = 2R$

11. Water flows along a horizontal pipe whose cross-section is not constant. The pressure is 1 cm of Hg, where the velocity is 35 cm $^{-1}$. At a point where the velocity is 65 cms^{-1}, the pressure will be

(a) 0.98 cm of Hg (b) 8.9 cm of Hg
(c) 0.5 cm of Hg (d) 1 cm of Hg

12. Water flows through a pipe of varying cross-section. Then, the ratio of the speeds of water at two points 1 and 2, where the radii of the pipe are r_1 and r_2 is

(a) $\frac{r_2^2}{r_1^2}$ (b) $\frac{r_2}{r_1}$ (c) $\frac{r_1^2}{r_2^2}$ (d) $\frac{r_1}{r_2}$

13. A liquid flows in the tube from left to right as shown in figure. A_1 and A_2 are the cross-sections of the portions of the tube as shown. Then, the ratio of speeds $\frac{v_1}{v_2}$ will be

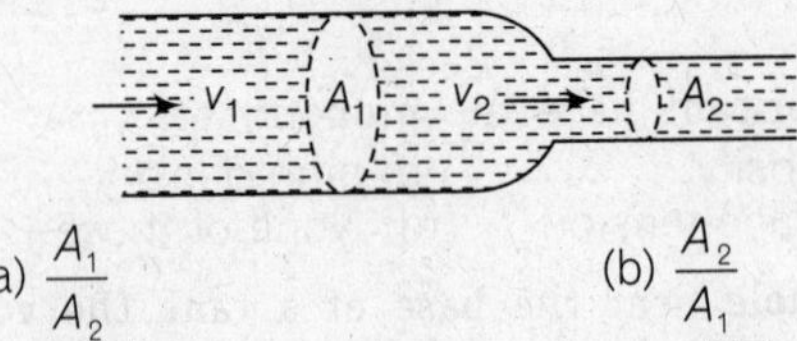

(a) $\frac{A_1}{A_2}$ (b) $\frac{A_2}{A_1}$

(c) $\frac{\sqrt{A_2}}{\sqrt{A_1}}$ (d) $\frac{\sqrt{A_1}}{\sqrt{A_2}}$

14. A tank of height 5 m is full of water. There is a hole of cross-sectional area 1cm^2 in its bottom. The initial volume of water that will come out from this hole per second is

(a) 10^{-3} m^3/s
(b) 10^{-4} m^3/s
(c) 10 m^3/s
(d) 10^{-2} m^3/s

15. A tank is filled with water upto a height H. Water is allowed to come out of a hole P in one of the walls at a depth h below the surface of water (see figure). Express the horizontal distance x in terms of H and h.

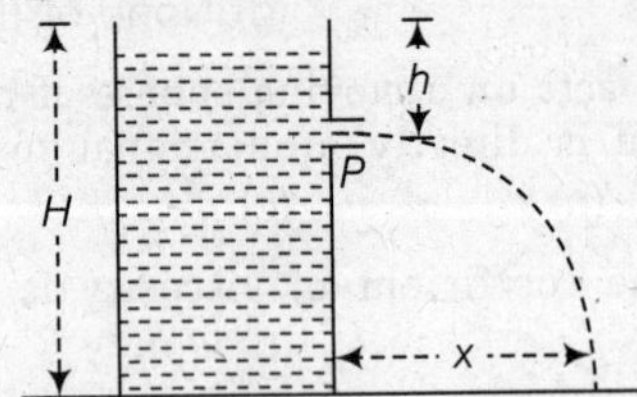

(a) $x = \sqrt{h(H-h)}$ (b) $x = \sqrt{\left[\frac{h(H-h)}{2}\right]}$

(c) $x = 2\sqrt{h(H-h)}$ (d) $x = 4\sqrt{h(H-h)}$

Answers

Level I

1. (a)	**2.** (b)	**3.** (c)	**4.** (a)	**5.** (c)	**6.** (a)	**7.** (c)	**8.** (c)	**9.** (c)	**10.** (a)
11. (a)	**12.** (c)	**13.** (c)	**14.** (c)	**15.** (c)					

Level II

1. (a)	**2.** (a)	**3.** (d)	**4.** (c)	**5.** (c)	**6.** (b)	**7.** (b)	**8.** (d)	**9.** (c)	**10.** (b)
11. (a)	**12.** (a)	**13.** (b)	**14.** (a)	**15.** (c)					

Hints and Solutions

Level II

3. The magnitude of viscous force depends on the shape and size of the body, its speed and the viscosity of the fluid. According to Stoke's law,

$$F = 6\pi\eta r v$$

$$\Rightarrow \quad \frac{F_1}{F_2} = \frac{r_1}{r_2} \qquad (\because \eta = \text{constant and } v_1 = v_2)$$

$$\frac{F_1}{F_2} = \frac{r}{4r} = \frac{1}{4}$$

4. Terminal velocity

$$v \propto r^2$$

$$\therefore \quad \frac{v'}{v} = \frac{(2R)^2}{(R)^2} \Rightarrow v' = 4v$$

5. The terminal velocity is given by v, where $v \propto r^2$ (r = radius of the sphere)

The mass of the sphere can be given by $m = \frac{4}{3}\pi r^3 \rho$, thus $m \propto r^3$.

So, according to the question, $\frac{m_1}{m_2} = \frac{1}{8} = \left(\frac{r_1}{r_2}\right)^3 \Rightarrow \frac{r_1}{r_2} = \frac{1}{2}$

and since, $\frac{v_1}{v_2} = \left(\frac{r_1}{r_2}\right)^2 = \left(\frac{1}{2}\right)^2 = \frac{1}{4} \Rightarrow \frac{v}{nv} = \frac{1}{4}$

$$\Rightarrow \quad n = 4$$

6. Terminal velocity $v \propto r^2$

For second lead sphere mass becomes 8 times *i.e.*, radius becomes two times $\left[m = \left(\frac{4}{3}\right)\pi r^3 \rho\right]$

$\therefore$ Terminal velocity becomes $(2)^2 v_0 = 4v_0$

7. According to Bernoulli's theorem,

$$p + \frac{1}{2}\rho v^2 = \text{constant}$$

So, when the pressure is lowest, the velocity is highest.

8. The velocity of outflow $v = \sqrt{2gh}$

This expression is independent of the density of the liquid.

9. Bernoulli's theorem states that for all points along a streamline in an incompressible and non-viscous fluid flowing steadily, the total energy per unit volume (pressure energy + kinetic energy + potential energy) remains constant *i.e.*,

$$p + \frac{1}{2}\rho v^2 + \rho g h = \text{Constant}$$

10. Thrust on the bottom of the cylinder $= (\pi R^2) H \rho g$

Thrust on the wall of the cylinder $= (2\pi R H)\left(\frac{H\rho g}{2}\right)$

$$\therefore \quad (\pi R^2) H\rho g = (2\pi R H)\left(\frac{H\rho g}{2}\right)$$

Solving, we get $H = R$

11. In horizontal pipe,

$$p_1 + \frac{1}{2}\rho v_1^2 = p_2 + \frac{1}{2}\rho v_2^2 \qquad \text{...(i)}$$

Given, $v_1 = 35 \times 10^{-2}$ m/s

$v_2 = 65 \times 10^{-2}$ m/s

$\rho = 1000$ kg/m^3

$p_1 = \rho_m g h_1 = 13600 \times 9.8 \times 10^{-2}$

$p_2 = 13600 \times 9.8 \times h$

From Eq. (i), we have

$$13600 \times 9.8 \times 10^{-2} + \frac{1}{2} \times 1000 \times (0.35)^2$$

$$= 13600 \times 9.8 \times h + \frac{1}{2} \times 1000 \times (0.65)^2$$

$$h = 0.887 \times 10^{-2} \text{ m} = 0.98 \text{ cm}$$

Solving, we get pressure = 0.98 cm of Hg

12. According to the equation of continuity,

$$A_1 v_1 = A_1 v_2$$

$$\Rightarrow \quad \frac{v_1}{v_2} = \frac{A_2}{A_1} = \frac{r_2^2}{r_1^2}$$

13. According to the equation of continuity,

$$A_1 v_1 = A_2 v_2$$

$$\therefore \quad \frac{v_1}{v_2} = \frac{A_2}{A_1}$$

14. Velocity of outflow, $v = \sqrt{2gh}$

$$\therefore \quad v = \sqrt{2 \times 10 \times 5} = 10 \text{ m/s}$$

Volume of liquid flowing out

$V = v \times$ area of hole

$= 10 \times 10^{-4} = 10^{-3}$ m^3/s

15. The pressure at the free surface of the liquid and also at outside of point P is atmospheric. Hence, there will be no effect of atmospheric pressure on the flow of liquid from hole P. The liquid on the free surface has no kinetic energy but only potential energy. On the other hand, the liquid coming out of the hole has both kinetic and potential energies. Let v be the velocity of efflux of the liquid coming out from the hole. According to Bernoulli's theorem, we have

$$p + 0 + \rho g H = p + \rho g (H - h) + \frac{1}{2}\rho v^2$$

$$\therefore \quad v = \sqrt{2gh} \qquad \text{...(i)}$$

After coming from the hole, the liquid adopts a parabolic path. If it takes t s in falling through a vertical distance $(H - h)$, then

$$(H - h) = \frac{1}{2}g t^2 \qquad \left(\because s = ut + \frac{1}{2}g t^2\right)$$

$$\therefore \quad t = \sqrt{\left\{2\frac{(H-h)}{g}\right\}} \qquad \text{...(ii)}$$

From Eqs. (i) and (ii),

$$x = vt = 2\sqrt{\{h(H-h)\}}$$

17

Thermometry

Heat

Heat is that mode of energy transfer which takes place due to difference in temperatures.

The sum total of the KE portion of the total internal energy of a body, may be called its thermal energy.

Temperature

It is that physical dimension of a body that determines the degree of hotness of that body and the direction of flow of heat when two bodies are kept in contact.

Temperature Scales

The centigrade (°C), Fahrenheit (°F), Kelvin (K), Reaumer (°R) and Rankine (°Ra) are commonly used temperature scales.

Various Temperature Scales with LFP and UFP

Temperature Scale	°C	°F	K	°R	°Ra	Another Scale
LFP	0	32	273	0	492	T_L
UFP	100	212	373	80	672	T_U
Number of divisions (N)	100	180	100	80	180	$T_U - T_L$

All these temperatures are related to each other by the following relationship

$$\frac{C-0}{100-0}=\frac{F-32}{212-32}$$

$$=\frac{K-273}{373-273}=\frac{R-0}{80-0}=\frac{Ra-492}{672-492}=\frac{T-T_L}{T_U-T_L}$$

or
$$\frac{C-0}{100}=\frac{F-32}{180}=\frac{k-273}{100}=\frac{R-0}{80}$$

$$=\frac{Ra-492}{180}=\frac{T-T_L}{T_U-T_L}$$

In general, whenever we are to go from any known scale to any unknown scale, then we follow the equation

$$\frac{\left(\begin{array}{c}\text{Temperature on}\\ \text{known scale}\end{array}\right)-\left(\begin{array}{c}\text{LFP for}\\ \text{known scale}\end{array}\right)}{(\text{UFP - LFP})_{\text{known scale}}}$$

$$=\frac{\left(\begin{array}{c}\text{Temperature on}\\ \text{unknown scale}\end{array}\right)-\left(\begin{array}{c}\text{LFP for}\\ \text{unknown scale}\end{array}\right)}{(\text{UFP} - \text{LFP})_{\text{unknown scale}}}$$

$$\therefore \quad \frac{C-0^\circ}{100^\circ-0^\circ}=\frac{F-32^\circ}{212^\circ-32^\circ}=\frac{R-0^\circ}{80^\circ-0^\circ}=\frac{^\circ Ra-492^\circ}{672^\circ-492^\circ}$$

$$=\frac{K-273.15}{373.15-273.15}$$

or
$$\frac{C}{5}=\frac{F-32}{9}=\frac{R}{4}=\frac{Ra-492}{9}=\frac{K-273}{5}$$

Different Thermometers

Constant-Volume Gas Thermometer

If p_0, p_{100}, p_{tr} and p_t are the pressures of gas at temperatures 0°C, 100°C, triple point of water and unknown temperature (t°C) respectively keeping the volume constant, then

$$t=\left(\frac{p-p_0}{p_{100}-p_0}\times 100\right)^\circ\text{C} \quad \text{or} \quad T=\left(273.16\frac{p}{p_{tr}}\right)\text{K}$$

Platinum Resistance Thermometer

If R_0, R_{100}, R_{tr} and R_t are the resistances of a platinum wire at temperatures 0°C, 100°C, triple point of water and unknown temperature (t° C) respectively, then

$$t=\left(\frac{R_t-T_0}{R_{100}-R_0}\times 100\right)^\circ\text{C}$$

or
$$T=\left(\frac{R_T}{R_{tr}}\times T_{tr}\right)\text{K}=\left(\frac{R_t}{R_{tr}}\times 273.16\right)\text{K}$$

Mercury Thermometer

In this thermometer, the length of a mercury column from some fixed point is taken as thermometric property. Thus,

$$t=\left(\frac{l_t-l_0}{l_{100}-l_0}\right)\times 100^\circ\text{C}$$

or
$$T=\left(\frac{l_t}{l_{tr}}\times 273.16\right)\text{K}$$

Ranges of Different Thermometers

Thermometer	Lower Limit	Upper Limit
Mercury thermometer	–30°C	300°C
Gas thermometer	–268°C	1500°C
Platinum resistance thermometer	–200°C	1200°C
Thermo-couple thermometer	–200°C	1600°C
Radiation thermometer	800°C	–6000°C

Pyrometers

It is a non-contacting thermometer which intercepts and measures thermal radiation known as radiometry. It can measure upto 800°C based on the principle Stefans law.

$$E \propto T^4 \text{ or } E = \sigma T^4$$

Where, σ is Stefans Boltzmann constant.

Practice Questions

Level I

1. Expression for an ideal gas measured by a thermometer is given by $\theta = \dfrac{P_t - P_0}{P_{100} - P_0} \times 100$, then temperature $\theta°$ is

(a) Kelvin (K) (b) Celsius (°C)
(c) Fahrenheit (°F) (d) Reaumer (°R)

2. What is the range of measurement of temperature with the help of mercury thermometer?

(a) ~260°C (b) ~360°C (c) ~500°C (d) ~100°C

3. The temperature of the Sun can be measured by

(a) Platinum thermometer
(b) Gas thermometer
(c) Vapour pressure thermometer
(d) None of the above

4. The range of platinum resistance thermometer is

(a) –200°C to 1200°C (b) –200°C to 1500°C
(c) 0°C to 1200°C (d) –273°C to 500°C

5. Correct value of 0°C on Kelvin scale is

(a) 272.85 K (b) 273.15 K
(c) 273.2 K (d) 273 K

6. Temperature on which Celsius scale and Fahrenheit scale gives same reading that is

(a) 0° (b) 30°
(c) 40° (d) – 40°

7. Boiling point of water on Kelvin scale is

(a) 373 K (b) 230 K
(c) 100 K (d) 273 K

8. Minimum possible temperature is

(a) 0°C (b) 0°F
(c)– 273° C (d) None of these

9. Relationship between Celsius and Fahrenheit scales is

(a) $C = \dfrac{9}{5}(F - 32)$ (b) $C = 9(F - 32)$

(c) $C = \dfrac{5}{9}(F - 32)$ (d) None of these

10. Ratio of the temperature of a body on Celsius scale and Fahrenheit scale is 1 : 3. The temperature of body is

(a) –26.66° C (b) 73°C
(c) 40°C (d) 26.66°C

Level II

1. In the Celsius temperature scale, the absolute zero of temperature is at

(a) 0°C (b) –32°C (c) 100°C (d) –273.15°C

2. One of the following thermometers, the one which can be used for measuring a rapidly changing temperature is a

(a) thermo-couple thermometer
(b) gas thermometer
(c) platinum resistance thermometer
(d) vapour pressure thermometer

3. The temperature of an iron block is 140°F. Its temperature on the Celsius scale is

(a) 60° (b) 160° (c) 140° (d) 132°

4. A mountain climber finds that water boils at 80°C. The temperature of this boiling water is .... Fahrenheit.

(a) 50° (b) 150° (c) 176° (d) 200°

5. If the temperature of a patient is 40°C his temperature on the Fahrenheit scale will be

(a) 104°F (b) 72°F (c) 96°F (d) 100°F

6. Maximum density of H_2O is at the temperature

(a) 32°F (b) 39.2°F
(c) 42°F (d) 4°F

7. The resistance of a resistance thermometer has values 2.71Ω and 3.70Ω at 10°C and 100°C, respectively. The temperature at which the resistance is 3.26Ω is

(a) 40°C (b) 50°C
(c) 60°C (d) 70°C

8. The temperature coefficient of resistance of the material of a wire is 0.00125 per °C. Its resistance at 300 K is 1Ω. At what temperature will the resistance of the wire will be 2Ω?

(b) 1154 K (c) 1100 K
(c) 1400 K (d) 1127 K

9. The two fixed points of a thermometer are wrongly marked as 5°C and 95°C.It shows a reading of 41°C in a room. The correct room temperature is

(a) 40°C (b) 40.5°C
(c) 41°C (d) 41.5°C

Answers

Level I

1. (b)	**2.** (b)	**3.** (d)	**4.** (a)	**5.** (b)	**6.** (d)	**7.** (a)	**8.** (c)	**9.** (c)	**10.** (d)

Level II

1. (d)	**2.** (a)	**3.** (a)	**4.** (c)	**5.** (a)	**6.** (b)	**7.** (c)	**8.** (d)	**9.** (a)

Hints and Solutions

Level I

6. Let x be the temperature at which Centigrade and Fahrenheit scale give the same reading. Then,

$$\frac{x-32}{9}=\frac{x}{5} \Rightarrow 5x-160=9x$$

$$\Rightarrow 4x=-160 \Rightarrow x=-40°C$$

Level II

3. $$\frac{140-32}{9}=\frac{C}{5}$$

$$\Rightarrow \frac{700-160}{9}=C$$

$$\Rightarrow C=60°C$$

4. $$\frac{F-32}{9}=\frac{80}{5} \Rightarrow F-32=144$$

$$\Rightarrow F=176°F$$

5. Temperature on Fahrenheit scale

$$= \text{Temperature on Celsius scale} \times (9/5)+32$$

$$=\frac{40\times 9}{5}+32=104°F$$

6. Maximum density of water is at 4°C.

Now $$\frac{F-32}{180}=\frac{C}{100}$$

$$\Rightarrow \frac{F-32}{180}=\frac{4}{100}$$

Solving, we get $F=39.2°F$

7. $$R_t=R_0(1+\alpha t)$$

$$2.71=R_0(1+\alpha\times 10) \quad \text{...(i)}$$

$$3.70=R_0(1+\alpha\times 100) \quad \text{...(ii)}$$

$$3.26=R_0(1+\alpha t) \quad \text{...(iii)}$$

Solving Eqs. (i) and (ii),

$$\frac{2.71}{3.70}=\frac{R_0(1+\alpha\times 10)}{R_0(1+\alpha\times 100)}$$

$$2.71(1+\alpha\times 100)=3.7(1+\alpha\times 10)$$

$$2.7+100\times\alpha\times 2.7=3.7+3.7\times 10\alpha$$

$$270\,\alpha-37\,\alpha=3.7-2.7$$

$$\alpha=\frac{1}{233}$$

and $R_0=2.59$

From Eq. (iii),

$$3.26=R_0(1+\alpha t)$$

$$3.26=2.59\left(1+\frac{1}{233}\times t\right)$$

$$\therefore \quad t=60.1\ °C$$

8. $R_t=R_0(1+\alpha t)$

$t=300\text{K}=27°C$ and $\alpha=0.00125/°C$

$$1=R_0(1+0.00125\times 27) \quad \text{...(i)}$$

$$2=R_0(1+0.00125\times t) \quad \text{...(ii)}$$

Solving Eqs. (i) and (ii), we get $t=854°\ C$

$$\therefore \quad t=(854+273)=1127\text{K}$$

9. $$\frac{C}{100}=\frac{F-(\text{LEP})}{(\text{UFP})-(\text{LEP})}$$

Where, C = actual temperature, F = reading on faulty thermometer, (LEP) = Lower Fixed Point and (UFP) = Upper Fixed Point. Hence,

$$\frac{C}{100}=\frac{41-5}{95-5}=\frac{36}{90}$$

$$C=\frac{36\times 100}{90}=40°C$$

18

Calorimetry

Calorimetry

It means measurement of heat, when a body at higher temperature is brought in contact with another body at lower temperature, the heat lost by the hot body is equal to the heat gained by the colder body and provided no heat is allowed to escape to the surrounding. A device in which heat measurement can be made is called a calorimeter.

1 calorie is the quantity of heat required to raise the temperature of 1 g of water by 1°C.

Principle of Calorimetry

When two bodies at different temperatures are placed in contact with each other or mixed with each other (liquid-in-liquid, solid-in-liquid), the heat will pass from the body at higher temperature to the body at lower temperature until both bodies reach a common temperature. This state is called as thermal equilibrium.

At this state,

Heat lost by one body = Heat gained by the other body

Let two bodies of masses m_1 and m_2, specific heats S_1 and S_2 and at temperatures θ_1 and θ_2 are brought in contact with each other. Assuming $\theta_1 > \theta_2$, heat will flow from body 1 to body 2. If θ is the common temperature of two bodies at the state of thermal equilibrium, then (assuming no heat is gained or lost from or to the surroundings).

Heat lost by body 1 = Heat gained by body 2

$$m_1 s_1(\theta_1 - \theta) = m_2\ s_2\ (\theta - \theta_2)\ (\theta_2 < \theta < \theta_1)$$

Determination of the Temperature of a Mixture on the Basis of the Principle of Calorimetry

Let mass, temperature and specific heat of two bodies A and B are m_A, θ_A and s_A and m_B, θ_B and s_B, respectively. θ_A is greater than θ_B.

Let final temperature be θ°C by taking these two bodies in contact. It will be clean that the temperature of body A down from θ_A to θ and the temperature of body B up from θ_B to θ.

Heat loss by body $A = m_A s_A (\theta_A - \theta)$

Heat gain by body $B = m_B s_B (\theta - \theta_B)$

Now, according to principle of mixture,

$$m_A s_A (\theta_A - \theta) = m_B s_B (\theta - \theta_B)$$

$$\Rightarrow \quad \theta = \frac{m_A s_A \theta_A + m_B s_B \theta_B}{m_A s_A + m_B s_B}$$

Specific Heat

The amount of heat required to raise the temperature of 1 g of substance by 1°C is called the specific heat. It is represented by s. Its unit is cal / g°C or J/g° C.

$$s = \frac{Q}{m \times \Delta t}$$

Specific Heat Capacities of Gases

Specific Heat at Constant Volume

The specific heat of a gas at constant volume is defined as the quantity of heat required to raise the temperature of unit mass of gas through 1°C or 1 K when its volume is kept constant *i.e.*,

$$C_V = \frac{(\Delta Q)_V}{m\Delta T}$$

If instead of unit mass, 1 mole of gas is considered, the specific heat is called molar specific heat is called molar specific heat at constant volume and is represented by C_V.

$$\therefore \quad C_V = Mc_V = \frac{M(\Delta Q)_V}{m\Delta T} = \frac{1(\Delta Q)_V}{n\Delta T} \quad \left[\because n = \frac{m}{M}\right]$$

Specific Heat at Constant Pressure

The specific heat of a gas at constant pressure is defined as the quantity of heat required to raise the temperature of unit mass of gas through 1K when its pressure is kept constant *i.e.*,

$$c_p = \frac{(\Delta Q)_p}{m\Delta T}$$

If instead of unit mass, 1 mole of gas is considered, the specific heat is called molar specific heat at constant pressure and is represented by C_p.

$$\therefore \quad C_p = Mc_p = \frac{M(\Delta Q)_p}{m\Delta T} \quad \ldots\text{(i)}$$

$$= \frac{1}{n}\frac{(\Delta Q)_p}{\Delta T} \quad [\because n = m/M]$$

Specific heat of a gas at constant pressure is greater than the specific heat at constant volume

i.e., $C_p > C_V$.

C_p and C_V are related to each other according to relation,

$$C_p - C_V = \frac{R}{j} \quad \ldots\text{(ii)}$$

Eq. (ii) is called Mayer's relation.

If C_p and C_V are measured in the units of work and R is also in the units of work (or energy), then Eq. (ii) becomes,

$$C_p - C_V = R$$

For monoatomic gas,

$$C_p = \frac{5}{2}R,\ C_V = \frac{3}{2}R$$

For diatomic gas, $C_p = \frac{7}{2}R,\ C_V = \frac{5}{2}R$

For polyatomic or triatomic gas,

$$C_V = 3R,\ C_p = 4R$$

Latent Heat

At constant temperature, the amount of heat taken by 1 g of a substance to change its state is called latent heat of substance.

It is represented by L, its unit is cal/g or J/kg.

It is of two types

1. Latent Heat of Fusion

At constant temperature, the amount of heat taken by 1 g of a substance to change its state from solid to liquid is called latent heat of fusion. Latent heat of fusion of ice is 80 cal/g.

2. Latent Heat of Vapourization

At constant temperature, the amount of heat taken by 1g of substance to change its state from liquid to vapour is called latent heat of vapourization. Latent heat of vapourization of water is 536 cal/g.

Practice Questions

Level I

1. Essential heat for increasing 1°C temperature of 1 kg substance is called ...... of that substance.

(a) latent heat (b) specific heat
(c) heat capacity (d) water equivalent

2. Dimensional formula of latent heat is

(a) $[M^0L^2T^{-2}]$ (b) $[MLT^{-2}]$
(c) $[ML^2T^{-2}]$ (d) $[ML^2T^{-1}]$

3. SI unit of specific heat is

(a) cal/g (b) Jule/°C
(c) kcal/°C (d) Jule /kg°C

4. Weight of 5 L benzene is

(a) more in summer with respect to winter
(b) some both the summer and winter
(c) more in winter with respect to summer
(d) None of the above

5. On increasing pressure the freezing point of water

(a) increases
(b) decreases
(c) stable
(d) first increases than decreases

6. Specific heat is equal to

(a) $\frac{H}{mt}$ (b) Hmt (c) $\frac{Ht}{m}$ (d) $\frac{Hm}{t}$

7. Which of the following have more specific heat?

(a) Mercury (b) Water (c) Alcohol (d) Benzene

8. In a close room a sprinkling water decreases the room temperature due to

(a) temperature of water is less than temperature of room
(b) water is insulator of heat
(c) value of latent heat of water vapour is more
(d) specific heat of water is high

9. What is the name of heat that changes 1 kg ice into water?

(a) Latent heat of melting
(b) Molar specific heat
(c) Latent heat of vapourization
(d) Heat capacity

10. Which of the following gives more pain on burning of a human skin?

(a) Hot water (b) Hot air
(c) Boiling water (d) Hot steam

Level II

1. If the atmospheric temperature and the dew point are nearly equal

(a) relative humidity is nearly 100%
(b) relative humidity is zero
(c) relative humidity is 50%
(d) nothing can be said about relative humidity

2. For hydrogen gas $C_p - C_V = a$ and for oxygen gas $C_p - C_V = b$. So, the relation between a and b is given by

(a) $a = 16b$
(b) $16a = b$
(c) $a = 4b$
(d) $a = b$

3. Boiling water is changing into steam. Under this condition the specific heat of water is
(a) zero (b) one
(c) infinite (d) less than one

4. Four students found set of C_p and C_V (in cal/deg. mole) as given below. Which of the following set is correct?
(a) $C_V = 4, C_p = 2$ (b) $C_V = 4$, $C_p = 1$
(c) $C_V = 3, C_p = 4$ (d) $C_p = 5, C_V = 3$

5. Heat required to convert 1 g of ice at 0°C into steam at 100°C is
(a) 100 cal (b) 0.01 kcal
(c) 716 cal (d) 1 kcal

6. A copper block of mass 50 g is heated to 100°C and placed in a block of ice at 0°C. The specific heat of copper is 0.1 cal/g/°C and latent heat of ice is 80 cal/g. The amount of ice melted is
(a) 6.15 g (b) 6.2 g
(c) 6.25 g (d) 6.3 g

7. 420 J of energy supplied to 10 g of water will raise its temperature by nearly
(a) 1°C (b) 4.2°C (c) 10°C (d) 42°C

8. 540 g of ice at 0°C is mixed with 540 g of water at 80°C. The final temperature of the mixture is
(a) 0°C (b) 4°C
(c) 80°C (d) less than 0°C

9. 70 cal are required to raise the temperature of 2 moles of an ideal gas at constant pressure from 30°C to 35°C. The amount of heat required (in calories) to raise the temperature of the same gas through the same range (30°C to 35°C) at constant volume is
(a) 30 (b) 50 (c) 70 (d) 90

10. The heat required to raise temperature from 30°C to 35°C for 2 moles of an ideal gas is 70 cal. At constant pressure, then heat required for the same gas to raise the temperature for the same range but at constant volume will be
(a) 30 cal (b) 50 cal
(c) 70 cal (d) None of these

Answers

Level I

1. (b)	**2.** (a)	**3.** (b)	**4.** (c)	**5.** (b)	**6.** (a)	**7.** (b)	**8.** (c)	**9.** (a)	**10.** (d)

Level II

1. (a)	**2.** (d)	**3.** (c)	**4.** (d)	**5.** (c)	**6.** (c)	**7.** (c)	**8.** (a)	**9.** (b)	**10.** (b)

Hints and Solutions

Level II

2. Both are diatomic gases and $C_p - C_V = R$ for all gases.

3. $Q = ms\Delta T$

$\therefore \quad s = \dfrac{Q}{m \cdot \Delta T}$

As, $\Delta T = 0$, hence $s = \infty$

4. $C_p - C_V = R$, where $R = 2$ cal/deg. mole

5. Q= Heat required to convert ice into water at 0°C + Heat required to raise the temperature of water from 0°C to 100°C + Heat required to convert water at 100°C to steam at 100°C

$= mL_1 + msT + mL_2$

$= 1 \times 80 + 1 \times 1 \times 100 + 1 \times 536 = 716$ cal.

6. $50 \times 0.1 \times 30 = m \times 80$

$m = \dfrac{50 \times 0.1 \times 100}{80} = 6.25$ g

7. $H = \dfrac{420}{42} = 100$ cal.

So, $10 \times 1 \times T = 100 \Rightarrow T = 10°C$

8. $540 \times 80 + 540 \times T = 540(80 - T)$

$\Rightarrow \quad 540[80 + T] = 540[80 - T]$

$\Rightarrow \quad 80 + T = 80 - T$

$T = 0°C$

9. Here, $\mu C_p \,\Delta T = 70$

$\Rightarrow \quad 2 \times C_p \times 5 = 70$

$\Rightarrow \quad C_p = 7$

$\therefore \quad C_V = C_p - R = 7 \text{ cal mol}^{-1}\text{K}^{-1} - 2 \text{ cal mol}^{-1}\text{K}^{-1}$

$= 5 \text{ cal mol}^{-1}\text{K}^{-1}$

Heat required to heat the gas at constant volume

$= 2 \times 5 \times 5$

$= 50$ cal.

10. We know that, $Q = nC_p \,\Delta T$

$\therefore \quad C_p = \dfrac{Q}{n\Delta T} = \dfrac{70}{2 \times 5} = 70$ cal/K

Further, $C_p - C_V = R$

$\Rightarrow \quad C_V = C_p - R = 7 - 2 = 5$ cal/K

Now $\quad Q = n\,C_V \Delta T = 2 \times 5 \times 5 = 50$ cal

19

Thermal Expansion

Thermal Expansion

Expansion on heating of a substance is called its thermal expansion.

Linear Expansion (α)

The coefficient of linear expansion α of a substance is defined as the fractional increase in length of a rod of that substance per unit rise of temperature, *i.e.*,

$$\alpha = \frac{\text{Increase in length}}{\text{Original length} \times \text{Rise in temperature}} = \frac{\Delta L}{L_0 t}$$

$$L_t = L_0 (1 + \alpha t)$$

α is measured in $^\circ C^{-1}$ or K^{-1}.

Superficial Expansion (β)

The coefficient of superficial expansion (β) of a substance is defined as the fractional increase in area of a piece of that substance per degree rise of temperature,

$$i.e., \beta = \frac{\text{Increase in area}}{\text{Original volume} \times \text{Rise in temperature}}$$

$$= \frac{\Delta A}{A_o t}; \quad A_t = A_0 (1 + Bt)$$

Note $\beta = 2\alpha$ *i.e.*, the coefficient of superficial expansion is twice the coefficient of linear expansion.

Cubical Expansion (γ)

The coefficient of cubical or volume expansion (γ) of a substance is the fractional increase in volume of a sample of that substance per degree rise in temperature,

$$\gamma = \frac{\text{Increase in volume}}{\text{Original volume} \times \text{Rise in temperature}} = \frac{\Delta V}{V_0}$$

$$V_t = V_0 (1 + \gamma t);$$

Note $\gamma = 3\alpha$

i.e., Coefficient of cubical expansion of a solid is three times its coefficient of linear expansion.

γ is a characteristic of the substance but is not strictly a constant. It depends in general on temperature. It is seen that γ becomes constant only at a high temperature.

β and γ are both measured in $^0C^{-1}$ or K^{-1}

Liquids have two types of volume expansion.

1. **Real Expansion** (γ_r) is the actual increase in the volume of a liquid.
2. **Apparent Expansion** (γ_a) is the apparent increase in the volume of a liquid *i.e.*, when no notice is taken of the expansion of the container vessel.

Real expansion of liquid = Apparent expansion of liquid + Expansion of vessel

In symbols, $\gamma_r = \gamma_a + \gamma_g$

Where, γ_g = Coefficient of volume expansion of vessel which is generally made up of glass (g).

Thermal Expansion of Gases

There are two coefficients of expansion for a gas viz., the pressure and the volume coefficient.

Pressure Coefficient (γ_p)

It is defined as the increase in pressure per unit pressure per unit degree rise of temperature at constant volume.

$$\gamma_p = \frac{p_t - p_0}{p_0 \times t} \quad \text{(At constant volume)}$$

$$\Rightarrow \quad p_t = p_0 [1 + \gamma_p t]$$

Volume Coefficient (γ_v)

It is defined as the increase in volume per unit volume per unit degree rise of temperature at constant pressure.

$$\gamma_v = \frac{V_t - V_0}{V_0 \times t} \quad \text{(At constant pressure)}$$

$$\Rightarrow \quad V_t = V_0 (1 + \gamma_v t)$$

Practice Questions

Level I

1. A small gap is left between the two railway tracks because
(a) it save iron
(b) increase the strength of iron
(c) easy to make small piece of iron
(d) it provides space of thermal expansion for tracks

2. If β be the coefficient of superficial expansion of a metal, then coefficient of its cubical expansion will be
(a) $\frac{\beta}{2}$ (b) $\frac{2\beta}{3}$ (c) $\frac{3\beta}{2}$ (d) 3β

3. Expansion is the rod due to heating does not depends upon its
(a) initial length (b) solidness or hollowness
(c) material of rod (d) increase in temperature

4. The density of water will be maximum, if its temperature is
(a) 0°C (b) 4°C
(c) 100°C (d) 32°C

5. On heating of bimetallic strip of a dimetal will be
(a) bend towards a strip of maximum value of α
(b) straight
(c) bend towards a strip of minimum value of α
(d) forming a shape of spring

6. Relationship among α, β and γ are
(a) $\alpha:\beta:\gamma=1:1:1$ (b) $\alpha:\beta:\gamma=1:2:3$
(c) $\alpha:\beta:\gamma=3:2:1$ (d) $\alpha:\beta:\gamma=2:3:1$

7. Coefficient of pressure expansion and cubical expansion for an ideal gas are
(a) equal (b) zero
(c) not equal (d) None of these

8. SI unit of universal gas constant is
(a) erg°C^{-1} (b) Jule-mole^{-1}Kelvin^{-1}
(c) dyne°C^{-1} (d) mole Kelvin^{-1}

9. A hole is there in a metal plate. Upon heating the plate, the diameter of hole would
(a) increase
(b) decrease
(c) remain the same
(d) may increase or decrease

10. When a copper ball is heated, the largest percentage increase will occur in its
(a) volume
(b) diameter
(c) area
(d) None of the above

Level II

1. A liquid with coefficient of volume expansion γ is filled in a container of a material having the coefficient of linear expansion α. If the liquid overflows on heating
(a) $\gamma=3\alpha$ (b) $\gamma>3\alpha$
(c) $\gamma<3\alpha$ (d) $\gamma>3\alpha^3$

2. Two spheres of same size are made of the same metal but one is hollow and the other is solid. They are heated to same temperature, then
(a) both spheres will expand equally
(b) hollow sphere will expand more than the solid one
(c) solid sphere will expand more than the hollow one
(d) None of the above

3. The coefficient of apparent expansion of a liquid in a copper vessel is C and in a silver vessel is S. The coefficient of volume expansion of copper is γ_c. What is the coefficient of linear expansion of silver?
(a) $(C+\gamma_c+S)/3$
(b) $(C-\gamma_c+S)/3$
(c) $(C+\gamma_c-S)/3$
(d) $(C-\gamma_c-S)/3$

4. A crystal has a coefficient of expansion 13×10^{-7} in one direction and 231×10^{-7} in every direction at right angles to it. Then, the cubical coefficient of expansion is
(a) 462×10^{-7} (b) 244×10^{-7}
(c) 475×10^{-7} (d) 257×10^{-7}

5. Two straight metallic strips each of thickness t and length l are rivetted together. Their coefficients of linear expansions are α_1 and α_2. If they are heated through temperature ΔT, the bimetallic strip will bend to form an arc of radius
(a) $t/\{(\alpha_1+\alpha_2)\Delta T\}$ (b) $t/\{(\alpha_2-\alpha_1)\Delta T\}$
(c) $t(\alpha_1+\alpha_2)\Delta T$ (d) $t(\alpha_2-\alpha_1)\Delta T$

6. A metal wire of length L and area of cross-section A is fixed between rigid supports at negligible tension. If this is cooled, the tension in the wire will be
(a) proportional to L
(b) inversely proportional to L
(c) independent of L
(d) proportional to square of L

7. On heating a liquid of coefficient of cubical expansion α in a container having coefficient of linear expansion $\alpha/3$, the level of liquid in the container will
(a) rise
(b) fall
(c) will remain almost stationary
(d) it is difficult to say

8. A thin copper wire of length L increase in length by 1% when heated from temperature T_1 to T_2. What is the percentage change in area when a thin copper plate having dimensions $2L\times L$ is heated from T_1 to T_2?
(a) 1 (b) 3 (c) 2 (d) 4

Answers

Level I

1. (d) **2.** (c) **3.** (a) **4.** (b) **5.** (c) **6.** (b) **7.** (a) **8.** (b) **9.** (a) **10.** (a)

Level II

1. (b) **2.** (a) **3.** (c) **4.** (c) **5.** (b) **6.** (c) **7.** (c) **8.** (c)

Hints *and* Solutions

Level II

3. $\gamma_r = C + \gamma_c = S + \gamma_s$

$\therefore \quad \gamma_s = C + \gamma_c - S$

Now, $\alpha = \dfrac{\gamma_s}{3} = (C + \gamma_c - S)/3$

4. $\gamma = \alpha_1 + \alpha_2 + \alpha_3$

$= 13 \times 10^{-7} + 231 \times 10^{-7} + 231 \times 10^{-7}$

$= 475 \times 10^{-7}$

5. Let the angle subtended by the arc formed be θ. Then,

$$\theta = \frac{l}{r}$$

$$\Rightarrow \quad \theta = \frac{\Delta l}{\Delta r} = \frac{l_2 - l_1}{r_1 - r_2}$$

$$\therefore \quad \theta = \frac{l(\alpha_2 - \alpha_1)\Delta T}{t}$$

$$\Rightarrow \quad \frac{l}{r} = \frac{l(\alpha_2 - \alpha_1)\Delta T}{t}$$

So, $$r = \frac{t}{(\alpha_2 - \alpha_1)\Delta T}$$

6. We know that, $T = \gamma A \alpha \Delta T$

So, the tension is independent of L.

8. $\beta = 2\alpha$

$\therefore$ Percentage increase in area = 2%.

20

Thermodynamics

Thermodynamics

It is that branch of Science, which deals with transformation of heat energy into mechanical energy or other form of energy.

First Law of Thermodynamics

According to this law, the heat given to a system (ΔQ) is equal to the sum of increase in its internal energy (ΔU) and the work done (ΔW) by the system against the surroundings.

Mathematically, $\Delta Q = \Delta U + \Delta W$

Sign Convention

ΔQ = Positive when heat is supplied

= Negative when heat is rejected

ΔU = Positive when temperature decreases

= Negative when temperature decreases

ΔW = Positive when work is done by the system (expansion)

= Negative when work is done on system (compression)

Second Law of Thermodynamics

It is stated in different forms. *Two most common statements are as below*

1. Clausius Statement

It is impossible for a self-acting machine, working in a cyclic process, to transfer heat from a colder body to a hotter body without he aid of an external agency.

2.Kelvin-Planck's Statement

It is impossible to design an engine which extracts heat from a reservoir and fully converts it into work without producing any other effect.

Simply, the second law of thermodynamics implies that no heat engine can have efficiency η equal to 1 (or 100%).

Thermodynamic Processes

Isochoric Process

- It is that thermodynamic process in which volume remains constant.

  In an isochoric process for a given mass of gas,

$$p \propto T \text{ or } \frac{p}{T} = \text{Constant}$$

- Work done in an isochoric process,

$$\Delta W = \int p dV = 0$$

- Molar specific heat of a gas under isochoric condition, $C_V = \frac{f}{2} R$, where f is the number of degrees of freedom per molecule.
- As, $\Delta W = 0$, hence according to first law of thermodynamics, we have

$$(\Delta Q)_V = \Delta U = \mu C_V \Delta T = \frac{\mu R}{(\gamma - 1)} \Delta T$$

Isobaric Process

- It is that process in which pressure remains constant.

  As in an isobaric process for a given mass of gas,

$$V \propto T \text{ or } \frac{V}{T} = \text{Constant}$$

- Work done in an isobaric process,

$$\Delta W = \int p dV = P \int_{V_i}^{V_f} dV$$

$$= P(V_f - V_i) = p\Delta V$$

- Molar specific heat of a gas under isobaric condition,

$$C_p = \left(\frac{f}{2} + 1\right) R = C_V + R$$

Isothermal Process

- It is that process in which temperature remains constant.
- Molar specific heat of a gas under isothermal condition,

$$C = \frac{\Delta Q}{m \cdot \Delta T} = \frac{\Delta Q}{m(0)} = \infty$$

- Work done in an isothermal process,

$$\Delta W = \int_{V_i}^{V_f} p dV$$

$$= \mu RT \log\left(\frac{V_f}{V_i}\right)$$

- As per first law of thermodynamics, since $\Delta T = 0$, hence $\Delta U = 0$ and we have $\Delta Q = \Delta W$. Thus, heat supplies to the system in an isothermal process is entirely used to do work against external surroundings.

Adiabatic Process

- It is that process in which there is no exchange of heat of the system with its surroundings. Thus, in an adiabatic process p, V and T change but $\Delta Q = 0$ or entropy remains constant $\left(\Delta S = \frac{\Delta Q}{T} = 0\right)$.

  The equation of state for an adiabatic process pV^γ = Constant

  or $TV^{\gamma-1}$ = Constant

  or $T^\gamma p^{1-\gamma}$ = Constant

- Molar specific heat of a gas under adiabatic condition,

$$C = \frac{\Delta Q}{m\Delta T} = \frac{0}{m\Delta T} = 0$$

- Work done in an adiabatic process,

$$\Delta W = \int_{V_i}^{V_f} p dV$$

$$= \frac{\mu R}{(\gamma - 1)}(T_i - T_f)$$

$$= -\frac{\mu R}{(\gamma - 1)}\Delta T$$

ENGINE

Heat Engine It is a device which a system undergoes a cyclic process resulting in conversion of heat into work. If Q_1 is the heat absorbed from the heat source (hotter reservoir), Q_2 is the heat released to the sink (colder reservoir) and the work output of the engine in one cycle is W, then the efficiency of the engine,

$$\eta = \frac{W}{Q_1} = 1 - \frac{Q_2}{Q_1}$$

Carnot's Engine It is a theoretical, ideal heat engine working in a reversible cyclic process operating between two temperatures T_1 (heat source) and T_2 (heat sink). The Carnot's cycle consists of two isothermal processes connected by two adiabatic processes as shown in figure. The efficiency of a Carnot's cycle is given by,

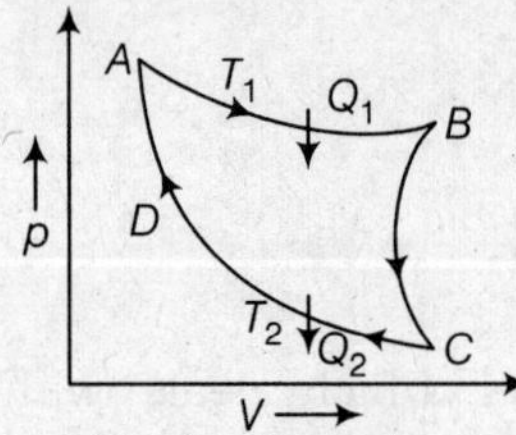

$$\eta = \frac{W}{Q_1} = 1 - \frac{Q_2}{Q_1} = 1 - \frac{T_2}{T_1}$$

Thus, efficiency does not depend on nature or quantity of the working substance.

Refrigerator or Heat Pump

The coefficient of performance of a refrigerator is defined as the ratio of the heat extracted from the cold reservoir (Q_2) to the work needed to be done (W) on the refrigerator.

Thus, coefficient of performance,

$$\beta = \frac{Q_2}{W} = \frac{Q_2}{Q_1 - Q_2} = \frac{T_2}{T_1 - T_2}$$

Where, T_2 = Temperature of colder body (contents of refrigerator)

and T_1 = Temperature of hot reservoir (the surroundings)

Entropy

If a small amount of heat ΔQ is given to a thermodynamic system maintained at a temperature T, then the change in the entropy of the system is given by

$$\Delta S = \frac{\Delta Q}{T} \qquad \Rightarrow S_f - S_i = \int_i^f \frac{\Delta Q}{T}$$

Practice Questions

Level I

1. **A constant quantity is adiabatic process is**
(a) temperature (b) volume
(c) heat (d) pressure

2. **The concept of internal energy was first introduced by**
(a) First law of thermodynamics
(b) Stefan's law
(c) Wien's law
(d) Second law of thermodynamics

3. **Internal energy of gas in a cyclic process is**
(a) increase (b) decrease
(c) zero (d) constant

4. **Which quantity is constant in isothermal process?**
(a) Pressure (b) Internal energy
(c) External energy (d) Volume

5. **In isothermal process**
(a) p, V and T changes
(b) V and T changes
(c) p and V changes
(d) p and T changes

6. **Coefficient of performance (β) is called**
(a) efficiency of steam engine
(b) efficiency of refrigerator
(c) efficiency of Carnot engine
(d) None of the above

7. **When the temperature of a source is increasing, then efficiency of Carnot engine is**
(a) decreases
(b) increases
(c) first increases then decreases
(d) unchanged

8. **The efficiency of Carnot engine depends only upon**
(a) temperature of source
(b) functioning part
(c) temperature of sink
(d) temperature of source and sink

9. **Relationship between temperature and volume of a gas for an adiabatic process is**
(a) $TV^{\gamma-1}$ = Constant
(b) $T^{\gamma-1}V^{\gamma-1}$ = Constant
(c) $T^{\gamma-1}V$ = Constant
(d) $TV^{1-\gamma}$ = Constant

10. **In adiabatic process of a gas there is**
(a) flow of heat
(b) constant temperature
(c) not flow of heat
(d) constant volume

11. **In adiabatic process, the gas follows**
(a) Pascal's law (b) Poisson's law
(c) Boyle's law (d) None of these

12. **When an ideal gas placed in vacuum inside a container is allowed to expand, then**
(a) internal energy decreases, temperature increases
(b) internal energy increases, temperature decreases
(c) both internal energy and temperature increases
(d) neither internal energy decreases nor temperature

13. **Heat added to a system is equal to**
(a) a change in its internal kinetic energy
(b) a change in its internal potential energy
(c) work done by it
(d) sum of above all the three

14. **The internal energy U is a unique function of any state because change in U**
(a) does not depend upon path
(b) depends upon path
(c) corresponds to an adiabatic process
(d) corresponds to an isothermal process

15. **The area under a curve in p-V diagram represents**
(a) the condition of a system
(b) work done on or by the system
(c) work done in cyclic process
(d) a thermodynamic process

Level II

1. **The Physics underlying the operation of a refrigerator most closely resembles the Physics underlying**
(a) heat engine
(b) melting of ice
(c) the freezing of water
(d) the vapourization of water

2. **Which statement is incorrect?**
(a) All reversible cycles have same efficiency
(b) Reversible cycle has more efficiency than an irreversible one
(c) Carnot cycle is a reversible one
(d) Carnot cycle has the maximum efficiency in all cycles

3. **The second law of thermodynamics implies**
(a) whole of the heat can be converted into mechanical energy
(b) no heat engine can be 100% efficient
(c) every heat engine has an efficiency of 100%
(d) a refrigerator can reduce the temperature to absolute zero

4. **A refrigerator is**
(a) heat engine
(b) an electric motor
(c) heat engine working backward
(d) air cooler

5. The efficiency of a Carnot engine working between the source at absolute temperature T_1 and the sink at an absolute temperature T_2 is

(a) $\frac{T_2}{T_1} \times 100$ (b) $\left(\frac{1}{T_1 \times T_2}\right) \times 100$

(c) $\left(\frac{T_1}{T_2} - 1\right) \times 100$ (d) $\left(1 - \frac{T_2}{T_1}\right) \times 100$

6. 110 J of heat are added to a gaseous system whose internal energy is 40 J, then the amount of external work done is

(a) 150 J (b) 70 J (c) 110 J (d) 40 J

7. Which of the following parameters does not characterize the thermodynamic state of matter?

(a) Temperature (b) Pressure
(c) Work (d) Volume

8. If Q, E and W denote respectively the heat added, change in internal energy and the work done in a closed cycle process, then

(a) $W = 0$ (b) $Q = W = 0$
(c) $E = 0$ (d) $Q = 0$

9. A Carnot engine work between temperatures 727°C and 27°C. The efficiency of engine is

(a) 0% (b) 100% (c) 30% (d) 70%

10. The efficiency of a Carnot engine working between steam point and ice point is

(a) 16.8% (b) 26.81% (c) 36.8% (d) 46.8%

11. A Carnot engine working between 300 K and 600 K has a work output of 800 J per cycle. The amount of heat energy supplied to the engine from the source in each cycle is

(a) 800 J (b) 1600 J (c) 3200 J (d) 6400 J

12. A Carnot engine whose sink is at a temperature of 300 K has an efficiency of 40%. By how much should the temperature of the source be increased so as to increase the efficiency to 60%?

(a) 380 K (b) 325 K (c) 250 K (d) 275 K

13. If ΔU and ΔW represent the increase in internal energy and work done by the system respectively in a thermodynamical process, which of the following is true?

(a) $\Delta U = -\Delta W$, in an adiabatic process
(b) $\Delta U = \Delta W$, in an isothermal process
(c) $\Delta U = \Delta W$, in an adiabatic process
(d) $\Delta U = -\Delta W$, in an isothermal process

14. The first law of thermodynamics is a special case of

(a) Newton's law
(b) the law of conservation of energy
(c) Charle's law
(d) the law of heat exchanging

15. An electric fan is switched on in a closed room. The air in the room is

(a) cooled
(b) heated
(c) maintains the temperature
(d) heated or cooled depending on the atmospheric pressure

Answers

Level I

1. (c)	**2.** (a)	**3.** (d)	**4.** (b)	**5.** (c)	**6.** (b)	**7.** (b)	**8.** (d)	**9.** (a)	**10.** (c)
11. (b)	**12.** (d)	**13.** (a)	**14.** (a)	**15.** (b)					

Level II

1. (a)	**2.** (a)	**3.** (b)	**4.** (c)	**5.** (d)	**6.** (b)	**7.** (c)	**8.** (c)	**9.** (d)	**10.** (b)
11. (b)	**12.** (c)	**13.** (a)	**14.** (b)	**15.** (b)					

Hints and Solutions

Level II

6. $dQ = dU + dW$

$\Rightarrow dW = dQ - dU \quad \therefore dW = 110 - 40 = 70$ J

9. $T_1 = 727 + 273 = 1000$K

$T_2 = 27 + 273 = 300$ K

$$\eta = 1 - \frac{T_2}{T_1} = 1 - \frac{300}{1000} = \frac{700}{1000} \times 100 = 70\%$$

10. T_2 = Ice point = 0 + 273 = 273 K

T_1 = Steam point = 100 + 273 = 373 K

$$\eta = 1 - \frac{273}{373} = \frac{100}{373} \times 100 = 26.81\%$$

11. $\therefore \frac{T_2}{T_1} = \frac{Q_2}{Q_1} \Rightarrow Q_1 = Q_2 \times \frac{T_1}{T_2}$

$$\therefore Q_1 = 800 \times \frac{600}{300} = 1600 \text{ J}$$

12. $\frac{40}{100} = 1 - \frac{300}{T_1}$

$\Rightarrow T_1 = 500$ K

For 60% efficiency,

$$\frac{60}{100} = 1 - \frac{300}{T_1} \Rightarrow T_1 = 750 \text{ K}$$

So, the temperature should be increased $= 750 - 500 = 250$ K

21

Kinetic Theory of Gases

Physical Properties of Gases

Matter is found in three states solid, liquid and gas.

- Gases have some special properties different from solid and liquid
- Gases can be compressed easily.
- They have neither a definite volume nor a definite shape.

Charles' Law

At constant pressure, the volume of given mass of the gas is directly proportional to its absolute temperature.

$$V \propto T \quad \text{(at constant pressure)}$$

$$V_t = V_0\,(1 + \alpha t)$$

Where, α = Volume coefficient

(for gases $\alpha = \frac{1}{273}$ per °C)

$$\therefore \quad V_t = V_0\left(1 + \frac{t}{273}\right)$$

$$\Rightarrow \quad \frac{V_1}{T_1} = \frac{V_2}{T_2}$$

Boyle's Law

At constant temperature, the volume of the given mass of a gas is inversely proportional to its pressure.

$$p \propto \frac{1}{V} \quad \text{(at constant temperature)}$$

$$pV = \text{Constant or } p_1V_1 = p_2V_2$$

Pressure's Law or Gay-Lussac's Law

At constant volume, pressure of the gas is directly proportional to its absolute temperature.

$$p \propto T \quad \text{(at constant volume)}$$

$$p_t = p_0\,(1 + \beta t)$$

Where, β = Pressure coefficient

(for gases $\beta = \frac{1}{273}$ per °C)

$$\therefore \quad p_t = p_0\left(1 + \frac{t}{273}\right)$$

$$\Rightarrow \quad \frac{p_1}{T_1} = \frac{p_2}{T_2}$$

Ideal Gases

Ideal gas is that imaginary gas which obey Boyle's, Charle's and Pressure's law in all conditions.

Since, ideal gas equation is $pV = RT$,

where R = Universal gas constant.

If p_1, V_1, T_1 and p_2, V_2, T_2 are the pressure, volume and temperature of gas 1 and 2, respectively. Then,

$$\frac{p_1V_1}{T_1} = \frac{p_2V_2}{T_2}$$

Van der Waal's Equation

Practically gases do not obey ideal gas equation, so to express the behaviour of real gases, van der Waal's equation was given

$$\left(p + \frac{a}{V^2}\right)(V - b) = RT$$

Where, a and b are constants. Which has different values for different gas.

Gaseous Pressure

Gas applies a pressure on the walls of the container, this pressure is called gaseous pressure.

$$p = \frac{1}{3}\frac{mn}{V}\overline{v}^2,\; p = \frac{1}{2}\rho\overline{v}^2$$

Where, m = Mass of one molecule,

n = Number of molecules of the gas,

V = Volume of the vessel,

$\overline{v}^2$ = Mean square velocity

$\rho = \frac{mn}{V}$ is density of gas

Various Speeds of Gas Molecules

Most probable speed $v_{MP} = \sqrt{\left(\frac{2RT}{M}\right)} = \sqrt{\left(\frac{2kT}{m}\right)}$

Mean speed $\bar{v} = \frac{\Sigma v}{n} = \sqrt{\left(\frac{8\ RT}{M\pi}\right)} = \sqrt{\left(\frac{8\ kT}{m\pi}\right)}$

$v_{rms} = \sqrt{\left(\frac{3RT}{M}\right)} = \sqrt{\left(\frac{3RT}{mN}\right)} = \sqrt{\left(\frac{3kT}{m}\right)}$

Relation between Temperature and Molecular Kinetic Energy

Let the mass of 1 mole of a gas be M and the mean square velocity of its molecules by $\bar{v}^2$, then the kinetic energy of 1 mole of the gas,

$$\frac{1}{2}M\bar{v}^2 = \frac{1}{2}M\left(\frac{3\ RT}{M}\right) = \frac{3}{2}RT$$

Average kinetic energy of one molecule $= \frac{\left(\frac{3}{2}\right)RT}{N}$

$$= \frac{3}{2}\left(\frac{R}{N}\right)T$$

$\therefore \quad \frac{R}{N} = k$ (constant)

$\therefore$ Average kinetic energy of one molecule $= \frac{3}{2}kT$

Degrees of Freedom

Degrees of freedom of a gas are the number of independent motions, that a molecules can have. Degree of freedom = (3 × number of atoms in the molecule – number of relations between the molecules).

Total Degree of Freedom

	Translatory	Rotatory	Total	C_V	$C_p = C_V + R$	$r = 1 + \frac{2}{f}$ or $r = \frac{C_p}{C_V}$
Monoatomic	3	0	3	3/2 R	5/2 R	5/3
Diatomic	3	2	5	7/2 R	7/2 R	1.4
Polyatomic	3	3	6	3R	4R	1.33

Mean Free Path

The mean free path is the average distance travelled between two successive collisions with other molecules.

Mean free path, $\lambda = \frac{1}{\sqrt{2}\pi d^2 n}$

Where, n = Number of molecules per unit volume
d = Molecular diameter

Practice Questions

Level I

1. Which of the following quantities will be zero at 0K?
(a) Kinetic energy of molecules
(b) Vibrating Kinetic energy of molecules
(c) Potential energy of molecules
(d) (a) and (b)

2. RMS velocity of a gas molecules at pressure p be v_{rms}. If pressure becomes doubled, then RMS velocity will be
(a) 0.5 v_{rms} (b) 4 v_{rms}
(c) 2 v_{rms} (d) 2 v_{rms}

3. SI unit of a gas constant is
(a) calorie /°C (b) Jule / mole
(c) Jule / mole-K (d) Jule / kg

4. The temperature of a gas is determined from
(a) most probable velocity of molecules
(b) RMS velocity of molecules
(c) maximum velocity of molecules
(d) average velocity of molecules

5. Natural gas behaves like an ideal gas at
(a) low temperature and high pressure
(b) high temperature and high pressure
(c) low temperature and low pressure
(d) high temperature and low pressure

6. An ideal gas follows
(a) only Boyle's law
(b) Avogadro's law
(c) only Charle's law
(d) Both of Boyle's and Charle's laws

7. Mean kinetic energy of a gas molecules at temperature 300 K will be (take $R = 8.31$ J/mole-K, $N = 6.02 \times 10^{23}$)
(a) 6.21×10^{-21} J (b) 6×10^{-21} J
(c) 6×10^{-19} J (d) 7.21×10^{-22} J

8. Perfect gases behaves like an ideal gas at
(a) low temperature and high pressure
(b) high temperature and high pressure
(c) high temperature and low pressure
(d) low temperature and low pressure

9. A gas molecule of mass m is directly proportional to RMS velocity at given temperature is
(a) m^0 (b) $\sqrt{m}$
(c) m (d) $m^{-\frac{1}{2}}$

10. .... energy of an ideal gas will be zero.
(a) Kinetic (b) Potential
(c) Both (a) and (b) (d) None of these

11. At a given volume and temperature, the pressure of gas
(a) varies inversely as its mass
(b) varies linearly as its mass
(c) varies inversely as the square of its mass
(d) is independent of its mass

12. Pressure exerted by a perfect gas is equal to
(a) mean kinetic energy per unit volume
(b) 2/3 of mean kinetic energy per unit volume
(c) half of mean kinetic energy per unit volume
(d) 1/3 of mean kinetic energy per unit volume

13. Equation $pV = RT$ shows behaviour of perfect gas at
(a) high temperature and high density
(b) low temperature and low density
(c) high temperature and low density
(d) low temperature and high density

14. The temperature of a gas increased from 27°C to 927°C. RMS velocity of a gas molecules will be
(a) half (b) $\sqrt{\frac{927}{27}}$ times
(c) unchaned (d) doubled

Level II

1. At a given temperature, the ratio of root mean square velocities of hydrogen molecule and helium atom will be
(a) $1:\sqrt{2}$ (b) $\sqrt{2}:1$
(c) 1:2 (d) 2 : 1

2. The value of C_V for 1 mole of neon gas is
(a) $\frac{9R}{2}$ (b) $\frac{7R}{2}$
(c) $\frac{5R}{2}$ (d) $\frac{3R}{2}$

3. Mean kinetic energy per degree of freedom of gas molecule is
(a) $\frac{3KT}{2}$ (b) KT
(c) $\frac{1}{2}KT$ (d) $\frac{5KT}{2}$

4. At what temperature is the kinetic energy of a gas molecule double that of its value is 27°C?
(a) 54°C (b) 300°C
(c) 327°C (d) 108°C

5. The temperature at which the root mean square velocity of a molecule will be double of its value at 100°C is
(a) 1492°C (b) 1219°C
(c) 546°C (d) 273°C

6. If f denotes the degree of freedom of a gas, the ratio of two specific heats $\frac{C_p}{C_V}$ is given by
(a) $\frac{1}{f}+1$ (b) $\frac{2}{f}+1$
(c) $\frac{1}{f}-1$ (d) $\frac{2}{f}-1$

7. According to the kinetic theory of gases, the root mean velocity of gas molecules is directly proportional to
(a) T (b) $\sqrt{T}$
(c) T^2 (d) $T^{3/2}$

8. The rms velocity of nitrogen molecules at NTP is
(a) 492 m/s (b) 517 m/s
(c) 546 m/s (d) 819 m/s

9. The molecular weight of a gas is 44. The volume occupied by 2.2 g of this gas at 0°C and 2 atm pressure will be
(a) 0.56 L (b) 1.2 L
(c) 1.4 L (d) 5.6 L

10. To what temperature should the hydrogen at room temperature (27°C) be heated at constant pressure so that, the rms velocity of its molecules becomes double of its previous value?
(a) 1200°C (b) 927°C (c) 600°C (d) 108°C

11. The rms speed of the molecules of a gas in a vessel is 400 m/s. If half of the gas leaks out at constant temperature, the rms speed of the remaining molecules will be
(a) 800 m/s (b) $400\sqrt{2}$ m/s
(c) 400 m/s (d) 200 m/s

12. When volume of a system is increased two times and temperature is decreased to half of its initial temperature, then pressure becomes
(a) 2 times (b) 4 times
(c) $\frac{1}{4}$ times (d) $\frac{1}{2}$ times

13. A perfect gas at 27°C is heated at constant pressure to 327°C. If original volume of gas at 27°C is V, then volume at 327°C is
(a) V (b) $3V$ (c) $2V$ (d) $\frac{V}{2}$

14. The velocity of molecules of a gas at temperature 120 K is v. At what temperature will the velocity be $2v$?
(a) 120 K (b) 240 K
(c) 480 K (d) 1120 K

15. When temperature of an ideal gas is increased from 27°C, to 227°C, its rms speed changes from 400 m/s to v_s. The v_s is
(a) 516 m/s (b) 450 m/s
(c) 310 m/s (d) 746 m/s

16. If 2 mole of diatomic gas and 1 mole of monoatomic gas are mixed, then the ratio of specific heats is
(a) $\frac{7}{3}$ (b) $\frac{5}{4}$ (c) $\frac{19}{13}$ (d) $\frac{15}{19}$

17. At what temperature will the oxygen molecules have the same root mean square velocity as hydrogen molecules at 200 K?
(a) 800 K (b) 1600 K (c) 3200 K (d) 6500 K

18. The temperature of a gas pressure p and volume V is 27°C. Keeping its volume constant, if its temperature is raised to 927°C, then its pressure will be
(a) $2p$ (b) $3p$ (c) $4p$ (d) $6p$

19. To what temperature should the hydrogen at 327°C be cooled at constant pressure, so that the root mean square velocity of its molecules become half of its previous value?
(a) 123°C (b) – 123°C (c) 100°C (d) 0°C

20. The quantity of heat required to raise 1 mole through 1°C for a monoatomic gas at constant volume is
(a) $\frac{R}{2}$ (b) $\frac{3R}{2}$ (c) $\frac{5R}{2}$ (d) $\frac{7R}{2}$

Answers

Level I

1. (d)	**2.** (d)	**3.** (c)	**4.** (b)	**5.** (d)	**6.** (d)	**7.** (c)	**8.** (c)	**9.** (b)	**10.** (b)
11. (b)	**12.** (b)	**13.** (d)	**14.** (d)						

Level II

1. (b)	**2.** (d)	**3.** (c)	**4.** (c)	**5.** (b)	**6.** (b)	**7.** (b)	**8.** (b)	**9.** (a)	**10.** (b)
11. (c)	**12.** (c)	**13.** (c)	**14.** (c)	**15.** (a)	**16.** (c)	**17.** (c)	**18.** (c)	**19.** (b)	**20.** (b)

Hints and Solutions

Level II

1. $v_{rms} = \sqrt{\frac{3RT}{M}}, \frac{V_{rms} \text{ of } H_2}{V_{rms} \text{ of He}}$

$$= \sqrt{\frac{M \text{ of He}}{M \text{ of } H_2}} = \sqrt{\frac{4}{2}} = \frac{\sqrt{2}}{1}.$$

2. Neon is a monoatomic gas, $C_V = \frac{3R}{2}$ for monoatomic gases.

4. Kinetic energy is proportional to absolute temperature.

$$\frac{2E}{E} = \frac{T}{300} \Rightarrow T = 600 \text{ K} = (600-273)°\text{C} = 327°\text{C}$$

5. $\bar{c} = \frac{3RT}{M} \Rightarrow \frac{T_2}{T_1} = \left(\frac{\bar{c}_2}{\bar{c}_1}\right)^2$

$$T_1 = (273+100) \text{ K}$$
$$T_2 = (273+100)(2)^2 = 1492 \text{ K}$$
$$= (1492-273) = 1219°\text{C}$$

9. Number of moles of gas $= \frac{2.2}{44} = \frac{1}{20}$ mole

1 mole of a gas occupies 22.4 L at NTP.

$$pV = nRT, \frac{p_1V_1}{p_2V_2} = \frac{n_1}{n_2}$$
$$\Rightarrow V_2 = \frac{p_1}{p_2} \times \frac{n_2}{n_1}$$
$$V_1 = \frac{22.4}{20 \times 2} \Rightarrow V_2 = 0.56 \text{ L}$$

10. $\left(\frac{v_1}{v_2}\right)^2 = \frac{T_1}{T_2} \Rightarrow \frac{(273+27)}{(273+t)}$

$$\Rightarrow \left(\frac{v_1}{2v_1}\right)^2 = \frac{300}{(273+t)}$$
$$\Rightarrow 273 + t = 1200$$
$$\therefore t = 927°\text{C}$$

11. $\left(\frac{v_1}{v_2}\right)^2 = \frac{T_1}{T_2}$, v_1 and v_2 are rms velocities. Velocity is a function of temperature. Temperature is constant. Velocity remains constant.

12.
$$pV = RT$$
$$p_1V_1 = RT_1 \text{ and } V_2 = 2V_1, T_2 = \frac{T_1}{2}, p_2 = ?$$
$$\frac{p_1V_1}{p_2V_2} = \frac{T_1}{T_2} \Rightarrow \frac{p_1}{p_2} \cdot \frac{V_1}{2V_1} = \frac{2T_1}{T_1} \Rightarrow \frac{p_1}{p_2} = 4$$
$$\therefore p_2 = \frac{p_1}{4} = \text{One-fourth of initial pressure}$$

13. $T_1 = 300$ K, $T_2 = 600$ K, $p_1 = p_2 = p$

Let $V_1 = V$

$$\frac{p_1V_1}{T_1} = \frac{p_2V_2}{T_2} \Rightarrow \frac{p \cdot V}{300} = \frac{p \cdot V_2}{600}$$
$$\Rightarrow V_2 = 2V$$

14. $(v_{rms})^2 \propto$ absolute temperature

$$\left(\frac{v_2}{v_1}\right)^2 = \frac{T_2}{T_1}$$
$$\Rightarrow \left(\frac{2v}{v}\right)^2 = \frac{T_2}{120}$$
$$\therefore T_2 = 120 \times 4 = 480 \text{ K}$$

15. $(v_{rms})^2 \propto$ Absolute temperature

$$\left(\frac{v_2}{v_1}\right)^2 = \frac{T_2}{T_1}$$
$$\Rightarrow \frac{v_2}{400} = \sqrt{\frac{273+227}{273+27}} = \sqrt{\frac{500}{300}} = \sqrt{\frac{5}{3}}$$
$$\therefore v_2 = 400 \times \sqrt{\frac{5}{3}}$$
$$= 4000 \times \sqrt{1.67} = 516 \text{ m/s}$$

16. We know that,

$$(C_V)_{mix} = \frac{\mu_1 (C_v)_1 + \mu_2 (C_v)_2}{\mu_1 + \mu_2} \quad ...(i)$$

and $$(C_p)_{mix} R + (C_V)_{mix} \quad ...(ii)$$

$$(C_V)_{mix} = \frac{1 \times \frac{3R}{2} + 2 \times \frac{5R}{2}}{1+2} = \frac{13R}{6}$$

$$(C_p)_{mix} = R + \frac{13R}{6} = \frac{19R}{6}$$

$$\frac{(C_p)_{mix}}{(C_V)_{mix}} = \frac{19R}{6} \times \frac{6}{13R} = \frac{19}{13}$$

17. $v_{rms} = \sqrt{\frac{3RT}{M}}$, Temperature of $H_2, T_{H_2} = 200\,K$

Temperature of $O_2, T_{O_2} = ?$

$$\frac{3RT_{O_2}}{M_{O_2}} = \frac{3RT_{H_2}}{M_{H_2}},$$

$$M_{O_2} = 32, M_{H_2} = 2$$

$$T_{O_2} = T_{H_2} \times \frac{M_{O_2}}{M_{H_2}}$$

$$= 200 \times \frac{32}{2} = 3200\,K$$

18. By Charle's law, $\frac{p_1}{T_1} = \frac{p_2}{T_2}$, $T_1 = 27 + 273$

$\Rightarrow$ $T_1 = 300\,K$

and $T_2 = 927 + 273 = 1200\,K$

$\therefore$ $p_2 = \frac{p_1 T_2}{T_1} = p \times \frac{1200}{300} = 4p$

$$p_2 = 4p$$

19. We know that, rms velocity, $\bar{c} = \sqrt{\frac{3RT}{M}}, \frac{\bar{c}_1}{\bar{c}_2} = \sqrt{\frac{T_1}{T_2}}$

$$c_1 = c \quad \text{and} \quad c_2 = \frac{1}{2}c$$

$$T_1 = 327 + 273 = 600\,K, \frac{c}{\frac{1}{2}c} = \sqrt{\frac{600}{T_2}}$$

or $T_2 = \frac{600}{4} = 150\,K = (150 - 273)°c = -123°c$

20. For monoatomic gas, $C_V = \frac{3}{2}R$

Mass = 1 mole

Heat = (Mass) (Specific heat C_V) (Temperature change)

$$= (1)\, C_v (1) = \frac{3R}{2}$$

22

Periodic Motion and Oscillations

Periodic Motion

A motion which repeats itself over and over again after a regular interval of time is called a periodic motion.

Examples of Periodic Motion

(i) The motion of any planet around the Sun in an elliptical orbit is periodic. The period of revolution of Mercury is 87.97 days.

(ii) The motion of the Moon around the Earth is periodic. Its time period is 27.3 days.

(iii) The motion of Halley's comet around the Sun is periodic. It appears on the Earth after every 76 yr.

(iv) The motion of the hands of a clock is periodic.

(v) The heart beats of a human being are periodic. The periodic times is about 0.8 s for a normal person.

Oscillatory Motion

If a body moves back and forth repeatedly about its mean position, its motion is said to be oscillatory or vibratory or harmonic motion.

Examples of Oscillatory Motion

(i) The swinging motion of the pendulum of a wall clock.

(ii) The oscillations of a mass suspended from a spring.

(iii) The motion of the piston of an automobile engine.

(iv) The vibrations of the string of a guitar.

(v) When a freely suspended bar magnet is displaced from its equilibrium position along North-South line and released, it executes oscillatory motion.

Note Every oscillatory motion is necessarily periodic but every periodic motion need not be oscillatory. Justify.

Time Period

It is the least interval of time after which the periodic motion of a body repeats itself.

Frequency

It is defined as the number of periodic motions executed by body per second.

It is denoted by ν. Clearly, $\nu = 1/T$. SI unit of ν is hertz (denoted by Hz), where 1 Hz = 1 oscillation per second = 1 cps = $1 s^{-1}$. Note that the frequency ν is not necessarily an integer.

Relationship between Time Period and Frequency

If T be the time period of a body, then its frequency

$$\nu = \frac{1}{T}$$

$$\Rightarrow \quad \nu T = 1$$

Angular Frequency

Angular frequency of a body executing periodic motion is equal to the product of frequency of the body with factor 2π. *i.e.,*

Angular frequency,

$$\omega = \nu \times 2\pi = 2\pi\nu = 2\pi / T$$

SI unit of ω is rad/s.

Angular Simple Periodic Motion

$$T = \frac{2\pi}{\omega}$$

$$\Rightarrow \quad \omega = \frac{2\pi}{T}$$

$$\Rightarrow \quad \nu = \frac{1}{T} = \frac{\omega}{2\pi}$$

Displacement

In general, the name displacement is given to a change in physical quantity under consideration with time in a periodic motion. Thus, displacements represent changes in physical quantities with time such as position, angle, pressure, electric and magnetic fields etc.

Examples

(i) **In a Loaded Spring** When a body is oscillating under the action of a spring, the displacement variable is its deviation from the mean position of the oscillation, with time.

(ii) **In a Simple Pendulum** The displacement variable is its angular deviation from the vertical during oscillations, with time.

(iii) **During the Propagation of Sound Wave in Air** The displacement variable is the local change in pressure, with time.

(iv) **During the Propagation of Electromagnetic Waves** The displacement variables are electric and magnetic fields which vary periodically, with time.

Displacement variable is measured as a function of time and it can have both positive and negative values. The displacement of an oscillating particle can be represented by x and y depending upon, whether the physical quantity changes along x-axis or y-axis.

Displacement can be represented by a mathematical function of time. In a simple periodic motion, the displacement can be given by

$$y = f(t) = a\sin\omega t \quad \Rightarrow \quad x = f(t) = a\cos\omega t$$

Where, a is called amplitude of oscillation or maximum displacement.

Periodic Function

These are those functions which are used to represent periodic motion.

A function $f(t)$ is said to be periodic, if

$$f(t) = f(t + T) = f(t + 2T)$$

Since, sine and cosine functions are the examples of periodic functions, therefore, a particle performing a periodic motion must return to its initial position after one period of the motion. If T is the period of this periodic motion, then for periodic motion

$$y = a\sin\omega t = a\sin\omega(t + T)$$

$$\Rightarrow \quad x = a\cos\omega t = a\cos\omega(t + T)$$

We know that the value of sine or cosine function repeats after a period of 2 π radian.

$$\therefore \quad \omega(t + T) = \omega t + 2\pi \Rightarrow \omega T = 2\pi$$

$$\Rightarrow \quad \omega = \frac{2\pi}{T} = 2\pi\nu \qquad \left[\because \frac{1}{T} = \nu\right]$$

Where, ω is called angular frequency.

The linear combination of sine and cosine functions is also a periodic function as discussed below.

Let a linear combination of sine and cosine functions be given by

$$x = f(t) = a\sin\omega t + b\cos\omega t$$

Taking, $a = R\cos\phi$ and $b = R\sin\phi$

Then, $x = R\cos\phi\sin\omega t + R\sin\phi\cos\omega t = R\sin(\omega t + \phi)$

It represents a periodic function of time period T and amplitude R, where

$$R = \sqrt{a^2 + b^2} \quad \text{and} \quad \tan\phi = \frac{b}{a}$$

We have $R^2 \quad (\cos^2\phi + \sin^2\phi) = a^2 + b^2$

$$\Rightarrow \quad R = \sqrt{a^2 + b^2}$$

Dividing them, we have, $\tan\phi = \dfrac{b}{a}$

Note The combination of any number of periodic functions will also be a periodic one, whose time period will be the minimum time period of the periodic functions used in the combinations.

Function

If x be any independent variable and y be a dependent variable, then y is called function of x and is represented by

$$y = f(x)$$

Variable

A physical quantity which accepts different values, called variable and further *it is divided into two parts*

(i) Independent Variable

A variable which accept any value under its limit.

(ii) Dependent Variable

A variable whose values depends upon the values of independent variable.

e.g., In $y = f(x)$

x = Independent variable

y = Dependent variable

Harmonic Function and Periodic Function

A function which can be represented by a single sine or cosine function is a harmonic function otherwise non-harmonic.

A periodic function can be expressed as the sum of sine and cosine functions of different time periods with suitable coefficients.

Simple Harmonic Motion (SHM)

It is a special type of periodic motion, in which a particle moves to and fro repeatedly about a mean (*i.e.*, equilibrium) position under a restoring force, which is always directed towards the mean (*i.e.*, equilibrium) position and whose magnitude at any instant is directly proportional to the displacement of the particle from the mean (*i.e.*, equilibrium) position at that instant.

Examples of Simple Harmonic Motion

(i) Oscillations of a loaded spring.

(ii) Vibrations of a tuning fork.

(iii) Vibrations of the balance wheel of a watch.

(iv) Oscillations of a freely suspended magnet in a uniform magnetic field.

Some Important Features of SHM

(i) The motion of the particle is periodic.

(ii) It is the oscillatory motion of simplest kind in which the particle oscillates back and forth about its mean position with constant amplitude and fixed frequency.

(iii) Restoring force acting on the particle is proportional to its displacement from the mean position.

(iv) The force acting on the particle always opposes the increase in its displacement.

(v) A simple harmonic motion can always be expressed in terms of a single harmonic function of sine or cosine.

Equation of Simple Harmonic Motion

Differential Equation of SHM In SHM, the restoring force acting on the particle is proportional to its displacement. Thus,

$$F = -kx$$

The negative sign shows that F and x are oppositely directed. Here, k is spring factor or force constant.

By Newton's second law,

$$F = m\frac{d^2x}{dt^2}$$

Where, m is the mass of the particle and $\frac{d^2x}{dt^2}$ is its acceleration.

$$\therefore \quad m\frac{d^2x}{dt^2} = -kx \Rightarrow \frac{d^2x}{dt^2} = -\frac{k}{m}x$$

Put $\frac{k}{m} = \omega^2$,

Then $\frac{d^2x}{dt^2} = -\omega^2 x$

$$\Rightarrow \frac{d^2x}{dt^2} + \omega^2 x = 0 \quad \text{...(i)}$$

This is the differential equation of SHM. Here, ω is the angular frequency.

The possible solution of Eq. (i) may be of the form,

$$x = A\cos(\omega t + \phi_0)$$

Then, $\frac{dx}{dt} = -\omega A\sin(\omega t + \phi_0)$

and $\frac{d^2x}{dt^2} = -\omega^2 A\cos(\omega t + \phi_0) = -\omega^2 x$

$$\Rightarrow \frac{d^2x}{dt^2} + \omega^2 x = 0$$

Which is same as Eq. (i), hence, the solution of the Eq. (i), is

$$x = A\cos(\omega t + \phi_0) \quad \text{...(ii)}$$

It gives displacement of the harmonic oscillator at any instant t.

Here, A is the amplitude of the oscillating particle.

$\phi = \omega t + \phi_0$, is the phase of the oscillating particle.

ϕ_0 is the initial phase (at $t = 0$) or epoch.

Displacement in SHM

The displacement of a particle executing SHM is, in general, expressed as $y = A\sin(\omega t + \phi_0)$,

where A is the amplitude of SHM, ω the angular frequency (Where, $\omega = \frac{2\pi}{T} = 2\pi\nu$) and ϕ the initial phase of SHM.

However, displacement may also be expressed as $x = A\cos(\omega t + \phi_0)$.

Time Period of SHM

The time taken by a particle to complete one oscillation is called time period. It is denoted by T.

Acceleration in SHM, $a = -\omega^2 x$, hence

$$|a| = \omega^2 |x|$$

$$\Rightarrow \quad \omega = \sqrt{\frac{|a|}{|x|}}$$

$\therefore$ Time period of SHM,

$$T = \frac{2\pi}{\omega} = 2\pi\sqrt{\frac{|x|}{|a|}}$$

$$= 2\pi\sqrt{\frac{\text{Displacement}}{\text{Acceleration}}}$$

Velocity in SHM

The velocity of a particle executing SHM at an instant is defined as the time rate of change of its displacement at that instant.

Velocity $v = \omega\sqrt{A^2 - x^2}$

At the mean position $(x = 0)$, during its motion $v = A\omega = v_{max}$ and at the extreme positions $(x = \pm A)$ $v = 0$.

Velocity amplitude $= v_{max} = A\omega$

Acceleration in SHM

The acceleration of a particle executing SHM at an instant is defined as the time rate of change of velocity at that instant.

Acceleration, $a = -\omega^2 x$

The acceleration is also a variable. At the mean position $(x = 0)$, acceleration $a = 0$ and at the extreme position $(x = \pm A)$, the acceleration is $a_{max} = -A\omega^2$.

$\therefore$ Acceleration amplitude $a_{max} = A\omega^2$.

Energy in SHM

If a particle of mass m is executing SHM, then at a displacement x from the mean position, the particle possesses potential and kinetic energy.

At any displacement x,

Potential energy, $U = \frac{1}{2}m\omega^2 x^2 = \frac{1}{2}kx^2$

Kinetic energy, $K = \frac{1}{2}m\omega^2(A^2 - x^2) = \frac{1}{2}k(A^2 - x^2)$

Total energy,

$$E = U + K = \frac{1}{2}m\omega^2 A^2 = 2\pi^2 m\nu^2 A^2$$

It there is no friction, the total mechanical energy, $E = K + U$, of the system always remains constant even though K and U change.

OTHER IMPORTANT TERMS RELATED WITH SHM

Amplitude The maximum displacement of the oscillating particle on either side of its mean position is called its amplitude. It is denoted by A. Thus, $x_{max} = \pm A$.

Oscillation or Cycle One complete back and forth motion of a particle starting and ending at the same point is called a cycle or oscillation or vibration.

Time Period The time taken by a particle to complete one oscillation is called its time period. Or, it is the smallest time interval after which the oscillatory motion repeats. It is denoted by T.

Frequency It is defined as the number of oscillations completed per unit time by a particle. It is denoted by ν (nu).

Frequency is equal to the reciprocal of time period. That is,

$$\nu = \frac{1}{T}$$

Clearly, the unit of frequency is $(\text{second})^{-1}$ or s^{-1}. It is also expressed as cycles per second (cps) or hertz (Hz).

SI unit of Frequency $= S^{-1}$ = cps = Hz.

Angular Frequency It is the quantity obtained by multiplying frequency ν by a factor of 2π. It is denoted by ω.

Thus, $\omega = 2\pi\nu = \frac{2\pi}{T}$

SI unit of angular frequency = rad s^{-1}.

Comparison between Simple Harmonic Motion and Uniform Circular Motion

S.No.	Simple Harmonic Motion (SHM)	Symbol	Uniform Circular Motion (UCM)
1.	Mean position	O	Centre of circle
2.	Amplitude	A	Radius of circle
3.	Angular frequency	ω	Angular velocity
4.	Phase	$(\omega t + \phi_0)$	Angle made by radius analogous to amplitude (A)

Energy in Different Position of Displacement in SHM

x	0	$\frac{a}{2}$	a	$-\frac{a}{2}$	$-a$	0
U	0	$\frac{E}{4}$	E	$\frac{E}{4}$	E	0
K	E	$\frac{3E}{4}$	0	$\frac{3E}{4}$	0	E

Phase

Phase of a vibrating particle at any instant is a physical quantity which completely expresses the position and direction of motion of the particle at that instant with respect to its mean position.

In oscillatory motion, the phase of a vibrating particle is the argument of sine or cosine function involved to represent the generalized equation of motion of the vibrating particle. If the displacement of a particle at the instant of time t is represented by the equation.

$$\underset{\text{Displacement}}{x(\pm)} = \underset{\text{Amplitude}}{A}\sin(\overbrace{\underset{\text{Angular Frequency}}{\omega t} + \underset{\text{Phase Constant}}{\phi_0}}^{\text{Phase}})$$

Then, the quantity $(\omega t + \phi_0)$ is called phase of oscillation at time t.

Simple Pendulum

A simple pendulum, in practice, consists of a heavy but small sized metallic bob suspended by a light, inextensible and flexible string. The motion of a simple pendulum is simple harmonic, whose time period and frequency are given by $T = 2\pi\sqrt{\frac{l}{g}}$ and $n = \frac{1}{2\pi}\sqrt{\frac{g}{l}}$, where l is the effective length of the string and g is acceleration due to gravity.

Note As, $T \propto \sqrt{l}$

So, $\frac{T_2}{T_1} = \sqrt{\frac{l_2}{l_1}}$

Also, $T \propto \frac{1}{\sqrt{g}}$

So, $\frac{T_2}{T_1} = \sqrt{\frac{g_1}{g_2}}$

Similarly, $\frac{\nu_2}{\nu_1} = \sqrt{\frac{g_1}{g_2}} = \sqrt{\frac{l_1}{l_2}}$ [as $\nu = \frac{1}{T}$]

Effective Length

The distance between point of suspension and centre of gravity (G) of a pendulum is called effective length and is denoted by l.

Point of Suspension

The point of contact of a pendulum is known as point of suspension.

Second's Pendulum

A pendulum whose time period is 2 s is called second's pendulum.

Using, $T = 2\pi\sqrt{\frac{l}{g}}$

$\Rightarrow$ $T^2 = 4\pi^2\left(\frac{l}{g}\right)$

$$\Rightarrow \qquad l = \frac{gT^2}{4\pi^2}$$

Putting $T = 2$ s, we get effective length

$$l = \frac{9.8 \times 4}{4 \times (3.14)^2} = 0.993 \text{ m} \simeq 1.0 \text{ m}$$

Note Maximum limit of time period of a simple pendulum on the Earth is 84.6 min (not infinity) when effective length of a pendulum become infinity.

Time Period of Spring Pendulum

Time period of spring pendulum is written as

$$T = 2\pi\sqrt{\frac{m}{k}}$$

and frequency, $\nu = \dfrac{1}{T} = \dfrac{1}{2\pi}\sqrt{\dfrac{k}{m}}$

General Features on Spring Pendulum

(i) Time period of spring pendulum depends upon suspended mass (m)

$$T \propto \sqrt{m}$$

(ii) Time period of spring pendulum is independent from acceleration due to gravity (g).

(iii) $T \propto \dfrac{1}{\sqrt{k}}$

(iv) If mass of spring be M and mass of suspended body be m, then the time period

$$T = 2\pi\sqrt{\frac{m + \frac{M}{3}}{k}}$$

(v) If length of spring becomes n times, then the force constant becomes $\dfrac{k}{n}$ and then

$$T' = 2\pi\sqrt{\frac{m}{\frac{k}{n}}} = \sqrt{n}T$$

i.e., time period will becomes $\sqrt{n}$ times.

(vi) If spring divided by n equal parts, then the force constant of each part will be nk and if a body of mass m is suspended in one part then the time period will be

$$T' = 2\pi\sqrt{\frac{m}{nk}} = \frac{T}{\sqrt{n}}$$

Series Combination of Springs

If two springs of spring constants k_1 and k_2 are joined in series (horizontally and vertically), then their equivalent spring constant k_s is given by

$$\frac{1}{k_s} = \frac{1}{k_1} + \frac{1}{k_2}$$

$$\Rightarrow \qquad k_s = \frac{k_1 k_2}{k_1 + k_2}$$

$$\therefore \qquad T = 2\pi\sqrt{\frac{m}{k_s}}$$

$$= 2\pi\sqrt{\frac{m(k_1 + k_2)}{k_1 k_2}}$$

k_1
m
k_2

(a)

Parallel Combination of Springs

If the two springs of spring constants k_1 and k_2 are jointed in parallel as shown, then their equivalent spring constant $k_p = k_1 + k_2$, hence

$$T = 2\pi\sqrt{\frac{m}{k_p}}$$

$$= 2\pi\sqrt{\frac{m}{(k_1 + k_2)}}$$

k_1 k_2
m

(b)

Note The force constant of a spring k is inversely proportional to the length of the spring *i.e.*,

$$k \propto \frac{1}{l}$$

The Phase Relationship between the Displacement (x), Velocity (v) and Acceleration (a) in SHM

1. (i) Acceleration (a) leads displacement (x) by $\dfrac{\pi}{2}$.

   (ii) Acceleration (a) lags behind the velocity (v) by $\dfrac{\pi}{2}$.

   (iii) Acceleration (a) differs in phase with displacement (x) by π.

2. (i) When $x = \dfrac{A}{2}$, $v = 0.86\, v_{\text{max}}$

   (ii) When $x = \dfrac{A}{2}$, in this condition kinetic energy is 75% and potential energy is 25% of total energy of SHM.

Some Other Important Points Conserving SHM

SHM is also represented by

$$x = A\sin\omega t + B\cos\omega t$$
$$= A_R \sin(\omega t + \phi_0)$$

Where, $A_R = \sqrt{A^2 + B^2}$ and $\tan\phi_0 = \dfrac{B}{A}$

Practice Questions

Level I

1. The correct relation between the acceleration and the displacement in Simple Harmonic Motion (SHM) is
(a) Acceleration ∝ Displacement
(b) Acceleration ∝ $\dfrac{1}{\text{Displacement}}$
(c) Acceleration ∝ – Displacement
(d) Acceleration ∝ $-\dfrac{1}{\text{Displacement}}$

2. The magnitude of acceleration for a particle executing simple harmonic motion at maximum displacement position is
(a) minimum (b) maximum
(c) zero (d) None of these

3. The velocity at mean position of a particle executing simple harmonic motion will be
(a) maximum (b) minimum
(c) zero (d) not change

4. The time period of a simple pendulum will become doubled when its effective length be
(a) double (b) four times
(c) halves (d) one fourth

5. If the length of a simple pendulum is multiplied by 4, then its oscillating frequency will be
(a) doubled (b) four times
(c) one fourth (d) halves

6. The potential energy of a particle executing simple harmonic motion at equilibrium condition from distance x will be
(a) $\frac{1}{2}m\omega^2x^2$ (b) $\frac{1}{2}m\omega^2(a^2-x^2)$
(c) $\frac{1}{2}m\omega^2a^2$ (d) zero

7. The kinetic energy of a particle in simple harmonic motion represented by $k = k_0\cos^2\omega t$. The maximum values of potential energy is
(a) k (b) $\frac{k_0}{2}$ (c) k_0 (d) zero

8. The time period of a simple pendulum is
(a) infinity at poles
(b) maximum at longitude than poles
(c) maximum at poles than longitude
(d) same at both places

9. The phase difference between the velocity and the acceleration of a body in simple harmonic motion is
(a) $\frac{\pi}{2}$ (b) π (c) 2π (d) 0

10. Equation of motion of a particle is $\frac{d^2x}{dt^2}+\omega^2x=0$, where ω^2 is a constant. The value of time period will be
(a) $2\pi\omega^2$ (b) $\frac{2\pi}{\omega}$ (c) $2\pi\omega$ (d) $\frac{2\pi}{\omega^2}$

11. A particle executes SHM. Then, the graph of velocity as a function of displacement is
(a) a straight line (b) a circle
(c) an ellipse (d) a hyperbola

12. If a graph is drawn for acceleration *versus* displacement of SHM. It is a
(a) straight line (b) circle
(c) ellipse (d) hyperbola

13. A particle performing SHM starts from mean position. The phase of that particle is $\frac{\pi}{2}$ when it has
(a) maximum displacement (b) maximum velocity
(c) maximum energy (d) maximum kinetic energy

14. A spring-mass system oscillates with a frequency ν. If it takes in an elevator slowly accelerating upwards, the frequency will
(a) increase (b) decrease
(c) remain same (d) become zero

15. The tension in the string of a simple pendulum is
(a) constant
(b) maximum in the extreme position
(c) zero in the mean position
(d) None of the above

16. The kinetic energy of a particle executing SHM is 16 J. When it is in its mean position. If the amplitude of oscillation is 25 cm and the mass of the particles is 5.12 kg, the time period of its oscillation in second is
(a) $\pi/5$ (b) 2π (c) 5π (d) 20π

17. Two simple pendulums of length 5 m and 10 m respectively are given small linear displacement in one direction at the same time. They will be again in the same phase when the pendulum of shorter length has completed oscillations
(a) 1 (b) 2 (c) 3 (d) 4

18. A hollow sphere is filled with water through a small hole in it. It is then hung by a long thread and made to oscillate. As the water slowly flows out of the hole at the bottom, the period of oscillation of the sphere
(a) continuously decreases
(b) continuously increases
(c) first decreases and then increases
(d) first increases and then decreases

19. A spring of force constant k is cut into two parts such that one piece is double the length of the other. Then, the long piece will have a force constant of
(a) $\left(\frac{2}{3}\right)k$ (b) $\left(\frac{3}{2}\right)k$ (c) $3k$ (d) $6k$

20. Two simple harmonic motions are represented by $y_1 = 4\sin\left(4\pi t+\frac{\pi}{2}\right)$ and $y_2 = 3\cos(4\pi t)$. The resultant amplitude is
(a) 7 (b) 1 (c) 5 (d) $(2+\sqrt{3})$

Level II

1. A simple harmonic motion is represented by equation $x = 10\sin(20t + 0.5)$, here displacement and time are in metre and second respectively, then its amplitude will be
(a) 20 m (b) 100 m (c) 10 m (d) 10π

2. The equation of motion of a particle executing SHM is given by $x = A\cos(\omega t + \phi)$, where x = Displacement and $\omega = \frac{2\pi}{T}$. At initial position ($t = 0, x = 1$) its initial velocity be π cm/s, then its amplitude will be (angular frequency of particle in rad/s)
(a) $\sqrt{2}$ cm (b) 1.5 cm
(c) 2 cm (d) 1 cm

3. Ths initial phase of a particle in question number 2 will be
(a) 2π or $\frac{7\pi}{4}$ (b) $\frac{3\pi}{4}$ or $\frac{7\pi}{4}$
(c) $\frac{3\pi}{4}$ or 2π (d) None of these

4. Which of the following given relation between the acceleration a and the displacement y shows SHM
(a) $a = 0.5y$ (b) $a = -20y$
(c) $a = -3y^2$ (d) $a = 400y^2$

5. If the effective length of a simple pendulum become halves, then the time period will be
(a) $\frac{1}{\sqrt{2}}$ times (b) $\frac{1}{4}$ times
(c) $\frac{1}{3}$ times (d) doubled

6. If the effective length of a simple pendulum is increased by 50% ,then time period will be
(a) 2 times (b) $\sqrt{1.5}$ times
(c) 4 times (d) None of these

7. If the length of a spring became n times, then its force constant will
(a) nk (b) $\frac{n}{k}$ (c) $\frac{k}{n}$ (d) $\frac{k^2}{n}$

8. What is the length of a simple pendulum which ticks seconds?
(a) 0.9 m (b) 1.5 m (c) 0.99 m (d) 0.92 m

9. The kinetic energy and potential energy of a simple pendulum are T and V, respectively. If the angular velocity is ω and amplitude is r, then the ratio of T and V is
(a) $\frac{r + x}{x^2}$ (b) $\frac{r^2 - x^2}{x^2}$
(c) $\frac{(r + x)(r - x)}{x}$ (d) $\frac{r - x}{x}$

10. A block rests on a horizontal table which is executing SHM in the horizontal plane with an amplitude A. When the block is just start to slip, the frequency of oscillation will be (coefficient of friction $= \mu$)
(a) $\frac{1}{2\pi}\sqrt{\frac{\mu}{g}}$ (b) $\frac{1}{2\pi}\sqrt{\frac{\mu g}{A}}$
(c) $\frac{1}{2\pi}\sqrt{\frac{\mu A}{g}}$ (d) None of these

11. The displacement of SHM is given by $y = 5\cos(10t + 0.6)$.
What is the initial phase of the SHM?
(a) 5 rad (b) 10 rad
(c) 0.6 rad (d) None of these

12. A system is subjected to two SHMs given by $y_1 = 6\cos\omega t$ and $y_2 = 8\cos\omega t$.
The resultant amplitude of SHM is given by
(a) 2 (b) 10
(c) 14 (d) 20

13. All other factors of SHM remaining unchanged, the displacement is halved. What happens to the corresponding acceleration?
(a) One-fourth (b) Halved
(c) Doubled (d) Four times

14. If the length of a pendulum is quadrupled, its time period is
(a) quadrupled (b) halved
(c) doubled (d) unchanged

15. A body executing SHM has amplitude of 4 cm. What is the distance at which the body has equal value of both KE and PE?
(a) $2\sqrt{2}$ cm (b) $\frac{1}{\sqrt{2}}$ cm
(c) $\sqrt{2}$ cm (d) $\frac{\sqrt{2}}{6}$ cm

16. What is the nature of graph between displacement (y) and acceleration (a) of SHM?
(a) Straight line (b) Parabola
(c) Hyperbola (d) Ellipse

17. Two springs of force constants k_1 and k_2 are connected in series. The spring constant of the combination is
(a) $k_1 + k_2$ (b) $\frac{k_1 + k_2}{2}$ (c) $\frac{k_1 + k_2}{k_1 k_2}$ (d) $\frac{k_1 k_2}{k_1 + k_2}$

18. If two springs force constants k_1 and k_2 are connected is parallel, then their equivalent spring constant $k_p = k_1 + k_2$. The time period of the combination is
(a) $2\pi\sqrt{\frac{m}{(k_1 + k_2)}}$ (b) $2\pi\sqrt{\frac{k_1 + k_2}{m}}$
(c) $2\pi\sqrt{\frac{k_p}{m}}$ (d) None of these

19. A body executing SHM with maximum acceleration 24 m/s ^{2} and maximum velocity is 16 m/s. The amplitude of SHM is
(a) $\frac{32}{3}$ m (b) $\frac{64}{9}$ m (c) $\frac{1024}{9}$ m (d) $\frac{3}{32}$ m

20. The value of acceleration due to gravity of a planet $\left(\frac{1}{9}\right)$th times of values on the Earth. If time period of a simple pendulum on the Earth be 1.0 s, then what will be the time period on that planet?
(a) 1 s (b) 3 s (c) 5 s (d) 6 s

Answers

Level I

1. (c)	**2.** (b)	**3.** (b)	**4.** (b)	**5.** (d)	**6.** (a)	**7.** (c)	**8.** (b)	**9.** (a)	**10.** (b)
11. (c)	**12.** (a)	**13.** (a)	**14.** (c)	**15.** (d)	**16.** (a)	**17.** (b)	**18.** (d)	**19.** (b)	**20.** (a)

Level II

1. (c)	**2.** (a)	**3.** (b)	**4.** (b)	**5.** (a)	**6.** (b)	**7.** (c)	**8.** (c)	**9.** (b)	**10.** (b)
11. (c)	**12.** (c)	**13.** (b)	**14.** (c)	**15.** (a)	**16.** (a)	**17.** (d)	**18.** (a)	**19.** (a)	**20.** (b)

Hints and Solutions

Level II

Sol. (Q.Nos. 2 and 3) $x = A\cos(\omega t + \phi)$

At $t = 0, x = 1$ cm

$\therefore \quad 1 = A\cos(\omega \times 0 + \phi)$

$\Rightarrow \quad A\cos\phi = 1 \quad$ ...(i)

Now velocity, $v = \frac{dx}{dt} = \frac{d}{dt}[A\cos(\omega t + \phi)]$

$= -A\omega\sin(\omega t + \phi)$

If $t = 0, v = \pi$ cm/s

$\pi = -A(\pi)\sin(\omega \times 0 + \phi)$

$A\sin\phi = 1 \quad$ ...(ii)

Adding Eqs. (i) and (ii), we have

$(A\sin\phi)^2 + (A\cos\phi)^2 = (-1)^2 + (1)^2$

$\Rightarrow \quad A = \sqrt{2}$ cm

Now, Eqs. (ii) ÷ (i), we have

$$\frac{A\sin\phi}{A\cos\phi} = \frac{-1}{1} = -1 \Rightarrow \tan\phi = -1$$

$\therefore \quad \phi = \frac{3\pi}{4}$ or $\frac{7\pi}{4}$

4. We know that,

$a \propto (-y)$, so $a = -20y$

5. $\because \quad T = 2\pi\sqrt{\frac{l}{g}}$

Here, $l_1 = \frac{1}{2}$, then $T_1 = 2\pi\sqrt{\frac{l}{2g}} = \frac{T}{\sqrt{2}} = \frac{1}{\sqrt{2}} \times T$

6. We know that, $\frac{T_2}{T_1} = \sqrt{\frac{l_2}{l_1}} = \sqrt{\frac{1.5 l_1}{l_1}} \Rightarrow T_2 = \sqrt{1.5}\, T_1$

8. As simple pendulum ticks seconds, so it is seconds pendulum when $T = 2$s.

$\therefore \quad T = 2\pi\sqrt{\frac{l}{g}}$

$$\Rightarrow \quad l = \frac{gT^2}{4\pi^2} = \frac{9.8 \times 4}{4 \times (3.14)^2} = 0.99 \text{ m}$$

9. $T = \frac{1}{2}mv^2 = \frac{1}{2}m\omega^2(r^2 - x^2)$, $V = \frac{1}{2}m\omega^2 x^2$

So, $\quad \frac{T}{V} = \frac{r^2 - x^2}{x^2}$

Restoring force on block $= m\omega^2 A = \mu mg$

Acceleration in block $= \mu g$

$\therefore$ Frequency of oscillation

$$\nu = \frac{1}{2\pi}\sqrt{\frac{\text{Acceleration}}{\text{Displacement}}} = \frac{1}{2\pi}\sqrt{\frac{\mu g}{A}}$$

12. The phase difference between the SHM is $\phi = 0$

Therefore, resultant amplitude is given by

$$A = \sqrt{A_1^2 + A_2^2 + 2A_1A_2\cos\phi}$$

$$= \sqrt{A_1^2 + A_2^2 + 2A_1A_2} = A_1 + A_2 = 6 + 8 = 14$$

15. Here, KE = PE, $\frac{1}{2}m\omega^2(A^2 - y^2) = \frac{1}{2}m\omega^2 y^2$

$$y = \frac{A}{\sqrt{2}} \Rightarrow y = 2\sqrt{2} \text{ cm}$$

16. The relation between y and a is $a = -\omega^2 y$. It is the equation of a straight line.

17. $\frac{1}{k_s} = \frac{1}{k_1} + \frac{1}{k_2} \Rightarrow k_s = \frac{k_1k_2}{k_1 + k_2}$

18. $k_p = k_1 + k_2$

$\therefore T = 2\pi\sqrt{\frac{m}{k_p}} = 2\pi\sqrt{\frac{m}{(k_1 + k_2)}}$

19. $a_{max} = r\omega^2$ and $v_{max} = r\omega$

$\therefore \quad \frac{v_{max}^2}{a_{max}} = \frac{r^2\omega^2}{r\omega^2} = r \Rightarrow$ amp $(r) = \frac{16 \times 16}{24} = \frac{32}{3}$ m

20. Time period of the surface of the Earth,

$$T_1 = 2\pi\sqrt{\frac{l}{g_1}}$$

Time period in the planet, $T_2 = 2\pi\sqrt{\frac{l}{g_2}}$

$\therefore \quad \frac{T_2}{T_1} = \sqrt{\frac{g_1}{g_2}}$

$\because \quad g_2 = \frac{g_1}{9} \Rightarrow \frac{g_1}{g_2} = 9$

$\therefore \quad \frac{T_2}{T_1} = \sqrt{9} = 3$

$\therefore \quad T_2 = 3T_1 = 3 \times 1 = 3$ s

23

Wave Motion

Wave Motion

It is a periodic disturbance through which energy is transferred from one place to another without the transfer of material medium.

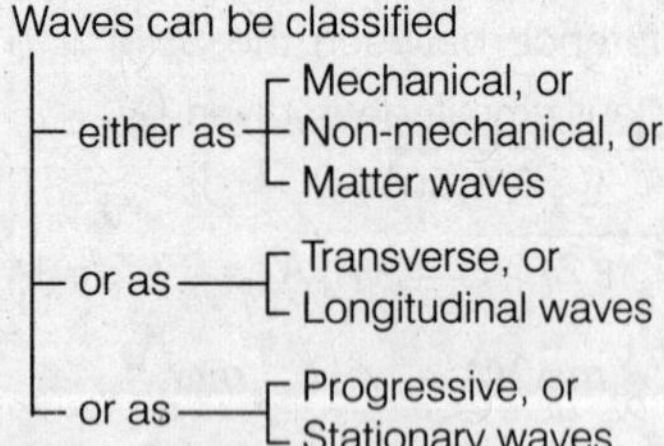

Mechanical Waves

These waves require material medium for propagation, like water, sound, seismic waves etc.

Non-mechanical Waves

These waves do not require any material medium for propagation like electromagnetic waves *e.g.*, heat waves, light waves, x-rays etc.

Matter Waves

These waves the waves in which matter *i.e.*, electrons, protons, neutrons, atoms or molecules move. Electron waves are used in electron microscopes.

Transverse Waves

These are those in which oscillation of wave particles take place in a direction perpendicular to the direction of motion (called propagation) of the wave.

Longitudinal Waves

These are those in which oscillations of wave particles take place in the direction of wave propagation *e.g.*, sound waves.

Some Important Terms Connected with Wave Motion

Amplitude

The amplitude of a wave is the magnitude of maximum displacement of the particles from their equilibrium position, as the wave passes through them.

It is represented by r. As r is a magnitude only, it is a positive quantity, even if the displacement is negative.

Wavelength

Wavelength of a wave is the length of one wave. It is equal to the distance travelled by the wave during the time, anyone particle of the medium completes one vibration about its mean position.

When, particle 1 completes one vibration about its mean position, the disturbance goes from particle 1 to particle 5. Hence, the distance between particles 1 and 5 is one wavelength (λ). As particles 1 and 5 are vibrating in the same phase, we may also define wavelength as the distance between two nearest particles of the medium, vibrating in the same phase.

As stated already, in transverse wave motion, λ = distance between the centres of two consecutive crests or distance between the centres of two consecutive troughs. Also, wavelength can be taken as the distance in which one crest and one trough are contained.

Similarly, in a longitudinal wave motion, λ = distance between the centres of two consecutive compressions or distance between the centres of two consecutive rarefactions. Also, wavelength can be taken as the distance in which one compression and one rarefaction are contained.

Angular Wave Number

Angular wave number of a wave is also called propagation constant of the wave.

It is 2π times the number of waves that can be accommodated per unit length.

The propagation constant or angular wave number of a wave is represented by k. Thus,

$$k = \frac{2\pi}{\lambda}$$

SI unit of k is radian m^{-1} or simply m^{-1}.

Frequency

We know that frequency of vibration of a particle is defined as the number of vibrations completed by particle in one second.

As one vibration is equivalent to one wavelength, therefore, we may define.

Frequency of a wave as the number of complete wavelengths traversed by the wave in one second.

It is represented by v and is measured in hertz.

Angular frequency of the wave is 2π times the frequency of the wave.

It is represented by ω and is measured in rad s^{-1}. Thus, $\omega = 2\pi\nu$

Time Period

We know that time period of vibration of a particle is defined as the time taken by the particle to complete one vibration about its mean position. As one vibration is equivalent to one wavelength, therefore,

Time period of a wave is equal to time taken by the wave to travel a distance equal to one wavelength.

It is represented by T.

Relations between ν and T

By definition, Time for completing ν vibrations = 1 s

Time for completing one vibration $= \frac{1}{\nu}$ s

i.e., $T = \frac{1}{\nu} \Rightarrow \nu = \frac{1}{T} \Rightarrow \nu T = 1$

Phase

Phase means stage of motion.

One period (T), or one wavelength (λ) corresponds to a phase difference of 2π. Two waves are said to be 'in phase' if their maximum and minimum occur at the same time. If the maximum of one wave occurs, when the minimum of the other wave occurs, they are said to be 'out of phase'.

Start of a Cycle (Zero phase): It is the time when the periodically varying quantity passes through a zero value from the negative to the positive side.

Path difference The distance between any two particles of the wave measured in the direction of propagation of wave is called path difference between them.

Phase and Phase Difference

Phase is the argument of the sine or cosine function representing the wave. Thus phase,

$$\phi = 2\pi\left(\frac{t}{T} - \frac{x}{\lambda}\right)$$

The relation between phase difference ($\Delta\phi$) and time interval Δt is

$$\Delta\phi = \frac{2\pi}{T}\Delta t$$

Thus in time period T, the phase of a particle changes by 2π.

The relation between phase difference ($\Delta\phi$) and path difference (Δx) is

$$\Delta\phi = -\frac{2\pi}{\lambda}\Delta x$$

The negative sign indicates that farther the particle is located from the origin in the positive X-direction, the more it lags behind in phase. Clearly, the phase difference between two particles located at separation λ is 2π.

Characteristics of Wave Motion

From what we have studied above, we can sum up the characteristics of wave motion as follows

- Wave motion is a sort of disturbance which travels through a medium.
- A material medium is essential for the propagation of mechanical waves. The medium must possess three properties, *viz.* elasticity, inertia and minimum friction amongst the particles of the medium.
- When a wave motion passes through a medium, particles of the medium only vibrate simple harmonically about their mean position. They do not leave their position and move with the disturbance.
- There is a continuous phase difference amongst successive particles of the medium *i.e.,* particle 2 starts vibrating slightly later than particle 1 and so on.
- The velocity of the particles during their vibration is different at different positions.

For example, all the particles cross their mean position with maximum velocity and at extreme positions, their velocity is zero.

- The velocity of wave motion through a particular medium is constant. It depends only on the nature of the medium. The velocity of wave motion does not depend upon its frequency or wavelength or intensity.
- Energy is propagated alongwith the wave motion without any net transport of the medium.

Speed of the Travelling Wave

$$v = \nu\lambda = \frac{\lambda}{T}$$

Velocity = Frequency × Time period

$$v = \frac{\omega}{k} = \frac{2\pi\nu}{\frac{2\pi}{\lambda}} = \nu\lambda$$

Where, $k = \frac{2\pi}{\lambda}$ wave number

Progression of Waves

Wave Equation A plane progressive harmonic wave travelling along positive X-direction may be represented as

(i) $y = A\sin(\omega t - kx)$, where $k = \frac{2\pi}{\lambda}$

(ii) $y = A\sin 2\pi\left(\frac{t}{T} - \frac{x}{\lambda}\right)$

(iii) $y = A\sin\frac{2\pi}{T}(vt - x)$

Where, v is the wave-velocity, λ the wavelength, A the amplitude of the oscillating particles of the medium and y is the displacement of the particle located at position x at any instant t.

If the wave is travelling along negative X-direction, the minus sign is replaced by plus sign in the above equations. Thus

(i) $y = A\sin(\omega t + kx)$, where $k = \dfrac{2\pi}{\lambda}$

(ii) $y = A\sin 2\pi\left(\dfrac{t}{T} + \dfrac{x}{\lambda}\right)$

(iii) $y = A\sin\dfrac{2\pi}{\lambda}(vt + x)$

In $y = A\sin(\omega t \pm kx)$ A is known as argument and $(\omega t \pm kx)$ is known as

The coefficient of t, ω is known as angular frequency.

$$\omega = 2\pi\nu = \frac{2\pi}{T}$$

The coefficient of x, k is known as wave number that is

$$k = \frac{2\pi}{\lambda}$$

Velocity of a Wave $v = \dfrac{dy}{dt} = \omega A\cos(\omega t - kx)$

$$= \omega A\sqrt{1 - \sin^2(\omega t - kx)}$$

$$= \omega\sqrt{A^2 - y^2}$$

(a) $v_{max} = \omega A$, when $y = 0$

(b) $v_{min} = 0$, when $y = A$

Intensity of a Wave

It is the power transferred per unit area to the surface perpendicular to the propagation direction.

$$I = 2\pi a^2 \nu^2 \rho v$$

Where, a is the amplitude of the vibration's and ν is the frequency of vibration and v is the velocity of wave.

Practice Questions

Level I

1. Distance between two consecutive crests is

(a) λ (b) $\dfrac{\lambda}{2}$ (c) $\dfrac{\lambda}{4}$ (d) 2λ

2. Distance between a compression and adjoining rarefaction in a pressure wave is

(a) λ (b) $\dfrac{\lambda}{2}$ (c) $\dfrac{\lambda}{4}$ (d) $\dfrac{\lambda}{3}$

3. The propagation constant of a wave is also called its

(a) wave number (b) wavelength
(c) frequency (d) angular wave number

4. Which of the following is carried by the waves from one place to another?

(a) Mass (b) Velocity
(c) Wavelength (d) Energy

5. A wave of frequency 1000 Hz travels between X and Y, a distance of 600 m in 2 s. How many wavelengths are there in distance XY?

(a) 3.3 (b) 300 (c) 180 (d) 2000

6. A source produces 50 crests and 50 troughs in 0.5 s. What is the frequency of the wave?

(a) 100 Hz (b) 150 Hz (c) 50 Hz (d) 125 Hz

7. One hertz is equivalent to

(a) one cycle per second (b) one second
(c) one meter per second (d) one second per meter

8. In a long spring which of the following type of waves can be generated.

(a) Longitudinal only (b) Transverse only
(c) Both (a) and (b) (d) Electromagnetic only

9. The frequency of a wave travelling at a speed of 500 ms^{-1} is 25Hz. Its time period is

(a) 20 s (b) 0.05 s (c) 25 s (d) 0.04 s

10. If the amplitude of sound is doubled and the frequency reduced to one fourth, the intensity of sound at the same point will be

(a) increasing by a factor of 2
(b) decreasing by a factor of 2
(c) decreasing by a factor of 4
(d) unchanged

11. Two waves having the intensities in the ratio of 9 : 1 produce interference. The ratio of maximum to the minimum intensity is equal to

(a) 2 : 1 (b) 4 : 1 (c) 9 : 1 (d) 10 : 8

12. A 440 Hz sound wave travels with a speed of 340 m/s. What is the wavelength of the wave?

(a) 15×10^5 m (b) 0.77 m
(c) 1.3 m (d) 1.1 m

13. Of the following properties of a wave, the one that is independent of the other is its

(a) amplitude (b) velocity
(d) wavelength (d) frequency

14. The relation between frequency n, wavelength λ and velocity of propagation v of the wave is

(a) $n = v\lambda$ (b) $n = \dfrac{\lambda}{v}$ (c) $n = \dfrac{1}{v}$ (d) $n = \dfrac{v}{\lambda}$

15. The diagram below shows the propagation of a wave. Which points are in phase?

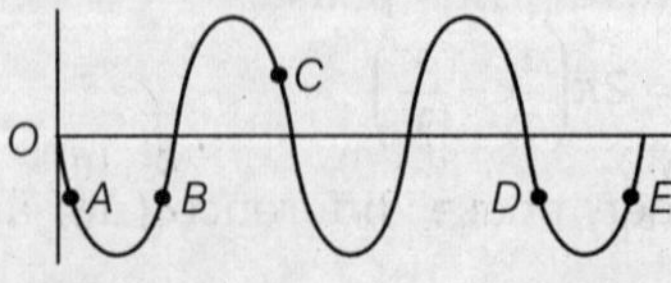

(a) A, B (b) B, C
(c) B, D (d) E, B

Level II

1. Which of the following is transmitted by a wave?
(a) Amplitude (b) Velocity
(c) Energy (d) Momentum

2. Which one of the following does not represent a travelling wave?
(a) $y = f(x - vt)$ (b) $y = y_m \sin k(x + vt)$
(c) $y = y_m \log(x - vt)$ (d) $y = f(x^2 - vt^2)$

3. The displacement represented by $y(x, t) = a\cos(kx + \omega t)$ represents
(a) transverse wave propagating in $+x$ direction
(b) transverse wave propagating in $-x$ direction
(c) longitudinal wave propagating in $+x$ direction
(d) longitudinal wave propagating in $-x$ direction

4. The equation $y = a \sin \frac{2\pi}{\lambda}(vt - x)$ is expression for
(a) stationary wave of single frequency along x-axis
(b) a simple harmonic motion
(c) a progressive wave of single frequency along x-axis
(d) the resultant of two SHM's of slightly different frequencies

5. It is possible to distinguish between transverse and longitudinal waves by studying the property of
(a) interference (b) diffraction
(c) reflection (d) polarization

6. A sine wave travelling to right is represented by the equation $y = y_m \sin(kx - \omega t)$. The velocity of wave is given by
(a) $\frac{k}{\omega}$ (b) ωt
(c) $\frac{\omega}{k}$ (d) kt

7. Two sound waves having a phase difference of 60° have path difference of
(a) 2λ (b) $\frac{\lambda}{2}$
(c) $\frac{\lambda}{6}$ (d) $\frac{\lambda}{3}$

8. If $x = a\sin\left(\omega t + \frac{\pi}{6}\right)$ and $x' = a\cos\omega t$, then what is the phase difference between the two waves?
(a) $\frac{\pi}{3}$ (b) $\frac{\pi}{6}$ (c) $\frac{\pi}{2}$ (d) π

9. The equation of a sound wave is $y = 0.0015 \sin(62.4x + 316t)$. Find the wavelength of this wave
(a) 0.2 unit
(b) 0.1 unit
(c) 0.3 unit
(d) Cannot be calculated

10. The equation of a wave travelling in a string can be written as $y = 3\cos\pi(100t - x)$. Its wavelength is
(a) 100 cm (b) 2 cm
(c) 5 cm (d) None of these

11. The equation of a transverse wave is given by $y = 10\sin\pi(0.01x - 2t)$ Where, y and x are in cm and t is in second. Its frequency is
(a) $10\ \text{s}^{-1}$ (b) $2\ \text{s}^{-1}$
(c) $1\ \text{s}^{-1}$ (d) $0.01\ \text{s}^{-1}$

12. Equation of a wave motion (with t in seconds and x and y are in metre) is given by $y = 7\sin\left(7\pi t - 0.4\pi x + \frac{\pi}{3}\right)$

The velocity of waves is given by
(a) $17.5\ \text{ms}^{-1}$ (b) $49\pi\ \text{ms}^{-1}$
(c) $\frac{49}{\pi}\ \text{ms}^{-1}$ (d) $0.28\pi\ \text{ms}^{-1}$

13. The frequency of a sinusoidal wave $y = 0.40\cos[2000t + 0.080]$ would be
(a) 100π Hz (b) 2000 Hz (c) 20 Hz (d) $\frac{1000}{\pi}$ Hz

14. Equation of progressive wave is given by $y = 4\sin\left[\pi\left(\frac{t}{5} - \frac{x}{9}\right) + \frac{\pi}{6}\right]$

Then, which of the following is correct?
(a) $v = 5$ cm (b) $\lambda = 18$ m
(c) $a = 0.04$ cm (d) $f = 50$ Hz

15. The displacement y of a particle in a medium can expressed as

$$y = 10^{-6}\sin\left(100t + 20x + \frac{\pi}{4}\right)\ \text{m}.$$

Where, t is in second and x in metre. The speed of wave is
(a) 2000 m/s (b) 5 m/s
(c) 20 m/s (d) 5π m/s

Answers

Level I

1. (a)	**2.** (b)	**3.** (d)	**4.** (d)	**5.** (d)	**6.** (a)	**7.** (a)	**8.** (c)	**9.** (d)	**10.** (c)
11. (b)	**12.** (b)	**13.** (a)	**14.** (d)	**15.** (d)					

Level II

1. (a)	**2.** (c)	**3.** (b)	**4.** (c)	**5.** (d)	**6.** (c)	**7.** (c)	**8.** (a)	**9.** (b)	**10.** (b)
11. (c)	**12.** (a)	**13.** (d)	**14.** (b)	**15.** (b)					

Hints and Solutions

Level I

10. Intensity $\propto$ (Amplitude)^2
and also Intensity $\propto$ (Frequency)^2
Therefore, intensity becomes $\frac{2^2}{4^2} = \frac{1}{4}$ th

11. As intensity of wave $\propto$ (amplitude)^2

$$\frac{I_1}{I_2} = \frac{9}{1} = \frac{a_1^2}{a_2^2}$$

$$\Rightarrow \quad \frac{a_1}{a_2} = \frac{3}{1}$$

$$\frac{I_{max}}{I_{min}} = \frac{(a_1 + a_2)^2}{(a_1 - a_2)} = \frac{16}{4}$$

$\Rightarrow$ Ratio is 4 : 1.

Level II

7. Phase difference $= \frac{2\pi}{\lambda} \times$ Path difference

$\Rightarrow$ Path difference $= \frac{\lambda}{2\pi} \times$ Phase difference

$$= \frac{\lambda}{2\pi} \times \frac{\pi}{3} = \frac{\lambda}{6}$$

8. $x = a\sin\left(\omega t + \frac{\pi}{6}\right)$

and $x' = a\cos\omega t = a\sin\left(\omega t + \frac{\pi}{2}\right)$

$\therefore$ Phase difference $= \left(\frac{\pi}{2}\right) - \left(\frac{\pi}{6}\right) = \frac{\pi}{3}$

9. We know that, $y = a\sin 2\pi\left[\frac{x}{\lambda} + \frac{t}{T}\right]$

Comparing with given equation, we get

$$\frac{2\pi}{\lambda} = 62.4$$

$$\Rightarrow \quad \lambda = \frac{2\pi}{62.4} = 0.1 \text{ unit}$$

10. Given equation is
$y = 3\cos\pi(100t - x) = 3\cos(100\pi t - \pi x)$
Standard equation is
$y = a\cos(\omega t \pm kx)$
Where, $k = 2\frac{\pi}{\lambda}$
Comparing, we have $k = \pi$

$$\therefore \quad \lambda = \frac{2\pi}{k} = \frac{2\pi}{\pi} = 2 \text{ cm}$$

11. The given equation is,

$$y = 10\sin\pi(0.01x - 2t) = 10\sin 2\pi\left(\frac{0.01x}{2} - t\right)$$

We know that, $y = a\sin 2\pi\left(\frac{t}{T} - \frac{x}{\lambda}\right)$

$$\therefore \quad T = 1 \Rightarrow n = \frac{1}{T} = 1\text{ s}^{-1}$$

12. We know that,

$$y = a\sin\left[\frac{2\pi}{\lambda}(vt - x) + \phi_0\right]$$

Given that, $y = 7\sin\left[7\pi t - 0.4\pi x + \frac{\pi}{3}\right]$

Comparing the two equations, we have

$$\frac{2\pi}{\lambda}v = 7\pi \text{ and } \frac{2\pi}{\lambda} = 0.4\pi \Rightarrow \lambda = 5$$

$$\therefore \quad v = \frac{7\lambda}{2} = \frac{35}{2} = 17.5 \text{ m/s}$$

13. $y = 0.40\cos[2000t + 0.080]$
We know that, $y = a\cos(2\pi\nu t + \phi)$
Comparing these equations, we have

$$2\pi\nu = 2000$$

$$\nu = \frac{2000}{2\pi}$$

$$\nu = \frac{1000}{\pi} \text{ Hz}$$

14. The standard equation of a progressive wave is

$$y = a\sin\left[2\pi\left(\frac{t}{T} - \frac{x}{\lambda}\right) + \phi\right]$$

The given equation can be written as

$$y = 4\sin\left[2\pi\left(\frac{t}{10} - \frac{x}{18}\right) + \frac{\pi}{6}\right]$$

$$\therefore \quad a = 4 \text{ cm}, \; T = 10, \lambda = 18 \text{ and } \phi = \frac{\pi}{6}$$

15. Given that, $y = 10^{-6}\sin\left(100t + 20x + \frac{\pi}{4}\right)$

The standard equation is

$$y = a\sin\frac{2\pi}{\lambda}(vt - x + \phi)$$

Comparing these two equations, we get

$$\frac{2\pi v}{\lambda} = 100 \text{ and } \frac{2\pi}{\lambda} = 20$$

$$\therefore \quad 20v = 100 \Rightarrow v = 5 \text{ m/s}$$

24

Superposition of Waves

Principle of Superposition of Waves

When two or more than two waves of similar type propagate in a medium simultaneously, then resultant displacement of any particle of the medium is equal to the vector sum of displacements produced by individual waves in that particle.

$$y = y_1 + y_2 + y_3 + \ldots$$

Reflection of a Wave

When a wave is reflected from a rigid boundary or a closed end, it is reflected back with a phase reversal or phase difference of π radians but reflection at an open boundary takes place without any phase change.

Stationary Waves

When two progressive waves of equal amplitude and frequency, travelling in opposite directions along a straight line superpose each other, the resultant wave does not travel in either direction and is called a stationary or standing wave. At some points, the particles of the medium always remain at rest. These are called nodes. At some other points, the amplitude of oscillation is maximum. These are called antinodes.

Consider a plane progressive harmonic wave travelling along positive X-direction.

$$y_1 = A \sin(\omega t - kx) \quad \text{(incident wave)}$$

If this wave is reflected from a free end, then

$$y_2 = A \sin(\omega t + kx) \quad \text{(reflected wave)}$$

The stationary wave formed by the superposition of the incident and reflected waves will be

$$y = y_1 + y_2 = 2A \cos kx \sin \omega t$$

In this case, the points $x = 0, \frac{\lambda}{2}, \lambda\ \frac{3\lambda}{2}, \ldots$, will be antinodes

and the points $x = \frac{\lambda}{4}, \frac{3\lambda}{4}, \frac{5\lambda}{4}$, will be antinodes.

If the wave is reflected from a rigid end, then

$$y_2 = -A \sin(\omega t + kx)$$

The equation of the stationary wave will be

$$y = -2A \sin kx \cos \omega t$$

In this case, the points $x = 0, \frac{\lambda}{2}, \lambda, \frac{3\lambda}{2}, \ldots$, will be nodes and the points $x = \frac{\lambda}{4}, \frac{3\lambda}{4}, \frac{5\lambda}{4}, \ldots$, will be antinodes.

Separation between two successive nodes or antinodes $= \frac{\lambda}{2}$.

Separation between a node and nearest antinode $= \frac{\lambda}{4}$.

PROPERTIES OF STANDING WAVE

- At nodes, the displacement of the particles remains minimum, strain is maximum, pressure a density variations are maximum.
- At antinodes, the displacement of the particles remains maximum, strain is minimum, press density variations are minimum.
- The distance between two consecutive nodes or two consecutive antinodes $= \frac{\lambda}{2}$
- The distance between a node and adjoining antinode $= \frac{\lambda}{4}$
- All the particles between two nodes vibrate in same phase. Particles on two sides of a node opposite phase.
- n consecutive nodes are separated n by $\left((n - l)\frac{\lambda}{2}\right)$.

Interference of Waves

It is the simplest example of superposition of waves, in which two waves of same frequency (or same wavelength) travelling along same path superimpose. If at a given position (x being constant) displacement due to two waves be

$$y_1 = A_1 \sin \omega t$$

and

$$y_2 = A_2 \sin(\omega t + \phi)$$

Then, resultant displacement

$$y = y_1 + y_2 = A \sin(\omega t + \theta)$$

Where, $A = \sqrt{A_1^2 + A_2^2 + 2A_1 A_2 \cos \phi}$

and $\tan\theta = \dfrac{A_2 \sin\phi}{A_1 + A_2 \cos\phi}$

At those points where phase difference $\phi = 0°$ or $2n\pi$, *i.e.*, an integer multiple of 2π ($n = 1, 2, 3...$),

$$A = A_1 + A_2 = A_{max}$$

This is known as constructive interference.

At those points where $\phi = (2n-1)\pi$, *i.e.*, phase difference is an odd multiple of π and hence

$$A = A_1 \sim A_2 = A_{min}$$

This is known as destructive interference.

If I_1 and I_2 be the intensities due to the two waves, then resultant intensity

$$I = I_1 + I_2 + 2\sqrt{I_1 I_2}\cos\phi$$

$$I_{max} = I_1 + I_2 + 2\sqrt{I_1 I_2}$$

and $I_{min} = I_1 + I_2 - \sqrt{I_1 I_2}$

Beats

When two interacting waves have slightly different frequencies the resultant disturbance at any point due to the superposition periodically fluctuates causing waxing and waning in the resultant intensity. The waxing and waning in the resultant intensity of two superposed waves of slightly different frequency are known as beats.

Let the displacement produced at a point by one wave be $y_1 = A\sin(2\pi f_1 t - \phi_1)$

And the displacement produced at the point produced by the other wave of equal amplitude as $y_2 = A\sin(2\pi f_2 t - \phi_2)$

By the principle of superposition, the resultant displacement is

$$y = y_1 + y_2 = A\sin(2\pi f_1 t - \phi_1) + A\sin(2\pi f_2 t - \phi_2)$$

$$y = 2A\sin\left\{2\pi\left(\frac{f_1 + f_2}{2}\right)t - \left(\frac{\phi_1 + \phi_2}{2}\right)\right\} \cos 2\pi\left(\frac{f_1 - f_2}{2}\right)t$$

$$y = R\sin\left\{2\pi\left(\frac{f_1 + f_2}{2}\right)t - \left(\frac{\phi_1 + \phi_2}{2}\right)\right\}$$

Where, $R = 2A\cos 2\pi\left(\dfrac{f_1 - f_2}{2}\right)t$

The time for one beat is the time between consecutive maxima or minima.

First maxima would occur when

$$\cos 2\pi\left(\frac{f_1 - f_2}{2}\right)t = +1, \text{ then } 2\pi\left(\frac{f_1 - f_2}{2}\right)t = 0$$

$$\therefore \quad t = 0$$

For second maxima would occur when

$$\cos 2\pi\left(\frac{f_1 - f_2}{2}\right)t = -1, \text{ then}$$

$$2\pi\left(\frac{f_1 - f_2}{2}\right)t = \pi \Rightarrow t = \frac{1}{f_1 - f_2}$$

The time for one beat $= \left(\dfrac{1}{f_1 - f_2} - 0\right) = \dfrac{1}{f_1 - f_2}$

Similarly, it may also be shown that time between two consecutive minima is $\dfrac{1}{f_1 - f_2}$.

Hence, frequency of beat *i.e.*, number of beats in one second or beat frequency $= f_1 - f_2$.

Practice Questions

Level I

1. The principle of superposition in wave motion tells that in a motion in which two or more waves are simultaneously producing their displacement in a particle, then the resultant

(a) amplitude is the sum of the individual amplitudes
(b) velocity is the sum of the individual velocities
(c) displacement is the sum of the individual displacements
(d) phase is the sum of the individual phases

2. When a wave is reflected from the boundary of another medium, the wavelength

(a) increases (b) decreases
(c) remains constant (d) None of these

3. To demonstrate the phenomenon of interference, we need

(a) two sources which emit radiation of nearly the same frequency
(b) two sources which emit radiation of exactly the same frequency
(c) two sources which emit radiation of exactly the same frequency and have a definite phase relationship
(d) two sources which emit radiation of exactly the same wavelength

4. The complete destructive interference of two sound waves takes place when the two waves are travelling in the same direction

(a) with the same frequency and amplitude and are in phase
(b) with the same frequency and amplitude and are in opposite phase
(c) with the same frequency and amplitude
(d) with the same frequency and opposite phase

5. When two coherent waves interfere, there is

(a) loss in energy
(b) gain in energy
(c) redistribution of energy which changes with time
(d) redistribution of energy which does not change with time

6. If two tuning forks A and B are sounded together, they produce 4 beats per second. A is then slightly loaded with wax, they produce two beats when sounded again. The frequency of A is 256. The frequency of B will be
(a) 250 (b) 252 (c) 260 (d) 262

7. The phenomenon of beat is
(a) a characteristic property of light waves
(b) a characteristic property of water waves
(c) a characteristic property of sound waves
(d) a particular case of the phenomenon of interference

8. For production of beats the two sources must have
(a) different frequencies and same amplitude
(b) different frequencies
(c) different frequencies, same amplitude and same phase
(d) different frequencies and same phase

9. When beats are produced by two progressive waves of same amplitude and of nearly the same frequencies, then corresponding to each of the constituent waves the maximum loudness is heard
(a) two times (b) four times (c) same (d) 8 times

10. In stationary waves
(a) energy is uniformly distributed
(b) energy is maximum at nodes and minimum at antinodes
(c) energy is minimum at nodes and maximum at antinodes
(d) alternating maxima and minima of energy are produced at nodes and antinodes

Level II

1. Two waves of equal frequencies have their amplitudes in the ratio 3 : 5. They superimpose on each other. The ratio of maximum to minimum intensities of resultant wave is
(a) 16 : 1 (b) 3 : 5
(c) 9 : 25 (d) $\sqrt{3} : \sqrt{5}$

2. Two waves of intensities I and $4I$ produce interference. Then, the intensities at constructive and destructive interference respectively are
(a) $3I, 5I$ (b) $5I, 3I$
(c) $I, 9I$ (d) $9I, I$

3. Two sound waves of relative intensities 400 : 1 show interference. The ratio of intensities at the maxima to minima is close to
(a) $\frac{11}{9}$ (b) $\frac{401}{399}$ (c) $\frac{21}{19}$ (d) $\sqrt{\frac{401}{399}}$

4. Two sources of intensities I and $4I$ and waves, which interfere to produce a resultant intensity I_0 at a point of phase difference $\frac{\pi}{2}$. I_0 is equal to
(a) $5I$ (b) $4I$
(c) $3I$ (d) I

5. Beats are produced by two progressive waves. Maximum loudness at the waxing is x times the loudness of each wave. The value of x is
(a) 1 (b) $\sqrt{2}$
(c) 2 (d) 4

6. A wave represented by equation $y = a\cos(kx - \omega t)$ is superposed with another wave to form a stationary wave such that the point $x = 0$ is a node. The equation for the other wave is
(a) $a\sin(kx + \omega t)$ (b) $-a\cos(kx + \omega t)$
(c) $-a\cos(kx - \omega t)$ (d) $-a\sin(kx - \omega t)$

7. If two waves of same frequency and same amplitude respectively, on superposition produce a resultant disturbance of the same amplitude, the waves differ in phase by
(a) π (b) $\frac{2\pi}{3}$ (c) $\frac{\pi}{3}$ (d) 3π

8. Beats are produced by frequencies f_1 and $f_2 (f_1 > f_2)$. The duration of time between two successive maxima or minima is equal to
(a) $\frac{1}{f_1 + f_2}$ (b) $\frac{2}{f_1 - f_2}$ (c) $\frac{2}{f_1 + f_2}$ (d) $\frac{1}{f_1 - f_2}$

9. A couple of tuning forks produces two beats in the time interval of 0.4 s, so the beat frequency is
(a) 8 Hz (b) 5 Hz
(c) 2 Hz (d) 4 Hz

10. Two adjacent piano keys are struck simultaneously. The notes emitted by them have frequencies, n_1 and n_2. The number of beats heard per second is
(a) $\frac{(n_1 - n_2)}{2}$ (b) $\frac{(n_1 + n_2)}{2}$
(c) $n_1 - n_2$ (d) $2(n_1 - n_2)$

Answers

Level I

1. (c)	**2.** (c)	**3.** (c)	**4.** (b)	**5.** (d)	**6.** (b)	**7.** (d)	**8.** (c)	**9.** (b)	**10.** (c)

Level II

1. (a)	**2.** (d)	**3.** (a)	**4.** (a)	**5.** (d)	**6.** (b)	**7.** (b)	**8.** (d)	**9.** (b)	**10.** (c)

Hints and Solutions

Level II

1. Given $\frac{a_1}{a_2} = \frac{3}{5}$

$\Rightarrow \quad \frac{\sqrt{I_1}}{\sqrt{I_2}} = \frac{3}{5} \qquad (\because I_1 \propto a^2)$

We know that intensity is maximum when $\cos\phi = 1$

$\therefore \quad I_{max} = (\sqrt{I_1} + \sqrt{I_2})^2$

and intensity is minimum when $\cos\phi = 0$

$$I_{min} = (\sqrt{I_1} - \sqrt{I_2})^2$$

$$\therefore \quad \frac{I_{max}}{I_{min}} = \frac{(\sqrt{I_1} + \sqrt{I_2})^2}{(\sqrt{I_1} - \sqrt{I_2})^2} = \frac{\left(\sqrt{\left(\frac{I_1}{I_2}\right)} + 1\right)^2}{\left(\sqrt{\frac{I_1}{I_2}} - 1\right)^2}$$

$$= \left[\frac{\left(\frac{3}{5}\right) + 1}{\left(\frac{3}{5}\right) - 1}\right]^2 = \frac{64}{4} = 16:1$$

2. The intensity at constructive interference will be maximum

$$I_{max} = [\sqrt{I_1} + \sqrt{I_2}]^2 = [\sqrt{(4I)} + \sqrt{I}]^2 = 9I$$

The intensity at destructive interference will be

$$I_{min} = [\sqrt{I_1} - \sqrt{I_2}]^2 = [\sqrt{(4I)} - \sqrt{I}]^2 = I$$

Therefore, the intensity at constructive and destructive interference will be $9I : I$.

3. $I \propto a^2$

At maxima, $a' = a_1 + a_2$

At minima, $a'' = a_1 - a_2$

Given that relative intensities are 400 : 1 *i.e.*, amplitudes are in the ratio 20 : 1.

$\therefore$ Ratio of intensities at maxima

$$= \frac{(20+1)^2}{(20-1)} = \frac{(21)^2}{(19)^2} \simeq \frac{11}{9}$$

4. $R^2 = a_1^2 + a_2^2 + 2a_1 a_2 \cos\theta$

$$\Rightarrow I_0 = I + 4I + 2\sqrt{I}\sqrt{4I}\cos\left(\frac{\pi}{2}\right)$$

$$\Rightarrow I_0 = I + 4I + 0 = 5I$$

5. Let a be the amplitude of each wave.

At maximum, resultant amplitude $= a + a = 2a$

$\therefore$ Intensity $= 4a^2$

Intensity of each wave $= a^2$

$\therefore$ Maximum loudness $= x \times$ Loudness of each

$\Rightarrow \quad 4a^2 = x \times a^2 \quad \Rightarrow \quad x = 4$

6. $y = y_1 + y_2 = a\cos(kx - \omega t) - a\cos(kx + \omega t)$

This gives $y = 0$ for $x = 0$

7. Resultant amplitude R is given by

$$= [a_1^2 + a_2^2 + 2a_1 a_2 \cos\theta]^{\frac{1}{2}}$$

$$= [a^2 + a^2 + 2a^2\cos\theta]^{\frac{1}{2}}$$

But $\quad R = a$

$$\therefore \quad a = [2a^2(1 + \cos\theta)]^{\frac{1}{2}} = \left[4a^2\cos^2\left(\frac{\theta}{2}\right)\right]^{\frac{1}{2}}$$

$$a = 2a\cos\left(\frac{\theta}{2}\right)$$

$$\Rightarrow \quad \cos\left(\frac{\theta}{2}\right) = \frac{1}{2}$$

$$\Rightarrow \quad \frac{\theta}{2} = \frac{\pi}{3}$$

$$\Rightarrow \quad \theta = \frac{2\pi}{3}$$

25

Vibration in String

Velocity of Transverse Wave Along a Stretched String

When a string stretched between two points is plucked in a direction perpendicular to its length, transverse vibrations are set up in the string. This is due to the fact that tension in the string tends to bring it back to its mean positions but due to its inertia the string overshoots and goes to other extreme. The velocity of transverse waves in a stretched string is given by

$$v = \sqrt{\left(\frac{T}{m}\right)}$$

Where, T is tension in the string and m is mass per unit length of the string.

Again, $m =$ Volume of the unit length × Density

$= \pi r^2 \times 1 \times d$ (r = Radius of wire)

$= \pi \dfrac{D^2}{4} \cdot d$ (D = Diameter of wire)

Frequency of a Vibrating String

Let us consider the case of a string of length l fixed between two points NN as shown in figure. The string will vibrate in such a way that fixed points of the strings are nodes (because not free to move) while point of plucking as antinode. Let this string be plucked in the middle at a point A and it vibrates transversely only in one segment. At the two ends, there will be nodes while in the middle there will be an antinode (a point of maximum displacement). The velocity of the transverse wave is given by

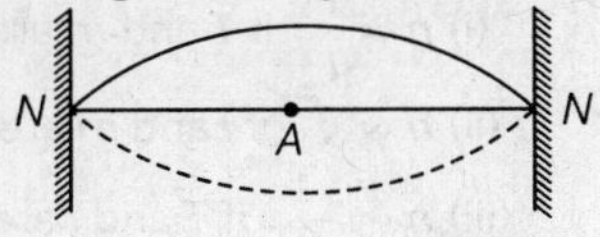

$$v = \sqrt{\left(\frac{T}{m}\right)} \quad \ldots\text{(i)}$$

If n is the frequency of vibration of the string and λ is the wavelength of the wave, then

$$v = n\lambda \quad \ldots\text{(ii)}$$

On comparing Eqs. (i) and (ii), we get

$$n\lambda = \sqrt{\left(\frac{T}{m}\right)}$$

$$\Rightarrow \quad n = \frac{1}{\lambda}\sqrt{\left(\frac{T}{m}\right)} \quad \ldots\text{(iii)}$$

When the string vibrates in one loop, then

$$NN = l = \frac{\lambda}{2}$$

$$\therefore \quad n = \frac{1}{2l}\sqrt{\left(\frac{T}{m}\right)} \quad \ldots\text{(iv)}$$

This is known as the fundamental frequency.

Eq. (iv) shows that

1. The frequency of the vibration is inversely proportional to the string's length.
2. The frequency is directly proportional to the square root of the tension.
3. The frequency varies inversely as the square root of mass per unit length.

These are known as the laws of vibrating strings.

Harmonics and Overtones

Let us consider the case of a string fixed at the two ends plucked. The progressive waves generated in the string travel to both ends. As the two ends are fixed, no displacement is possible at these two ends and the waves are reflected with phase change. The two waves interfere and produce stationary waves with nodes at fixed ends as shown in figure. The frequency of vibration will depend upon the number of nodes formed between two fixed ends of the string.

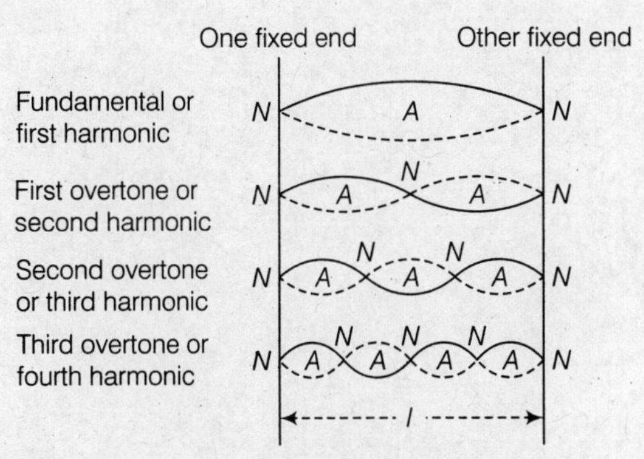

When the string is plucked in the middle, it vibrates with nodes at the ends and antinode in the middle. The tone emitted under this condition is known as fundamental or first harmonic and the frequency n_1 is given by

$$n_1 = \frac{v}{\lambda_1} = \frac{1}{\lambda_1}\sqrt{\left(\frac{T}{m}\right)}$$

But $\frac{\lambda_1}{2} = l \Rightarrow \lambda_1 = 2l$

$$n_1 = \frac{1}{2l}\sqrt{\left(\frac{T}{m}\right)} \quad \text{...(i)}$$

If the wire is plucked at one-fourth of its length, the string vibrates in two segments. In this case, there is one more node at the middle points. If λ_2 is the wavelength in this case, then

$$\frac{\lambda_2}{2} + \frac{\lambda_2}{2} = l \text{ i.e., } \lambda_2 = l$$

The frequency of vibrations of string n_2 is given by

$$n_2 = \frac{v}{\lambda_2} = \frac{1}{l}\sqrt{\left(\frac{T}{m}\right)} = 2n_1 \quad \text{...(ii)}$$

This is called first overtone or second harmonic.

Now, when the wire vibrates in these segments, the wavelength λ_3 is given by

$$\frac{\lambda_3}{2} + \frac{\lambda_3}{2} + \frac{\lambda_3}{2} = l \text{ i.e., } \frac{3\lambda_3}{2} = l$$

$$\Rightarrow \quad \lambda_3 = \frac{2l}{3}$$

The frequency n_3 of vibration in this case is

$$n_3 = \frac{1}{\lambda_3}\sqrt{\left(\frac{T}{m}\right)} = \frac{3}{2l}\sqrt{\left(\frac{T}{m}\right)} = 3n_1 \quad \text{...(iii)}$$

This is called second overtone or third harmonic.

Similarly, when the string vibrates in four segments, then

$$\frac{\lambda_4}{2} + \frac{\lambda_4}{2} + \frac{\lambda_4}{2} + \frac{\lambda_4}{2} = l, \text{ i.e., } \frac{4\lambda_4}{2} = l$$

$$\Rightarrow \quad \lambda_4 = \frac{l}{2}$$

$$\therefore \quad n_4 = \frac{1}{\lambda_4}\sqrt{\left(\frac{T}{m}\right)} = \frac{4}{2l}\sqrt{\left(\frac{T}{m}\right)} = 4n_1 \quad \text{...(iv)}$$

This is called as third overtone or fourth harmonic.

Hence, fundamental and harmonics are in the following ratio

$$n_1 : n_2 : n_3 : \; = 1:2:3: \ldots$$

Plucking in the Middle When the string is plucked in the middle, all the modes of vibrations are possible in which the middle point is an antinode. In this case, as is obvious all the odd harmonics are possible.

Hence, the possible frequencies are n_1, n_3, n_5,...etc.

Important Points

- The string has many natural frequencies which are integral multiples of fundamental frequency. When the string is excited with a tuning fork or any vibrating body, the string will be in resonance with the fork if anyone of its natural frequencies coincides with it.
- If M is the total mass of the string and l is its total length, then mass per unit length $m = \frac{M}{l}$. The natural frequency is given by

$$n = \frac{1}{2l}\sqrt{\left(\frac{T}{\frac{M}{l}}\right)} = \frac{1}{2}\sqrt{\left(\frac{T}{Ml}\right)}$$

- If r be the radius of the string and p be its density, then

$$n = \frac{1}{2l}\sqrt{\left(\frac{T}{\pi r^2 p}\right)} = \frac{1}{2lr}\sqrt{\frac{t}{\pi p}}$$

- If the string is vibrating in nth harmonic, its frequency will be $n \times n_1$. *i.e.*, number of loops in the string or antinodes will be n while total number of nodes will be $(n+1)$ including two at the ends.
- When a string is made by joining two strings of different lengths, cross-sections and densities and having same tension throughout, then joint will be a node.
- *Following are the laws of stretched string*

  (i) $n \propto \frac{1}{l}$ if T and m are constant.

  (ii) $n \propto \sqrt{T}$ if l and m are constant.

  (iii) $n \propto \frac{1}{\sqrt{m}}$ if T and l are constant.

These laws are known as Mersenne's laws.

Practice Questions

Level I

1. When tension of string increases, then frequency of transverse vibration
(a) increases (b) remain constant
(c) decreases (d) first increases, then decreases

2. The length of string of a sonometer is increase, then frequency of them
(a) increases
(b) decreases
(c) remain constant
(d) sometime increases and sometime decreases

3. The length of a stretched string of a sonometer is doubled and tension is halved. The frequency will
(a) increased (b) halved
(c) less than halved (d) remain constant

4. The number of loops in a stretched string be P and tension acted an it be T (while length of string is constant), then the relation between P and T will be
(a) $\frac{P^2}{T}$ = Constant (b) $\frac{P}{T}$ = Constant
(c) $P^2 \times T$ = Constant (d) $\frac{T}{P^2}$ = Constant

5. If vibration frequency of a string is doubled. Then, tension in the string will be
(a) halved (b) triplet (c) doubled (d) Four times

6. A uniform string whose length be l, mass be m and tension be T. The frequency of its vibration will be
(a) $\frac{1}{2l}\sqrt{\frac{T}{m}}$ (b) $\frac{1}{l}\sqrt{\frac{T}{m}}$
(c) $\frac{1}{m}\sqrt{\frac{T}{2l}}$ (d) $\frac{1}{2}\sqrt{\frac{T}{lm}}$

7. In a stretched string under tension. If frequency of vibration of its area of cross-section of wire increased by 50%, then tension should be increased by
(a) 100% (b) 150% (c) 50% (d) 125%

8. A stretched string fixed at both the ends with strong base producing 15 beats. If wavelength be 2 m, then length of the string will be
(a) 14 m (b) 13 m (c) 14.4 m (d) 14.2 m

9. Velocity of waves in a string depends upon
(a) length of the string
(b) tension on the string
(c) density of the surrounding medium
(d) temperature of atmosphere

10. Two identical wires of different materials are stretched by the same tension, velocity of transverse waves in both the string is
(a) same (b) different (c) zero (d) infinite

Level II

1. If frequency of vibration of string is increased by a factor two, then tension in string will be
(a) half (b) double (c) one-fourth (d) four times

2. The length of a stretched string is doubled and the tension is increased four times.The frequency will
(a) become twice (b) reduced to half
(c) remain constant (d) become one-fourth

3. In a stretched string under tension and fixed at both the ends, the area of cross-section of its wire is halved and tension is doubled. The frequency becomes
(a) twice (b) eight times
(c) half (d) four times

4. In stretched string under tension and fixed at both the ends, the length and the radius both are doubled. The frequency becomes
(a) double (b) half
(c) one-fourth (d) one-sixteenth

5. There are two strings of equal length and diameter but the densities are in the ratio 1 : 2. They are stretched by a tension T. The ratio of frequencies will be
(a) $\sqrt{2}:1$ (b) 1 : 4 (c) 1 : 2 (d) 2 : 1

6. In a stretched string under tension and fixed at both ends,there will be
(a) antinodes at both ends and atleast one node in between
(b) nodes at both ends and atleast one antinode in between
(c) nodes at both the ends and no antinode in between
(d) antinode at both the ends and no node in between

7. The frequencies of the harmonics of the string are
(a) unrelated (b) of the same pitch
(c) in the ratio 1 : 2 : 3 (d) in the ratio 1 : 3 : 5

8. A 5.5 m length of string has a mass of 0.035 kg. If the tension in the string is 77 N, the speed of a wave the string is
(a) 110 m/s (b) 165 m/s (c) 77 m/s (d) 102 m/s

9. A stretched string of length l fixed at both ends can sustain stationary waves of wavelength λ given by
(a) $\lambda = \frac{n^2}{2l}$ (b) $\lambda = \frac{l^2}{2n}$ (c) $\lambda = \frac{2l}{n}$ (d) $\lambda = \frac{2}{n}$
Here, n is a whole number.

10. If the length of the wire of a sonometer is halved, the value of the resonant frequency will be
(a) double (b) half
(c) four times (d) eight times

11. A uniform metal wire of density ρ, cross-sectional area A and length l is stretched with a tension T. The speed of transverse wave in the wire is given by
(a) $\sqrt{\left(\frac{Tl}{\rho A}\right)}$ (b) $\sqrt{\left(\frac{T\rho}{Al}\right)}$ (c) $\sqrt{\left(\frac{T}{\rho l}\right)}$ (d) $\sqrt{\left(\frac{T}{A\rho}\right)}$

12. Two wires made up of the material are of equal lengths but their diameters are in the ratio 1 : 2. On stretching each of these two strings by the same tension, the ratio between the fundamental frequencies of these strings is

(a) 1 : 4 (b) 1 : 2 (c) 2 : 1 (d) 4 : 1

13. The radius, density and tension of a string A are twice the radius, density and tension of another string B. If the lengths of the string are equal, the ratio of their frequencies of their vibration (*i.e.*, $\frac{n_A}{n_B}$) will be

(a) 1 (b) 2 (c) 1/2 (d) 1/4

14. Two stretched wires of same material of lengths l and $2l$ vibrate with frequencies 100 Hz and 150 Hz, respectively. The ratio of their tensions is

(a) 2 : 3 (b) 3 : 2
(c) 1 : 9 (d) 1 : 3

15. To increase the frequency by 20%, the tension in the string vibrating on a sonometer has to be increased by

(a) 44% (b) 33%
(c) 22% (d) 11%

Answers

Level I

1. (a) **2.** (b) **3.** (c) **4.** (c) **5.** (d) **6.** (a) **7.** (d) **8.** (a) **9.** (b) **10.** (b)

Level II

1. (d) **2.** (c) **3.** (a) **4.** (c) **5.** (a) **6.** (b) **7.** (c) **8.** (a) **9.** (c) **10.** (a)
11. (d) **12.** (c) **13.** (c) **14.** (c) **15.** (a)

Hints and Solutions

Level II

8. $$v = \sqrt{\left(\frac{T}{m}\right)}$$

Here, $T = 77$ N and $m = \frac{0.035}{55} = \frac{7}{1100}$

$$\therefore \quad v = \sqrt{\left(\frac{77 \times 1100}{7}\right)} = 110 \text{ m/s}$$

9. Both the ends will behave as nodes. So, nth mode of vibration

$$n \times \left(\frac{\lambda}{2}\right) = l$$

Where, $n = 1, 2, 3...$

$$\therefore \quad \lambda = \left(\frac{2l}{n}\right)$$

10. $n = \frac{1}{2l}\sqrt{\left(\frac{T}{m}\right)}$

When the length is halved, then

$$n' = \frac{1}{2\left(\frac{l}{2}\right)}\sqrt{\left(\frac{T}{m}\right)} = 2\left[\frac{1}{2l}\sqrt{\frac{T}{m}}\right] = 2n$$

11. Volume of wire = Al

Mass of the wire = $Al \times \rho$

$\therefore$ Mass per unit length = $\left(Al \times \frac{\rho}{l}\right) = A\rho$

Now, $$v = \sqrt{\left(\frac{T}{m}\right)} = \sqrt{\left(\frac{T}{A\rho}\right)}$$

12. $n \propto \left(\frac{1}{D}\right)$, where D = Diameter

$$\therefore \quad n_1 \propto \left(\frac{1}{D}\right) \text{ and } n_2 \propto \left(\frac{1}{2D}\right)$$

$$\frac{n_1}{n_2} = \frac{2D}{D} = \frac{2}{1} \Rightarrow n_1 : n_2 = 2 : 1$$

13. $$n_B = \frac{1}{2l}\sqrt{\left(\frac{T}{\pi r^2 \rho}\right)}$$

$$n_A = \frac{1}{2l}\sqrt{\left[\frac{2T}{\pi(2r)^2 2\rho}\right]} = \frac{1}{2l} \times \frac{1}{2}\sqrt{\left(\frac{T}{\pi r^2 \rho}\right)}$$

$$\therefore \quad \frac{n_A}{n_B} = \frac{1}{2}$$

14. $100 = \frac{1}{2l}\sqrt{\left(\frac{T}{m}\right)}$, $150 = \frac{1}{2 \times (2l)}\sqrt{\left(\frac{T'}{m}\right)}$

$$\therefore \quad \frac{100}{150} = 2\sqrt{\left(\frac{T}{T'}\right)} \Rightarrow \frac{T}{T'} = \frac{1}{9}$$

$$\therefore \quad T : T' = 1 : 9$$

15. We know that, $v \propto \sqrt{T}$.

Let tension has to be increased by x%, then

$$\frac{v + 20\% \text{ of } v}{v} = \sqrt{\frac{T + x\% \text{ of } T}{T}}$$

$$\frac{6}{5} = \sqrt{\left(1 + \frac{x}{100}\right)}$$

$$\frac{36}{25} = 1 + \frac{x}{100} \Rightarrow x = 44\%$$

Thus, tension has to be increased by 44%.

26

Speed of Sound

Sound

It is a variation in an elastic medium at a frequency and intensity that is capable of being heard by human ear.

Velocity of Sound

(i) Velocity of sound in an extended solid (Earth's crust) of bulk modulus K, modulus of rigidity η and density ρ is given by

$$v = \sqrt{\frac{K + \frac{4}{3}\eta}{\rho}}$$

The factor $K + \left(\frac{4}{3}\right)\eta$ is called elongational elasticity.

(ii) Velocity of sound in a long rod of Young's modulus Y and density ρ is given by

$$v = \sqrt{\frac{Y}{\rho}} = 5300 \text{ m/s in steel}$$

(iii) Velocity of sound in a liquid of bulk modulus K and density ρ is given by

$$v = \sqrt{\frac{K}{\rho}} = 1450 \text{ m/s in water}$$

(iv) Velocity of sound in a gaseous medium of bulk modulus K and density ρ is given by

$$v = \sqrt{\frac{K}{\rho}}$$

According to Newton, when sound travels through gas, the changes taking place in the medium are isothermal in nature. So, Newton's formula for the speed of sound is

$$v = \sqrt{\frac{K_{\text{iso}}}{\rho}} = \sqrt{\frac{p}{\rho}}, \text{ where } p = \text{Pressure of the gas.}$$

At 0°C, $p = 1.01 \times 10^5 \text{ Nm}^{-2}$

$\rho = 1.293 \text{ kg-m}^{-3}$

$$\therefore \quad v_{\text{air}} = \sqrt{\frac{1.01 \times 10^5}{1.293}} = 280 \text{ m/s}$$

Which is less than velocity of sound in air is 332 m/s.

So, correction should be need.

Laplace's Correction

According to Laplace, the changes in p and V of a gas, when sound waves are propagated through it are adiabatic.

$$v = \sqrt{\frac{K_{\text{adiabatic}}}{\rho}}$$

$$v = \sqrt{\frac{\gamma P}{\rho}}$$

$= 332$ m/s in air at 0°C.

$K_{\text{adiabatic}}$ = Adiabatic volume elasticity

i.e., Bulk Modulus of gas

$$\gamma = \frac{C_p}{C_V}$$

ρ = Density of gas

$$v = \sqrt{\frac{\gamma RT}{M}}$$

R = Gas constant

T = Absolute temperature of gas

M = Molecular weight of gas

$\therefore \quad v \propto \sqrt{T},$

if γ, R and M are same *i.e.*, same gas at different absolute temperatures.

$\gamma = 1.4$ for air

$\gamma = 1.33$ for water vapour

Effect of Different Physical Quantities on Velocity of Sound

Effect of Density

The velocity of sound at given ρ and γ is inversely proportional to the square root of the density or molecular weight of gases. *i.e.*

$$v \propto \sqrt{\frac{1}{\rho}} \Rightarrow v \cdot \sqrt{\rho} = \text{Constant}$$

(i) $\frac{v_1}{v_2} = \sqrt{\frac{\rho_2}{\rho_1}}$

(ii) $\frac{v_H}{v_O} = \sqrt{\frac{\rho_O}{\rho_H}} = \sqrt{\frac{M_O}{M_H}} = \frac{\sqrt{32}}{2} = 4$

$\therefore \quad v_H = 4v_O$

Effect of Temperature

$$v = \sqrt{\frac{vp}{\rho}} = \sqrt{\frac{\gamma\, p\, v}{m}} = \sqrt{\frac{\gamma\,\mu\, RT}{M}} = \sqrt{\frac{\gamma\,\mu\, RT}{\mu M}}$$

$$= \sqrt{\frac{\gamma\, R\, T}{M}}$$

Clearly, $v \propto \sqrt{T}$, because for given gas γ and M = Constant.

(i) Hence, the temperature for a given gas increased by n^2 times, then the speed of sound becomes n times *i.e.*, $T_1 = n^2 T$, where $n^2 = 1, 2, 3, \ldots$

(ii) When increase in temperature is very least, then

$$\frac{v'}{v_0} = \sqrt{\frac{T'}{T_0}} = \sqrt{\frac{273 + t}{273 + 0}} = \left[1 + \frac{t}{273}\right]^{\frac{1}{2}}$$

Using binomial theorem,

$$\frac{v'}{v_0} = 1 + \frac{t^0}{546}$$

$$\Rightarrow \quad v' = v_0 \left(1 + \frac{1}{546}\right)$$

$\Rightarrow v' = [332 + 0.61]\ (t°C)$ m/s

From this formula, it is clear that when the temperature increases from 0°C to 1°C in air, the speed of sound increases by 0.61 m/s approx.

Effect of Pressure

Velocity of sound in independent of pressure at constant temperature.

$$v = \sqrt{\frac{\gamma p}{\rho}} = \sqrt{\frac{\gamma\, RT}{M}} \quad \left[\begin{array}{l}\therefore p = \frac{RT}{V} \\ \text{and } \rho V = M\end{array}\right]$$

Effect of Relative Humidity

Since, velocity of sound is inversely proportional to the square root of density. Hence, the velocity of sound is more in moist air with respect to dry air.

Velocity of Sound in Moist Air

$$v_{\text{moist air}} = v_{\text{dry air}} \times \sqrt{1 + \frac{0.325\, p}{P}}$$

p = Saturation vapour pressure at 0°C

P = Atmospheric pressure

Effect of Wind

Velocity of sound is increase in the direction of velocity of air but decrease in the opposite direction.

If exact velocity of sound be v and velocity of air be w, then

(i) velocity of sound in direction of air, $v' = v + w$

(ii) velocity of sound in opposite direction of air, $v'' = v - w$

Note The frequency, Amplitude, phase, lowelness, pitch and quality does not effect the velocity of sound.

Relation between Speed of Sound in a Jar and rms of Molecules of the Same Gas

Velocity of sound in a gas

$$v = \sqrt{\frac{\gamma p}{\rho}}$$

rms of molecules of the same gas,

$$v_{\text{rms}} = \sqrt{\bar{v}^2} = \sqrt{\frac{3p}{\rho}} \quad \left[\therefore P = \frac{1}{3}\rho \bar{v}^2\right]$$

$$\therefore \quad \frac{v}{v_{\text{rms}}} = \sqrt{\frac{\gamma}{3}}$$

Note Speed of sound is maximum in solid and minimum in gas.

i.e., $v_{\text{solid}} > v_{\text{liquid}} > v_{\text{air}}$

Practice Questions

Level I

1. The speed of sound in air does not depend upon

(a) pressure (b) density
(c) temperature (d) humidity

2. When sound waves enters from air to water, then which of the following be constant?

(a) Time period (b) Wavelength
(c) Frequency (d) Velocity

3. If the value of wavelength to be halves, then the speed of sound would be

(a) halves (b) doubled
(c) four times (d) unchanged

4. The speed of sound is maximum in

(a) air (b) vacuum
(c) water (d) iron

5. **The speed of sound in gases depends upon**
(a) wavelength of sound
(b) density and elasicity of gas
(c) frequency and amplitude of sound
(d) intensity of sound

6. **Supersonic plane travels with the speed**
(a) less than the speed of sound
(b) more than the speed of sound
(c) equal to the speed of sound
(d) on the speed of sound

7. **The speed of sound in a gas is directly proportional to**
(a) T (b) T^{-1}
(c) T^2 (d) $T^{\frac{1}{2}}$

8. **The ratio of the velocities of sound in air at 16 atmospheric pressure and 4 atmospheric pressure would be**
(a) 1 : 1 (b) 3 : 1
(c) 1 : 4 (d) 4 : 1

9. **Production of sound wave in a gas is**
(a) longitudinal
(b) transverse
(c) electromagnetic
(d) None of the above

10. **The speed of sound in air will be increases with increase in temperature 1°C.**
(a) 0.33 m/s (b) 0.61 m/s
(c) 0.5 m/s (d) zero

11. **The velocity of sound in gases are independent of**
(a) humidity (b) temperature
(c) pressure (d) All of these

12. **If v_m be the speed of sound in moist air and v_d be the speed of sound in dry air, then at constant temperature and pressure**
(a) $v_m > v_d$ (b) $v_m v_d = 1$
(c) $v_m = v_d$ (d) $v_m < v_d$

13. **Usually velocity of sound is more in solid in comparison with gases because**
(a) density of solid is more but elasticity in less
(b) elasticity of solid is more but density is less
(c) elasticity and density both are less in solids
(d) elasticity and density both are more in solids

14. **The ratio of the velocity of sound (v) in a gas and rms velocity (v_{rms}) of molecules of the same gas at constant temperature will be (γ = Ratio of specific heat of gas)**
(a) $\sqrt{\frac{3}{\gamma}}$ (b) $\frac{1}{\sqrt{3\gamma}}$ (c) $\sqrt{3\gamma}$ (d) $\sqrt{\frac{\gamma}{3}}$

Level II

1. **Which of the following properties of sound is affected by change in air temperature?**
(a) Amplitude (b) Frequency
(c) Wavelength (d) Intensity

2. **Which of the following statements is wrong?**
(a) Sound travels in a straight line
(b) Sound travels as waves
(c) Sound is a form of energy
(d) Sound travels faster in vacuum than in air

3. **Sound waves do not show the phenomenon of**
(a) interference (b) diffraction
(c) refraction (d) polarisation

4. **The velocity of sound is maximum in**
(a) Air (b) Water
(c) Iron (d) Vacuum

5. **The velocity of sound in air is not affected by change in**
(a) moisture content of the air
(b) the temperature of the air
(c) the atmospheric pressure
(d) the composition of the air

6. **The speed of sound in air at NTP is 300 m/s. If air pressure becomes four times, then the speed of sound will be**
(a) 150 m/s (b) 300 m/s
(c) 600 m/s (d) 1200 m/s

7. **The velocity of sound in air at 4 atmosphere and that at 1 atmosphere pressure would be**
(a) 1 : 1 (b) 4 : 1
(c) 1 : 4 (d) 3 : 1

8. **The velocity of sound in air is independent of change in**
(a) pressure (b) density
(c) temperature (d) humidity

9. **A source of frequency 500 Hz emits waves of wavelength 0.2 m. How long does it take the waves to travel 300 m?**
(a) 75 s (b) 60 s
(c) 12 s (d) 3 s

10. **Human ears can sense sound waves travelling in air having wavelength of**
(a) 10^{-3}m (b) 10^{-2}m
(c) 1 m (d) 10^2m

11. **Which of the following statements is wrong?**
(a) Sound travels in straight line
(b) Sound is form of energy
(c) Sound travels in the form of waves
(d) Sound travels faster in vacuum than in air

12. **Voice of a friend is recognized by its**
(a) pitch (b) quality
(c) intensity (d) velocity

13. **Velocity of sound in air is**
(a) 300 m/s (b) 3.8×10^{10} m/s
(c) 3×10^8 m/s (d) 9×10^{19} m/s

14. **The velocity v of a sound wave travelling in a gas pressure p and density d is given by**
(a) $v = \sqrt{\left(\frac{p}{d}\right)}$ (b) $v = \sqrt{\left(\frac{\gamma p}{d}\right)}$
(c) $v = \gamma\sqrt{\left(\frac{p}{d}\right)}$ (d) $v = \sqrt{\left(\frac{p}{\gamma d}\right)}$

15. **The Laplace's correction in the expression for the velocity of sound given by Newton is needed because sound waves**
(a) are longitudinal (b) propagate isothermally
(c) propagate adiabatically (d) are of long wavelengths

16. **Velocity of sound in a gas is proportional to**
(a) square root of adiabatic elasticity
(b) adiabatic elasticity
(c) square root of isothermal elasticity
(d) isothermal elasticity

17. **With the rise of temperature, the velocity of sound**
(a) decreases
(b) increases
(c) remains the same
(d) is independent of temperature

18. **Velocity of sound is**
(a) directly proportional to absolute temperature ($v \propto T$)
(b) $v \propto \sqrt{T}$
(c) $v \propto \frac{1}{\sqrt{T}}$
(d) $v \propto \frac{1}{T}$

19. **The velocity of sound at 0°C is 330 m/s. At what temperature the velocity of sound will be 660 m/s?**
(a) 519°C (b) 900°C
(c) 1200°C (d) 819°C

20. **The ratio of the speeds of sound at 300 K in nitrogen gas and helium gas would be**
(a) $\sqrt{\frac{2}{7}}$ (b) $\sqrt{\frac{3}{5}}$ (c) $\sqrt{\frac{1}{7}}$ (d) $\sqrt{\frac{6}{5}}$

21. **The frequency and speed of sound wave are ν and v, respectively. If frequency leads to become 4ν, then the speed of sound wave will be**
(a) v (b) $4v$
(c) $2v$ (d) $\frac{v}{4}$

22. **Two sound waves of wavelengths 5 m and 6 m produces 30 beats in 3 s, then speed of sound will be**
(a) 300 m/s (b) 320 m/s
(c) 310 m/s (d) 330 m/s

23. **The density of air at 10^5 N/m^2 atmospheric pressure be 1.29 kg/m^3, then which of the following will be velocity of sound in air? [for air $\gamma = 1.41$]**
(a) 332 m/s (b) 330.6 m/s
(c) 33 m/s (d) None of these

24. **The wavelength of a wave be 0.60 cm and velocity be 300 m/s, then which of the following will be the frequency of the wave?**
(a) 10000 Hz (b) 100 Hz
(c) 50000 Hz (d) 30000 Hz

Answers

Level I

1. (a)	**2.** (c)	**3.** (a)	**4.** (d)	**5.** (b)	**6.** (b)	**7.** (d)	**8.** (a)	**9.** (a)	**10.** (b)
11. (c)	**12.** (a)	**13.** (d)	**14.** (d)						

Level II

1. (c)	**2.** (d)	**3.** (d)	**4.** (c)	**5.** (c)	**6.** (b)	**7.** (a)	**8.** (a)	**9.** (d)	**10.** (c)
11. (d)	**12.** (b)	**13.** (a)	**14.** (b)	**15.** (c)	**16.** (a)	**17.** (b)	**18.** (b)	**19.** (d)	**20.** (b)
21. (a)	**22.** (a)	**23.** (b)	**24.** (c)						

Hints and Solutions

Level II

19. We know that,
$V \propto \sqrt{T}$

Let velocity of sound at temperature t = 660 m/s

$$\therefore \quad \frac{v_1}{v_0} = \sqrt{\frac{273+t}{273}}$$

$$\Rightarrow \quad \frac{660}{330} = \sqrt{\frac{273+t}{273}}$$

$$\Rightarrow \quad 2 = \sqrt{\frac{273+t}{273}}$$

On squaring both sides,

$$4 = \frac{273+t}{273}$$

$$\Rightarrow \quad t = 273(4-1) = 819°\text{C}$$

22. $n_1 - n_2 = \frac{30}{3} = 10 \Rightarrow \left[\frac{v}{\lambda_1} - \frac{v}{\lambda_2}\right] = 10$

$\Rightarrow v\left[\frac{1}{5} - \frac{1}{6}\right] = 10$ by the condition of question.

$$\therefore \quad v = 300 \text{ m/s}$$

24. Here, Frequency of the move $n = \frac{300\text{ m/s}}{0.60 \times 10^{-2}\text{m}} = 50000\text{ Hz}$

27

Vibration in Air Column

Longitudinal Stationary Wave

It is produced in

1. Organ pipe 2. Resonance tube

1. Organ Pipes

An organ pipe is a cylindrical tube of uniform cross-section in which a gas (usually air) is trapped as a column (*i.e.*, bounded medium). One end of an organ pipe is always open while the other may be closed or open giving rise to closed it becomes a cavity.

As organ pipe contains gas (air), the waves in it are longitudinal. And as the medium is bounded the incident wave travelling along the axis of the tube will be reflected back from the other end resulting in stationary wave *i.e.*, the mechanical waves in an organ pipe are always longitudinal stationary.

Now if in an organ reflection is from closed end which is rigid (*i.e.*, hard boundary), the closed end will be a node as particles at node are permanently at rest and if reflection is from open ends (*i.e.*, free end or soft boundary), where particles are free to move, there will be an antinode, *i.e.*, in an organ pipe, closed end is always a node while free end an antinode.

Open Pipe

If both ends of a pipe are open and a system of air is directed against an edge, standing longitudinal waves can be set up in the tube. The open ends are a displacement antinodes and pressure nodes

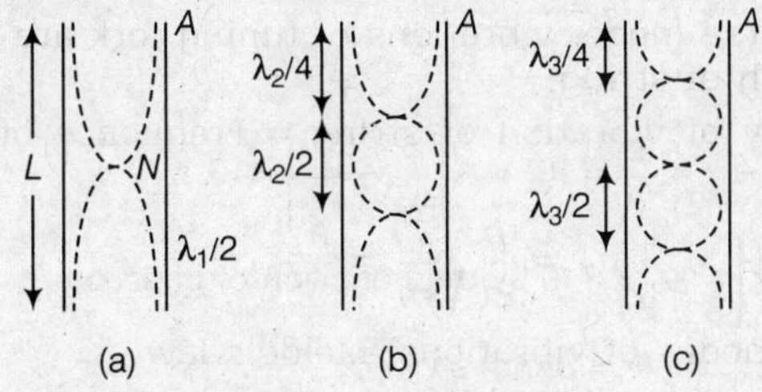

(i) For fundamental mode of vibrations,

$$L = \frac{\lambda_1}{2}$$

$$\therefore \quad \lambda_1 = 2L$$

$$v = \lambda_1 f_1$$

$$\therefore \quad v = 2Lf_1$$

$$\Rightarrow \quad f_1 = \frac{v}{2L} \quad \text{...(i)}$$

(ii) For the second harmonic or first overtone,

$$L = \lambda_2 \text{ or } \lambda_2 = L$$

$$v = \lambda_2 f_2$$

$$\therefore \quad v = Lf_2$$

$$\Rightarrow \quad f_2 = \frac{v}{L} = \frac{2v}{2L} = 2f \quad \text{...(ii)}$$

(iii) For the third harmonic or second overtone,

$$L = 3 \times \frac{\lambda_3}{2}$$

$$\therefore \quad \lambda_3 = \frac{2}{3} L$$

$$v = \lambda_3 f_3$$

$$\therefore \quad v = \frac{2}{3} Lf_3$$

$$\Rightarrow \quad f_3 = \frac{3v}{2L} \quad \text{...(iii)}$$

From Eqs. (i), (ii) and (iii),

we get $f_1 : f_2 : f_3 : \ldots = 1 : 2 : 3 : \ldots$

i.e., for a cylindrical tube, open at both ends, the harmonics excitable in the tube are all integral multiples of its fundamental.

$\therefore$ In the general case, $\lambda = \frac{2L}{n}$, where $n = 1, 2, \ldots$

Frequency $= \frac{v}{\lambda} = \frac{nv}{2L}$, where $n = 1, 2, \ldots$

Closed Pipe

If one end of a pipe is closed the reflected wave is 180° out of phase with the incoming wave. Thus, the displacement of the small volume elements at the closed end must always be zero. Hence, the closed end must be a displacement node and pressure antinode.

(i) This represents the fundamental mode of vibration,

$$L = \frac{\lambda_1}{4}$$

$$\therefore \quad \lambda_1 = 4L$$

If f_1 is the fundamental frequency, then the velocity of sound waves is given as,

$$v = \lambda_1 f_1$$

$$\therefore \quad v = 4Lf_1$$

$$\Rightarrow \quad f_1 = \frac{v}{4L}$$

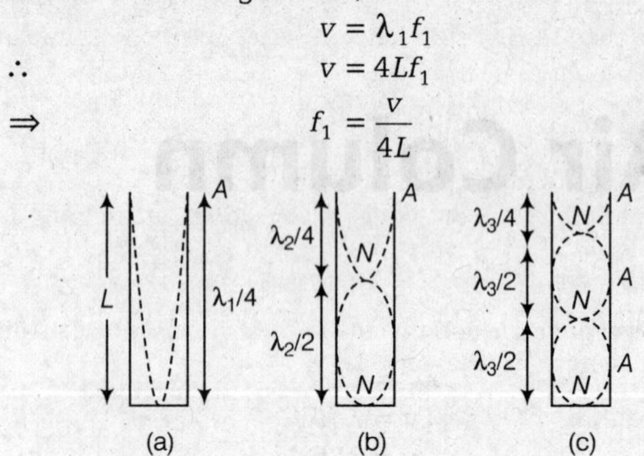

(ii) This is the third harmonic or first overtone,

$$L = 3 \times \frac{\lambda_2}{4}$$

$$\therefore \quad \lambda_2 = \frac{4}{3}L$$

$$v = \lambda_2 f_2$$

$$\therefore \quad v = \frac{4}{3}Lf_2 \Rightarrow f_2 = 3\frac{v}{4L} = 3f_1$$

(iii) This is the fifth harmonic or second overtone,

$$L = 5 \times \frac{\lambda_3}{4}$$

$$\therefore \quad \lambda_3 = \frac{4}{5}L$$

$$v = \lambda_3 f_3$$

$$\therefore \quad v = \frac{4}{5}Lf_3 \Rightarrow f_3 = \frac{5v}{4L} = 5f_1$$

$$f_1 : f_2 : f_3 : \ldots = 1 : 3 : 5 : \ldots$$

In general, $\lambda = \frac{4l}{(2n+1)}$, where $n = 0, 1, 2, \ldots$

Velocity of sound $= v$

Frequency $= \frac{(2n+1)v}{4L}$, where $n = 0, 1, 2, \ldots$

Due to finite momentum of air molecules in organ pipes reflection takes place not exactly at open end but some what it so in an organ pipe antinode is not formed exactly at free end but above it at a distance $e = 0.6r$ (called end correction or Rayleigh correction) with r being the radius of pipe. So, for closed organ pipe $L = L + 0.6r$, while for open $L = L + 2 \times 0.6r$ (as both ends are open) so that

$$f_c = \frac{v}{4(L + 0.6r)}, \text{ while } f_0 = \frac{v}{4(L + 1.2r)}$$

This is why for a given v and L narrower the pipe higher will the frequency or pitch and shriller will be the sound.

Note

- In a pipe open at both the ends, the frequency of fundamental note produced is twice as that produced by a closed pipe of the same length.
- An open pipe produces all the harmonics, while in a closed pipe,the even harmonics are absent.

End Correction

Antinode is not obtained at exact open end but slightly above it. The distance between open and a called end correction.

It is denoted by e.

- Length of air column, $n \propto \left(\frac{1}{l}\right)$
- Radius of air column, $n \propto \left(\frac{1}{r}\right)$
- Temperature of air column, $n \propto \sqrt{T}$
- Pressure of air inside air column, $n \propto \sqrt{p}$
- Density of air, $n \propto \left(\frac{1}{\sqrt{\rho}}\right)$
- Velocity of sound in air column, $n \propto v$

2. Resonance Tube

It tube is a closed organ pipe in which length of air column can be changed by changing liquid column in it.

For first resonance $\frac{\lambda}{4} = l_1 + e$

For second resonance $\frac{3\lambda}{4} = l_2 + e$

Velocity of sound $v = n\lambda = 2n(l_2 - l_1)$

End correction $e = \frac{l_2 - 3l_1}{2}$

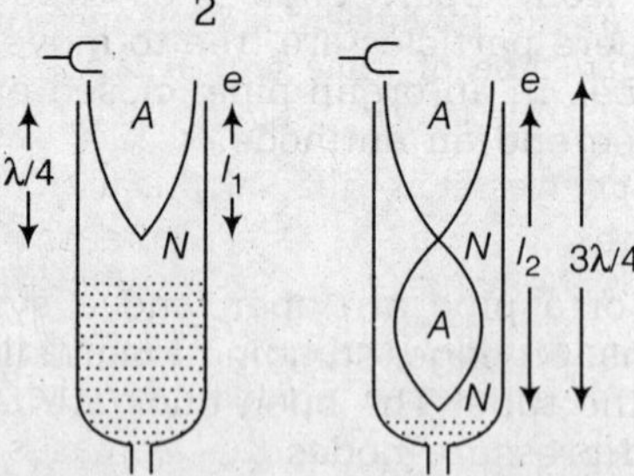

In tranverse mode, vibrations of tuning fork are at 90° to the length of string.

Frequency of vibration of string = Frequency of tunning fork

$$n_T = \frac{p}{2l}\sqrt{\frac{T}{m}} = \frac{n_L}{2}$$

In both modes of vibrations, Melde's law p^2T = constant, is obeyed.

Practice Questions

Level I

1. **Which of the following gives good quality of sound?**
(a) Open organ pipe (b) Damped oscillator
(c) Both (a) and (b) (d) Closed organ pipe

2. **If the end of an open organ pipe is suddenly closed, then what will be the effect an fundamental frequency?**
(a) fundamental frequency becomes one-fourth
(b) fundamental frequency becomes three-fourth
(c) fundamental frequency becomes halved
(d) fundamental frequency becomes one-third

3. **Both the ends of open organ pipe generates**
(a) only even harmonics (b) only odd harmonics
(c) Both (a) and (b) (d) None of these

4. **A closed organ pipe produces harmonics only**
(a) even
(b) odd
(c) sometime even and sometime odd
(d) (a) and (b)

5. **The ratio of fundamental frequencies of closed and open organ pipes of same length is**
(a) 1 : 3 (b) 1 : 2
(c) 3 : 1 (d) 2 : 1

6. **A vibrating damped oscillator taken over a resonance tube, then in first resonance position antinode shows at**
(a) the bottom of the pipe
(b) over the end of the pipe
(c) the end of the pipe
(d) the surface of water

7. **Generation of all overtones from closed organ pipe is**
(a) even (b) odd
(c) Both (a) and (b) (d) None of these

8. **The resonance generater at a end of a closed organ pipe, when length of the pipe is**
(a) $\frac{\lambda}{8}$ (b) λ (c) $\frac{\lambda}{2}$ (d) $\frac{\lambda}{4}$

9. **If r be the radius of resonance tube, then end correction will be**
(a) 0.04 r (b) 0.6 r (c) 0.04 r (d) r

10. **The frequency of tones generated by an organ pipe is inversely proportional to the**
(a) length of the pipe
(b) tones
(c) fundamental note
(d) None of the above

Level II

1. **For an open organ pipe of length l the wavelength of the fundamental note is equal to**
(a) l (b) $\frac{l}{2}$ (c) $\frac{l}{4}$ (d) $2l$

2. **The ratio of the fundamental frequency of an open and closed organ pipe of same length is**
(a) 2 : 1 (b) 1 : 2 (c) 1 : 1 (d) 4 : 1

3. **As an empty vessel is filled with water, its frequency**
(a) increases (b) decreases
(c) remains the same (d) None of these

4. **If the temperature increases, then what happens the frequency of the sound produced by the organ pipe?**
(a) Increases (b) Decreases
(c) Unchanged (d) Not definite

5. **If n_1 is the resonant frequency of a pipe open at both ends and n_2 the resonant frequency of pipe open one end only. Both are vibrating in the fundamental mode and both pipes are of same length, then**
(a) $n_1 = n_2$ (b) $2n_1 = n_2$
(c) $n_1 = 2n_2$ (d) $3n_1 = 4n_2$

6. **A resonating column of air contains**
(a) stationary longitudinal waves
(b) stationary transverse waves
(c) transverse progressive waves
(d) longitudinal progressive waves

7. **Resonance is an example of**
(a) tuning fork (b) free vibration
(c) damped vibration (d) forced vibration

8. **With an opened end organ pipe of length l, the fundamental tone has a frequency**
(a) $\left(\frac{v}{2l}\right)$ and only even harmonics are present
(b) $\left(\frac{v}{2l}\right)$ and only odd harmonics are present
(c) $\left(\frac{v}{2l}\right)$ and even as well as odd harmonics are present
(d) $\left(\frac{v}{4l}\right)$ and only odd harmonics are present

9. **With a closed end organ pipe of length l, the fundamental tone has a frequency**
(a) $\left(\frac{v}{2l}\right)$ and all harmonics are present
(b) $\left(\frac{v}{4l}\right)$ and all harmonics are present
(c) $\left(\frac{v}{4l}\right)$ and only odd harmonics are present
(d) $\left(\frac{v}{4l}\right)$ and only even harmonics are present

10. There are two open organ pipes of exactly the same length and material but different radii. The frequencies of their fundamental notes will be
(a) wider pipe has lower frequency
(b) narrower pipe has lower frequency
(c) both the pipes have same frequency
(d) None of the above

11. A cylindrical tube, open at both ends, has a fundamental frequency n in air. The tube is dipped vertically in water so that half of it is in water. The fundamental frequency of the air column is now
(a) $\frac{n}{2}$ (b) $\frac{3n}{4}$
(c) n (d) $2n$

12. A tuning fork of frequency n is held near the open end of a tube which is closed at the other end and the length of the tube is adjusted until resonance occurs. If the two shortest lengths that produce resonance are l_1 and l_2, the speed of the sound is
(a) $n(l_2 - l_1)$ (b) $\frac{n(l_2 - l_1)}{2}$
(c) $2n(l_2 + l_1)$ (d) $2n(l_2 - l_1)$

13. An air column in a pipe, which is closed at one end, will be in resonance with a vibrating tuning fork of frequency 264 Hz, if the length of the column (in cm) is
(a) 31.25 (b) 62.50 (c) 93.75 (d) 125

14. In the open organ pipe, the fundamental frequency is 30 vibrations/s. If the organ pipe is closed, then the fundamental frequency will be
(a) 10 vibrations/s (b) 20 vibrations/s
(c) 30 vibrations/s (d) 15 vibrations/s

15. If an open organ pipe is sounded with a tuning fork having frequency 256 Hz resonance occurred at 35 cm and 105 cm, the velocity of sound is
(a) 360 m/s (b) 512 m/s
(c) 524 m/s (d) All of these

16. An organ pipe sounds a fundamental note of frequency of 230 Hz. If the speed of sound in air is 330 m/s, then the length of the pipe is nearly
(a) 0.25 m (b) 0.50 m (c) 0.75 m (d) 2.00 m

17. The end correction of a resonance column is 1.0 cm. If the shortest length resonating with a tuning fork is 15.0 cm, the next resonating length is
(a) 31 cm (b) 45 cm
(c) 46 cm (d) 47 cm

18. A closed tube has a frequency n. If its length is doubled and radius is halved, its frequency will become
(a) $\frac{n}{3}$ (b) $\frac{n}{2}$
(c) n (d) $2n$

19. A closed organ pipe and an open organ pipe have their first overtone identical in frequency. Their lengths are in the ratio
(a) 1 : 2 (b) 2 : 3
(c) 3 : 4 (d) 4 : 5

20. If λ_1, λ_2 and λ_3 are the wavelengths of the waves giving resonance with the fundamental, first and second overtones respectively of a closed organ pipe. Then, the ratio of wavelengths $\lambda_1 : \lambda_2 : \lambda_3$ is
(a) 1 : 3 : 5 (b) 1 : 2 : 3
(b) 5 : 3 : 1 (d) $1 : \frac{1}{3} : \frac{1}{5}$

21. The fundamental frequencies of an open and a closed tube, each of same length L with v as the speed of sound in air, respectively are
(a) $\frac{v}{2L}$ and $\frac{v}{L}$ (b) $\frac{v}{L}$ and $\frac{v}{2L}$
(c) $\frac{v}{2L}$ and $\frac{v}{4L}$ (d) $\frac{v}{4L}$ and $\frac{v}{2L}$

22. The vibrations of four air columns are represented in the figure below. The ratio of frequencies $n_p : n_q : n_r : n_s$ is

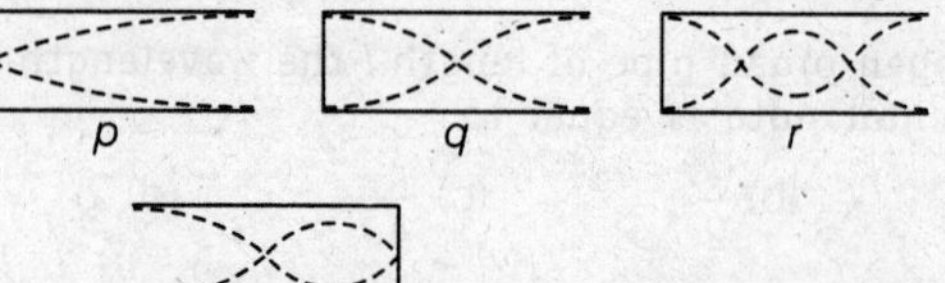

(a) 12 : 6 : 3 : 4 (b) 1 : 2 : 4 : 3
(c) 4 : 2 : 3 : 1 (d) 6 : 2 : 3 : 4

Answers

Level I

1. (a)	**2.** (c)	**3.** (c)	**4.** (b)	**5.** (b)	**6.** (b)	**7.** (b)	**8.** (c)	**9.** (a)	**10.** (a)

Level II

1. (d)	**2.** (a)	**3.** (a)	**4.** (a)	**5.** (c)	**6.** (a)	**7.** (d)	**8.** (c)	**9.** (c)	**10.** (c)
11. (c)	**12.** (d)	**13.** (c)	**14.** (d)	**15.** (a)	**16.** (c)	**17.** (d)	**18.** (b)	**19.** (c)	**20.** (d)
21. (c)	**22.** (b)								

Hints and Solutions

Level II

5. $n_1 = \frac{v}{2l}$ and $n_2 = \frac{v}{4l}$

$\therefore \quad n_1 = 2n_2$

11. For open pipe, $n = \frac{v}{2l}$

For closed pipe, $n' = \frac{v}{4l'} = \frac{v}{4\left(\frac{l}{2}\right)} = \frac{v}{2l}$

$\therefore \quad n' = n$

12. $n = \frac{v}{4l_1}$ and $n = \frac{3v}{4l_2}$

$\therefore \quad v = 4nl_1$ and $3v = 4nl_2$

$\Rightarrow \quad 2v = 4n(l_2 - l_1)$

$\Rightarrow \quad v = 2n(l_2 - l_1)$

13. Fundamental frequency for closed pipe

$\eta = \frac{v}{4l}$

$264 = \frac{v}{4l_1}$

$\therefore \quad l_1 = \frac{330 \times 100}{4 \times 264} = 31.25$

$l_2 = 3 \times 31.25 = 93.75$

14. $30 = v/2l$

For closed organ pipe,

$$n = \frac{v}{4l} = \frac{1}{2}\left(\frac{v}{2l}\right) = \frac{1}{2}(30) = 15 \text{ vibrations/s}$$

15. $v = 2n(l_2 - l_1) = 2 \times 256 \times (1.05 - 0.35)$

$= 2 \times 256 \times 0.70 = 360$ m/s

16. In case of fundamental mode, $l = \frac{\lambda}{2}$

Here, $\lambda = \frac{330}{230}$

$\therefore \quad l = \frac{330}{(230 \times 2)} = 0.72 \text{ m} \approx 0.75 \text{ m}$

17. For second resonance, $l = \frac{3\lambda}{4}$

$\lambda = (15 + 1) \times 4 = 64$ cm

$\therefore \quad l = \frac{3 \times 64}{4} = 48$ cm

Length of the tube = l – End correction = 48 – 1 = 47 cm

18. $n = \frac{v}{4l}$ and $n' = \frac{v}{4(2l)}$

$n' = \frac{n}{2}$

19. For first overtone of closed pipe, $n_2 = \frac{3v}{4l_1}$

For first overtone of open pipe, $n_2 = \frac{2v}{2l_2}$

$\therefore \quad \frac{3v}{4l_1} = \frac{2v}{2l_2}$

$\Rightarrow \quad \frac{l_1}{l_2} = \frac{3}{4}$

20. The first three wavelengths of closed organ pipes are shown in figure.

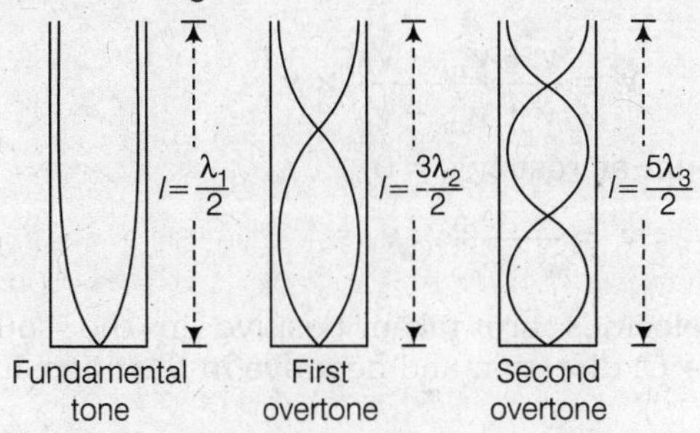

Here, $l = \frac{\lambda_1}{2} \Rightarrow \lambda_1 = 2l$

$l = \frac{3\lambda_2}{2} \Rightarrow \lambda_2 = \left(\frac{2l}{3}\right)$

$l = \frac{5\lambda_3}{2} \Rightarrow \lambda_3 = \left(\frac{2l}{5}\right)$

$\therefore \quad \lambda_1 : \lambda_2 : \lambda_3 = 2l : \frac{2l}{3} : \frac{2l}{5}$

$\Rightarrow \quad \lambda_1 : \lambda_2 : \lambda_3 = 1 : \frac{1}{3} : \frac{1}{5}$

21. For an open pipe, fundamental frequency is $n_0 = \frac{v}{2L}$

For closed pipe, fundamental frequency is $n_c = \frac{v}{4L}$

22. $n_p = \frac{v}{4l}$, $n_q = \frac{v}{2l}$, $n_r = \frac{2v}{2l}$ and $n_s = \frac{3v}{4l}$

$\therefore \quad n_p : n_p : n_r : n_s = 1 : 2 : 4 : 3$

28

Doppler Effect

Doppler Effect in Sound

The phenomenon of the change in apparent pitch of sound due to relative motion between the source of sound and the observer is called Doppler effect. If v, v_0, v_s and v_m are the velocities of sound, observer, source and medium (in the direction of sound) respectively, then the apparent frequency is given by

$$\nu' = \frac{v + v_m - v_0}{v + v_m - v_s} \times \nu$$

For the medium at rest ($v_m = 0$),

$$\nu' = \frac{v - v_0}{v - v_s} \times \nu$$

Here, the velocities are taken positive in the source to observer ($S \to O$) direction and negative in the opposite ($O \to S$) direction.

Special Cases

***Case* I.** When the source moves towards the stationary observer,

$$\nu' = \frac{v}{v - v_s} \times \nu \qquad (\nu' > \nu)$$

***Case* II.** When the source moves away from the stationary observer,

$$\nu' = \frac{v}{v + v_s} \times \nu \qquad (\nu' < \nu)$$

***Case* III.** When the observer moves towards the stationary source,

$$\nu' = \frac{v + v_0}{v} \times \nu \qquad (\nu' > \nu)$$

***Case* IV.** When the observer moves away from the stationary source,

$$\nu' = \frac{v - v_0}{v} \times \nu \qquad (\nu' < \nu)$$

***Case* V.** When both source and observer move towards each other,

$$\nu' = \frac{v + v_0}{v - v_s} \times \nu \qquad (\nu' > \nu)$$

***Case* VI.** When both source and observer move away each other,

$$\nu' = \frac{v - v_0}{v + v_s} \times \nu \qquad (\nu' < \nu)$$

***Case* VII.** When sources moves towards observer and observer away from the source,

$$\nu' = \frac{v - v_0}{v - v_s} \times \nu$$

***Case* VIII.** When source moves away from observer and observer towards the source,

$$\nu' = \frac{v + v_0}{v + v_s} \times \nu$$

Application of Doppler's Effect

- It is used to find the location of a moving aeroplane in the air.
- It is used to find the velocity of submarine inside water.

MASTER FORMULA

In order to solve numerical problems related to Doppler's effect, the following formula should be keep in memory.

$$\nu' = \left(\frac{v \pm v_0}{v \pm v_s}\right) \nu$$

Here, look at the following points

- Here, sources are taken to be left and the audience in right side.
- When source and audience both are constant, then the values of v_0 and v_s taken to be zero.
- Take $v_0 = + v_0$, when audiences are moving towards left.
- Take $v_0 = - v_0$, when audiences are moving towards right.
- Take $v_s = + v_s$, when sources are moving towards left of the audiences.
- Take $v_s = - v_s$, when sources are moving towards audiences.

Practice Questions

Level I

1. The law applicable for determining the apparent change in frequency, when a source and an observer are in motion is

(a) Doppler's law (b) Huygen's law
(c) Newton's law (d) Galileo's law

2. Doppler's effect in sound is produced when the source and observer are

(a) moving (b) in relative motion
(c) stationary (d) resonance phenomenon

3. The Doppler's effect is not observed if

(a) the source and observer both are at rest
(b) the source is still and the observer is in motion
(c) the source is in motion and observer is still
(d) the source and observer both are in motion

4. The Doppler's effect is applicable for

(a) light waves only (b) sound waves only
(c) Both (a) and (b) (d) None of these

5. Change in frequency due to Doppler's effect is produced, when

(a) the source and the observer are moving in the same direction
(b) the source and the observer are both at rest
(c) there is a relative motion between the source and the observer
(d) resultant motion between the source and the observer

6. To a stationary man the frequency of a sound source moving towards the man appears to be

(a) lower than the original frequency
(b) same as the original frequency
(c) higher than the original frequency
(d) lower as well higher than the original frequency depending upon the speed of the source

7. When a source of sound is in motion towards a stationary observer, the effect observed is

(a) increase in velocity of sound
(b) decrease in velocity of sound
(c) increase in frequency of sound
(d) increase in velocity as well as frequency of sound

8. The observer is moving away from a stationary source of sound emitting waves of constant frequency, the apparent frequency will

(a) increase
(b) decrease
(c) first increase and then decrease
(d) first decrease and then increase

9. A source of sound and an observer are moving away from each other. The apparent pitch will

(a) decrease (b) increase
(c) same as actual frequency (d) None of these

10. In case if two engines cross each other, the observer will notice

(a) a fall in pitch
(b) an increase in pitch
(c) no change in pitch of the sounding body
(d) resonance

Level II

1. An observer approaches a source of sound with a velocity v_0. Sound travels with a velocity v. If n be the pitch of the source of sound, the apparent pitch of the sound heard by the observer is

(a) $\left(\frac{v}{v+v_0}\right)n$ (b) $\left(\frac{v+v_0}{v}\right)n$ (c) $\left(\frac{v-v_0}{v}\right)n$ (d) $\left(\frac{v}{v-v_0}\right)n$

2. A source of sound is moving away from the stationary observer with a velocity v_s. Velocity of sound is v. If n be the pitch of the source of sound, then the apparent pitch of sound heard by the observer is

(a) $\left(\frac{v-v_s}{v}\right)n$ (b) $\left(\frac{v+v_s}{v}\right)n$ (c) $\left(\frac{v}{v+v_s}\right)n$ (d) $\left(\frac{v}{v-v_s}\right)n$

3. Velocity of sound is v. A source moves away from the observer with a velocity v_s and the observer moves towards the source with a velocity v_0. If n be the pitch of the source of sound, then the apparent pitch of sound heard by observer is

(a) $\left(\frac{v+v_0}{v+v_s}\right)n$ (b) $\left(\frac{v-v_0}{v+v_s}\right)n$
(c) $\left(\frac{v-v_0}{v-v_s}\right)n$ (d) $\left(\frac{v+v_0}{v-v_0}\right)n$

4. A sound source is moving towards a stationary observer with $\left(\frac{1}{10}\right)$ of the speed of sound. The ratio of apparent to real frequency is

(a) $\frac{10}{9}$ (b) $\frac{11}{10}$
(c) $\left(\frac{11}{10}\right)^2$ (d) $\left(\frac{9}{10}\right)^2$

5. Suppose that the speed of sound in air at a given temperature is 400 m/s. An engine blows a whistle at 1200 Hz frequency. It is approaching an observer at the speed of 100 m/s. What is the apparent frequency as heard by the observer?

(a) 600 Hz (b) 1200 Hz
(c) 1500 Hz (d) 1600 Hz

6. The frequency of a train whistle is 360 Hz. As the train passes through a station the frequency appears to be 400 Hz to a man who is standing on the station platform. If the speed of sound in air is 340 m/s, the speed of train is

(a) 20 m/s (b) 34 m/s
(c) 36 m/s (d) 39 m/s

7. A source of frequency 512 cyclic/s moves towards a listener with a speed of 100 m/s. If the velocity of sound in air is 350 m/s, the frequency heard by listener is

(a) 7168 s^{-1} (b) 7.168 s^{-1}
(c) 716.8 s^{-1} (d) 71.68 s^{-1}

8. An object producing a pitch of 400 Hz is moving towards a stationary person with a velocity of 200 m/s. The velocity of sound is 300 m/s. The frequency of sound heard by stationary person is

(a) 96 Hz (b) 240 Hz
(c) 1200 Hz (d) 960 Hz

9. At what speed should a source of sound move so that observer finds the apparent frequency equal to half of the original frequency?

(a) $\frac{v}{2}$ (b) $2v$
(c) $\frac{v}{4}$ (d) v

10. Two persons A and B each carrying a source of sound of frequency n, are standing a few metres apart in a quiet field. A starts moving towards B with a speed v_0. If v be the speed of sound, the number of beats heard per second by A will be

(a) $\frac{nv_0}{v}$ (b) $\frac{nv}{v_0}$ (c) nv_0v (d) $\frac{2nv}{v_0}$

11. An engine driver moving towards a wall with a velocity 50 m/s emits a note of 1.2 kHz. Speed of sound in air is 350 m/s. The frequency of the note after reflection from the wall as heard by the engine driver is

(a) 1.2 kHz (b) 1.6 kHz
(c) 0.24 kHz (d) 2.4 kHz

12. A siren emitting sound of 1000 Hz is moving away from us towards a high hill with velocity 10 m/s. The frequency of sound reflected from the hill will be ($v = 330$ m/s)

(a) 100 Hz (b) 130 Hz
(c) 1031.25 Hz (d) 1200 Hz

Answers

Level I

1. (a)	2. (b)	3. (a)	4. (c)	5. (c)	6. (c)	7. (c)	8. (b)	9. (a)	10. (a)

Level II

1. (b)	2. (c)	3. (a)	4. (a)	5. (d)	6. (b)	7. (c)	8. (c)	9. (d)	10. (a)
11. (b)	12. (c)								

Hints and Solutions

Level II

4. $n' = n\left(\frac{v}{v - v_s}\right) \quad \therefore \quad \frac{n'}{n} = \left[\frac{v}{v - \left(\frac{v}{100}\right)}\right] = \frac{10}{9}$

5. When engine is approaching the observer

$$n' = \left(\frac{v}{v - v_s}\right)n = \left(\frac{400}{400 - 100}\right) \times 1200 = 1600 \text{ Hz}$$

6. $n' = \left(\frac{v}{v - v_s}\right)n$

$$400 = \left(\frac{340}{340 - v_s}\right)360$$

$\Rightarrow \quad 400 \times 340 - 400v_s = 340 \times 360$

$\Rightarrow \quad 340[400 - 360] = 400v_s$

$\Rightarrow \quad \frac{340 \times 40}{400} = v_s \Rightarrow v_s = 34$ m/s

7. $n' = \left(\frac{v}{v - v_s}\right)n = \left(\frac{350}{350 - 100}\right)512 = \frac{350 \times 512}{250} = 716.8 \text{ s}^{-1}$

8. $n' = \left(\frac{v}{v - v_s}\right)n = \left(\frac{300}{300 - 200}\right) \times 400 = 1200$ Hz

9. Here, $n' = \frac{nv}{(v + v_s)}$

($\therefore$ The given situation corresponds when source moves away from observer.)

$$\frac{n}{2} = \frac{nv}{(v + v_s)} \Rightarrow 2v = v + v_s \Rightarrow v_s = v$$

10. The apparent frequency received by A due to the source of B is given by

$$n' = n\left(\frac{v + v_0}{v}\right) \text{(Observer moving towards source)}$$

A also hears the sound of his source whose frequency is n.

$\therefore$ Beat frequency $= n' - n = n\left(\frac{v + v_0}{v}\right) - n = \frac{nv_0}{v}$

11. $n' = \left(\frac{v + v_0}{v - v_s}\right)n$

$$\therefore n' = \left(\frac{350 + 50}{350 - 50}\right)1.2 = \frac{400}{300} \times 1.2 \simeq 1.6 \text{ kHz}$$

12.

S — v_S → Stationary observer; Hill; ← v_S — S (image)

$$n' = \frac{nv}{v - v_s} = \frac{1000 \times 330}{330 - 10} = 1031.25 \text{ Hz}$$

29

Musical Sound and Ultrasound

Musical Sound

A musical sound consists of quick, regular and periodic succession of compressions and rarefactions without a sudden change in amplitude. It produces pleasing effect on the ears.

Noise

A noise consists of slow, irregular and non-periodic succession of compressions and rarfractions, that may have a sudden change in amplitude. It produces non-pleasing effect on the ears.

Intensity of Sound (*I*)

The intensity of sound at any point may be defined as the amount of sound energy passing per unit time per unit area around that point in a perpendicular direction.

Zero Level or Threshold of Hearing (I_0)

The lowest intensity of sound that can be perceived by the human ear is called threshold of hearing.

For a sound of frequency 1 kHz, it is found that the threshold of hearing is $10^{-12}\ \text{W/m}^2$.

Characteristics of a Musical Sound

These are

Pitch It is the characteristics of musical sound that helps the listener in distinguishing a shrill note from a grave (flat or dull) one. It depends on frequency.

Quality It is the characteristics of the musical sound that distinguishes between two sounds of same pitch and loudness from one another. It depends on the number or intensity of overtones.

Loudness The sensation of hearing which enables us to distiguish between a loud and a faint sound, is called loudness. It depends on intensity.

Units of Loudness

The unit of loudness of a sound is bel. The loudness of a sound is said to be 1 bel, if its intensity is 10 times that of the threshold of hearing.

The loudness of a sound of intensity I is given by

$$L = \log_{10} \frac{I}{I_0}$$

Where, I_0 is threshold of hearing. It is called Weber-Fechner law.

The practical and a smaller unit to loudness is decibel (dB).

$$1 \text{ decibel} = \frac{1}{10} \text{ bel}$$

In decibels, the loudness of a sound of intensity I is given by

$$L = 10 \log_{10} \frac{I}{I_0}$$

Reverberation

The persistence of a sound in a big hall due to repeated reflections from the walls, ceiling and floor of the wall is known as reverberation.

A short reverberation is desirable in a concert hall, where music is being played, as it boosts the sound level. But excessive reverberation is highly undesirable, because sound becomes blurred, distorted and confusing due to overlapping of different sounds.

To reduce reverberation, the roof and walls of the auditorium are generally covered with sound absorbent materials like compressed fibre board, rough plaster or draperies. The seat materials are also selected on the basis of their sound absorbing properties.

Interval between Two Notes

The ratio of the frequencies of two notes is called interval between them. Two notes are said to be in unison if their frequencies are equal, that is interval between them is 1 : 1. *Some other common intervals found useful in producing musical sound are as follows*

(a) Octave (1 : 2)

(b) Majortone (8 : 9)

(c) Minortone (9 : 10)

(d) Semitone (15 : 16)

The interval between any two notes is obtained by multiplying the various intervening intervals.

Musical Scale

A series of notes arranged such that their fundamental frequencies have definite ratios is called a musical scale.

Major Diatonic Scale

The eight notes of major diatonicscale starting with 256 as keynote along with their Helmholtz and Indian notation are as below

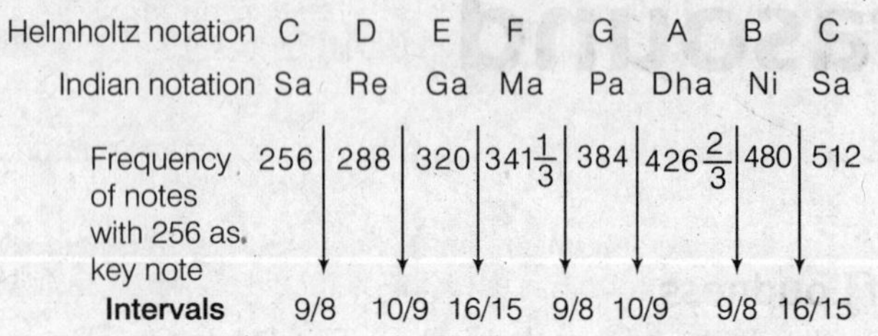

Frequency Range of Sound Waves

(i) Infrasonic Wave

Sounds of frequencies below 20 Hz are called infrasonic wave. Our ears are not able to hear this range of sounds.

(ii) Audible Wave

Sounds of frequencies betwen 20 Hz to 20000 Hz are called audible wave. Our ears able to hear this range of sounds.

(iii) Ultrasonic Wave

Frequencies higher than 20000 Hz are called ultrasonic wave (ultrasound). Ears of human being are not able to hear this range of sounds but some animals ears like bats, dog, cat etc., are able to hear this range of sound.

Note The wavelength of ultrasonic wave in air is less than 1.66 cm.

Use of Ultrasonic Wave (Ultrasound)

- Determination of the velocity of sound in liquid.
- Ultrasound can be used to detect cracks and flows in metal blocks.
- In study of crystals.
- To measurement of depth of echo.
- In chemical effect.
- In industrial use.
- In symbol of vision.
- Utilize by medical physician.

Practice Questions

1. Intensity of sound has
(a) an objective existence (b) a subjective existence
(c) no existence (d) All are true

2. Loudness of sound has
(a) an objective existence (b) a subjective existence
(c) no existence (d) All are true

3. Pitch of a sound depends upon its
(a) wavelength
(b) frequency
(c) amplitude
(d) periodicity and regularity

4. Loudness of sound depends upon its
(a) wavelength (b) frequency
(c) amplitude (d) overtones

5. Quality of sound depends upon its
(a) wavelength (b) frequency
(c) amplitude (d) overtone

6. Loudness of sound is measured in
(a) bel (b) erg
(c) cycles/s (d) weber

7. Intensity of sound is proportional to
(a) A^2 (b) $\left(\frac{1}{A^2}\right)$
(c) A (d) A^4

8. Pitch of a note is directly proportional to
(a) frequency of a body
(b) loudness
(c) size
(d) amplitude

9. Decibel is
(a) musical instrument
(b) musical note
(c) measure of sound level
(d) the wavelength of noise

10. The relationship between the objective measurement of intensity of sound I and the subjective response called loudness L is given by
(a) $L = I$ (b) $L = K \log I$
(c) $I = K \log L$ (d) $L = K \log I^2$

11. The intensity level of a sound having intensity I is defined in terms of I_0 the threshold intensity of hearing as
(a) intensity level $= \frac{I}{I_0}$ decibels
(b) intensity level $= I \times I_0$ decibels
(c) intensity level $\left(\frac{I}{I_0}\right) \times 100$ decibels
(d) intensity level $= 10 \log_{10} \left(\frac{I}{I_0}\right)$ decibels

12. **A musical scale is constructed by providing intermediate frequencies between a note and its octave which**
(a) form an arithmetic progression
(b) form a geometric progression
(c) bear a simple ratio with their neighbours
(d) form a harmonic progression

13. **In a harmonium the intermediate notes between a note and its octave form**
(a) an arithmetic progression
(b) a geometric progression
(c) a harmonic progression
(d) an exponential progression

14. **Those persons who have sweeter sound have**
(a) greater number of overtones
(b) lesser number of overtones
(c) no overtone
(d) Neither more nor less overtones

15. **In the musical *sa, re, ga,...***
(a) the frequency of the note is *sa* > *re* > *ga*
(b) the frequency of the note is *sa* < *ga*
(c) the frequency of all the notes is same
(d) the frequency decreases in the sequence *sa, re, ga*

16. **On the diatonic scale when *sa* = 24, then other notes are**
(a) 27, 30, 32, 36, 40, 45, 48
(b) 24, 32, 35, 38, 40, 45, 48
(c) 27, 29, 30, 32, 35, 38, 48
(d) 30, 32, 34, 36, 40, 45, 48

17. **An air box attached to a musical instrument increases the**
(a) pitch of the sound
(b) intensity of the sound
(c) quality of the sound
(d) shrillness of the sound

18. **Major diatonic scale is so called because**
(a) the interval major tone is repeated larger number of times
(b) major frequencies are used
(c) major issues are involved
(d) minor issues are less in number

19. **The same notes being played on the Sitar and Veena differ in**
(a) pitch (b) quality
(c) Both (a) and (b) (d) None of these

20. **The walls of the halls built for music concerns should**
(a) amplify sound (b) reflect sound
(c) transmit sound (d) absorb sound

21. **Decibal is unit of**
(a) intensity of light (b) X-rays radiation capacity
(c) sound loudness (d) energy of radiation

22. **The term reverberation time is generally understood to be the reverberation time at which of the following frequencies?**
(a) 2048 Hz (b) 512 Hz (c) 1024 Hz (d) 256 Hz

23. **When we hear a sound, we can identify its source from**
(a) amplitude of sound
(b) intensity of sound
(c) wavelength of sound
(d) overtones present in the sound

24. **Radar waves are sent towards a moving aeroplane and the reflected waves are received by radar. When aeroplane is moving towards radar, then the wavelength of reflected wave**
(a) decreases (b) increases
(c) remains same (d) Either (a) or (b)

Answers

1. (a)	**2.** (b)	**3.** (b)	**4.** (c)	**5.** (d)	**6.** (a)	**7.** (a)	**8.** (a)	**9.** (c)	**10.** (b)
11. (d)	**12.** (c)	**13.** (b)	**14.** (a)	**15.** (b)	**16.** (a)	**17.** (b)	**18.** (a)	**19.** (b)	**20.** (d)
21. (c)	**22.** (a)	**23.** (d)	**24.** (a)						

30

Gauss' Theorem

Electric Flux

The electric flux through a surface held inside an electric field represents the total number of electric lines of force crossing the surface in a direction normal to the surface.

Electric flux is a scalar quantity and is denoted by ϕ.

Thus, electric flux linked with a surface in an electric field may be defined as the surface integral of the electric field over that surface.

The unit of electric flux is Nm^2C^{-1}.

Note The electric flux through a surface is denoted by ϕ, while the electric flux through a closed surface is denoted by Φ. Thus, if the surface S is a closed surface, then the total electric flux through the closed surface is given by

$$\Phi = \oint_S \mathbf{E} \cdot d\mathbf{S} = \oint_S E_n dS$$

If $\theta = 0 \Rightarrow \phi = E\, dS$, $\theta = 90° \Rightarrow \phi = 0$, $\theta = 180° \Rightarrow \phi = -Eds$

Gauss' Theorem

It states that the total electric flux through a closed surface enclosing a charge is equal to $\frac{1}{\varepsilon_0}$ times the magnitude of the charge enclosed.

Here, ε_0 is the absolute permittivity of the free space.

If a closed surface S encloses an electric charge q, then according to Gauss' theorem, the total electric flux through the closed surface is given by

$$\Phi = \frac{q}{\varepsilon_0} \quad \text{...(i)}$$

By definition, the total electric flux through the closed surface S is given by

$$\Phi = \int_S \vec{E} \cdot d\vec{S}$$

Where, $\vec{E}$ is electric field at the area element $d\vec{S}$.

Therefore, Gauss' theorem may be expressed as

$$\int_S \vec{E} \cdot d\vec{S} = \frac{q}{\varepsilon_0} \quad \text{...(ii)}$$

Hence, Gauss' theorem may also be stated as below

If a closed surface enclosed a charge, then surface integral of the electric field (due to the enclosed charge) over the closed surface is equal to $\frac{1}{\varepsilon_0}$ times the charge enclosed.

Note If inside a closed surface $q_1, -q_2, -q_3$ and q_4, charges are enclosed the net charge will be q_{net}

$q_{net} = q_1 - q_2 - q_3 + q_4$

If a charge is outside a closed surface, then total electric flux passing through that closed surface is zero.

Applications of Gauss' Theorem

S.No.	System	Electric Field Intensity
1.	A ring of charge	$E = \frac{1}{4\pi\varepsilon_0} \frac{qx}{(R^2 + x^2)^{\frac{3}{2}}}$
2.	A disc of charge	$E = \frac{\sigma}{2\varepsilon_0}\left[1 - \frac{x}{\sqrt{x^2 + R^2}}\right]$
3.	Infinite sheet of charge	$E = \frac{\sigma}{2\varepsilon_0}$
4.	Infinitely long line of charge	$E = \frac{\lambda}{2\pi\varepsilon_0 r}$
5.	Finite line of charge	$E_{\perp} = \frac{\lambda}{4\pi\varepsilon_0 x}(\sin\alpha + \sin\beta)$ $E_{11} = \frac{\lambda}{4\pi\varepsilon_0 x}(\cos\alpha - \cos\beta)$
6.	Charged spherical shell 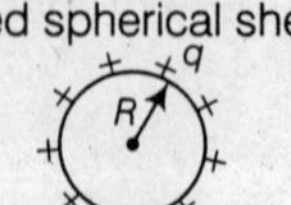	(a) Inside, $0 \le r \le R$, $E = 0$ (b) Outside, $r \ge R$, $E = \frac{q}{4\pi\varepsilon_0 r^2}$
7.	Solid sphere of charge	(a) Inside, $0 \le r \le R$, $E = \frac{\rho r}{3\varepsilon_0}$ (b) Outside, $r \ge R$, $E = \frac{\rho R}{3\varepsilon_0}\left(\frac{R}{r}\right)^2$

Potential energy of conductor per unit volume,

$$V = \frac{\sigma^2}{2\varepsilon_0} = \frac{1}{2}\varepsilon_0 E^2$$

Variation of E and V

(i) Point charge

(a) $E \propto \frac{1}{r^2}$ (b) $V \propto \frac{1}{r}$

(ii) Dipole

(a) $E \propto \frac{1}{r^3}$ (b) $V \propto \frac{1}{r^2}$

(iii) Sphere

(a) $E \propto \frac{1}{r^2}$ (b) $V \propto \frac{1}{r}$

(iv) Cylender

(a) $E \propto \frac{1}{r}$ (b) $V \propto \log \frac{1}{r}$

(v) Plane sheet

(a) $E \propto \frac{1}{\varepsilon_0}$ (b) $V \propto \varepsilon_0$

Practice Questions

Level I

1. According to Gauss' law

(a) $\phi_E = \frac{q}{\varepsilon_0}$ (b) $\phi_E = \frac{\varepsilon_0}{q}$

(c) $\phi_E = \frac{1}{\varepsilon_0 q}$ (d) $\phi_E = q\varepsilon_0$

2. If a point charge q is enclosed in a closed surface, then the electric flux of the surface will be

(a) $\frac{2q}{\varepsilon_0}$ (b) $\frac{q}{\varepsilon_0}$

(c) 0 (d) None of these

3. If an area A is placed in an electric field, then the electric flux ϕ passing through the area A is given by

(a) $\phi = E \times A$ (b) $\phi = E \cdot A$

(c) $\phi = EA$ (d) $\phi = \frac{E}{A}$

4. For a given surface, Gauss' law is written is such a way that $\oint \vec{\mathbf{E}} \cdot dA = 0.1$, for which we conclude that

(a) $\vec{\mathbf{E}}$ on the surface will be zero

(b) flux in the surface is going outside only

(c) $\vec{\mathbf{E}}$ on the every point of the surface is perpendicular to the label

(d) total electric flux passing through the surface is zero

5. The tendency of compression due to charging one drop of liquid is

(a) increases (b) remains constant

(c) decreases (d) None of these

6. A hollow sphere of radius r m and charge on it is q C. The electric potential at the centre of them will be

(a) zero (b) $\frac{qr}{4\pi\varepsilon_0}$ (c) $\frac{q}{4\pi\varepsilon_0 r^2}$ (d) $\frac{q}{4\pi\varepsilon_0 r}$

7. The distance r along with variation of potential V is an electric field $E = 0$ will be

(a) $V \propto r$

(b) $V \propto \frac{1}{r^2}$

(c) $V \propto \frac{1}{r}$

(d) The value of V does not depend on r

8. The electric potential inside a positively charged hollow spherical conductor will be

(a) zero

(b) positive and disimilar

(c) positive and similar

(d) negative and similar

9. At the centre of charged hollow spherical conductor

(a) the electric field and potential both are zero

(b) the electric field will be zero but not potential

(c) the potential will be zero but not eletric field

(d) both of the electric field and potential does not zero

10. The dimensional formula of the electric flux density is

(a) $[MLT^{-3}A^{-1}]$ (b) $[ML^2T^2A^{-3}]$

(c) $[MLT^{-3}A]$ (d) $[M^{-1}LT^{-3}A^{-1}]$

Level II

1. Electric field varies as r^{-3} due to

(a) a point charge

(b) an infinite line charge

(c) an electric dipole

(d) an infinite plane sheet of charge

2. Electric field varies as r^{-1} due to

(a) a point charge

(b) a quadrupole

(c) an infinite line charge

(d) an infinite plane sheet of charge

3. The electric field inside a spherical shell of uniform surface charge density is
(a) zero
(b) uniform
(c) non-uniform
(d) proportional to distance from the centre

4. A spherical shell of radius R has a charge $+q$ units. The electric field due to the shell at a point
(a) inside is zero and varies as r^{-1} outside it
(b) inside is constant and varies as r^{-2} outside it
(c) inside is zero and varies as r^{-2} outside it
(d) inside is constant and varies r^{-1} outside it

5. A sphere of charge of radius R has uniform volume charge density. The electric field due to the sphere of charge at a point
(a) inside varies as r^{-2} and as r outside it
(b) inside varies as r and as r^{-2} outside it
(c) inside is zero and varies as r outside it
(d) inside is constant and varies as r^{-2} outside it

6. A charge q is placed at the corner of a cube of side a. The electric flux through the cube is
(a) $\frac{q}{\varepsilon_0}$ (b) $\frac{q}{3\varepsilon_0}$
(c) $\frac{q}{6\varepsilon_0}$ (d) $\frac{q}{8\varepsilon_0}$

7. If the electric flux through a closed surface is zero, then
(a) the electric field must be zero everywhere on the surface
(b) the electric field may be zero everywhere on the surface
(c) the charge inside the surface must be zero
(d) the charge in the vicinity of the surface must be zero

8. An electric dipole is placed inside a hollow sphere at its centre. Then,
(a) the electric flux through the sphere is zero
(b) the electric field is zero at every point on the surface of the sphere
(c) the electric field is non-zero at every point on the surface of sphere
(d) the electric field is non-zero at every point on the surface of the sphere

9. The surface density of charges at the surface of the two spherical conductor of radii R_1 and R_2 are equal. The ratio of the electric field intensities on surfaces be
(a) $\frac{R_1^2}{R_2^2}$ (b) $\frac{R_1}{R_2}$ (c) 1:1 (d) $\frac{R_2^2}{R_1^2}$

10. R_1 and R_2 are the radii of two spheres. Charge on it are q_1 and q_2, respectively. If potential on the surface of the spheres be same, then the ratio of q_1 and q_2 will
(a) $R_1 : R_2$ (b) $R_2^2 : R_1^2$
(c) $R_2 : R_1$ (d) None of these

11. The surface density of charges at the surface of two spherical conductor of radii R_1 and R_2 are equal, the ratio of potentials on its surfaces will be
(a) $R_1^2 : R_2^2$ (b) $R_1 : R_2$ (c) 1:1 (d) $R_2 : R_1$

12. An electric charge of 17.7×10^{-4} C is equally spread on a thin layer of area 200 m^2. The electric field intensity in air at a distance of 20 cm from it will
(a) $2 \times 10^5 \frac{N}{C}$ (b) $5 \times 10^5 \frac{N}{C}$
(c) $3 \times 10^5 \frac{N}{C}$ (d) None of these

13. A metallic hollow sphere of radius 30 cm and charge on it is 500μC. What will be the electric field intensity at 1 m apart from the centre of sphere?
(a) $4.5 \times 10^6 \frac{N}{C}$ (b) $2.5 \times 10^6 \frac{N}{C}$
(c) $5 \times 10^6 \frac{N}{C}$ (d) $5.5 \times 10^6 \frac{N}{C}$

14. Surface charged density of an equally charged spherical conductor of radius 1.2 m is $16 \mu C m^{-2}$. The charge on sphere and net electric flux passing through the sphere will be
(a) 2.9×10^{-4} C and 1.88×10^7 Nm^{2}C^{-1}
(b) 2.9×10^{-4} C and 3.28×10^7 Nm^{2}C^{-1}
(c) 1.88×10^{-4} C anc 2.9×10^7 Nm^{2}C^{-1}
(d) None of the above

15. The electric potential on the surface of a nucleus ($z = 50$) of radius 9×10^{-15} m will be
(a) 80V (b) 9V (c) 9×10^{16} V (d) 8×10^6 V

Answers

Level I

1. (a)	2. (b)	3. (b)	4. (d)	5. (c)	6. (d)	7. (d)	8. (c)	9. (b)	10. (a)

Level II

1. (c)	2. (c)	3. (a)	4. (c)	5. (b)	6. (d)	7. (b)	8. (d,a)	9. (d)	10. (a)
11. (b)	12. (b)	13. (a)	14. (b)	15. (d)					

Hints and Solutions

Level II

10. $V_1 = \frac{1}{4\pi\varepsilon_0}\frac{q_1}{R_1}$

and $$V_2 = \frac{1}{4\pi\varepsilon_0}\frac{q_2}{R_2}$$

$\because$ $$V_1 = V_2$$

$\therefore$ $$\frac{q_1}{R_1} = \frac{q_2}{R_2}$$

$\Rightarrow$ $$\frac{q_1}{q_2} = \frac{R_1}{R_2}$$

11. Surfaces density of charge,

$$\sigma = \frac{q_1}{4\pi R_1^2} = \frac{q_2}{4\pi R_2^2}, \ V_1 = \frac{1}{4\pi\varepsilon_0}\frac{q_1}{R_1}$$

and $$V_2 = \frac{1}{4\pi\varepsilon_0}\frac{q_2}{R_2}$$

$\therefore$ $$\frac{V_1}{V_2} = \frac{q_1}{q_2} \times \frac{R_2}{R_1} = \frac{\sigma 4\pi R_1^2}{\sigma 4\pi R_2^2} \times \frac{R_2}{R_1} = \frac{R_1}{R_2}$$

12. Here, $q = 17.7 \times 10^{-4}$ C and area of layer,

$$A = 200 \text{ m}^2$$

$\therefore$ Surface density of charge on layer,

$$\sigma = \frac{q}{A} = \frac{17.7 \times 10^{-4}}{200}$$

$$= 8.85 \times 10^{-6} \frac{\text{C}}{\text{m}^2}$$

Near electric field intensity at 20 cm apart from it.

$$E = \frac{\sigma}{2\varepsilon_0} = \frac{8.85 \times 10^{-6}}{2 \times 8.85 \times 10^{-12}} = 5 \times 10^5 \frac{\text{N}}{\text{C}}$$

13. Here, $R = 30$ cm $= 0.30$ m

$$q = 500\,\mu\text{ C} = 500 \times 10^{-6}\text{ C} = 5 \times 10^{-4}\text{ C}$$

Here, $r = 1\text{m} > R$, hence observing point outside the sphere.

$\therefore$ $$E = \frac{1}{4\pi\varepsilon_0}\left(\frac{q}{r^2}\right) = 9 \times 10^9\left(\frac{5 \times 10^{-4}}{1^2}\right)$$

$$= 4.5 \times 10^6 \frac{\text{N}}{\text{C}}$$

14. Here, $r = 1.2$ m

$$\sigma = 16\,\mu\text{Cm}^{-2} = 16 \times 16^{-6}\text{ Cm}^{-2}$$

$$\sigma = \frac{q}{4\pi r^2}$$

$\therefore$ $$q = \sigma \times 4\pi r^2$$

$$= 16 \times 10^{-6} \times 4 \times \frac{22}{7} \times (1.2)^2$$

$$= 2.9 \times 10^{-4}\text{ C}$$

$$\phi = \frac{q}{\varepsilon_0} = \frac{2.9 \times 10^{-4}}{8.85 \times 10^{-12}}$$

$$= 3.28 \times 10^7\text{ Nm}^2\text{C}^{-1}$$

15. Here, $V = \frac{1}{4\pi\varepsilon_0}\frac{q}{R}$, where $q = Ze$

Here, $Z = 50$

$$e = 1.6 \times 10^{-19}\text{ C}$$

$$R = 9 \times 10^{-15}\text{ m}$$

$\therefore$ $$V = \frac{9 \times 10^9 \times 50 \times 1.6 \times 10^{-19}}{9 \times 10^{-15}}$$

$$= 8 \times 10^6\text{ V}$$

31

Electrical Capacitance

Conductors and Insulators

Conductors are those through which electric charge can easily flow, while insulators are those through which electric charge is difficult to flow.

Dielectric and Electric Polarization

A dielectric is an insulating material in which all the electrons are tightly bound to the nuclei of the atoms. Thus, there are no free electrons to carry current. Hence, electrical conductivity of a dielectric is very low.

Polar and Non-polar Dielectrics

We know that in an atom, the negative charge in the form of electron cloud is distributed around the nucleus having equal positive charge. As such, in an atom or molecule of a dielectric, the centres of gravity of the positive and negative charges may or may not coincide and likewise the atoms or molecules of the dielectric are termed as non-polar or polar.

Non-polar Dielectric

A dielectric, in the atoms or molecules of which, the centres of gravity of positive and negative charges coincide, is called a non-polar dielectric.

Polar Dielectric

A dielectric in the atoms or molecules of which, the centres of gravity of positive and negative charges do not coincide, is called a polar dielectric.

Electric Polarization

The stretching of atoms of a dielectric slab under the action of an applied electric field.

Due to polarization, equal and opposite induced charges are developed on the two faces of the slab and an electric field E_p, called the electric field due to polarization is produced. It opposes the applied electric field (E_0). As a result, due to the polarization of the dielectric, the strength of the electric field gets reduced inside it.

The reduced value of electric field in a polarized dielectric is given by

$$E = E_0 - E_p$$

Dielectric constant

$$K = \frac{E_0}{E}$$

Polarization Density

The induced dipole moment developed per unit volume in a dielectric slab on placing it inside the electric field is called polarization density.

Dielectric Constant

The ratio of the strength of the applied electric field to the strength of reduced value of electric field on inserting the dielectric slab between the plates of a capacitor is called the dielectric constant of the slab.

Dielectric Strength

The maximum value of electric field (or potential gradient) that can be applied to the dielectric without its electric breakdown is called dielectric strength of the dielectric.

Loss of Energy

If Δu is the loss of energy due to the combination of two conductors.

$$\Delta u = \frac{1}{2}\frac{C_1 C_2}{C_1 + C_2}(V_1 - V_2)^2$$

Parallel Plate Capacitor

If magnitude of charge on each plate of a parallel plate capacitor be Q and overlapping area of plates be A, then

(i) Electric field between the plates

$$E = \frac{\sigma}{\varepsilon_0} = \frac{Q}{\varepsilon_0 A}$$

(ii) Potential difference between the plates

$$V = Ed = \frac{\sigma d}{\varepsilon_0} = \frac{Q}{\varepsilon_0 A}$$

Where,
d = Separation between the two plates

(iii) Capacitance, $C = \frac{Q}{V} = \frac{\varepsilon_0 A}{d}$

If a dielectric medium of dielectric constant K is completely filled between the plates of a capacitor, then its capacitance becomes

$$C' = \frac{K\varepsilon_0 A'}{d} = KC$$

If a dielectric slab/sheet of thickness t (where $t < d$) is introduced between the plates of capacitor, then

$$C' = \frac{\varepsilon_0 A}{\left(d - t + \frac{t}{K}\right)}$$

Magnitude of attractive force between the plates of a parallel plate capacitor is given by

$$F = \frac{\sigma^2 A}{2\varepsilon_0} = \frac{Q^2}{2A\varepsilon_0} = \frac{CV^2}{2d}$$

The energy density between the plates of a capacitor

$$u = \frac{U}{\text{Volume}} = \frac{1}{2}\varepsilon_0 E^2$$

Electrical Capacitance

Capacitance of a conductor is the amount of charge needed in order to raise the potential of the conductor by unity. Mathematically, capacitance $C = \frac{Q}{V}$

Electrical capacitance is a scalar. SI unit of capacitance is 1 farad (1F), where $1\text{F} = \frac{1\text{C}}{1\text{V}}$. Its dimensional formula is $[M^{-1}L^{-2}T^4A^2]$.

Capacitance of an isolated spherical conductor (solid or hollow) is given by

$$C = 4\pi\varepsilon_0 R = \frac{R}{9 \times 10^9}$$

The electrostatic potential energy of a charged conductor having capacitance C, charge Q and a potential V is given by

$$U = \frac{1}{2}QV = \frac{1}{2}CV^2 = \frac{Q^2}{2C}$$

Distribution of Charges between Two Conductors at Different Potential.

Let Q_1, V_1, C_1 = Charge, potential and capacitance of 1st conductor

Q_2, V_2, C_2 = Charge, potential and capacitance of 2nd conductor

If potential V is common to both the conductors.

Then, $Q_1 + Q_2 = Q'_1 + Q'_2$

[From principle of conservation of charge]

$$\Rightarrow \quad C_1V_1 + C_2V_2 = C_1V + C_2V$$

$$V(C_1 + C_2) = C_1V_1 + C_2V_2$$

$$\therefore \quad V = \frac{C_1V_1 + C_2V_2}{C_1 + C_2}$$

Capacitance of a Spherical Capacitor

$$C = 4\pi\varepsilon_0 K\left(\frac{ab}{b - a}\right)$$

a = Inner radius

b = Outer radius

K = Dielectric constant between the capacitors.

Capacitance of a Cylindrical Capacitor

$$C = \frac{2\pi\varepsilon_0 Kl}{\log_e \frac{b}{a}}$$

l = Length of the capacitor

a = Radius of inner cylinder

b = Radius of outer cylinder

Grouping of Capacitors

Series Grouping of Capacitors

In series arrangement, charge on each plate of each capacitor has same magnitude, equal to the charge supplied by the battery.

The potential difference is distributed inversely in the ratio of capacitors, *i.e.*,

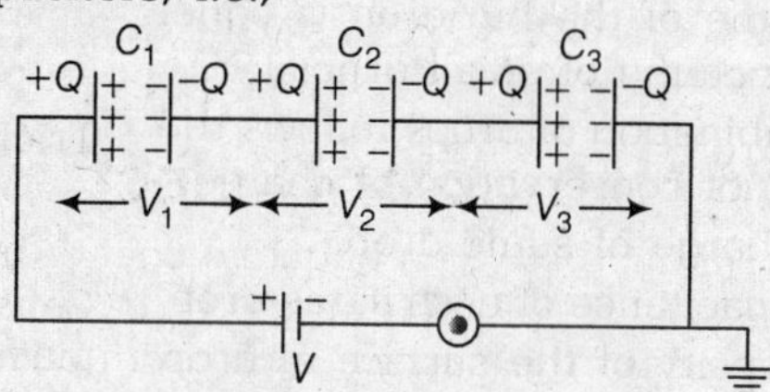

$$V = V_1 + V_2 + V_3 + \ldots$$

and $V_1 : V_2 : V_3 \ldots = \frac{1}{C_1} : \frac{1}{C_2} : \frac{1}{C_3}$

The equivalent capacitance C_s is given by

$\frac{1}{C_s} = \frac{1}{C_1} + \frac{1}{C_2} + \frac{1}{C_3} + \ldots + \frac{1}{C_n}$ for n number of capacitance

$$C_s = \frac{C}{n}$$

Parallel Grouping of Capacitors

In parallel arrangement the potential across each capacitor is exactly same. Charges on different capacitors are different. In fact, the charge is distributed on the ratio of capacitance.

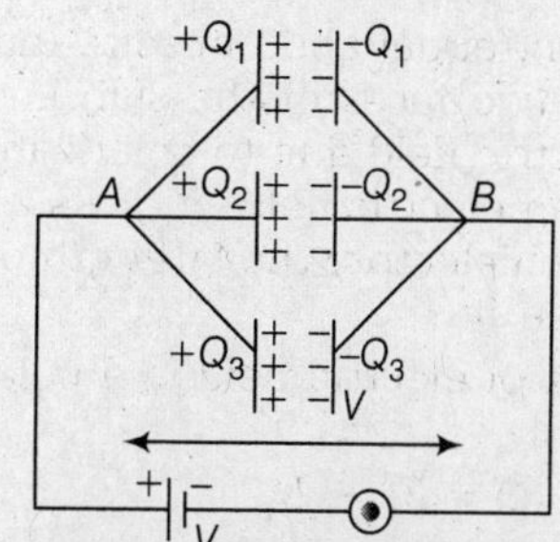

i.e., $$Q = Q_1 + Q_2 + Q_3 + \ldots$$

and $Q_1 : Q_2 : Q_3 \ldots = C_1 : C_2 : C_3 \ldots$

The equivalent capacitance is given by

$C_p = C_1 + C_2 + C_3 + \ldots + C_n$ for n number of capacitance

$C_P = nC$

Note

$$C_s = \frac{C}{n} \Rightarrow C_p = nC \Rightarrow \frac{C_p}{C_s} = nC \times \frac{n}{C} = n^2$$

$\therefore$ $C_p = C_s \times n^2$

Principle of Van de Graaff Generator
Electric discharge takes place in air or gases easily at pointed conductors and that a hollow conductor continues accepting charge through its inner surface irrespective of the fact, howsoever large its potential may grow.

Combination of Drops

- When small drops are joined together to forms a big drop, then the volume of the big drop is equal to total volume of small drops.
- The combination of drops follows the principle of conservation of charge.

If Q = Charge of same drop
C = Capacitance of each same drop
σ = Density of the surface of drop
U = Energy of each equal drop
V = Potential of each equal drop
n = Number of drops
r = Radius of each equal drop
R = Radius of big drop
Q' = Charge of big drop
C' = Capacitance of big drop
σ' = Density of big drop
U' = Energy of big drop
V' = potential of big drop

Then,
(a) $Q' = nQ$
(b) $V' = n^{\frac{2}{3}} V$
(c) $C' = n^{\frac{1}{2}} C$
(d) $R = n^{\frac{1}{3}} r$
(e) $\sigma' = n^{\frac{1}{3}} \sigma$
(f) $U' = n^{\frac{5}{3}} U$

TRICKS

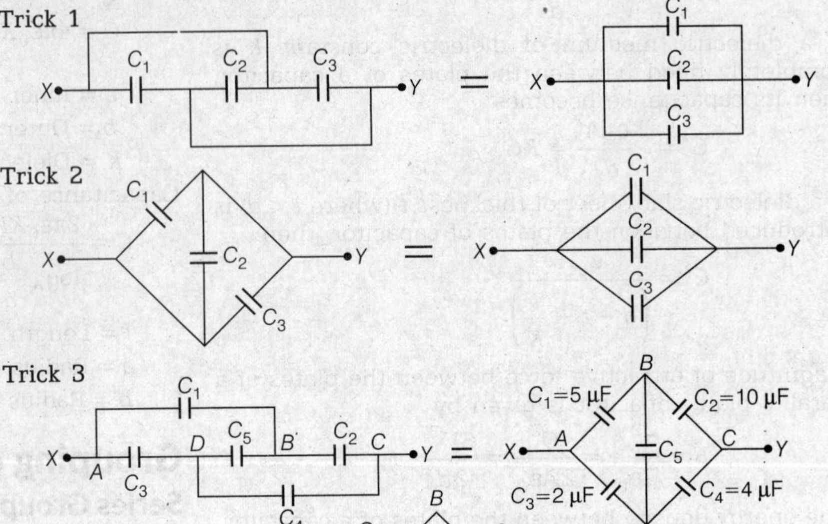

Trick 4

Consider that three metallic plates 1, 2 and 3, each of surface area A, are placed at a distance d apart from each other and the two outer plates (1 and 2) are connected to each other as shown in figure. Then, the arrangement of the conductors behaves as a parallel combination of two subcapacitors. Each subcapacitor has plate area A and plate separation d. The capacitance of the arrangement of the conductors is given by $C = \frac{2\varepsilon_0 A}{d}$.

Trick 5

Consider that four metallic plates 1, 2, 3 and 4, each of surface area A, are placed at a distance d apart from each other and the two outer plates (1 and 4) and the two inner plates (2 and 3) are connected to each other as shown in figure. Then, the arrangement of the conductors behaves as a parallel combination of two subcapacitors. Each subcapacitor has plate area A and plate separation d. The capacitance of the arrangement of the conductors is given by $C = \frac{2\varepsilon_0 A}{d}$.

Trick 6

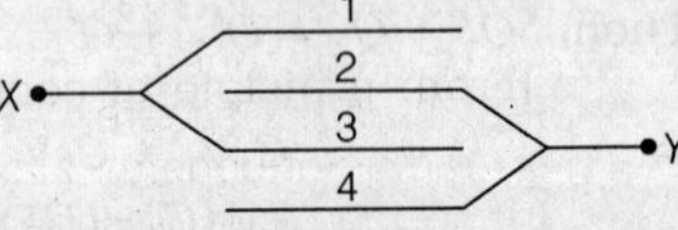

Consider that four metallic plates 1, 2, 3 and 4, each of surface area A, are placed at a distance d apart from each other and the two alternate plates (1 and 3) and the plates (2 and 4) are connected to each other separately as shown in figure. Then, the arrangement of the conductors behaves as a parallel combination of three subcapacitors. Each subcapacitor has plate area A and plate separation d. The capacitance of the arrangement of the conductors is given by $C = \frac{3\varepsilon_0 A}{d}$.

Practice Questions

Level I

1. SI unit of electrical capacitance is
(a) volt (b) farad
(c) ampere (d) newton

2. Coulomb/volt is equal to
(a) farad (b) gauss
(c) henry (d) current

3. If the distance between the plates of a parallel plate capacitor is increased the net capacitance will
(a) increase (b) decrease
(c) remains same (d) None of these

4. When a conductor is held in an electric field, the field inside the conductor is always
(a) positive (b) negative
(c) constant (d) zero

5. Charge on a capacitor is doubled. Its capacity becomes k times, where
(a) $k=2$ (b) $k=1$ (c) $k=\frac{1}{2}$ (d) $k=4$

6. Electrical capacity of Earth is
(a) 1 F (b) 1μ F
(c) 711 μ F (d) 9×10^9 μ F

7. When air in between the plates of a capacitor is replaced by mica of dielectric constant 6, its capacity
(a) remains unaffected (b) reduced to $\frac{1}{6}$th
(c) becomes 6 times (d) None of these

8. When a number of capacitors are connected in series between two points, all the capacitors possess same
(a) capacity (b) potential
(c) charge (d) None of these

9. When a number of capacitors are connected in parallel between two points, the equivalent capacitance
(a) increases (b) decreases
(c) remains the same (d) None of these

10. A condenser is charged to double its initial potential. The energy stored in the condenser becomes x times, where x is equal to
(a) 2 (b) 4
(c) 1 (d) $\frac{1}{2}$

11. The capacitance of a spherical conductor in air is directly proportional to the
(a) mass of sphere
(b) volume of sphere
(c) radius of sphere
(d) surface area of sphere

12. A capacitor provides infinite resistance for
(a) direct current
(b) alternating current
(c) direct as well as alternating current
(d) None of the above

13. The capacitance of a parallel plate capacitor does not depend upon
(a) area of the plates
(b) distance between the plates
(c) charge on the plate
(d) None of the above

14. The energy required to charge a parallel plate condenser of plate separation d and plate area of cross-secton A such that the uniform electric field between the plates is E, is
(a) $\frac{1}{2}\varepsilon_0\frac{E^2}{Ad}$ (b) $\varepsilon_0\frac{E^2}{Ad}$
(c) $\varepsilon_0 E^2 Ad$ (d) $\frac{1}{2}\varepsilon_0 E^2 Ad$

15. Which of the following relations is correct?
(a) $V=\frac{q}{C}$ (b) $C=qV$ (c) $V=C\times q$ (d) $q=\frac{V}{C}$

16. The capacitance of a parallel plate condenser is given by
(a) $C=QV$ (b) $C=\frac{KA}{(9\times10^9\cdot4\pi d)}$
(c) $C=\frac{Kd}{(9\times10^9\cdot4\pi A)}$ (d) $C=\frac{A}{(9\times10^9\cdot4\pi Kd)}$

17. The energy stored in a capacitor of capacity C and potential V is given by
(a) $\frac{CV}{2}$ (b) $\frac{CV^2}{2}$ (c) $\frac{C^2V}{2}$ (d) $\frac{C^2V^2}{2}$

18. A parallel plate capacitor is made by stacking n equally spaced plates connected alternately. If the capacitance between any two plates is C, then the resulting capacitance is
(a) C (b) nC (c) $(n-1)C$ (d) $(n+1)C$

19. Two condensers of capacitance C_1 and C_2 respectively are connected in parallel. The equivalent capacitance of the system is
(a) C_1+C_2 (b) $\frac{C_1C_2}{(C_1+C_2)}$
(c) C_1-C_2 (d) $\left(\frac{1}{C_1}\right)+\left(\frac{1}{C_2}\right)$

20. Two condensers of capacitance C_1 and C_2 respectively are connected in series. The equivalent capacitance of the system is
(a) C_1+C_2 (b) C_1-C_2
(c) $\frac{C_1C_2}{(C_1+C_2)}$ (d) $\frac{(C_1+C_2)}{C_1C_2}$

21. The plate separation in a parallel plate condenser is d and plate area is A. If it is charged to V volts, then the work done in increasing the plate separation to $2d$ will be
(a) $\frac{\varepsilon_0AV^2}{2d}$ (b) $\frac{\varepsilon_0A^2V}{2d}$ (c) $\frac{\varepsilon_0AV^2}{d}$ (d) $\frac{\varepsilon_0A^2V}{d}$

22. A condenser of capacity C_1 is charged to V volt. The energy stored in it is U. It is connected in parallel to another condenser of capacity C_2. The energy loss in this process will be

(a) $\frac{UC_1}{C_1+C_2}$ (b) $\frac{UC_2}{C_1+C_2}$

(c) $\left(\frac{C_1}{C_1+C_2}\right)^2 U$ (d) $\frac{UC_1C_2}{C_1+C_2}$

23. The electric energy density between the plates of a charged condenser is

(a) $\frac{q^2}{2\varepsilon_0 A^2}$ (b) $\frac{q}{2\varepsilon_0 A^2}$

(c) $\frac{q^2}{2\varepsilon_0 A}$ (d) $\frac{q^2}{2\varepsilon_0^2 A^2}$

24. The capacity of a parallel plate condenser is C. If a dielectric of relative permittivity K and thickness equal to one-fourth of the plate separation is placed between the plates, then its capacity becomes C'. The value of $\frac{C'}{C}$ will be

(a) $\frac{4K}{3K+1}$ (b) $\frac{5K}{4K+1}$

(c) $\frac{2K}{K+1}$ (d) $\frac{K}{2(K+1)}$

25. The capacity of a parallel plate condenser is C. Its capacity when the separation between the plates is halved will be

(a) $4C$ (b) $2C$

(c) $\frac{C}{2}$ (d) $\frac{C}{4}$

Level II

1. A capacitor of capacitance 1 μF is charged to 1 kV. The energy stored in capacitor in joules is

(a) 5 (b) 0.5

(c) 0.005 (d) 50

2. A 60 μF capacitor has charge on each plate 3×10^{-8} C, then the energy stored is

(a) 1.2×10^{-4} J (b) 7.5×10^{-6} J

(c) 15×10^{-6} J (d) 2.4×10^{-4} J

3. Two capacitors of capacitances 2 μF and 6μF are in series, the effective capacitance of the system in μF will be

(a) 8 (b) 2

(c) $\frac{3}{2}$ (d) $\frac{2}{3}$

4. If a 2.0μF condenser is charged to 200 V and its plates are connected by a wire, the heat produced in the wire is

(a) 4×10^{-4} J (b) 4×10^{-2} J

(c) 4×10^{-5} J (d) 2.5×10^{-2} J

5. A condenser is charged through a potential difference of 200 V and possesses charge of 0.1 C. When discharged it would release an energy

(a) 1 J (b) 2 J

(c) 10 J (d) 20 J

6. A parallel plate capacitor has a capacitance of 50 μF in air and 110 μF when immersed in an oil. The dielectric constant K of the oil is

(a) 0.45 (b) 0.55

(c) 1.10 (d) 2.20

7. The capacity of a parallel plate condenser is 5μF. When a glass plate is placed between the plates of the condenser, its potential difference reduces to $\left(\frac{1}{8}\right)$ of the original value. The value of the relative dielectric constant of glass is

(a) 1.6 (b) 5

(c) 8 (d) 40

8. Two condensers of capacity 0.3 μF and 0.6 μF respectively are connected in series. The combination is connected across a potential of 6 V. The ratio of energies stored by the condensers will be

(a) $\frac{1}{2}$ (b) 2 (c) $\frac{1}{4}$ (d) 4

9. Force acting upon a charged particle kept between the plates of a charged condenser is F. If one of the plates of the condenser is removed, force acting on the same particle become

(a) 0 (b) $\frac{F}{2}$ (c) F (d) $2F$

10. A capacitor of capacitance 2 μF is charged to a potential difference of 200 V. After disconnecting from the battery, it is connected in parallel with an another uncharged capacitor. The common potential is 20 V. The capacitance of the second capacitor is

(a) 2μF (b) 4μF (c) 18 μF (d) 16μF

11. Two capacitors each of capacitance 1 μF are connected in parallel and then charged by 200 V DC supply. The total energy of their charges in joules is

(a) 0.01 (b) 0.02 (c) 0.04 (d) 0.06

12. A parallel plate capacitor has a capacity C. The separation between the plates is doubled and a dielectric medium is introduced between the plates. If the capacity now becomes $2C$, the dielectric constant of the medium is

(a) 2 (b) 1 (c) 4 (d) 8

13. A capacitor is charged by a battery and the energy stored is U. The battery is now removed and the separation distance between the plates is doubled. The energy stored now is

(a) $\frac{U}{2}$ (b) U (c) $2U$ (d) $4U$

14. The number of ways one can arrange three identical capacitors to obtain distinct effective capacitances is

(a) 8 (b) 6 (c) 4 (d) 3

15. The equivalent capacity between the points A and B in the following figure will be

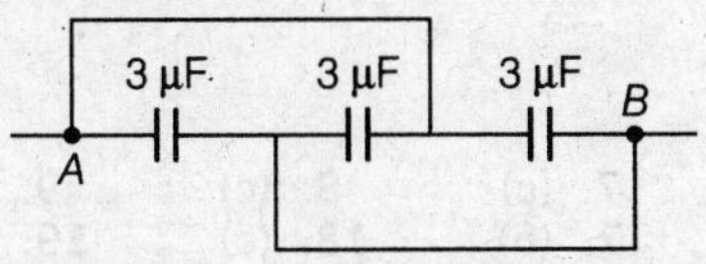

(a) 9 μF (b) 1 μF (c) 4.5 μF (d) 6 μF

16. The effective capacitance between points X and Y shown in figure, assuming $C_2 = 10 \mu F$ and that the

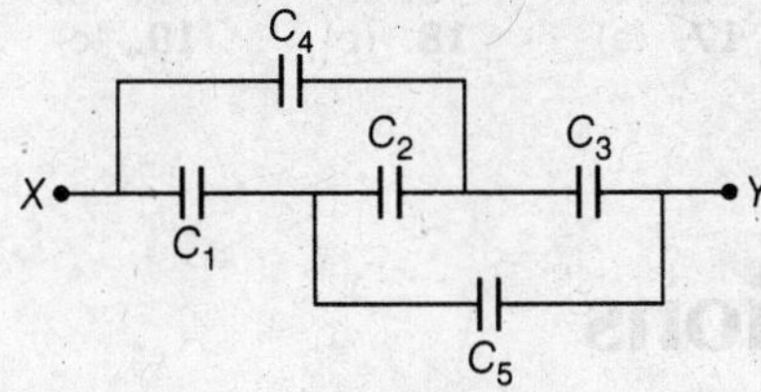

other capacitors are all 4.00 μF is

(a) 8 μF (b) 6 μF (c) 2.5 μF (d) 4 μF

17. Referring to figure, the effective capacitance between A and B will be

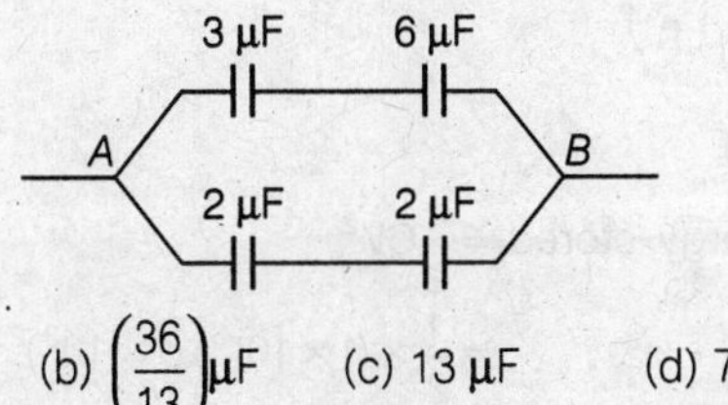

(a) 3 μF (b) $\left(\frac{36}{13}\right)$ μF (c) 13 μF (d) 7 μF

18. Four metallic plates, each with a surface area of one side A, are placed at a distance d apart from each other. The two inner plates are connected to point B and the other two plates to another point A as shown in figure. Then, the capacitance of the system is

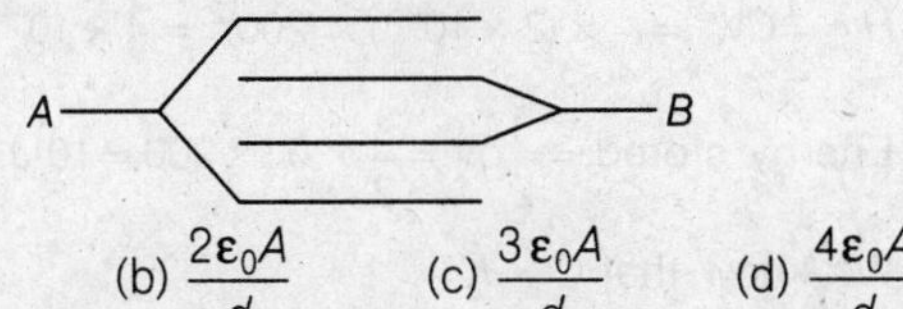

(a) $\frac{\varepsilon_0 A}{d}$ (b) $\frac{2\varepsilon_0 A}{d}$ (c) $\frac{3\varepsilon_0 A}{d}$ (d) $\frac{4\varepsilon_0 A}{d}$

19. Four metallic plates of each with a surface area of one side A, are placed at a distance d from each other. The alternate plates are connected to points A and B as shown in figure. The equivalent capacitance of the system will be

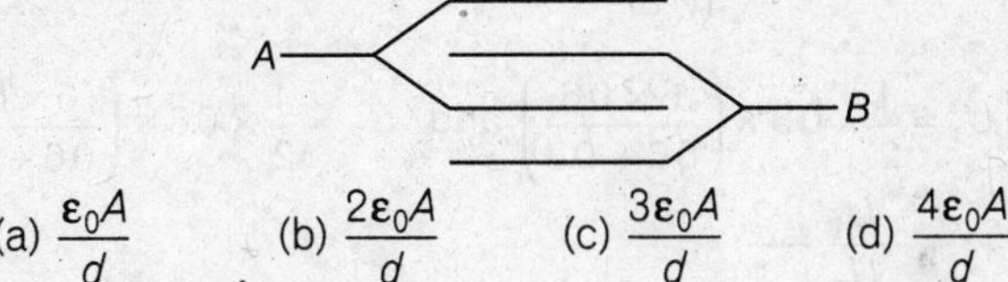

(a) $\frac{\varepsilon_0 A}{d}$ (b) $\frac{2\varepsilon_0 A}{d}$ (c) $\frac{3\varepsilon_0 A}{d}$ (d) $\frac{4\varepsilon_0 A}{d}$

20. Four capacitors are connected in a circuit as shown in figure. The effective capacitance between points A and B will be

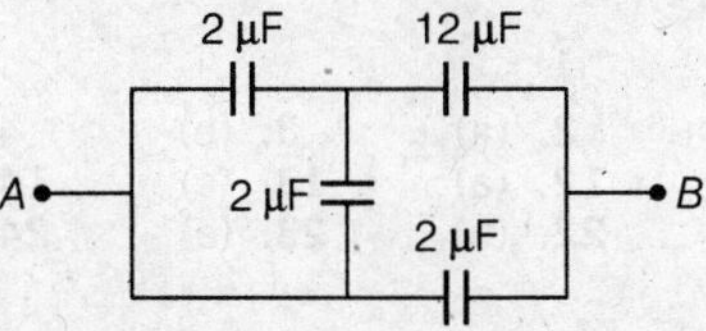

(a) $\frac{28}{9}$ μF (b) 4 μF
(c) 5 μF (d) 18 μF

21. Total capacitance of the system of capacitors in figure. between A and B is

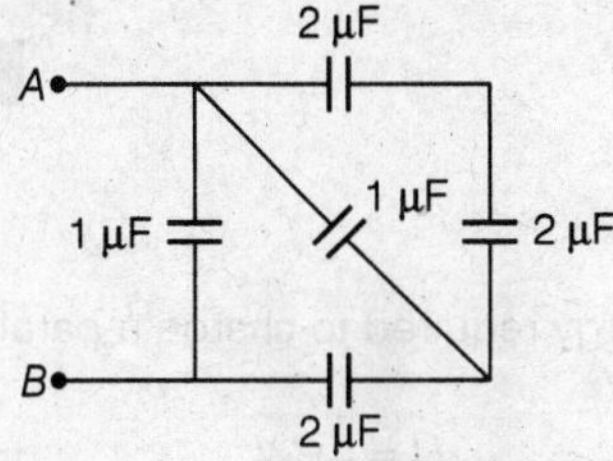

(a) 1μF (b) 2μF
(c) 3μF (d) 4μF

22. In the circuit of figure, find the charge of the condenser having capacity 3 μF

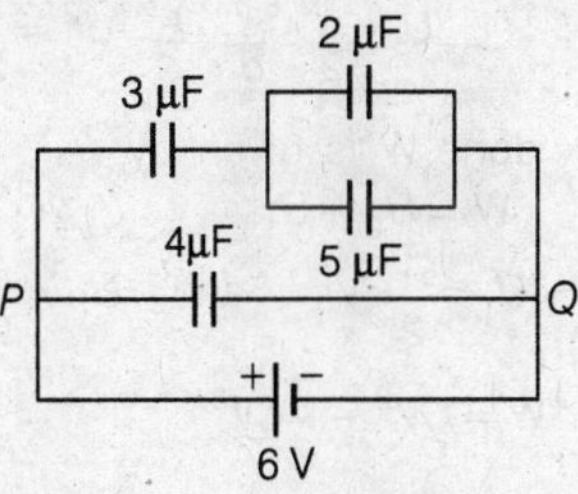

(a) 4.5 μC (b) 12.6 μC
(c) 7 μC (d) 30 μC

23. The potential difference across the capacitance of 2μF in figure is

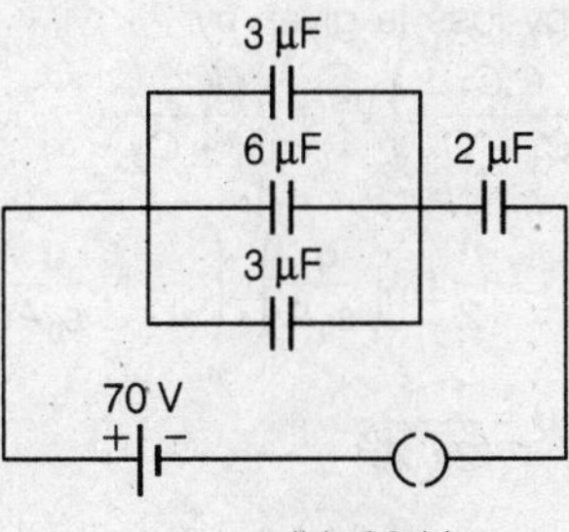

(a) 10 V (b) 60 V
(c) 28 V (d) 56 V

Answers

Level I

1. (b)	**2.** (a)	**3.** (b)	**4.** (d)	**5.** (b)	**6.** (c)	**7.** (c)	**8.** (c)	**9.** (a)	**10.** (b)
11. (c)	**12.** (a)	**13.** (c)	**14.** (d)	**15.** (a)	**16.** (b)	**17.** (b)	**18.** (c)	**19.** (a)	**20.** (c)
21. (a)	**22.** (b)	**23.** (a)	**24.** (a)	**25.** (b)					

Level II

1. (b)	**2.** (b)	**3.** (c)	**4.** (b)	**5.** (c)	**6.** (d)	**7.** (c)	**8.** (b)	**9.** (b)	**10.** (c)
11. (c)	**12.** (c)	**13.** (c)	**14.** (c)	**15.** (a)	**16.** (d)	**17.** (a)	**18.** (b)	**19.** (c)	**20.** (c)
21. (b)	**22.** (b)	**23.** (b)							

Hints and Solutions

Level I

14. The energy required to charge a parallel plate condenser is given by,

$$U = \frac{1}{2} C V^2$$

As, $C = \frac{\varepsilon_0 A}{d}$

and $V = E \cdot d$

$\therefore$ $U = \frac{1}{2} \cdot \frac{\varepsilon_0 A}{d} \cdot E^2 \cdot d^2 = \frac{1}{2} \varepsilon_0 E^2 \, A d$

21. The work done W is given by,

$$W = U_2 - U_1$$

Here, $U_1 = \frac{1}{2} C V^2$ and $U_2 = \frac{1}{2}\left(\frac{C}{2}\right)(2V)^2 = CV^2$

$\therefore$ $W = CV^2 - \frac{1}{2} CV^2$

$$= \frac{1}{2} CV^2 = \frac{1}{2}\left(\frac{\varepsilon_0 A}{d}\right) V^2 = \frac{\varepsilon_0 A V^2}{2d}$$

22. $U = \frac{1}{2} C_1 V^2$

The energy loss is given by,

$$\Delta E = \frac{1}{2}\left(\frac{C_1 C_2}{C_1 + C_2}\right) V^2 = \frac{U C_2}{C_1 + C_2}$$

23. $u = \frac{1}{2} \varepsilon_0 E^2 = \frac{1}{2} \varepsilon_0 \left(\frac{q}{\varepsilon_0 A}\right)^2 \left(\because E = \frac{q}{\varepsilon_0 A}\right)$

$\therefore$ $u = \frac{q^2}{2 \varepsilon_0 A^2}$

24. $C = \frac{\varepsilon_0 A}{d}$

and $C' = \dfrac{\varepsilon_0 A}{d - \frac{d}{4}\left(1 - \frac{1}{K}\right)} = \dfrac{4 \varepsilon_0 A}{3d + \left(\frac{d}{K}\right)} = \dfrac{4 \varepsilon_0 A K}{d(3K + 1)}$

$$= \frac{4KC}{(3K + 1)}$$

$\therefore$ $\frac{C'}{C} = \left(\frac{4K}{3K + 1}\right)$

25. $C = \frac{\varepsilon_0 A}{d}$, When d is halved,

$$C' = \frac{\varepsilon_0 A}{\left(\frac{d}{2}\right)} = \frac{2 \varepsilon_0 A}{d} = 2C$$

Level II

1. Energy stored $= \frac{1}{2} CV^2$

$$= \frac{1}{2} \times (1 \times 10^{-6})(1 \times 10^3)^2 = 0.5$$

2. $E = \frac{1}{2} \times \frac{q^2}{C} = \frac{1}{2} \times \frac{(3 \times 10^{-8})^2}{60 \times 10^{-12}} = 7.5 \times 10^{-6}$ J.

3. $\frac{1}{C} = \frac{1}{C_1} + \frac{1}{C_2} = \frac{1}{2} + \frac{1}{6} = \frac{4}{6} \Rightarrow C = \frac{6}{4} = \frac{3}{2}$

4. $H = \frac{1}{2} CV^2 = \frac{1}{2} \times (2 \times 10^{-6}) \times (200)^2 = 4 \times 10^{-2}$ J

5. Energy stored $= \frac{1}{2} qV = \frac{1}{2} \times 0.1 \times 200 = 10$ J.

6. We know that $C \propto K$

$\therefore$ $\frac{C_1}{C_2} = K = \frac{110}{50} = 2.2$

7. $V = \frac{V_0}{K} \Rightarrow K = \frac{V_0}{V}$

$\therefore$ $K = \frac{V_0}{(V_0 8)} = 8$

8. $U_1 = \frac{1}{2} \times 0.3 \times \left(\frac{6 \times 0.6}{0.6 + 0.3}\right)^2$ and $U_2 = \frac{1}{2} \times 0.6 \times \left(\frac{6 \times 0.3}{0.6 + 0.3}\right)^2$

$\therefore$ $\frac{U_1}{U_2} = \frac{2}{1}$

9. $F = q\,E = q\left(\frac{\sigma}{\varepsilon_0}\right)$

For one plate,

$$F' = qE_1 = q\left(\frac{\sigma}{2\varepsilon_0}\right) = \frac{F}{2}$$

10. Let the capacity of the second condenser be C. As, charge is conserved, we have

$$\{(2 + C) \times 10^{-6}\}(20) = (2 \times 10^{-6})(200)$$

$$\Rightarrow \quad 2 + C = 20$$

$$\therefore \quad C = 18\mu F$$

11. Resultant capacitance $= (1 + 1) = 2\mu F$

Energy stored $= \frac{1}{2}CV^2$

$$= \frac{1}{2} \times (2 \times 10^{-6})(200)^2 = 0.04 \text{ J}.$$

12. $C = \frac{\varepsilon_0 A}{d}$ and $2C = \frac{K\varepsilon_0 A}{2d}$

$\therefore \quad K = 4$

13. For a capacitor energy stored is given by,

$$U = \frac{1}{2}\frac{q^2}{C} \qquad \text{...(i)}$$

Where, q = Charge stored

C = Capacitance

When battery is removed and then plate separation doubled, new charge $q' = q$

New capacitance, $C' = \frac{C}{2}$. $\qquad \left[\because C \propto \frac{1}{d}\right]$

Hence, energy stored in capacitor

$$U' = \frac{1}{2}\frac{q'^2}{C'} = \frac{1}{2}\frac{q^2}{\left(\frac{C}{2}\right)} = \frac{q^2}{C}$$

$$\Rightarrow \quad U' = 2U \qquad \text{[From Eq. (i)]}$$

14. The three identical capacitors can be arranged in 4 way to obtain distinct effective capacitance.

15. The equivalent arrangement of capacitors is shown in figure

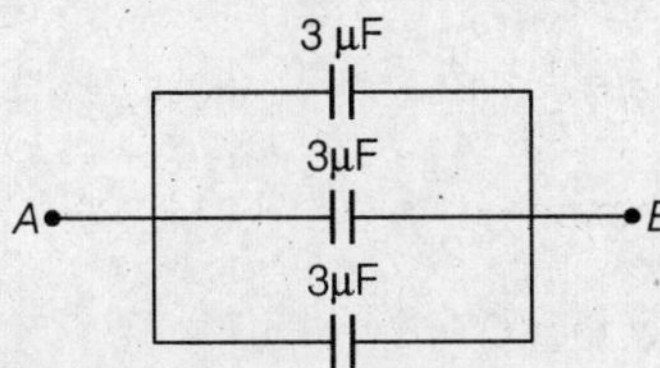

Net capacitance C is given by,

$$C = 3\mu F + 3\mu F + 3\mu F = 9\mu F$$

($\because$ Condensers are connected in parallel)

16. The equivalent circuit is shown in figure. It a battery is

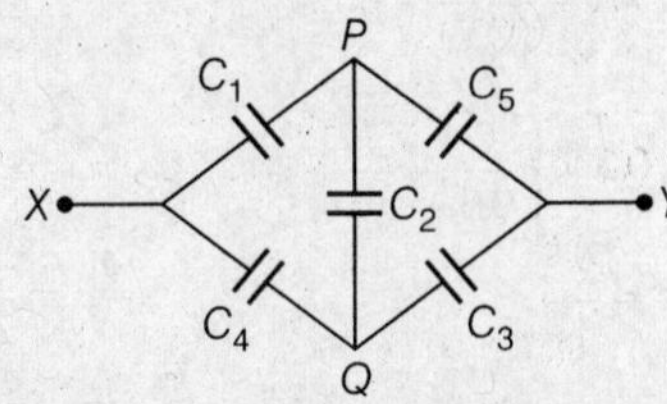

connected between X and Y, the points P and Q are at the same potential because $C_1 = C_4 = C_3 = C_5 = 4\mu F$

Hence, no charge flows through C_2. Now C_1 and C_5 are in series. Hence,

$$\frac{1}{C'} = \frac{1}{C_1} + \frac{1}{C_5}$$

$$\Rightarrow \quad C' = \frac{C_1C_5}{C_1 + C_5} = \frac{4 \times 4}{4 + 4} = 2\mu F$$

Similarly, C_4 and C_3 are in series and resultant capacitance C'' of these capacitors is also $2\mu F$. Further, C' of these capacitors and C'' parallel. Hence, net capacitance between points X and Y

$$= C' + C'' = 2\,\mu F + 2\,\mu F = 4\mu F$$

17. The upper two condensers of capacities $3\mu F$ and $6\mu F$ are in series. Their resultant capacitance C' will be

$$\frac{1}{C'} = \frac{1}{3} + \frac{1}{6} = \frac{3}{6} = \frac{1}{2}$$

$$\Rightarrow \quad C' = 2\mu F$$

Similarly, the lower two condensers of capacities $2\mu F$ and $2\mu F$ are in series. Their resultant capacitance C'' will be

$$\frac{1}{C''} = \frac{1}{2} + \frac{1}{2} = 1$$

$$\Rightarrow \quad C'' = 1\mu F$$

The effective capacitance between A and B will be

$$C = C' + C''$$

$$= 2 + 1 = 3\mu F$$

18. The two condensers in the middle are connected together *i.e.*, the connected plates act as a single conductor. In this way, effectively there are two capacitors connected in parallel. The capacity of each capacitor is given by

$$C = \frac{\varepsilon_0 A}{d}$$

Net capacitance between A and B is given by

$$C_{AB} = C + C = (2\varepsilon_0 \frac{A}{d})$$

19. The four plates are alternatively connected and form three capacitors in parallel. The capacity of each capacitor is $\left(\frac{\varepsilon_0 A}{d}\right)$. Hence, the net capacitance between A and B is given by,

$$C_{AB} = C + C + C = \left(\frac{3\varepsilon_0 A}{d}\right)$$

20. The given circuit is equivalent to the circuit shown in figure

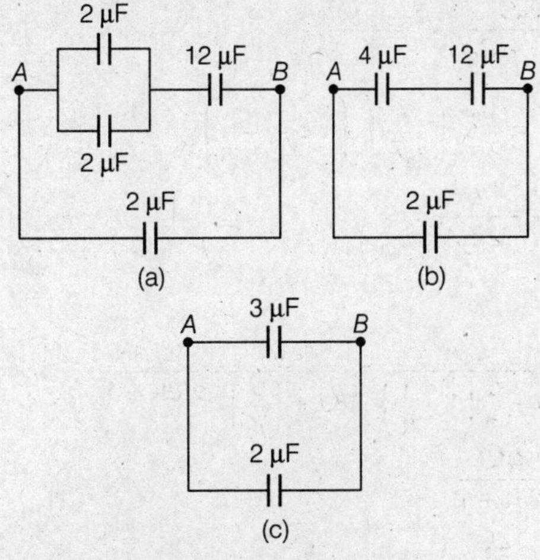

$$\therefore \quad C = C_1 + C_2 = 5\mu F$$

21. The simplified circuit is shown in figure

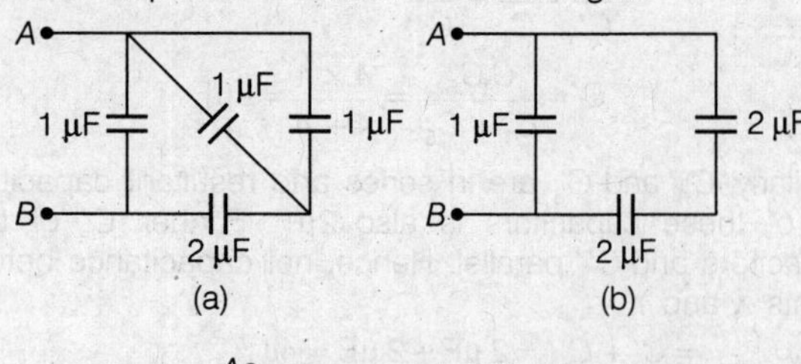

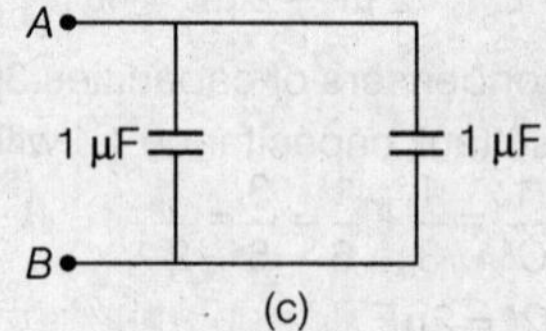

$\therefore \quad C_{AB} = C_1 + C_2 = 1\,\mu F + 1\,\mu F = 2\,\mu F$

22. The circuit is redrawn as shown in figure

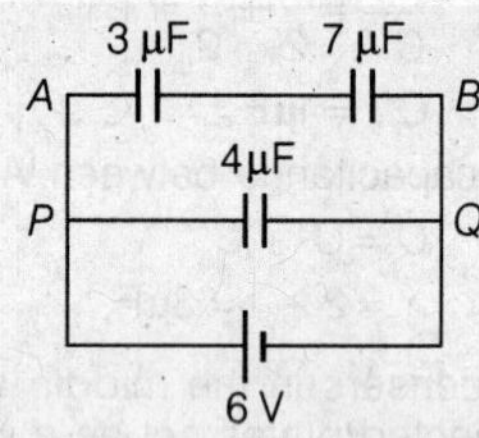

$$C_{AB} = \frac{3 \times 7}{3+7} = \frac{21}{10} = 2.1\,\mu F$$

The capacitor (3 μF and 7μF) are in series, so charge is same on both,

Now charge on 3 μF is given by

$$q = C_{AB} \times 6 = 2.1 \times 6 = 12.6\,\mu C$$

23. The equivalent circuit is shown in figure

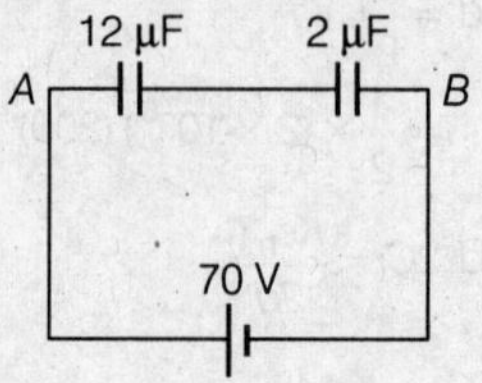

Now, $$C_{AB} = \frac{C_1 C_2}{C_1 + C_2} = \frac{12 \times 2}{12+2} = \frac{24}{14}$$

Both the condensers are in series and hence charge on both is same.

$$Q = C_{AB} \times V = \frac{24}{14} \times 70 = 120\,\mu C$$

Potential across 2μF condenser

$$V = \frac{Q}{C} = \frac{120\,\mu C}{2\,\mu F} = 60\text{ V}$$

32

Electric Conduction

Electric Current

It is defined as the rate of flow of electric charge through any section of a wire. It is denoted by I.

Thus, $$I = \frac{\text{Total charge flowing}}{\text{Time taken}}$$

If charge q flows in a time t through any section of a wire, then

$$I = \frac{q}{t} \quad \ldots\text{(i)}$$

If charge dq flows through a wire in small time dt, then

$$I = \frac{dq}{dt}$$

If n carriers of electricity, each having charge e cross any section of the conductor in time t, then

$$I = \frac{ne}{t} \quad \ldots\text{(ii)}$$

The direction in which the positive charge will flow gives the direction of conventional current. However, in metallic conductors, free electrons are carriers of electricity and hence electrons constitute the electric current. Therefore, the direction of electronic current is opposite to that of conventional current.

Although, a direction is associated with electric current, yet it is a scalar quantity. The reason is that the laws of ordinary algebra are used to add electric current. The laws of vector algebra do not apply to the addition of electric currents.

Unit of Electric Current

The SI unit of electric current is ampere. It is also the practical unit of current. It is denoted by A.

1 ampere (A)

$$= \frac{1 \text{ Coulomb (C)}}{1 \text{ Second (s)}} = 1 \text{coulomb per second } (\text{C s}^{-1})$$

The current through a wire is called one ampere, if one coulomb of charge flows through the wire in one second.

Note Number of electronic charge in one coulomb $= 6.25 \times 10^{18}$

Current Density

Consider that a current I is flowing through a conductor of area of cross-section A. The current through the conductor can be defined in terms of a vector quantity $\vec{j}$, called current density. If $\vec{E}$ is uniform electric field in the conductor, then current density is defined as a vector

$$\vec{j} = j\frac{\vec{E}}{E}$$

If the current flowing through the conductor is uniform over its cross-section, then current may be defined as

$$I = \vec{j} \cdot \vec{A}$$

Where, $\vec{A}$ is area vector representing the area of cross-section of the conductor. In case, the current flowing through the conductor is not uniform over its cross-section, then the current through a small area $d\vec{A}$ of the conductor is given by,

$$dI = \vec{j} \cdot d\vec{A}$$

Drift Velocity

It is defined as the average velocity with which the free electrons get drifted towards the positive end of the conductor under the influence of an external electric field applied.

The drift velocity of electrons is of the order of 10^{-4} m / s.

If V is the potential difference applied across the ends of the conductor of length l, the magnitude of electric field set up is

$$E = \frac{\text{Potential difference}}{\text{Length}} = \frac{V}{l}$$

The direction of this electric field is from positive end to negative end of conductor. Since, the charge on electron is $-e$, each free electron in the conductor experiences a force, $\vec{F} = -e\,\vec{E}$.

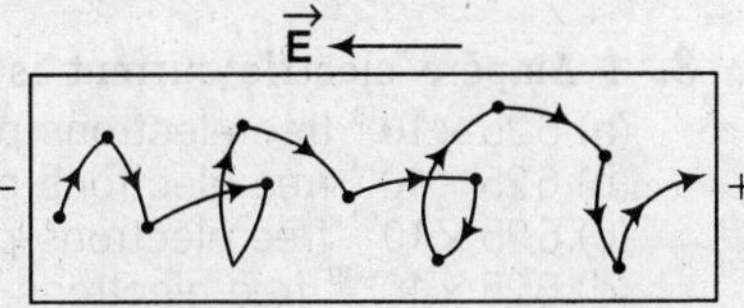

Here, the negative sign shows that the direction of force is opposite to that of electric field applied. If m is the mass of an electron, the acceleration of each electron is

$$\vec{a} = -\frac{e\,\vec{E}}{m} \quad \ldots\text{(i)}$$

The directions of motion of these free electrons are so randomly distributed that the average thermal velocity of the electrons is zero. If $\vec{u}_1, \vec{u}_2, \vec{u}_3, \ldots, \vec{u}_n$ are random thermal velocities of n free electrons in the metal conductor, then the average thermal velocity of electrons is

$$\frac{\vec{u}_1 + \vec{u}_2 + \vec{u}_3 + \ldots + \vec{u}_n}{n} = \vec{0} \qquad \ldots\text{(ii)}$$

At any instant of time, the velocity acquired by electron having thermal velocity $\vec{u}_1$ will be

$$\vec{v}_1 = \vec{u}_1 + \vec{a}\,\tau_1$$
$$\vec{v}_2 = \vec{u}_2 + \vec{a}\,\tau_2$$
$$\vec{v}_3 = \vec{u}_3 + \vec{a}\,\tau_3$$

....

The drift velocity is

$$\vec{v}_d = \frac{\vec{v}_1 + \vec{v}_2 + \vec{v}_3 + \ldots + v_n}{n}$$

$$= \left(\frac{\vec{u}_1 + \vec{u}_2 + \vec{u}_3 + \ldots}{n}\right) + \vec{a}\left(\frac{\tau_1 + \tau_2 + \tau_3 + \ldots + \tau_n}{n}\right)$$

$$\Rightarrow \boxed{\vec{v}_d = \vec{a}\,\tau} \qquad \text{[from Eq. (ii)]}$$

From, $\vec{v}_d = \dfrac{-e\,\vec{E}\,\tau}{m}$

Average drift speed, $v_d = \dfrac{e\,E}{m}\,\tau \qquad \ldots\text{(iii)}$

Where, τ = Average relaxation time.

Relation between Current and Drift Velocity

Consider a conductor of length l and area of cross-section A.

$\therefore$ Volume of the conductor $= Al$

If n be the number of free electrons per unit volume of the conductor and e be the charge on each electron than total charge on all the free electrons in the conductor

$$v_d = \frac{I}{n\,A\,e} = \frac{I}{ne} = \frac{I}{\pi r^2 ne}$$

Mobility

Mobility of charge carrier (μ), responsible for current is defined as the magnitude of drift velocity of charge per unit electric field applied, *i.e.*

$$\mu = \frac{\text{Drift velocity}}{\text{Electric field}} = \frac{v_d}{E} = \frac{q\,E\,\tau/m}{E} = \frac{q\,\tau}{\mu}$$

Where, τ is the average relaxation time of the charge, while drifting towards the opposite electrode and m is the mass of the charged particle.

Mobility of electron, $\mu_e = \dfrac{e\tau_e}{m_e}$

Note $I = \dfrac{e}{t} = \dfrac{1}{t} \times e = \nu e = \dfrac{\omega}{2\pi} e = \dfrac{ve}{2\pi r}$

Practice Questions

Level I

1. Which of the following is a scalar quantity?
(a) Electric current (b) Drift velocity
(c) Current density (d) All of these

2. SI unit of current density is
(a) $\dfrac{\text{Ampere}}{\text{Metre}}$ (b) $\dfrac{\text{Ampere}}{\text{Metre}^2}$
(c) Ampere $\times$ Metre^2 (d) $\dfrac{\text{Ampere}}{\text{Metre}^3}$

3. 1 Ampere electric current is equal to
(a) 6.25×10^{18} free electrons per second
(b) 6.25×10^{19} free electrons per second
(c) 6.25×10^{27} free electrons per second
(d) 6.25×10^{-19} free electrons per second

4. The dimensional formula of the current density is
(a) $[M^0L^{-3}A]$ (b) $[M^0L^{-2}A]$
(c) $[M^0LA^{-2}]$ (d) $[M^1L^{-3}A]$

5. Coulomb second^{-1} is also known as
(a) ohm (b) faraday
(c) henry (d) ampere

6. Which of the following relation is correct?
(a) $v_d = \dfrac{I}{n\,A\,e}$ (b) $v_d = \dfrac{In}{A\,e}$
(c) Both (a) and (b) (d) $v_d = \dfrac{e}{I\,n\,A}$

7. The value of drift velocity of the degree
(a) 10^{-6} m/s (b) 10^{-7} m/s
(c) 10^{-2} m/s (d) 10^{-4} m/s

8. SI unit of mobility is
(a) $m^2\,V^{-1}\,s^{-1}$ (b) $m\,V^{-1}\,s^{-2}$
(c) $m\,V^{-2}\,s^{-1}$ (d) $m^2\,V\,s^{-1}$

9. Which of the following relation is true?
(a) $v_d \propto \dfrac{1}{l}$ (b) $v_d \propto \dfrac{1}{r}$
(c) $v_d \propto \dfrac{1}{n}$ (d) $v_d \propto \dfrac{1}{J}$

10. 3 A of current is equal to
(a) $3\,J\,C^{-1}$ (b) $3\,C\,s^{-1}$
(c) $3\,V\,s^{-1}$ (d) $5\,J\,s^{-1}$

Level II

1. $1\,\mu A$ current is flowing in a wire if charge on an electron be 1.6×0^{-19}C, then the number of electron flowing per second through the wire will be

(a) 6.25×10^{12} (b) 6.25×10^{15}
(c) 6.25×10^{19} (d) 6.25×10^{21}

2. The current of $90\,\mu A$ is flowing in a wire till 30 s. The transfer of charge from the wire will be

(a) 6×10^{-10} C (b) 6×10^{-4} C
(c) 1.6×10^{4} C (d) 6×10^{-8} C

3. 90 C of charge flowing in a given wire till 1 h 15 min. The electric current flowing in the wire will be

(a) 1A (b) 0.2 A (c) 0.01 A (d) 0.02 A

4. An electron of radius 5×10^{-11}m is revolving around a circular orbit of a nucleus with velocity 2.2×10^{6} m/s in hydrogen atom. Then, its equivalent electric current will be

(a) 1 A
(b) 1.6×10^{-3} A
(c) 1.12×10^{-3} A
(d) 1.12×10^{-5} A

5. The current flowing through the area of cross-section $0.01\ m^2$ till the time 15 s. If current density be $10\ A/m^2$, then flowing net charge will be

(a) 1.5 C (b) 3 C
(c) 1C (d) 2.5 C

Answers

Level I

1. (a)	**2.** (b)	**3.** (a)	**4.** (b)	**5.** (d)	**6.** (a)	**7.** (d)	**8.** (a)	**9.** (c)	**10.** (b)

Level II

1. (a)	**2.** (b)	**3.** (d)	**4.** (c)	**5.** (a)

Hints and Solutions

Level II

1. Using, $I = ne$

$$\Rightarrow \quad n = \frac{I}{e} = \frac{1 \times 10^{-6}}{1.6 \times 10^{-19}} = 6.25 \times 10^{12}$$

2. Charge transfer from wire is

$$q = I \times t = 20 \times 10^{-6} \times 30 = 6 \times 10^{-4}\ C$$

3. Here, $q = 90C$

$t = 1$ h 15 min = 75 min = 4500 s.

$$\therefore \quad I = \frac{q}{t} = \frac{90}{4500} = \frac{1}{50} = 0.02\ A$$

4. Here, $v = 2.2 \times 10^{6}$ m/s,

$e = 1.6 \times 10^{-19}$ C,

$r = 5 \times 10^{-11}$m and

$t = 1$ s

$$\therefore \quad I = \frac{v_e}{2\pi r} = \frac{2.2 \times 10^{6} \times 1.6 \times 10^{-19}}{2 \times \frac{22}{7} \times 5 \times 10^{-11}}$$

$$= 1.12 \times 10^{-3}\ A$$

5. As, $\vec{J} = \frac{q}{tA}$

$$\Rightarrow \quad q = \vec{J}At = 10 \times 0.01 \times 15 = 1.5C$$

33

Ohms Law

Electric Current

It is defined as the time rate of flow of electric charge through a cross-section of the conductor. Instantaneous value of current at any instant is given by

$$I_{\text{ins}} = \lim_{x \to 0}\left(\frac{\Delta q}{\Delta t}\right) = \frac{dq}{dt}$$

SI unit of electric current is 1 ampere. It is a scalar quantity.

Ohm's Law

According to Ohm's law, physical conditions (temperature, mechanical strain etc.) remaining unchanged, the current flowing through a conductor is directly proportional to the potential difference across is ends.

Thus, $I \propto V$ or $V = IR$

Where, R is a constant known as the electrical resistance of a given conductor.

- The resistance of a conductor is directly proportional to its length l and inversely proportional to the area of cross-section A.

$$R = \rho\frac{l}{A}$$

Where, the constant ρ depends on the nature of the material. It is called the resistivity of the material.

- In terms of free electron density n and relaxation time τ, the resistance of a conductor is given by

$$R = \frac{ml}{ne^2\tau A}$$

- Resistance and resistivity of metallic conductors increase with increase in temperature. The relation is written as,

$$R_\theta = R_0\,(1 + \alpha\,\theta) \text{ and } \rho_\theta = \rho_\theta\,(1 + \alpha\,\theta)$$

$$\Rightarrow \quad \alpha = \frac{R_\theta - R_0}{R_0 \times \theta} = \frac{\rho_\theta - \rho_0}{\rho_0 \times \theta} \,/°\text{C}$$

The constant α is known as the temperature coefficient of resistance/resistivity of given material.

Series and Parallel Combinations of Resistors

Series Grouping

In series grouping of resistances same current I flows through all the resistance.

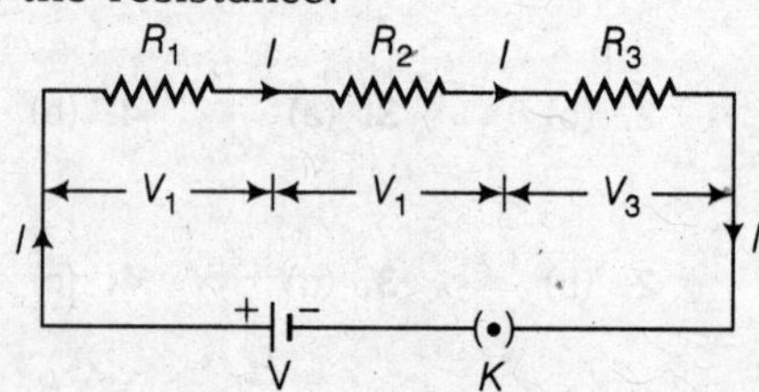

Total equivalent resistance in series grouping is equal to the sum of individual resistance. Thus,

$$R_s = R_1 + R_2 + R_3 + \dots + R_n$$
$$R_s = nR$$

Parallel Grouping

In parallel grouping, same potential difference V appears across each resistance.

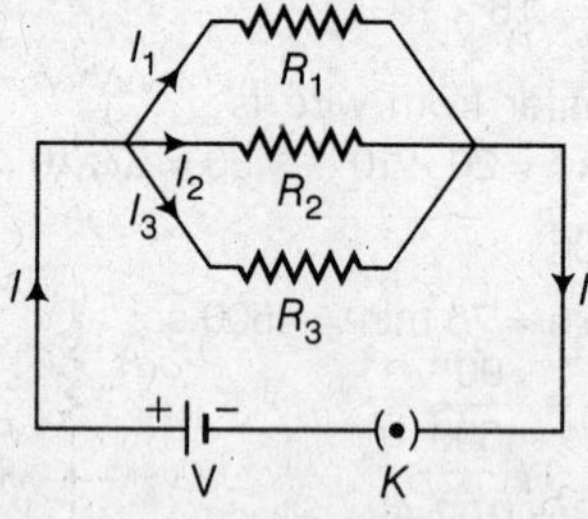

Equivalent resistance in parallel grouping R_p is given by,

$$\frac{1}{R_p} = \frac{1}{R_1} + \frac{1}{R_2} + \frac{1}{R_3} + \dots + \frac{1}{R_n} \Rightarrow R_p = \frac{R_1 R_2}{R_1 + R_2}$$

$$\Rightarrow R_p = \frac{R}{n}$$

Ratio of R_p and R_s

$$\frac{R_s}{R_p} = \frac{nR}{\frac{R}{n}} = n^2 \Rightarrow R_s = n^2 Rp$$

TRICKS

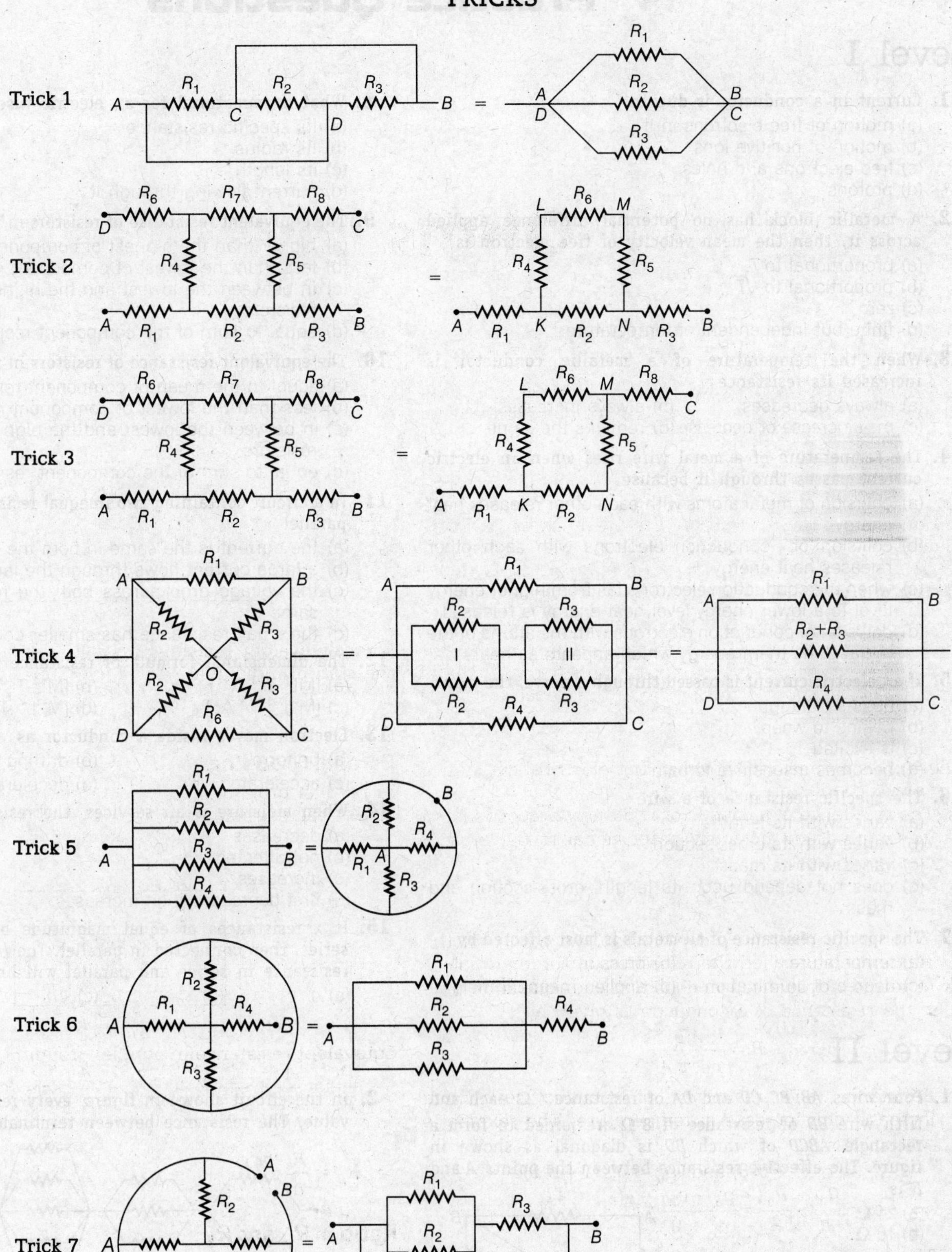
Trick 1
A
R_1
C
R_2
D
R_3
B
=
A
D
R_1
R_2
R_3
B
C
Trick 2
D
R_6
R_7
R_8
C
R_4
R_5
A
R_1
R_2
R_3
B
=
L
R_6
M
R_4
R_5
A
R_1
K
R_2
N
R_3
B
Trick 3
D
R_6
R_7
R_8
C
R_4
R_5
A
R_1
R_2
R_3
B
=
L
R_6
M
R_8
C
R_4
R_5
A
R_1
K
R_2
N
Trick 4
A
R_1
B
R_2
R_3
O
R_2
R_3
R_6
D
C
=
A
R_1
B
R_2
R_3
I
II
R_2
R_4
R_3
D
C
=
A
R_1
B
R_2+R_3
R_4
D
C
Trick 5
A
R_1
R_2
R_3
R_4
B
=
B
R_2
R_4
R_1
A
R_3
Trick 6
A
R_2
R_1
R_4
B
R_3
=
A
R_1
R_2
R_3
R_4
B
Trick 7
A
A
B
R_2
R_1
R_3
R_4
=
A
R_1
R_2
R_3
R_4
B

Practice Questions

Level I

1. **Current in a conductor is due to**
(a) motion of free electrons in it
(b) motion of positive ions
(c) free electrons and holes
(d) protons

2. **A metallic block has no potential difference applied across it, then the mean velocity of free electron is**
(a) proportional to T
(b) proportional to $\sqrt{T}$
(c) zero
(d) finite but independent of temperature

3. **When the temperature of a metallic conductor is increased its resistance**
(a) always decreases (b) always increases
(c) may increase or decrease (d) remains the same

4. **The temperature of a metal wire rises when an electric current passes through it because**
(a) collision of metal atoms with each other releases heat energy
(b) collision of conduction electrons with each other releases heat energy
(c) when the conduction electrons fall from higher energy level to a lower energy level heat energy is released
(d) collision of conduction electrons with the atoms of the metal gives them energy which appears as heat

5. **If an electric current is passed through a nerve, the man**
(a) begins to laugh
(b) begins to weep
(c) is excited
(d) becomes insensitive to pain

6. **The specific resistance of a wire**
(a) varies with its length
(b) varies with its cross-section
(c) varies with its mass
(d) does not depend upon its length, cross-section and mass

7. **The specific resistance of all metals is most affected by**
(a) temperature (b) pressure
(c) degree of illumination (d) applied magnetic field

8. **What is immaterial for an electric fuse?**
(a) Its specific resistance
(b) Its radius
(c) Its length
(d) current flowing through it

9. **The equivalent resistance of resistors in parallel is always**
(a) higher than the highest of component resistors
(b) less than the lowest of component resistors
(c) in between the lowest and the highest of component resistors
(d) equal to sum of the component resistors

10. **The equivalent resistance of resistors in series is always**
(a) equal to the mean of component resistors
(b) less than the lowest of component resistors
(c) in between the lowest and the highest of component resistors
(d) equal to sum of the component resistors

11. **In a circuit containing two unequal resistors connected in parallel**
(a) the current is the same in both the resistors
(b) a large current flows through the large resistor
(c) the voltage drop across both the resistances is the same
(d) the small resistance has smaller conductance

12. **The dimensional formula of resistance is**
(a) $[ML^2 T^{-3} A^{-2}]$ (b) $[ML^3 T^{-3} A^{-2}]$
(c) $[M^{-1}L^{-3} T^3 A^2]$ (d) $[M^{-1}L^{-2} T^3 A^2]$

13. **Electron moves inside a conductor as**
(a) uniform (b) drifting
(c) accelerated (d) decelerated

14. **When moisture is air services, the resistance**
(a) decreases
(b) not affected
(c) increases
(d) first decreases then increases

15. **If x resistances of equal magnitude be first joined in series, then connected in parallel. The ratio of equivalent resistance in series and parallel will be**
(a) n (b) x^4 (c) $\sqrt{n}$ (d) n^2

Level II

1. **Four wires AB, BC, CD and DA of resistance 4 Ω each and fifth wire BD of resistance of 8 Ω are joined to form a rectangle $ABCD$ of which BD is diagonal as shown in figure. The effective resistance between the points A and B is**
(a) 24 Ω
(b) 16 Ω
(c) $\frac{4}{3}$ Ω
(d) $\frac{8}{3}$ Ω

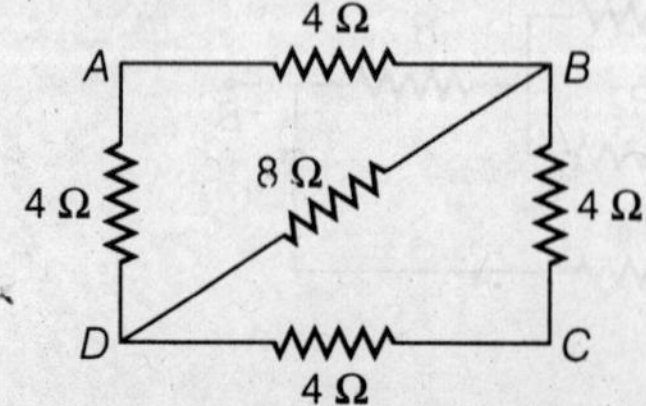

2. **In the circuit shown in figure, every resistance has 24 Ω value. The resistance between terminals P and Q is**

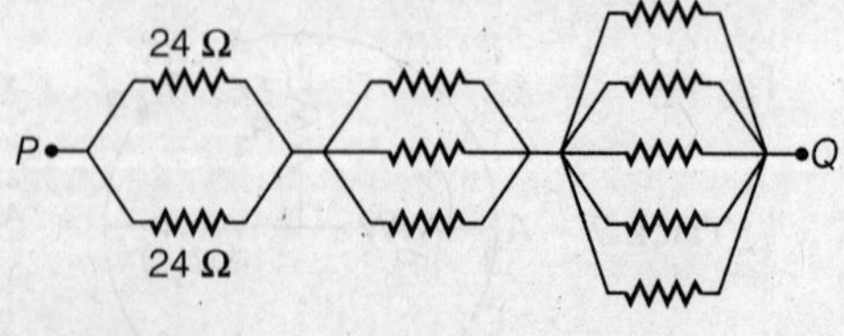

(a) 24.8 Ω (b) 32 Ω
(c) 36 Ω (d) 42 Ω

3. The current in the circuit of figure is

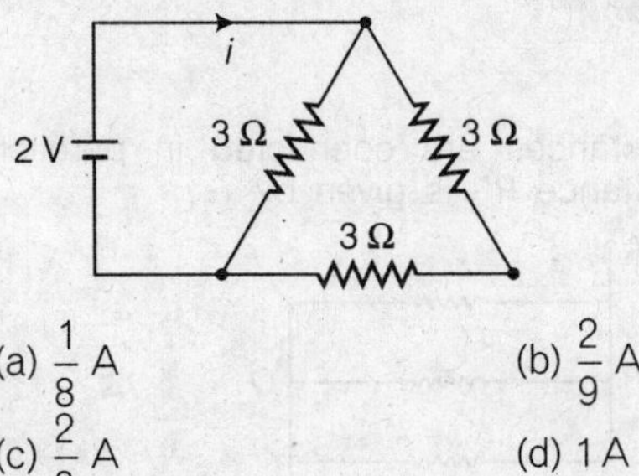

(a) $\frac{1}{8}$ A (b) $\frac{2}{9}$ A
(c) $\frac{2}{3}$ A (d) 1 A

4. What will be the equivalent resistance between the two points *A* and *D* of figure?

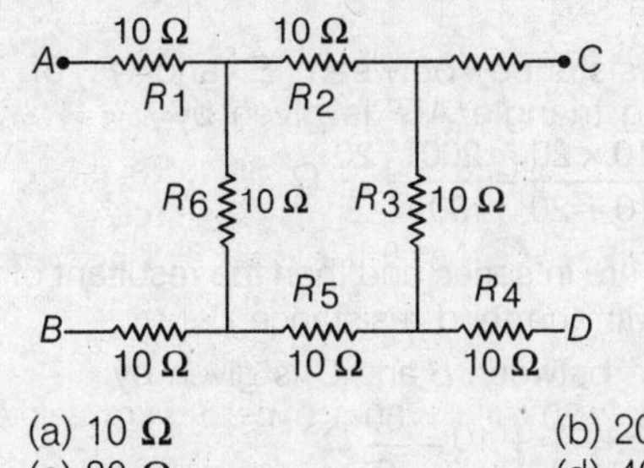

(a) 10 Ω (b) 20 Ω
(c) 30 Ω (d) 40 Ω

5. Three resistances each of 4 Ω are connected to form a triangle. The resistance between any two terminals is
(a) 12 Ω (b) 2 Ω
(c) 6 Ω (d) $\frac{8}{3}$ Ω

6. Find the resistance of the portion of the circuit between *A* and *B* in the circuit shown in figure.

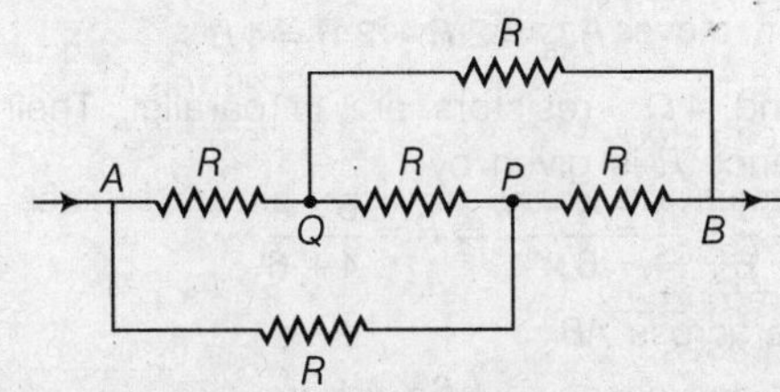

Points *A* and *P* are connected by a copper wire of negligible resistance. Similarly, points *B* and *Q* are also connected by a copper wire of neglible resistance

(a) 3 *R* (b) $\frac{R}{3}$ (c) $\frac{3R}{2}$ (d) $\frac{2R}{3}$

7. The effective resistance (in Ω) between *B* and *C* containing resistances as shown in figure is

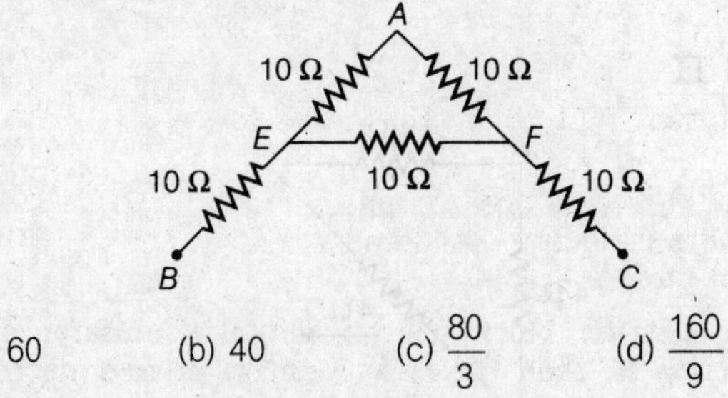

(a) 60 (b) 40 (c) $\frac{80}{3}$ (d) $\frac{160}{9}$

8. The ring shown in figure has zero resistance. The equivalent resistance between points *A* and *B* will be

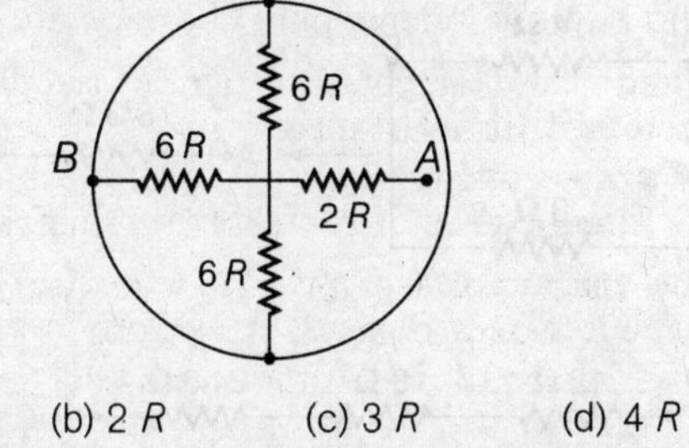

(a) *R* (b) 2 *R* (c) 3 *R* (d) 4 *R*

9. In the figure, the current passing through 6 Ω resistor is

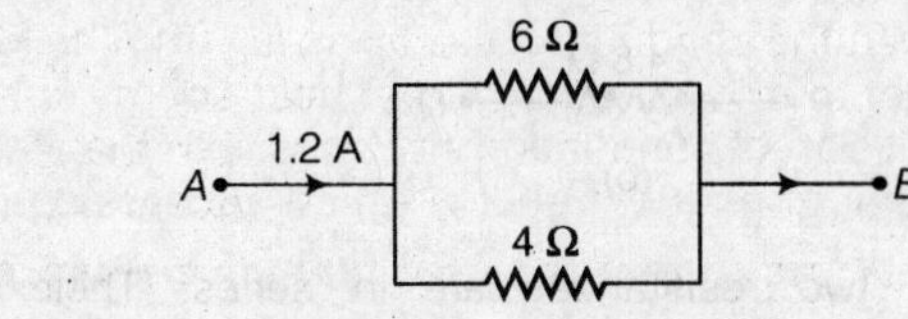

(a) 0.40 A (b) 0.48 A (c) 0.72 A (d) 0.80 A

10. In the given network, the equivalent resistance between *A* and *B* is

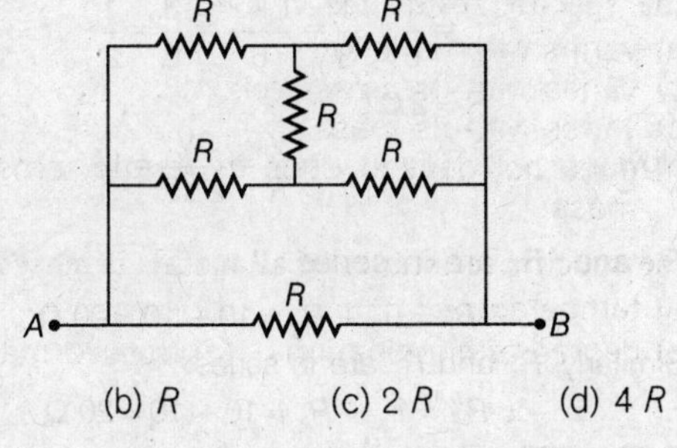

(a) $\frac{R}{2}$ (b) *R* (c) 2 *R* (d) 4 *R*

Answers

Level I

1. (a)	**2.** (c)	**3.** (b)	**4.** (d)	**5.** (c)	**6.** (d)	**7.** (a)	**8.** (c)	**9.** (b)	**10.** (d)
11. (c)	**12.** (a)	**13.** (b)	**14.** (a)	**15.** (d)					

Level II

1. (d)	**2.** (a)	**3.** (d)	**4.** (c)	**5.** (d)	**6.** (b)	**7.** (c)	**8.** (d)	**9.** (b)	**10.** (a)

Hints and Solutions

Level II

1.

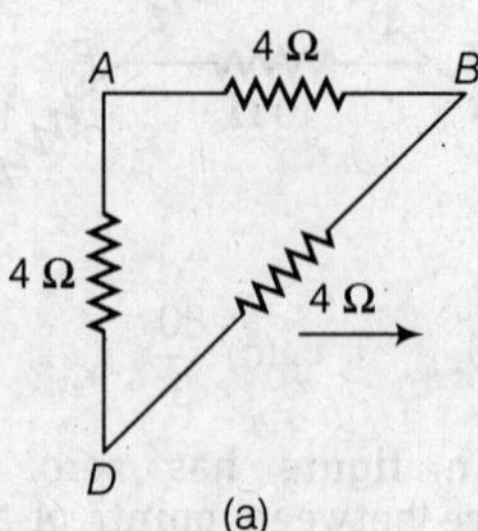

(a)

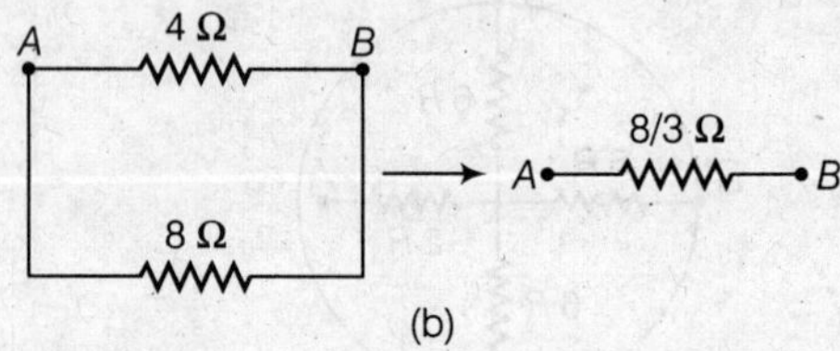

(b)

2.

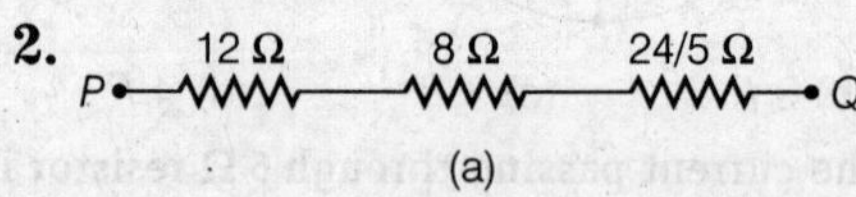

(a)

P —— 24.8 Ω —— Q

(b)

3. Here, two resistances are in series. Their equivalent resistance is $R_1 = 3 + 3 = 6\,\Omega$. The third resistance is in parallel. Hence, equivalent resistance is given by

$$\frac{1}{R} = \frac{1}{R_1} + \frac{1}{R_2}$$

$$= \frac{1}{6} + \frac{1}{3} = \frac{1+2}{6} = \frac{3}{6} = \frac{1}{2}$$

$\therefore \quad R = 2\Omega$

Now, $\quad i = \frac{V}{R} = \frac{2\text{V}}{2\,\Omega} = 1\text{A}$

4. R_2 and R_3 are in series.

$\therefore \quad R' = R_2 + R_3 = 10 + 10 = 20\,\Omega$

Similarly, R_5 and R_6 are in series.

$\therefore \quad R'' = R_5 + R_6 = 10 + 10 = 20\,\Omega$

Further, R' and R'' are in parallel.

$$R''' = \frac{R'R''}{R'+R''} = \frac{20 \times 20}{20+20} = 10\Omega$$

Resistance between A and D

$$= R_1 + R''' + R_4 = 10 + 10 + 10 = 30\,\Omega$$

5. The two resistances are connected in series and the resultant is connected in parallel with the third resistance.

$\therefore \quad R' = 4\,\Omega + 4\,\Omega = 8\,\Omega$ and $\frac{1}{R''} = \frac{1}{8} + \frac{1}{4} = \frac{3}{8}$

$\Rightarrow \quad R'' = \frac{8}{3}\Omega$

6. The three resistances are connected in parallel. Their equivalent resistance R' is given by

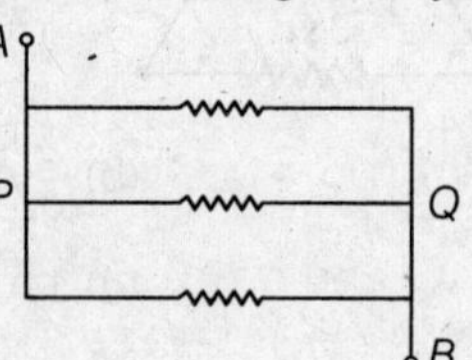

$$\frac{1}{R'} = \frac{1}{R} + \frac{1}{R} + \frac{1}{R} = \frac{3}{R} \quad \Rightarrow R' = \frac{R}{3}$$

7. The effective resistance between E and F of three resistance forming triangle AEF is given by

$$R_1 = \frac{10 \times 20}{10 + 20} = \frac{200}{30} = \frac{20}{3}\,\Omega$$

($\because$ Two resistances are in series and then the resultant of these two is in parallel with the third resistance.)

Effective resistance between B and C is given by

$$R = 10 + \frac{20}{3} + 10 = \frac{80}{3}\,\Omega$$

8. The three resistance of $6\,R$ resistance, each are connected in parallel. Their equivalent resistance is

$$\frac{1}{R'} = \frac{1}{6\,R} + \frac{1}{6\,R} + \frac{1}{6\,R} = \frac{3}{6\,R}$$

$\Rightarrow \quad R' = 2\,R$

This R' is series with $2\,R$ resistance. Hence, equivalent resistance between B and A will be

$$R_{AB} = 2\,R + 2\,R = 4\,R$$

9. $6\,\Omega$ and $4\,\Omega$ resistors are in parallel. Their equivalent resistance R is given by

$$\frac{1}{R} = \frac{1}{6} + \frac{1}{4} = \frac{4+6}{6 \times 4} \Rightarrow R = \frac{6 \times 4}{4+6}$$

Voltage across AB

$$V_{AB} = \left(\frac{6 \times 4}{4+6}\right) \times 1.2$$

Current i_1 through 6Ω resistor is given by

$$i_1 = V_{AB} \times \left(\frac{1}{R}\right) = \left[\left(\frac{6 \times 4}{6+4}\right) \times 12\right] \times \frac{1}{6}$$

$$\frac{4}{10} \times 12 = 0.48\text{ A.}$$

10. In the five resistances form a balanced Wheatstone bridge. Their effective resistance R_1 is given by

$$R_1 = \frac{2R \times 2R}{2R + 2R} = R$$

This is parallel with the resistance R between A and B. Therefore, total resistance between A and B

$$= \frac{R \times R}{R + R} = \frac{R}{2}$$

34

Electromotive Force and Electric Cells

Electromotive Force (Emf)

The emf of a cell is defined as work done by cell in moving a unit positive charge in the whole circuit including the cell once emf $E = W / q$.

Its SI units is joule/coulomb or volt.

Emf is the maximum potential difference between the two electrodes of the cell when no current is drawn from the cell. It is the characteristic property of cell and depends on the nature of electrodes and electrolyte used in cell and is independent of quantity of electrolyte, size of electrodes and distance between the electrodes.

Electrochemical Cell

An electrochemical cell is a device which transforms chemical energy into electrical energy. A cell is a source of constant emf but not a constant current.

Internal Resistance of Cell

The opposition offered by the electrolyte of the cell to the flow of electric current through it is called the internal resistance of the cell. The internal resistance of cell depends on.

- Distance between electrodes ($r \propto d$), larger is the separation between electrodes more is the length of electrolyte through which ions have to move, so more is internal resistance.
- Conductivity or nature of electrolyte $\left(r \propto \frac{1}{\sigma}\right)$
- Concentration of electrolyte ($r \propto c$), Temperature of electrolyte $\left(r \propto \frac{1}{T}\right)$.
- Nature and area of electrodes dipped in electrolyte $\left(r \propto \frac{1}{A}\right)$.

∴ The resistance offered by the electrolyte to the flow of current through the cell is called the internal resistance of the cell.

$$V = E - Ir$$

When a cell is charged by an external source V.

Then, $V = E + Ir$

Difference between Emf and Potential Difference

Emf of a Cell	Potential Difference
The emf of a cell is the maximum potential difference between the two electrodes of a cell when the cell is in the open circuit.	The potential difference between the two points is the difference of potential between these two points in a closed circuit.
Emf is independent of resistance of circuit and depends upon the nature of electrodes and electrolyte.	This depends upon the resistance between two points of the circuit and current flowing through the circuit.
The term emf is used for source of current.	Potential difference can be measured between any two points of circuit.
This is a cause.	It is an effect.

Combination of Cells

In Series

Suppose n cells are connected in series.

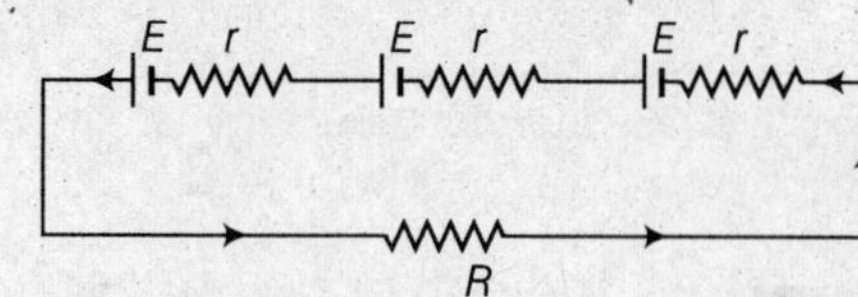

Net emf $= nE$
Total resistance $= nr + R$
Current, $i = \dfrac{nE}{nr + R}$

In Parallel

Suppose n cells are connected in parallel.
Net emf $= E$

Total resistance $= \dfrac{r}{n} + R$

$\Rightarrow \quad i = \dfrac{E}{R + \dfrac{r}{n}}$

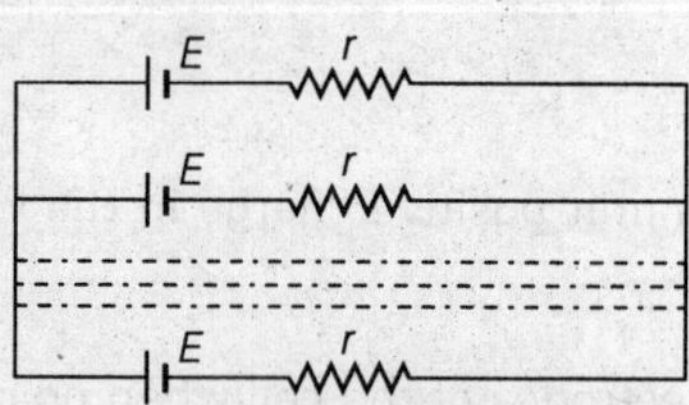

In Mixed Grouping

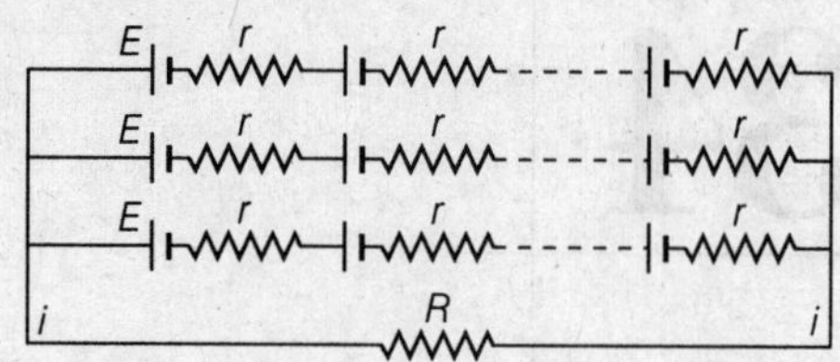

Net emf $= nE$

Net internal resistance $= \dfrac{nr}{m}$

External resistance $= R$

$$i = \frac{nE}{R + \dfrac{nr}{m}}$$

Note Net Emf's

(i) $E_1 \quad E_2 \quad E_3$ $\qquad E_{net} = E_1 + E_2 + E_3$

(ii) $E_1 \quad E_2 \quad E_3$ $\qquad E_{net} = E_1 + E_2 - E_3$

Practice Questions

Level I

1. Dimension of electromotive force is
(a) $[MLT^{-2}]$ (b) $[ML^2T^{-2}A^{-1}]$
(c) $[ML^2T^{-3}A^{-1}]$ (d) $[M^0L^1T^{-2}]$

2. Potential difference is measured in
(a) Ampere (A) (b) Coulomb (C)
(c) Volt (V) (d) Ohm (Ω)

3. The internal resistence of a cell depends upon
(a) nature of electrolyte
(b) concentration of electrolyte
(c) area of immerged electrode in the solution of electrolyte
(d) All of the above

4. The value of internal resistance in series combination of cells is
(a) increases (b) remains same
(c) decreases (d) None of these

5. The internal resistance in parallel combination of cells will
(a) decreases (b) increases
(c) remains same (d) None of these

6. If n cells emf E be connected in series then total emf will be
(a) En^2 (b) $\dfrac{E}{n}$ (c) $\dfrac{n}{E}$ (d) nE

7. A cell of emf E volt and internal resistance (r) ohm be joined to an external resistance of (r) ohm. The terminal voltage of the cell will be
(a) E volt (b) $\dfrac{E}{2}$ volt
(c) $2E$ volt (d) $\dfrac{E}{4}$ volt

8. In n cells each of internal resistance r be connected in parallel, then its internal resistance will be
(a) $\dfrac{r}{n}$ (b) $\dfrac{r}{n^2}$ (c) nr (d) n^2r

9. If internal resistance is equal to external resistance in mixed combination of cells, then the current in the external circuit will be
(a) minimum
(b) depends upon number of cells
(c) maximum
(d) None of the above

10. If n cells each of internal resistance r be connected in series, then total internal resistance will be
(a) $\dfrac{r}{n}$ (b) n^2r
(c) nr (d) None of these

Level II

1. Emf is most closely related to
(a) mechanical force (b) potential difference
(c) electric Field (d) magnetic field

2. Electromotive force is the force, which is able to maintain a constant
(a) current
(b) resistance
(c) power
(d) potential difference

3. A cell of emf E is connected with an external resistance R, then potential difference across cell is V. The internal resistance of cell will be
(a) $\frac{(E-V)R}{E}$ (b) $\frac{(E-V)R}{V}$
(c) $\frac{(V-E)R}{V}$ (d) $\frac{(V-E)R}{E}$

4. Two cells, each of emf E and internal resistance r are connected in parallel between the resistance R. The maximum energy given to the resistor will be, only when
(a) $R=\frac{r}{2}$ (b) $R=r$
(c) $R=2r$ (d) $R=0$

5. n identical cells each of emf E and internal resistance r are connected in series. An external resistance R is connected in series to this combination. The current through R is
(a) $\frac{nE}{R+nr}$ (b) $\frac{nE}{nR+r}$
(c) $\frac{E}{R+nr}$ (d) $\frac{nE}{R+r}$

6. A cell of internal resistance r is connected to an external resistance R. The current will be maximum in R, if
(a) $R=r$ (b) $R<r$ (c) $R>r$ (d) $R=\frac{r}{2}$

7. To get the maximum current from a parallel combination of n identical cells each of internal resistance r and external resistance R, when
(a) $R>>r$ (b) $R<<r$
(c) $R=r$ (d) None of these

8. When a resistance of 2Ω is connected across the terminals of a cell, the current is 0.5 A. When the resistance is increased to 5 Ω, the current is 0.25 A. The emf of the cell is
(a) 1.0 V (b) 1.5 V (c) 2.0 V (d) 2.5 V

9. 4 cells each of emf 2 V and internal resistance of 1Ω are connected in parallel to a load resistor of 2Ω. Then, the current through the load resistor is
(a) 2 A (b) 1.5 A (c) 1 A (d) 0.888 A

10. If six identical cells each having an emf of 6 V are connected in parallel, the emf of the combination is
(a) 1 V (b) 36 V (c) $\frac{1}{6}$ V (d) 6 V

11. The potential difference in open circuit for a cell is 2.2 V. When a 4 Ω resistor is connected between its two electrodes the potential difference becomes 2 V. The internal resistance of the cell will be
(a) 1Ω (b) 0.2 Ω
(c) 2.5 Ω (d) 0.4 Ω

12. The power dissipated in the circuit shown in the figure is 30 W. The value of R is

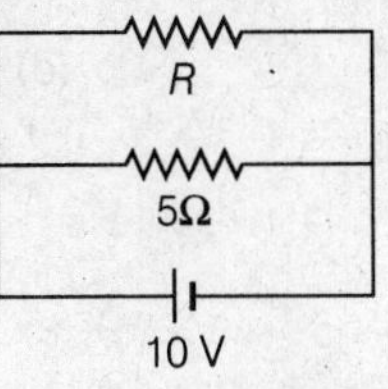

(a) 20 Ω (b) 15 Ω
(c) 10 Ω (d) 30 Ω

13. A cell whose emf is 2 V and internal resistance is 0.1Ω, is connected with a resistance of 3.9Ω. The voltage across the cell terminal will be
(a) 0.50 V (b) 1.90 V
(c) 1.95 V (d) 2.00 V

14. For driving a current of 2A for 6 min in a circuit, 1000 J of work is to be done. The emf of the source in the circuit is
(a) 1.38 V (b) 1.68 V
(c) 2.04 V (d) 3.10 V

15. Two batteries of emf 4 V and 8 V with internal resistances 1 Ω and 2 Ω are connected in a circuit with a resistance of 9 Ω as shown in figure. The current and potential difference between the points P and Q are

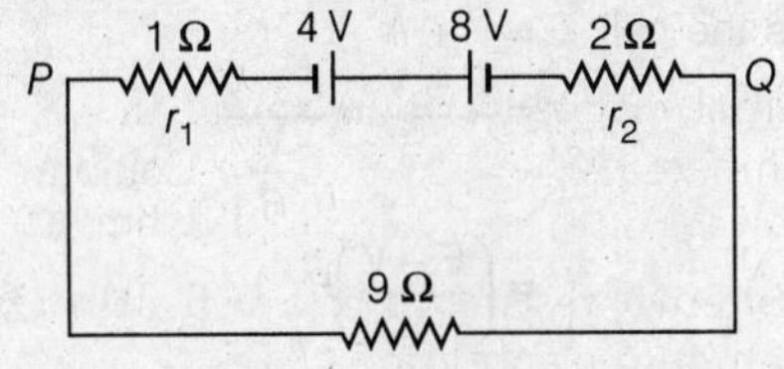

(a) $\frac{1}{3}$ A and 3V (b) $\frac{1}{6}$ A and 4V
(c) $\frac{1}{9}$ A and 9V (d) $\frac{1}{2}$ A and 12 V

16. In the shown circuit, what is the potential difference across A and B?

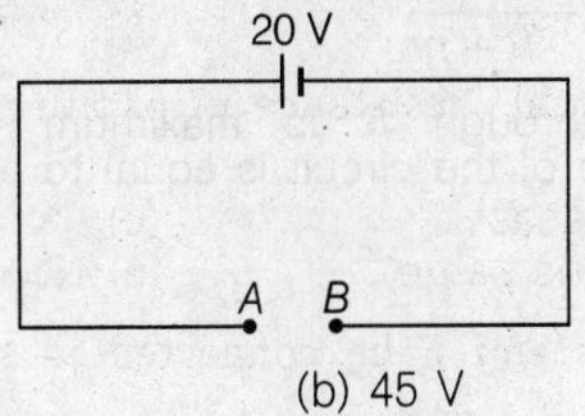

(a) 50 V (b) 45 V
(c) 30 V (d) 20 V

17. Two cells having emf 4V, 2V and internal resistances 1Ω, 1Ω are connected as shown in figure. Current through 6 Ω resistance is

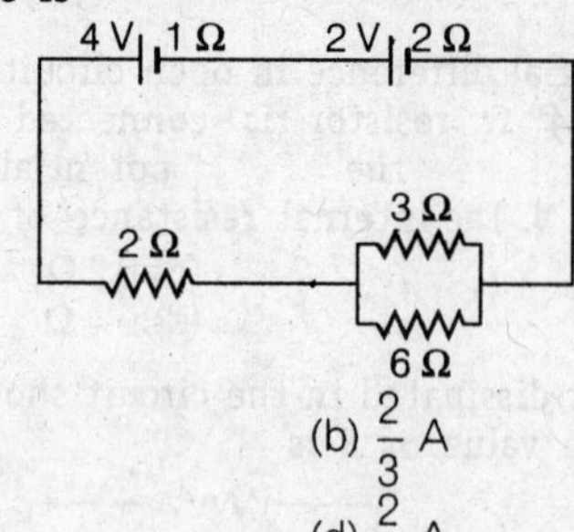

(a) $\frac{1}{3}$ A (b) $\frac{2}{3}$ A
(c) 1 A (d) $\frac{2}{9}$ A

18. A battery having emf 5 V and internal resistance 0.5Ω is connected with a resistance of 4.5Ω, then the voltage at the terminals of battery is
(a) 4.5 V (b) 4 V
(c) 0 V (d) 2 V

19. A cell of emf 6 V and resistance 0.5 Ω is short circuited. The current in the cell is
(a) 3 A (b) 12 A
(c) 24 A (d) 6 A

20. A storage cell is charged by 5 A DC for 18 h. Its strength after charging will be
(a) 18 AH (b) 5 AH
(c) 90 AH (d) 15 AH

Answers

Level I

1. (c)	**2.** (c)	**3.** (d)	**4.** (a)	**5.** (a)	**6.** (d)	**7.** (b)	**8.** (a)	**9.** (c)	**10.** (c)

Level II

1. (b)	**2.** (d)	**3.** (b)	**4.** (a)	**5.** (a)	**6.** (a)	**7.** (b)	**8.** (b)	**9.** (d)	**10.** (d)
11. (d)	**12.** (c)	**13.** (c)	**14.** (a)	**15.** (a)	**16.** (d)	**17.** (a)	**18.** (a)	**19.** (b)	**20.** (c)

Hints and Solutions

Level II

3. Let the current in the circuit $i = \frac{V}{R}$.

Across the cell, $E = V + ir$

$\Rightarrow \quad r = \frac{E - V}{i} = \frac{E - V}{\frac{V}{R}}$

$= \left(\frac{E - V}{V}\right)R$

4. For maximum energy, we have External resistance of the circuit

= Equivalent internal resistance of the circuit *i.e.*, $R = \frac{r}{2}$

5. Total emf = nE, Total resistance $R = nr$

$\Rightarrow \quad i = \frac{nE}{R + nr}$

6. Current through R is maximum when total internal resistance of the circuit is equal to external resistance.

7. Cells are joined in parallel when internal resistance is higher than external resistance. $[R << r]$

$$i = \frac{E}{R + \frac{r}{n}}$$

8. Since, $i = \left(\frac{E}{R + r}\right)$, we get

$$0.5 = \frac{E}{2 + r} \quad \ldots(i)$$

$$0.25 = \frac{E}{5 + r} \quad \ldots(ii)$$

Dividing Eq. (i) by (ii), we get $2 = \frac{5 + r}{2 + r}$

$\Rightarrow \quad r = 1\Omega$

$\therefore \quad 0.5 = \frac{E}{2 + 1}$

$\Rightarrow \quad E = 1.5\text{V}$

9. $I = \frac{E}{R + \frac{r}{4}} = \frac{2}{2 + \frac{1}{4}} = \frac{2}{2.25} = 0.888$ A

10. In parallel combination $E_{eq} = E = 6V$.

11. $E = 2.2V$, $R = 4\Omega$, $V = 2V$

$$r = \left(\frac{E}{V} - 1\right)R$$

$$R = \left(\frac{2.2}{2} - 1\right) \times 4 = 0.1 \times 4 = 0.4\Omega.$$

12. $P_{Total} = \frac{V^2}{R_{eq}}$

So, $R_{eq} = \frac{V^2}{P_{Total}}$

$= \frac{10 \times 10}{30} = \frac{10}{3}$

As, $R_{eq} = \frac{R_1 R_2}{R_1 + R_2}$

$\Rightarrow \frac{10}{3} = \frac{5R}{5 + R}$

$\Rightarrow R = 10\Omega$

13. The voltage across cell terminal will be given by

$$= \frac{E}{R + r} \times R = \frac{2}{3.9 + 0.1} \times 3.9 = 1.95 \text{ V}$$

14. Power $P = \frac{W}{t} = Vi$

$\Rightarrow$ Voltage $V = \frac{W}{it}$

$$= \frac{1000}{2 \times 6 \times 60} = 1.38 \text{ V}$$

15. Applying Kirchhoff's voltage law in the given loop.

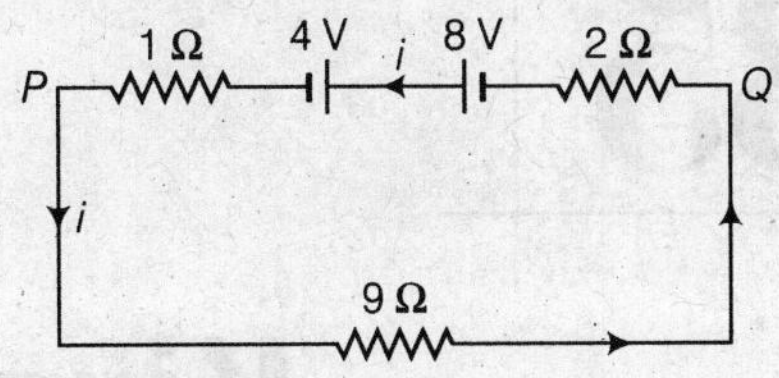

$$-2i + 8 - 4 - 1 \times i - 9i = 0$$

$\Rightarrow$ $i = \frac{1}{3}$ A

Potential difference across $PQ = \frac{1}{3} \times 9 = 3V$.

16. Because cell is in open circuit. So, the potential difference between A and B is 20 V.

17. Total $i = \frac{6}{2 + 2 + 2} = \frac{6}{6} = 1$ A

Current at 6Ω resistance $= \frac{3 \times 1}{3 + 6} = \frac{1}{3}$ A

18. Current $i = \frac{E}{R + r} = \frac{5}{4.5 + 0.5} = 1$ A

$V = E - ir = 5 - 1 \times 0.5$

$= 4.5$ V

19. Maximum current flows momentarily $i = \frac{E}{r} = \frac{6}{0.5} = 12$ A

20. Strength $= 5 \times 18 = 90$ AH

35

Kirchhoff's Law and Wheatstone Bridge

Kirchhoff's Law

This law is used to solve a problem regarding electrical circuit. *The law has two parts*

1. Kirchhoff's First Law (or Current Law or Junction Rule)

In any electrical network, the algebraic sum of currents meeting at a junction is always zero *i.e.*, $\Sigma I = 0$

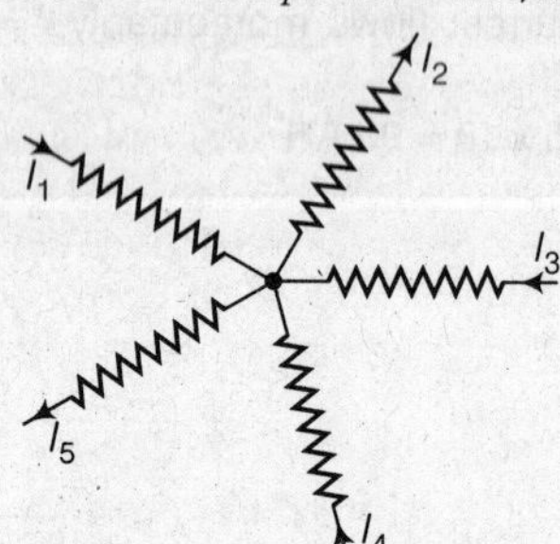

$$I_1 - I_2 + I_3 + I_4 - I_5 = 0$$

$$\Rightarrow \quad I_1 + I_3 + I_4 = I_2 + I_5$$

The sum of currents flowing towards a junction is equal to sum of currents leaving the junction.

By convention the current directed towards the junction is positive while those directed away from the junction is taken as negative.

The first law is in accordance with conservation of charge.

The charges do not accumulate at a junction. The total charge entering a junction is equal to total charge leaving the junction.

2. Kirchhoff's Second Law (or Voltage Law or Loop Rule)

The algebraic sum of all the potential drops and emf's along any closed path in a network is zero. *i.e.*, $\Sigma V = 0$

The second law is in accordance with conservation of energy.

According to second law, the electric energy given to the charge by a source of emf is lost in passing through resistance.

The change in potential in covering a resistance in the direction of current is negative ($-IR$) while in opposite direction it is positive.

(a) $V_A - IR = V_B$; $V_B - V_A = IR$

(b) $V_B + IR = V_A$; $V_A - V_B = IR$

The potential falls along direction of current. The potential fall is taken as negative while potential rise is taken as positive. The emf of source is taken as positive when it is traversed from negative to positive terminal while it is taken as negative when it is traversed from positive to negative irrespective of the direction of current.

(a) $V_A - E = V_B$; $V_B - V_A = -E$

(b) $V_B + E = V_A$; $V_A - V_B = E$

If there are n loops their will be $(n-1)$ equations according to loop rule.

The algebraic sum of products of currents and resistances in a closed loop is equal to sum of emf's applied in the circuit. *i.e.*, $\Sigma E = \Sigma IR$

Note

- Kirchhoff's first law based on the law of conservation of charge.
- Kirchhoff's second law based on the law of conservation of energy.

Example

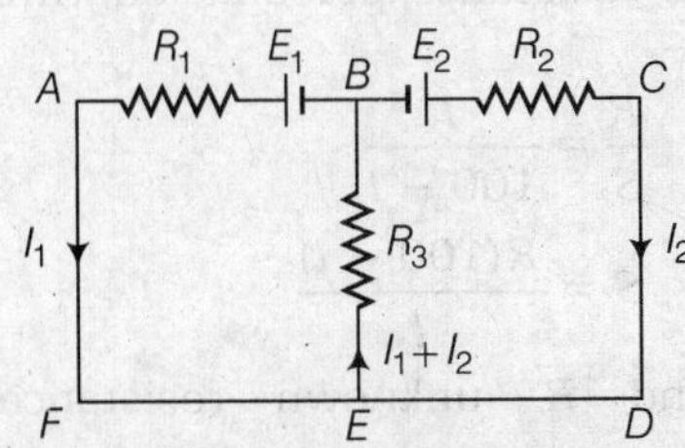

Suppose that due to the battery of emf E_1, current I_1 flows through the resistor R_1 and that due to E_2, the current I_2 flows through the resistor R_2. Then, according to Kirchhoff's first law, current $(I_1 + I_2)$ will flow through the resistor R_3 as shown in above figure.

In closed part $ABEFA$ of the circuit

$$I_1R_1 + (I_1 + I_2)R_3 = E_1$$

In closed part $BCDEB$ of the circuit

$$I_2R_2 + (I_1 + I_2)R_3 = E_2$$

Wheatstone Bridge

It is an arrangement of four resistances used to determine one of these resistances quickly and accurately in terms of the remaining three resistances. This method was first suggested by a British physicist Sir Charles F. Wheatstone in 1843.

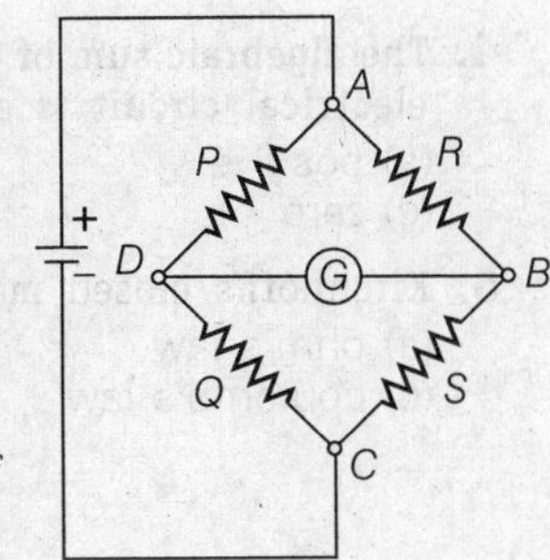

A wheatstone bridge consists of four resistances P, Q, R and S; connected to form the arms of a quadrilateral $ABCD$. A battery of emf E is connected between points A and C and a sensitive galvanometer between B and D, as shown in above figure.

Let S be the resistance to be measured. The resistance R is so adjusted that there is no deflection in the galvanometer. The bridge is said to balanced when the potential difference across the galvanometer is zero, so that there is no current through the galvanometer. In the balanced condition of the bridge,

$$\frac{P}{Q} = \frac{R}{S}$$

Unknown resistance, $S = \frac{Q}{P} . R$

Knowing the ratio of resistances P and Q and the resistance R, we can determine the unknown resistance S. That is why the arms containing the resistances P and Q are called ratio arms, the arm AD containing R standard arm and the arm CD containing S the unknown arm.

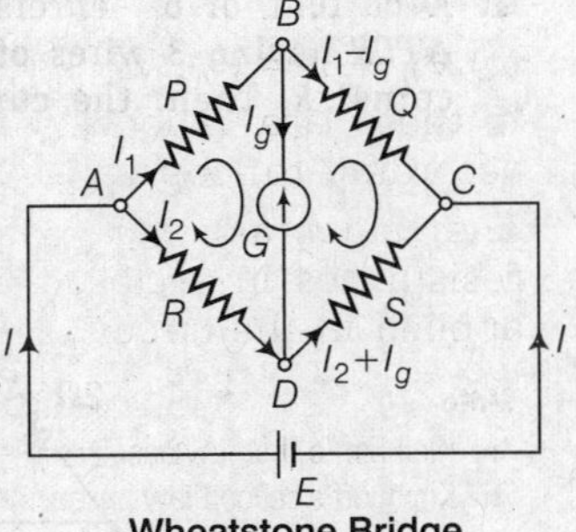

Wheatstone Bridge

Note While solving the problem related to Wheatstone bridge it is an important to first verify whether the Wheatstone balancing condition is applicable or not.

If Wheatstone balancing is proved, then we can solve the problem by using Ohm's law. If Wheatstone balancing is not existing there, we can solve the problem by using Kirchhoff's law.

e.g., For balanced Wheatstone bridge,

$$\frac{P}{Q} = \frac{R}{S}$$

If $P = Q = R = S = r$ (say), then

$$R_{eq} = \frac{(P + Q)(R + S)}{(P + Q) + (R + S)} = \frac{(r + r)(r + r)}{(r + r) + (r + r)} = \frac{4r^2}{4r} = r\,\Omega$$

Metre Bridge or Slide Wire Bridge

It is the simplest practical application of the Wheatstone bridge that is used to measure an unknown resistance.

Principle

Its working is based on the principle of Wheatstone bridge. When the bridge is balanced,

$$\frac{P}{Q} = \frac{R}{S}$$

Construction

It consists of usually one metre long magnanin wire of uniform cross-section, stretched along a metre scale fixed over a wooden board and with its two ends soldered to two L-shaped thick copper strips A and C. Between these two copper strips, another copper strip is fixed so as to provide two gaps ab and a_1b_1. A resistance box R.B. is connected in the gap ab and the unknown resistance S is connected in the gap a_1b_1. A source of emf E is connected across AC. A movable jockey and a galvanometer are connected across BD, as shown in figure.

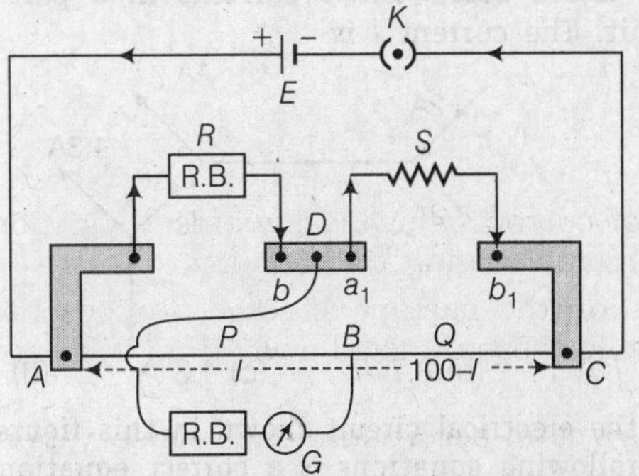

Measurement of Unknown Resistance by a Metre Bridge

Working

After taking out a suitable resistance R from the resistance box, the jockey is moved along the wire AC till there is no deflection in the galvanometer. This is the balanced condition of the Wheatstone bridge. If P and Q are the resistances of the parts AB and BC of the wire, then for the balanced condition of the bridge, we have

$$\frac{P}{Q} = \frac{R}{S}$$

Unknown Resistance

Let total length of wire $AC = 100$ cm and $AB = l$ cm, then $BC = (100 - l)$ cm. Since, the bridge wire is of uniform cross-section, therefore

Resistance of wire ∝ Length of wire

$$\therefore \quad \frac{P}{Q} = \frac{\text{Resistance of } AB}{\text{Resistance of } BC} = \frac{\sigma l}{\sigma(100 - l)} = \frac{l}{100 - l}$$

Where, σ is the resistance per unit length of the wire. Hence,

$$\frac{R}{S} = \frac{l}{100 - l}$$

$$\therefore \quad S = \frac{R(100 - l)}{l}$$

Knowing l and R, unknown resistance S can be determined.

Practice Questions

Level I

1. Which of the following represent Kirchhoff's first law?
(a) Law of conservation of momentum
(b) Law of conservation of charge
(c) Law of conservation of energy
(d) None of the above

2. Kirchhoff's second law represents the law of conservation of
(a) charge
(b) energy
(c) momentum
(d) None of the above

3. Wheatstone bridge is used to measure
(a) emf (b) current
(c) resistance (d) charge

4. The algebraic sum of the currents meeting at a point in an electrical circuit is always
(a) positive (b) negative
(c) zero (d) infinity

5. Kirchhoff's closed mesh law is extended form of
(a) ohm's law (b) lenz's conservation law
(c) coulomb's law (d) None of these

Level II

1. The figure below shows currents in a part of electric circuit. The current i is

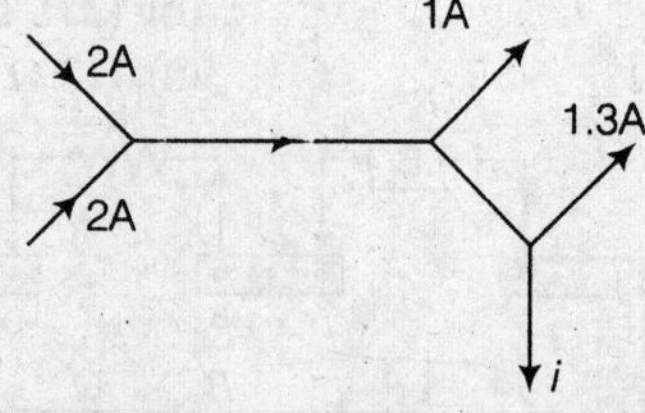

(a) 1.7 A (b) 3.7 A (c) 1.3 A (d) 1 A

2. See the electrical circuit shown in this figure. Which of the following equations is a correct equation for it?

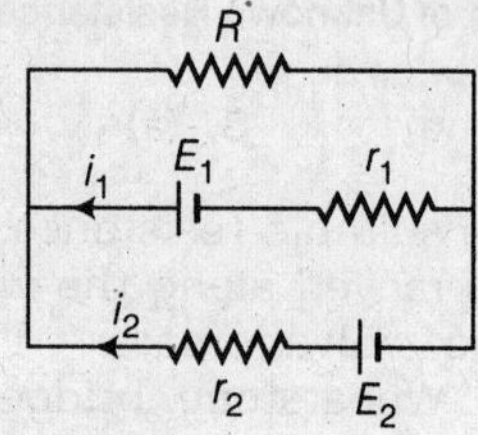

(a) $E_1 - (i_1 + i_2)R - i_1r_1 = 0$
(b) $E_2 - i_2r_2 - E_1 - i_1r_1 = 0$
(c) $-E_2 - (i_1 + i_2)R + i_2r_2 = 0$
(d) $E_1 - (i_1 + i_2)R + i_1r_1 = 0$

3. Consider the circuit shown in the figure. The current I_3 is equal to

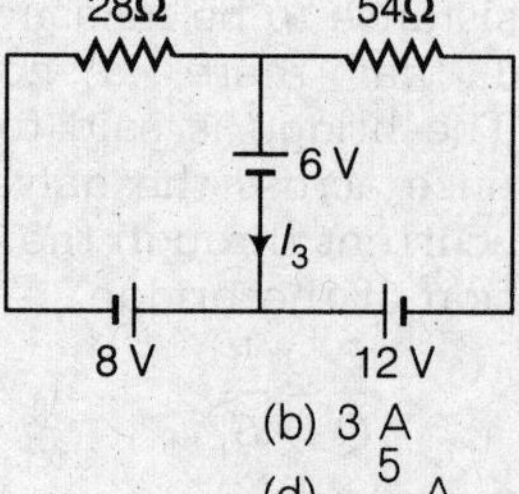

(a) 5 A (b) 3 A
(c) −3 A (d) $-\frac{5}{6}$ A

4. A current of 6 enters one corner P of an equilateral ΔPQR having 3 wires of resistances 2 Ω each and by the corner R. Then, the current I_1 I_2 are

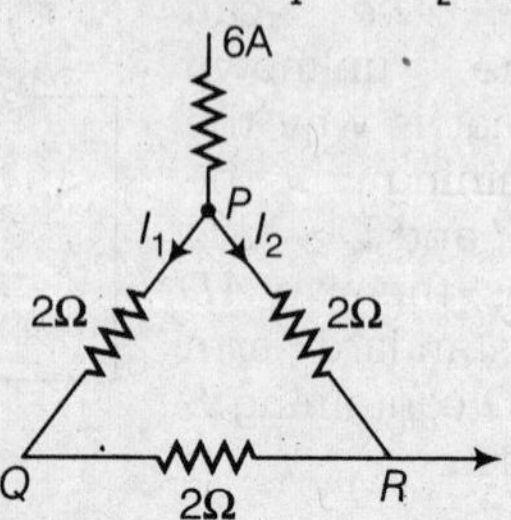

(a) 2 A, 4 A (b) 4 A, 2 A (c) 1A, 2 A (d) 2 A, 3 A

5. Five resistances are connected as shown in figure. The effective resistance between the points *A* and *B* is

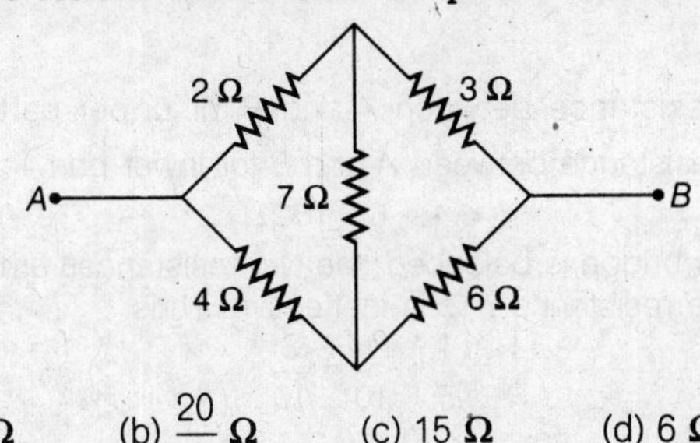

(a) $\frac{10}{3}\ \Omega$ (b) $\frac{20}{3}\ \Omega$ (c) 15 Ω (d) 6 Ω

6. Each of the resistances in the network shown in figure is equal to *R*. The resistance between the terminals *A* and *B* is

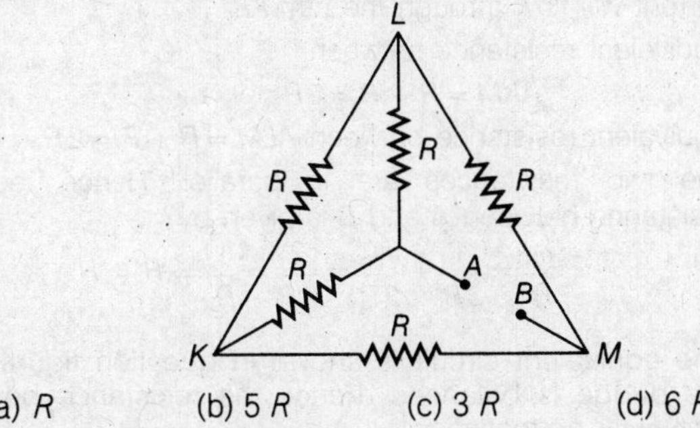

(a) *R* (b) 5 *R* (c) 3 *R* (d) 6 *R*

7. The equivalent resistance between the points *X* and *Y* of the following figure is

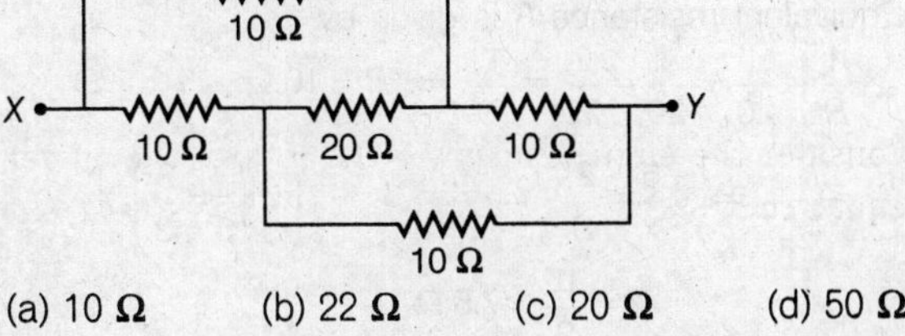

(a) 10 Ω (b) 22 Ω (c) 20 Ω (d) 50 Ω

8. In the circuit given, the correct relation to a balanced Wheatstone bridge is

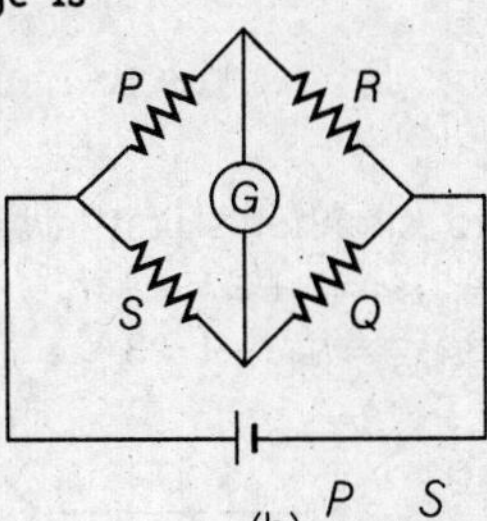

(a) $\frac{P}{Q} = \frac{R}{S}$ (b) $\frac{P}{Q} = \frac{S}{R}$

(c) $\frac{P}{R} = \frac{S}{Q}$ (d) None of these

9. In a metre bridge, with a standard resistance of 5 Ω in the left gap, the ratio of balancing lengths on the meter bridge wire is 2:3. The unknown resistance is

(a) 7.5 Ω (b) 15 Ω

(c) 10 Ω (d) 3.3 Ω

10. Figure is a metre bridge set up with null deflection

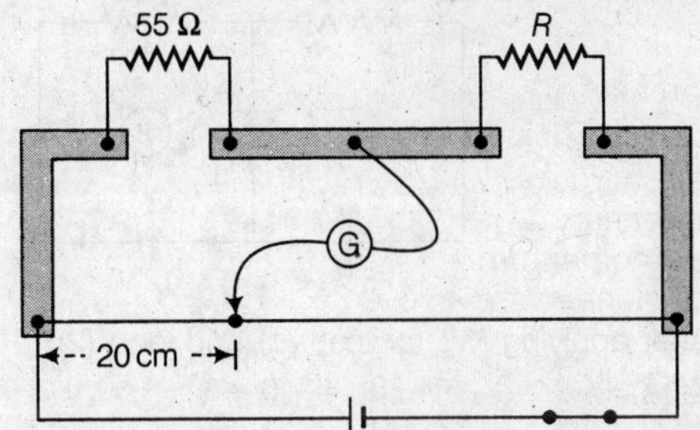

in the galvanometer. The value of the unknown resistance *R* is

(a) 55 Ω (b) 13.75 Ω

(c) 220 Ω (d) 110 Ω

Answers

Level I

1. (b)	**2.** (b)	**3.** (c)	**4.** (c)	**5.** (a)

Level II

1. (a)	**2.** (a)	**3.** (d)	**4.** (a)	**5.** (a)	**6.** (a)	**7.** (a)	**8.** (a)	**9.** (a)	**10.** (c)

Hints and Solutions

Level II

1. According to Kirchhoff's first law

At junction A, $i_{AB} = 2 + 2 = 4\text{A}$

At junction B, $i_{AB} = i_{BC} - 1 = 3\text{A}$

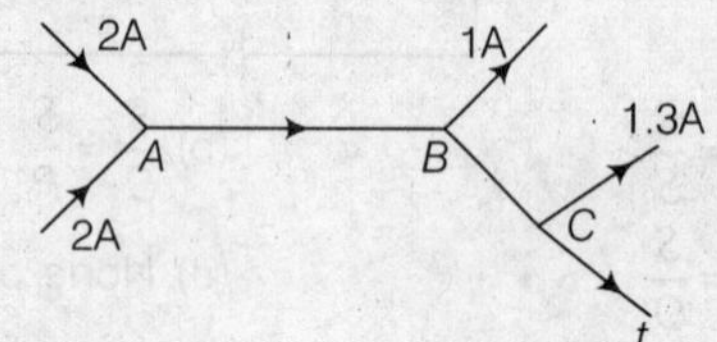

At junction C, $i = i_{BC} - 1.3 = 3 - 1.3 = 1.7\text{ A}$

2. According to Kirchhoff's voltage law only option (a) is correct.

3. Suppose current through different paths of the circuit is as follows

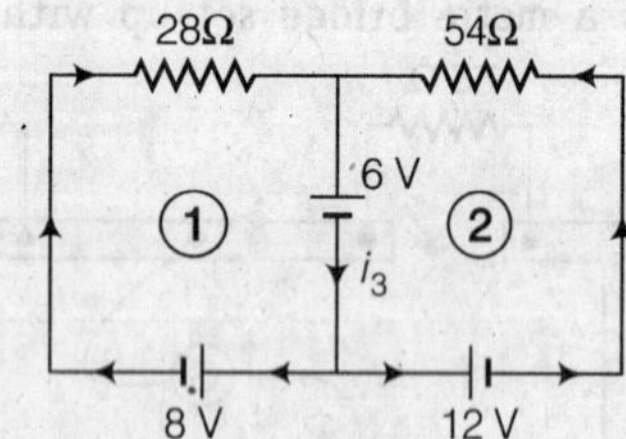

After applying KVL for loop (1) and loop (2).

We get, $\quad 28i_1 = -6 - 8$

$\Rightarrow \quad i_1 = -\frac{1}{2}\text{A}$

and $\quad 54i_2 = -6 - 12$

$\Rightarrow \quad i_2 = -\frac{1}{3}\text{A}$

Hence, $\quad i_3 = i_1 + i_2 = -\frac{5}{6}\text{A}$

4. $I_1 = \frac{2}{2+4} \times 6 = 2\text{ A}$

$\therefore \quad I_2 = 4\text{ A}$

5. Resistance between A and B for upper part $= 2 + 3 = 5\,\Omega$

Resistance between A and B for lower part

$$= 4 + 6 = 10\,\Omega$$

As bridge is balanced, the two resistances are in parallel and the resistance $7\,\Omega$ is ineffective. Thus,

$$\frac{1}{R} = \frac{1}{5} + \frac{1}{10} = \frac{3}{10}$$

$$\Rightarrow \quad R = \left(\frac{10}{3}\right)\Omega$$

6. The equivalent circuit is shown in question figure.

Since, the Wheatstone's bridge is balanced, therefore no current will flow through the arm KL.

Equivalent resistance between

$$AKM = R + R = 2R$$

Equivalent resistance between $ALM = R + R = 2R$

The two resistances are in parallel. Hence, equivalent resistance between A and B is given by

$$\frac{1}{R'} = \frac{1}{2R} + \frac{1}{2R} = \frac{2}{2R} = \frac{1}{R} \Rightarrow R' = R$$

7. The equivalent circuit is shown in question figure. Since, the bridge is balanced, hence the resistance between B and D is ineffective.

Resistance of part $ABC = 10 + 10 = 20\,\Omega$

Resistance of part $ADC = 10 + 10 = 20\,\Omega$

Equivalent resistance R is given by

$$\frac{1}{R} = \frac{1}{20} + \frac{1}{20} = \frac{2}{20} = \frac{1}{10} \quad \Rightarrow R = 10\,\Omega$$

9. $\frac{P}{Q} = \frac{l_1}{l_2} \quad \Rightarrow \quad \frac{5}{x} = \frac{2}{3} \qquad \left(\because \frac{l_1}{l_2} = \frac{2}{3}\right)$

$\therefore \quad x = \frac{15}{2} = 7.5\,\Omega$

10. As bridge is balanced, so $\frac{55}{R} = \frac{20}{80} = \frac{1}{4}$

$\therefore \quad R = 55 \times 4$

$\quad = 220\,\Omega$

36

Potentiometer

Principle

The principle of potentiometer states that when a constant current is passed through a wire of uniform area of cross-section, the potential drop across any portion of the wire is directly proportional to the length of that portion.

A potentiometer consists of a number of segments of wire of uniform area of cross-section stretched over a wooden board between two thick copper strips. Each segment of wire is 100 cm long. The wire is usually of constantan or manganin. A meter rod is fixed parallel to its length. An auxiliary or driver battery connected across the two end terminals sends current through the wire, which is kept constant by using a rheostat.

Theory

Let V be potential difference across certain portion of wire, whose resistance is R. If I is the current through the wire, then

$$V = IR$$

We know that, $R = \rho \frac{l}{A}$

Where, l, A ρ are length, area of cross-section and resistivity of the material of wire respectively.

$$\therefore \quad V = I \rho \frac{l}{A}$$

If a constant current is passed through the wire of uniform area of cross-section, then I and A are constants. Since, for a given wire, ρ is also constant, we have

$$V = \text{Constant} \times l \Rightarrow V \propto l$$

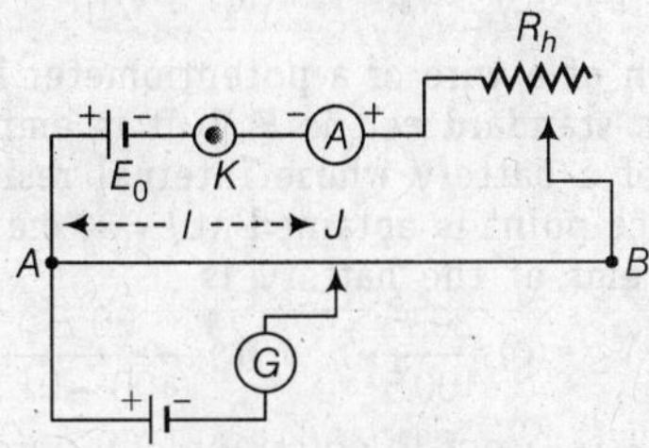

Hence, if a constant current flows through a wire of uniform area of cross-section, then potential drop along the wire is directly proportional to the length of the wire.

- If with a given potentiometer arrangements, we obtain balancing lengths l_1 and l_2 for cells of emfs E_1 and E_2, then $\frac{E_1}{E_2} = \frac{l_1}{l_2}$
- Internal resistance of the cell $r = \left(\frac{l_1 - l_2}{l_2}\right) R = \left(\frac{E}{V} - 1\right) R$

Practice Questions

Level I

1. emf of a cell can be measured by

(a) voltmeter
(b) ammeter
(c) potentiometer
(d) meter bridge

2. If emf's of two cells are E_1 and E_2, then the relation with the balancing length in from a potentiometer is

(a) $E_1 \times E_2 = l_1 \times l_2$
(b) $\frac{E_1}{E_2} = \frac{l_2}{l_1}$
(c) $\frac{E_1}{E_2} = \frac{l_1}{l_2}$
(d) $\frac{E_1}{E_2} = \frac{l_1^2}{l_2^2}$

3. In a potentiometer if the galvanometer shows zero reading. This means
(a) there is no current in the circuit
(b) there is no current in the potentiometer
(c) there is no current in galvanometer
(d) None of the above

4. If the length of the wire is increased in a potentiometer, then the effect on the balancing length will
(a) balancing long the will be achieved at longer length
(b) balancing length will be achieved at shorter length
(c) there is no effect on the balancing length
(d) None of the above

5. If the length of the wire is increased in a potentiometer, then the sensitivity of the potentiometer will
(a) increase (b) decrease
(c) remain same (d) None of these

Level II

1. A potentiometer consists of a wire of length 400 cm and of resistance 10 Ω. It is connected to a cell of emf 2 V having negligible internal resistance. Calculate the potential difference per unit length of the wire
(a) 5 V/m (b) 0.5 V/m
(c) 50 V/m (d) None of these

2. A potentiometer consists of a wire of length 4 m and resistance 10 Ω. It is connected to a cell of emf 2 V. The potential difference per unit length of the wire will be
(a) 0.5 V/m (b) 2 V/m (c) 5 V/m (d) 10 V/m

3. The length of a wire of a potentiometer is 100 cm and the emf of its standard cell is E V. It is employed to measure the emf of a battery whose internal resistance is 0.5 Ω. If the balance point is obtained at $l = 30$ cm from the positive end, the emf of the battery is
(a) $\frac{30E}{100}$ (b) $\frac{30E}{100.5}$ (c) $\frac{30E}{(100-0.5)}$ (d) $\frac{30(E-0.5i)}{100}$
Where, i is current in potentiometer wire.

4. In a potentiometer experiment, the balancing length with a cell is 560 cm. When an external resistance of 10 Ω is connected in parallel to the cell, the balancing length changes by 412 cm. The internal resistance of the cell (in Ω) is
(a) 3.6 (b) 2.4
(c) 1.2 (d) 0.6

5. A potentiometer has uniform potential gradient. The specific resistance of the material of the potentiometer wire is 10^{-7} Ω-m and the current passing through it is 0.1 A, cross-section of the wire is 10^{-6} m^2. The potential gradient along the potentiometer wire is
(a) 10^{-8} V/m
(b) 10^{-2} V/m
(c) 10^{-6} V/m
(d) 10^{-4} V/m

Answers

Level I

1. (c)	2. (c)	3. (c)	4. (a)	5. (a)

Level II

1. (b)	2. (a)	3. (a)	4. (c)	5. (b)

Hints and Solutions

Level II

1. Length of wire = 400 cm = 4 m

Current flowing, $i = \frac{E}{R} = \frac{2}{10} = 0.2\text{ A}$

Resistance of unit length of wire $= \frac{10}{4} = 2.5\text{N}$

Potential difference per unit length of the wire
$$= 0.2 \times 2.5 = 0.5\text{ V/m}$$

2. Current in the wire $= \left(\frac{2}{10}\right) = 0.2\text{ A}$

Potential difference per unit length $= iR = \frac{0.2 \times 10}{4} = 0.5\text{ V/m}$

3. Using the principle of potentiometer, we have
$$V \propto l \Rightarrow \left(\frac{V}{E}\right) = \left(\frac{l}{L}\right)$$

Here, V = emf of battery, E = emf of standard cell, l = balancing length and L = length of potentiometer wire.

$$\therefore \quad V = \frac{El}{L} = \frac{E \times 30}{100} = \frac{30E}{100}$$

4. The internal resistance is given by $r = \frac{R(l_1 - l_2)}{l_2}$

Here, $l_1 = 560\text{ cm}$ and $l_2 = 500\text{ cm}$

$$\therefore \quad r = \frac{10 \times 60}{500} = 1.2\ \Omega$$

5. If k be the potential gradient, then
$$k = \frac{i\rho}{A} = \frac{0.1 \times 10^{-7}}{10^{-6}} = 10^{-2}\text{ V/m}$$

37

Heating Effect of Electric Current

What happens when you switch on an electric iron? Within a few seconds the plane bottom plate of electric iron gets heated up. Where does this heat come from? This heat is produced by the heating effect of electric current. When electric current flows through the resistance element, the flowing charges suffer resistance. Work has to be done to overcome this resistance which is converted into heat energy. The complete sequence is, electrical energy does work which converts into heat energy.

If Q amount of charge flows through a potential difference of V, then

Work done is $\quad W = QV \quad$ ...(i)

But $\quad I = \dfrac{Q}{t}$

$\therefore \quad Q = I \times t \quad$ ...(ii)

From Eqs. (i) and (ii), $\quad W = VIt$

Also by Ohm's law, $\quad V = IR$

$$W = (IR)It = I^2Rt$$

This work is converted into heat energy (H).

$$\therefore \quad H = I^2Rt$$

$\Rightarrow$ Heat energy, $H \propto I^2$ and $H \propto R$ and $H \propto t$

Note The above effect is also called joule's heating effect.

Electric Power

The rate at which energy is used by an electrical appliance is called the electric power of that appliance.

Therefore, Power $= \dfrac{\text{Work}}{\text{Time}}$, Power $= \dfrac{\text{Energy}}{\text{Time}}$

$\Rightarrow \quad P = \dfrac{W}{t}$, where $W = I^2Rt = \dfrac{V^2}{R}t = VIt$

$\Rightarrow \quad P = I^2R$ [in terms of I and R]

$\Rightarrow \quad P = \dfrac{V^2}{R}$ [in terms of V and R]

$\Rightarrow \quad P = V \times I$ [in terms of V and I]

SI unit of power is watt (W). Power is a scalar quantity.

Important Points

- When resistances are connected in series.
  In this case, the current in each resistance will be the same.
  We have, $P \propto V$ and $P \propto R$
  This shows that in series connections, the potential difference and power consumed will be more in larger resistance.
- When resistances are connected in parallel.
  In this case, the potential difference V across each resistance is same. We have, $P \propto \left(\dfrac{1}{R}\right)$ and $i \propto \left(\dfrac{1}{R}\right)$
  This shows that in parallel connections, the current and power consumed will be more in smaller resistance.
- Power consumed when resistance is changed from R to $\left(\dfrac{R}{n}\right)$ keeping potential difference same.
  We know that, $P = \dfrac{V^2}{R}$
  When resistance is changed from R to $\left(\dfrac{R}{n}\right)$ keeping V same, then
  $$P' = \frac{V^2}{\frac{R}{n}} = \frac{nV^2}{R} = nP$$
  Therefore, the power consumed changes from P to n P.
- Ratio of power dissipated when n equal resistances are connected first in series and then in parallel with a voltage source.
  Power dissipated in series combination is given by
  $$P_s = \frac{V^2}{nR}$$
  Power dissipated in parallel combination is given by
  $$P_p = \frac{V^2}{\left(\frac{R}{n}\right)} = \frac{nV^2}{R} \therefore \frac{P_p}{P_s} = n^2 \text{ or } P_p = n^2P_s$$
  Therefore, the power consumed by n equal resistors in parallel is n^2 times that of the power consumed in series provided the potential difference remains the same.

Long Distance Power Transmission

The loss in a power transmission line is given

Power loss $= PL = i^2 R$

Where, i is current flowing through the line.

Let the power be transmitted at voltage V, then loss is given by

$$PL = \frac{P^2}{V^2} \times R \qquad \left(\because P = Vi \text{ or } i = \frac{P}{V}\right)$$

For a power line, P and R constant. Therefore, $PL \propto \left(\frac{1}{V^2}\right)$

This shows that if the power is transmitted a voltage, then power loss will be small and *vice-versa* the power is transmitted at high voltage.

Ex. Two bulbs of 25W and 100W are joined to each other in (i) series and (ii) parallel. Again, connect these combinations to the main power supply. Which bulb will glow more brightness in the given two combinations?

Sol. More amount of heat transfer per second in a bulb gives more brightness.

Resistance R_1 of a bulb of 25 W $= \frac{V^2}{25}$

and resistance R_2 of a bulb of 100 W $= \frac{V^2}{100}$

(i) When both the bulb connected in series, then current flowing in each bulb will be same.

Hence, Power in a bulb of 25 W per second,

$$P_1 = I^2 R_1$$

Similarly, per second power in bulb of 100 W

$$P_2 = I^2 R_2$$

$$\therefore \quad \frac{P_1}{P_2} = \frac{I^2 R_1}{I^2 R_2} = \frac{\frac{V^2}{25}}{\frac{V^2}{100}} = \frac{4}{1} \Rightarrow P_1 = 4P_2$$

Thus, bulb of 25 W glows with more brightness.

(ii) In parallel combination the potential difference of each bulb will be same. Hence,

$$P'_1 = \frac{V^2}{R_1}, \quad P'_2 = \frac{V^2}{R_2}$$

$$\therefore \quad \frac{P'_1}{P'_2} = \frac{V^2/R_1}{V^2/R_2} = \frac{R_2}{R_1} = \frac{V^2/100}{V^2/25} = \frac{1}{4} \Rightarrow 4P'_1 = P'_2$$

In this case, bulb of 100 W will glows with more brightness.

Practice Questions

Level I

1. An expression for rate of heat generated, if a current of I ampere flows through a resistance of $R\ \Omega$, is

(a) I^2Rt (b) I^2R (c) V^2R (d) IR

2. One kilowatt hour is equal to

(a) 36×10^5 J (b) 36×10^3 J
(c) 10^3 J (d) 10^5 J

3. Which of the following is not equal to watt?

(a) $(\text{Amp})^2 \times \text{Ohm}$ (b) Amp/Volt
(c) Amp × Volt (d) Joule/Second

4. Two bulbs are fitted in a room in the domestic electric installation. One of them glows brighter than the other. Then,

(a) the brighter bulb has smaller resistance
(b) the brighter bulb has larger resistance
(c) both the bulbs have the same resistance
(d) None of the above

5. The heating element of an electric heater should be made of a material having

(a) high specific resistance and high melting point
(b) high specific resistance and low melting point
(c) low specific resistance and low melting point
(d) low specific resistance and high melting point

6. Two electric bulbs whose resistance's are in the ratio 1:2 are connected in parallel to a constant voltage source. The power dissipated in them have the ratio

(a) 1 : 2 (b) 1 : 1
(c) 2 : 1 (d) 1 : 4

7. If two bulbs of 25 W and 100 W, rated at 220V, are connected in series across a 440 V supply

(a) 25 W bulb will fuse (b) 100 W bulb will fuse
(c) Both will fuse (d) None will fuse

8. The filament of bulb is of

(a) mercury (b) copper
(c) tungsten (d) None of these

9. Fuse wire should have

(a) low resistance, high melting point
(b) low resistance, low melting point
(c) high resistance, low melting point
(d) high resistance, high melting point

10. If a high power heater is connected to electric mains, then the bulbs in the house become dim because there is a

(a) current drop (b) potential drop
(c) no current drop (d) no potential drop

11. The electric current passing through a metallic wire produces heat because of

(a) collision of conduction electrons with each other
(b) collisions of the atoms of the metal with each other
(c) collision of the conduction electron with the atoms of the metallic wire
(d) None of the above

12. When a metal is heated, its resistance

(a) decreases (b) increases
(c) may increase or decrease (d) remains constant

Level II

1. If two wires having resistances R and $2R$ both are joined in series and in parallel, then ratio of heat generated in this situation, applying the same voltage is

(a) 2 : 1 (b) 1 : 2
(c) 2 : 9 (d) 9 : 2

2. A 60 W bulb operates on 220V supply. The current flowing through the bulb is

(a) $\frac{11}{3}$ A (b) $\frac{3}{11}$ A
(c) 3 A (d) 6 A

3. A hot electric iron has a resistance of 80Ω and is used on a 200V source. The electrical energy spent, if it is used for two hours, will be

(a) 8000 Wh (b) 2000 Wh
(c) 1000 Wh (d) 800 Wh

4. Two electric bulbs (60W and 100W respectively) are connected in series. The current passing through them is

(a) more in 100W bulb (b) more in 60W bulb
(c) same in both (d) None of these

5. A heater draws a current of 2A when connected to a 250 V source. The rate of energy dissipation is

(a) 500 W (b) 1000 W
(c) 250 W (d) 125 W

6. A bulb rated at (100W – 200V) is used on a 100V line. The current in the bulb is

(a) $\frac{1}{4}$ A (b) 4 A (c) $\frac{1}{2}$ A (d) 2 A

7. If three bulbs 60W, 100W and 200W are connected in parallel, then

(a) 200 W bulb will glow more
(b) 60 W bulb will glow more
(c) 100 W bulb will glow more
(d) All the bulbs will glow equally

8. Three electric bulbs of rating 60W each are joined in series and then connected to electric mains. The power consumed by these three bulbs will be

(a) 180W (b) 60W
(c) 20W (d) $\frac{20}{3}$ W

9. Two bulbs of 500W and 200W are manufactured to operate on 220V line. The ratio of heat produced in 500W and 200W, in two cases, when firstly they are joined in parallel and secondly in series, will be

(a) $\frac{5}{2}, \frac{2}{5}$ (b) $\frac{5}{2}, \frac{5}{2}$
(c) $\frac{2}{5}, \frac{5}{2}$ (d) $\frac{2}{5}, \frac{2}{5}$

10. An electric bulb is rated 60W, 220V. The resistance of its filament is

(a) 708Ω (b) 870Ω (c) 807Ω (d) 780Ω

11. An electric bulb of 100W is connected to a supply of electricity of 220V. Resistance of the filament is

(a) 484Ω (b) 100Ω (c) 22000Ω (d) 242Ω

12. If current in an electric bulb changes by 1%, then the power will change by

(a) 1% (b) 2% (c) 4% (d) $\frac{1}{2}$%

13. What must be the efficiency of an electric kettle marked 500 W, 230 V, if it was found to bring 1 kg of water at 15°C to boiling point in 15 min? (Given, specific heat capacity of water = 4200 J/kg°C)

(a) 79% (b) 81%
(c) 72% (d) 69%

14. 3 identical bulbs are connected in series and these together dissipate a power P. If now the bulbs are connected in parallel, then the power dissipated will be

(a) $\frac{P}{3}$ (b) $3P$ (c) $9P$ (d) $\frac{P}{9}$

15. An electric bulb is rated 220V and 100W. Power consumed by it when operated on 110V is

(a) 50 W (b) 75 W
(c) 90 W (d) 25 W

16. A 25 W, 220 V bulb and a 100 W, 220 V bulb are connected in series across a 220 V lines. Which electric bulb will glow more brightly?

(a) 25 W bulb
(b) 100 W bulb
(c) First 25 W and then 100 W
(d) Both with same brightness

17. When two resistances R_1 and R_2 are connected in series, they consume 12W power. When they are connected in parallel, they consume 50W power. What is the ratio of the powers of R_1 and R_2

(a) $\frac{1}{4}$ (b) 4 (c) $\frac{3}{2}$ (d) 3

18. Two electric bulbs whose resistances are in the ratio of 1 : 2 are connected in parallel to a constant voltage source. The powers dissipated in them have the ratio

(a) 1 : 2 (b) 1 : 1 (c) 2 : 1 (d) 1 : 4

19. Three electric bulbs of 200W, 200W and 400W are shown in figure. The resultant power of the combination is

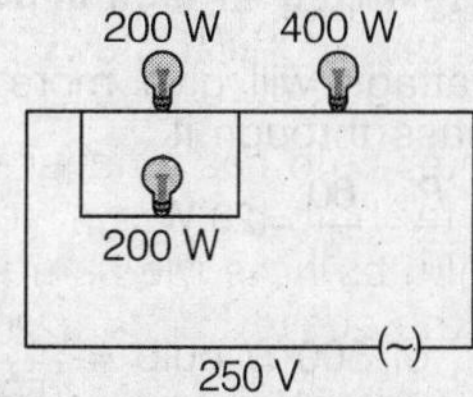

(a) 800W (b) 400W (c) 200W (d) 600W

20. Forty electric bulbs are connected in series across a 220V supply. After one bulb is fused, the remaining 39 are connected again in series across the same supply. The illumination will be

(a) more with 40 bulbs than with 39
(b) more with 39 bulbs than with 40
(c) equal in both the cases
(d) in the ratio of $49^2 : 39^2$

Answers

Level I

1. (a)	**2.** (a)	**3.** (b)	**4.** (a)	**5.** (a)	**6.** (c)	**7.** (a)	**8.** (c)	**9.** (c)	**10.** (a)
11. (c)	**12.** (b)								

Level II

1. (c)	**2.** (b)	**3.** (c)	**4.** (c)	**5.** (a)	**6.** (a)	**7.** (a)	**8.** (c)	**9.** (a)	**10.** (c)
11. (a)	**12.** (b)	**13.** (a)	**14.** (c)	**15.** (d)	**16.** (a)	**17.** (c)	**18.** (c)	**19.** (c)	**20.** (b)

Hints and Solutions

Level II

1. Heat $H = \dfrac{V^2 t}{R}$

$\Rightarrow \quad H \propto \dfrac{1}{R}$ (If V, t Constant)

$\Rightarrow \quad \dfrac{H_S}{H_P} = \dfrac{R_P}{R_S} = \dfrac{\left(\dfrac{R \times 2R}{3R}\right)}{(R + 2R)} = \dfrac{2}{9}$

2. $P = Vi \Rightarrow i = \dfrac{P}{V} = \dfrac{60}{220} = \dfrac{3}{11}$ A

3. Energy $= \dfrac{V^2}{R} t = \dfrac{200 \times 200 \times 2}{80} = 1000$ Wh

4. Because in series current is same.

5. $P = Vi = 250 \times 2 = 500$ W

6. $P = \dfrac{V^2}{R} \Rightarrow 100 = \dfrac{(200)^2}{R}$

$\Rightarrow \quad R = \dfrac{4 \times 10^4}{10^2} = 400\Omega$

Now, $\quad i = \dfrac{V}{R} = \dfrac{100}{400} = \dfrac{1}{4}$ A

7. $P_{\text{consumed brightness}} \propto P_{\text{rated}} \propto \dfrac{1}{R}$ *i.e.*, In parallel combination bulb of greater wattage will give more bright light and more current will pass through it.

8. In series $P' = \dfrac{P}{n} = \dfrac{60}{3} = 20$ W

9. Resistance R_1 of 500 W bulb $= \dfrac{(220)^2}{500}$

Resistance R_2 of 200 W bulb $= \dfrac{(220)^2}{200}$

When joined in parallel the potential difference across both the bulbs will be same.

Ratio of heat produced $= \dfrac{\dfrac{V^2}{R_1}}{\dfrac{V^2}{R_2}} = \dfrac{R_2}{R_1} = \dfrac{5}{2}$

When joined in series, the same current will flow through both the bulbs.

Ratio of heat produced $= \dfrac{i^2 R_1}{i^2 R_2} = \dfrac{R_1}{R_2} = \dfrac{2}{5}$

10. $R = \dfrac{V^2}{P} = \dfrac{(220)^2}{60} = 807\Omega$

11. $\dfrac{V^2}{R} = P$

$\Rightarrow \quad R = \dfrac{V^2}{P} = \dfrac{220 \times 220}{100} = 484\Omega$

12. $P = i^2 R \Rightarrow \dfrac{\Delta P}{P} = \dfrac{2\Delta i}{i}$ $\quad [R \to \text{Constant}]$

$\Rightarrow$ Per cent change in power $= 2 \times$ Per cent change in current $= 2 \times 1 = 2\%$

13. Heat produced $H = vit$

$= pt$

Where $\quad p = VI$

$\therefore \quad H = 500 \times 15 \times 60$

$= 45 \times 10^4$ J

Heat observed by water

= Mass × Specific heat capacity × Rise in temperature

$= 1 \times 4200 \times (100 - 15)$

$= 42 \times 10^3 \times 85$

$\therefore \quad$ Efficiency $= \dfrac{\text{Heat absorbed}}{\text{Heat produced}} \times 100$

$= \dfrac{85 \times 42 \times 10^3}{45 \times 10^4} \times 100$

$= 79\%$

14. When bulbs are connected in series,

$P = \dfrac{V^2}{R'} = \dfrac{V^2}{3R}$

When bulbs are connected in parallel,

$P' = \dfrac{V^2}{R''} = \dfrac{V^2 \times 3}{R}$

$= 3 \times 3P = 9P$

15. Resistance of the bulb $= \dfrac{V^2}{P_{Rated}}$

$$= \frac{220 \times 220}{100} = 484\Omega$$

When connected with 110V, the power consumed

$$P_{Consumed} = \frac{V^2}{R}$$

$$= \frac{110 \times 110}{484} = 25 \text{ W}$$

16. The resistance of 25W bulb is greater than 100W bulb. So, for the same current, heat produced will be more 25W bulb. So, it will glow more brightly.

17. $\dfrac{1}{P_1} + \dfrac{1}{P_2} = \dfrac{1}{12} \Rightarrow P_1 + P_2 = 50$

On solving these equations,

$$P_1 = 30 \text{ and } P_2 = 20$$

$$\therefore \quad \frac{P_1}{P_2} = \frac{3}{2}$$

18. We know that, $\dfrac{P_1}{P_2} = \dfrac{R_2}{R_1} = \dfrac{2}{1}$

19. Bulbs A and B are in parallel, their effective power is $P' = P_A + P_B$

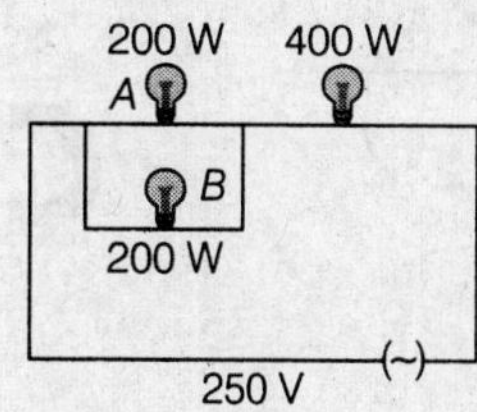

$$= 200 + 200 = 400 \text{ W}$$

P' and bulb C are in series, the resultant power of the combination is

$$P_R = \frac{P' \times P_C}{P' + P_C} = \frac{400 \times 400}{400 + 400} = 200 \text{ W}$$

20. When 1 bulb fuses, the total resistance of the circuit decreases, hence the current increases. Since, $P = i^2R$, therefore illumination increases.

38

Chemical Effect of Current

Chemical Effect of Current

Electric current can produce chemical change. This ability of current is called chemical effect. This effect is shown by DC only. AC current can't produce chemical effect.

Faraday's Laws of Electrolysis

Faraday's laws of electrolysis are quantitative relationships based on the electrochemical researches published by Michael Faraday in 1834.

Faraday's Ist Law of Electrolysis

The mass of a substance altered at electrode during electrolysis is directly proportional to the quantity of electricity transferred at that electrode.

Quantity of electricity refers to the quantity of electrical charge, typically measured in coulomb.

$$m \propto q$$

$$\Rightarrow \quad m = zq \quad \ldots(i)$$

Where, z is a electrochemical constant

But $\quad q \propto it$

$$\therefore \quad m = z\,it \quad \ldots(ii)$$

From Eqs. (i) and (ii), $z = \frac{m}{q}$

Faraday's IInd Law of Electrolysis

For a given quantity of DC electricity (electric charge), the mass of an elemental material altered at an electrode is directly proportionally to the element's equivalent weight.

$$m \propto E$$

$$\therefore \quad \frac{m_1}{m_2} = \frac{E_1}{E_2} \quad (\text{if } q_1 = q_2)$$

$$\frac{m_1}{m_2} = \frac{z_1}{z_2} \text{ and } \frac{m_1}{m_2} = \frac{E_1}{E_2} \quad (\text{If } q_1 = q_2)$$

$$\Rightarrow \quad \frac{z_1}{z_2} = \frac{E_1}{E_2} = \ldots = \frac{E}{z} = \text{constant}$$

Where, $\frac{E}{z} = F =$ Faraday's constant

Faraday Constant

(i) It is equal to the amount of charge required to liberate the mass of a substance at an electrode during electrolysis, equal to its chemical equivalent in gram (*i.e.,* one gram equivalent)

(ii) One faraday = 1F = 96500 C/g equivalent.

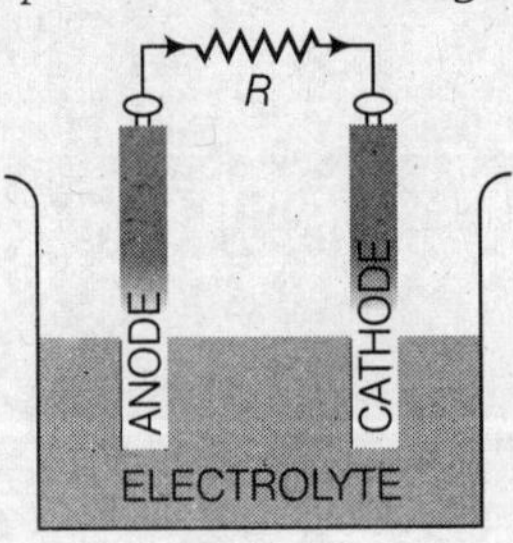

Electrochemical Cell

An electrochemical cell is a device which by converting chemical energy into electrical energy maintains the flow of charge in a circuit. It usually consists of two electrodes of different materials and an electrolyte. The electrode at higher potential is called anode and the one at lower potential is cathode.

Primary Cells

The cells which cannot be recharged electrically are called primary cells. Here the original state of cell cannot be brought back by passing electrical energy through cell from external source after cell is discharged.

e.g., Voltaic cell, Daniel cell, Leclanche cell, Manganese-alkaline cell, Mercury button cell etc.

Secondary Cells

The cells in which chemical process is reversible are called secondary cells. Here, original chemical state of cell can be brought back by passing electrical energy through cell from external source.

e.g., Lead acid accumulator, alkali cells etc.

Practice Questions

Level I

1. Faraday is a unit of
(a) charge (b) current
(c) capacitance (d) resistance

2. 1 Faraday is equal to
(a) 96500 A (b) 96500 N
(c) 96500 C (d) 96500 V

3. Voltmeter is used to measure
(a) current (b) EMF
(c) resistance (d) mass of ions

4. Chemical equivalent is equal to
(a) $\frac{\text{Atomic weight}}{\text{Valency}}$ (b) Atomic weight × Valency
(c) $\frac{\text{Valency}}{\text{Atomic weight}}$ (d) None of these

5. Ampere hour (Ah) is a unit of
(a) power (b) capacitance of a cell
(c) charge (d) resistance

6. For electroplating a spoon, it is placed in the voltameter at the position of
(a) cathode
(b) anode
(c) between cathode and anode
(d) anywhere in solution

7. Faraday constant (F) in terms of chemical equivalent W and electrochemical equivalent Z is
(a) $F = \frac{W}{Z}$ (b) $F = WZ$
(c) $F = \frac{Z^2}{W}$ (d) $F = \frac{Z}{W}$

8. Same current (I) from in many voltameters for the same time (t). If m be the mass of material on electrode and Z be the electrochemical equivalent, then
(a) $\frac{ZIt}{m}$ = constant (b) $\frac{It}{Zm}$ = constant
(c) $\frac{Z}{mIt}$ = constant (d) $\frac{I}{Zmt}$ = constant

9. The electric current flowing inside electrolyte by
(a) electrons
(b) only anions
(c) only cations
(d) (b) and (c)

10. Which of the following used for electrolyte?
(a) Alternating current (AC)
(b) Direct current (DC)
(c) Both (a) and (b)
(d) None of the above

Level II

1. The current of 1.6 A is flowing in a voltameter made by copper. The number of Cu^{++} ions accumulated per minute at cathode will be
(a) 3×10^{20}
(b) 1.6×10^{19}
(c) 1.5×10^{20}
(d) 3.2×10^{19}

2. The current of 0.5 A is flowing through a copper voltameter upto 10 min. The amount of copper accumulated at cathode is 0.1 g. The electrochemical equivalent of copper will be
(a) 3.3×10^{-5} kg C^{-1}
(b) 3.3×10^{-10} kg C^{-1}
(c) 3.3×10^{-7} kg C^{-1}
(d) 3.3×10^{-9} kg C^{-1}

3. The necessary electric current for accumulating 0.972 g chromium in 3 h will be (electrochemical equivalent of Cr $= 0.00018$ g C^{-1})
(a) 1 A (b) $\frac{3}{4}$ A (c) 0.5 A (d) 1.5 A

4. If 9.6×10^7 C of electric charge releases equivalent to 1 kg of material than time taken to release 2×10^{-5} kg copper from a copper sulphate solution flowing 0.15 A of current will be (Atomic weight of copper $= 64$)
(a) 402 s (b) 300 s (c) 500 s (d) 942 s

5. A copper voltameter connected with a resistance coil of 100 Ω. An stable current flowing upto 10 min through them which accumulate 0.1 g copper. What will be the heat generated in the coil?
(a) 10532.5 J (b) 12032.5 J
(c) 15302.5 J (d) None of these

Answers

Level I

1. (c)	**2.** (c)	**3.** (b)	**4.** (a)	**5.** (b)	**6.** (a)	**7.** (a)	**8.** (a)	**9.** (d)	**10.** (b)

Level II

1. (a)	**2.** (c)	**3.** (c)	**4.** (a)	**5.** (c)

Hints and Solutions

Level II

1. $q = It = n \times (2e)$

$$\Rightarrow \quad n = \frac{It}{2e} = \frac{1.6 \times 60}{2 \times 1.6 \times 10^{-19}}$$

$$= 3 \times 10^{20}$$

2. $m = ZIt$

$$Z = \frac{m}{It}$$

$$= \frac{0.1 \times 10^{-3}}{0.5 \times 10 \times 60} = \frac{10^{-4}}{300}$$

$$= 3.3 \times 10^{-7} \text{ kg C}^{-1}$$

3. Here, $I = \frac{m}{Zt} = \frac{0.972}{0.00018 \times 3 \times 60 \times 60} = 0.5 \text{ A}$

4. Chemical equivalent of copper $= \frac{64}{2} = 32$

$\because$ 32 kg releases copper 9.65×10^7C electric charge.

$\therefore$ 2×10^{-5} kg will releases copper

$$= \frac{9.65 \times 10^7 \times 2 \times 10^{-5}}{32} = 60.3$$

$$\therefore \quad \text{Time} = \frac{\text{Charge}}{\text{Current}} = \frac{60.3}{0.15} = 402\text{s}$$

5. $I = \frac{m}{Zt}$

$$= \frac{0.1 \times 10^{-3}}{3.3 \times 10^{-7} \times 600} = 0.505 \text{ A}$$

$H = I^2 Rt$

$$= (0.505)^2 \times 100 \times 60 \times 10 = 15302.5 \text{ J}$$

39

Instruments

Moving Coil Galvanometer

It is a device used to detect current in a circuit. It is based on the principle that a current carrying coil placed in a magnetic field experiences a torque, the magnitude of which depends on the strength of current. It consists of a coil of wire of area A and N turns carrying current I to be measured. It is suspended in a radial magnetic field so that its plane always remains parallel to $\vec{B}$ $(\sin\theta = 1)$ by a suspension fibre of torsion constant k. In equilibrium position,

Restoring torque = Deflecting torque

$$\Rightarrow \quad k\alpha = NIBA \Rightarrow \alpha = \frac{NBA}{k} \cdot I$$

*i.e.,*Deflection of coil ∝ Current in the coil.

Figure of Merit of a Galvanometer

It is the current which produces a deflection of one scale division in the galvanometer. It is given by

$$G = \frac{I}{\alpha} = \frac{k}{NBA}$$

Current Sensitivity of a Galvanometer

It is the deflection produced in a galvanometer when a unit current flows through it.

$$\text{Current sensitivity} = \frac{\alpha}{I} = \frac{NBA}{k}$$

Voltage Sensitivity of a Galvanometer

It is the deflection produced in a galvanometer when a unit potential difference is applied across its ends.

$$\text{Voltage sensitivity} = \frac{\alpha}{v} = \frac{\alpha}{IR} = \frac{NBA}{kR}$$

Conversion of a Galvanometer into an Ammeter

An ammeter is an instrument used to measure electric current in a circuit. A galvanometer of resistance G can be converted into an ammeter of range $0 - I$ by connecting a small resistance S in parallel with it. The value of small resistance, called shunt, is given by

$$S = \frac{I_g}{I - I_g} \times G$$

Where, I_g is the current with which galvanometer gives full-scale deflection.

Total resistance of an ammeter,

$$R_A = \frac{GS}{G + S}$$

An ammeter is a low resistance device and is connected in series in a circuit.

Conversion of Galvanometer into a Voltmeter

A voltmeter is used to measure potential difference between any two points of a circuit. A galvanometer of resistance G can be converted into a voltmeter of range $0 - V$ by connecting a large resistance R in series with it. The value of R, is given by

$$R = \frac{V}{I_g} - G$$

Total resistance of a voltmeter,

$$R_V = G + R$$

A voltmeter is a high resistance device and is always connected parallel to the conductor across potential difference, is to be measured.

Practice Questions

Level I

1. To convert a galvanometer into an ammeter, we connect
(a) low resistance in parallel
(b) high resistance in series
(c) high resistance in parallel
(d) low resistance in series

2. A galvanometer acting as a voltmeter will have
(a) a high resistance in parallel with its coil
(b) a high resistance in series with its coil
(c) a low resistance in parallel with its coil
(d) a low resistance in series with its coil

3. To convert a galvanometer into a voltmeter,
(a) a high resistance is connected in parallel
(b) a low resistance is connected in series
(c) a low resistance is connected in parallel
(d) a high resistance is connected in series

4. A candidate connects a moving coil voltmeter V and a moving coil ammeter A and resistance R as shown in figure.

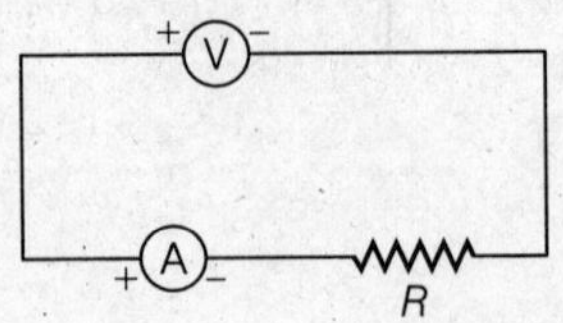

If the voltmeter reads 20 V and the ammeter reads 4 A, then R is
(a) equal to 5Ω
(b) greater than 5Ω
(c) less than 5Ω
(d) greater or less than 5Ω depending upon its material

5. The resistance of an ideal ammeter is
(a) very low (b) very high
(c) infinity (d) can have any value

6. The resistance of an ideal voltmeter is
(a) very high (b) nearly zero
(c) very low (d) None of these

Level II

1. A galvanometer having a resistance of 8Ω is shunted by a wire of resistance 2Ω. If the total current is 1A, the part of it passing through the shunt will be
(a) 1.2 A (b) 0.8 A (c) 0.5 A (d) 0.3 A

2. A galvanometer has a coil of resistance 100Ω and gives full scale deflection for 30 mA current. If it is to work as a voltmeter of 30 V range, the resistance required to be added will be
(a) 500Ω (b) 900Ω (c) 1000Ω (d) 1800Ω

3. A galvanometer of resistance 50Ω is connected to a battery of 3 V along with a resistance of 2950Ω in series. A full scale deflection of 30 divisions is obtained in the galvanometer. In order to reduce this deflection to 20 divisions, the resistance in series should be
(a) 4450Ω (b) 5050Ω (c) 5550Ω (d) 6050Ω

4. The resistance of an ammeter is 13Ω and scale is graduated for a current upto 100 A. After an additional shunt has been connected to this ammeter, it becomes possible to measure current upto 750 A by this meter. The value of shunt resistance is
(a) 0.2 Ω (b) 2 Ω (c) 20 Ω (d) 2 kΩ

5. A galvanometer of resistance G is shunted in such away that the current passing through galvanometer is $\left(\frac{I}{n}\right)$ part of total current. Then, the resistance of shunt will be
(a) nG (b) $\frac{G}{(n-1)}$ (c) $\frac{(n-1)}{G}$ (d) $\frac{G}{n}$

6. An ammeter of resistance 0.81Ω can measure the current upto 1 A is connected to the shunt. What will be the resistance of the shunt for measuring 10 A of current?
(a) 0.08Ω (b) 0.09Ω
(c) 0.05Ω (d) None of these

7. A shunted galvanometer having a resistance of 99Ω. If only 1% part of current passing through the galvanometer of the total current, then the resistance of shunt will be
(a) 0.5Ω (b) 1.5Ω (c) 1Ω (d) 2Ω

8. The range of a voltmeter having a resistance of $G\Omega$ is V Volt. What will be the resistance require to convert this voltmeter into nV volt range in series?
(a) nG (b) $\frac{G}{(n-1)}$ (c) $\frac{G}{n}$ (d) $G(n-1)$

Answers

Level I

1. (a) 2. (b) 3. (d) 4. (a) 5. (a) 6. (a)

Level II

1. (b) 2. (b) 3. (a) 4. (b) 5. (b) 6. (b) 7. (c) 8. (d)

Hints and Solutions

Level II

1. Let I be the total current and I_s be the current that passes through the shunt. Then,

$$(I - I_s) \times G = I_s \times S$$

Here, $I = 1\text{A}$, $G = 8\Omega$ and $S = 2\Omega$

$$\Rightarrow \quad I_s = \frac{I \times G}{G + S} = \frac{1 \times 8}{8 + 2} = 0.8\text{A}$$

2. Given that, $G = 100\Omega$,

$$I_g = 30\text{mA} = 30 \times 10^{-3}\text{A},$$

$$V = 30\text{V},$$

$$R = \frac{V}{I_g} - G$$

$$= \frac{30}{30 \times 10^{-3}} - 100$$

$$= 10^3 - 100 = 900\Omega$$

3. The current for full scale deflection,

$$I_g = \frac{E}{R + G} = \frac{3}{2950 + 50}$$

$$= \frac{3}{3000} = 10^{-3}\text{A}$$

The current required for a deflection of 20 divisions,

$$I_g{}' = I_g \times \frac{20}{30}$$

$$= 10^{-3} \times \frac{20}{30}$$

$$= \frac{2}{3} \times 10^{-3}\text{A}$$

If R' is the required resistance, then

$$I_g{}' = \frac{E}{R' + G}$$

$$\therefore \quad \frac{2}{3} \times 10^{-3} = \frac{3}{R' + 50}$$

$$\Rightarrow \quad R' + 50 = \frac{3 \times 3}{2 \times 10^{-3}} = 4500$$

$$\Rightarrow \quad R' = 4500 - 560$$

$$= 4450\Omega$$

4. The ammeter can be considered as a galvanometer having a resistance of 13Ω and which can allow a maximum current of 100A to pass through it.

Thus, $G = 13\Omega$, $I_g = 100\text{A}$ and $I = 750\text{A}$

The value of the required shunt is given by

$$S = \frac{I_g G}{I - I_g} = \frac{100 \times 13}{750 - 100} = \frac{100 \times 13}{650} = 2\Omega$$

5. If S be the resistance of shunt and I be the total current, then current flowing in a galvanometer $= \frac{I}{n}$

Current flowing through the shunt $= I - \frac{I}{n}$

$$\therefore \quad \frac{I}{n} \times G = \left(I - \frac{I}{n}\right)S$$

$$\Rightarrow \quad S = \frac{G}{n} \times \left(\frac{n}{n-1}\right) = \frac{G}{n-1}$$

6.

$$I_g = I\frac{S}{G + S}$$

$$1 = \frac{10 \times S}{0.81 + S}$$

$$0.81 + S = 10S$$

$$\Rightarrow 10S - S = 0.81$$

$$\therefore \quad S = \frac{0.81}{9} = 0.09\Omega$$

7. $I_g = \frac{I}{100}$ From $I_g = I\frac{S}{G + S}$,

$$\frac{I}{100} = I \times \frac{S}{99 + S}$$

$$\Rightarrow \quad 99 + S = 100S$$

$$\Rightarrow \quad 99S = 99$$

$$\therefore \quad S = 1\Omega$$

8. The maximum current flowing through the coil of voltmeter

$$I = \frac{V}{G} = \frac{nV}{G + R}$$

$$\Rightarrow \quad G + R = nG$$

$$R = nG - G = G(n - 1)$$

40

Magnetic Effects of Current

Oersted Observation

A compass needle suffers a deflection when it is placed near a wire carrying an electric current. When the direction of current is reversed, the direction of deflection of the needle also reverses. This conclusively proves that a current carrying conductor produces a magnetic field around it. This is called magnetic effect of current.

Oersted's Experiment

Oersted found experimentally that a magnetic field is established around a current carrying conductor just as it occurs around a magnet.

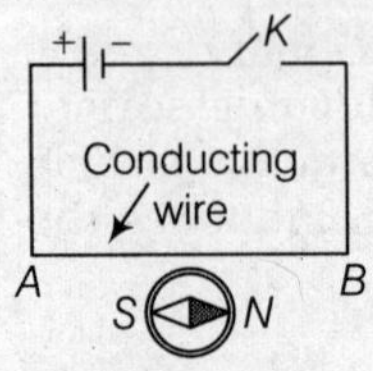

No current, key is open

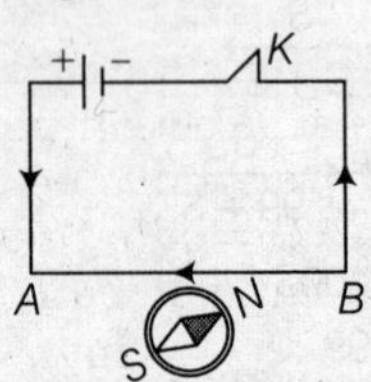

When key is pressed needle suffers deflection

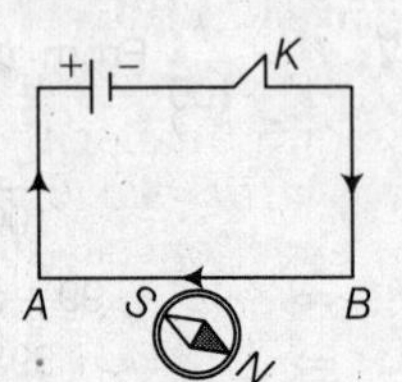

When key is pressed it suffers deflection in opposite direction

Biot-Savart Law

According to this law, the magnetic field due to a current carrying element $d\vec{l}$ carrying current I at a point P at distance r from it is given by

$$dB = \frac{\mu_0}{4\pi} \frac{Idl\sin\theta}{r^2}$$

In vector notation, $d\vec{B} = \frac{\mu_0 I}{4\pi} \cdot \frac{d\vec{l} \times \vec{r}}{r^3}$

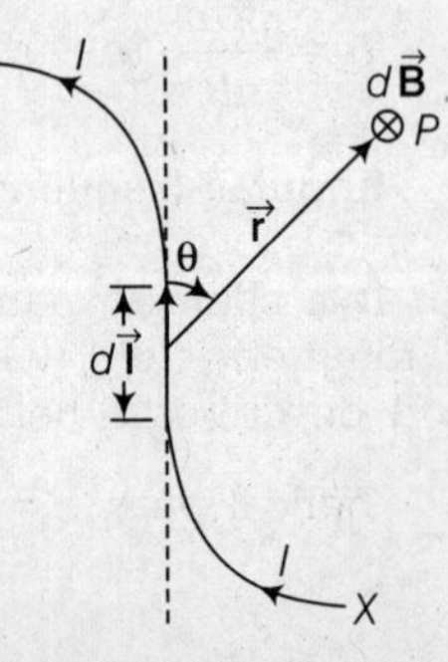

Here, θ is the angle between $d\vec{l}$ and $\vec{r}$ and $\mu_0 = 4\pi \times 10^{-7}$ Tm A^{-1}, is the permeability of free space. The direction of $d\vec{B}$ is sam e as that of $d\vec{l} \times \vec{r}$ and is given by right-hand screw rule.

Magnetic Field Due to Straight Current Carrying Conductor

The magnetic field at a point at perpendicular distance a from a straight conductor carrying current I is given by

$$B = \frac{\mu_0 I}{4\pi a} (\sin\phi_1 + \sin\phi_2)$$

Where, ϕ_1 and ϕ_2 are the angles which the perpendicular from the observation point to the conductor makes with the lines joining the ends of the conductor to the observation point.

The magnetic field due to a straight conductor of infinite length $\left(\phi_1 = \phi_2 = \frac{\pi}{2}\right)$ is given by $B = \frac{\mu_0 I}{2\pi a}$

Rules for Finding the Direction of Magnetic Field Due to Straight Current Carrying Conductor.

Right Hand Thumb Rule If we hold the straight conductor in the grip of our right hand in such a way that the extended thumb points in the direction of current, then the direction of curl of fingers will give the direction of the magnetic field.

Maxwell's Cork Screw Rule If a right handed screw be rotated along a wire so that it advances in the direction of current, then the direction in which the thumb rotates gives the direction of the magnetic field.

Magnetic Field of a Circular Current Loop

The magnetic field of a circular current loop of radius a carrying current I is

(i) At the centre of the loop, $B = \frac{\mu_0 I}{2a}$

(ii) At an axial point at distance r from the centre,

$$B = \frac{\mu_0 I a^2}{2(r^2 + a^2)^{3/2}}$$

Rules for Finding the Direction of Magnetic Field Due to Circular Current Loop

Right Hand Thumb Rule If we curl the fingers of our right hand around the circular wire with the fingers pointing in the direction of the current, then the extended thumb gives the direction of the magnetic field.

Clock Rule This rule gives the polarity of any face of the circular current loop. If the current round any face of the coil is in anti-clockwise direction, it behaves like a North pole. If the current flows in the clockwise direction, if behaves like a South pole.

Ampere's Circuital Law

The line integral of the magnetic field $\vec{B}$ around any closed path is equal to μ_0 times the total current I threading the closed path

$$\oint \vec{B} \cdot d\vec{l} = \mu_0 I$$

In a simplified form, the law states that if field $\vec{B}$ is directed along the tangent to every point on the perimeter L of a closed curve and its magnitude is constant along the curve, then

$$BL = \mu_0 I$$

Magnetic Field of a Straight Solenoid

A solenoid is a long insulated wire wound in the form of a helix. Its length is very large as compared to its diameter. The magnetic field of a straight solenoid carrying current I and having n turns per unit length is given by

(i) $B = \mu_0 nI$

(At a point well inside the solenoid)

(ii) $B_{\text{end}} = \frac{1}{2}\mu_0 nI$

(At either end of the solenoid)

Magnetic Field of a Toroidal Solenoid

A solenoid bent into the form of a closed ring is called a toroidal solenoid. The magnetic field inside the toroidal solenoid has a constant magnitude and tangential direction. It is given by

$$B = \mu_0 nI$$

Where, I is the current in the windings and n is the number of turns per unit length. The field lines are concentric circles.

Rules for Finding the Direction of Force on a Charge Moving Perpendicular to a Magnetic Field.

Fleming's Left Hand Rule Stretch the thumb and the first two fingers of the left hand mutually perpendicular to each other. If the forefinger points in the direction of the magnetic field, central finger in the direction of current, then the thumb gives the direction of force on the charged particle.

Right Hand Palm Rule Open the right hand and place it so that tips of the fingers point in the direction of the field $\vec{B}$ and thumb in the direction of velocity $\vec{v}$ of positive charge, then the palm faces towards the force $\vec{F}$.

Definition of Magnetic Field

The magnetic field at a point may be defined as the force acting on a unit charge moving with a unit velocity at right angles to the direction of the field.

SI Unit of Magnetic Field is Tesla

One tesla is that magnetic field in which a charge of 1 coulomb moving with a speed of 1 ms^{-1} at right angles to the field experiences a force of 1 newton.

1 tesla (T) = 1 N A^{-1} m^{-1}, 1 gauss G = 10^{-4}T

Force on a Moving Charge in Uniform Magnetic Field

The magnetic force $\vec{F}_m$ acting on a charge q moving with a velocity $\vec{v}$ in magnetic field $\vec{B}$ is given by

$$\vec{F}_m = q[\vec{v} \times \vec{B}]$$

The direction of force $\vec{F}_m$ is given by rule of vector product.

The force F_m is zero, if either (a) $\vec{B} = 0$ or

(b) $\vec{v} = 0$ or (c) $q = 0$ *i.e.*, the particle is neutral particle or $\theta = 0°$ or $180°$ *i.e.*, motion of charged particle is parallel or anti-parallel to the magnetic field.

The force $\vec{F}_m$ is maximum having a value $F_m = qvB$ when $\theta = 90°$ *i.e.*, charged particle is moving in a direction perpendicular to that of magnetic field.

Thus, magnetic field B may be defined by the relation

$$B = \frac{F_m}{qv\sin\theta}$$

Thus, SI unit 1 T = 1 NA^{-1} m^{-2}.

Motion of a Charged Particle in a Uniform Magnetic Field

1. (i) If a charge particle enters a uniform magnetic field B with a velocity v in a direction perpendicular to that of B (*i.e.*, $\theta = 90°$), then the charged particle experiences a force $F_m = qvB$. Under its influence the particle describes a circular path such that

Radius of circular path $r = \dfrac{mv}{qB}$

In general $r = \dfrac{mv}{qB} = \dfrac{p}{qB}$

$$= \frac{\sqrt{2mK}}{qB} = \frac{\sqrt{2mqV}}{qB} = \frac{1}{B}\sqrt{\frac{2mV}{q}}$$

Where, $p = mv =$ Momentum of charged particle,
$K =$ Kinetic energy of charged particle and
$V =$ Accelerating potential difference.

(ii) The period of revolution of charged particle $T = \dfrac{2\pi m}{qB}$, the frequency of revolution $\nu = \dfrac{qB}{2\pi m}$ or

angular frequency $\omega = \dfrac{qB}{m}$.

2. (i) If a charged particle is moving at an angle θ to the magnetic field (where θ is other than 0°, 90° or 180°), it describes a helical path, where radius of

helical path $r = \dfrac{mv\sin\theta}{qB}$.

(ii) Revolution period $T = \dfrac{2\pi m}{qB}$

or frequency $\nu = \dfrac{qB}{2\pi m}$

(iii) Moreover, pitch (the linear distance travelled during one complete revolution) of helical path is given by

$$p = v\cos\theta \cdot T = \frac{2\pi m v\cos\theta}{qB}$$

3. If the direction of a $\vec{v}$ is parallel or anti-parallel to $\vec{B}$, $\theta = 0$ or $\theta = 180°$ and therefore $F = 0$. Hence, the trajectory of the particle is a straight line.
If the velocity of the charged particle is not perpendicular to the field, we will break the velocity in parallel ($v_{||}$) and perpendicular ($v_{\perp}$) components.

$$r = \frac{mv_{\perp}}{qB}$$

Pitch $p = (v_{||})T$

Cyclotron

It is a device used to accelerate charged particles like protons, deutrons, α-particles, etc. to very high energies. Here, charged particles move along a spiral path under the action of a perpendicular magnetic field and gain energy as they cross an alternating electric field again and again.

Cyclotron Frequency

In a cyclotron, the frequency of the applied alternating electric field is equal to the frequency of revolution of the charged particle. This frequency is called cyclotron frequency.

It is given by, $f_c = \dfrac{qB}{2\pi m}$

Where, m is the mass and q is the charge of the positive ion. The cyclotron frequency is independent of both the velocity of the particle and the radius of its orbit.

Force on a Current Carrying Conductor in a Magnetic Field

A conductor of length l carrying current I held in a magnetic field $\vec{B}$ at an angle θ with it, experiences a force given by

$$F = IlB\sin\theta$$

In vector notation, $\vec{F} = I(\vec{l} \times \vec{B})$

The direction of $\vec{F}$ is perpendicular to both $\vec{l}$ and $\vec{B}$ and is given by Fleming's left hand rule.

The force is maximum when $\theta = 90°$ and zero when $\theta = 0°$ or $180°$.

$$F_{max} = IlB$$

Force between Two Parallel Infinitely Long Current Carrying Conductors

The force per unit length between two long parallel conductors carrying currents I_1 and I_2 and separated by distance r is given by

$$f = \frac{\mu_0}{2\pi}\frac{I_1 I_2}{r}$$

The force is attractive when the currents are in the same direction and repulsive when the currents are in opposite directions.

Torque on Current Carrying Coil in a Magnetic Field

A rectangular coil of area A, carrying current I and capable of rotation about an axis perpendicular to the field $\vec{B}$ experiences a torque,

$$\tau = NIBA\sin\theta = m\,B\sin\theta$$

Where, N = Number of turns in the coil, $m = NIA$ = Magnetic dipole moment, θ = Angle which the normal to the plane of the coil makes with the field $\vec{B}$.

In vector rotation, $\vec{\tau} = \vec{m} \times \vec{B}$

Torque is minimum when the plane of the coil is perpendicular to the magnetic field ($\theta = 0°$).

Torque is maximum when the plane of the coil is parallel to the magnetic field ($\theta = 90°$).

$$\tau_{max} = NIBA.$$

Practice Questions

Level I

1. An electric charge in uniform motion produces
(a) an electric field
(b) a magnetic field
(c) Both (a) and (b)
(d) no such field at all

2. The unit of magnetic induction B is
(a) weber
(b) weber/metre^2
(c) newton/ (amp×metre)
(d) newton/metre

3. The magnetic field at a point due to a current carrying conductor is directly proportional to
(a) resistance of the conductor
(b) thickness of the conductor
(c) current flowing through the conductor
(d) distance from the conductor

4. Ampere's circuital law is equivalent to
(a) Biot-Savart law (b) Coulomb's law
(c) Faraday's law (d) Kirchhoff's law

5. Two free parallel wires carrying currents in the opposite directions
(a) attract each other
(b) repel each other
(c) do not affect each other
(d) get rotated perpendicular to each other

6. Two parallel wires carrying currents in the same direction attract each other because of
(a) potential difference between them
(b) mutual inductance between them
(c) electric forces between them
(d) magnetic forces between them

7. The magnetic effect of electric current was first discovered by
(a) Fleming (b) Orested
(c) Ampere (d) Faraday

8. The dimension of magnetic field is
(a) $[MA^{-1}T^{-2}]$ (b) $[M^{-1}L^{-1}A^{-1}T^{-2}]$
(c) $[MA^{-2}T^{-2}]$ (d) None of these

9. Unit of $\frac{\mu_0}{\epsilon_0}$ is
(a) ohm-metre (b) weber-metre
(c) tesla (d) ohm

10. If current flowing through storing, then storing will
(a) compressed (b) oscillated
(c) extended (d) remains same

11. A circular coil of n turns and radius r carries a current I. The magnetic field at the centre is
(a) $\frac{\mu_0 nI}{r}$ (b) $\frac{\mu_0 nI}{2r}$ (c) $\frac{2\mu_0 nI}{r}$ (d) $\frac{\mu_0 nI}{4r}$

12. The magnetic field at a perpendicular distance of 2 cm from an infinite straight current carrying conductor is 2×10^{-6} T. The current in the wire is
(a) 0.1 A (b) 0.2 A (c) 0.4 A (d) 0.8 A

13. A positive charge is moving towards an observer. The direction of magnetic induction lines is
(a) clockwise (b) anti-clockwise
(c) right (d) left

14. The force acting on a charge q moving with a velocity $\vec{v}$ in a magnetic field of induction $\vec{B}$ is given by
(a) $q/(\vec{v} \times \vec{B})$ (b) $(\vec{v} \times \vec{B})/q$
(c) $q(\vec{v} \times \vec{B})$ (d) $q(\vec{v} \cdot \vec{B})$

15. A charge q is moving with a velocity $\vec{v}$ parallel to a magnetic field $\vec{B}$. Force on the charge due to magnetic field is
(a) $q\,\vec{v}\,\vec{B}$ (b) $\frac{q\vec{B}}{\vec{v}}$ (c) zero (d) $\frac{\vec{B}\vec{v}}{q}$

16. The magnetic field dB due to a small current element dl at a distance r and element carrying current i is
(a) $dB = \frac{\mu_0 i}{4\pi}\left(\frac{dl \times \vec{r}}{r}\right)$ (b) $dB = \frac{\mu_0 i^2}{4\pi}\left(\frac{dl \times \vec{r}}{r^2}\right)$
(c) $dB = \frac{\mu_0 i^2}{4\pi}\left(\frac{dl \times \vec{r}}{r}\right)$ (d) $dB = \frac{\mu_0 i}{4\pi}\left(\frac{dl \times \vec{r}}{r^3}\right)$

17. If a copper wire carries a direct current, the magnetic field associated with the current will be
(a) outside the wire
(b) inside the wire
(c) Both (a) and (b)
(d) Neither (a) nor (b)

18. A circular coil carrying current behaves as a
(a) bar magnet (b) horse shoe magnet
(c) magnetic shell (d) solenoid

19. A long solenoid has n turns per metre and current I A is flowing through it. The magnetic field induction at the ends of the solenoid is
(a) zero (b) $\mu_0 nI/2$ (c) $\mu_0 nI$ (d) $2\mu_0 NI$

20. A coil of wire has an area of 600 sq cm and has 500 turns. If it carries 1.5 A current, its magnetic dipole moment is
(a) 5 Am^2 (b) 15 Am^2
(c) 30 Am^2 (d) 45 Am^2

Level II

1. In a current carrying long solenoid, the field produced does not depend upon
(a) number of turns per unit length
(b) current flowing
(c) radius of the solenoid
(c) All of the above

2. The magnetic induction at any point due to a long straight wire carrying a current is
(a) proportional to the distance from the wire
(b) inversely proportional to the distance from wire
(c) inversely proportional to the square of the distance from the wire
(d) does not depend on distance

3. An arc of a circle of radius R subtends an angle $\frac{\pi}{2}$ at the centre. It carries a current i. The magnetic field at the centre will be
(a) $\frac{\mu_0 i}{2R}$ (b) $\frac{\mu_0 i}{8R}$
(c) $\frac{\mu_0 i}{4R}$ (d) $\frac{2\mu_0 i}{5R}$

4. The direction of magnetic lines of forces close to a straight conductor carrying current will be
(a) along the length of the conductor
(b) radially outward
(c) circular in a plane perpendicular to the conductor
(d) helical

5. A circular coil of radius R carries an electric current. The magnetic field due to the coil at a point on the axis of the coil located at a distance r from the centre of the coil, such that $r >> R$, varies as

(a) $\frac{1}{r}$ (b) $\frac{1}{r^{3/2}}$ (c) $\frac{1}{r^2}$ (d) $\frac{1}{r^3}$

6. The magnetic induction due to an infinitely long straight wire carrying a current i at a distance r from wire is given by

(a) $|\vec{\mathbf{B}}| = \left(\frac{\mu_0}{4\pi}\right)\frac{2i}{r}$ (b) $|\vec{\mathbf{B}}| = \left(\frac{\mu_0}{4\pi}\right)\frac{r}{2i}$

(c) $|\vec{\mathbf{B}}| = \left(\frac{4\pi}{\mu_0}\right)\frac{2i}{r}$ (d) $|\vec{\mathbf{B}}| = \left(\frac{4\pi}{\mu_0}\right)\frac{r}{2i}$

7. The magnetic field at a distance r from a long wire carrying current i is 0.4 T. The magnetic field at a distance $2r$ is

(a) 0.2 T (b) 0.8 T (c) 0.1 T (d) 1.6 T

8. A current I flows along the length of an infinitely long, straight and thin-walled pipe. Then,

(a) The magnetic field at all points inside the pipe is the same but not zero
(b) The magnetic field at any point inside the pipe is zero
(c) The magnetic field is zero only on the axis of the pipe
(d) The magnetic field is different at different points inside the pipe

9. The magnetic field at the centre of current carrying coil is

(a) $\frac{\mu_0 ni}{2r}$ (b) $\frac{\mu_0 ni}{2\pi r}$ (c) $\frac{\mu_0 ni}{4r}$ (d) $\mu_0 ni$

10. Energy in a current carrying coil is stored in the form of

(a) electrical energy (b) magnetic field
(c) heat (d) None of these

11. The magnetic field at the centre of coil of n turns, bent in the form of a square of side $2l$, carrying current i, is

(a) $\frac{\sqrt{2}\mu_0 ni}{\pi l}$ (b) $\frac{\sqrt{2}\mu_0 ni}{2\pi l}$ (c) $\frac{\sqrt{2}\mu_0 ni}{4\pi l}$ (d) $\frac{2\mu_0 ni}{\pi l}$

12. Which of the following gives the value of magnetic field according to Biot-Savart's law

(a) $\frac{i\Delta l \sin\theta}{r^2}$ (b) $\frac{\mu_0}{4\pi}\frac{i\Delta l \sin\theta}{r^2}$

(c) $\frac{\mu_0}{4\pi}\frac{i\Delta l \sin\theta}{r^2}$ (d) $\frac{\mu_0}{4\pi} i\Delta l \sin\theta$

13. One tesla is equal to

(a) 10^7 gauss (b) 10^{-4} gauss
(c) 10^4 gauss (d) 10^{-8} gauss

14. A current carrying wire in the neighbourhood produces

(a) no field (b) electric field
(c) magnetic field (d) (b) and (c)

15. Magnetic field due to a ring having n turns at a distance x on its axis is proportional to (if r = Radius of ring)

(a) $\frac{r}{(x^2 + r^2)}$ (b) $\frac{r^2}{(x^2 + r^2)^{3/2}}$

(c) $\frac{nr^2}{(x^2 + r^2)^{3/2}}$ (d) $\frac{n^2 r^2}{(x^2 + r^2)^{3/2}}$

16. A charged particle is moving with velocity v in a magnetic field of induction B. The force on the particle will be maximum, when

(a) v and B are in the same direction
(b) v and B are in opposite direction
(c) v and B are perpendicular
(d) v and B are at an angle of 45°

17. An electron and a proton enter a magnetic field perpendicularly. Both have same kinetic energy. Which of the following is true?

(a) Trajectory of electron is less curved
(b) Trajectory of proton is less curved
(c) Both trajectories are equally curved
(d) Both move in straight-line path

18. A charge moves in a circle perpendicular to a magnetic field. The time period of revolution is independent of

(a) magnetic field
(b) charge
(c) mass of the particle
(d) velocity of the particle

19. An electron is moving along positive x-axis. To get it moving on an anti-clockwise circular path in x-y plane, a magnetic field is applied

(a) along positive y-axis (b) along positive z-axis
(c) along negative y-axis (d) along negative z-axis

20. A moving charge will gain energy due to the application of

(a) electric field (b) magnetic field
(c) Both (a) and (b) (d) None of these

21. A particle of mass m and charge q enters a magnetic field B perpendicularly with a velocity v. The radius of the circular path described by it will be

(a) $\frac{Bq}{mv}$ (b) $\frac{mq}{Bv}$

(c) $\frac{mB}{qv}$ (d) $\frac{mv}{Bq}$

22. The radius of circular path of an electron when subjected to a perpendicular magnetic field is

(a) $\frac{mv}{Be}$ (b) $\frac{me}{Be}$

(c) $\frac{mE}{Be}$ (d) $\frac{Be}{mv}$

23. Cyclotron is used to accelerate

(a) electrons (b) neutrons
(c) positive ions (d) negative ions

24. Motion of a moving electron is not affected by

(a) an electric field applied in the direction of motion
(b) magnetic field applied in the direction of motion
(c) electric fuel applied perpendicular to the direction of motion
(d) magnetic field applied perpendicular to the direction of motion

25. When a charges particle enters a uniform magnetic field, its kinetic energy

(a) remains constant (b) increases
(c) decreases (d) becomes zero

Answers

Level I

1. (c)	**2.** (b)	**3.** (c)	**4.** (a)	**5.** (b)	**6.** (d)	**7.** (b)	**8.** (a)	**9.** (d)	**10.** (a)
11. (b)	**12.** (b)	**13.** (b)	**14.** (c)	**15.** (c)	**16.** (d)	**17.** (a)	**18.** (c)	**19.** (b)	**20.** (d)

Level II

1. (a)	**2.** (b)	**3.** (b)	**4.** (c)	**5.** (d)	**6.** (a)	**7.** (a)	**8.** (b)	**9.** (a)	**10.** (b)
11. (a)	**12.** (c)	**13.** (c)	**14.** (c)	**15.** (c)	**16.** (c)	**17.** (b)	**18.** (d)	**19.** (b)	**20.** (a)
21. (b)	**22.** (a)	**23.** (c)	**24.** (b)	**25.** (a)					

Hints and Solutions

Level II

1. Here, $B = \mu_0 ni$

Where, n is number of turns per unit length $= \dfrac{N}{l}$

3. $B = \dfrac{\mu_0}{4\pi}\dfrac{\theta i}{r} = \dfrac{\mu_0}{4\pi} \times \dfrac{\pi}{2} \times \dfrac{i}{R} = \dfrac{\mu_0 i}{8R}$

8. Applying Ampere's law $\oint B dl = \mu_0 i$ to any closed path inside the pipe we find no current is enclosed. Hence, $B = 0$

17. We have $qvB = \dfrac{mv^2}{r} \Rightarrow r = \dfrac{mv}{qB} = \dfrac{\sqrt{2mK}}{qB}$

For same kinetic energy K, we have $r \propto \sqrt{m}$

Hence, path of proton will have larger r and is therefore less curved.

19. To move the electron in x-y plane, force on it must be acting in the y-direction initially. The direction of $\vec{F}$ is known, and the direction of v is known, hence by applying Fleming's left hand rule, the direction of magnetic field is also determined.

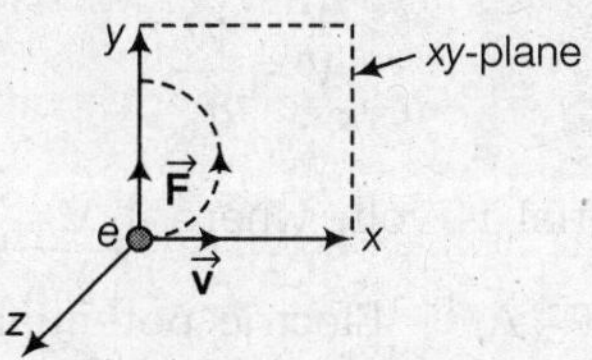

20. A moving charge gains energy in electric field only because in magnetic field energy remains constant.

41

Electric Potential

Electric Potential

Electric potential at a point in an electric field is defined as the amount of work done in bringing a unit positive charge, without any acceleration, from infinity to that point, along any arbitrary path.

Mathematically, if W work is to be done to bring a test charge q_0 from infinity to a point, then the potential of that point, is

$$V = \frac{W}{q_0}$$

SI unit of potential is volt, where $1\ \text{V} = \frac{1\ \text{J}}{1\ \text{C}}$. Its dimensional formula is $[\text{ML}^2\text{T}^{-3}\text{A}^{-1}]$. Electric potential is a state function and does not depend on the path followed.

Electric Potential Due to a Point Charge

Potential due to a point charge Q, at a distance r is given by

$$V = \frac{1}{4\pi\varepsilon_0} \cdot \frac{Q}{r}$$

- At the centre of the line joining two equal and opposite charges, $V = 0$ but $E \neq 0$.
- At the centre of the line joining two equal and like charges, $E = 0$ but $V \neq 0$.
- If four identical charges q each are placed at the four vertices of a square, then the net electric field at the centre of the square is zero, but $V = \frac{\sqrt{2}q}{\pi\varepsilon_0 a}$

Electric Potential Due to a System of Charges

If a number of charges $q_1, q_2, q_3, \ldots$ are present in space, then the electric potential at any point will be

$$V = V_1 + V_2 + V_3 + \ldots$$

$$= \frac{1}{4\pi\varepsilon_0}\left[\frac{q_1}{r_1} + \frac{q_2}{r_2} + \frac{q_3}{r_3} + \ldots\right] = \frac{1}{4\pi\varepsilon_0}\sum_{i=1}^{n}\left(\frac{q_i}{r_i}\right)$$

Electric Potential Due to an Electric Dipole

At any general point,

$$V = \frac{1}{4\pi\varepsilon_0} \cdot \frac{p\cos\theta}{r^2}$$

On the dipole axis, $\theta = 0°$

and $$V = \frac{1}{4\pi\varepsilon_0} \cdot \frac{p}{r^2}$$

On the equitorial axis $\theta = 90°$ and $V = 0$

Electric Potential Due to Some Common Charge Distributions

Potential at a point distant r from an infinitely long wire having linear charge density λ, is

$$V = \frac{\lambda}{2\pi\varepsilon_0} \cdot \ln r$$

For a charged conducting sphere/shell having total charge Q and radius R, the potential at a point distant r from the centre of the sphere/shell is

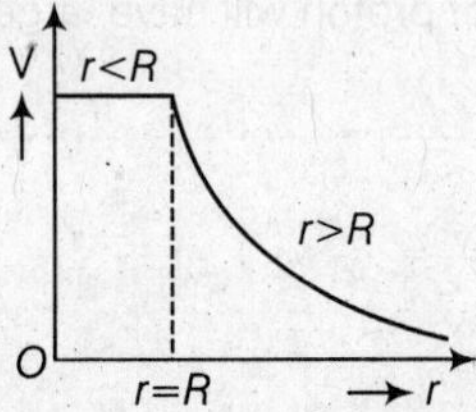

(i) $V = \frac{Q}{4\pi\varepsilon_0 r}$, for $r > R$

(ii) $V = \frac{1}{4\pi\varepsilon_0} \frac{Q}{r}$, for $r = R$

(iii) $V = \frac{Q}{4\pi\varepsilon_0 R}$, for $r \leq R$

For a charged non-conducting (dielectric) sphere of radius R, the charge Q is uniformly distributed over the entire volume.

Hence,

(i) $V = \frac{Q}{4\pi\varepsilon_0 r}$, for $r > R$

(ii) $V = \frac{Q}{4\pi\varepsilon_0 R}$, for $r = R$ and

(iii) $V = \dfrac{Q}{4\pi\varepsilon_0}\left[\dfrac{3R^2 - r^2}{2R^3}\right]$, for $r < R$

At the centre of the sphere ($r = 0$),

$$V = \frac{3Q}{8\pi\varepsilon_0 R}$$

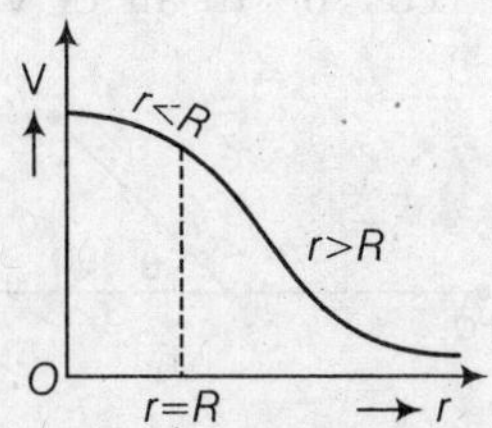

Electric Potential Energy

The electric energy of a system of charges is the work that has been done in bringing those charges from infinity to near each other to form the system. For two point charges q_1 and q_2 separated by distance r_{12}, the potential energy is given by $U = \dfrac{1}{4\pi\varepsilon_0}\dfrac{q_1 q_2}{r_{12}}$

Electric potential energy is a scalar quantity. In the above formula, the values of q_1 and q_2 are used with proper signs. If there are more than two charges in a system, then the electric energy is calculated for each pair and then all energies so obtained, are added algebraically.

e.g., For a system of three charges q_1, q_2 and q_3 are placed at three corners of a triangle (figure), then the electric potential energy of the system will be given by

$$U = U_{12} + U_{23} + U_{31}$$

$$= \frac{1}{4\pi\varepsilon_0}\left[\frac{q_1 q_2}{r_{12}} + \frac{q_2 q_3}{r_{23}} + \frac{q_1 q_3}{r_{31}}\right]$$

In general, for a system of n charges, the electric potential energy is given by

$$U = \frac{1}{2}\Sigma \frac{q_1 q_j}{4\pi\varepsilon_0 r_{ij}} \; [i \neq j]$$

$\left(\dfrac{1}{2}\right.$ is used as each term in summation will appear twice.$\left.\right)$

Relation between E and V

Because E is force per unit charge and V is work per unit charge. E and V are related in the same way as work and force. If $\Delta V = (V_B - V_A)$ is the increase in potential over a short displacement Δs, $\Delta V = -E\Delta s$.

Where, the negative sign indicates that works is done against the field. If α is the angle between E and Δs, we have

$$\Delta V = -E(\Delta s)\cos\alpha = -E\Delta x \quad (\text{along } \vec{E})$$

Where, $\Delta x = \Delta s \cos\alpha$ is the component of $\Delta\vec{s}$ along $\vec{E}$.

Therefore, $E = -\dfrac{\Delta V}{\Delta x}$

For small changes, above expression may be written as $E = \dfrac{-dV}{dx}$

Thus, the electric field intensity E is the negative gradient of potential. This means that decrease in potential is along the direction of E. The SI unit of E is, therefore volt per metre (Vm^{-1}).

Equipotential Surface

For a given charge distribution, an equipotential surface is the locus of the all the points having the same electric potential. For a point charge or a spherical charge distribution, equipotential surfaces are concentric spheres as shown in figure.

For a uniform electric field, the equipotential surfaces are planes perpendicular to the direction of electric field.

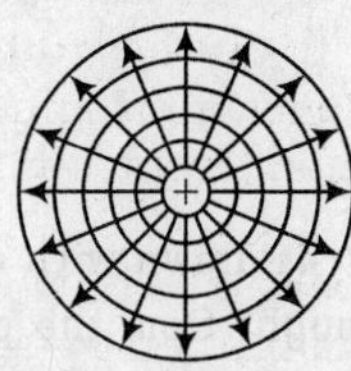

There is no component of electric field along an equipotential surface.

As a result, work done in moving a charge along an equipotential surface, is always zero.

i.e., $dW = \vec{E}\cdot d\vec{l}$

$dW = E\,dl\cos\theta = 0$

$\therefore \quad \cos\theta = 0$

or $\quad \theta = 90°$. So, $\vec{E} \perp d\vec{l}$

- Equipotential surface may be planar, solid etc. But equipotential surface can never be point size.
- Equipotential surface is single valued. So, equipotential surfaces never cross each other.
- Electric field is always perpendicular to equipotential surface.

Electrostatic Potential Energy of a System of Two Point Charges in an Electrostatic Field

Electrostatic potential energy of a charge q, placed at a point in an electric field, is equal to work done in bringing the given charge from infinity to that point. Hence, electrostatic potential energy is $U = qV$, where V is the electric potential at the point.

For a system of two point charges q_1 and q_2 separated by a distance r,

$$W = U = \frac{1}{4\pi\varepsilon_0}\frac{q_1 q_2}{r_{22}}$$

+q_2(At infinity)
(r_1) (r_2)
+q_1 +q_2
r_{12}

Work Done by Electric Dipole

$$W = PE\,(1-\cos\theta)$$

Work done is stored in the form of potential energy in dipole. *i.e.*, stored potential energy in electric dipole is

$$E_P = W = PE\,(1-\cos\theta)$$

Explanation of $W = E_P = PE(1-\cos\theta)$

(i) If $\theta = 0°$, then $\cos\theta = 1$,

$W = E_p = PE\,(1-1) = 0$

(ii) If $\theta = 90°$, then $\cos\theta = 0$, $W = E_p = PE$

(iii) If $\theta = 180°$, then $\cos 180° = -1$

$\therefore\ W = E_P = 2\,PE$

Electric Field and Potential Due to Electric Dipole

Suppose, a point P placed away at distance r from the middle point of a dipole. The value of electric field E at point $P(r, \theta)$ due to dipole will be

$$E = \frac{1}{4\pi\varepsilon_0}\frac{P}{r^3}\sqrt{1+3\cos^2\theta},\ \text{(In air or vacuum)}$$

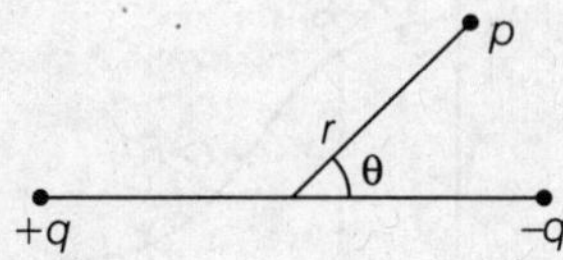

Practice Questions

Level I

1. A circle of radius r is drawn with charge $+q$ at the centre. A charge q_0 is brought from the point B to C. Then, work done is

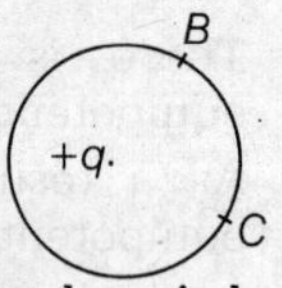

(a) positive
(b) negative
(c) infinite
(d) zero

2. Work done in carrying a charge Q once round a circle radius r with charge Q at the centre of the circle is

(a) $\frac{1}{4\pi\varepsilon_0}\cdot\frac{Q}{r}$ (b) $\frac{Q\cdot Q}{4\pi\varepsilon_0 r}$

(c) zero (d) $\frac{Q\cdot Q}{2r}$

3. If a point charge q moves round in a circle about a charge, then the work done by the charge is

(a) zero (b) $\frac{1}{4\pi\varepsilon_0}\frac{q}{r}$ (c) $\frac{1}{4\pi\varepsilon_0}\cdot\frac{q^2}{r}$ (d) $\frac{1}{4\pi\varepsilon_0}\frac{q^2}{r^2}$

4. It is possible to have a positively charged body at

(a) zero potential (b) negative potential
(c) positive potential (d) All of these

5. Electric potential of Earth is taken to be zero, because Earth is a good

(a) insulator (b) conductor
(c) semi-conductor (d) dielectric

6. What is not true for equipotential surface for a unifom electric field?

(a) Equipotential surface is flat
(b) Equipotential surface is spherical
(c) Electrical lines of force are perpendicular to the equipotential surface
(d) Work done is zero

7. Which of the following is not the property of equipotential surfaces?

(a) They do not cross each other
(b) They are concentric spheres for uniform electric field
(c) Rate of change of potential with distance on them is zero
(d) They can be imaginary spheres

8. If an electron is brought toward an another electron, the electric potential energy of the system

(a) increases (b) decreases
(c) becomes zero (d) remains the same

9. A hollow metallic sphere of radius 10 cm is charged such that potential of its surface is 70 V. The potential at the centre of the sphere would be

(a) 0 V (b) 7 V (c) 70 V (d) 700 V

10. Two equal and opposite charges ($+q$ and $-q$) are situated at x distance from each other. The value of potential at very far point will depend

(a) q (b) x (c) qx (d) q/x

Level II

1. The unit of intensity of electric field is

(a) Newton/Coulomb (b) Joule/Coulomb
(c) Volt-metre (d) Newton/metre

2. Equal charges are given to two spheres of different radii. The potential will

(a) be more on the smaller sphere
(b) be more on the bigger sphere
(c) be equal on both the spheres
(d) depend on the nature of the materials of the spheres

3. Two equal charges q are placed at a distance of $2a$ and a third charge $-2q$ is placed at the mid-point. The potential energy of the system is

(a) $\frac{q^2}{8\pi\varepsilon_0 a}$ (b) $\frac{6q^2}{8\pi\varepsilon_0 a}$ (c) $-\frac{7q^2}{8\pi\varepsilon_0 a}$ (d) $\frac{9q^2}{8\pi\varepsilon_0 a}$

4. The figure shows some of the electric field lines corresponding to an electric field. The figure suggests

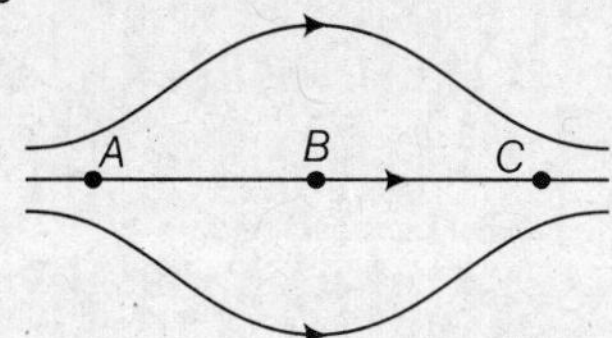

(a) $E_A > E_B > E_C$ (b) $E_A = E_B = E_C$
(c) $E_A = E_C > E_B$ (d) $E_A = E_C < E_B$

5. The electric potential at a point in free space due to a charge Q C is $Q \times 10^{11}$ V. The electric field at the point is
(a) $4\pi\varepsilon_0 Q \times 10^{20}$ V/m (b) $12\pi\varepsilon_0 Q \times 10^{22}$ V/m
(c) $4\pi\varepsilon_0 Q \times 10^{22}$ V/m (d) $12\pi\varepsilon_0 Q \times 10^{20}$ V/m

6. A charge of 5C is given a displacement of 0.5 m. The work done in the process is 10 J. The potential difference between the two points will be
(a) 2 V (b) 0.25 V (c) 1 V (d) 25 V

7. The electric potential V is given as a function of distance x m by $V = (5x^2 + 10x - 9)$ V. Value of electric field at $x = 1$ is
(a) -20 V/m (b) 6 V/m
(c) 11 V/m (d) -23 V/m

8. As shown in the figure, charges $+q$ and $-q$ are placed at the vertices B and C of an isosceles triangle. The potential at the vertex A is

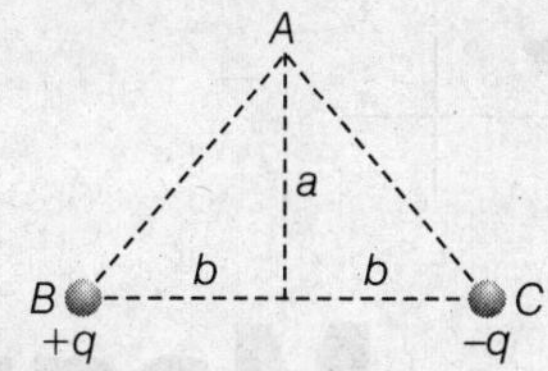

(a) $\frac{1}{4\pi\varepsilon_0} \cdot \frac{2q}{\sqrt{a^2 + b^2}}$ (b) zero

(c) $\frac{1}{4\pi\varepsilon_0} \cdot \frac{q}{\sqrt{a^2 + b^2}}$ (d) $\frac{1}{4\pi\varepsilon_0} \cdot \frac{(-q)}{\sqrt{a^2 + b^2}}$

9. Electric potential at any point is $V = -5x + 3y + \sqrt{15}z$, then the magnitude of the electric field is
(a) $3\sqrt{2}$ (b) $4\sqrt{2}$ (c) $5\sqrt{2}$ (d) 7

10. The work done in bringing a 20 C charge from point A to B for distance 0.2 m is 2 J. The potential difference between the two points will be (in V)
(a) 0.2 (b) 8
(c) 0.1 (d) 0.4

Answers

Level I

1. (d)	**2.** (c)	**3.** (a)	**4.** (d)	**5.** (b)	**6.** (b)	**7.** (b)	**8.** (a)	**9.** (c)	**10.** (c)

Level II

1. (a)	**2.** (a)	**3.** (c)	**4.** (c)	**5.** (c)	**6.** (a)	**7.** (a)	**8.** (b)	**9.** (d)	**10.** (c)

Hints *and* Solutions

Level II

2. $V = \frac{kq}{R}$ i.e., $V \propto \frac{1}{R}$

$\therefore$ Potential on smaller sphere will be more.

3. $U_{system} = \frac{1}{4\pi\varepsilon_0} \frac{(q)(-2q)}{a} + \frac{1}{4\pi\varepsilon_0} \frac{(-2q)(q)}{a} + \frac{1}{4\pi\varepsilon_0} \frac{(q)(q)}{2a}$

$U_{system} = -\frac{7q^2}{8\pi\varepsilon_0 a}$

5. Electric potential at a distance r due to point charge Q is $V = \frac{kQ}{r}$ and electric field at the same point $E = \frac{kQ}{r^2}$

$\Rightarrow \quad E = \frac{kQ}{(kQ/V)^2} = \frac{V^2}{kQ} = \frac{(Q \times 10^{11})^2}{kQ}$

$= 4\pi\varepsilon_0 Q \times 10^{22}$ V/m $\quad \left[\because k = \frac{1}{4\pi\varepsilon_0}\right]$

6. Since, $W = qV \Rightarrow 10 = 5 \times V \Rightarrow V = 2$ V

7. $E = -\frac{dV}{dx} = -\frac{d}{dx}(5x^2 + 10x - 9) = -10x - 10$

$\therefore \quad (E)_{x=1} = -10 \times 1 - 10 = -20$ V/m

9. $E_x = -\frac{dV}{dx} = -(-5) = 5;$

$E_y = -\frac{dV}{dy} = -3$

and $\quad E_z = -\frac{dV}{dz} = -\sqrt{15}$

$E_{net} = \sqrt{E_x^2 + E_y^2 + E_z^2}$

$= \sqrt{(5)^2 + (-3)^2 + (-\sqrt{15})^2} = 7$

10. By using $W = Q \cdot \Delta V \Rightarrow \Delta V = \frac{2}{20} = 0.1$ V

42

Magnetic Dipole and Earths Magnetism

Magnetic Pole

The preferred regions of attraction near the two ends of a magnet, where the magnetic force due to bar magnet is maximum, are called the poles of the magnet.

A bar magnet has the following properties.

1. Attractive Property

A magnet can attract small pieces of magnetic substances like iron, steel, cobalt, nickel etc. The attraction is maximum at poles. It may be pointed out that the poles are situated near the ends of the magnet and not exactly at the ends.

2. Directive Property

A magnet when suspended freely, aligns itself approximately along geographical N-S line, such that North pole of the magnet is towards the North of the Earth and the South pole is towards the South of the Earth.

3. Unlike Poles Attract and Like Poles Repel

If the S-pole of a magnet is brought near the N-pole of another magnet, they are found to attract each other.

On the other hand, if the N-pole of a magnet is brought near the N-pole of another magnet (or S-pole of a magnet is brought near the S-pole of another magnet), they are found to repel each other.Therefore, unlike poles attract each other and like poles repel each other.

4. Magnetic Poles Exist in Pairs

If a magnet is cut into two equal parts transverse to its length, N and S-poles of the magnet do not get separated. Each of the two parts is found to be a magnet having North and South poles at the two ends as. Further, each part of the magnet possesses the pole strength same as that of the original magnet.

On the other hand, if the magnet is cut into two equal parts along the length of the magnet, each part is found to be a magnet having pole strength exactly half of the pole strength of the original magnet.

The important difference in electricity and magnetism is that in electricity, an isolated charge exists, whereas in magnetism, an isolated magnetic pole *i.e.,* monopole does not exist.

5. Inductive Property

When a piece of a substance,such as soft iron, steel, cobalt, nickel etc., is placed near a bar magnet, it acquires magnetism. The magnetism, so acquired is called induced magnetism.

6. Repulsion is the Surest Test for Distinguishing between a Magnet and a Piece of Iron.

The pole a magnet attracts a piece of iron as well as the unlike pole of an other magnet. Therefore, when the magnet used for distinguishing between a magnet and a piece of iron is brought near the two ends of a specimen, it will show attraction in it is an iron rod, but will show repulsion at one end, if it is a magnet. Thus, repulsion is the surest test to distinguish between a magnet and a piece of iron.

Magnetic Dipole and Magnetic Dipole Moment

A bar magnet has two magnetic poles. It is sometimes also called as magnetic dipole.

Magnetic Dipole

An arrangement of two magnetic poles of equal and opposite strengths the separated by a finite distance is called a magnetic dipole.

The two poles of a magnetic dipole (or a magnet), called North and South poles, are always of equal strength and of opposite nature. Further, such two magnetic poles always exist in pair. In other words, an isolated North or a South pole does not exist.

Magnetic Length

The distance between the two poles of a bar magnet is called the magnetic length of the magnet.

Magnetic length is a vector from S-pole of the magnet to its N-pole and is denoted by $2\vec{l}$.

Since, the magnetic poles are situated within the magnet, the distance between its two magnetic poles called its magnetic length is always less than its geometric length.

Magnetic Dipole Moment

The product of the strength of either pole and the magnetic length of the magnet is called magnetic dipole moment.

It is a vector quantity and is represented by $\vec{M}$. Its direction is same as that of $2\vec{l}$ *i.e.,* from S-pole of the magnet to its N-pole. Thus,

$$\vec{M} = m(2\vec{l})$$

In SI, the unit of magnetic dipole moment is ampere-metre^2(A - m^2).

Note As said above, the term 'magnetic dipole' is also often used for a bar magnet *i.e.,* for an arrangement of two equal and unlike magnetic poles separated by certain distance.

Current Look As a Magnetic Dipole

Consider a circular coil carrying current I. Suppose that the current flows in anti-clockwise direction,when seen from below in figure. The magnetic field lines due to each elementary portion of the circular coil will be of the shape of circular loops near that portion and almost straight near the centre of the circular coil. From Biot-Savart's law (or right hand thumb rule), it follows that the magnetic field lines seem to enter at the lower face of the coil and leave at its upper face. Thus, the lower face of the coil, through which magnetic field lines enter, behaves as the South pole, while the upper face, through which the field lines leave, behaves as the North pole. Hence, the current carrying circular coil behaves as a magnetic dipole.

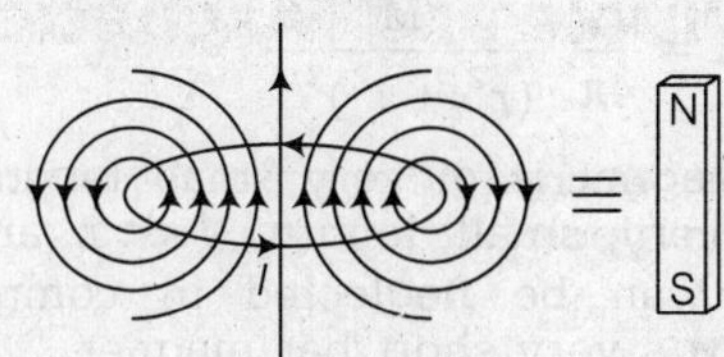

It is found that magnetic dipole moment of the current loop

(i) is directly proportional to strength of current through the loop *i.e.,*

$$M \propto I$$

(ii) is directly proportional to area of the current loop *i.e.,*

$$M \propto A$$

Combining equations, we have

$$M \propto IA$$

$$\Rightarrow \quad M = kIA$$

Where, K is the constant of proportionality. The constant of proportionality k is found to be equal to 1,when current is measured in ampere, area in metre^2 and magnetic dipole moment in ampere-metre^2. Thus,

$$M = IA$$

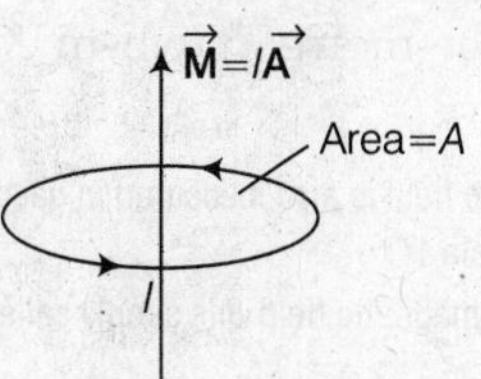

Since, the upper face of the current loop behaves as North pole and the lower face as South pole, the magnetic dipole moment vector $\vec{M}$ acts perpendicular to the plane of the current loop and in upward direction as shown in figure. If $\vec{A}$ is area vector representing the area of the current loop, then equation may be expressed as

$$\vec{M} = I\vec{A}$$

In case, the current carrying circular coil has n turns, then

$$M = nIA$$

The factor nI is called ampere turns of the circular current loop. Thus,

Magnetic dipole moment of current loop

= Ampere turns × Area of the coil

The equation has been obtained for a circular current loop. In fact, it is true for planar current loop of any shape.

Atom As a Magnetic Dipole

In an atom, electrons revolve around the nucleus and as such the circular orbits of electrons may be considered as the small current loops. Due to this, an atom possesses magnetic dipole moment and hence behaves as a magnetic dipole.

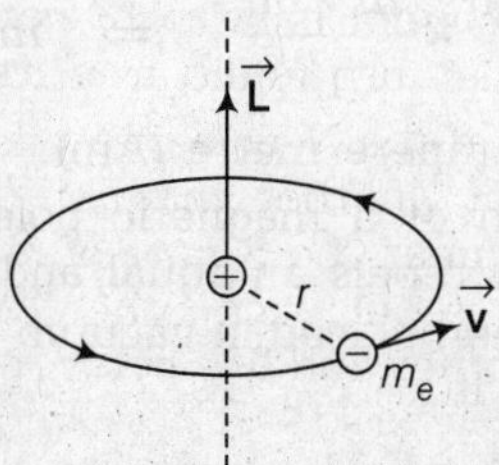

Magnetic Field

The space around a magnet (or a conductor carrying current), in which its magnetic effect can be experienced, is called the magnetic field.

The magnetic field in a region is said to be uniform, if the magnitude of its strength and direction is same at all the points in that region.

A uniform magnetic field is represented by equidistant parallel arrows.

The SI unit of strength of magnetic field (also known as magnetic induction or magnetic induction field or magnetic flux density) is tesla (T). It can be measured in terms of force on a charge moving inside the magnetic field or by using the concept of magnetic flux linked with a surface.

1 tesla (T) = 1 newton-ampere^{-1}-metre^{-1} ($NA^{-1}m^{-1}$)

= 1 weber-metre^{-1} (wb-m^{-2})

Note

- The strength of magnetic field is also measured in gauss (G). 1 gauss (G) = 10^{-4} tesla (T)
- Usually, the strength of magnetic field B is simply called magnetic field.

Coulomb's Law in Magnetism

In 1785, by making use of his torsion balance, coulomb discovered the law earning force between two magnetic poles.

Suppose that two magnetic poles of strengths m_1 and m_2 are placed a distance part. Then, force of attraction or repulsion between the two poles is found to be directly proportional to the product of their pole strengths an inversely proportional the square of the distance between them *i.e.*,

$$F \propto \frac{m_1 m_2}{r^2} \quad \Rightarrow \quad F = k\frac{m_1 m_2}{r^2} \quad \text{...(i)}$$

In SI, the constant of proportionality,

$$k = \frac{\mu_0}{4\pi} = 10^{-7} \text{ Wb A}^{-1}\text{m}^{-1}$$

$$\therefore \quad F = \frac{\mu_0}{4\pi}\cdot\frac{m_1 m_2}{r^2} = 10^{-7} \times \frac{m_1 m_2}{r^2}$$

Here, μ_0 is called the absolute permeability of free space.

Unit of Magnetic Pole Strength

Suppose that $m_1 = m_2 = m$ (say)

$$r = 1 \text{ m and } F = 10^{-7}\text{ N}$$

From Eq. (i), we have

$$10^{-7} = 10^{-7} \times \frac{m \times m}{1^2} \quad \Rightarrow \quad m^2 = 1$$

$$\Rightarrow \quad m = \pm 1 \text{ ampere metre (Am).}$$

Therefore, strength of a magnetic pole is said to be one ampere metre, if it repels an equal and similar pole with a force of 10^{-7} N, when placed in vacuum (or air) at a distance of one metre from it.

Magnetic Field on Axial Line of a Bar Magnet

Consider a bar magnet N-S, whose each pole is strength m. Let $2l$ be magnetic length of the magnet and O be its centre. Let P be a point on the axial line of the magnet at a distance r from the centre of the magnet.

m m $\vec{B}_{axial}$
S O N $\vec{B}_2$ P $\vec{B}_1$ X
l l
r

$$\therefore \quad \vec{B}_{axial} = \frac{\mu_0}{4\pi}\cdot\frac{2\vec{M}r}{(r^2 - l^2)^2} \quad \text{(along PX)}$$

It may be noted that the direction of magnetic field due to a bar magnet at a point on its axial line is from S-pole to N-pole *i.e.*, same as that of magnetic dipole moment of the bar magnet. Therefore, equation may be expressed as

$$\vec{B}_{axial} = \frac{\mu_0}{4\pi}\cdot\frac{2\vec{M}r}{(r^2 - l^2)^2}$$

When bar magnet is of very small length. For a magnet of very small length, $l << r$ and hence in equation l^2 can be neglected in comparison to r^2. Therefore, for a very short bar magnet,

$$\vec{B}_{axial} = \frac{\mu_0}{4\pi}\cdot\frac{2M}{r^3} \quad \text{(along } PX)$$

Magnetic Field on Equitoral Line of a Bar Magnet

Consider a bar magnet N-S, whose each pole is of strength m. Let $2l$ be the magnetic length of the bar magnet and O be its centre. Let P be a point on the equatorial line of the magnet at a distance r from the centre of the magnet

$$\Rightarrow \quad B_{axial} = \frac{\mu_0}{4\pi}\cdot\frac{2Mr}{(r^2 + l^2)^{3/2}} \quad \text{(along } PX')$$

Here, $M = 2ml$ is magnetic dipole moment of the bar magnet.

It may be noted that direction of magnetic field due to a bar magnet on its equatorial line is from N-pole to S-pole of the magnet *i.e.*, in a direction opposite to that of the magnetic dipole moment of the magnet. Therefore, equation may be expressed as

$$\vec{B}_{equi} = \frac{\mu_0}{4\pi}\cdot\frac{\vec{M}}{(r^2 + l^2)^{3/2}}$$

When bar magnet is of very small length. For a bar magnet of very small length, $l << r$ and hence in equation l^2 can be neglected in comparison tor^2. Therefore, for a very short bar magnet.

$$\vec{B}_{equi} = \frac{\mu_0}{4\pi}\cdot\frac{M}{r^3} \quad \text{(along } PX')$$

Note From equations and it follows that magnetic field at a point at a certain distance on the equitorial line of a short bar magnet is just one half of that at the same distance on its axial line.

Torque on a Bar Magnetic Field

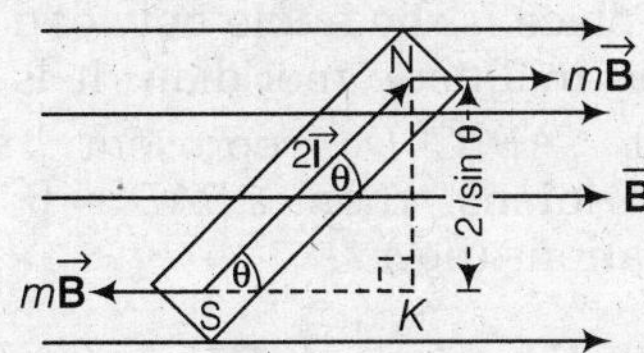

Hence, the magnetic dipole moment of a magnetic dipole is numerically equal to the torque acting on the dipole, when placed perpendicular to the direction of a uniform magnetic field of unit strength.

In vector notation,

$$\vec{\tau} = \vec{M} \times \vec{B}$$

If the vectors $\vec{M}$ and $\vec{B}$ are in the plane of paper, then torque vector $\vec{\tau}$, which acts in the direction of $\vec{M} \times \vec{B}$ will be perpendicular to the plane of the paper and in inward direction.

Unit of Magnetic Dipole Moment From the equation, we have

$$M = \frac{\tau}{B\sin\theta}$$

Therefore, unit of $M = \frac{\text{Newton metre}}{\text{tesla}}$

$$= \text{NmT}^{-1} = \text{JT}^{-1}$$

Therefore, magnetic dipole moment may be measured as newton metre tesla^{-1} (NmT^{-1}) or as joule tesla^{-1}(JT^{-1}).

Potential Energy of a Bar Magnet Placed in a Magnetic Field

Let a bar magnet of dipole moment M be placed in a uniform magnetic field of strength B, such that the magnet makes an angle θ with the direction of the field.

The work done in rotating the magnet is stored inside the magnet as its potential energy (U). Thus, potential energy of the magnet inside the magnetic field,

$$U = MB(\cos\theta_1 - \cos\theta_2)$$

Suppose that the magnet is initially perpendicular to the direction of the magnetic field *i.e.*, $\theta_1 = 90°$. Then, potential energy of the magnet in any position making angle θ with the direction of the field can be obtained by setting $\theta_1 = 90°$ and $\theta_2 = \theta$ in the equation *i.e.*,

$$U = MB(\cos 90° - \cos\theta)$$

or $$U = -MB\cos\theta$$

In vector notation, $U = -\vec{M}\cdot\vec{B}$

Special Cases

Let us find the potential energy of the dipole in following cases

(i) When $\theta = 0°$, $U = -MB\cos 0° = -MB$ (Minimum)

(ii) When $\theta = 90°$, $U = -MB\cos 90° = 0$

(iii) When $\theta = 180°$,

$$U = -MB\cos 180° = MB \text{ (Maximum)}$$

Thus, a magnetic dipole possesses minimum potential energy, when $\vec{M}$ and $\vec{B}$ are like parallel and maximum potential energy. When $\vec{M}$ and $\vec{B}$ are antiparallel.

Gauss' Law in Magnetism

According to Gauss' law in electrostatic, the surface integral of electric field $\vec{E}$ over a closed surface S is equal to $\frac{1}{\epsilon_0}$ times the total charge q enclosed by the surface i.e.,

$$\oint \vec{E}\cdot d\vec{S} = \frac{q}{\epsilon_0}$$

An isolated magnetic pole does not exist. In other words, a surface may enclose a magnetic dipole *i.e.*, a pair of equal and opposite magnetic poles so that net pole strength enclosed by the surface is zero. Therefore, the magnetic analogue of Gauss' law in electrostatic may be stated as

$$\oint_S \vec{B}\cdot d\vec{S} = 0$$

i.e., surface integral of magnetic field $\vec{B}$ over a closed surface S is always zero. It is called Gauss' Law in magnetism.

Following are a few direct consequences of Gauss' law in magnetism

1. If a number of magnetic field lines are leaving a closed surface, an equal number of field lines must also be entering the surface.
2. Isolated magnetic poles do not exist *i.e.*, magnetic poles exist in unlike pairs of equal strengths.

Magnetic Field Lines

The magnetic field line is the path along which an isolated North pole will tend to move, if it is free to do so.

Since, an isolated magnetic pole does not exist, a small magnetic needle is used to plot the field lines of a magnetic field. The magnetic field lines do not exist in reality. The concept of magnetic field lines was developed to visualise the strength of the magnetic field in different regions of the field. The regions, where the magnetic field lines are close enough (crowded), the magnetic field is considered as quite strong there.

Properties of Magnetic Field Lines

The following are a few important properties of magnetic field lines

1. The magnetic field lines are closed continuous loops extending through the body of the magnet.
2. Outside the body of the magnet, the magnetic field lines run from North pole to South pole of the magnet.

3. The tangent to the magnetic field line at any point gives the direction of magnetic field at that point.
4. No two magnetic field lines can intersect each other.
5. The magnetic field lines dilate laterally and contract longitudinally.

Earth's Magnetism

Figure Represents the magnetic field lines around the Earth. The axis of rotation of Earth is called geographic axis and the points, where it passes through the surface of Earth, are called geographic poles. The points N and S represent the geographic North and South poles. The great circle on the Earth's surface perpendicular to the geographic axis is called equator.

A vertical plane passing through the geographic axis is called the geographic meridian.

The axis of the huge magnet assumed to be lying inside the Earth is called magnetic axis of the Earth and the points, where the magnetic axis cuts the Earth's surface are called Earth's magnetic poles. The points N′ and S′ indicate the magnetic North and South of the Earth. The great circle on the Earth's surface perpendicular to the magnetic axis is called magnetic equator.

A vertical plane passing through the magnetic axis of the Earth is called magnetic meridian.

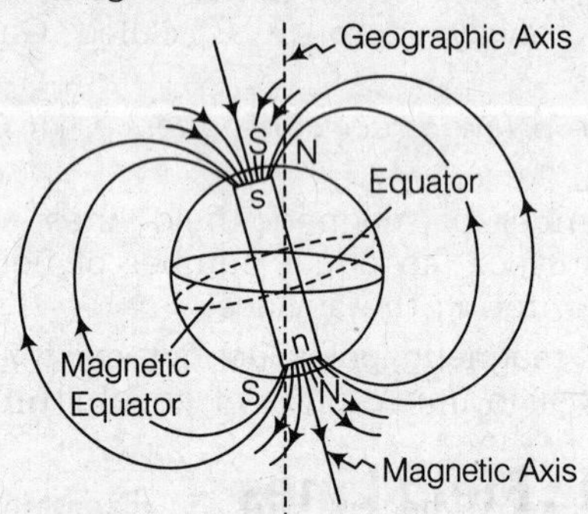

Magnetic Elements

The physical quantities, which determine the intensity of Earth's total magnetic field completely (both in magnitude and direction), are called magnetic elements.

Following are three magnetic elements of Earth.

1. Magnetic Declination

Declination at a place is the angle between the geographic meridian and the magnetic meridian. It is denoted by θ.

If $ABCD$ and $AB'C'D$ represent magnetic and geographical meridians, then $\angle BAB' = \theta$ represents the magnetic declination. (fig.)

2. Magnetic Inclination or Dip

Dip at a place is defined as the angle made by the direction of the Earth's total magnetic field with the horizontal direction. It is denoted by δ.

Suppose that a small bar magnet is suspended freely at point A and it points in direction AP. Then, AP is the direction of the intensity of Earth's total magnetic field (B). The line AP lines in magnetic meridian. Consider that AB is a horizontal line in the magnetic meridian. Then, $\angle BAP = \delta$ represents the dip at point A.

3. Horizontal Component of Earth's Magnetic Field

It is the component of Earth's magnetic field along the horizontal direction. It is denoted by B_H.

From point P, drop PL perpendicular to AB and PM perpendicular to AD. Then, AL and AM represent horizontal component (B_H) and vertical component (B_V) of Earth's total magnetic field. In right angled ΔALP.

$$B = \sqrt{B_H^2 + B_V^2}$$

or $$\tan\delta = \frac{B_V}{B_H}$$

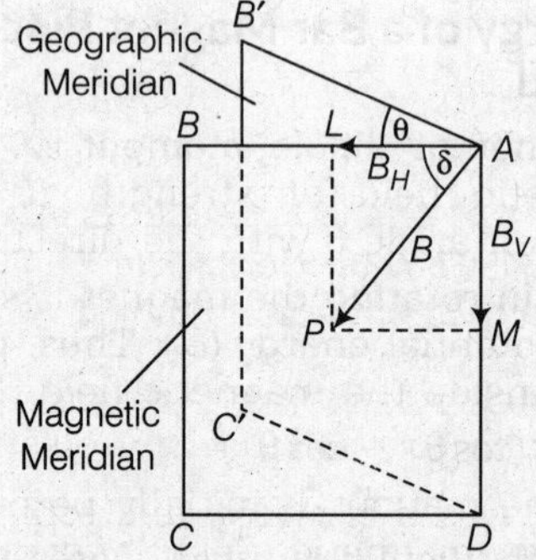

Practice Questions

Level I

1. The magnetic moment is a
(a) scalar quantity (b) vector quantity
(c) constant (d) None of these

2. The magnetic moment has dimensions of
(a) $[LA]$ (b) $[L^2A]$
(c) $[LT^{-1}A]$ (d) $[L^2T^{-1}A]$

3. The magnet of pole strength m and magnetic mom cut into two pieces along its axis. The magnetic mom pole strength of either part is
(a) $\frac{M}{2}, \frac{m}{2}$ (b) $M, \frac{m}{2}$
(c) $\frac{M}{2}, m$ (d) M, m

4. Two magnets each of magnetic moment M are placed so also form a cross at right angles to each other. The magnetic moment of the system is
(a) $0.5M$ (b) M (c) $\sqrt{2}M$ (d) $2M$

5. The magnetic field due to a small magnetic dipole of magnetic moment M at a point on the axis of the dipole and at a distance r from it is given by
(a) $\frac{\mu_0}{4\pi}\cdot\frac{M}{r^3}$ (b) $\frac{\mu_0}{4\pi}\cdot\frac{M}{r^2}$
(c) $\frac{\mu_0}{4\pi}\cdot\frac{2M}{r^3}$ (d) $\frac{\mu_0}{4\pi}\cdot\frac{2M}{r^2}$

6. If the magnetic dipole is rotated through an angle θ wrt to the direction of the magnetic field B, then the work done will be
(a) $MB(1-\cos\theta)$ (b) $MB\cos\theta$
(c) $MB(1-\sin\theta)$ (d) $MB\sin\theta$

7. The direction of magnetic field lines of a bar magnet is
(a) from South pole to North pole
(b) from North pole to South pole
(c) across the bar magnet
(d) from South pole to North pole inside the magnet and from North pole to South pole outside the magnet

8. A magnetic needle is placed on a cork floating in a still lakein the Northern hemisphere. Does the needle together with the cork move towards the North of the lake?
(a) Yes
(b) No
(c) May or may not move
(d) Nothing can be said

9. The effect due to uniform magnetic field on a freely suspended magnetic needle is as follows
(a) both torque and net force are present
(b) torque is present but no net force
(c) force is present but no net torque
(d) both torque and net force are absent

10. Angle between magnetic meridian and geographical meridian is called
(a) angle of dip (b) angle of declination
(c) angle of depression (d) (a) and (b)

11. At which place on the Earth, the Earth's magnetic field becomes horizontal?
(a) Magnetic pole (b) Geographical pole
(c) Magnetic meridian (d) Magnetic equator

12. Which of the following relation is correct in magnetism?
(a) $B = \sqrt{B_V^2 + B_H^2}$ (b) $B = B_V + B_H$
(c) $B_V = \sqrt{B^2 + B_H^2}$ (d) $B_H = \sqrt{B^2 + B_V^2}$

13. Magnetic lines of force
(a) always intersect
(b) are always closed
(c) tend to crowd far away from the poles of magnet
(d) do not pass through vacuum

14. The magnetic field lines due to a bar magnet are correctly shown in

(a) 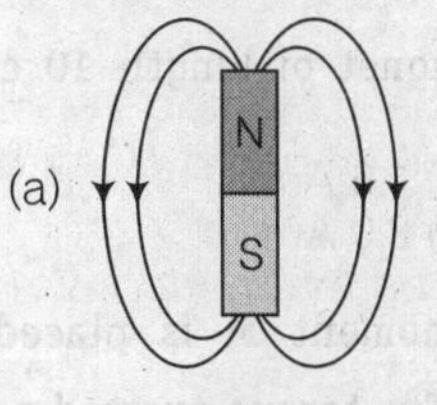

(b) 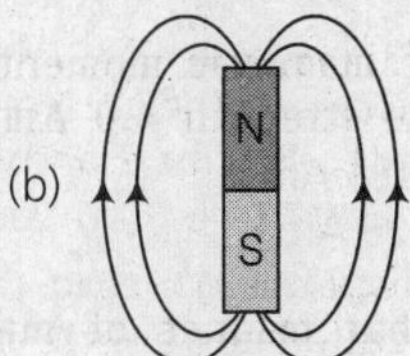

(c) 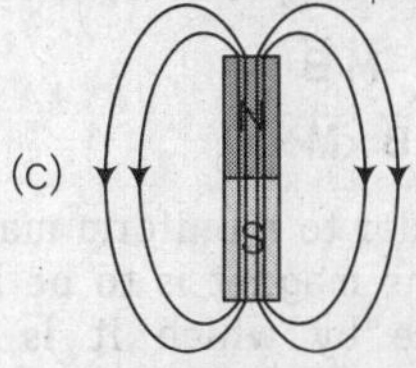

(d) 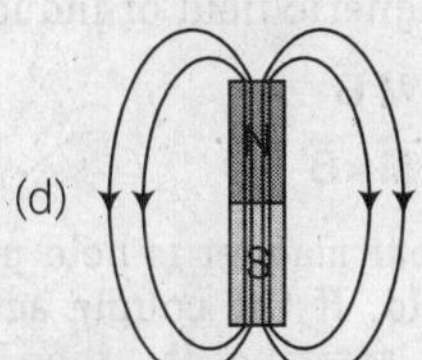

15. A magnet of magnetic moment M is rotated though 360° in a magnetic field H. The work done will be
(a) MH (b) $2MH$ (c) $2\pi MH$ (d) Zero

16. If a magnet is hanged with its magnetic axis, then it stops in
(a) magnetic meridian (b) geometric meridian
(c) angle of dip (d) None of these

17. Earth's magnetic field always has a horizontal component except at or horizontal component of Earth's magnetic field remains zero at
(a) equator (b) magnetic poles
(c) a latitude of 60° (d) an altitude of 60°

18. A dip needle in a plane perpendicular to magnetic meridian will remain
(a) vertical
(b) horizontal
(c) in any direction
(d) at an angle of dip to the horizontal

19. At magnetic poles of Earth, angle of dip is
(a) zero (b) 45° (c) 90° (d) 180°

20. The lines of force due to Earth's horizontal component of magnetic field are
(a) parallel straight lines (b) concentric circles
(c) elliptical (d) parabolic

Level II

1. What happens to the force between magnetic poles when their pole strength and the distance between them are both doubled?
(a) Force increases to two times the previous value
(b) No change
(c) Force decreases to half the previous value
(d) Force increases to four times the previous value

2. A magnet of magnetic moment M is situated with its axis along the direction of a magnetic field of strength B. The work done in rotating it by an angle of 180° will be
(a) $-MB$ (b) $+MB$ (c) 0 (d) $+2MB$

3. A permanent magnet
(a) attracts all substances
(b) attracts only magnetic substances
(c) attracts magnetic substances and repels all non-magnetic substances
(d) attracts non-magnetic substances and repels all magnetic substances

4. The magnetic moment of a magnet of length 10 cm and pole strength 4.0 Am will be
(a) 0.4 Am^2 (b) 1.6 Am^2
(c) 20 Am^2 (d) 8.0 Am^2

5. A bar magnet of magnetic moment $\vec{M}$ is placed in a magnetic field of induction $\vec{B}$. The torque exerted on it is
(a) $\vec{M}\cdot\vec{B}$ (b) $-\vec{M}\cdot\vec{B}$
(c) $\vec{M}\times\vec{B}$ (d) $\vec{B}\times\vec{M}$

6. A bar magnet is held perpendicular to a uniform magnetic field. If the couple acting on the magnet is to be halved by rotating it, then the angle by which it is to be rotated is
(a) 30° (b) 45°
(c) 60° (d) 90°

7. Weber/m² is equal to
(a) volt (b) henry
(c) tesla (d) All of these

8. Two magnets, each of magnetic moment M are placed so as to form a cross at right angles to each other. The magnetic moment of the system will be
(a) $2M$ (b) $\sqrt{2}M$
(c) $0.5M$ (d) M

9. The ultimate individual unit of magnetism in any magnet is called
(a) North pole (b) South pole
(c) Dipole (d) Quadrupole

10. The vertical component of Earth's magnetic field is zero. The Earth's magnetic field always has a vertical component except at the
(a) magnetic poles (b) geographical poles
(c) every place (d) magnetic equator

11. The angle between the magnetic meridian and geographical meridian is called
(a) angle of dip
(b) angle of declination
(c) magnetic moment
(d) power of magnetic field

12. At a place, if the Earth's horizontal and vertical components of magnetic fields are equal, then the angle of dip will be
(a) 30° (b) 90°
(c) 45° (d) 0°

13. If the angles of dip at two places are 30° and 45° respectively, then the ratio of horizontal components of Earth's magnetic field at the two places will be
(a) $\sqrt{3}:\sqrt{2}$ (b) $1:\sqrt{2}$
(c) $1:\sqrt{3}$ (d) $1:2$

14. If magnetic lines of force are drawn by keeping magnet vertical, then number of neutral points will be
(a) one (b) two
(c) four (d) five

15. The angle of dip at the magnetic equator is
(a) 0° (b) 45°
(c) 30° (d) 90°

16. At which place, Earth's magnetism becomes horizontal?
(a) Magnetic pole
(b) Geographical pole
(c) Magnetic meridian
(d) Magnetic equator

17. A compass needle will show which of the following directions at the Earth's magnetic pole?
(a) Vertical
(b) No particular direction
(c) Bent at 45° to the vertical
(d) Horizontal

18. The vertical component of the Earth's magnetic field is zero at a place where the angle of dip is
(a) 0° (b) 45°
(c) 60° (d) 90°

19. The magnetic field of Earth is due to
(a) motion and distribution of some material in and outside the Earth
(b) interaction of cosmic rays with the current of Earth
(c) a magnetic dipole buried at the centre of the Earth
(d) induction effect of the Sun

20. When the N-pole of a bar magnet points towards the South and S-pole towards the North, the null points are at the
(a) magnetic axis
(b) magnetic centre
(c) perpendicular divider of magnetic axis
(d) N and S-poles

Answers

Level I

1. (b)	**2.** (b)	**3.** (a)	**4.** (c)	**5.** (c)	**6.** (a)	**7.** (d)	**8.** (b)	**9.** (b)	**10.** (b)
11. (b)	**12.** (a)	**13.** (b)	**14.** (d)	**15.** (d)	**16.** (a)	**17.** (b)	**18.** (a)	**19.** (c)	**20.** (a)

Level II

1. (b)	**2.** (d)	**3.** (b)	**4.** (a)	**5.** (c)	**6.** (c)	**7.** (c)	**8.** (b)	**9.** (c)	**10.** (d)
11. (b)	**12.** (c)	**13.** (a)	**14.** (a)	**15.** (a)	**16.** (d)	**17.** (a)	**18.** (a)	**19.** (a)	**20.** (a)

Hints *and* Solutions

Level II

2. Work done $= MB(\cos\theta_1 - \cos\theta_2)$

$$\theta_1 = 0° \text{ and } \theta_2 = 180°$$

$$\Rightarrow \quad W = MB(\cos 0° - \cos 180°) = 2MB$$

4. $M = mL = 4 \times 10 \times 10^{-2}$

$$= 0.4 \text{ A m}^2$$

6. $\tau = MB\sin\theta$

$$\Rightarrow \quad \tau \propto \sin\theta$$

$$\Rightarrow \quad \frac{\tau_1}{\tau_2} = \frac{\sin\theta_1}{\sin\theta_2}$$

$$\Rightarrow \quad \frac{\tau}{\tau/2} = \frac{\sin 90°}{\sin\theta_2}$$

$$\Rightarrow \quad \sin\theta_2 = \frac{1}{2}$$

$$\Rightarrow \quad \theta_2 = 30°$$

$\therefore$ Angle of rotation $= 90° - 30° = 60°$

7. Magnetic flux $\phi = BA$

$$\Rightarrow \quad B = \frac{\phi}{A} = \frac{\text{weber}}{\text{m}^2} = \text{tesla}$$

8.

$$\Rightarrow M_{\text{net}} = \sqrt{M^2 + M^2} = \sqrt{2}M$$

10. At magnetic equator, the angle of dip is 0°. Hence, the vertical component

$$V = I\sin\phi = 0$$

12.

$$B_V = B_H \tan\phi,$$

If $\quad B_V = B_H,$

Then, $\quad \tan\phi = 1$ or $\phi = 45°$.

13. The horizontal components are

$$(B_H)_1 = B\cos\phi_1 \text{ and } (B_H)_2 = B\cos\phi_2$$

$$\because \quad \frac{(B_H)_1}{(B_H)_2} = \frac{\cos 30°}{\cos 45°}$$

$$\Rightarrow \quad \frac{(B_H)_1}{(B_H)_2} = \frac{\sqrt{3}/2}{1/\sqrt{2}}$$

$$\therefore \quad \frac{(B_H)_1}{(B_H)_2} = \frac{\sqrt{3}}{\sqrt{2}}$$

43

Classification of Magnetic Materials

Magnetic Intensity
(Magnetising Field Intensity)

It is the number of ampere-turns (nI) flowing round the unit length of the solenoid required to produce a given magnetising field.

Thus, $H = nI$.

Also, $B_0 = \mu_0\, nI = \mu H$

$$\therefore \quad H = \frac{B_0}{\mu_0}$$

SI unit of H is Am^{-1} and its dimensions are $[L^{-1}A]$.

Magnetisation (Intensity of Magnetisation)

It is the magnetic moment developed per unit volume of a meterial when placed in a magnetising field. It is a vector quantity.

$$M = \frac{m}{V}$$

Its SI unit is Am^{-1} or $N\,Wb^{-1}$ or $Nm^{-1}T^{-1}$.

Magnetic Induction

It is the total number of magnetic lines of force crossing per unit area through a magnetic material. Its SI unit is tesla (T).

$$B = \mu_0 (H + M)$$

Magnetic Permeability

It is the ratio of the magnetic induction to the magnetising field intensity.

$$\mu = \frac{B}{H}$$

Its SI unit is $Tm\,A^{-1}$ or $Wbm^{-1}\,A^{-1}$.

Relative Permeability

It is the ratio of the permeability of the material to the permeability of free space.

$$\mu_r = \frac{\mu}{\mu_0}$$

Magnetic Susceptibility

It is the ratio of the intensity of magnetisation (M) induced to the magnetising field intensity (H).

$$\chi_m = \frac{M}{H}$$

It can be shown that $\mu = \mu_0 (1 + \chi_m)$

and $\mu_r = 1 + \chi_m$

Curie's Law

The magnetic susceptibility of a paramagnetic substance varies inversely with its absolute temperature.

$$\chi_m \propto \frac{1}{T}$$

$$\Rightarrow \quad \chi_m = \frac{C}{T}$$

Where, C is curie constant.

Curie Temperature The temperature above which a ferromagnetic substance becomes paramagnetic is called Curie temperature (T_C). The modified Curie law for ferromagnetic substances above the Curie temperature is

$$\chi_m = \frac{C'}{T - T_C} \quad (T > T_C)$$

S.No.	Property	Diamagnetic Substances	Paramagnetic Substances	Ferromagnetic Subtances
1.	Cause of magnetism	Orbital motion of electrons	Spin motion of electrons	Formation of domains
2.	Explanation of magnetism	On the basis of orbital motion of electrons	On the basis of spin and orbital motion of electrons	On the basis of domains formed
3.	State of magnetisation	These are weekly magnetised in a direction opposite to that of applied magnetic field	These get weekly magnetised in the direction of applied magnetic field	These get strongly magnetised in the direction of applied magnetic field
		S n s N	N s n S	N s n S
4.	When the material in the form of liquid is filled in the U-tube and placed between pole pieces	Liquid level in that limb gets depressed N S Liquid	Liquid level in that limb rises up N S Liquid	Liquid level in that limb rises up very much N S Liquid
5.	The value of magnetic induction B	$B < B_0$ (Where, B_0 is the magnetic induction in vaccum)	$B > B_0$	$B >> B_0$
6.	Magnetic susceptibility χ	Low and negative $\|\chi\| \approx 1$	Low but positive $\chi \approx 1$	Positive and high $\chi \approx 10^2$
7.	Dependence of χ on temperature	Does not depend on temperature (except Bi at low temperature) χ T	On cooling, these get converted to ferromagnetic materials at Curie temperature χ T	These get converted into paramagnetic materials at Curie temperature χ T_C T
8.	Relative permeability (μ_r)	$\mu_r < 1$	$\mu_r > 1$	$\mu_r >> 1$ $\mu_r = 10^2$
9.	Intensity of magnetisation (I)	I is in a direction opposite to that of H and its value is very low	I is in the direction of H but value is low.	I is in the direction of H and value is very high
10.	Magnetic moment (M)	Very low ($\simeq 0$)	Very low	Very high
11.	Examples	Cu, Ag, Au, Zn, Bi, Sb, NaCl, H_2O air and diamond etc.	Al, Mn, Pt, Na, $CuCl_2$, O_2 and crown glass	Fe, Co, Ni, Cd, Fe_3O_4 etc.

Practice Questions

Level I

1. Which of following is not a unit of the intensity of magnetisation?

(a) Am^{-1} (b) $J\ T^{-1}\ m^{-3}$
(c) $NT^{-1}\ m^{-2}$ (d) $A\ T^{-1}\ m^{-2}$

2. Which of the following is not unit of magnetic induction?

(a) T (b) $Wb\ m^2$
(c) $J\ A^{-1}\ m^{-2}$ (d) $N\ A^{-1}\ m^{-1}$

3. Which of the following relation is not correct?

(a) $B = \mu_0 (I + H)$ (b) $B = \mu_0 (1 + \chi_m) H$
(c) $I = \dfrac{B - \mu_0 H}{\mu_0}$ (d) $\chi_m = \mu - 1$

4. Which of the following relation is not correct?

(a) $\chi_m = \dfrac{I}{H}$ (b) $\mu_0 = \mu_0 (1 + \chi_m) H$
(c) $\mu_0 = \mu (1 + \chi_m)$ (d) $\mu_r = 1 + \chi_m$

5. Which of the following is ferromagnetic?

(a) Aluminium (b) Quartz
(c) Nickel (d) Bismuth

6. An example of a ferromagnetic substance is

(a) aluminium (b) nickel
(c) gold (d) copper

7. Which of the following is paramagnetic?

(a) Antimony (b) Silver
(c) Marble (d) Alnico

8. If the permanent magnetic moment of the atoms of a substance is zero, then substance is called

(a) diamagnetic (b) paramagnetic
(c) ferromagnetic (d) anti-ferromagnetic

9. The susceptibility of a diamagnetic substance

(a) decreases with temperature
(b) does not vary with temperature
(c) first decreases and then increases with increase of temperature
(d) increases with temperature

10. The magnetic permeability is maximum for

(a) paramagnetic (b) ferromagnetic
(c) diamagnetic (d) non-magnetic

11. Susceptibility is positive and small for a

(a) paramagnetic (b) ferromagnetic
(c) diamagnetic (d) non-magnetic

12. Susceptibility is positive and large for a

(a) paramagnetic (b) ferromagnetic
(c) non-magnetic (d) diamagnetic

13. A uniform magnetic field (parallel to the plane of the paper) existed in space initially directed from left to right. When bar of soft iron is placed in the field parallel to it, the line of force passing through it, will be represented by

(a) 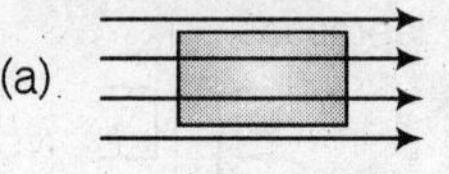 (b) 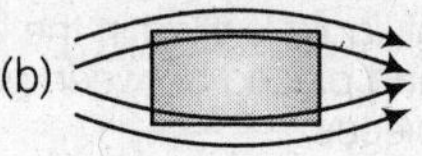

(c) 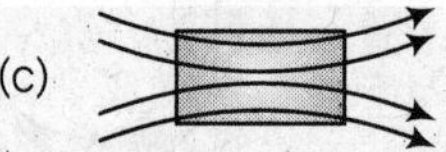 (d) 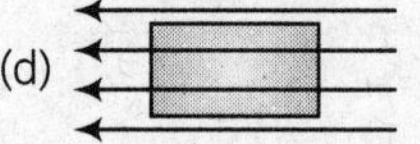

14. At Curie point, a ferromagnetic material becomes

(a) non-magnetic (b) diamagnetic
(c) paramagnetic (d) strongly ferromagnetic

15. Above Curie temperature, ferromagnetic specimen

(a) remains ferromagnetic (b) becomes ferromagnetic
(c) becomes paramagnetic (d) becomes diamagnetic

16. The diamagnetic materials are

(a) strongly repelled by a magnet
(b) strongly attracted by a magnet
(c) feebly repelled by a magnet
(d) feebly attracted by a magnet

17. The substance, in which the magnetic moment of a single atom is not zero, is called

(a) diamagnetic (b) paramagnetic
(c) ferromagnetic (d) ferrite

18. The relative permeability of a diamagnetic material is

(a) equal to unity (b) more than unity
(c) less than unity (d) zero

19. In which type of material, the magnetic susceptibility does not depend on the temperature?

(a) Diamagnetic (b) Paramagnetic
(c) Ferrite (d) Ferromagnetic

20. Curie temperature of iron is the temperature below which, it is

(a) super conducting (b) ferromagnetic
(c) diamagnetic (d) paramagnetic

Level II

1. For a paramagnetic material, the dependence of the magnetic susceptibility χ_m on the absolute temperature T is given by

(a) $\chi_m \propto T$ (b) $\chi_m \propto \dfrac{1}{T}$
(c) $\chi_m = e^{kT}$ (d) $\chi_m =$ Constant

2. Tesla is the unit of

(a) electric flux
(b) electric field
(c) magnetic induction
(d) magnetic flux

3. If a diamagnetic substance is brought near North or South pole of a bar magnet, it is
(a) attracted by both the poles
(b) repelled by both the poles
(c) attracted by the North pole and repelled by the South pole
(d) repelled by the North pole and attracted by the South pole

4. A diamagnetic material in a magnetic field moves
(a) perpendicular to the field
(b) from weaker to stronger parts
(c) from stronger to weaker parts
(d) None of the above

5. The magnetic moment of a diamagnetic atom is
(a) equal to zero
(b) equal to one
(c) between zero and one
(d) much greater than one

6. If the susceptibility of dia, para and ferro magnetic materials are χ_d, χ_p, χ_f respectively, then
(a) $\chi_d < \chi_p < \chi_f$ (b) $\chi_d < \chi_f < \chi_p$
(c) $\chi_f < \chi_d < \chi_p$ (d) $\chi_f < \chi_p < \chi_d$

7 A paramagnetic substance of susceptibility 3×10^{-4} is placed in a magnetic field of 4×10^{-4} Am^{-1}. Then, the intensity of magnetisation in the units of Am^{-1} is
(a) 1.33×10^{8} (b) 0.75×10^{-8}
(c) 12×10^{-8} (d) 14×10^{-8}

8. Relative permeability of iron is 5500, then its magnetic susceptibility will be
(a) 5500×10^{7} (b) 5500×10^{-7}
(c) 5501 (d) 5499

9. An example of a diamagnetic substance is
(a) aluminium (b) copper
(c) iron (d) nickel

10. Curie's law can be written as
(a) $\chi \propto (T - T_c)$ (b) $\chi \propto \frac{1}{T - T_c}$
(c) $\chi \propto \frac{1}{T}$ (d) $\chi \propto T$

11. The given figure represents a material which is

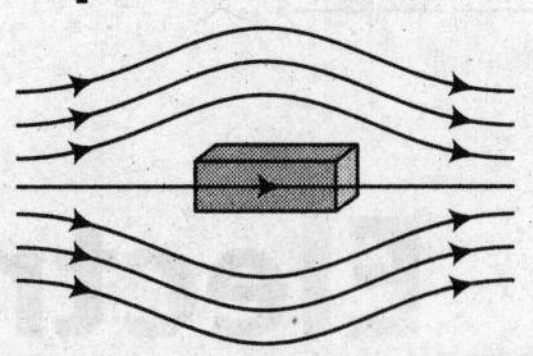

(a) paramagnetic (b) diamagnetic
(c) ferromagnetic (d) None of these

12. For an isotropic medium B, μ, H and M are related as (where B, μ_0, H and M have their usual meanings in the context of magnetic material)
(a) $(B - M) = \mu_0 H$ (b) $M = \mu_0 (H + M)$
(c) $H = \mu_0 (H + M)$ (d) $B = \mu_0 (H + M)$

13. Iron would become paramagnetic at about
(a) 200°C (b) 400°C
(c) 600°C (d) 800°C

14. The relative magnetic permeability of ferromagnetic materials is of the order of
(a) 10 (b) 100
(c) 1000 (d) 10000

15. Which one of the following is not a characteristics of diamagnetism?
(a) The diamagnetic material are repelled by a bar magnet
(b) The magnetic susceptibility of the material is small and negative
(c) The origin of diamagnetism is the spin of electrons
(d) The material move from a region of strong magnetic field to weak magnetic field

Answers

Level I

1. (d)	**2.** (d)	**3.** (d)	**4.** (c)	**5.** (c)	**6.** (b)	**7.** (a)	**8.** (a)	**9.** (b)	**10.** (b)
11. (a)	**12.** (b)	**13.** (c)	**14.** (c)	**15.** (c)	**16.** (c)	**17.** (b)	**18.** (c)	**19.** (a)	**20.** (b)

Level II

1. (b)	**2.** (c)	**3.** (b)	**4.** (c)	**5.** (a)	**6.** (a)	**7.** (c)	**8.** (d)	**9.** (b)	**10.** (c)
11. (b)	**12.** (d)	**13.** (d)	**14.** (d)	**15.** (c)					

Hints and Solutions

Level II

8. $\chi_m = (\mu_r - 1)$

$\chi_m = [5500 - 1] = 5499$

44

Electromagnetic Induction

Magnetic Flux

The number of magnetic lines of force crossing a surface normally is called magnetic flux linked with the surface. If the normal drawn to the surface area A makes angle θ with the field $\vec{B}$, then the magnetic flux is

$\phi = BA\cos\theta = \vec{B}\cdot\vec{A}$

Magnetic flux is a scalar quantity. Its dimensions are $[ML^2A^{-1}T^{-2}]$.

SI Unit of Magnetic Flux is Weber (Wb)

It is the flux produced when a uniform magnetic field of 1 T crosses normally an area $1\,m^2$. The CGS unit of magnetic flux is Maxwell.

1 weber $= 10^8$ maxwell

Electromagnetic Induction

It is the phenomenon of production of induced emf (and hence induced current) due to a change of magnetic flux linked with a closed circuit. The term electromagnetic induction means inducing electricity by magnetism.

Faraday's Laws of Electromagnetic Induction

First Law

Whenever the magnetic flux linked with a closed circuit changes, an emf is induced in it which lasts only so long as the change in flux is taking place.

Second Law

The magnitude of induced emf is equal to the rate of change of magnetic flux linked with the closed circuit. Mathematically,

$$|\varepsilon| = \frac{d\phi}{dt}$$

Lenz's Law

It states that the direction of induced current is such that it opposes the cause which produces it *i.e.*, it opposes the change in flux.

Mathematical Form of the Laws of Electromagnetic Induction

For a coil of one turn, induced emf is given by

$$\xi = -\frac{d\phi}{dt} = -\frac{\phi_2 - \phi_1}{t}$$

For a coil of N turns, $\xi = -N\frac{d\phi}{dt} = -N\frac{\phi_2 - \phi_1}{t}$.

The negative sign shows that induced emf opposes the change in flux. It is an accordance with Lenz's law.

Fleming's Right Hand Rule

It gives the direction of induced emf. If we stretch the thumb and the first two fingers of our right mutually perpendicular to each other and if the forefinger points in the direction of the magnetic field, thumb in the direction of motion of the conductor, then the central finger points in the direction of current induced in the conductor.

Motional emf

The emf induced across the ends of a conductor due to its motion in a magnetic field is called motional emf. It is produced due to the magnetic Lorentz force acting on the free electrons of the conductor. If a conductor of length l moves with velocity v in a magnetic field B perpendicular to both its length and the direction of the magnetic field, then the emf induced across its ends is given by $\xi = Blv$

Induced current, $I = \frac{\xi}{R} = \frac{Blv}{R}$

Force necessary to move the conductor,

$$F = \frac{B^2 l^2 v}{R}$$

Power dissipated as Joule heating loss,

$$P = Fv = \frac{B^2 l^2 v^2}{R}$$

Self-Induction

It is phenomenon of production of induced emf in a coil when a changing current passes through it.

Self-Inductance or Coefficient of Self-Induction

(L) When a current I flows through a coil, flux linked with it is $\phi = LI$

$$\text{Induced emf, } \xi = -\frac{d\phi}{dt} = -L\frac{dI}{dt}$$

Thus, self-inductance of a coil is the induced emf set up in it when the current passing through it changes at the unit rate. It is a measure of the opposition of the coil to the flow of current through it.

Self-Inductance of a Long Solenoid

The self-inductance of a long solenoid of length l, area of cross-section A and having N turns is

$$L = \frac{\mu_0 N^2 A}{l} = \mu_0 n^2 lA, \text{ where } n = \frac{N}{l}$$

When the solenoid is wound over a soft iron core of relative permeability μ_r, $L = \mu_r \mu_0 n^2 lA$. The value of self-inductance depends on the number of turns in the solenoid, its area of cross-section and the relative permeability of its core material.

Mutual Induction

It is the phenomenon of production of induced emf in one coil when the current through the neighbouring coil changes at the unit rate.

Mutual Inductance or Coefficient of Mutual Induction (M)

If a current I flowing through one coil generates flux ϕ in the neighbouring coil, then $\phi = MI$

$$\text{Induced emf, } \xi = -\frac{d\phi}{dt} = -M\frac{dI}{dt}$$

Thus, mutual inductance of two coils may be defined as the induced emf set up in one coil when the current in the neighbouring coil changes at the unit rate.

Mutual Inductance of Two Long Solenoids

The mutual inductance of two long co-axial solenoids wound over one another is

$$M = \frac{\mu_0 N_1 N_2 A}{l} = \mu_0 n_1 n_2 Al = \mu_0 \ n_1 \ n_2 \ \pi r_1^2 \ l$$

When n_1, n_2 are the number of turns per unit length of the solenoids, l is their common length and $A = \pi r_1^2 =$ cross-sectional area of the inner solenoid.

> **HENRY**
>
> It is SI unit for both self and mutual inductances. Inductance is one henry if an induced emf of 1 volt is set up when the current changes at the rate of 1 ampere per second.
>
> 1 Henry (H) $= 1\ \text{VsA}^{-1} = 1\ \text{Wb A}^{-1}$

Coefficient of Coupling

It gives a measure of the manner in which two coils are coupled together. If L_1 and L_2 are the self-inductances of the two coils and M is the mutual inductance, then the coefficient of coupling

$$K = \sqrt{\frac{M}{L_1 L_2}}$$

The value of K lies between 0 and 1.

Practice Questions

Level I

1. The SI unit of magnetic flux is

(a) Gauss (b) Oersted (c) Ttesla (d) Weber

2. In electromagnetic induction, the induced emf is independent of

(a) change of flux
(b) time
(c) number of turns in the coil
(d) resistance of the coil

3. Magnitude of emf produced in a coil, when a magnet is inserted into it does not depend upon

(a) number of turns in the coil
(b) resistance of the coil
(c) speed of the magnet
(d) magnetic moment of magnet

4. A magnet is moved towards a coil, first quickly and then slowly. The induced emf produced is

(a) larger in first case
(b) smaller in first case
(c) equal in both cases
(d) larger or smaller, depending upon resistance of the coil

5. Refer to the figure. Deflection in the galvanometer (G) occurs, when

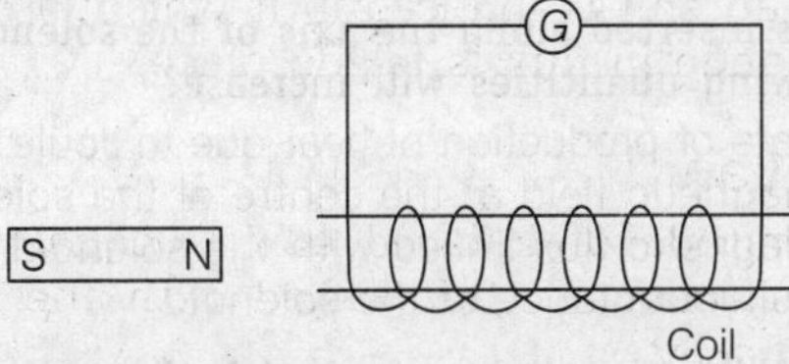

(a) the magnet is pushed into the coil
(b) the magnet is rotated into the coil
(c) the magnet is stationary at the centre of the coil
(d) the number of turns in the coil is reduced

6. Faraday's law of electromagnetic induction is related to the law of conservation of

(a) charge (b) angular momentum
(c) mass (d) energy

7. Lenz's law is a consequence of the law of conservation of
(a) charge only (b) momentum only
(c) energy only (d) energy and momentum

8. The direction of induced emf is given by
(a) Fleming's left hand rule
(b) Fleming's right hand rule
(c) Lenz's law
(d) Biot-Savart's law

9. In electromagnetic induction, the induced charge is independent of
(a) time (b) change of flux
(c) resistance of the coil (d) None of these

10. An electron moves along the line AB, which lies in the same plane as a circular loop of conducting wires. What will be the direction of the current induced in the loop, if any?

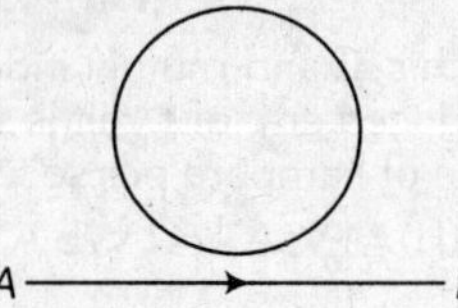

(a) No current will be induced
(b) The current will be clockwise
(c) The current will be anti-clockwise
(d) The current will change direction as the electron passes by

11. In a solenoid, if number of turns is doubled, then self-inductance will become
(a) half (b) doubled
(c) 1/4 times (d) quadruped

12. When the number of turns and length of a solenoid are doubled keeping the area of cross-section same, the inductance
(a) remains the same
(b) becomes four times
(c) is doubled
(d) is halved

13. A dynamo works on the principle of
(a) electromagnetic induction
(b) induced current
(c) induced magnetism
(d) Faraday's effect

14. Electric fan works on the principle of
(a) electric dynamo (b) electric motor
(c) Both of these (d) None of these

15. The device that does not work on the principle of mutual induction is
(a) induction coil (b) tesla coil
(c) transformer (d) motor

Level II

1. An induction furnace works on the principle of
(a) eddy currents (b) Faraday's laws
(c) self-induction (d) mutual induction

2. Dimensions of coefficient of self-induction is
(a) $[ML^2T^{2}A^{-2}]$ (b) $[ML^2T^{-3}A^{-2}]$
(c) $[ML^2T^{-3}]$ (d) None of these

3. The self-inductance of a straight conductor is
(a) zero (b) infinity
(c) very large (d) very small

4. Two pure inductors each of self-inductance L are connected in parallel but are well separated from each other. Then, the total inductance is
(a) L (b) $2L$ (c) $L/2$ (d) $L/4$

5. A constant current is passed through a solenoid. If an iron rod is inserted along the axis of the solenoid, which of the following quantities will increase?
(a) Rate of production of heat due to Joule heating
(b) Magnetic field at the centre of the solenoid
(c) Magnetic flux linked with the solenoid
(d) Self-inductance of the solenoid

6. A metallic ring is attached with the wall of a room. When the North pole of a magnet is brought near to it, the induced current in the ring will be

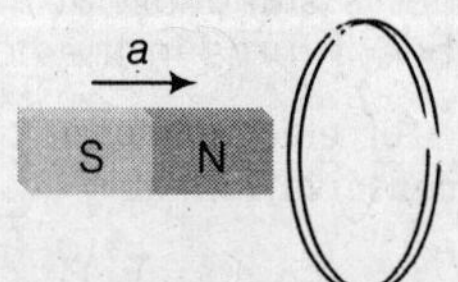

(a) first clockwise, then anti-clockwise
(b) in clockwise direction
(c) in anti-clockwise direction
(d) first anti-clockwise, then clockwise

7. The magnetic flux linked with a coil of N turns of area of cross-section A held with its plane parallel to the field B is
(a) $\frac{NAB}{2}$ (b) NAB (c) $\frac{NAB}{4}$ (d) 0

8. A coil having 500 square loops each of side 10 cm is placed normal to a magnetic flux which increases at the rate of 1.0 T/s. The induced emf (in V) is
(a) 0.1 (b) 0.5 (c) 1 (d) 5

9. The formula for induced emf in a coil due to change in magnetic flux through the coil is (here A = area of the coil, B = magnetic field)
(a) $e = -A \cdot \frac{dB}{dt}$ (b) $e = -B \cdot \frac{dA}{dt}$
(c) $e = -\frac{d}{dt}(A \cdot B)$ (d) $e = -\frac{d}{dt}(A \times B)$

10. Lenz's law is expressed by the following formula (here e = induced emf, ϕ = magnetic flux in one turn and N = number of turns)
(a) $e = -\phi \frac{dN}{dt}$ (b) $e = -N \frac{d\phi}{dt}$
(c) $e = -\frac{d}{dt}\left(\frac{\phi}{N}\right)$ (d) $e = N \frac{d\phi}{dt}$

11. A square loop of side 22 cm is converted into circular loop in 0.4 s. A uniform magnetic field of 0.2 T directed normal to the loop, then the emf induced in the loop is
(a) 6.6×10^{-3} V
(b) 6.6×10^{-5} V
(c) 4.6×10^{-4} V
(d) 4.60×10^{-8} V

12. Two coils of self-inductance L_1 and L_2 are placed closer to each other so that total flux in one coil is completely linked with other. If M is mutual inductance between them, then
(a) $M = L_1L_2$ (b) $M = L_1/L_2$
(c) $M=\sqrt{L_1L_2}$ (d) $M=(L_1L_2)^2$

13. The average power dissipation in pure inductance is
(a) $\frac{1}{2}LI^2$ (b) $2LI^2$ (c) $\frac{1}{4}LI^2$ (d) Zero

14. If a current of 3.0 A flowing in the primary coil is reduced to zero in 0.001 s, then the induced emf in the secondary coil is 15000 V. The mutual inductance between the two coils is
(a) 0.5 H (b) 5 H (c) 1.5 H (d) 10 H

15. An emf of 12 V is induced in a given coil when the current in it changes at the rate of 48 A /min. The self-inductance of the coil is
(a) 0.25 H (b) 15 H
(c) 1.5 H (d) 9.6 H

Answers

Level I

1. (d)	**2.** (d)	**3.** (b)	**4.** (a)	**5.** (a)	**6.** (d)	**7.** (c)	**8.** (b,c)	**9.** (a)	**10.** (c)
11. (d)	**12.** (c)	**13.** (a)	**14.** (b)	**15.** (d)					

Level II

1. (a)	**2.** (a)	**3.** (a)	**4.** (c)	**5.** (b,c,d)	**6.** (c)	**7.** (d)	**8.** (d)	**9.** (c)	**10.** (b)
11. (a)	**12.** (c)	**13.** (d)	**14.** (b)	**15.** (b)					

Hints and Solutions

Level II

8. $e = N\left(\frac{\Delta B}{\Delta t}\right)\cdot A\cos\theta$

$= 500\times1\times(100+10^{-2})^2\cos 0° = 5\text{ V}$

11. $e=\frac{d\phi}{dt}=\frac{Bd\,A}{dt}=\frac{2(\pi r^2-l^2)}{dt}=6.6\times10^{-3}\text{V}$

14. $e = M\frac{di}{dt}$

$\Rightarrow M=\frac{15000}{3}\times0.001=5\text{H}$

15. $L = e/di/dt = \frac{12}{48/60} = 15\text{ H}$

45

Alternating Current

Alternating Current

It is that current which varies in magnitude continuously and reverses its direction periodically. Its value at any instant is given by

$$I = I_0 \sin \omega t = I_0 \sin 2\pi f t$$

Where, I_0 is the peak value of AC or current amplitude. The frequency of AC supplied to our homes is 50 cycle/second. The average value of AC over a complete cycle is zero.

Direct Current

It is that current which flows with a constant magnitude in the same fixed direction.

Average or Mean Value of AC

It is that value of direct current which sends the same charge in a circuit in the same time as is sent by the given alternating current in the same circuit in its half time period.

$$I_{av} = \frac{2}{\pi} I_0 = 0.637\, I_0$$

Effective or Rms or Virtual Value of AC

It is that value of direct current which produces the same heating effect in a given resistor as is produced by the given alternating current when passed for the same time.

$$I_{rms} \text{ or } I_{eff} \text{ or } I_v = \frac{1}{\sqrt{2}} . I_0 = 0.707\, I_0$$

Alternating Voltage

It is that voltage whose magnitude varies continuously and direction reverses periodically with time. Its instantaneous, average and roof mean square values are respectively given by

$$\varepsilon = \varepsilon_0 \sin \omega t$$

$$\varepsilon_{av} = 0.637 \varepsilon_0$$

$$\varepsilon_{rms} = \frac{1}{\sqrt{2}} \varepsilon_0$$

Pure Resistive Circuit

Let an alternating voltage $V = V_0 \sin \omega t$ be applied across a pure resistance R. Then,

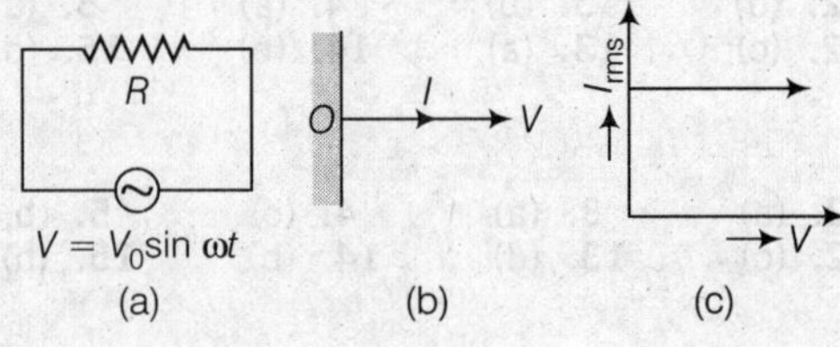

Current $I = \dfrac{V}{R}$ or $I_{rms} = \dfrac{V_{rms}}{R}$

Current and voltage are in the same phase *i.e.*, current is given by $I = I_0 \sin \omega t$.

Pure Inductive Circuit

Let an alternating voltage $V = V_0 \sin \omega t$ be applied across a pure inductance L. Then, the average power

$$= V_{rms} I_{rms} \cos \frac{\pi}{2} = 0$$

Such a current, for which average power as well as power factor is zero, is called as wattless current.

The inductance offers some opposition to the flow of AC. It is known as "Inductive reactance" $X_L = 2\pi \nu L = L\omega$. Thus, a pure inductance does not oppose the flow of DC ($\omega = 0$) but opposes the flow of AC.

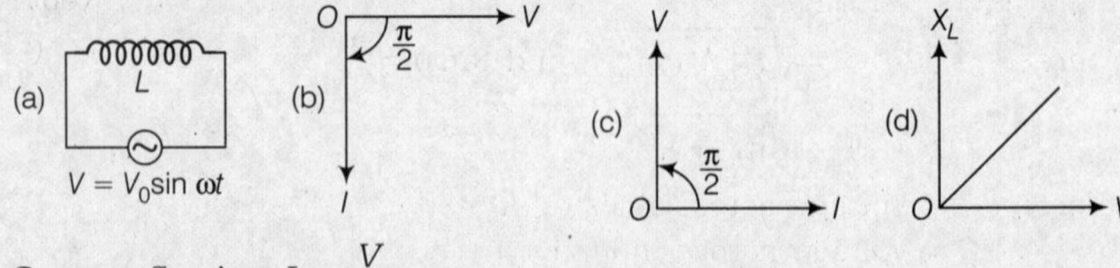

Current flowing $I = \dfrac{V}{X_L}$

The current decreases with an increase in frequency.

The current lags behind the voltage by $\dfrac{\pi}{2}$ (or voltage leads the current by $\dfrac{\pi}{2}$) and is, thus given by

$$I = I_0 \sin \left(\omega t - \frac{\pi}{2} \right)$$

Pure Capacitive Circuit

Let an alternating voltage $V = V_0 \sin \omega t$ be applied across a pure capacitance C. Then,

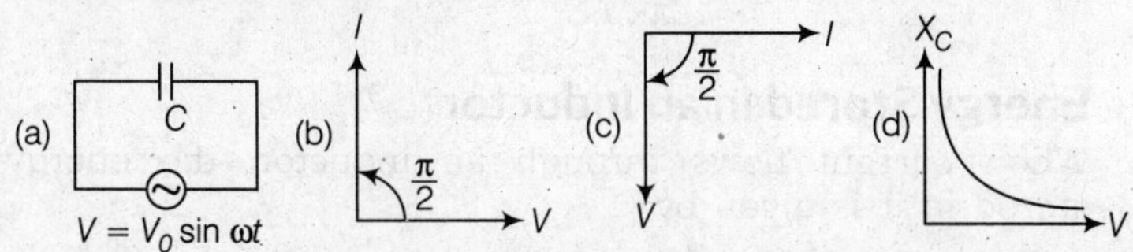

The capacitance offers some opposition to the flow of current but allows AC to pass through it. The opposition offered is known as the capacitive reactance.

$$X_C = \frac{1}{C\omega}\,\Omega = \frac{1}{C \times 2\pi\nu}\,\Omega$$

Current flowing $\quad I = \dfrac{V}{X_C}$

The current increases with an increase in frequency.

The current leads the voltage by $\frac{\pi}{2}$ (or voltage lags behind the current by $\frac{\pi}{2}$) and is, thus given by

$$I = I_0 \sin\left(\omega t + \frac{\pi}{2}\right)$$

Series *L-R* Circuit

The potential difference across a resistance in AC is in phase with current and it leads in phase by 90° with current across the inductor.

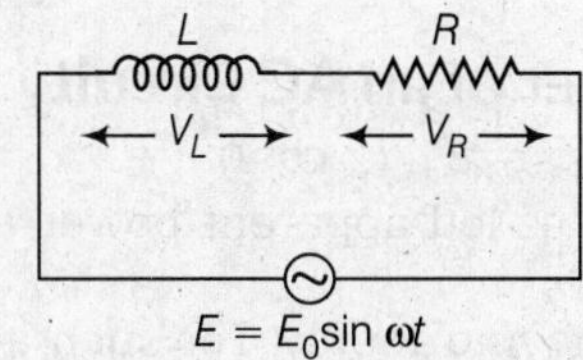

For $\quad E = E_0 \sin \omega t$

$$I = \frac{E_0}{Z}\sin(\omega t + \phi)$$

Where, $\quad Z = \sqrt{R^2 + (\omega L)^2} \quad$ and $\tan \phi = \dfrac{\omega L}{R}$

$$V = \sqrt{V_R^2 + V_L^2}$$

Where, V_R = Voltage across resistor R.

V_L = Voltage across inductor.

Current lags behind the voltage by ϕ.

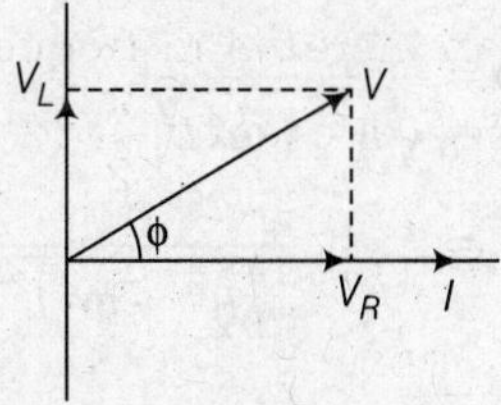

Series *R-C* Circuit

Potential difference across a capacitor in AC lags in phase by 90° with the current in the circuit.

For $\quad E = E_0 \sin \omega t,$

$$I = \frac{E_0}{Z}\sin(\omega t - \phi)$$

$E = E_0 \sin \omega t$

Where, $\quad Z = \sqrt{R^2 + \left(\dfrac{1}{\omega C}\right)^2} \quad$ and $\tan \phi = \dfrac{\frac{-1}{\omega C}}{R}$

Current leads the voltage by ϕ.

$$V^2 = V_R^2 + V_C^2 \Rightarrow V = \sqrt{V_R^2 + V_C^2}$$

Series *L-C* Circuit

For $E = E_0 \sin \omega t$, $I = \dfrac{E_0}{Z}\sin(\omega t - \phi)$

Where, $\quad Z = X_L - X_C$

and $\quad \tan \phi = \dfrac{X_L - X_c}{0} = \infty$

$E = E_0 \sin \omega t$

For $X_L > X_C$, $\phi = \dfrac{\pi}{2}$ and $X_L < X_C$, $\phi = -\dfrac{\pi}{2}$

If $X_L = X_C$ *i.e.*, at $\omega = \dfrac{1}{\sqrt{LC}}$, $Z = 0$ and I_0 becomes infinity. This condition is termed as the resonant condition and this frequency is termed as natural frequency of the circuit.

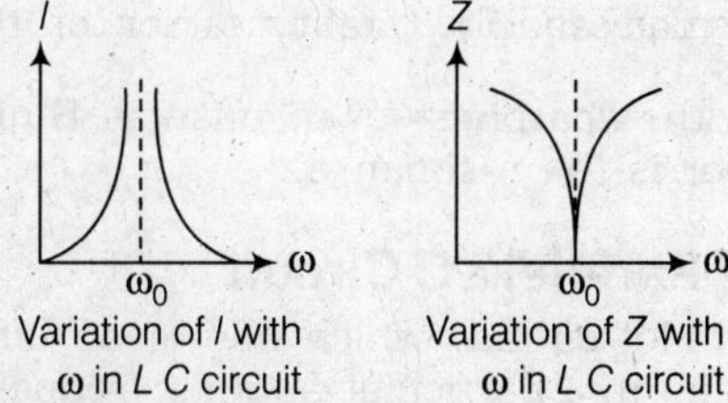

Variation of I with ω in $L\,C$ circuit

Variation of Z with ω in $L\,C$ circuit

Series *LCR* Circuit

For $\quad E = E_0 \sin \omega t$, $I = \dfrac{E_0}{Z}\sin(\omega t - \phi)$

Where, $\quad Z = \sqrt{R^2 + \left(\omega L - \dfrac{1}{\omega C}\right)^2}$

and $\tan\phi = \frac{X}{R} = \frac{X_L - X_C}{R}$

L C R

$E = E_0 \sin \omega t$

For $X_L > X_C$, current lags voltage.
$X_L < X_C$, current leads voltage
$X_L = X_C$, current and voltage are in phase.

If $X_L = X_C \Rightarrow \omega_0 = \frac{1}{\sqrt{LC}}$ *i.e.*, the natural frequency of the circuit is to the applied frequency, then the circuit is said to be in resonance.

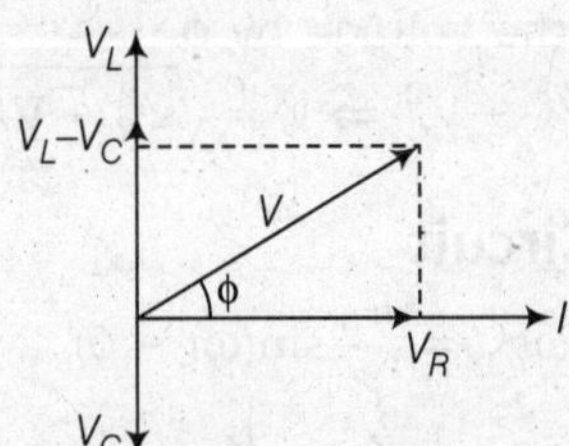

Phasor diagram for LCR series circuit for $x_L > x_c$

At resonance, the current in the circuit is maximum and the impedance in minimum. At resonance frequency, $\nu = \frac{1}{2\pi\sqrt{LC}}$.

Quality Factor

At resonance, $I_0 = \frac{E_0}{R}$

and $V_L = I_0 X_L = V_C = I_0 X_C$

i.e., $V_L = \frac{\omega L}{R} \times E_0 = \frac{1}{\omega RC} \times E_0 = QE_0$

Where, $Q = \frac{\omega L}{R}$

$\frac{1}{\omega RC}$ is termed as the Quality factor of the circuit. It determines the sharpness of resonance. Higher the value of Q, sharper is the resonance.

Resonant Parallel *LC* Circuit

The LC parallel circuit, which allows no current to flow corresponding to a particular angular frequency ω_0 of the AC source, is called LC parallel resonant circuit and angular frequency ω_0 is called the resonant angular frequency.

When the frequency of AC supply is such that the inductive reactance and capacitive reactance become equal ($X_L = X_C$), the impedance of the series LCR circuit becomes infinite. As such, no current flows in the circuit. Such a parallel LC circuit is called resonant parallel LC circuit and the frequency of the AC supply is called resonant frequency (f_0). The resonant frequency is given by

$$f_0 = \frac{1}{2\pi\sqrt{LC}}$$

Energy Stored in an Inductor

When current flows through an inductor, the energy stored in it is given by

$$U = \frac{1}{2} LI_0^2$$

Where, I_0 is final value of current in the inductor. The energy is stored inside an inductor in the form of magnetic field.

Energy Stored in a Capacitor

When a capacitor is charged, the energy stored in the capacitor is given by

$$U = \frac{1}{2} CE^2 = \frac{1}{2}\frac{q_0^2}{C} = \frac{1}{2} q_0 E$$

Where, E is maximum value of potential difference set up across the two plates of the capacitor.

The energy is stored inside the capacitor in the form of electric field between the plates of the capacitor.

LC Oscillations

When a charged capacitor discharges through an inductor, LC oscillations are produced. The frequency of the oscillations is given by $f = \frac{1}{2\pi\sqrt{LC}}$

Average Power of an AC Circuit

It is given by $P_{av} = E_v\, I_v \cos\phi$.

Where, $E_v\, I_v$ is called apparent power and $\cos\phi$ is called the power factor.

(i) AC circuit having R only. For such a circuit, $\phi = 0$ and power factor, $\cos\phi = 1$.

$\therefore$ $P_{av} = E_v\, I_v$

(ii) AC circuit having L only. For such a circuit $\phi = \frac{\pi}{2}$ and power factor, $\cos\phi = 0$.

$\therefore$ $P_{av} = 0$

(iii) AC circuit containing C only. For such a circuit and power factor, $\cos\phi = 0$.

$\therefore$ $P_{av} = 0$

(iv) AC circuit containing L and R. For such a circuit, $\tan\phi = \frac{\omega L}{R}$, so that power factor,

$$\cos\phi = \frac{R}{\sqrt{R^2 + \omega^2 L^2}}$$

$$\therefore \quad P_{av} = E_v I_v . \frac{R}{\sqrt{R^2 + \omega^2 L^2}}$$

(v) AC circuit containing C and R. For such a circuit,

$$\tan\phi = \frac{\frac{1}{\omega C}}{R}$$ so that power factor,

$$\cos\phi = \frac{R}{\sqrt{R^2 + \frac{1}{\omega^2 C^2}}}$$

$$\therefore \quad P_{av} = E_v\, I_v \cdot \frac{R}{\sqrt{R^2 + \frac{1}{\omega^2 C^2}}}$$

(vi) AC circuit containing L, C and R. For such a circuit,

$$\tan\phi = \frac{\sqrt{\omega L - \frac{1}{\omega C}}}{R}$$ so that power factor,

$$\cos\phi = \frac{R}{\sqrt{R^2 + \left(\omega L - \frac{1}{\omega C}\right)^2}}$$

$$P_{av} = E_v\, I_v \cdot \frac{R}{\sqrt{R^2 + \left(\omega L - \frac{1}{\omega C}\right)^2}}$$

Practice Questions

Level I

1. Choose the quantity whose SI unit is not ohm.
(a) Resistance (b) Reactance
(c) Capacitance (d) Impedance

2. Which of the following does not have the dimensions of time?
(a) RC (b) $\frac{L}{R}$ (c) $\frac{R}{L}$ (d) $\sqrt{LC}$

3. Q factor of resonance is given by
(a) $\frac{1}{R}\sqrt{\frac{L}{C}}$ (b) $\frac{1}{R}\sqrt{\frac{C}{L}}$ (c) $\frac{1}{L}\sqrt{\frac{R}{C}}$ (d) $\frac{1}{C}\sqrt{\frac{L}{R}}$

4. The power factor of an AC circuit is given by $\cos\phi$ is equal to
(a) $\frac{R}{Z}$ (b) $\frac{Z}{R}$ (c) $\frac{R}{X_L}$ (d) $\frac{R}{X_C}$

5. The average power dissipation in pure inductance is
(a) $\frac{1}{2}LI^2$ (b) $\frac{1}{4}LI^2$
(c) $2\,LI^2$ (d) zero

6. If a capacitor of capacitance C is connected in series with an inductor of inductance L, then the angular frequency is
(a) $\sqrt{LC}$ (b) LC (c) $\sqrt{\frac{L}{C}}$ (d) $\frac{1}{\sqrt{LC}}$

7. Impedance of an AC circuit, when a resistance R and an inductor of inductance L are connected in series with a supply of frequency f, is
(a) $\sqrt{R^2 + 2\pi^2 f^2 L^2}$ (b) $\sqrt{R^2 + 4\pi^2 f^2 L^2}$
(c) $\sqrt{R + 2\pi^2 f^2 L^2}$ (d) $\sqrt{R + 4\pi^2 f^2 L^2}$

8. A normal domestic electric supply is an alternating current, whose average value is
(a) zero
(b) half the peak value
(c) the peak value multiplied by $\frac{\pi}{2}$
(d) the peak value divided by $\frac{\pi}{2}$

9. The peak value of 220 V AC is
(a) 220 V (b) $\frac{220}{\sqrt{2}}$ V
(c) 440 V (d) $220\sqrt{2}$ V

10. The rms value of AC is related to peak value of AC by the equation
(a) $I_{rms} = \sqrt{2} I_0$ (b) $I_0 = \sqrt{2} I_{rms}$
(c) $I_{rms} = \frac{2I_0}{\pi}$ (d) $I_0 = \frac{2I_{rms}}{\pi}$

11. The equation of an AC voltage is $V = 200 \sin 50\pi t$. Then, the rms value of voltage is
(a) $100\sqrt{2}$ V (b) $200\sqrt{2}$ V
(c) 100 V (d) 400 V

12. In AC circuits, the AC meters measure
(a) rms values (b) peak values
(c) mean values (d) mean square values

13. An inductor
(a) allows AC to pass, but blocks DC
(b) allows DC to pass, but blocks AC
(c) allows both AC and DC to pass
(d) blocks DC

14. In an AC circuit containing inductance
(a) current lags the voltage by 90°
(b) current lags the voltage by 180°
(c) current leads the voltage by 90°
(d) None of the above

15. When AC flows through a capacitor, then the current
(a) leads emf by $\frac{\pi}{2}$
(b) lags emf by $\frac{\pi}{2}$
(c) is in phase with emf
(d) None of the above

16. A capacitor
(a) offers easy path to AC but blocks DC
(b) offers easy path to DC but blocks AC
(c) offers easy path to both AC and DC
(d) blocks AC

17. In an AC circuit, the current
(a) is always in phase with the emf
(b) always leads the emf
(c) always lags the emf
(d) any of the above, depending upon the elements (L, C or R) of the circuit

18. In an LCR series AC circuit, the current
(a) is always in phase with the voltage
(b) always lags the generator voltage
(c) always leads the generator voltage
(d) may lag behind or lead the voltage

19. The impedance of an AC (LCR) circuit is given by
(a) $\sqrt{R^2-(X_C+X_L)^2}$ (b) $\sqrt{R^2+(X_C-X_L)^2}$
(c) $\sqrt{R^2-(X_C-X_L)^2}$ (d) $\sqrt{R^2+(X_C+X_L)^2}$

Level II

1. An LCR circuit is connected to a source of AC current under resonant condition. The phase difference between the applied voltage and the current in the circuit is
(a) $\frac{\pi}{4}$ (b) $\frac{\pi}{2}$
(c) π (d) zero

2. For the current in LCR circuit to be maximum,
(a) $X_L=0$ (b) $X_C=0$
(c) $X_L=X_C$ (d) $R=X_L+X_C$

3. The average power of an AC circuit is
(a) E_vI_v (b) $E_vI_v\cos\phi$
(c) $E_vI_v\sin\phi$ (d) zero

4. The minimum and maximum values of power factor in an AC circuit are
(a) 0 and 1 (b) 1 and ∞
(c) 0 and ∞ (d) 0.1 and 1

5. L, C and R represent the physical quantities inductance, capacitance and resistance, respectively. The combination, which have the dimensions of frequency are
(a) $\frac{1}{RC}$ (b) $\frac{RL}{C}$ (c) $\frac{R}{LC}$ (d) $\frac{C}{L}$

6. In an oscillating circuit, the restoring force is must. In an LC circuit, the restoring force is provided by
(a) a capacitor
(b) an inductance
(c) a resistance
(d) None of the above

7. In AC circuit, the power is consumed only in
(a) inductance (b) capacitance
(c) resistance (d) All of these

8. The power in AC circuit is given by $P=E_vI_v\cos\phi$. The value of power factor $\cos\phi$ in series LCR circuit at resonance is
(a) zero (b) 1
(c) $\frac{1}{2}$ (d) $\frac{1}{\sqrt{2}}$

9. The inductive reactance of an inductor of $\frac{L}{\pi}$ H at 50 Hz frequency is
(a) $\frac{50}{\pi}\,\Omega$ (b) $\frac{\pi}{50}\,\Omega$
(c) $100\,\Omega$ (d) $50\,\Omega$

10. An oscillator circuit consists of an inductance of 0.5 mH and a capacitor of 20 μF. The resonant frequency of the circuit in nearly
(a) 15.92 Hz
(b) 159.2 Hz
(c) 1592 Hz
(d) 15910 Hz

11. Reactance of a capacitor of capacitance CμF for AC frequency $\frac{400}{\pi}$ Hz is 25 Ω. The value C is
(a) 50 μF (b) 25 μF
(c) 100 μF (d) 75 μF

12. In a LCR circuit capacitance is changed from C to $2C$. For the resonant frequency to remain unchanged, the inductance should be change from L to
(a) $4L$ (b) $2L$
(c) $\frac{L}{2}$ (d) $\frac{L}{4}$

13. In an LCR series AC circuit, the voltage across each of the components, L, C and R is 50 V. The voltage across the LC combination will be
(a) 50 V (b) $50\sqrt{2}$ V
(c) 100 V (d) 0 V (zero)

14. An inductance of $\left(\frac{200}{\pi}\right)$ mH, a capacitance of $\left(\frac{10^{-3}}{\pi}\right)$ F and a resistance of 10 Ω are connected in series with an AC source 220 V, 50 Hz. The phase angle of the circuit is
(a) $\frac{\pi}{6}$ (b) $\frac{\pi}{4}$
(c) $\frac{\pi}{2}$ (d) $\frac{\pi}{3}$

15. A resistance of 40 Ω and an inductance of 95.5 mH are connected in series in a 50 cycle/s AC ciruit. The impedance of this combination is very nearly
(a) 30 Ω (b) 40 Ω
(c) 50 Ω (d) 60 Ω

16. A circuit has a resistance of 11 Ω, an inductive reactance of 25 Ω and a capacitative resistance of 18 Ω. It is connected to an AC source of 260 V and 50 Hz. The current through the circuit (in A) is
(a) 11 (b) 15
(c) 18 (d) 20

17. A 0.7 H inductor is connected across a 120 V - 60 Hz AC source. The current in the inductor will be very nearly

(a) 4.55 A (b) 0.355 A
(c) 0.455 A (d) 3.55 A

18. There is a $5\,\Omega$ resistance in an AC circuit. Inductance of 0.1 H is connected with it in series. If equation of AC emf is $5 \sin 50t$, then the phase difference between current and emf is

(a) $\frac{\pi}{2}$ (b) $\frac{\pi}{6}$
(c) $\frac{\pi}{4}$ (d) 0

19. A coil of $200\,\Omega$ resistance and 1.0 H inductance is connected to an AC source of frequency $\frac{200}{2\pi}$ Hz. Phase angle between potential and current will be

(a) 30° (b) 90°
(c) 45° (d) 0°

20. In *LCR* circuit the potential difference between the terminals of the inductance is 60 V, between the terminals of the capacitor is 30 V and that between the terminals of resistance i s 40 V. The supply voltage will be equal to

(a) 50 V (b) 70 V (c) 130 V (d) 10 V

Answers

Level I

1. (c)	**2.** (c)	**3.** (a)	**4.** (a)	**5.** (d)	**6.** (d)	**7.** (b)	**8.** (d)	**9.** (d)	**10.** (b)
11. (a)	**12.** (a)	**13.** (b)	**14.** (a)	**15.** (a)	**16.** (a)	**17.** (d)	**18.** (b)	**19.** (b)	

Level II

1. (d)	**2.** (c)	**3.** (b)	**4.** (a)	**5.** (a)	**6.** (b)	**7.** (c)	**8.** (b)	**9.** (c)	**10.** (c)
11. (a)	**12.** (c)	**13.** (d)	**14.** (b)	**15.** (c)	**16.** (d)	**17.** (c)	**18.** (c)	**19.** (c)	**20.** (a)

Hints and Solutions

Level II

9. $X_L = 2\pi\nu L = 2 \times \pi \times 50 \times \frac{1}{\pi} = 100\,\Omega$

10. $\nu_0 = \frac{1}{2\pi\sqrt{LC}} = \frac{1}{2 \times 3.14\sqrt{5 \times 10^{-4} \times 20 \times 10^{-6}}}$

$\nu_0 = \frac{10^4}{6.28} = 1592$ Hz

11. $X_C = \frac{1}{2\pi\nu C} \Rightarrow C = \frac{1}{2\pi\nu X_C}$

$= \frac{1}{2 \times \pi \times \frac{400}{\pi} \times 25} = 50\,\mu\text{F}$

12. $\nu_0 = \frac{1}{2\pi\sqrt{LC}}$

If C changes to $2C$, then for keeping ν_0 constant L must change to $\frac{L}{2}$.

13. Net voltage across LC combination $= V_L - V_C = 0$ V

14. Phase difference between E and $I = \theta$

$\therefore \quad \tan\theta = \frac{X_L - X_C}{R}$

Now, $X_L = 2\pi fL = 2\pi \times 50 \times \left(\frac{200}{\pi} \times 10^{-3}\right) = 20\,\Omega$

$X_C = \frac{1}{2\pi fC} = \frac{\pi}{2\pi \times 50 \times 10^{-3}} = 10\,\Omega$

$R = 10\,\Omega$

$\therefore \quad \tan\theta = \frac{20 - 10}{10} = \frac{10}{10} = 1 = \tan\frac{\pi}{4}$

$\therefore \quad \theta = \frac{\pi}{4}$. The current will lag by $\frac{\pi}{4}$.

15. $Z = \sqrt{R^2 + (2\pi\nu L)^2}$

$= \sqrt{(40)^2 + 4\pi^2 \times (50)^2 \times (95.5 \times 10^{-3})^2} = 50\Omega$

16. $Z = \sqrt{R^2 + (X_L - X_C)^2} = \sqrt{(11)^2 + (25 - 18)^2} = 13\,\Omega$

Current $i = \frac{260}{13} = 20$ A

17. $i = \frac{V}{X_L} = \frac{120}{2 \times 3.14 \times 60 \times 0.7} = 0.455$ A

18. $\cos\phi = \frac{R}{Z} = \frac{R}{\sqrt{R^2 + \omega^2 L^2}} = \frac{5}{\sqrt{25 + (50)^2 \times (0.1)^2}}$

$= \frac{5}{\sqrt{25 + 25}} = \frac{1}{\sqrt{2}}$

$\therefore \quad \phi = \frac{\pi}{4}$

19. $\tan\phi = \frac{X_L}{R} = \frac{2\pi\nu L}{R} = \frac{2\pi \times \frac{200}{2\pi} \times 1}{200} = 1$

$\therefore \quad \phi = 45°$

20. $V = \sqrt{V_R^2 + (V_L - V_C)^2}$

$= \sqrt{(40)^2 + (60 - 30)^2} = 50$ V

46

AC Instruments

Wattless Current

In an AC circuit $R = 0 \Rightarrow \cos\phi = 0$, so $P_{av} = 0$ *i.e.,* in resistance less circuit the power consumed is zero. Such a circuit is called the wattless circuit and the current flowing is called the wattless current.

or

The component of current which does not contribute to the average power dissipation is called wattless current.

(i) The average of wattless component over one cycle is zero.

(ii) Amplitude of wattless current $= i_0 \sin\phi$ and rms value of wattless current

$$= i_{rms} \sin\phi = \frac{i_0}{\sqrt{2}} \sin\phi.$$

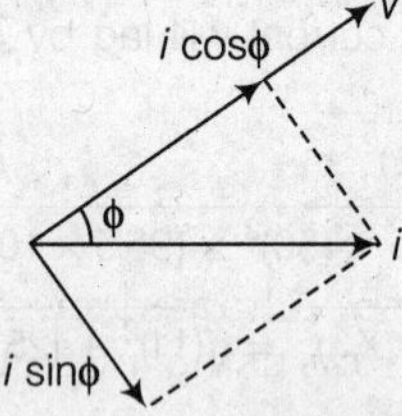

It is quadrature (90°) with voltage.

Choke Coil

Choke coil (or ballast) is a device having high inductance and negligible resistance. It is used to control current in AC circuits and is used in fluorescent tubes. The power loss in a circuit containing choke coil is least. It is based on the principle of wattless current.

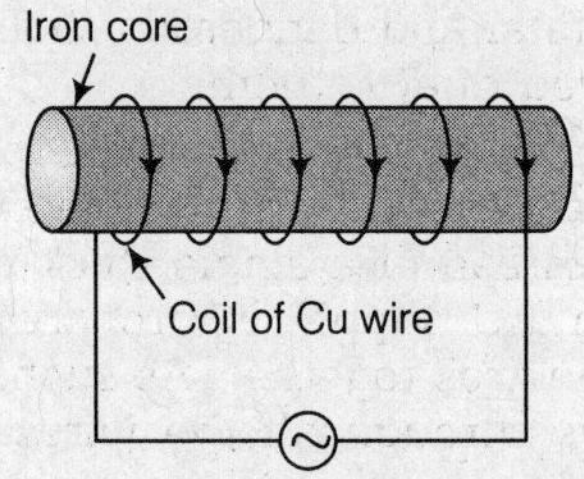

Choke Coil

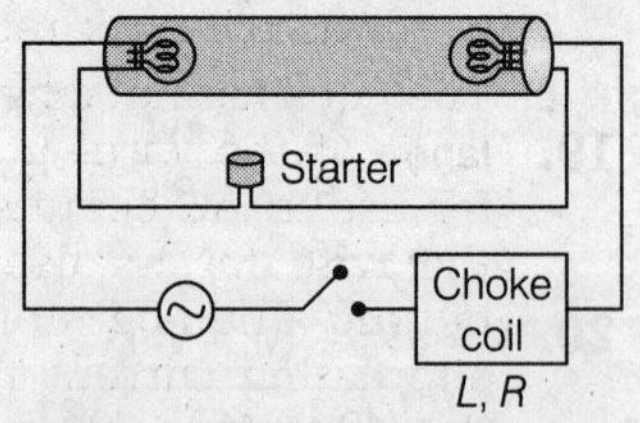

Application of Choke Coil

Choke coil is so named because it is used to choke or reduce the current in the circuit.

1. It consist of a Cu coil wound over a soft iron laminated core.
2. Thick Cu wire is used to reduce the resistance (R) of the circuit.
3. Soft iron is used to improve inductance (L) of the circuit.
4. The inductive reactance or effective opposition of the choke coil is given by
   $X_L = \omega L = 2\pi\nu L.$
5. For an ideal choke coil $r = 0$, therefore no electric energy is wasted *i.e.,* average power $P = 0$.
6. In actual practice choke coil is equivalent to a R-L circuit.
7. Choke coil for different frequencies are made by using different substances in their core.

For low frequency L should be large, thus iron core choke coil is used. For high frequency AC circuit, L should be small, so air cored choke coil is used.

AC Generator or Dynamo

It is a device which converts mechanical energy into alternating current energy.

Its working is based on electromagnetic induction.

The induced emf produced by the AC generator is given by $e = NBA\omega \sin\omega t = e_0 \sin\omega t$

There are four main parts of an AC generator

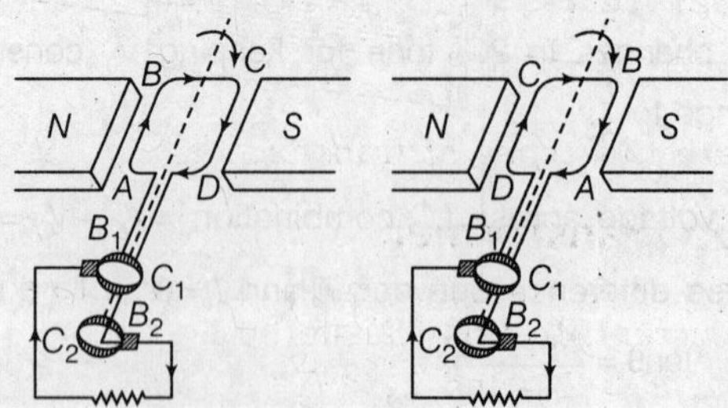

Working of AC Dynamo

1. **Armature** It is rectangular coil of insulated copper wire having a large number of turns.

2. **Field Magnets** These are two pole pieces of a strong electromagnet.
3. **Slip Rings** These are two hollow metallic rings.
4. **Brushes** These are two flexible metals or carbon rods, which remains slightly in contact with slip rings.

Note

An DC generator or dynamo contains split rings or commutator inspite of slip rings.

DC Motor

It is a device which converts electrical energy into mechanical energy.

Its working is based on the fact that when a current carrying coil is placed in uniform magnetic field a torque acts on it. Torque acting on a current carrying coil placed in uniform magnetic field

$$\tau = NBIA \sin\theta$$

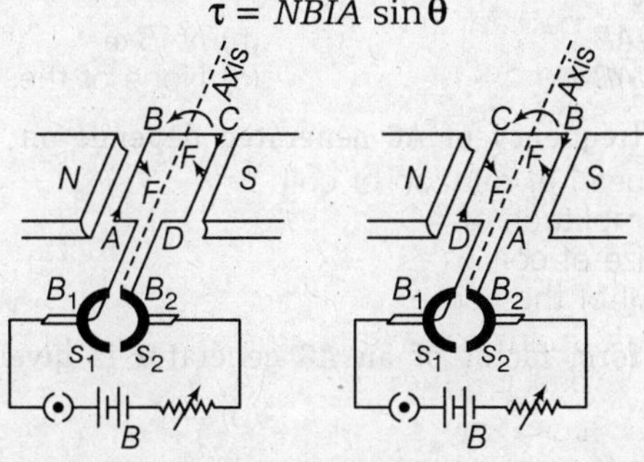

When armature coil rotates, a back emf is produced in the coil. Efficiency of a motor

$$(\eta) = \frac{\text{Back emf}}{\text{Applied emf}} = \frac{E}{V}$$

Transformer

It is a device which can change a low voltage of high current into a high voltage of low current and *vice-versa*. Its working is based on mutual induction.

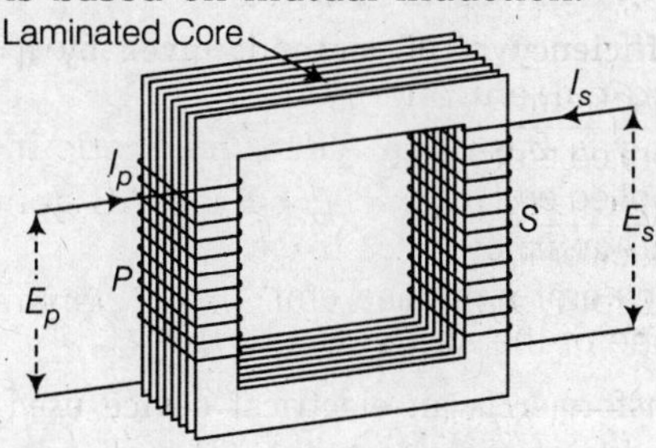

There are two types of transformers

Step-up Transformer

It convert a low voltage of high current into a high voltage of low current. In this transformer,

$N_s > N_p$, $E_s > E_P$ and $I_p < I_s$

Step-down Transformer

It converts a high voltage of low current into a low voltage of high current. In this transformer,

$N_s > N_p$, $E_s > E_P$ and $I_p < I_s$

Transformation Ratio

Transformation ratio $K = \frac{N_s}{N_p}$

$$= \frac{E_s}{E_p} = \frac{I_p}{I_s}$$

For step-up transformer, $K > 1$

For step-down transformer, $K < 1$

ENERGY LOSSES IN A TRANSFORMER

The main energy losses in a transformer are given below

- Iron loss
- Flux loss
- Hysteresis loss
- Humming loss

Other Uses of a Transformer

1. A step-down transformer is used for obtaining large current for electric welding.
2. A step-down transformer is used in induction furnace for melting the metals.
3. A step-up transformer is used for the production of X-rays.
4. Transformers are used in voltage regulators and stabilised power supplies.
5. Small transformers are used in radio sets, televisions, telephones, loudspeakers etc.

Advantages and Disadvantages of AC over DC

Advantages

1. The generation of AC is found to be economical than that of DC.
2. The alternating voltages can be easily stepped-up or stepped-down by using a transformer.
3. The alternating currents can be regulated by using a choke coil without any significant wastage of electrical energy.
4. The alternating voltages can be transmitted to distant places at a very small loss of the electric power.
5. Further, AC can be easily converted into DC by using rectifiers.

Disadvantages

1. The AC supply is more fatal and dangerous than DC in terms of shock received due to them.
2. The alternating current always flows on the outer layer of the wire. It is called skin effect. Therefore, for use in AC circuits; instead of a single thick wire, the wire for its use on AC supply is prepared by putting a number of thin wires together. As such, the alternating current flows through all the wires and the skin effect is avoided.
3. The alternating current cannot be used in electrolytic processes, such as electroplating, electrotyping etc.

Practice Questions

1. Which of the following quantities remain constant in a step-down transformer?

(a) Current (b) Voltage
(c) Power (d) None of these

2. AC power is transmitted from a power house at a high voltages

(a) the rate of transmission is faster at high voltages
(b) it is more economical due to less power loss
(c) power cannot be transmitted at low voltage
(d) a precaution against theft of transmission line

3. Armature current in DC motor will be maximum when the

(a) motor has acquired maximum speed
(b) motor has acquired intermediate speed
(c) motor has just started moving
(d) None of the above

4. Core of a dynamo is laminated because

(a) magnetic field increases
(b) magnetic saturation level in core increases
(c) residual magnetism in core decreases
(d) loss of energy in core due to eddy currents decreases

5. Quantity that remains unchanged in a transformer is

(a) voltage (b) current
(c) frequency (d) None of these

6. By increasing the number of turns in the coil, the strength of the magnetic field

(a) decrease
(b) increase
(c) first increases then decreases
(d) remains unchanged

7. If the current in the core decreases, the strength of the magnetic field

(a) decreases (b) increases
(c) remain same (d) None of these

8. The essential difference between an AC dynamo and DC dynamo is that

(a) AC dynamo has an electromagnet, but DC dynamo has a permanent magnet
(b) AC dynamo has slip rings, but DC dynamo has commutators
(c) AC dynamo has coil would on soft iron, but the coil in DC dynamo is wound on copper
(d) AC dynamo generates much high voltage

9. A rectangular coil *ABCD* is rotated anti-clockwise with a uniform angular velocity about the axis shown in the figure.

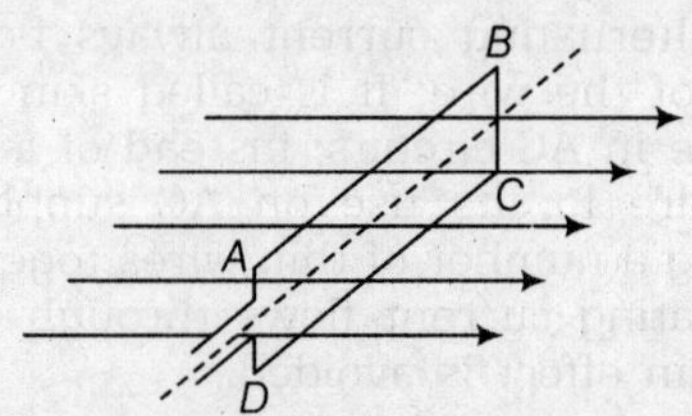

The axis of rotation of the coil as well as the magnetic field *B* are horizontal. The induced emf in the coil would be maximum, when the plane of the coil

(a) is parallel to the magnetic field
(b) is vertical
(c) makes an angle of 45° with the magnetic field
(d) makes an angle of 30° with the magnetic field

10. Split ring commutators are used in which of the following device?

(a) AC dynamo (b) DC dynamo
(c) AC motor (d) All of these

11. The peak value of alternating emf in a generator is given by $e_0 =$

(a) NAB (b) $NAB\omega$
(c) $NABv$ (d) None of these

12. The frequency of AC generated depends on

(a) speed of rotation of coil
(b) amplitude of AC
(c) size of coil
(d) All of the above

13. The form factor of an AC generator is given by

(a) $\frac{I_{av}}{I_0}$ (b) $\frac{I_0}{I_{av}}$
(c) $\frac{I_{av}}{I_v}$ (d) $\frac{I_v}{I_{av}}$

14. In which of the following appliances, Fleming's right hand rule for direction of induced current is not applicable?

(a) AC generator (b) DC generator
(c) Induction motor (d) Transformer

15. The split ring arrangement is used in

(a) AC generator (b) DC generator
(c) choke coil (d) transformer

16. The efficiency of DC motor is given by $\eta =$

(a) $\frac{\text{Back emf}}{\text{Applied emf}}$
(b) $\frac{\text{Applied emf}}{\text{Back emf}}$
(c) Back emf × Applied emf
(d) None of the above

17. A transformer is an electrical device used for

(a) producing direct current
(b) producing alternating current
(c) changing DC into AC
(d) changing AC voltages

18. The relation $\frac{E_S}{E_P} = \frac{n_S}{n_P}$ is applicable only to

(a) AC generator
(b) DC generator
(c) induction coil
(d) step-up/step-down transformer

19. **A battery of 12 V is connected to primary of a transformer with turns ratio $\frac{n_S}{n_P}=10$. Voltage across secondary would be**
(a) 120 V (b) 1.2 V
(c) 12 V (d) zero

20. **A dynamo converts**
(a) mechanical energy into sound energy
(b) mechanical energy into electrical energy
(c) electrical energy into mechanical energy
(d) None of the above

21. **Power is transmitted from a power station at a very high AC voltage, because**
(a) the rate of transmission is faster at high voltage
(b) it is more economical due to less power loss
(c) power cannot be generated at low voltage
(d) theft of power is not possible at high voltage

22. **Wattless current is possible, only in**
(a) resistive circuit
(b) non-resistive circuit
(c) *LR*-circuit
(d) *LCR*-circuit

23. **Energy stored in the choke coil in the form of**
(a) heat (b) electric energy
(c) magnetic energy (d) None of these

24. **The core of a transformer is liminated to reduce**
(a) copper loss (b) magnetic loss
(c) eddy current loss (d) hysteresis loss

25. **Ampere rule is used to find the**
(a) direction of current
(b) direction of magnetic field
(c) direction of motion of the conductor
(d) None of the above

26. **A dynamo is sometimes said to generate electricity. It actually acts as a source of**
(a) charge (b) magnetism
(c) emf (d) energy

27. **As the speed of an electric fan increases, current**
(a) increases
(b) decreases
(c) remains the same
(d) becomes maximum, when speed is maximum

28. **A motor**
(a) converts electrical energy into mechanical energy
(b) converts mechanical energy into electrical energy
(c) converts electrical energy into magnetic energy
(d) produces mechanical energy

29. **A choke coil has**
(a) high inductance and high resistance
(b) high inductance and low resistance
(c) low inductance and high resistance
(d) low inductance and high resistance

30. **In an induction coil, the secondary emf is**
(a) zero during break of the circuit
(b) very high during make of the circuit
(c) very high during the break of the circuit
(d) zero during make of the circuit

Answers

1. (c)	**2.** (b)	**3.** (c)	**4.** (d)	**5.** (c)	**6.** (b)	**7.** (a)	**8.** (b)	**9.** (a)	**10.** (b)
11. (b)	**12.** (a)	**13.** (d)	**14.** (d)	**15.** (b)	**16.** (a)	**17.** (d)	**18.** (d)	**19.** (d)	**20.** (b)
21. (b)	**22.** (b)	**23.** (c)	**24.** (c)	**25.** (b)	**26.** (c)	**27.** (b)	**28.** (a)	**29.** (b)	**30.** (c)

47

Electromagnetic Values

Electromagnetic Wave

An electromagnetic wave is a wave radiated by an accelerated charge and which propagates through space coupled electric and magnetic fields, oscillating perpendicular to each other and to the direction of propagation of the wave.

Principle of Production of Electromagnetic Waves

An accelerated charge produces electric and magnetic fields, which vary both in space and time. The two oscillating fields act as sources of each other and hence sustain each other. This results in the propagation of an electromagnetic wave through space.

Source of an Electromagnetic Wave

An accelerating charge produces electromagnetic waves. An electric charge oscillating harmonically with frequency ν, generates electromagnetic waves of the same frequency ν. An electric dipole is a basic source of electromagnetic waves.

An L-C circuit containing inductance L and capacitance C produces electromagnetic waves of frequency,

$$\nu = \frac{1}{2\pi\sqrt{LC}}$$

Mathematical Representation of Electromagnetic Waves

For a plane electromagnetic wave of frequency ν, wavelength λ, propagating along x-axis, the electric and magnetic fields may be represented as follows:

$$\vec{E} = E_y \hat{j} = E_0 \sin(kx - \omega t)\hat{j}$$

$$= E_0 \sin\left[2\pi\left(\frac{x}{\lambda} - \nu t\right)\right]\hat{j}$$

$$= E_0 \sin\left[2\pi\left(\frac{x}{\lambda} - \frac{t}{T}\right)\right]\hat{i}$$

$$E_x = E_z = 0$$

and $$\vec{B} = B_z \hat{k} = B_0 \sin(kx - \omega t)\hat{k}$$

$$= B_0 \sin\left[2\pi\left(\frac{x}{\lambda} - \nu t\right)\right]\hat{k} = B_0 \sin\left[2\pi\left(\frac{x}{\lambda} - \frac{t}{T}\right)\right]\hat{k}$$

$$B_x = B_y = 0$$

Here, E_0 and B_0 are the amplitudes of the electric and magnetic fields respectively.

Propagation constant,

$$k = \frac{2\pi}{\lambda} = \frac{\omega}{c}.$$

Basic Properties of Electromagnetic Waves

These are

(i) The EM waves are produced by accelerated charges and do not require any medium for their propagation.

(ii) The oscillations of $\vec{E}$ and $\vec{B}$ fields are perpendicular to each other as well as to the direction of propagation of the wave. So, the EM waves are transverse in nature.

(iii) The oscillations of $\vec{E}$ and $\vec{B}$ fields are in same phase.

(iv) All electromagnetic waves travel in free space with same speed c given by

$$c = \frac{1}{\sqrt{\mu_0 \varepsilon_0}} \simeq 3 \times 10^8 \text{ ms}^{-1}$$

In a material medium of refractive index μ, the speed of an electromagnetic wave is given by

$$v = \frac{1}{\sqrt{\mu\varepsilon}} = \frac{c}{\sqrt{\mu_r \varepsilon_r}} = \frac{c}{\mu}$$

(v) The ratio of the amplitudes of electric and magnetic fields is

$$\frac{E_0}{B_0} = c = \frac{1}{\sqrt{\mu_0 \varepsilon_0}}$$

(vi) The electromagnetic waves carry energy as they travel through space and this energy is shared equally by the electric and magnetic fields. The average energy of an electromagnetic wave is

$$u = u_E + u_B = \frac{1}{2}\left[\varepsilon_0 E_0^2 + \frac{B_0^2}{\mu}\right]$$

Momentum of an Electromagnetic Wave

If an electromagnetic wave transfers a total energy U to a surface in time t, then total linear momentum delivered to the surface is $p = \frac{U}{c}$

Intensity of an Electromagnetic Wave

The energy crossing per unit area per unit time in a direction perpendicular to the direction of propagation of the wave is called intensity of the wave.

$$\text{Intensity} = \frac{\text{Energy / Time}}{\text{Area}} = \frac{\text{Power}}{\text{Area}}$$

For an EM wave of average energy density u, $I = uc$

The Electromagnetic Spectrum

Name	Frequency Range (Hz)	Wavelength Range	Production	Detection	Main Properties and Uses
Radiowaves	10^4 to 10^8	> 0.1 m	Rapid acceleration and decelerations of electrons in aerials.	Receivers aerials.	Different wavelengths find specialised uses in radio communication.
Microwaves	10^9 to 10^{12}	0.1 m to 1 mm	Klystron valve or magneton valve.	Point contact diodes.	(a) Radar communication. (b) Analysis of fine details of molecular and atomic structure. (c) Since, $\lambda \simeq 3 \times 10^{-2}$ m, useful for demonstration of all wave properties on macroscopic scale.
Infrared	10^{11} to 5×10^{14}	1 mm to 700 nm	Vibration of atoms and molecules.	Thermopiles, Bolometers, Infrared, photographic film.	(a) Useful for elucidating molecular structure. (b) Less scattered than visible light by atmospheric particles useful for haze photography.
Visible light	4×10^{14} to 7×10^{14}	700 nm to 400 nm	Electrons in atoms emit light when they move from one energy level to a lower energy level.	Human eye, Photocells, Photographic film.	(a) Detected by stimulating nerve endings of human retina. (b) Can cause chemical reaction.
Ultraviolet	10^{16} to 10^{17}	400 nm to 1 nm	Inner shell electrons in atoms moving from one energy level to a lower level.	Photocells, Photographic film.	(a) Absorbed by glass. (b) Can cause many chemical reactions, *e.g.*, the tanning of the human skin. (c) Ionise atoms in atmosphere, resulting in the ionosphere.
X-rays	10^{16} to 10^{19}	1 nm to 10^{-3} nm	X-ray tubes or inner shell electrons.	Photographic film, Geiger tubes, Ionisation chamber.	(a) Penetrate matter (*e.g.*, radiography). (b) Ionise gases. (c) Cause fluorescence. (d) Cause photoelectric emission from metals. (e) Reflected and diffracted by crystals enabling ionic lattice spacing and N_A (or wavelength) to be measured.
Gamma rays	10^{18} to 10^{22}	< 10^{-3} nm	Radioactive decay of the nucleus.	Photographic film, Geiger tubes, Ionisation chamber.	Similar to X-rays.

Practice Questions

1. The SI unit of displacement current is
(a) H (b) A (c) F m^{-1} (d) C

2. The displacement current flows in the dielectric of a capacitor, when the potential difference across its plates
(a) is increasing with time
(b) is decreasing with time
(c) becomes zero
(d) attains a constant value

3. The displacement current is produced across the gap between the two plates of a capacitor, when the charge on the capacitor
(a) is zero (b) decreases
(c) increases (d) does not change

4. Electromagnetic waves are produced due to
(a) a charge at rest (b) a moving charge
(c) an accelerating charge (d) None of these

5. **Which of the following statements is a wrong one? Electromagnetic waves**
(a) are produced by accelerating charges
(b) are transverse in nature
(c) travel with the same speed irrespective of the nature of the medium
(d) travel with velocity of light in vacuum

6. **A magnetic field can be produced by**
(a) a charge at rest (b) a moving charge
(c) a changing electric field (d) both (b) and (c)

7. **The speed of electromagnetic waves is independent of**
(a) wavelength (b) frequency
(c) intensity (d) medium, in which it travels

8. **The speed of electromagnetic waves in vacuum is equal to**
(a) $\varepsilon_0 \mu_0$ (b) $\sqrt{\varepsilon_0 \mu_0}$ (c) $\frac{1}{\sqrt{\varepsilon_0 \mu_0}}$ (d) $\frac{1}{\varepsilon_0 \mu_0}$

9. **Dimensions of $\varepsilon_0 \mu_0$ is**
(a) $[LT^{-1}]$ (b) $[L^{-1}T]$ (c) $[L^2T^{-2}]$ (d) $[L^{-2}T^2]$

10. **In a plane electromagnetic wave, which of the following have zero average value?**
(a) Magnetic field (b) Magnetic energy
(c) Electric field (d) Electric energy

11. **Which scientist experimentally proved the existence of electromagnetic waves?**
(a) Sir JC Bose (b) Maxwell
(c) Marconi (d) Hertz

12. **Which of the following is not the property of light?**
(a) It requires a material medium for propagation
(b) It can travel through vacuum
(c) It involves transportation of energy
(d) It has finite speed

13. **Which of the following statements is true?**
(a) Both light and sound waves in air are transverse
(b) The sound waves in air are longitudinal, while the light waves are transverse
(c) Both light and sound waves in air are longitudinal
(d) Both light and sound waves can travel in vacuum

14. **When light passes from one medium to another, which one of the quantities remain unchanged?**
(a) Refractive index (b) Frequency
(c) Wavelength (d) Speed

15. **Which one of the following are not transverse waves?**
(a) Sound waves (b) Visible light waves
(c) γ-rays (d) X-rays

16. **Which one of the following has the longest wavelength?**
(a) Ultraviolet rays (b) Infrared rays
(c) Radio waves (d) X-rays

17. **Absorption of X-rays is maximum in which of the following material sheets of the same thickness?**
(a) Cu (b) Au (c) Be (d) Pb

18. **Which one is used in ionospheric propagation?**
(a) Ultraviolet rays (b) Infrared rays
(c) Radio waves (d) Light waves

19. **Ozone layer in atmosphere is useful, because it**
(a) stops ultraviolet rays
(b) absorbs pollutant gases
(c) stops green house effect
(d) stops increase in temperature of atmosphere

20. **Which of the following is independent of wavelength?**
(a) k (b) ω (c) ωk (d) k/ω

21. **Which of the following pairs of space and time varying E and B fields would generate a plane electromagnetic wave travelling along the Z-direction?**
(a) E_x, B_y (b) E_y, B_x
(c) E_x, B_z (d) E_z, B_x

22. **If an electromagnetic wave propagating through vacuum is described by $E = E_0 \sin(kx - \omega t)$, $B = B_0 \sin(kx - \omega t)$, then**
(a) $E_0 k = B_0 \omega$ (b) $E_0 B_0 = \omega k$
(c) $E_0 \omega = B_0 k$ (d) $E_0 B_0 = \omega / k$

23. **Red light differs from blue light in its**
(a) speed (b) frequency
(c) intensity (d) amplitude

24. **Among the following, longest wave is**
(a) radio wave (b) γ-ray
(c) micro wave (d) X-ray

25. **Which has the longest wavelength?**
(a) Radio waves (b) X-rays
(c) Ultraviolet rays (d) Infrared rays

26. **Infrared spectrum lies between**
(a) radio wave and micro wave region
(b) micro wave and visible region
(c) visible and ultraviolet region
(d) ultraviolet and X-rays

27. **Which of the following represents an infrared wavelength?**
(a) 10^{-4} cm (b) 10^{-5} cm (c) 10^{-6} cm (d) 10^{-7} cm

28. **Which of the following statements is wrong?**
(a) Ultraviolet rays have a wavelength longer than infrared rays
(b) Infrared rays travel with the same velocity as visible light
(c) Infrared can be focused by a lens and can be reflected by a mirror just as visible light
(d) Infrared rays have more heating power than visible light rays

29. **Finger prints on a piece of paper may be detected by sprinkling fluorescent powder on the paper and then looking it in the**
(a) dark light (b) sunlight
(c) Infrared light (d) ultraviolet light

Answers

1. (b)	**2.** (a,b)	**3.** (c)	**4.** (c)	**5.** (c)	**6.** (d)	**7.** (c)	**8.** (c)	**9.** (d)	**10.** (a,c)
11. (d)	**12.** (a)	**13.** (b)	**14.** (b)	**15.** (a)	**16.** (c)	**17.** (d)	**18.** (c)	**19.** (a)	**20.** (d)
21. (a,b)	**22.** (a)	**23.** (b)	**24.** (a)	**25.** (a)	**26.** (b)	**27.** (a)	**28.** [illegible]	**29.** (d)	

48

Reflection of Light

Light

The light is that form of energy which makes objects visible to our eyes. The branch of physics which deals with nature of light, its sources, properties, measurements, effects and vision is called optics. Light transmits as a wave whose energy is confined in the form of a small packets called photon.

The speed of light in vacuum is 3×10^8 ms^{-1} but different in different media.

Values of the speed of light in various media

Medium	Speed of Light (m/s)
Air	2.96×10^8
Water	2.25×10^8
Glass	2.00×10^8
Oil of tarpin	2.04×10^8

Image

If light rays coming from an object meet or appear to meet at a point after reflection or refraction, then this point is called image of the object.

There are two types of images

Real Image

The image obtained by the real meeting of light rays, is called a real image.

A real image is inverted and be obtained on a screen.

Virtual Image

The image obtained when light rays are not really meeting but appear to meet only, is called a virtual image.

- A virtual image is erect and cannot be obtained on a screen.
- Real and virtual both types of images can be photographed.

Reflection of Light

The phenomenon of rebouncing back of light into the same medium when it strikes on a smooth shining surface such as a plane mirror, is called reflection of light.

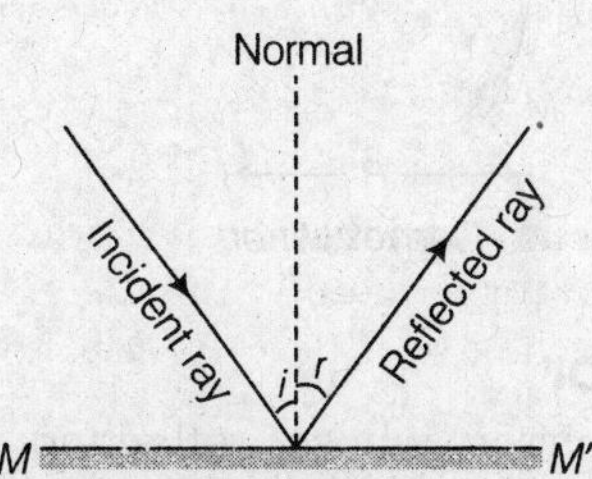

There are two laws of reflection

1. The angle of incidence is always equal to angle of reflection *i.e.,*

$$\angle i = \angle r$$

2. The incident ray, normal and reflected ray all lie in same plane.

Reflection from Plane Mirror

Size of image is always equal to size of object. The image in a plane mirror appear as far behind the mirror as the object is in front of it.

- If the object is displaced by a distance *a* towards or away from the mirror, then its image will be displaced by a distance *a* towards or away from the mirror.
- The minimum size of the mirror required to see the full image of an observer is half the height of the observer. If the plane mirror is rotated in the plane of incidence by an angle θ, then the reflected ray rotates by an angle 2θ.
- Focal length of plane mirror is infinity *i.e.,* power is zero.
- Linear magnification produced by plane mirror is 1.
- When two plane mirrors are kept facing each other at an angle θ and an object is placed between them, then

(i) Number of images $n = \dfrac{360°}{\theta} - 1$, if $\dfrac{360°}{\theta}$ is even or the object lies symmetrically.

(ii) Number of images $n = \left(\dfrac{360°}{\theta}\right)$, if $\dfrac{360°}{\theta}$ is odd or the object lies asymmetrically.

Reflection at Spherical Surface

Spherical mirrors are the mirrors in which reflecting side is spherical.

There are two types of spherical mirrors

(i) Convex mirror
(ii) Concave mirror

Convex Mirror

The spherical mirror whose reflecting surface outwardly leaned called convex mirror. It is also called diverging mirror.

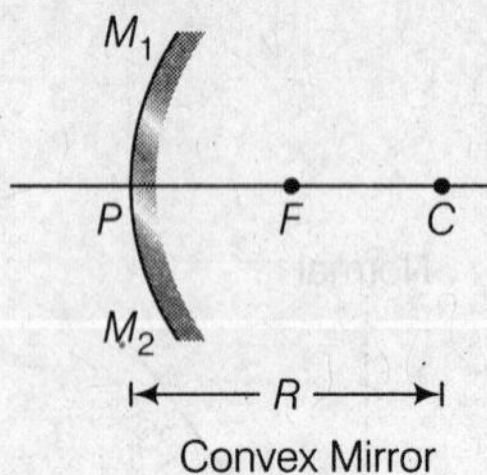

Concave Mirror

The spherical mirror whose reflecting surface inwardly leaned called concave mirror. It is also called converging mirror.

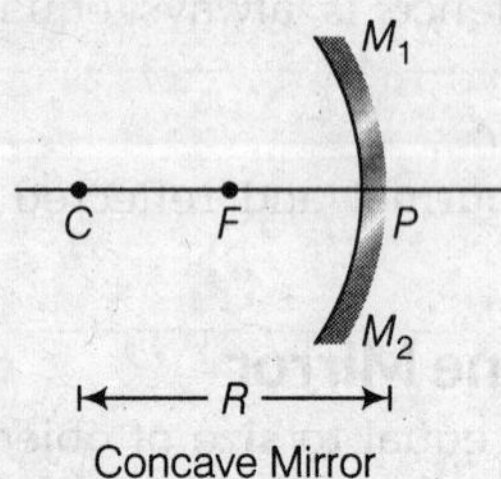

TERMS RELATED TO SPHERICAL MIRROR

Centre of Curvature (*C*) It is the centre of sphere of which the mirror is a part.

Radius of Curvature (*R*) It is the radius of the sphere of which the mirror is a part.

Pole (*P*) It is the geometrical centre of the spherical reflecting surface.

Principal Axis It is the straight line joining the centre of curvature to the pole.

Focus (*F*) When a narrow beam of rays of light, parallel to the principal axis and close to it (know as paraxial rays), is incident on the surface of a mirror, the reflected beam is found to converge (concave mirror) or appear to diverge (convex mirror) from a point principal axis. This point is called focus.

Focal Length (*f*) It is the distance of the pole and the principal focus. For spherical mirrors, $f = \frac{R}{2}$.

Rules for Ray Diagrams

(i) When a ray falls in the direction of centre of curvature of mirror, then it reflects back along the same path.
(ii) A ray, parallel to the principal axis will after reflection, pass through the focus.
(iii) A ray, passing through the focus is reflected parallel to the principal axis.

Observe the following diagrams to draw ray diagrams.

Ray Diagrams of Concave Mirror

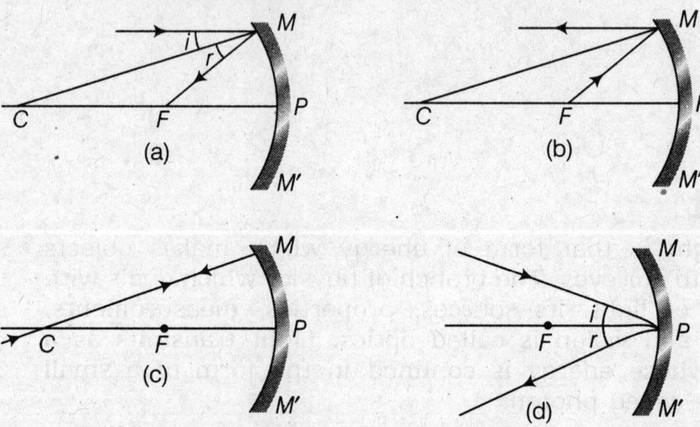

Ray Diagrams of Convex Mirror

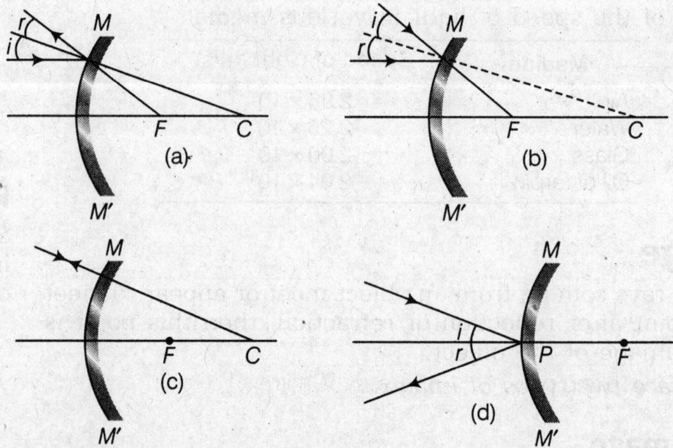

Reflection Through Concave Mirror

$F \rightarrow$ Principal focus
$P \rightarrow$ Pole of mirror
$C \rightarrow$ Centre of curvature
PC = Radius of curvature
PF = Focal length

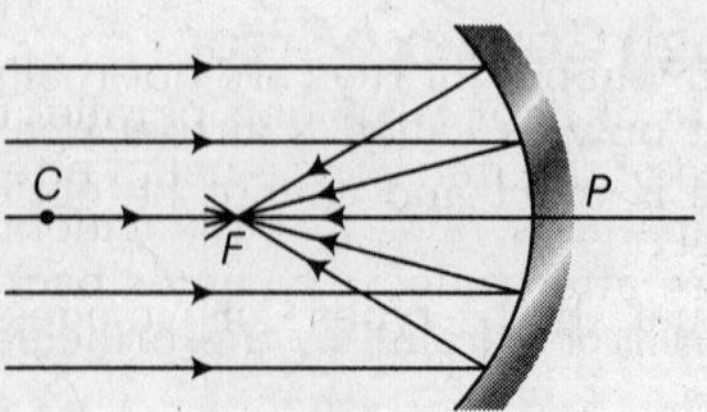

When a narrow beam of light travelling parallel to the principal axis is incident on the reflecting surface of the concave mirror, the beam after reflection converge at a point on the principal axis.

Image Formed by the Concave Mirror

Position of Object	Position of Image	Nature	Figure
At infinity	At the focus	Real, inverted and diminished.	F
Between infinity and centre of curvature	Between focus and centre of curvature	Real, inverted and small in size.	I, O, C, F
At centre of curvature	At centre of curvature	Real, inverted and of the same size.	C, F
Between focus and centre of curvature	Beyond centre of curvature	Real, inverted and enlarged.	C, F
At focus	At infinity	Real, inverted and enlarged.	F
Between focus and pole	Behind the mirror	Erect, virtual and enlarged.	F, O, I

Makeup and shaving mirrors are concave mirrors. When you place your face between the mirror and its focal point, you see an enlarged virtual image of yourself. Concave mirrors are also used in a new method for displaying the speed of a car.

Reflection Through Convex Mirror

When a narrow beam of light travelling parallel to the principal axis is incident on the reflecting surface of the mirror, the beam after reflection appear to diverge from a point on the principal axis. When a ray incident on convex mirror in the direction of centre of curvature after reflection comes back along the same path. When a ray incident on convex mirror parallel to the principal axis, after reflection, appears to come from the focus.

A ray appearing to pass through the focus is reflected parallel to the principal axis.

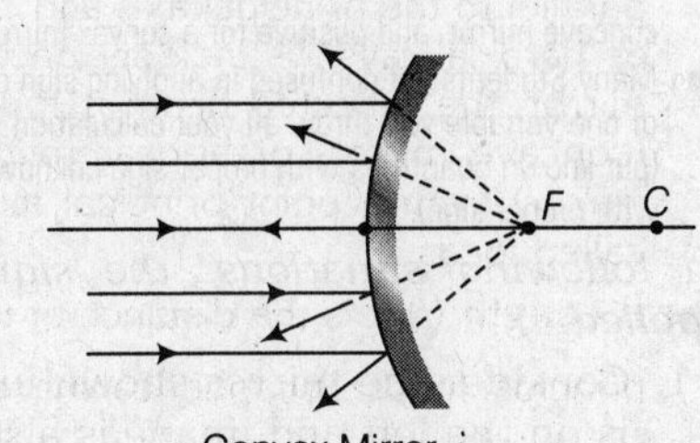

Convex Mirror

Image Formed by Convex Mirror

A convex mirror forms only virtual images for all positions of the real object. The image is always virtual, erect, smaller than the object and is located between the pole and the focus. The image becomes smaller and moves closer to the focus as the object is moved away from the mirror.

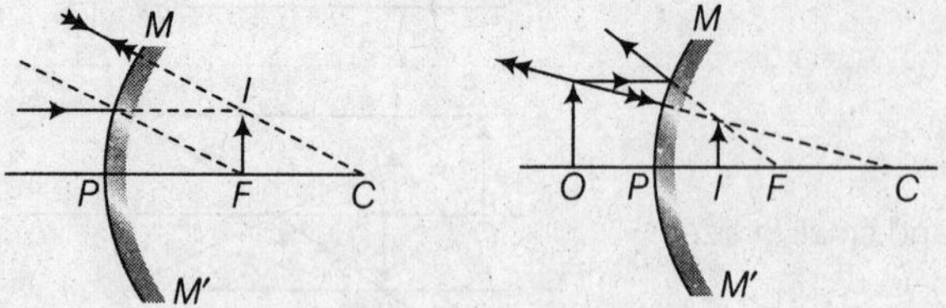

The virtual image is diminished in size and upright, relative to the object. A convex mirror form a virtual image of the object, no matter where in front of the mirror the object is placed. Because of the shape of convex mirrors, they give a wider field of view than do other types of mirrors. Therefore, they are often used for security purposes.

Sign Convention

1. Ali distances are measured from the pole.
2. The distance measured along the direction of propagation of light are taken as positive and the direction opposite to the propagation of light is taken as negative.
3. The distances (heights) measured above the principal axis *i.e.,* along positive Y-axis, are taken as positive while distances below the principal axis *i.e.,* along negative Y-axis are taken as negative.

   The sign convention can be summarised in the following figure.

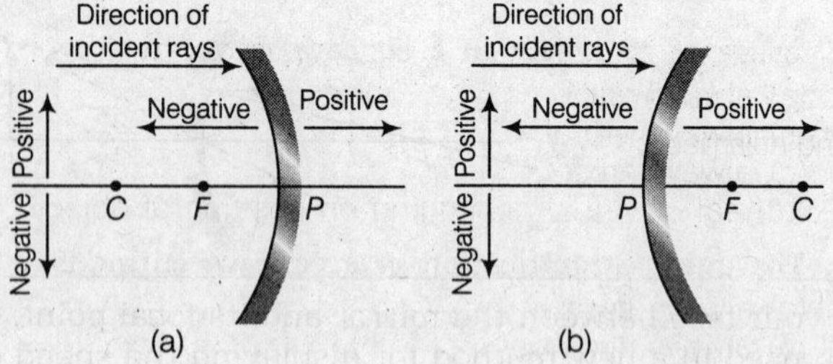

Note

- In this convention, the focal length (f) and radius of curvature (R) are negative for a concave mirror and positive for a convex mirror.
- Many Students get confused in applying sign convention and a small error in sign of one variable will throw all your calculation. Please study three points carefully (put known quantities with proper sign unknown quantity will come automatically with proper sign).

In following situations, the sign convention has been applied.

1. Consider the mirror shown in figure. Here, the object is on the left and image is also on the left. The mirror is a concave mirror. The incident ray is directed from left to right and so the positive X-axis is also from left to right.

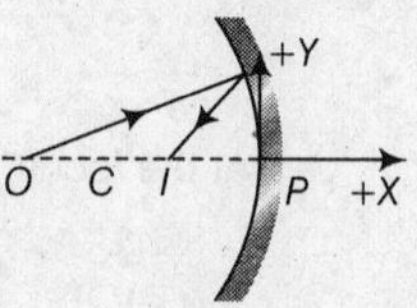

Here, object distance $u = -PO$,
image distance $v = -PI$,
radius of curvature $R = -PC$, focal length f = negative.

2. Consider the mirror shown in figure. Here, the object is on the left and image is on the right and the mirror concave. The incident ray is once again from left to right and so the positive X-axis.

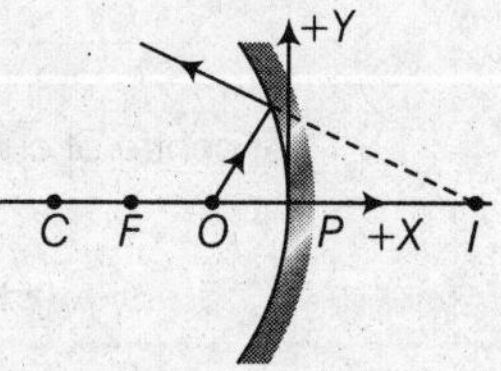

Here, object distance $u = -PO$,
image distance $v = +PI$,
radius of curvature $R = -PC$, focal length f = negative.

3. Consider the mirror shown in figure. Here, the object is virtual and on the left, image is also on the right and the mirror is a convex. The incident ray is from the right and the positive X-axis is from right to left.

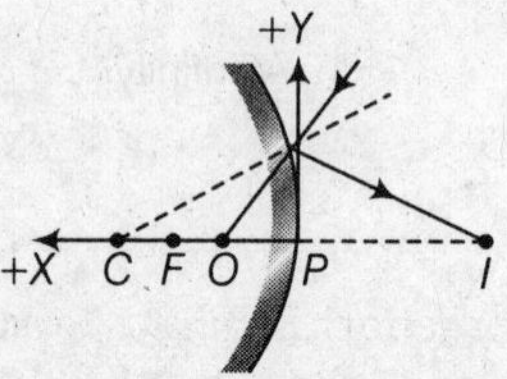

Here, object distance $u = +PO$,
image distance $v = -PI$, radius of curvature $R = +PC$, focal length f = positive.

MIRROR FORMULA

The relation between u, v and focal length f of a spherical mirror is known as mirror formula. *i.e.,*

$$\frac{1}{u} + \frac{1}{v} = \frac{1}{f}$$

Magnification

m = Height of the image (h') /Height of the object (h) and also, $m = -$ Image distance (v) /Object distance (u)

So, we can get $m = \frac{h'}{h} = -\frac{v}{u} = \frac{I}{O} = -\left(\frac{v-f}{f}\right) = -\left(\frac{f}{u-f}\right)$

Revision Fact

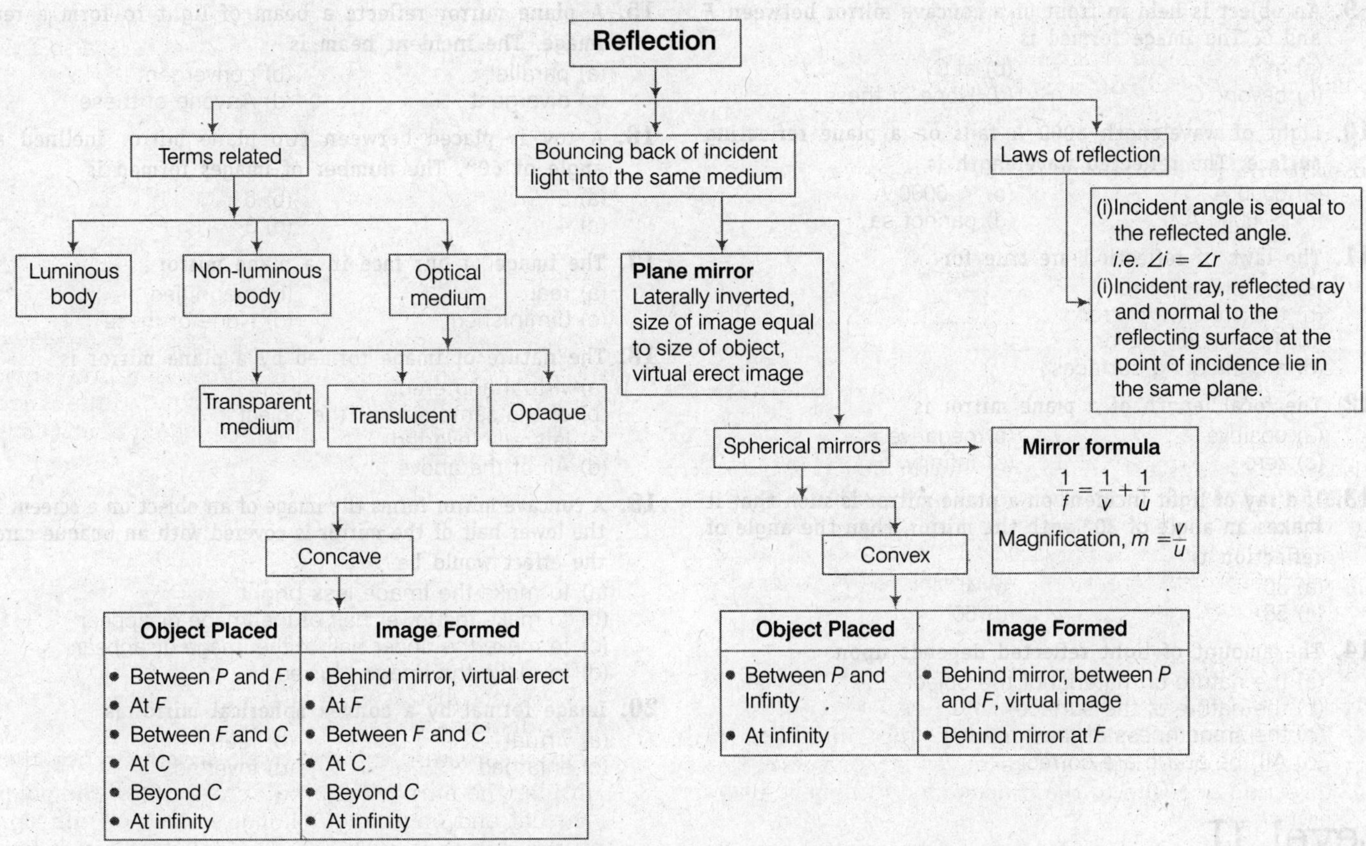

Practice Questions

Level I

1. Which is not true for the image formed in a plane mirror? The image is
(a) virtual
(b) erect
(c) laterally inverted
(d) closer to the mirror than the object

2. The relation between focal length f and radius of curvature R of a spherical mirror is
(a) $f = R$
(b) $f = \frac{R}{2}$
(c) $f = 2R$
(d) None of these

3. The correct mirror equation is
(a) $\frac{1}{f} = \frac{1}{v} + \frac{1}{u}$
(b) $\frac{1}{f} = \frac{1}{v} - \frac{1}{u}$
(c) $\frac{1}{f} = \frac{1}{u} - \frac{1}{v}$
(d) None of these

4. For any position of an object, image formed in a convex mirror is
(a) virtual
(b) erect
(c) smaller in size
(d) as far behind the mirror as the object is in front

5. Image of an object in a concave mirror is
(a) always real
(b) always virtual
(c) always erect
(d) real or virtual depending on position of object

6. The linear magnification of a concave mirror is
(a) always positive
(b) always negative
(c) positive or negative depending upon the position of the object
(d) cannot say

7. When an object is held between pole and focus of a concave mirror, the image formed is
(a) real and inverted
(b) real and enlarged
(c) virtual and diminished
(d) virtual and enlarged

8. The linear magnification of a convex mirror is
(a) always positive
(b) always negative
(c) sometimes positive and sometimes negative
(d) cannot predict

9. An object is held in front of a concave mirror between F and C. The image formed is
(a) at F (b) at C
(c) beyond C (d) None of these

10. Light of wavelength 6000 Å falls on a plane reflecting surface. The reflected wavelength is
(a) 6000 Å (b) < 6000 Å
(c) > 6000 Å (d) cannot say

11. The laws of reflection are true for
(a) the plane mirror
(b) the concave mirror
(c) the convex mirror
(d) all reflecting surfaces

12. The focal length of a plane mirror is
(a) positive (b) negative
(c) zero (d) infinity

13. If a ray of light incident on a plane mirror is such that it makes an angle of 30° with the mirror, then the angle of reflection is
(a) 30° (b) 45°
(c) 55° (d) 60°

14. The amount of light reflected depends upon
(a) the nature of material of the object
(b) the nature of the surface
(c) the smoothness of the surface
(d) All the above are correct

15. A plane mirror reflects a beam of light to form a real image. The incident beam is
(a) parallel (b) convergent
(c) divergent (d) Anyone of these

16. A toy is placed between two plane mirror inclined at angle of 60°. The number of images formed is
(a) 5 (b) 6
(c) 4 (d) 3

17. The image of our face in a plane mirror
(a) real (b) magnified
(c) diminished (d) None of these

18. The nature of image formed by a plane mirror is
(a) virtual and erect
(b) of the same size as the object
(c) laterally inverted
(d) All of the above

19. A concave mirror forms the image of an object on a screen. If the lower half of the mirror is covered with an opaque card, the effect would be
(a) to make the image less bright
(b) to make the lower half of the image disappear
(c) to make the upper half of the image disappear
(d) to make the image blurred

20. Image formal by a convex spherical mirror is
(a) virtual (b) real
(c) enlarged (d) inverted

Level II

1. A light bulb is placed between two plane mirrors inclined at an angle of 60°. The number of images formed are
(a) 6 (b) 2 (c) 5 (d) 4

2. A ray of light incidents on a plane mirror at an angle of 30°. The deviation produced in the ray is
(a) 30° (b) 60° (c) 90° (d) 120°

3. A ray of light is incidenting normally on a plane mirror. The angle of reflection
(a) will be 0°
(b) will be 90°
(c) will not be reflected
(d) None of the above

4. When light wave suffers reflection at the interface from air to glass, the change in phase of the reflected wave is equal to
(a) 0 (b) $\frac{\pi}{2}$ (c) π (d) 2π

5. Two plane mirrors are at right angles to each other. A man stands between them and combs his hair with his right hand. In how many of the images will he be seen using his right hand?
(a) None (b) 1 (c) 2 (d) 3

6. When a plane mirror is rotated through an angle θ, then the reflected ray turns through the angle 2θ, then the size of the image
(a) is doubled (b) is halved
(c) remains the same (d) becomes infinite

7. Focal length of a plane mirror is
(a) zero (b) infinite
(c) very less (d) indefinite

8. A light beam is being reflected by using two mirrors, as in a periscope used in submarines. If one of the mirrors rotates by an angle θ, the reflected light will deviate from its original path by the angle
(a) 2θ (b) 0°
(c) θ (d) 4θ

9. A convex mirror of focal length f forms an image which is $\frac{1}{n}$ times the object. The distance of the object from the mirror is
(a) $(n-1)f$ (b) $\left(\frac{n-1}{n}\right)f$ (c) $\left(\frac{n+1}{n}\right)f$ (d) $(n+1)f$

10. A square wire of side 1cm is placed perpendicular to the principal axis of a concave mirror of focal length 15 cm at a distance of 20 cm. The area enclosed by the image of the wire is
(a) 4 cm^2 (b) 6 cm^2
(c) 2 cm^2 (d) 9 cm^2

11. The focal length of a concave mirror is f and the distance from the object to the principle focus is x. The ratio of the size of the image to the size of the object is
(a) $\frac{f+x}{f}$ (b) $\frac{f}{x}$ (c) $\sqrt{\frac{f}{x}}$ (d) $\frac{f^2}{x^2}$

12. Given a point source of light, which of the following can produce a parallel beam of light?
(a) Convex mirror
(b) Concave mirror
(c) Concave lens
(d) Two plane mirrors inclined at an angle of 90°

13. What will be the height of image when an object of 2 mm is placed on the axis of a convex mirror at a distance 20 cm of radius of curvature 40 cm?
(a) 20 mm (b) 10 mm
(c) 6 mm (d) 1 mm

14. An object of length 6 cm is placed on the principal axis of a concave mirror of focal length f at a distance of $4f$. The length of the image will be
(a) 2 cm (b) 12 cm
(c) 4 cm (d) 1.2 cm

15. An object is placed 40 cm from a concave mirror of focal length 20 cm. The image formed is
(a) real, inverted and same in size
(b) real, inverted and smaller
(c) virtual, erect and larger
(d) virtual, erect and smaller

16. An object 2.5 cm high is placed at a distance of 10 cm from a concave mirror of radius of curvature 30 cm. The size of the image is
(a) 9.2 cm (b) 10.5 cm
(c) 5.6 cm (d) 7.5 cm

17. A convex mirror has a focal length f. A real object is placed at a distance f in front of it from the pole produces an image at
(a) infinity (b) f (c) $\frac{f}{2}$ (d) $2f$

18. A concave mirror gives an image three times as large as the object placed at a distance of 20 cm from it. For the image to be real, the focal length should be
(a) 10 cm (b) 15 cm (c) 20 cm (d) 30 cm

19. The focal length of a convex mirror is 20 cm, its radius of curvature will be
(a) 10 cm (b) 20 cm (c) 30 cm (d) 40 cm

20. A concave mirror of focal length 15 cm forms an image having twice the linear dimensions of the object. The position of the object when the image is virtual will be
(a) 22.5 cm (b) 7.5 cm (c) 30 cm (d) 45 cm

Answers

Level I

1. (c)	2. (b)	3. (a)	4. (d)	5. (d)	6. (c)	7. (d)	8. (a)	9. (c)	10. (a)
11. (d)	12. (d)	13. (d)	14. (d)	15. (b)	16. (a)	17. (d)	18. (d)	19. (a)	20. (d)

Level II

1. (c)	2. (d)	3. (a)	4. (c)	5. (c)	6. (c)	7. (b)	8. (a)	9. (a)	10. (d)
11. (b)	12. (b)	13. (d)	14. (a)	15. (a)	16. (d)	17. (c)	18. (b)	19. (d)	20. (b)

Hints and Solutions

Level II

1. Number of images $= \left(\frac{360°}{\theta} - 1\right)$

$= \left(\frac{360°}{60°} - 1\right) = 5$

2. $\delta = 180° - 60° = 120°$

3. $\angle i = \angle r = 0°$

4. When light is reflected from denser medium, a phase difference of π always occurs.

5. In two images man will see himself using left hand.

6. In plane mirror, size of the image is independent of the angle of incidence.

7. $f = \frac{R}{2}$ and $R = \infty$ for plane mirror.

8. When a mirror is rotated by an angle θ, the reflected ray deviates from its original path by angle 2θ.

9. $m = +\frac{1}{n} = -\frac{v}{u}$

$\Rightarrow \quad v = -\frac{u}{n}$

By using mirror formula, $\frac{1}{f} = \frac{1}{-\frac{u}{n}} + \frac{1}{u}$

$\Rightarrow \quad u = -(n-1)f$

10. Here, $u = -20$ cm, $f = -15$ cm

$\frac{1}{v} + \frac{1}{u} = \frac{1}{f}$

$\Rightarrow \quad \frac{1}{v} = \frac{1}{-15} - \frac{1}{-20} = -\frac{1}{15} + \frac{1}{20} = -\frac{1}{60}$

$\Rightarrow \quad v = -60$ cm, $u = -20$ cm

$\therefore \quad m = -\frac{v}{u} = -\frac{(-60)}{(-20)}$

$= -3$ cm or $|m| = 3$ cm

Each side of the square is now 3 cm, area = 9 cm^2

11. $\frac{I}{O} = \frac{f}{f-u}$; where $u = f + x$

$\therefore \quad \frac{I}{O} = -\frac{f}{x}$

12. Object should be placed on focus of concave mirror.

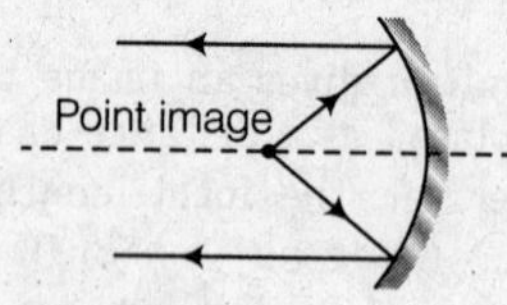

13. $\frac{I}{O} = \frac{f}{f-u} \Rightarrow \frac{I}{2} = \frac{200}{(200+200)} = \frac{1}{2}$

$\Rightarrow \quad I = 1$ mm

14. $\frac{I}{O} = \frac{f}{f-u} \Rightarrow \frac{I}{+6} = \frac{-f}{-f-(-4f)} \Rightarrow I = -2$ cm

15. Real, inverted and same in size because object is at the centre of curvature of the mirror.

16. $R = -30$ cm

$\Rightarrow \quad f = -15$ cm

$O = \pm 2.5$ cm, $u = -10$ cm

By mirror formula, $\frac{1}{-15} = \frac{1}{v} + \frac{1}{(-10)}$

$\Rightarrow \quad v = 30$ cm

Also, $\frac{I}{O} = -\frac{v}{u}$

$\Rightarrow \quad \frac{I}{(+2.5)} = -\frac{30}{(-10)}$

$\Rightarrow \quad I = +7.5$ cm

17. The image is magnified, real and inverted.

Here, focal length = f and $u = -f$

On putting these values in $\frac{1}{f} = \frac{1}{u} + \frac{1}{v}$

$\Rightarrow \quad \frac{1}{f} = -\frac{1}{f} + \frac{1}{v}$

$\Rightarrow \quad \frac{1}{f} + \frac{1}{f} = \frac{1}{v}$

$\Rightarrow \quad \frac{2}{f} = \frac{1}{v}$

$\therefore \quad v = \frac{f}{2}$

18. $m = \frac{f}{f-u}$

$\Rightarrow \quad -3 = \frac{f}{f-(-20)}$

$\Rightarrow \quad f = -15$ cm

19. $f = \frac{R}{2}$

$\Rightarrow \quad R = 40$ cm

20. $f = -15$ cm, $m = +2$ (Positive because image is virtual)

$\because \quad m = -\frac{v}{u}$

$\Rightarrow \quad v = -2u$

By using mirror formula,

$\frac{1}{-15} = \frac{2}{(-2u)} + \frac{1}{u}$

$\Rightarrow \quad u = -7.5$ cm

49

Refraction of Light Through Plane Surface

Refraction of Light Through a Plane Transparent Surface

In the figure, XY is section of a plane transparent surface of a denser medium. A ray of light PQ strikes the surface at Q and goes along QR in denser medium. It is bent towards normal. This bending of ray of light when it travels in different medium, is called refraction. The surface is said to have refracted the light.

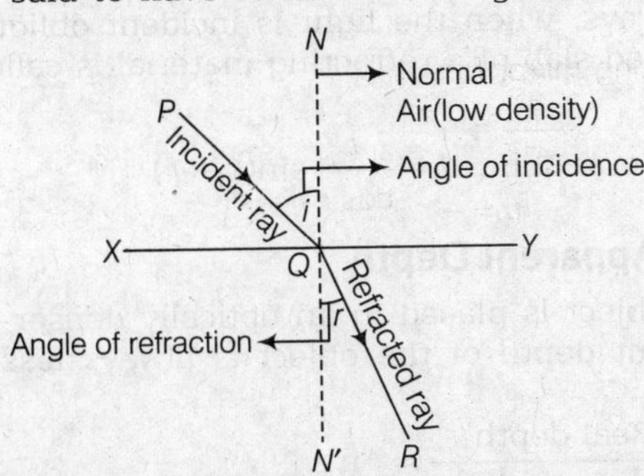

(i) **Transparent Surface** The plane surface which refracts light, is called transparent surface in the figure, XY is the section of a plane transparent surface.

(ii) **Point of Incidence** The point Q on the boundary of two media where the incident r strikes is called the point of incidence.

(iii) **Normal** A perpendicular drawn at the point of incidence is called normal. In the figure, NQN' is the normal on surface XY.

(iv) **Incident Ray** The ray of light which strikes the transparent surface at the point of incidence is called incident ray. Here, the ray PQ is the incident ray.

(v) **Refracted Ray** The ray of light on entering the second medium is called refracted ray. In the figure, QR is the refracted ray.

(vi) **Angle of Incidence** The angle between the incident ray and the normal is called angle of incidence ($\angle i$).

(vii) **Angle of Refraction** The angle between the refracted ray and the normal is called angle of refraction ($\angle r$).

(viii) **Plane of Incidence** The plane containing the normal and the incident ray is called plane of incidence. For the diagram, plane of paper is the plane of incidence.

(ix) **Plane of Refraction** The plane containing the normal and the refracted ray is called plane of refraction. For the diagram, plane of paper is the plane of refraction.

Refraction of Light

The phenomenon of deviation of light rays from its path when it travels from one transparent medium to another transparent medium, is called refraction of light.

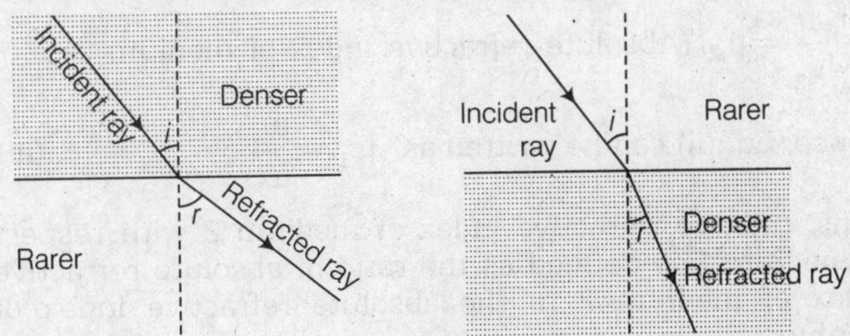

When a light ray travels from a denser medium to a rarer medium, it deviates away from the normal and when light ray travels from a rarer medium to a denser medium, it deviates towards the normal.

The cause of refraction is that the speed of light is different in different media.

In refraction, the speed of light and its wavelength change but its frequency remains unchanged, when light travels from one transparent medium to another transparent medium.

Laws of Refraction

There are two laws of refraction

(i) The incidence ray, the refracted ray and the normal at the point of incidence all three lie in the same plane.

(ii) The ratio of sine of angle of incidence to the sine of angle of refraction remains constant for a pair of media, *i.e.*,

$$\frac{\sin i}{\sin r} = \text{constant } ({}_1\mu_2)$$

This law is also called Snell's law (${}_1\mu_2$ is called refractive index of second medium with respect to the first medium).

Refractive Index

The ratio of speed of light in vacuum (c) to the speed of light in any medium (v) is called refractive index of the medium.

Refractive index of a medium,

$$\mu = \frac{c}{v}$$

Relative Refractive Index

When light passes from medium 1 to another medium 2, the refractive index of medium 2 with respect to medium 1 is written as ${}_2\mu_1$ and is called relative refractive index.

$${}_2\mu_1 = \frac{\text{Speed of light in medium 1}}{\text{Speed of light in medium 2}} = \frac{v_1}{v_2} \quad \text{...(i)}$$

On multiplying and dividing by c (speed of light in air) on RHS in Eq. (i), we get

$${}_2\mu_1 = \frac{cv_1}{cv_2} = \left(\frac{c}{v_2}\right) \times \left(\frac{v_1}{c}\right) = \frac{\dfrac{c}{v_2}}{\dfrac{c}{v_1}} \quad \text{...(ii)}$$

But $\frac{c}{v_1} = \mu_1$ (Absolute refractive index of medium 1) and

$\frac{c}{v_2} = \mu_2$ (Absolute refractive index of medium 2)

Hence, Eq. (ii) can be written as ${}_2\mu_1 = \frac{\mu_2}{\mu_1}$ ...(iii)

Thus, relative refractive index of medium 2 with respect to medium 1 is defined as the ratio of absolute refractive index of medium 2 to the absolute refractive index of medium 1.

Also, $${}_2\mu_1 = \frac{\sin i}{\sin r} \quad \text{...(iv)}$$

Comparing Eqs. (iii) and (iv), we get $\frac{\sin i}{\sin r} = \frac{\mu_2}{\mu_1}$

or $\mu_1 \sin i = \mu_2 \sin r$ ...(v)

We know, refractive index of medium 2 with respect to medium 1 is given by, ${}_2\mu_1 = \frac{v_1}{v_2}$ ...(vi)

Similarly, refractive index of medium 1 with respect to 2 is given by, ${}_1\mu_2 = \frac{v_2}{v_1}$ ...(vii)

Multiplying Eqs. (vi) and (vii), we get

$${}_2\mu_1 \times {}_1\mu_2 = \frac{v_1}{v_2} \times \frac{v_2}{v_1} = 1 \text{ or } {}_2\mu_1 = \frac{1}{{}_1\mu_2}$$

i.e., refractive index of medium 2 with respect to medium 1 is the reciprocal of refractive index of medium 1 with respect to medium 2.

e.g., Refractive index of water with respect to air,

For water, ${}_w\mu_a = \frac{4}{3}$ or 1.33, for glass, ${}_g\mu_a = \frac{3}{2} = 1.5$

When light goes from water to glass, Refractive index of glass with respect to water, ${}_g\mu_w = \frac{3/2}{4/3} = \frac{9}{8} = 1.125$

Principle of Reversibility of Light

It states that if light after suffering any number of reflections and refractions has its final path reversed, it travels back along the same path in the opposite direction. It leads to result that the refractive index of the medium b with respect to the medium a is equal to the reciprocal of the refractive index of the medium a with respect to the medium b

$${}^a\mu_b = \frac{1}{{}^b\mu_a}$$

Lateral Shift

The perpendicular distance between the incident and the emergent rays, when the light is incident obliquely on a parallel sided slab of a refracting material is called lateral shift.

$$\text{Lateral shift, } d = \frac{t}{\cos r}\sin(i - r)$$

Real and Apparent Depth

When an object is placed in an optically denser medium, the apparent depth of the object is always less than its real depth.

$$\frac{\text{Real depth}}{\text{Apparent depth}} = {}^a\mu_b$$

$$\text{Normal shift, } d = t\left(1 - \frac{1}{{}^a\mu_b}\right)$$

Total Internal Reflection

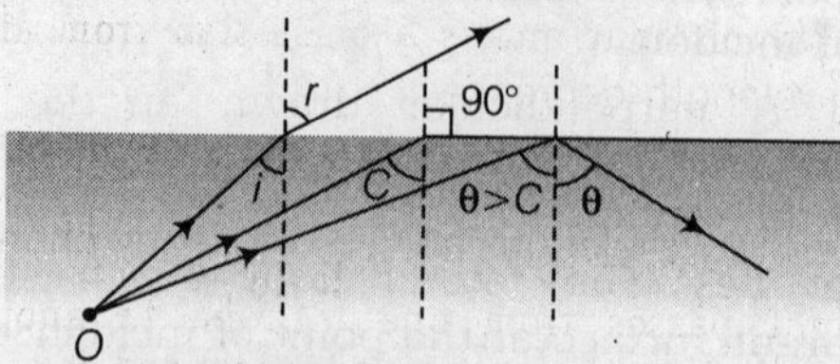

When a light ray travelling from a denser medium towards a rarer medium is incident at the interface at an angle of incidence greater than critical angle, then light rays reflected back into the denser medium. This phenomenon is called total internal reflection.

1. $\mu = \frac{1}{\sin C}$ = cosec C, where $\mu \rightarrow {}_{\text{Rarer}}\mu_{\text{Denser}}$

2. Conditions for TIR

(i) The ray must travel from denser medium to rarer medium.
(ii) The angle of incidence i must be greater than critical angle C.

3. Dependence of Critical Angle

(i) Colour of light (or wavelength of light) Critical angle depends upon wavelength as

$$\lambda \propto \frac{1}{\mu} \propto \sin C$$

(a) $\lambda_R > \lambda_V \Rightarrow C_R > C_V$

(b) $\sin C = \frac{1}{{}_R\mu_D} = \frac{\mu_R}{\mu_D} = \frac{\lambda_D}{\lambda_R} = \frac{v_D}{v_R}$ (for two media)

Temperature With temperature rise refractive index of the material decreases, therefore critical angle increases.

4. Promo Prism

A right angled isosceles prism, which is used in periscopes or binoculars. It is used to deviate light rays through 45°, 90° and 180° and also to erect the image.

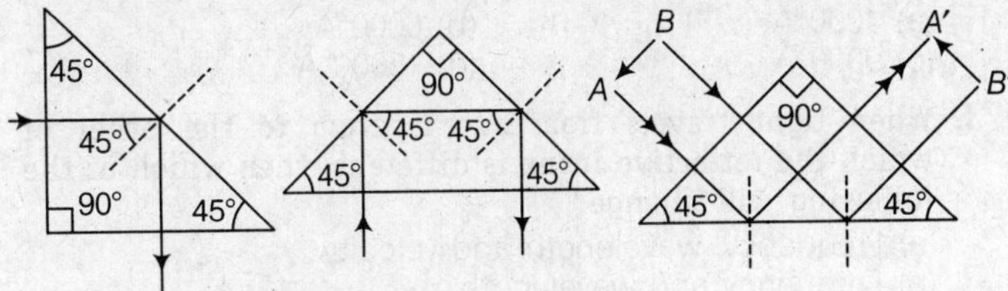

Practice Questions

Level I

1. Velocity of light is maximum in
(a) diamond (b) water
(c) glass (d) vacuum

2. In vacuum, the speed of light depends upon
(a) frequency
(b) wavelength
(c) velocity of the source of light
(d) None of the above

3. If v_c is the speed of light in vacuum and v_m is the speed of light in given medium, then the refractive index of medium is
(a) $\frac{v_m}{v_c}$ (b) $\frac{v_c}{v_m}$
(c) $v_m \times v_c$ (d) None of these

4. A ray of light travelling obliquely from denser to rarer medium
(a) bends towards the normal
(b) bends away from the normal
(c) deviates from its path
(d) None of the above

5. When a ray of light enters a glass slab from air,
(a) its wavelength decreases
(b) its wavelength increases
(c) its frequency increases
(d) neither its wavelength nor its frequency changes

6. When light passes from one medium to another, the physical quantity that remains unchanged is
(a) velocity (b) wavelength
(c) frequency (d) None of these

7. A monochromatic beam of light passes from a denser to a rarer medium as a result its
(a) velocity increases (b) velocity decreases
(c) frequency decreases (d) wavelength decreases

8. A well cut diamond appears bright because
(a) it emits light (b) it is radioactive
(c) of total reflection (d) of disperson

9. For total internal reflection, light must travel
(a) from rarer to denser medium
(b) from denser to rarer medium
(c) in air only
(d) in water only

10. Optical fibres are based on the phenomenon of
(a) reflection (b) refraction
(c) dispersion (d) total internal reflection

11. Total internal reflection can occur when light tends to pass from
(a) a denser to a rarer medium
(b) a rarer to a denser medium
(c) one medium to another of equal refractive index
(d) None of the above

12. Mirage is observed in a desert due to the phenomenon of
(a) interference (b) total reflection
(c) scattering (d) double refraction

13. Light appears to travel in straight lines, since
(a) it is not absorbed by the atmosphere
(b) it is reflected by the atmosphere
(c) its wavelength is very small
(d) its velocity is very large

14. If the light propagating along a straight line bends by a small but fixed angle, it may be due to
(a) reflection (b) refraction
(c) dispersion (d) diffraction

15. A small ink dot on a paper is seen through a glass slab of thickness 4 cm and refractive index 1.5. The dot appears to be raised by
(a) 1 cm (b) 2 cm (c) 3 cm (d) 1.33 cm

Level II

1. The refractive index of a piece of transparent quartz is the greatest for
(a) red light (b) violet light
(c) green light (d) yellow light

2. The refractive index of a certain glass is 1.5 for light whose wavelength in vacuum is 6000 Å. The wavelength of this light when it passes through glass is
(a) 4000 Å (b) 6000 Å
(c) 9000 Å (d) 15000 Å

3. When light travels from one medium to the other of which the refractive index is different, then which of the following will change?
(a) Frequency, wavelength and velocity
(b) Frequency and wavelength
(c) Frequency and velocity
(d) Wavelength and velocity

4. A light wave has a frequency of 4×10^{14} Hz and a wavelength of 5×10^{-7} m in a medium. The refractive index of the medium is
(a) 1.5 (b) 1.33 (c) 1.0 (d) 0.66

5. White light is incident normally on a glass slab. Inside the glass slab
(a) red light travels faster than other colours
(b) violet light travels faster than other colours
(c) yellow light travels faster than other colours
(d) All colours travel with the same speed

6. When light wave suffer reflection at the interface between air and glass, the change of phase of reflected wave is equal to
(a) zero (b) $\frac{\pi}{2}$ (c) π (d) 2π

7. Light travels through a glass plate of thickness t and having refractive index n. If c is the velocity of light in vacuum, the time taken by the light to travel this thickness of glass is
(a) $\frac{t}{nc}$ (b) tnc (c) $\frac{nt}{c}$ (d) $\frac{tc}{n}$

8. The refractive indices of glass and water with respect to air are $\frac{3}{2}$ and $\frac{4}{3}$ respectively. The refractive index of glass with respect to water will be
(a) $\frac{8}{9}$ (b) $\frac{9}{8}$
(c) $\frac{7}{6}$ (d) None of these

9. Monochromatic light of frequency 5×10^{14} Hz travelling in vacuum enters a medium of refractive index 1.5. Its wavelength in the medium is
(a) 4000 Å (b) 5000 Å
(c) 6000 Å (d) 5500 Å

10. Which of the following is a correct relation?
(a) ${}_a\mu_r = {}_a\mu_w \times {}_r\mu_w$ (b) ${}_a\mu_r \times {}_r\mu_w = {}_w\mu_a$
(c) ${}_a\mu_r \times {}_r\mu_a = 0$ (d) $\frac{{}_a\mu_r}{{}_w\mu_r} = {}_a\mu_w$

11. A mark at the bottom of a liquid appears to rise by 0.1 m. The depth of the liquid is 1 m. The refractive index of the liquid is
(a) 1.33 (b) $\frac{9}{10}$
(c) $\frac{10}{9}$ (d) 1.5

12. A ray of light is incident on a transparent glass slab of refractive index 1.62. The reflected and the refracted rays are mutually perpendicular. The angle of incidence is
(a) 58.3° (b) 50°
(c) 35° (d) 30°

13. A microscope is focused on a coin lying at the bottom of a beaker. The microscope is now raised up by 1 cm. To what depth should the water be poured into the beaker, so that coin is again in focus? (Refractive index of water is $\frac{4}{3}$)
(a) 1 cm (b) $\frac{4}{3}$ cm
(c) 3 cm (d) 4 cm

14. A fish at a depth of 12 cm in water is viewed by an observer on the bank of a lake. To what height the image of the fish is raised?
(a) 9 cm (b) 12 cm
(c) 3.8 cm (d) 3 cm

15. The wavelength of sodium light in air is 5890 Å. The velocity of light in air is 3×10^8 $^{-1}$. The wavelength of light in a glass of refractive index 1.6 would be close to
(a) 5890 Å (b) 3681 Å
(c) 9424 Å (d) 15078 Å

16. Critical angle of light passing from glass to air is minimum for
(a) red (b) green (c) yellow (d) violet

17. A diver at a depth of 12 m in water $\left(\mu = \frac{4}{3}\right)$ sees the sky in a cone of semi-vertical angle
(a) $\sin^{-1}\left(\frac{4}{3}\right)$ (b) $\tan^{-1}\left(\frac{4}{3}\right)$ (c) $\sin^{-1}\left(\frac{3}{4}\right)$ (d) 90°

18. Monochromatic light is refracted from air into the glass of refractive index μ. The ratio of the wavelength of incident and refracted waves is
(a) $1:\mu$ (b) $1:\mu^2$
(c) $\mu:1$ (d) $1:1$

19. Which of the following is not due to total internal reflection?
(a) Brilliance of diamond
(b) Working of optical fibre
(c) Difference between apparent and real depth of a pond
(d) Mirage on hot summer days

20. 'Mirage' is a phenomenon due to
(a) reflection of light
(b) refraction of light
(c) total internal reflection of light
(d) diffraction of light

Answers

Level I

1. (d)	**2.** (d)	**3.** (b)	**4.** (b)	**5.** (a)	**6.** (c)	**7.** (a)	**8.** (c)	**9.** (b)	**10.** (d)
11. (a)	**12.** (b)	**13.** (c)	**14.** (a, b)	**15.** (d)					

Level II

1. (b)	**2.** (a)	**3.** (d)	**4.** (a)	**5.** (a)	**6.** (c)	**7.** (c)	**8.** (b)	**9.** (a)	**10.** (d)
11. (c)	**12.** (a)	**13.** (d)	**14.** (d)	**15.** (b)	**16.** (d)	**17.** (c)	**18.** (c)	**19.** (c)	**20.** (c)

Hints and Solutions

Level II

1. $\mu \propto \frac{1}{\lambda}$, $\lambda_R > \lambda_V$

2. $\lambda_{\text{medium}} = \frac{\lambda_{\text{air}}}{\mu} = \frac{6000}{1.5} = 4000\ \text{Å}$

3. Velocity and wavelength change but frequency remains same.

4. $\mu = \frac{c}{v} = \frac{c}{\nu\lambda} = \frac{3 \times 10^8}{4 \times 10^{14} \times 5 \times 10^{-7}} = 1.5$

7. Time $= \frac{\text{Distance}}{\text{Speed}} = \frac{t}{c/n} = \frac{nt}{c}$

8. $${}_a\mu_g = \frac{3}{2},\ {}_a\mu_w = \frac{4}{3}$$

$\therefore$ $${}_w\mu_g = \frac{{}_a\mu_g}{{}_a\mu_w} = \frac{3/2}{4/3} = \frac{9}{8}$$

9. $\lambda_m = \frac{\lambda_a}{\mu} = \frac{c}{\nu\mu} = \frac{3 \times 10^8}{5 \times 10^{14} \times 1.5} = 4000\ \text{Å}$

10. $\frac{{}_a\mu_r}{{}_w\mu_r} = \frac{\mu_r/\mu_a}{\mu_r/\mu_w} = \frac{\mu_w}{\mu_a} = {}_a\mu_w$

11. Real depth = 1 m

Apparent depth = 1 – 0.1 = 0.9 m

Refractive index,

$$\mu = \frac{\text{Real depth}}{\text{Apparent depth}} = \frac{1}{0.9} = \frac{10}{9}$$

12. $\mu = \tan i$

$\Rightarrow i = \tan^{-1}\mu = \tan^{-1} 1.62 = 58.3°$

13. Suppose water is poured upto the height h.

So, $h\left(1 - \frac{1}{\mu}\right) = 1$

$\Rightarrow$ $h = 4$ cm

14. Apparent rise $= d\left(1 - \frac{1}{{}_a\mu_w}\right)$

$$= 12 \times \left(1 - \frac{3}{4}\right) = 3\ \text{cm}$$

15. $\lambda_g = \frac{\lambda_a}{\mu_g} = \frac{5890}{1.6} = 3681\ \text{Å}$

16. $${}_a\mu_g = \frac{1}{\sin C}$$

$\Rightarrow$ $$\sin C = \frac{1}{{}_a\mu_g}$$

As μ is maximum for violet colour, so $\sin C$ is minimum and hence critical angle C is minimum for violet colour.

17. Semi-vertical angle $= C = \sin^{-1}\left(\frac{1}{\mu}\right) = \sin^{-1}\left(\frac{3}{4}\right)$

18. $\lambda \propto \frac{1}{\mu} \Rightarrow \frac{\lambda_1}{\lambda_2} = \frac{\mu_2}{\mu_1} = \frac{\mu}{1}$

19. Real and apparent depth are explained on the basis of refraction only. TIR is not involved here.

50

Interference

Interference of Light Waves

When light waves from two coherent sources travelling in the same direction superpose each other, the intensity in the region of superposition gets redistributed, becoming maximum at some points and minimum at others. This phenomenon is called interference of light.

Constructive and Destructive Interference

If path difference $p = n\lambda$ or phase difference $\phi = 2n\pi$, the two waves are in same phase and so add up to give maximum of intensity. This is called constructive interference.

If $p = (2n-1)\dfrac{\lambda}{2}$ or $\phi = (2n-1)\pi$, the two superposing waves are out of phase, the resultant amplitude is equal to difference between their individual amplitudes and hence intensity is minimum. This is called destructive interference.

Young's Double Slit Experiment

In Young's double slit experiment, two identical narrow slits S_1 and S_2 are placed symmetrically with respect to narrow slit S illuminated with monochromatic light. The interference pattern is obtained on an observation screen placed at large distance D from S_1 and S_2.

The position of nth bright fringe from the centre of screen is

$$x_n = n\frac{D\lambda}{d}$$

The position of nth dark fringe from the centre of the screen is

$$x'_n = (2n-1)\frac{D\lambda}{2d}$$

Fringe width is the separation between two successive bright or dark fringes and is given by

$$\beta = \frac{D\lambda}{d}$$

Resultant Amplitude and Intensity of Interfering Waves

If a_1 and a_2 are the amplitudes and I_1 and I_2 are the intensities of two coherent waves having phase difference ϕ, then their resultant amplitude and intensity at the point of superposition are given by

$$a = \sqrt{a_1^2 + a_2^2 + 2a_1a_2\cos\phi}$$

and $$I = I_1 + I_2 + 2\sqrt{I_1I_2}\cos\phi$$

If amplitude of each wave is a_o and intensity I_0, then

$$I = 2ka_0^2(1+\cos\phi) = 2I_0(1+\cos\phi)$$
$$= 4I_0\cos^2\frac{\phi}{2}$$

The term $2\sqrt{I_1I_2}\cos\phi$ is called interference term.

(i) When $\cos\phi$ remains constant with time, the two sources are coherent. The intensity will be maximum at points for which $\cos\phi = +1$ and minimum at points for which $\cos\phi = -1$.

(ii) When $\cos\phi$ varies continuously with time, so that its average value is zero over the time interval of measurement, the resultant intensity at all points will be $I_1 + I_2$. No interference fringes are observed. The sources are incoherent.

$$\frac{I_{max}}{I_{min}} = \frac{(a_1+a_2)^2}{(a_1-a_2)^2} = \left(\frac{r+1}{r-1}\right)^2$$

where, $r = \dfrac{a_1}{a_2} = \sqrt{\dfrac{I_1}{I_2}}$ is the amplitude ratio of two waves. If w_1 and w_2 are the widths of the two slits, then

$$\frac{w_1}{w_2} = \frac{I_1}{I_2} = \frac{a_1^2}{a_2^2}$$

Coherent Sources

Two sources of light which continuously emit light waves of same frequency (or wavelength) with a zero or constant phase difference between them, are called coherent sources. Two independent source of light cannot act as coherent sources, they have to be derived from the same parent source.

Conditions for Substained Interference

- The two sources should continuously emit waves of same frequency or wavelength.
- The two sources of light should be coherent.
- The amplitudes of the interfering waves should be equal.
- The two sources should be narrow.
- The interfering waves must travel nearly along the same direction.
- The sources should be monochromatic.
- The interfering waves should be in the same state of polarisation.
- The distance between the two coherent sources should be small and the distance between the two sources and the screen should be large.

Practice Questions

Level I

1. Two Sources of wave are called coherent if
(a) both have the same amplitude of vibration
(b) both produce waves of the same wavelength
(c) both produce waves of the same wavelength having a constant phase difference
(d) both produce waves having the same velocity

2. Two coherent sources of light can be obtained by
(a) two different lamps
(b) two different lamps but of the same power
(c) two different lamps of same power and having the same colour
(d) None of the above

3. Two waves of the same frequency and intensity superimpose with each other in opposite phases. After the superposition, the
(a) intensity increases by 4 times
(b) intensity increases by 2 times
(c) frequency increases by 4 times
(d) None of the above

4. Two waves of the same frequency and same intensity are superimposed in the same phase. The intensity of the resultant wave at the central point will be
(a) equal to that of the individual wave
(b) twice that of the individual wave
(c) three times that of the individual wave
(d) four times that of the individual wave

5. In double slit experiment, the two slits are illuminated with two independent identical sources of light. What happens to the interference pattern?
(a) No interference pattern is produced
(b) The intensity of bright fringes gets doubled
(c) The intensity of bright fringes becomes four times
(d) Two sets of interference patterns are produced

6. Two waves have intensities in the ratio of 1:9. If these waves produce interference, then the ratio of maximum and minimum intensities is
(a) 3 : 1 (b) 4 : 1
(c) 9 : 1 (d) 16 : 1

7. When light wave suffers reflection at the interface between air and glass, the change of phase of the reflected wave is equal to
(a) zero (b) $\frac{\pi}{2}$
(c) π (d) 2π

8. Colours of thin films are due to
(a) dispersion of light (b) interference of light
(c) absorption of light (d) scattering of light

9. The phenomenon of interference is shown by
(a) longitudinal mechanical waves only
(b) transverse mechanical waves only
(c) non-mechanical transverse waves only
(d) All the above types of wave

10. Young's experiment established that
(a) light consists of waves
(b) light consists of particle
(c) light consists of neither particle nor wave
(d) light consists of both particle and wave

Level II

1. If a torch is used in place of mono chromatic light in young's experiment what will happen
(a) fringe will appear for moment then it will disappear
(b) fringes will or occur as from monochromatic light
(c) only bright fringes will appear
(d) No fringes will appear

2. In the interference pattern, energy is
(a) created at the position of maxima
(b) destroyed at the position of minima
(c) conserved but is redistributed
(d) None of the above

3. In Young's double slit interference experiment, the slit separation is made 3 fold. The fringe width becomes
(a) 1/3 times (b) 1/9 times
(c) 3 times (d) 9 times

4. The Young's experiment is performed with the lights of blue ($\lambda = 4360$ Å) and green colour ($\lambda = 5460$ Å), if the distance of the 4th fringe from the centre is x, then
(a) x (Blue) $= x$ (Green)
(b) x (Blue) $> x$ (Green)
(c) x (Blue) $< x$ (Green)
(d) $\frac{x(\text{Blue})}{x(\text{Gree})} = \frac{5460}{4360}$

5. In Young's double slit experiment with slit separation d, a monochromatic light of wavelength λ is used. The angular separation of the fringes is
(a) $\frac{d}{\lambda}$ (b) $\frac{\lambda}{d}$
(c) $\frac{2\lambda}{d}$ (d) $\frac{\lambda}{2d}$

6. In a Young's double slit experiment, the central point on the screen is
(a) bright
(b) dark
(c) first bright and then dark
(d) first dark and then bright

7. Young's experiment is performed in air and then performed in water, the fringe width
(a) will remain same
(b) will decrease
(c) will increase
(d) will be infinite

8. In Young's double slit experiment, if one of the slits is closed fully, then in the interference pattern
(a) a bright slit will be observed, no interference pattern will exist
(b) the bright fringes will become more bright
(c) the bright fringes will become fainter
(d) None of the above

9. In Young's double slit experiment, a glass plate is placed before a slit which absorbs half the intensity of light. Under this case
(a) the brightness of fringes decreases
(b) the fringe width decreases
(c) no fringes will be observed
(d) the bright fringes become fainter and the dark fringes have finite light intensity

10. In Young's experiment, the distance, between the slits is reduced to half and the distance between the slit and screen is doubled, then the fringe width
(a) will not change (b) will become half
(c) will be doubled (d) will become four times

11. In an interference experiment, the spacing between successive maxima or minima is
(a) $\frac{\lambda d}{D}$ (b) $\frac{\lambda D}{d}$ (c) $\frac{dD}{\lambda}$ (d) $\frac{\lambda d}{4D}$

12. In Young's experiment, one slit is covered with a blue filter and the other (slit) with a yellow filter. Then, the interference pattern
(a) will be blue (b) will be yellow
(c) will be green (d) will not be formed

13. Two sources give interference pattern which is observed on a screen, D distance apart from the sources. The fringe width is $2w$. If the distance D is now doubled, the fringe width will
(a) become $\frac{w}{2}$ (b) remain the same
(c) become w (d) become $4w$

14. In Young's double slit experiment, if the widths of the slits are in the ratio 4 : 9, the ratio of the intensity at maxima to the intensity at minima will be
(a) 169 : 25 (b) 81 : 16 (c) 25 : 1 (d) 9 : 4

15. In Young's double slit experiment, when wavelength used is 6000 and the screen is 40 cm from the slits, the fringes are 0.012 cm wide. What is the distance between the slits?
(a) 0.024 cm (b) 2.4 cm
(c) 0.24 cm (d) 0.2 cm

Answers

Level I

1. (c) **2.** (d) **3.** (d) **4.** (d) **5.** (a) **6.** (b) **7.** (c) **8.** (b) **9.** (d) **10.** (a)

Level II

1. (d) **2.** (c) **3.** (a) **4.** (b) **5.** (b) **6.** (a) **7.** (b) **8.** (a) **9.** (d) **10.** (d)
11. (b) **12.** (d) **13.** (d) **14.** (c) **15.** (d)

Hints and Solutions

Level II

1. If we use torch light in place of monochromatic light then overlapping of fringe pattern take place. Hence, no fringe will appear.

3. $\beta \propto \frac{1}{d} \Rightarrow$ If d becomes thrice, then β becomes $\frac{1}{3}$ times.

4. Distance of nth bright fringe $y_n = \frac{n\lambda D}{d}$, *i.e.,* $y_n \propto \lambda$

$$\therefore \quad \frac{x_{n_1}}{x_{n_2}} = \frac{\lambda_1}{\lambda_2}$$

$$\Rightarrow \quad \frac{x(\text{Blue})}{x(\text{Green})} = \frac{4360}{5460}$$

$$\therefore \quad x(\text{Green}) > x(\text{Blue})$$

5. Fringe width, $\beta = \frac{\lambda D}{d}$

Angular separation of the fringes is $\theta = \frac{\beta}{D} = \frac{\lambda D}{dD} = \frac{\lambda}{d}$

6. In the normal adjustment of Young's double slit experiment, path difference between the waves at central location is always zero. So, maxima is obtained at central position.

8. If one of slits is closed, then interference fringes are not formed on the screen but a fringe pattern is observed due to diffraction from slit.

10. $\beta = \frac{\lambda D}{d} \Rightarrow$ If D becomes twice and d becomes half, so β becomes four times.

12. For interference, λ of both the waves must be same.

13. $\beta \propto D$

14. Slit width ratio = 4 : 9

Hence, $I_1 : I_2 = 4 : 9$

$$\therefore \quad \frac{a_1^2}{a_2^2} = \frac{4}{9} \quad \Rightarrow \quad \frac{a_1}{a_2} = \frac{2}{3}$$

$$\therefore \quad \frac{I_{max}}{I_{min}} = \frac{(a_1 + a_2)^2}{(a_1 - a_2)^2} = \frac{25}{1}$$

15. $\beta = \frac{\lambda D}{d}$

$$\Rightarrow \quad d = \frac{\lambda D}{\beta} = \frac{6000 \times 10^{-10} \times (40 \times 10^{-2})}{0.012 \times 10^{-2}} = 0.2 \text{ cm}$$

51

Nuclear Fission and Fusion Reaction

Nuclear Fission

It is the process in which a heavy nucleus ($A > 230$) when excited gets split up into two smaller nuclei of nearly comparable masses. *e.g.*,

$$^{235}_{92}\text{U} + {}^{1}_{0}n \longrightarrow {}^{141}_{56}\text{Ba} + {}^{92}_{36}\text{Kr} + 3{}^{1}_{0}n + Q$$

Nuclear Reaction

It is a reaction which involves the change of stable nucleus of one element into the nucleus of another element.

RELATED TERMS

Thermal Neutrons These are the slow moving neutrons of energy 0.0253 eV, corresponding to the velocities of 2200 ms^{-1}.

Multiplication Factor The multiplication factor of a fissionable mass is defined as the ratio of the number of neutrons present at the beginning of a particular generation to the number of neutrons present at the beginning of the previous generation.

If $k > 1$, the chain reaction grows.

If $k = 1$, the chain reaction remains steady.

If $k < 1$, the chain reaction gradually dies out.

Critical Size and Critical Mass The size of the fissionable material for which multiplication factor is unity is called critical size and its mass is called critical mass of the material. The chain reaction in this case remains steady or sustained.

Thermonuclear Fusion

It is the process of fusion of two smaller nuclei into a heavier nucleus with the liberation of large amount of energy. *e.g.*,

$$^{2}_{1}\text{H} + {}^{2}_{1}\text{H} \longrightarrow {}^{4}_{2}\text{He} + 24\ \text{MeV}$$

These reactions require the extreme conditions of temperature and pressure, so that the reacting nuclei can overcome their electrostatic repulsion. For this reason, these reactions are called thermonuclear reactions.

Natural Radioactivity

It is the phenomenon of the spontaneous emission of α-, -β or γ-radiations from the nuclei of naturally occurring isotopes.

Artificial or Induced Radioactivity

It is the phenomenon of inducing radioactivity in certain stable nuclei by bombarding them by suitable high energy particles.

RELATED TERMS

Becquerel It is the SI unit of activity and is defined as the decay rate of one disintegration per second.

1 becquerel = 1 BQ = 1 decay/s

Curie One curie is the decay rate of 3.7×10^{10} disintegrations per second.

1 Ci (curie) = 3.70×10^{10} disintegrations/s

Rutherford One rutherford is the decay rate of 10^6 disintegrations per second.

1 Rd (rutherford) = 10^6 disintegrations/s

Nuclear Reactor

It is a device that can initiate a self-sustaining controlled chain reaction of a fissionable material. They are used at nuclear power plants for generating electricity and in propulsion of ships.

Key Components of Nuclear Reactor

Nuclear Fuel It is a material that can be burned by nuclear fission or fusion to derive nuclear energy. The common fuels used in nuclear reactor are ^{233}U, ^{235}U, ^{239}Pu etc. Uranium oxide pellets are inserted end-to-end into long hollow metal tubes constituting the fuel rods. When slow neutrons interact with the fuel, the fission starts and the energy is released.

Nuclear Reactor Core It is the portion of a nuclear reactor containing the nuclear fuel components where the nuclear reaction takes place.

Moderator It is a medium to slow down the fast moving secondary neutrons produced during the fission, *i.e.*, reduces the speed of fast neutrons. Heavy water, graphite, deuterium, paraffins etc., acts as moderator. It produces a slow moving thermal neutron.

Control Rods It is used in nuclear reactors to control the rate of fission of uranium and plutonium. They are made of chemical elements capable of absorbing many neutrons without fissioning themselves such as silver, indium and cadium. They are also called safety rods.

Coolant It is a fluid which flows through or around a device to prevent its overheating, transferring the heat produced by the device to other device that use or dissipate it.

Shielding The whole reactor is protected with concrete walls which are 2 to 2.5 m thick, so that the radiations emitted during nuclear reaction may not produce harmful effects on the persons working on the reactor.

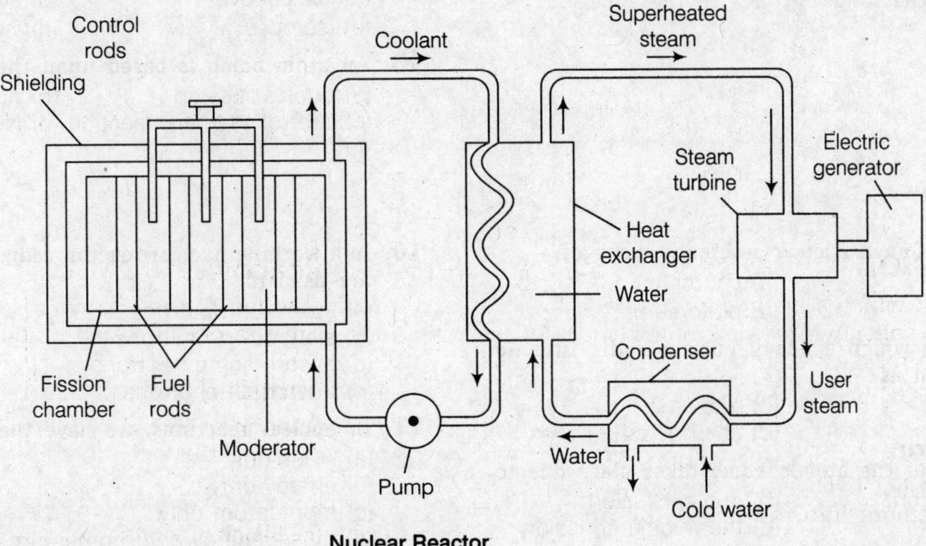

Nuclear Reactor

Thermal Reactor and Breeder Reactor

The nuclear reactors in which energy is produced by the fission of U^{235} by slow moving neutrons, are called thermal reactors.

The nuclear reactors in which energy is produced by the fission of Pu^{239} or U^{233}, are called breeder reactors. Pu^{239} is produced from U^{238} and U^{233} is produced from Th^{235}.

Practice Questions

Level I

1. Atomic power plant works on the principle of
(a) fission
(b) fusion
(c) thermal combustion
(d) combined effect of all the three

2. Which one of the following is not a radioactive element?
(a) Uranium (b) Thorium
(c) Radium (d) Cadmium

3. In nuclear reaction, there is conservation of
(a) mass only
(b) energy only
(c) momentum only
(d) mass, energy and momentum

4. What was the fissionable material used in the bomb dropped at Nagasaki (Japan) in the year 1945?
(a) Uranium (b) Plutonium
(c) Neptunium (d) None of these

5. In any fission process, the ratio $\frac{\text{Mass of fission products}}{\text{Mass of parent nucleus}}$ is
(a) greater than 1
(b) equal to 1
(c) less than 1
(d) depends on the mass of the parent nucleus

6. Enriched uranium is better as a fuel for a nuclear reactor because it has greater proportion of
(a) ^{233}U (b) ^{235}U (c) ^{238}U (d) ^{239}U

7. Hydrogen bomb is based upon the principle of
(a) nuclear fission
(b) nuclear fusion
(c) controlled nuclear fission
(d) None of the above

8. The main source of solar energy is
(a) nuclear fission (b) nuclear fusion
(c) combustion (d) None of these

9. Which of the following nuclei undergo fission when struck by thermal neutrons?
(a) U^{235} (b) U^{238}
(c) Pu^{239} (d) None of thsese

10. The equation given below shows the disintegration of the radioactive isotope of hydrogen
$^3_1T \longrightarrow\ ^3_2He + X$
Which one of the following is X in the equation?
(a) Electron
(b) Deutron
(c) Neutron
(d) Positron

11. A nuclear reactor harnesses nuclear energy by
(a) nuclear fusion
(b) spontaneous fission
(c) uncontrolled chain reaction
(d) controlled chain reaction

12. If a U-238 nucleus splits into two identical parts, the two nuclei so produced will be
(a) radioactive (b) stable
(c) isotopes (d) isobars

13. An atom bomb is based upon the principle of
(a) nuclear fission (b) nuclear fusion
(c) controlled chain reaction (d) None of these

Level II

1. The control rod in a nuclear reactor is made of
(a) uranium (b) cadmium
(c) graphite (d) plutonium

2. The process by which a heavy nucleus splits into light nuclei is known as
(a) fission (b) α-decay
(c) fusion (d) chain reaction

3. The explosion of the atomic bomb takes place due to
(a) nuclear fission (b) nuclear fusion
(c) scattering (d) thermionic emission

4. In nuclear reaction $_2He^4 + {}_zX^A \rightarrow {}_{z+2}Y^{A+3} + A$, A denotes
(a) electron (b) positron
(c) proton (d) neutron

5. Energy generation in stars is mainly due to
(a) chemical reactions (b) fission of heavy nuclei
(c) fusion of light nuclei (d) fusion of heavy nuclei

6. Which of the following is the fusion reaction
(a) $_1H^2 + {}_1H^2 \rightarrow {}_2He^4$
(b) $_0n^1 + {}_7N^{14} \rightarrow {}_6C^{14} + {}_1H^1$
(c) $_0n^1 + {}_{92}U^{238} \rightarrow {}_{93}Np^{239} + \beta^{-1} + \gamma$
(d) $_1H^3 \rightarrow {}_2He^3 + \beta^{-1} + \gamma$

7. If the speed of light were 2/3 of its present value, the energy released in a given atomic explosion will be decreased by a fraction
(a) 2/3 (b) 4/9 (c) 3/4 (d) 5/9

8. Why high temperature is required for fusion reaction?
(a) At high temperature, kinetic energy is sufficient to overcome repulsive force
(b) Atoms are ionised at high temperature
(c) Molecules break up at high temperature
(d) Nuclei break up at high temperature

9. During the nuclear fusion reaction,
(a) a heavy nucleus breaks into two fragments by itself
(b) a light nucleus bombarded by thermal neutrons breaks up
(c) a heavy nucleus bombarded by thermal neutrons breaks up
(d) two light nuclei combine to give a heavier nucleus and possibly other products

10. In a working nuclear reactor, cadmium rods (control rods) are used to
(a) speed up neutrons
(b) slow down neutrons
(c) absorb some neutrons
(d) absorb all neutrons

11. In nuclear reactions, we have the conservation of
(a) mass only
(b) energy only
(c) momentum only
(d) mass, energy and momentum

12. Fast neutrons can easily be slowed down by
(a) the use of lead shielding
(b) passing them through water
(c) elastic collisions with heavy nuclei
(d) applying a strong electric field

13. The mass equivalent of 931 MeV energy is
(a) 1.66×10^{-27} kg
(b) 6.02×10^{-24} kg
(c) 1.66×10^{-20} kg
(d) 6.02×10^{-27} kg

14. A chain reaction is continuous due to
(a) large mass defect
(b) large energy
(c) production of more neutrons in fission
(d) None of the above

15. Complete the equation for the following fission process $_{92}U^{235} + {}_0n^1 \rightarrow {}_{38}Sr^{90} + \ldots$
(a) $_{54}Xe^{143} + 3\ {}_0n^1$ (b) $_{54}Xe^{145}$
(c) $_{57}Xe^{142}$ (d) $_{54}Xe^{142} + {}_0n^1$

16. Boron rods in nuclear reactor are used as a
(a) moderator
(b) control rods
(c) coolants
(d) protective shield

17. In an atomic bomb, the energy is released due to
(a) chain reaction of neutrons and $_{92}U^{235}$
(b) chain reaction of neutrons and $_{92}U^{238}$
(c) chain reaction of neutrons and $_{92}P^{240}$
(d) chain reaction of neutrons and $_{92}U^{236}$

Answers

Level I

1. (a)	**2.** (d)	**3.** (d)	**4.** (b)	**5.** (c)	**6.** (b)	**7.** (b)	**8.** (b)	**9.** (c)	**10.** (a)
11. (d)	**12.** (b)	**13.** (a)							

Level II

1. (b)	**2.** (a)	**3.** (a)	**4.** (d)	**5.** (c)	**6.** (a)	**7.** (b)	**8.** (a)	**9.** (d)	**10.** (c)
11. (d)	**12.** (b)	**13.** (a)	**14.** (c)	**15.** (a)	**16.** (b)	**17.** (a)			

Hints and Solutions

Level II

4. The given equation is ${}_2He^4 + {}_ZX^A \to {}_{Z+2}Y^{A+3} + A$

Applying charge and mass conservation,

$$4 + A = A + 3 + x \Rightarrow x = 1$$

$$\Rightarrow \quad 2 + Z = Z + 2 + n \Rightarrow n = 0$$

Hence, A is a neutron.

5. Energy of stars is due to the fusion of light hydrogen nuclei into He. In this process, much energy is released.

6. ${}_1H^2 + {}_1H^2 \to {}_2He^4 + 24\,\text{MeV}$

7. Energy $\propto c^2$; $\therefore$ Decrease in energy $\propto \frac{4}{9}$.

8. For fusion high temperature of the order of 10^7 K to 10^8 K is required.

10. Cadmium rods absorb the neutrons, so they are used to control the chain reaction process.

11. No energy and mass enters or goes out of the system of the reaction and no external force is assumed to act.

12. Heavy water is used as moderators in nuclear reactions to slow down the neutrons.

13. $m = \frac{E}{c^2} = \frac{931 \times 1.6 \times 10^{-13}}{(3 \times 10^8)^2} = 1.66 \times 10^{-27}$ kg

14. Due to the production of neutrons, a chain of nuclear fission is established which continues until the whole of the source substance is consumed.

15. ${}_{92}U^{235} + {}_0n^1 \to {}_{38}Sr^{90} + {}_{54}Xe^{143} + 3\,{}_0n^1$.

52

Digital Electronics

Digital Circuit

Any circuit that responds to discrete value of input voltage and produce discrete output voltage level. Usually two levels are used, one as reference voltage as grounded or zero and another as supply voltage.

Logic Gate

There are number of questions which have only two answers either YES or NO. Similarly, there are number of objects which can remain in either two states only. As, electric bulb can either be ON or OFF.

Similarly, a diode can either be conducting or non-conducting for conducting state-1 (*i.e.*, ON) and for non-conducting state-0(*i.e.*, OFF) is provided. This is known as the logic gate of electronic circuit while state-1 and state-0 are the logic states.

There are following types of fundamental logic gates.

OR Gate

It is a digital circuit having two or more inputs but only one output. It gives a high output if either input A or B or both are high (1) otherwise it gives low output (0). It is described by Boolean expression, $A + B = Y$

Logic Symbol of OR Gate

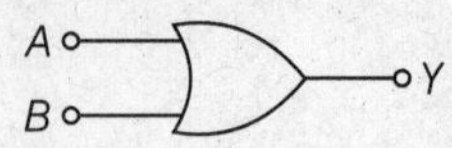

Truth Table of OR Gate

A	B	Y
0	0	0
0	1	1
1	0	1
1	1	1

AND Gate

It is a digital circuit having two or more inputs but only one output. It gives a high output (1) if inputs A and B are both high (1) otherwise it gives low output (0). It is described by the Boolean expression, $A \cdot B = Y$

Logic Symbol of AND Gate

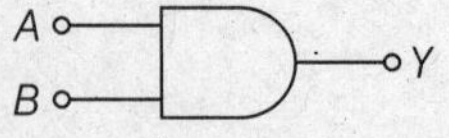

Truth Table of AND Gate

A	B	Y
0	0	0
0	1	0
1	0	0
1	1	1

NOT Gate

It is a digital circuit having only one input and one output. It gives a high output (1) if the input A is low (0) and *vice-versa*. It is described by the Boolean expression, $\overline{A} = Y$

Logic Symbol of NOT Gate

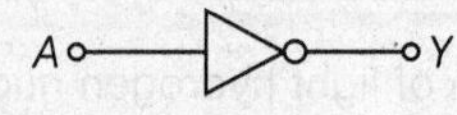

Truth Table of Not Gate

A	Y
0	1
1	0

NAND Gate

It is obtained by connecting the output of an AND gate to the input of a NOT gate. Its input is high if both inputs A and B are not high. It is described by the Boolean expression, $\overline{A \cdot B} = Y$

Logic Symbol of NAND Gate

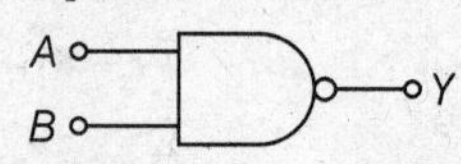

Truth Table of Nand Gate

A	B	Y
0	0	1
0	1	1
1	0	1
1	1	0

NOR Gate

It is obtained by connecting the output of an OR gate to the input of a NOR gate. Its output is high if neither input A nor input B is high. It is described by the Boolean expression, $\overline{A + B} = Y$

Logic Symbol of NOR Gate

A
B
Y

Truth Table of NOR Gate

A	B	Y
0	0	1
0	1	0
1	0	0
1	1	0

Decimal and Binary Number System

1. **Decimal Number System** In a decimal number system, we have ten digits, *i.e.*, 0, 1, 2, 3, 4, 5, 6, 7, 8, 9.
   A decimal number system has a base of ten (10).

e.g., 1971

$= 1000 + 900 + 70 + 1$

$= 1 \times 10^3 + 9 \times 10^2 + 7 \times 10^1 + 1 \times 10^0$

MSD LSD

LSD = Least significant digit

MSD = Most significant digit

2. **Binary Number System** A number system which has only two digits *i.e.,* 0 (Low) and 1 (High) is known as binary system. The base of binary number system is 2.
   (i) Each digit in binary system is known as a bit and a group of bits is known as a byte.
   (ii) The electrical circuit which operates only in these two states *i.e.,* (ON or High) and 0 (OFF or Low) are known as digital circuits.
3. **Decimal to Binary Conversion**
   (i) Divide the given decimal number by 2 and the successive quotients by 2 till the quotient becomes zero.
   (ii) The sequence of remainders obtained during divisions gives the binary equivalent of decimal number.
   (iii) The most significant digit (or bit) of the binary number, so obtained is the last remainder and the least significant digit (or bit) is the first remainder obtained during the division.

e.g., Binary equivalence of 61

		Remainder
2	61	
2	30	1 LSD
2	15	0
2	7	1
2	3	1
2	1	1
	0	1 MSD

$\Rightarrow (61)_{10} = (111101)_2$

4. **Binary to Decimal Conversion** The least significant digit in the binary number is the coefficient of 2 with power zero. As, we move towards the left side of LSD, the power of 2 goes on increasing.

e.g., $(11111100101)_2$

$$= 1 \times 2^{10} + 1 \times 2^9 + 1 \times 2^8 + 1 \times 2^7 + 1 \times 2^6 + 1 \times 2^5 + 0 \times 2^4 + 0 \times 2^3 + 1 \times 2^2 + 0 \times 2^1 + 1 \times 2^0$$

$= 2021$

Practice Questions

1. Which represents NAND gate?

(a) 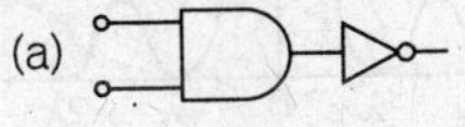
(b) 
(c) 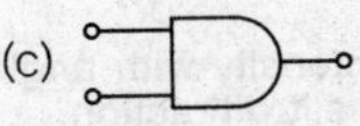
(d)

2. The given truth table is of

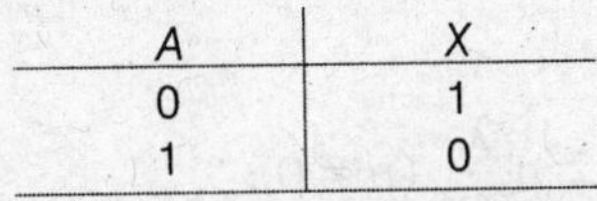

A	X
0	1
1	0

(a) OR gate (b) AND gate
(c) NOT gate (d) None of these

3. The Boolean equation of NOR gate is

(a) $C = A + B$ (b) $C = \overline{A + B}$
(c) $C = A \cdot B$ (d) $C = \overline{A \cdot B}$

4. This symbol represents

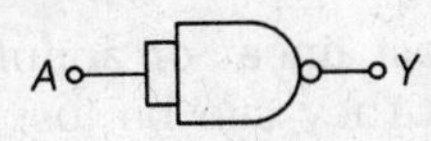

(a) NOT gate (b) OR gate
(c) AND gate (d) NOR gate

5. Which logic gate is represented by following diagram?

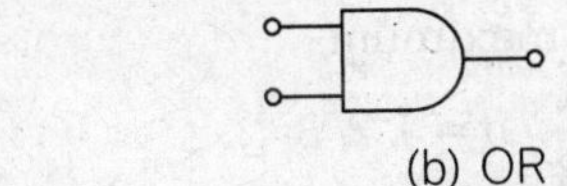

(a) AND (b) OR
(c) NOR (d) XOR

6. Symbol represents

(a) NAND gate
(b) NOR gate
(c) NOT gate
(d) XNOR gate

7. Boolean expression for OR gate is

(a) $A + B = Y$ (b) $A \cdot B = Y$
(c) $\overline{A \cdot B} = Y$ (d) $\overline{A + B} = Y$

8. Boolean expression for NAND gate is

(a) $\overline{A \cdot B} = Y$ (b) $A \cdot B = Y$
(c) $\overline{A + B} = Y$ (d) $A + B = Y$

9. Boolean expression for NOT gate is

(a) $Y = \overline{A \cdot B}$ (b) $A + B = Y$
(c) $\overline{A} = Y$ (d) None of these

Answers

1. (a)	2. (c)	3. (b)	4. (a)	5. (a)	6. (b)	7. (a)	8. (a)	9. (c)

53

Diffraction

Diffraction of Light

The phenomenon of bending of light around the corners of small obstacles or apertures and their consequent spreading into the regions of geometrical shadow is called diffraction of light.

Diffraction at a Single Slit

A plane wave of wavelength λ on passing through a narrow slit of width d suffers diffraction producing a central bright fringe ($\theta = 0°$), flanked on both sides by minima and maxima. The intensity of secondary maxima decreases with the increase in distance from the centre.

For nth minimum,

$d \sin\theta_n = n\lambda$, $n = 1, 2, 3, \ldots$

For nth secondary maximum,

$d \sin\theta_n = (2n+1)\dfrac{\lambda}{2}$, $n = 1, 2, 3, \ldots$

Angular position of nth minimum,

$$\theta_n = \frac{n\lambda}{d}$$

Distance of nth minimum from the centre of the screen, $x_n = n\dfrac{D\lambda}{d}$

Angular position of nth secondary maximum,

$$\theta'_n = (2n+1)\frac{\lambda}{2d}$$

Distance of nth secondary maximum from the centre of the screen,

$$x'_n = (2n+1)\frac{D\lambda}{2d}$$

Width of a secondary maximum, $\beta = \dfrac{D\lambda}{d}$

Width of central maximum, $\beta_0 = 2\beta = \dfrac{2D\lambda}{d}$

Angular spread of central maximum on either side of the centre of the screen is

$$\theta = \pm\frac{\lambda}{d}$$

Total angular spread of the central maximum is

$$2\theta = \frac{2\lambda}{d}$$

For diffraction to be more pronounced, the size of the slit should be comparable to the wavelength of light used.

Intensity Distribution Curve If we plot a graph between the intensities of maxima and minima against the diffraction angle θ, we get a graph of the type shown in figure. It has a broad central maximum in the direction ($\theta = 0°$) of incident light. On either side of the central maximum, it has secondary maxima of decreasing intensity at positions, $\theta = \pm(2n+1)\dfrac{\lambda}{2d}$

Varitation of intensity with angle θ in single slit diffraction.

and minima at positions, $\theta = \pm n\dfrac{\lambda}{d}$ $(n \neq 0)$.

The intensities of secondary maxima relating to the intensity of central maximum are in ratio,

$$1 : \frac{1}{21} : \frac{1}{61} : \frac{1}{121} \ldots$$

Thus, the intensity of the first secondary maximum is just 4% of that of the central maximum.

Limit of Resolution The smallest linear or angular separation between two point objects at which they can be just resolved by an optical instrument is called the limit of resolution of the instrument.

Resolving Power It is the ability of an optical instrument to resolve or separate the images of two nearby point objects, so that they can be distinctly seen. It is equal to the reciprocal of the limit of resolution of the optical instrument.

Diffraction as a Limit on Resolving Power All optical instruments like lens, telescope, microscope, etc., act as apertures. Light on passing through them undergoes diffraction. This puts the limit on their resolving power.

Rayleigh's Criterion for Resolution The images of two point objects are just resolved when the central maximum of the diffraction pattern of one falls over the first minimum of the diffraction pattern of the other.

Resolving Power of a Microscope The resolving power of a microscope is defined as the reciprocal of the smallest distance *d* between two point objects at which they can be just resolved when seen in the microscope.

$$\text{RP of a microscope} = \frac{1}{d} = \frac{2\mu \sin\theta}{\lambda}$$

Where, θ is half the angle of cone of light from each point object and μ is the refractive index of the medium between the object and the objective.

The factor $\mu \sin\theta$ is called Numerical Aperture (NA).

Resolving Power of a Telescope The resolving power of a telescope is defined as the reciprocal of the smallest angular separation $d\theta$ between two distant objects whose images can be just resolved by it.

$$\text{RP of a telescope} = \frac{1}{d\theta} = \frac{D}{1.22\lambda}$$

Where, *D* is the diameter of the telescope objective and λ is the wavelength of light used.

Resolving Power of the Human Eye The human eye can see two point objects distinctly if they subtend at the eye, an angle equal to one minute of arc. This angle is called the limit of resolution of the eye. The reciprocal of this angle equals the resolving power of the eye.

Practice Questions

Level I

1. The phenomenon of diffraction of light was discovered by

(a) Huygens (b) Newton (c) Fresnel (d) Grimaldi

2. Conditions of diffraction is

(a) $\frac{a}{\lambda} = 1$ (b) $\frac{a}{\lambda} >> 1$

(c) $\frac{a}{\lambda} << 1$ (d) None of these

3. The condition for obtaining secondary maxima in the diffraction pattern due to single slit is

(a) $a \sin\theta = n\lambda$ (b) $a \sin\theta = (2n-1)\frac{\lambda}{2}$

(c) $a \sin\theta = (2n-1)\lambda$ (d) $a \sin\theta = \frac{n\lambda}{2}$

4. The diffraction effect can be observed in

(a) sound waves
(b) light waves
(c) ultrasonic waves
(d) sound as well as light waves

5. The width of the diffraction band varies

(a) inversely as the wavelength
(b) directly as the width of the slit
(c) directly as the distance between the slit and the screen
(d) inversely as the size of the source from which the slit is illuminated

6. In the diffraction pattern of a straight slit

(a) all bands are uniformly bright
(b) all bands are uniformly wide
(c) central band is narrower
(d) central band is wider

7. In single slit diffraction pattern,

(a) central fringe has negligible width than others
(b) all fringes are of same width
(c) central fringes do not exist
(d) None of the above

8. The limit of resolution of an optical instrument arises on account of

(a) reflection (b) diffraction
(c) polarisation (d) interference

9. Red light is generally used to observe diffraction pattern from single slit. If blue light is used instead of red light, then diffraction pattern

(a) will be more clear (b) will contract
(c) will expanded (d) will not be visualised

10. In the experiment of diffraction at a single slit, if the slit width is decreased, the width of the central maximum

(a) increases both in Fresnel and Fraunhoffer diffraction
(b) decreases both in Fresnal and Fraunhoffer diffraction
(c) increases in Fresnel diffraction, but decreases in fraunhoffer diffraction
(d) decreases in Fresnel diffraction, but increases in Fraunhoffer diffraction

Level II

1. Consider Fraunhoffer diffraction pattern obtained with a single slit at normal incidence. At the angular position of first diffraction minimum, the phase difference between the wavelets from the opposite edges of the slit is

(a) $\pi/4$ (b) $\pi/2$ (c) π (d) 2π

2. The angular width of the central maximum of the diffraction pattern in a single slit (of width *a*) experiment, with λ as the wavelength of light is

(a) $\frac{3\lambda}{2a}$ (b) $\frac{\lambda}{2a}$ (c) $\frac{2\lambda}{a}$ (d) $\frac{\lambda}{a}$

3. In Fresnel diffraction, if the distance between the disc and the screen is decreased, the intensity of central bright spot will
(a) increase (b) decrease
(c) remain constant (d) None of these

4. The bending of beam of light around corners of obstacles is called
(a) reflection (b) diffraction
(c) refraction (d) interference

5. In the diffraction of light of wavelength λ through single slit of width d, the angle between the principal maxima and first minima will be
(a) $\frac{\lambda}{d}$ (b) $\frac{\lambda}{2d}$ (c) $\frac{\lambda}{4d}$ (d) $\frac{\pi}{2}$

6. A diffraction pattern is obtained using a beam of red light. What happens if the red light is replaced by blue light?
(a) No change
(b) Diffraction bands become narrower and crowded together
(c) Band become broader and farther apart
(d) Bands disappear altogether

7. Diffraction and interference of light suggest
(a) nature of light is electromagnetic
(b) wave nature
(c) nature is quantum
(d) nature of light is transverse

8. Diffraction effects are easier to notice in the case of sound waves than in the case of light waves because
(a) sound waves are longitudinal
(b) sound is perceived by the ear
(c) sound waves are mechanical waves
(d) sound waves are of longer wavelength

9. Direction of the first secondary maximum in the Fraunhoffer diffraction pattern at a single slit is given by (a is the width of the slit)
(a) $a\sin\theta = \frac{\lambda}{2}$ (b) $a\cos\theta = \frac{3\lambda}{2}$
(c) $a\sin\theta = \lambda$ (d) $a\sin\theta = \frac{3\lambda}{2}$

10. Angular width (β) of central maximum of a diffraction pattern on a single slit does not depend upon
(a) distance between slit and screen
(b) wavelength of light used
(c) width of the slit
(d) frequency of light used

11. A single slit of width 0.20 mm is illuminated with light of wavelength 500 nm. The observing screen is placed 80 cm from the slit. The width of the central bright fringe will be
(a) 1 mm (b) 2 mm
(c) 4 mm (d) 5 mm

Answers

Level I

1. (a)	2. (a)	3. (b)	4. (d)	5. (c)	6. (d)	7. (d)	8. (b)	9. (b)	10. (a)

Level II

1. (d)	2. (c)	3. (b)	4. (b)	5. (a)	6. (b)	7. (b)	8. (d)	9. (d)	10. (a)
11. (c)									

Hints and Solutions

Level I

9. $\lambda_{Blue} < \lambda_{Red}$. Therefore, fringe pattern will contract because fringe width $\propto \lambda$.

Level II

1. To have the first minimum, the path difference between the waves from A and B is $BD = \frac{a}{2} \cdot \sin\theta = \frac{\lambda}{2}$. The path difference between the waves from A and C at the same point should be λ or phase difference is 2π.

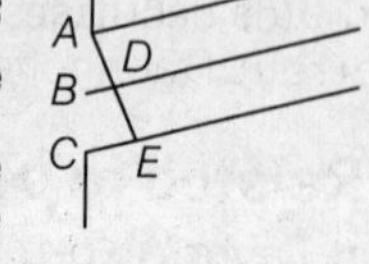

3. $A = n\pi d\lambda \Rightarrow nd = \frac{A}{\pi\lambda}$ = constant

$\Rightarrow n \propto \frac{1}{d}$ (n = Number of blocked HPZ)

On decreasing d, n increases, hence intensity decreases.

6. As, $\lambda_{Blue} < \lambda_{Red}$ and width of diffraction bands is directly proportional to λ, therefore diffraction bands become narrower and crowded.

9. For nth secondary maxima, path difference

$d\sin\theta = (2n+1)\frac{\lambda}{2} \Rightarrow a\sin\theta = \frac{3\lambda}{2}$

10. For single slit diffraction pattern, $d\sin\theta = \lambda$

($\because d$ = Slit width)

Angular width $= 2\theta = 2\sin^{-1}\left(\frac{\lambda}{d}\right)$

It is independent of D, *i.e.*, distance between screen and slit.

11. Width of central bright fringe

$$= \frac{2\lambda D}{d} = \frac{2 \times 500 \times 10^{-9} \times 80 \times 10^{-2}}{0.20 \times 10^{-3}} = 4 \times 10^{-3} \text{ m} = 4 \text{ mm}$$

54

Semiconductor and Devices

Materials

On the basis of its electrical nature, *materials are categorised in three types*

1. Conductor

It is that type of materials, which have number of free electrons to conduct the electricity. The metals are good conductor of electricity.

2. Insulator

It is that type of materials, which do not have the free electrons volume and hence it does not conduct the electricity at all. The free electrons are also known as conduction electrons.

The materials such as wood, plastic, rubber etc., are the insulators.

3. Semiconductor

It is that type of materials, which do not have free electrons at the normal temperature but has the free electrons at the increased temperature and hence behaves like a conductor. The whole electronic system is based on semiconductor devices. The materials such as Si, Ge, As etc., are the semiconductors.

The active elements are such as voltage source, current source, etc, while a battery, resistor, inductors etc., are the passive elements. There are two energy bands involved in the semiconductor activities, naming valence band and conduction band. A pure semiconductor is neither a *n*-type nor a *p*-type. Both *p*-type and *n*-type semiconductor is electrically neutral. *Semiconductor are of two types*

(i) Intrinsic Semiconductor

A semiconductor in its pure state is called intrinsic semiconductor. It is also known as undoped semiconductor. Germanium (Ge) and Silicon (Si) are the important examples of intrinsic semiconductor.

(ii) Extrinsic Semiconductor

A semiconductor doped with a suitable impurity to increase its conductivity, is called extrinsic semiconductor. On the basis of doped impurity, *extrinsic semiconductors are of two types*

(a) *n*-type Semiconductor Extrinsic semiconductor doped with pentavalent impurity like As, Sb, Bi etc., in which negatively charge electrons work as charge carrier, is called *n*-type semiconductor.

Every pentavalent impurity atom donate one electron in the crystal, therefore it is called a donor atom. In this, majority charge carriers are electrons and minority charge carriers are holes.

(b) *p*-type Semiconductor Extrinsic semiconductor doped with trivalent impurity like Al, B etc., in which positively charged holes works as charge carriers is called *p*-type semiconductor.

Every trivalent impurity atom has a tendency to accept one electron called as acceptor atom. In this, majority charge carriers are holes and minority charge carriers are electrons.

Doping

The process of adding impurities to semiconductor materials are called doping. It is done to increase the conductivity of semiconductors.

p-n Junction

When a semiconductor material such as silicon or germanium is doped with impurity in such a way that one side is doped with trivalent impurity and other side is doped with pentavalent impurity, we obtain a *p-n* junction.

It is used as a rectifier, which converts an alternating current into direct current.

Terms Related to *p-n* Junction

Depletion Layer At *p-n* junction, a region is created, where there is no charge carriers. This region is called depletion layer. The width of this region is of the order of 10^{-6} m.

Potential Barrier The potential difference across the depletion layer is called potential barrier. Potential barrier for Ge is 0.3 V and for Si is 0.7 V.

Forward Biasing In this biasing, the p-side is connected to positive terminal and n-side to negative terminal of a battery. In this biasing, forward current flows due to majority charge carriers. The width of depletion layer decreases.

Reverse Biasing In this biasing, the p-side is connected to negative terminal and n-side to positive terminal of a battery.

Breakdown Voltage When reverse bias voltage is continuously increased for a certain reverse voltage, then current through the p-n junction will increase abruptly. This reverse bias voltage is known as breakdown voltage.

Types of Junction Diode

LED (Light Emitting Diode)

It is a specially designed diode made of gallium-arsenide or gallium-indium phosphide, etc. when used in forward biased, it emits almost monochromatic light.

LEDs are used in electronic gadgets as indicator of light.

The symbol of a LED is shown in the figure.

p n

Zener Diode

It is a highly doped p-n junction diode, which is not damaged by high reverse current. It is always used in reverse bias in breakdown voltage region and is chiefly used as a voltage regulator. The symbol of Zener diode is shown in the figure

n p

Photo Diode

It is a special p-n junction diode fabricated with a transparent window to allow light to fall on the diode. It is used in reverse biasing. When light (photon of energy, $h\nu$ greater than the energy gap E_g) is incident on photodiode, electron-hole pairs are generated due to the absorption of photons.

Due to electric field of the junction, electrons and holes are separated before they recombine. Electrons are collected on n-side and holes are collected on p-side giving rise to an emf. If external circuit is completed using some load, a photocurrent flows.

The symbol of a photodiode is shown in the figure.

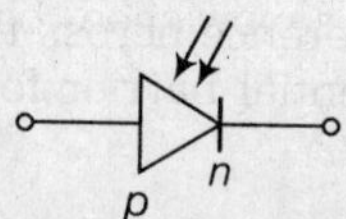

Transistor

A junction transistor is three terminal semiconductor device consisting of two p-n junctions formed by placing a thin layer of doped semiconductor (p-type or n-type) between two thick similar layers of opposite type. A transistor has three doped regions forming two p-n junction between them.

Transistors are of two types

1. n-p-n
2. p-n-p

A junction transistor is formed by sandwiching a thin layer of a p-type semiconductor between two layers of n-type semiconductor or by sandwiching a thin layer of n-type semiconductor between two layers of p-type semiconductor. There are three terminals in it, naming emitter (E), base (B) and collector (C). It is used as an amplifier in the circuits.

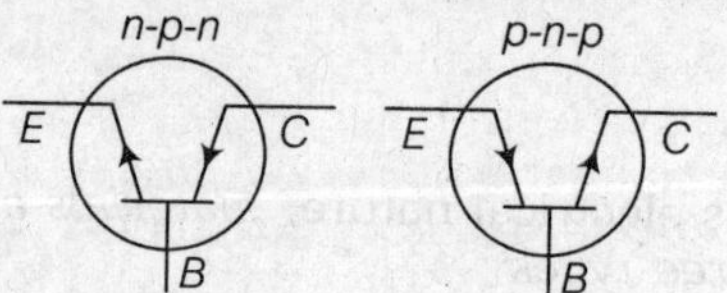

Transistor symbols

Note Diode valves and triode valves are used as rectifiers and amplifiers respectively.

Action of Transistor

When the emitted-base junction is forward biased, majority charge carriers are pushed from emitter to base. Few electrons and holes recombine in the base region. Most of the majority charge carriers cross over to the reversed biased collector. Collector current I_C is always slightly less than the emitter current.

$$I_E = I_C + I_B$$

Where, I_B is base current.

Three Configurations of a Transistor

A transistor can be used in one of the following three configurations

(i) Common base (CB) circuit

(ii) Common emitter (CE) circuit

(iii) Common collector (CC) circuit

Parameters of transistor in Common Base (CB) configuration

(a) Input Characteristics

$$\text{The input resistance, } R = \left(\frac{\Delta V_{\text{EB}}}{\Delta I_E}\right)_{V_{\text{CB}}}$$

(b) Output Characteristics

$$\text{The output resistance, } R_O = \left(\frac{\Delta V_{\text{CB}}}{\Delta I_C}\right)_{I_E}$$

(c) Current Amplification Factor

$$\text{AC current gain, } \alpha = \left(\frac{\Delta I_C}{\Delta I_B}\right)_{V_{\text{CB}}}$$

Parameters of transistor in Common Emitter (CE) configuration

(a) **Input Characteristics**

The input resistance, $R_i = \left(\frac{\Delta V_{EB}}{\Delta I_B}\right)_{V_{CE}}$

(b) **Output Characteristics**

The output resistance, $R_o = \left(\frac{\Delta V_{CB}}{\Delta I_C}\right)_{I_B}$

(c) **AC Current Gain**

$$\beta = \left(\frac{\Delta I_C}{\Delta I_B}\right)_{V_{CB}}$$

Transistor as an Amplifier

An amplifier is a circuit which is used for increasing the voltage, current or power of alternating form. A transistor operates as an amplifier when its emitter-base junction is forward biased, while collector-base junction is reverse biased. Transistor biased in this way is said to be in active state.

Common Base Transistor Amplifier

(i) **DC Current Gain** It is defined as the ratio of collector current to the emitter current.

$$\alpha_{DC} = \frac{I_C}{I_E}$$

(ii) **AC Current Gain** It is defined as the ratio of the small change in collector current to the small change in emitter current.

$$\alpha_{AC} = \frac{\Delta I_C}{\Delta I_E}$$

(iii) **Voltage Gain** It is defined as the ratio of the small change in output voltage to the small change in input voltage.

$$A_v = \frac{\Delta V_{CB}}{\Delta V_{EB}} = \frac{\Delta I_C \times R_o}{\Delta I_E \times R_i}$$

$$\Rightarrow \quad A_v = \alpha_{AC} \cdot \frac{R_o}{R_i} = A_i \times A_r$$

(iv) **Power Gain** It is defined as the ratio of output power to input power.

$$A_P = \frac{\Delta V_{CB}}{\Delta V_{EB}} \times \frac{\Delta Ic}{\Delta I_E}$$

$$= A_v \cdot A_i = A_V \cdot \alpha_{AC} = \alpha_{AC}^2 \cdot \frac{R_0}{R_i}$$

Practice Questions

Level I

1. In a p-type semiconductor, the majority charge carriers are

(a) electrons (b) holes
(c) neutrons (d) protons

2. The impurity atoms with which pure silicon should be dopped to make a p-type semiconductor are those of

(a) phosphorus (b) boron
(c) aluminium (d) (b) and (c)

3. If germanium has to be doped with a donor impurity, the foreign atom should be

(a) tetravalent (b) pentavalent
(c) trivalent (d) None of these

4. A hole in p-type semiconductor is

(a) an excess electron
(b) a missing electron
(c) a missing atom
(d) a donor level

5. An n-type semiconductor is formed

(a) when germanium crystal is doped with an impurity containing three valence electron
(b) when germanium crystal is doped with an impurity containing five valence electron
(c) from pure germinium
(d) from pure silicon

6. A typical example of a semiconductor is

(a) platinum (b) germinium
(c) quartz (d) mica

7. Resistance of a p-n function in forward bias is

(a) zero (b) low
(c) high (d) infinite

8. In an intrinsic semiconductor

(a) only electrons are responsible for the blow of current
(b) only holes are responsible for the blow of current
(c) both holes and electrons carry current and their number is the same
(d) None of the above

9. The reverse biassing in a p-n junction diode

(a) decreases the potential barrier
(b) increase the potential barrier
(c) increase the number of minority charge carriers
(d) increase the number of majority charge carries

10. A transistor is made of

(a) intrinsic semiconductors
(b) doped semiconductors
(c) a metal piece sandwiched between two intrinsic semiconductors
(d) None of the above

11. In a transistor, the base is
(a) an insulator
(b) a conductor of low resistance
(c) a conductor of high resistance
(d) an extrinsic semiconductor

12. In a transistor
(a) both the emitter and the collector are equally doped
(b) emitter is more heavily doped than the collector
(c) the base is made very thin and is lightly doped
(d) (b) and (c)

13. In a transistor,
(a) length of emitter is greater than that of collector
(b) length of collector is greater than that of emitter
(c) both collector and emitter have the same length
(d) None of the above

14. In a transistor, the emitter current is
(a) slightly more than the collector current
(b) slightly less than the collector current
(c) equal to the collector current
(d) equal to the base current

15. In the use of transistor as an amplifier
(a) the emitter-base junction is forward baised and the collector-base junction is reverse biased
(b) both the junctions are forward biased
(c) any of the two junctions may be forward biased
(d) None of the above

16. The positive charge carriers in semiconductor are
(a) positive ions
(b) protons
(c) positrons
(d) holes

Level II

1. When *n-p-n* transistor is used as an amplifier,
(a) electrons move from base to collector
(b) holes move from emitter to base
(c) electrons move from collector to base
(d) holes move from base to emitter

2. The phase difference between input and output voltages of a CE circuit is
(a) 0° (b) 90° (c) 180° (d) 270°

3. The emitter-base junction of a transistor is ...... biased while the collector-base junction is ...... biased.
(a) reverse, forward (b) reverse, reverse
(c) forward, forward (d) forward, reverse

4. In an *n-p-n* transistor the collector current is 24mA. If 80% of electrons reach collector its base current in mA is
(a) 36 (b) 26
(c) 16 (d) 6

5. In the case of constants α and β of a transistor
(a) $\alpha = \beta$ (b) $\beta < 1, \alpha > 1$
(c) $\alpha\,\beta = 1$ (d) $\beta > 1, \alpha < 1$

6. For a common base configuration of *p-n-p* transistor $\frac{I_C}{I_E} = 0.96$, then maximum current gain in common configuration will be
(a) 12 (b) 24
(c) 6 (d) 5

7. Least doped region in a transistor is
(a) either emitter or collector
(b) base
(c) emitter
(d) collector

8. The transistors provide good power amplification when they are used in
(a) common collector configuration
(b) common emitter configuration
(c) common base configuration
(d) None of the above

9. For a transistor the parameter $\beta = 99$. The value of the parameter α is
(a) 0.9 (b) 0.99
(c) 1 (d) 9

10. In a *p-n-p* transistor the base is the *n*-region. Its width relative to the *p*-region is
(a) smaller (b) larger
(c) same (d) not related

11. The symbol given in figure represents

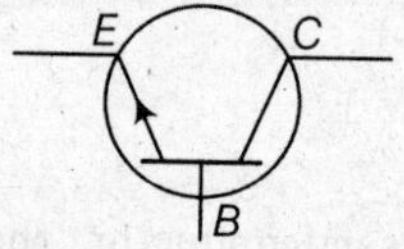

(a) *n-p-n* transistor
(b) *p-n-p* transistor
(c) forward biased *p-n* junction diode
(d) reverse biased *n-p* junction diode

12. For a transistor, in a common emitter arrangement, the alternating current gain β is given by
(a) $\beta = \left(\frac{\Delta I_C}{\Delta I_B}\right)_{V_C}$ (b) $\beta = \left(\frac{\Delta I_B}{\Delta I_C}\right)_{V_C}$
(c) $\beta = \left(\frac{\Delta I_C}{\Delta I_E}\right)_{V_C}$ (d) $\beta = \left(\frac{\Delta I_E}{\Delta I_C}\right)_{V_C}$

13. An *n-p-n* transistor having current gain of 50 is to be used to make an amplifier of power gain of 300. What will be the voltage gain of the amplifier?
(a) 8.5 (b) 6
(c) 4 (d) 3

14. The concentrations of impurities in a transistor are
(a) equal for the emitter, base and collector region
(b) least for the emitter region
(c) larger for the emitter region
(d) largest for the base region

15. In the CB mode of a transistor, when the collector voltage is changed by 0.5 volt. The collector current changes by 0.05 mA. The output resistance will be

(a) 10 kΩ (b) 20 kΩ
(c) 5 kΩ (d) 2.5 kΩ

16. Relation between α and β is

(a) $\beta = \frac{\alpha}{1-\alpha}$ (b) $\alpha = \frac{\beta}{1-\beta}$
(c) $\alpha = \frac{1-\beta}{\beta}$ (d) $\beta = \frac{1-\alpha}{\alpha}$

Answers

Level I

1. (b)	**2.** (d)	**3.** (b)	**4.** (b)	**5.** (b)	**6.** (b)	**7.** (b)	**8.** (c)	**9.** (b)	**10.** (b)
11. (d)	**12.** (d)	**13.** (b)	**14.** (a)	**15.** (a)	**16.** (d)				

Level II

1. (a)	**2.** (c)	**3.** (d)	**4.** (d)	**5.** (d)	**6.** (b)	**7.** (b)	**8.** (b)	**9.** (b)	**10.** (a)
11. (a)	**12.** (a)	**13.** (b)	**14.** (c)	**15.** (a)	**16.** (a)				

Hints and Solutions

Level II

3. The emitter-base junction is forward biased while collector base junction is reversed biased.

4. Given, $i_C = \frac{80}{100} \times i_E$

$\Rightarrow$ $24 = \frac{80}{100} \times i_E \Rightarrow i_E = 30\text{ mA}$

By using $i_E = i_B + i_C$

$\Rightarrow$ $i_B = 30 - 24 = 6\text{ mA}$

5. α is the ratio of collector current and emitter current, while β is the ratio of collector current and base current.

6. $\beta = \frac{\alpha}{1-\alpha} = \frac{0.96}{1-0.96} = 24$

7. In transistor, base is least doped.

9. $\alpha = \frac{\beta}{1+\beta} = \frac{99}{1+99} = 0.99$

13. Power gain = Voltage gain × Current gain

$\text{Voltage gain} = \frac{\text{Power gain}}{\text{Current gain}} = \frac{300}{50} = 6$

15. Here,

$\Delta V_C = 0.5\text{V}, \Delta i_C = 0.05\text{ mA} = 0.05 \times 10^{-3}\text{ A}$

Output resistance is given by

$$R_{out} = \frac{\Delta V_C}{\Delta i_C} = \frac{0.5}{0.05 \times 10^{-3}} = 10^4\ \Omega = 10\text{ k}\Omega$$

Communication

Communication System

The act of transmission and reception of information from one place to another place is called communication. Historically, it may be noted that

- Long distance communication started with the advent of telegraphy and the first telegraph cable for USA-Europe communication link came up in 1850.
- Marconi was the first to establish radio transmission in 1901. The famous Indian physicist JC Bose made significant contributions in this field.
- Coast to Coast telephone service in USA started in the year 1915. Coaxial cables with multiple channel were laid in 1941.
- Satellite communication started in 1962 with the launching of Telstar satellite. The first geostationary satellite, Early Bird was launched in 1965.
- Optical fibre communication started in USA in the year 1970. Transatlantic optical fibre cables were laid in 1988. Since then, the entire field of communication has been revolutionised.

Types of Communication System

A communication system contains three main parts

1. Transmitter

It process and encode the information and make it suitable for transmission. The message signal for communication can be analog signals or digital signals. An analog signal can be converted suitably into a digital signal and *vice-versa*. An analog signal, in which current or voltage value varies continuously with time. A digital signal is a discontinuous function of time such a signal is usually in the form of pulses.

2. Receiver

It receives and decode the signal. *The block diagram of a generalised communication system is shown below*

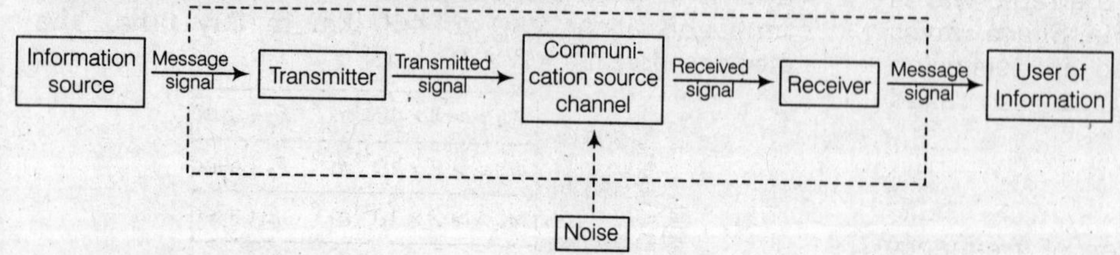

3. Communication Channel

The medium, through which information propagate from transmitter to receiver is called communication channel.

Terms Used in Communication System

Transducer

Any device, that converts physical signal into electrical signal, is called a transducer. *e.g.,* A microphone converts speech signals into electrical signals.

Noise

The disturbance or distortion in the transmission and processing of message signals in a communication is referred as noise.

Attenuation

The loss of strength of a signal during its propagation through the communication channel, is referred as attenuation.

Amplification

The process of increasing the strength of the transmitted signal using some suitable electronic circuit is called amplification.

Range

It is the largest distance between the transmitter and receiver, where the signal is received with high strength.

Bandwidth

It refers usually to the range of frequencies over which, the communication system works.

Repeater

It is a combination of receiver, amplifier and transmitter. Its function is to extend the range of communication.

Propagation of Electromagnetic Waves

In radio wave communication between two places, the electromagnetic waves are radiated out by the transmitter antenna at one place, which travel through the space and reach the receiving antenna at the other place.

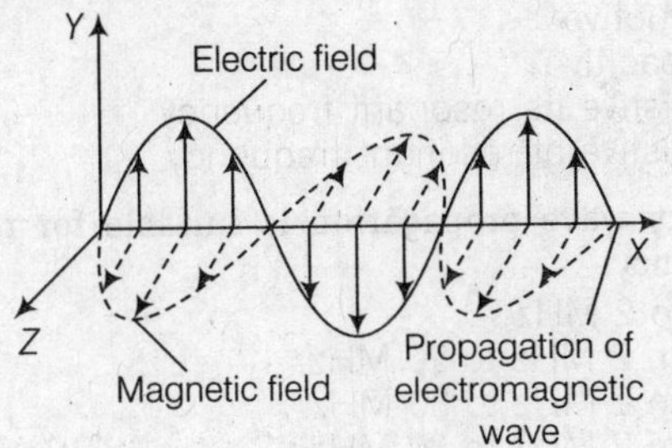

Types of Propagation of Electromagnetic Waves

Ground Wave Propagation

In ground wave propagation, the radio waves (AM) travel along the surface of Earth. These waves are called ground waves or surface waves. Infact, these waves are not confined to surface of the Earth but are guided along the Earth's surface and they follow the curvature of the Earth.

The ground wave propagation is used for low frequency (LF) band and medium frequency band (*i.e.,* 2 MHz) but not for high frequency (HF) band. It is used for local broadcasting.

Sky Wave Propagation

Sky waves are the AM radio waves, which are received after being reflected from ionosphere. The propagation of radiowaves signals from one point to another *via* reflection from ionosphere is known as sky wave propagation. It is suitable for radio waves of frequency between 2 to 30 MHz. It is used for a long distance (*i.e.,* 65 to 400 km) radio communication.

Space Wave Propagation

It is the method of wave propagation in which the radio waves emitted from the transmitter antenna, reaches the receiving antenna through space. These radio waves are called space waves. The space waves are the radio waves of frequency range from 54 MHz to 4.2 GHz. Space waves travel in straight lines. These are used in television communication and radar communication. It is also called Line of Sight Communication (Los).

Microwave Propagation

- Microwaves are electromagnetic waves of frequency 1 to 300 GHz, greater than those of TV signals. The wavelength of microwaves is of the order of a few mm.
- Microwave communication is used in radar to locate the flying objects in space.
- These waves can be transmitted as beam signals in a particular direction, much better than radio waves.
- There is no diffraction of microwaves around corners of an obstacle which happens to lie along its passage.

Earth's Atmosphere

The gaseous envelope surrounding the Earth is called Earth's atmosphere.

It contains the following layers

1. Troposphere

This region extends upto a height of 12 km from the Earth's surface.

2. Stratosphere

This region extends from 12 to 50 km. In this region, most of the atmospheric ozone is concentrated from 30 to 50 km. This layer is called ozone layer.

3. Mesosphere

This region extends from 50 to 80 km.

4. Ionosphere

This region extends from 80 to 400 km. In ionosphere, the electron density is very large in a region beyond 110 km from Earth's surface, which extends vertically for a few kilometres. This layer is called Kennelly Heaviside layer. In ionosphere, a layer having large electron density is found at height 250 km from the Earth's surface, called appleton layer.

Layers of Earth's Atmosphere

There are four main layers in the Earth's atmosphere having high density of electrons and positive ions, produced due to ionisation by the high energy particles coming from sun the star or cosmos.

These layers play their effective role in space communication. These layers are D, E, F_1 and F_2.

D-layer is at a virtual height of 65 km from surface of the Earth and having electron density $\approx 10^9 \text{ m}^{-3}$.

E-layer is at a virtual height of 100 km from the surface of Earth, and having electron density $\approx 2 \times 10^{11} \text{ m}^{-3}$.

F_1-layer is at a virtual height of 180 km from the surface of the Earth, having electron density $\approx 3 \times 10^{11} \text{ m}^{-3}$.

F_2-layer is at a vertical height of about 300 km in night time and about 250 to 400 km in day time. The electron density $\approx 8 \times 10^{11} \text{ m}^{-3}$.

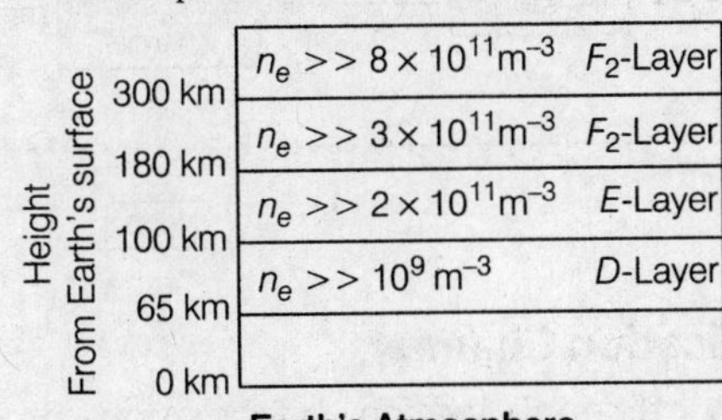

Earth's Atmosphere

 Practice Questions

1. **The waves relevant to telecommunications are**
(a) visible light (b) infrared
(c) ultraviolet (d) microwave

2. **Modem is a device used for**
(a) modulating signals
(b) converting analog signals to digital signals
(c) Either of the above
(d) None of the above

3. **Modern communication systems use**
(a) analog circuits
(b) digital circuits
(c) combination of analog and digital circuits
(d) None of the above

4. **For television broadcasting the frequency employed is normally**
(a) 30-300 MHz (b) 30-300 GHz
(c) 30-300 kHz (d) 30-300 Hz

5. **The audio signal**
(a) can be sent directly over the air for distance
(b) cannot be sent directly over the air for large distance
(c) possess very high frequency
(d) None of the above

6. **The absorption of radio waves by the atmosphere depends on**
(a) their distance from the transmitter
(b) the polarisation of the wave
(c) their frequency
(d) the polarisation of the atmosphere

7. **Radio wave of constant amplitude can be generated with**
(a) filter (b) rectifier
(c) FET (d) oscillator

8. **The space waves which are affected seriously by atmospheric conditions are**
(a) MFO (b) HF (c) VHF (d) UHF

9. **Which of the following is not transducer?**
(a) Loudspeaker (b) Amplifier
(c) Microphone (d) All of these

10. **Antenna is**
(a) inductive
(b) capacitive
(c) resistive its resonant frequency
(d) resistive at resonant frequency

11. **The sky wave propagation is suitable for radio waves of frequency**
(a) upto 2 MHz
(b) from 2 MHz to 20 MHz
(c) from 2 MHz to 30 MHz
(d) from 2 MHz to 80 MHz

12. **Long distance short wave radio broadcasting uses**
(a) ground wave
(b) ionospheric wave
(c) direct wave
(d) sky wave

13. **Through which mode of propagation the radiowaves can be sent from one place to another**
(a) ground wave propagation
(b) sky wave propagation
(c) space wave propagation
(d) All of the above

14. **Communication system may be**
(a) electrical (b) electronic
(c) optical (d) Any of these

15. **Short wave band are used for transmission of radio waves to a large distance because short waves are reflected from**
(a) ionosphere
(b) lithosphere
(c) troposphere
(d) None of the above

Answers

1. (d)	**2.** (b)	**3.** (b)	**4.** (a)	**5.** (b)	**6.** (c)	**7.** (d)	**8.** (d)	**9.** (b)	**10.** (a)
11. (c)	**12.** (b)	**13.** (d)	**14.** (d)	**15.** (a)					

56

Human Eye

Human Eye

The human eye has been called the most complex organ in our body. It's amazing that something so small can have so many working parts.

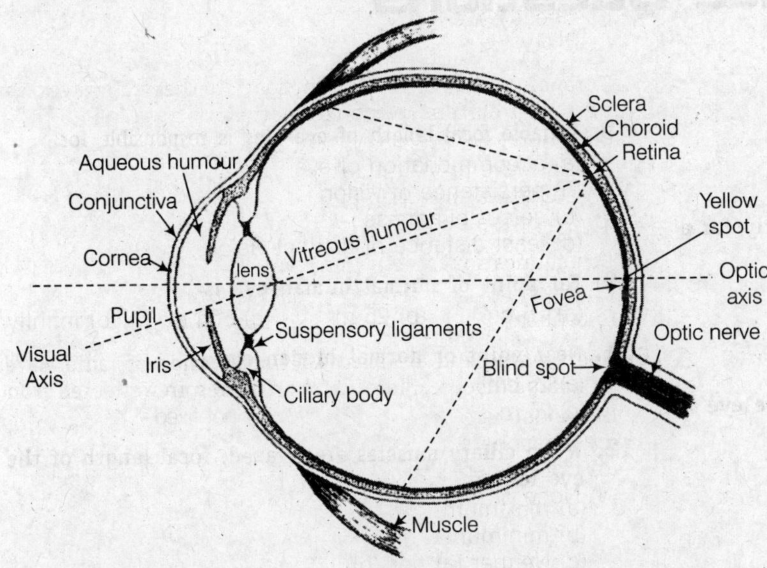

There are many part of human eye which are given below

Eye Lens Overall behaves as a convex lens of $\mu = 1.437$.

Retina Real and inverted, image of an object, obtained at retina, brain sense it erect.

Yellow Spot It is the most sensitive part, the image formed at yellow spot is brightest.

Blind Spot Optic nerves go to brain through blind spot. It is not sensitive for light.

Ciliary Muscles Eye lens is fixed between these muscles. It's both radius of curvature can be changed by applying pressure on it through ciliary muscles.

Power of Accommodation The ability of eye to see near objects as well as far objects is called power of accommodation.

Range of Vision For healthy eye it is 25 cm (near point) to ∞ (far point).

A normal eye can see the objects, clearly only if they are at a distance greater than 25 cm. This distance is called least distance of distinct vision and is represented by *D*.

Persistence of Vision It is 1/10 s *i.e.,* if time interval between two consecutive light pulses is lesser than 0.1 s, eye cannot distinguish them separately.

Binocular Vision The seeing with two eyes is called binocular vision.

Resolving Limit The minimum angular separation between two objects, so that they are just resolved is called resolving limit. For eye it is $1' = \left(\frac{1}{60}\right)^{\circ}$.

Defects of Vision

Myopia or Short Sightedness

It is a defect of eye due to which a person can see near by objects clearly but cannot see far away objects clearly.

In this defect, the far point of eye shifts from infinity to a nearer distance.

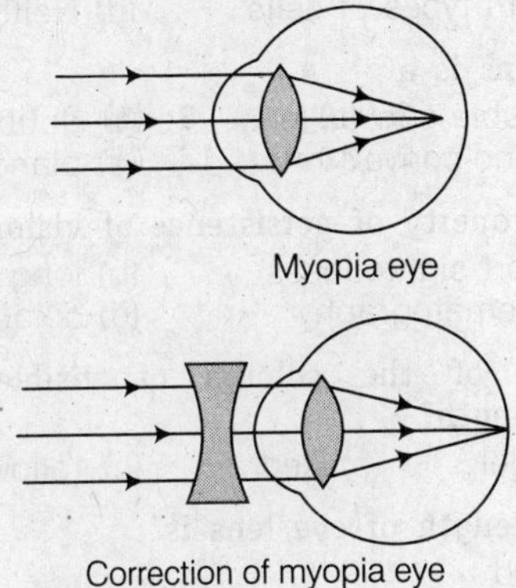

Note This defect can be removed by using a concave lens of appropriate power.

Hypermetropia or Long Sightedness

It is a defect of eye due to which a person can see far away objects clearly but cannot see nearby objects clearly.

In this defect, the near point of eye shifts away from the eye.

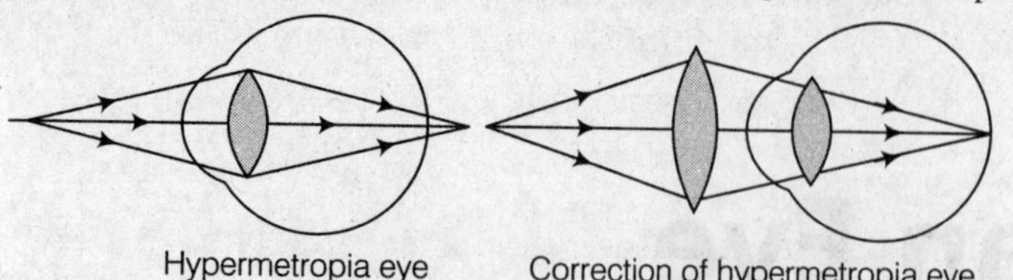

Note This defect can be removed by using a convex lens of appropriate power.

Astigmatism

In this defect, a person cannot focus on horizontal and vertical lines at the same distance at the same time.

Note This defect can be removed by using suitable cylindrical lenses.

Colour Blindness

In this defect, a person is unable to distinguish between few colours.

- The reason of this defect is the absence of cone cells sensitive for few colours.
- This defect cannot be removed.

Cataract

In this defect, an opaque, white membrane is developed on cornea due to which a person loses power of vision partially or completely. This defect can be removed by removing this membrane through surgery.

Practice Questions

Level I

1. The size of the pupil of the eye is adjusted by
(a) cornea (b) retina
(c) iris (d) blind spot

2. When we enter a cinema hall, we cannot see properly for a short time. This is because
(a) pupil does not open
(b) pupil does not close
(c) adjustment of the size of pupil takes some time
(d) None of the above

3. When we go out in bright sunlight, the pupil of the eye
(a) contracts
(b) expands
(c) sometimes contracts and sometimes expands
(d) neither contracts nor expands

4. Which cells respond to colour of light?
(a) Rod shaped cells (b) Cone shaped cells
(c) Both types of cells (d) Neither of the two

5. Eye lens is a
(a) double convex lens (b) double concave lens
(c) plano-convex lens (d) plano-concave lens

6. The property of persistence of vision is used in
(a) short sightedness (b) long sightedness
(c) cinematography (d) colour vision

7. Which of the colours of visible light has minimum wavelength?
(a) Violet (b) Red (c) Yellow (d) Green

8. Focal length of eye lens is
(a) fixed
(b) variable
(c) sometimes fixed and sometimes variable
(d) Cannot say

9. Variable focal length of eye lens is responsible for
(a) accommodation of eye
(b) persistence of vision
(c) colour blindness
(d) least distance of distinct vision

10. Far point of normal human eye is
(a) 25 cm (b) 25 m (c) 500 m (d) infinity

11. Near point of normal human eye is
(a) 25 cm (b) 25 mm
(c) 25 m (d) not fixed

12. When ciliary muscles are relaxed, focal length of the eye lens is
(a) maximum
(b) minimum
(c) Neither (a) nor (b)
(d) Cannot say

13. A concave lens of suitable focal length is used for correcting a
(a) myopic eye
(b) hypermetropic eye
(c) Both (a) and (b)
(d) Neither (a) nor (b)

14. Ability of the eye to see objects at all distances is called
(a) binocular vision (b) myopia
(c) hypermetropia (d) accommodation

15. For the myopic eye, the defect is cured by
(a) convex lens
(b) concave lens
(c) cylindrical lens
(d) toric lens

Level II

1. Image formed on retina of eye is proportional to
(a) size of object
(b) area of object
(c) $\frac{\text{size of object}}{\text{size of image}}$
(d) $\frac{\text{size of image}}{\text{size of object}}$

2. The numerical aperture for a human eye is of the order of
(a) 1
(b) 0.1
(c) 0.01
(d) 0.001

3. The sensation of vision in the retina is carried to the brain by
(a) ciliary muscles
(b) blind spot
(c) cylindrical lens
(d) optic nerve

4. When the power of eye lens increases, the defect of vision is produced. The defect is known as
(a) short sightedness
(b) long sightedness
(c) colour blindness
(d) None of the above

5. A man is suffering from colour blindness for green colour. To remove this defect, he should use goggles of
(a) green colour glasses
(b) red colour glasses
(c) smoky colour glasses
(d) None of the above

6. In an eyepiece, field lens and eye lens have focal lengths 7.5 cm and 7.3 cm. To eliminate spherical aberration, distance between them would be
(a) 0.2 cm (b) 0.4 cm (c) 0.1 cm (d) 0.5 cm

7. The impact of an image on the retina remains for
(a) 0.1 s
(b) 0.5 s
(c) 10 s
(d) 15 s

8. A person uses spectacles of power +2D. He is suffering from
(a) short sightedness or myopia
(b) long sightedness or hypermetropia
(c) presbyopia
(d) astigmatism

9. A person suffering from 'presbyopia' (myopia and hypermetropia both defects) should use
(a) a concave lens
(b) a convex lens
(c) a bifocal lens whose lower portion is convex
(d) a bifocal lens whose upper portion is convex

10. To remove myopia (short sightedness) a lens of power 0.66 D is required. The distant point of the eye is approximately
(a) 100 cm
(b) 151 cm
(c) 50 cm
(d) 25 cm

Answers

Level I

1. (c)	2. (c)	3. (a)	4. (b)	5. (a)	6. (c)	7. (a)	8. (b)	9. (a)	10. (d)
11. (a)	12. (a)	13. (a)	14. (d)	15. (b)					

Level II

1. (a)	2. (d)	3. (d)	4. (a)	5. (d)	6. (a)	7. (a)	8. (b)	9. (c)	10. (b)

Hints and Solutions

Level II

4. In short sightedness, the focal length of eye lens decreases and so the power of eye lens increases.

5. Colour blindness is a genetic disease and still cannot be cured.

6. $d = f_1 - f_2 = 7.5 - 7.3 = 0.2$ cm

8. Power of the lens given positive so defect is hypermetropia.

9. A bifocal lens consist of both convex and concave lenses with lower part is convex.

10. Far point of the eye = Focal length of the lens

$$= \frac{100}{P} = \frac{100}{0.66} \approx 151 \text{ cm}$$

57

Photometry

Photometry

Photometry is a branch of optics in which we study the measurement of light energy.

Solid Angle

(i) Solid angle $= \dfrac{\text{Normal area}}{(\text{Distance})^2} = \dfrac{\Delta A}{r^2}$

When $\Delta A = r^2$, then solid angle, $\omega = 1$.

(ii) The SI unit of solid angle is steradian.

(iii) The surface area of a sphere is $4\pi r^2$. Therefore, whole sphere made a solid angle at their centre is

$$\omega = \frac{4\pi r^2}{r^2} = 4\pi$$

Luminous Flux

The magnitude of light emitted from a light source in one second is called luminous flux. In other word, we can say light emitted per second from a light source is called luminous flux.

Luminous flux is only a part of perfect radiation which is visible range ($\lambda = 3800$ Å to 7800 Å)

Luminous flux is denoted by ϕ and its SI unit is 'lumen'.

Luminous Intensity

The luminous intensity in a direction of point light source is equal to emission of luminous flux from a unit solid angle in the given direction. Usually, luminous intensity is denoted by I.

If $\Delta\phi$ be the emission of luminous flux in solid angle $\Delta\omega$ from a point source, then luminous intensity of source $I = \dfrac{\Delta\phi}{\Delta\omega}$. The unit of luminous intensity is 'lumen per steredian' and is also known as 'candela'.

$$1 \text{ candela} = \frac{1 \text{ lumen}}{\text{steradian}}$$

The dimension of candela and lumen is $[M^1L^2T^{-3}]$.

Relation between Luminous Intensity and Luminous Flux

$$I = \frac{\phi}{4\pi} \quad \Rightarrow \quad \phi = 4\pi I$$

Intensity of Illumination

The amount of light falls normally at unit area around a point is called intensity of illumination of that point and is denoted by E.

Relation between Intensity of Illumination (*E*) and Luminous Intensity (*I*)

If ϕ be the luminous flux of a point light source at the centre of a sphere of radius r, then

$$E = \frac{\phi}{A} = \frac{\phi}{4\pi r^2} = \frac{4\pi I}{4\pi r^2} = \frac{I}{r^2}$$

The SI unit of intensity of illumination is metre-candela or lux.

$$1 \text{ lux} = \frac{1 \text{ cd}}{(1 \text{ m})^2}$$

CGS unit of intensity of illumination is centimetre candela or Phot.

$$1 \text{ Phot (cm candela)} = \frac{1 \text{ cd}}{(1 \text{ cm})^2}$$

$$1 \text{ Phot} = 10^4 \text{ Lux}$$

Inverse Square Law

This law states that the intensity of illumination generated from a source of light at a point is inversely proportional to the square of distance between that point to the source. If d be the distance from point to source, then intensity of illumination at that point will be

$$E \propto \frac{1}{d^2} \quad \Rightarrow \quad E = \frac{P}{d^2}$$

Here, P is a constant which is illuminating power of the source.

Lambert's Cosine Law

According to this law, the intensity of illumination of light at a point is directly proportional to the cosine of the angle of incidence of light at that point.

i.e., $\quad E \propto \cos\theta$

At normal incident, $\theta = 90°$

$\therefore \quad \cos\theta = \cos 90° = 1$ (maximum)

i.e., illumination in this direction will maximum.

Principle of Photometer

Let S_1 and S_2 be two point source of light which is situated at the distances d_1 and d_2 respectively from a screen. If luminous intensity of sources S_1 and S_2 be respectively I_1 and I_2 and intensity of illumination be E_1 and E_2 respectively, then

$$E_1 = \frac{I_1}{d_1^2} \text{ and } E_2 = \frac{I_2}{d_2^2}$$

On same intensity of illumination,

$$E_1 = E_2$$

$$\Rightarrow \quad \frac{I_1}{d_1^2} = \frac{I_2}{d_2^2} \quad \Rightarrow \quad \frac{I_1}{I_2} = \frac{d_1^2}{d_2^2}$$

Practice Questions

Level I

1. Lux is an international unit of
(a) illumination (b) efficiency
(c) luminous flux (d) luminous intensity

2. Candela is an international unit of
(a) illumination (b) luminous intensity
(c) luminous flux (d) None of these

3. Unit of luminous flux is
(a) candela power (b) lumen
(c) lumen/watt (d) None of these

4. The unit of illuminating power is
(a) candela power (b) lumen
(c) lux (d) candela

5. Unit of efficiency is
(a) lumen (b) candela power
(c) lux (d) lumen/watt

6. 1 phot is equal to
(a) 10^4 lux (b) 10^9 lux
(c) 10^2 lux (d) 10 lux

7. A pin hole camera works on the principle of
(a) refraction
(b) reflection
(c) linear propagation of light
(d) None of the above

Level II

1. Luminous intensity of an illuminating tube of 40 watt is 300 candela. The value of luminous flux of tube will be
(a) 1200 lumen (b) 1000 lumen
(c) 1200 π lumen (d) 1400 lumen

2. The maximum illumination on a screen is 25 lux at a distance of 2 m apart from a lamp. The emission of whole flux from the lamp will be
(a) 1000 lumen (b) 1256 lumen
(c) 1056 lumen (d) None of these

3. Luminous intensity of a light source is 100 candela. The illuminating density on a surface situated 2m apart from light source will be
(a) 25 lux (b) 30 lux (c) 75 lux (d) 20 lux

4. A lamp is suspended at the height of 6m above a table. On decreasing 2m height of lamp, percentage increase in intensity of illumination will be
(a) 120% (b) 110%
(c) 113% (d) 125%

5. One candela is equal to
(a) one candela power (b) $\frac{59}{60}$ candela power
(c) $\frac{1}{60}$ candela power (d) 10 candela power

Answers

Level I

1. (a)	**2.** (b)	**3.** (b)	**4.** (a)	**5.** (d)	**6.** (a)	**7.** (c)

Level II

1. (c)	**2.** (b)	**3.** (a)	**4.** (d)	**5.** (a)

Hints and Solutions

Level II

1. Luminous flux (ϕ) = $4\pi \times$ Luminous intensity I)
$= 4\pi \times 300 = 1200\ \pi$ lumen

2. Illumination $(E) = \frac{I}{r^2} \Rightarrow 25 = \frac{I}{2^2}$
$\Rightarrow \quad I = 25 \times 4 = 100$ candela
$\therefore \quad \phi = 4\pi \times I = 4 \times 3.14 \times 100 = 1256$ lumen

58

Particle Nature of Light

Photoelectric Effect

The phenomenon of emission of electrons from a metal surface, when light of appropriate frequency is incident on it, is called photoelectric effect. The electrons emitted during photoelectric current, are called photoelectrons. In photoelectric effect, it should be noted that one photon interacts with one electron and not more than one electrons.

Terms of Photoelectric Effect

Work Function (ϕ) The minimum energy required to eject an electron from a metal surface, is called its work function. It is given by $\phi = h\nu_0$
Where, h = Planck's constant and ν_0 = Threshold frequency.

Note The minimum frequency of incident light that can eject photoelectron from a metal surface, is called its threshold frequency. It is denoted by ν_0.

Threshold Wavelength (λ_0) The maximum wavelength of incident light than can eject photoelectron from a metal surface, is called its threshold wavelength. It is denoted by λ_0.

Work function, $\phi = h\nu_0 = \dfrac{hc}{\lambda_0}$

Where, h = Planck's constant.

Stopping Potential (V_s) The negative potential given to the anode of a photoelectric cell for which photoelectric current becomes zero, is called the stopping potential or cut-off potential. It is denoted by V_0.
Maximum kinetic energy of photoelectrons is given by

$$E_K = eV_0$$

Where, e is the charge of an electron.

Laws of Photoelectric Effect

- The rate of emission of photoelectrons from a metal surface is directly proportional to the intensity of incident light.
- The maximum kinetic energy of photoelectrons does not depend on the intensity of incident light.
- Maximum kinetic energy of emitted photoelectrons increases with increase in frequency of incident light.
- If the frequency of incident light is below than a certain minimum value called threshold frequency, then no emission of photoelectrons takes place from the metal surface.
- There is no time lag between the incidence of light and emission of photoelectrons from the metal surface.

Einstein's Photoelectric Equation

Einstein explained photoelectric effect on the basis of Max Planck quantum theory. According to which light is emitted from a source in the form of packets or bundles of energy, called quanta or photon. The energy of each photon is give by

$$E = h\nu$$

where, h = Planck's constant,
ν = Frequency of incident light.

Kinetic energy of emitted photoelectron is given by

$$E_K = h\nu - \phi \text{ or } E_K = \frac{1}{2}mv^2 = h(\nu - \nu_0)$$

This is called Einstein's photoelectric equation,

The Photocell

The photocell is the arrangement which converts light energy into electric energy. This is based on the phenomenon of photoelectric effect. *The photoelectric cells are of three types.*

(i) Photoemissive cell
(ii) Photovoltaic cell
(iii) Photoconductive cell

Photoemissive cells are of two types

(a) Vacuum type (b) Gas filled type

Practice Questions

Level I

1. **Photoelectric effect is an example of**
(a) elastic collision
(b) inelastic collision
(c) two-dimensional collision
(d) oblique collision

2. **If the work function of the metal is ϕ and the frequency of incident light is ν, there is no emission of photoelectrons when**
(a) $\nu < (\phi / h)$
(b) $\nu = (\phi / h)$
(c) $\nu > (\phi / h)$
(d) $\nu \geq (\phi / h)$

3. **Einstein's photoelectric equation states that $E_K = h\nu - \phi$. In this equation, E_K refers to**
(a) KE of all the emitted electrons
(b) mean KE of the emitted electrons
(c) maximum KE of the emitted electrons
(d) minimum KE of the emitted electrons

4. **Photoelectric effect experiment establishes that light consists of**
(a) particles
(b) energy packets
(c) wave
(d) wave fronts

5. **In a photoelectric experiment, if both the intensity and frequency of the incident light are doubled, then the saturation photoelectric current**
(a) remains constant
(b) is halved
(c) is doubled
(d) becomes four times

6. **The electrons are emitted in a photoelectric effect from a metal surface**
(a) only if the frequency of radiation is above a certain threshold value
(b) only if the temperature of the surface is high
(c) at a rate that is independent of the nature of metal
(d) with a maximum velocity proportional to the frequency of incident radiation

7. **By increasing the intensity of incident light on the surface of a metal**
(a) kinetic energy of the photoelectrons increases
(b) number of emitted electrons increases
(c) kinetic energy and number of electrons increases
(d) no effect

8. **The minimum energy required to remove an electron is called**
(a) stopping potential
(b) KE
(c) work function
(d) None of these

9. **The maximum energy of the electrons released in photocell is independent of**
(a) frequency of incident light
(b) intensity of incident light
(c) nature of cathode surface
(d) None of the above

10. **Photocell is a device to**
(a) store photons
(b) measure light intensity
(c) convert photon energy into mechanical energy
(d) store electrical energy for replacing storage batteries

Level II

1. **Photoelectric effect shows**
(a) wave nature of electrons
(b) particle nature of light
(c) Both (a) and (b)
(d) None of the above

2. **A light whose frequency is equal to 6×10^{14} Hz is incident on a metal whose work function is 2eV. ($h = 6.63 \times 10^{-34}$ Js, 1eV $= 1.6 \times 10^{-19}$ J). The maximum energy of the electrons emitted will be**
(a) 2.49 eV
(b) 4.49 eV
(c) 0.49 eV
(d) 5.49 eV

3. **The surface of a metal is illuminated with the light of 400 nm. The kinetic energy of the ejected photoelectrons was found to be 1.68 eV. The work function of the metal is ($hc = 1240$ eV-nm)**
(a) 3.09 eV
(b) 1.41 eV
(c) 1.51 eV
(d) 1.68 eV

4. **The work function of a metallic substance is 5 eV. The threshold frequency is approximately**
(a) 1.6×10^{7} Hz
(b) 8.68×10^{15} Hz
(c) 9.68×10^{17} Hz
(d) 1.2×10^{15} Hz

5. **The threshold wavelength of sodium metals is 6780 Å. The work function of metal will be**
(a) 1.83 eV
(b) 2.75 eV
(c) 2.95 eV
(d) 3.25 eV

Answers

Level I

1. (b) **2.** (b) **3.** (c) **4.** (c) **5.** (b) **6.** (a) **7.** (a) **8.** (c) **9.** (d) **10.** (a)

Level II

1. (b) **2.** (c) **3.** (b) **4.** (d) **5.** (a)

Hints and Solutions

Level II

2. Frequency of light $= 6 \times 10^{14}$ Hz

Energy in electron volt

$$= \frac{6 \times 10^{14} \times 6.63 \times 10^{-34}}{1.6 \times 10^{-19}} = 2.49 \text{ eV}$$

Work function of the metal $= 2$ eV

$\therefore$ Maximum kinetic energy of photoelectrons $= 0.49$ eV.

4. Using formula,

$$\phi = h\nu_0 \Rightarrow \nu_0 = \frac{\phi}{h} = \frac{5 \text{ eV}}{h}$$

$$\therefore \quad \nu_0 = \frac{5 \times 1.6 \times 10^{-19}}{6.63 \times 10^{-34}}$$

$$= 1.2 \times 10^{15} \text{ Hz}$$

5. Using formula,

$$\phi = \frac{hc}{\lambda_0}$$

$$\therefore \quad \phi = \frac{6.63 \times 10^{-34} \times 3 \times 1.8}{6780 \times 10^{-10}}$$

$$= 2.93 \times 10^{-19} \text{ J}$$

$$= 1.83 \text{ eV}$$

59

Wave Nature of Light

Photons

According to Planck's quantum theory of radiation, an electromagnetic wave travels in the form of discrete packets of energy called quanta. One quantum of light radiation is called a photon.

The main features of photons are as follows

(i) A photon travels with the speed of light.

(ii) The frequency of a photon does not change as it travels from one medium to another.

(iii) The speed of a photon changes as it travels through different media due to the change in its wavelength.

(iv) The rest mass of a photon is zero *i.e.*, a photon cannot exist at rest.

(v) Energy of a photon, $E = h\nu = \frac{hc}{\lambda}$.

(vi) Momentum of a photon, $p = mc = \frac{h\nu}{\lambda} = \frac{h}{\lambda}$.

(vii) From Einstein's mass-energy relationship, the equivalent mass m of a photon is given by $E = mc^2 = h\nu$ or $m = \frac{h\nu}{c^2}$

Dual Nature of Radiation

Light has dual nature. It manifests itself as a wave in diffraction, interference, polarisation, etc., while it shows particle nature in photoelectric effect, Compton scattering etc.

Dual Nature of Matter

As, there is complete equivalence between matter (mass) and radiation (energy) and the principle of symmetry is always obeyed, de-Broglie suggested that moving particles like protons, neutrons, electrons, etc., should be associated with waves known as de-Broglie waves and their wavelength is called de-Broglie wavelength. The de-Broglie wavelength of a particle of mass m moving with velocity v is given by $\lambda = \frac{h}{p} = \frac{h}{mv}$.

Where, h is the Planck's constant. The de-Broglie wavelength is independent of the charge and nature of the material particles. It has significantly measurable values for subatomic particles like electrons, protons, etc., due to the small masses. For macroscopic objects of evenday life, the de-Broglie wavelength is extreme small, quite beyond measurement.

Davisson and Germer Experiment The electron diffraction experiment has verified and confirmed the wave nature of electrons.

De-Broglie Wavelength of an Electron The wavelength associated with an electron accelerated through a potential difference of volts is given by

$$\lambda = \frac{h}{\sqrt{2meV}} = \frac{1.227}{\sqrt{V}} \text{ nm}$$

Electron Microscope It is a device that exploit the wave nature of electrons to provide high resolving power. It is used to investigate the structural details of bacteria, viruses, etc. It has proved to be a powerful tool of investigation for research in science, technology, metallurgy, industry, medicine etc.

Practice Questions

Level I

1. Which one of the following statements about photon is incorrect?

(a) Photon's rest mass is zero
(b) Momentum of photon is $\frac{h\nu}{c}$
(c) Photon's energy is $h\nu$
(d) Photons exert no pressure

2. The momentum of photon is

(a) $\frac{h}{\lambda}$ (b) $\frac{\lambda}{h}$ (c) λh (d) zero

3. If we consider electrons and photons of same wavelength, then they will have same

(a) energy (b) velocity
(c) momentum (d) angular momentum

4. The mass of a photon at rest is

(a) zero (b) 1.67×10^{-35} kg
(c) 1 amu (d) 9×10^{-31} kg

5. Energy of photon cannot be expressed as

(a) $h\nu$ (b) $h\,c\,\lambda$ (c) $\frac{hc}{\lambda}$ (d) $h\,c\,\bar{\nu}$

6. If a photon has velocity c and frequency ν, then which of the following represents its wavelength?

(a) $\frac{hc}{E}$ (b) $\frac{h\nu}{c}$ (c) $\frac{h\nu}{c^2}$ (d) $h\nu$

7. The energy of a photon of wavelength λ is

(a) $h\,c\,\lambda$ (b) $\frac{h\,c}{\lambda}$
(c) $\frac{\lambda}{h\,c}$ (d) $\frac{h\,\lambda}{c}$

8. A photon is motion has a mass

(a) $\frac{c}{h\,\nu}$ (b) $\frac{h}{\nu}$
(c) $h\,\nu$ (d) $\frac{h\,\nu}{c^2}$

9. The energy E and the momentum p of photon is given by $E = h\,\nu$ and $p = \frac{h}{\lambda}$, the velocity of photon will be

(a) $\frac{E}{p}$ (b) $E\,p$
(c) $\left(\frac{E}{p}\right)^2$ (d) $\left(\frac{E}{p}\right)^{1/2}$

10. Wave is associated with matter,

(a) when it is stationary
(b) when it is in motion with any velocity
(c) when it is in motion with velocity of light
(d) None of the above

11. Dual nature of radiation is shown by

(a) diffraction and reflection
(b) refraction and diffraction
(c) photoelectric effect alone
(d) photoelectric effect and diffraction

12. The de-Broglie wave corresponding to a particle of mass m and velocity v has a wavelength associated with it

(a) $\frac{h}{m\,v}$ (b) $h\,m\,v$
(c) $\frac{m\,h}{v}$ (d) $\frac{m}{h\,v}$

Level II

1. What is the momentum of a photon having frequency 1.5×10^{13} Hz?

(a) 3.3×10^{-29} kg-m/s (b) 3.3×10^{-34} kg-m/s
(c) 6.6×10^{-34} kg-m/s (d) 6.6×10^{-30} kg-m/s

2. The energy of a photon of light of wavelength 450 nm is

(a) 4.4×10^{-19} J (b) 2.5×10^{-19} J
(c) 1.25×10^{-17} J (d) 2.5×10^{-17} J

3. The kinetic energy of an electron gets tripled, then the de-Broglie wavelength associated with it changes by a factor

(a) $\frac{1}{3}$ (b) $\sqrt{3}$ (c) $\frac{1}{\sqrt{3}}$ (d) 3

4. A particle of mass 1 mg has the same wavelength as an electron moving with a velocity of 3×10^{6} $^{-1}$. The velocity of the particle is

(a) 3×10^{-31} ms^{-1} (b) 2.7×10^{-21} ms^{-1}
(c) 2.7×10^{-18} ms^{-1} (d) 9×10^{-2} ms^{-1}
(Mass of electron $= 9.1 \times 10^{-31}$ kg)

5. If an electron and a photon propagate in the form of waves having the same wavelength, it implies that they have the same

(a) energy (b) momentum
(c) velocity (d) angular momentum

6. The de-Broglie wavelength is proportional to

(a) $\lambda \propto \frac{1}{v}$ (b) $\lambda \propto \frac{1}{m}$
(c) $\lambda \propto \frac{1}{p}$ (d) $\lambda \propto p$

7. The de-Brogile wavelength λ associated with an electron having kinetic energy E is given by the expression

(a) $\frac{h}{\sqrt{2mE}}$
(b) $\frac{2h}{mE}$
(c) $2mhE$
(d) $\frac{2\sqrt{2mE}}{h}$

Answers

Level I

1. (d) **2.** (a) **3.** (c) **4.** (a) **5.** (b) **6.** (a) **7.** (b) **8.** (d) **9.** (a) **10.** (b)
11. (c) **12.** (a)

Level II

1. (a) **2.** (a) **3.** (c) **4.** (c) **5.** (b) **6.** (c) **7.** (a)

Hints and Solutions

Level II

1. $p = \frac{hv}{c} = \frac{6.6 \times 10^{-34} \times 1.5 \times 10^{13}}{3 \times 10^{8}}$

$= 3.3 \times 10^{-29}$ kg-m/s

2. $E = \frac{hc}{\lambda} = \frac{6.62 \times 10^{-34} \times 3 \times 10^{8}}{450 \times 10^{-9}}$

$= 4.4 \times 10^{-19}$ J

3. For an electron,

de-Broglie wavelength, $\lambda = \frac{h}{\sqrt{2mK}}$

where, h = Planck's constant, m = Mass of an electron,
K = Kinetic energy of an electron

Since h, m remains the same.

$\therefore \quad \lambda \propto \frac{1}{\sqrt{K}}$

$\Rightarrow \quad \frac{\lambda}{\lambda'} = \sqrt{\frac{K'}{K}} = \sqrt{\frac{3K}{K}}$

$\Rightarrow \quad \lambda' = \frac{\lambda}{\sqrt{3}}$

4. de-Broglie wavelength, $\lambda = \frac{h}{mv}$

As, both particle and electron having same wavelength, therefore their momentum will be equal.

$m_p v_p = m_e v_e$

$\Rightarrow \quad v_p = \frac{m_e v_e}{m_p} = \frac{9.1 \times 10^{-31} \times 3 \times 10^{6}}{10^{-6}}$

$\Rightarrow \quad v_p = 2.7 \times 10^{-18}$ m/s

5. If an electron and a photon propagates in the form of waves having the same wavelength, it implies that they have same momentum. This is according to de-Broglie equation, $p \propto \frac{1}{\lambda}$

6. $\lambda = \frac{h}{p} \Rightarrow \lambda \propto \frac{1}{p}$

7. $\frac{1}{2} mv^2 = E \Rightarrow mv = \sqrt{2mE}$;

$\therefore \quad \lambda = \frac{h}{mv} = \frac{h}{\sqrt{2mE}}$

60

Structure of Atom

Atom as a Constituent of Every Element

Every element has characteristic atoms. Atoms of different elements contain electrons, which are completely identical. Atom as a whole is electrically neutral and therefore contains equal amount of positive and negative charges.

Rutherford's Atomic Model

- The entire positive charge and almost entire mass of the atom is concentrated at its centre in a very tiny region of the order of 10^{-15} m, called nucleus.
- The negatively charged electrons revolve around the nucleus in different orbits.
- The total positive charge on nucleus is equal to the total negative charge on electrons. Therefore, atom as an over all is neutral.
- The centripetal force required by electrons for revolution is provided by the electrostatic force of attraction between the electrons and the nucleus.

Bohr's Atomic Model

- Electrons can revolve in certain non-radiating orbits called stationary orbits for which the angular momentum of electrons is an integer multiple of $\frac{h}{2\pi}$.

$$mvr = \frac{nh}{2\pi}$$

where, $n = 1, 2, 3, \ldots$, called principal quantum numbers and h is Planck's constant.

- The radiation of energy occurs only when an electron jumps from one permitted orbit to another permitted orbit.
- The absorption or emission of energy can occur only by the transition of electron from lower to higher energy or *vice-versa*, energy of emitted photon $h\nu = E_2 - E_1$ where, E_1 and E_2 are energies of electron in orbits.

Bohr's Theory of Hydrogen Atom

An electron having charge $-e$ revolves with speed v in a circular orbit of radius r round the nucleus having charge $+e$.

For a circular orbit,

$$\frac{mv^2}{r} = \frac{kZe^2}{r}$$

From quantisation of angular momentum,

$$L = mvr = \frac{nh}{2\pi}$$

On solving the above two equations, we get

Radius of nth orbit,

$$r = \frac{n^2h^2}{4\pi^2 mkZe^2}$$

Speed of electron in nth orbit,

$$v = \frac{2\pi ke^2}{nh} = \alpha\frac{c}{n} = \frac{1}{137}\cdot\frac{c}{n}$$

where, $\alpha = \frac{2\pi ke^2}{ch}$ is fine structure constant.

Total energy of an electron in nth orbit is

$$E_n = \text{KE} + \text{PE}$$

$$= \frac{kZe^2}{2r} - \frac{kZe^2}{r} = -\frac{kZe^2}{2r}$$

$$\Rightarrow \quad E_n = -\frac{2\pi^2 mk^2Z^2e^4}{n^2h^2}$$

$$= -\frac{Z^2Rhc}{n^2} = -\frac{13.6Z^2}{n^2}\ \text{eV}$$

Where, $R = \frac{2\pi^2 mk^2e^4}{ch^3}$

$$= 1.0973 \times 10^7\ \text{m}^{-1}$$

is the Rydberg's constant.

Spectral Series of Hydrogen Atom

Whenever an electron makes a transition from a higher energy level n_2 to a lower energy level n_1, the difference of energy appears in the form of a photon of frequency ν given by

$$\nu = \frac{2\pi^2 mk^2 Z^2 e^4}{h^3}\left[\frac{1}{n_1^2} - \frac{1}{n_2^2}\right]$$

Wave number,

$$\bar{\nu} = \frac{1}{\lambda} = \frac{\nu}{c} = \frac{2\pi^2 mk^2 Z^2 e^4}{ch^3}\left[\frac{1}{n_1^2} - \frac{1}{n_2^2}\right]$$

$$\Rightarrow \quad \bar{\nu} = \frac{1}{\lambda} = RZ^2\left[\frac{1}{n_1^2} - \frac{1}{n_2^2}\right]$$

Different spectral series for hydrogen atom are as follows

(i) **Lyman Series** Here, $n_2 = 2, 3, 4, \ldots$ and $n_1 = 1$. This series lies in the ultraviolet region

$$\bar{\nu} = \frac{1}{\lambda} = R\left[\frac{1}{1^2} - \frac{1}{n_2^2}\right],\ n_2 = 2, 3, 4, \ldots$$

(ii) **Balmer Series** Here, $n_2 = 3, 4, 5, \ldots$ and $n_1 = 2$. This series lies in the visible region

$$\bar{\nu} = \frac{1}{\lambda} = R\left[\frac{1}{2^2} - \frac{1}{n_2^2}\right],\ n_2 = 3, 4, 5, \ldots$$

(iii) **Paschen Series** Here, $n_2 = 4, 5, 6, \ldots$ and $n_1 = 3$. This series lies in the infrared region

$$\bar{\nu} = \frac{1}{\lambda} = R\left[\frac{1}{3^2} - \frac{1}{n_2^2}\right],\ n_2 = 4, 5, 6, \ldots$$

(iv) **Brackett Series** Here, $n_2 = 5, 6, 7, \ldots$ and $n_1 = 4$. This series lies in the infrared region

$$\bar{\nu} = \frac{1}{\lambda} = R\left[\frac{1}{4^2} - \frac{1}{n_2^2}\right],\ n_2 = 5, 6, 7, \ldots$$

(v) **Pfund Series** Here, $n_2 = 6, 7, 8, \ldots$ and $n_1 = 5$. This series lies in the infrared region

$$\bar{\nu} = \frac{1}{\lambda} = R\left[\frac{1}{5^2} - \frac{1}{n_2^2}\right],\ n_2 = 6, 7, 8, \ldots$$

Other Important Definitions

Energy Level Diagram It is a diagram in which the energies of the different stationary states of an atom are represented by parallel horizontal lines, drawn according to some suitable energy scale.

Failure of Bohr's Model This model is applicable only to hydrogen like atoms and fails in case of higher atoms. It could not explain the fine structure of the spectral lines in the spectrum of hydrogen atom.

Excitation Energy It is defined as the energy required by an electron of an atom to jump from its ground state to any one of its excited states.

Ionisation Energy It is defined as the energy required to remove an electron from an atom, *i.e.,* the energy required to take an electron from its ground state to the outermost orbit ($n = \infty$).

Excitation Potential It is that accelerating potential which gives to a bombarding electron sufficient energy to excite the target atom by raising one of its electrons from an inner to an outer orbit.

Ionisation Potential It is that accelerating potential which gives to a bombarding electron sufficient energy to ionise the target atom by knocking one of its electrons completely out of the atom.

Practice Questions

Level I

1. In Bohr model of hydrogen atom, which of the following is quantised?

(a) Linear velocity of electron
(b) Angular velocity of electron
(c) Linear momentum of electron
(d) Angular momentum of electron

2. For an electron in the second orbit of hydrogen, what is the moment of momentum as per the Bohr's model?

(a) $2\pi h$ (b) πh (c) $\frac{h}{\pi}$ (d) $\frac{2h}{\pi}$

3. The angular momentum of an electron in the second excited state of a helium ion (He^+) is the moment of momentum as per the Bohr's model?

(a) $\frac{h}{\pi}$ (b) $\frac{h}{2\pi}$ (c) $\frac{3h}{2\pi}$ (d) $\frac{2h}{\pi}$

4. According to Bohr theory, relation between main quantum number n and radius of orbit r is

(a) $r \propto n$ (b) $r \propto \frac{1}{n}$
(c) $r \propto n^2$ (d) $r \propto \frac{1}{n^2}$

5. In Bohr's model, the atomic radius of the first orbit is r_0. Then, the radius of the third orbit is

(a) $\frac{r_0}{9}$ (b) r_0
(c) $9r_0$ (d) $3r_0$

6. When hydrogen atom is in its first excited level, its radius is

(a) same (b) half
(c) twice (d) four times

7. The ground state energy of hydrogen atom is -13.6 eV. What is the potential energy of the electron in this state?
(a) 0 eV (b) -27.2 eV
(c) 1 eV (d) 2 eV

8. For ionising an excited hydrogen atom, the energy required (in eV) will be
(a) a little less than 13.6 eV
(b) 13.6 eV
(c) more than 13.6 eV
(d) 3.4 eV or less

9. If the energy of hydrogen atom in nth orbit is E_n, then the energy in nth orbit of a singly ionised helium atom will be
(a) $4E_n$ (b) $\frac{E_n}{4}$
(c) $2E_n$ (d) $\frac{E_n}{2}$

10. Rutherford's α-particle experiment shows that the atoms have
(a) electrons (b) neutrons
(c) nucleus (d) protons

11. Rutherford α-scattering experiment concludes that
(a) electrons are revolving around the nucleus
(b) there is heavy mass at centre
(c) electrons are scattered in space
(d) velocity of all electrons is same

12. Bohr's theory was modified by
(a) Rutherford and Soddy (b) Planck
(c) Hund (d) Sommerfeld

13. Rutherford's model of the atom was unstable, because
(a) nuclei will breakdown
(b) electrons move in circular orbits
(c) orbiting electrons radiate energy
(d) electrons are repelled by the nucleus

14. If E_P and E_K represents potential and kinetic energies of the orbital electrons, then
(a) $E_K = -\frac{E_P}{2}$ (b) $E_K = -E_P$
(c) $E_K = -2E_P$ (d) None of these

15. The ionisation potential of hydrogen is
(a) 13.6 V (b) 8.24 V
(c) -10.36 V (d) 14.24 V

Level II

1. In the Bohr's hydrogen atom model, the radius of the stationary orbit is directly proportional to (n = Principal quantum number)
(a) n^{-1} (b) n
(c) n^{-2} (d) n^2

2. In the nth orbit the energy of an electron $E_n = -\frac{13.6}{n^2}$ eV for hydrogen atom. The energy required to take the electron from first orbit to second orbit will be
(a) 10.2 eV (b) 12.1 eV
(c) 13.6 eV (d) 3.4 eV

3. First Bohr radius of an atom with $Z = 82$ is R. Radius of its third orbit is
(a) $9R$ (b) $6R$ (c) $3R$ (d) R

4. The size of an atom is of the order of
(a) 10^{-8} m (b) 10^{-10} m
(c) 10^{-12} m (d) 10^{-14} m

5. Which one of the series of hydrogen spectrum is in the visible region?
(a) Lyman series (b) Balmer series
(c) Paschen series (d) Brackett series

6. The Rutherford α-particle experiment shows that most of the α-particles pass through almost unscattered while some are scattered through large angles. What information does it give about the structure of the atom?
(a) Atom is hollow
(b) The whole mass of the atom is concentrated in a small centre called nucleus
(c) Nucleus is positively charged
(d) All of the above

7. For a hydrogen atom, in which of the following transitions will the wavelength emitted photon be minimum?
(a) $n = 5$ to $n = 4$ (b) $n = 4$ to $n = 3$
(c) $n = 3$ to $n = 2$ (d) $n = 2$ to $n = 1$

8. Calculate the highest frequency of the emitted photon in the paschen series of spectral lines of the hydrogen atom.
(a) 3.7×10^{14} Hz (b) 9.1×10^{15} Hz
(c) 10.23×10^{14} Hz (d) 29.7×10^{15} Hz

9. The angular momentum of electron in nth orbit is given by
(a) nh (b) $\frac{h}{2\pi n}$
(c) $n\frac{h}{2\pi}$ (d) $n^2\frac{h}{2\pi}$

10. The radius of electron's second stationary orbit in Bohr's atom is R. The radius of the third orbit will be
(a) $3R$ (b) $2.25R$
(c) $9R$ (d) $\frac{R}{3}$

11. The ratio between Bohr radii are
(a) 1 : 2 : 3 (b) 2 : 4 : 6
(c) 1 : 4 : 9 (d) 1 : 3 : 5

12. An electron of an atom transits from n_1 to n_2. In which of the following maximum frequency of photon will be emitted?
(a) $n_1 = 1$ to $n_2 = 2$
(b) $n_1 = 2$ to $n_2 = 1$
(c) $n_1 = 2$ to $n_2 = 6$
(d) $n_1 = 6$ to $n_2 = 2$

13. The Rydberg constant R for hydrogen is

(a) $R=-\left(\frac{1}{4\pi\varepsilon_0}\right)\cdot\frac{2\pi^2me^2}{ch^2}$ (b) $R=\left(\frac{1}{4\pi\varepsilon_0}\right)\cdot\frac{2\pi^2me^4}{ch^2}$

(c) $R=\left(\frac{1}{4\pi\varepsilon_0}\right)^2\cdot\frac{2\pi^2me^4}{c^2h^2}$ (d) $R=\left(\frac{1}{4\pi\varepsilon_0}\right)^2\cdot\frac{2\pi^2me^4}{ch^3}$

14. The wavelength of the first line of Balmer series is 656. The Rydberg constant for hydrogen is about

(a) 1.09×10^7 per m
(b) 1.09×10^8 per m
(c) 1.09×10^9 per m
(d) 1.09×10^5 per m

Answers

Level I

1. (d)	**2.** (c)	**3.** (c)	**4.** (c)	**5.** (c)	**6.** (d)	**7.** (b)	**8.** (d)	**9.** (a)	**10.** (c)
11. (b)	**12.** (d)	**13.** (c)	**14.** (a)	**15.** (a)					

Level II

1. (d)	**2.** (a)	**3.** (a)	**4.** (b)	**5.** (b)	**6.** (d)	**7.** (d)	**8.** (a)	**9.** (c)	**10.** (b)
11. (c)	**12.** (b)	**13.** (d)	**14.** (a)						

Hints *and* Solutions

Level II

1. Bohr radius, $r=\frac{\varepsilon_0 n^2h^2}{\pi Zme^2}$; $\therefore r\propto n^2$

2. $n=2$ $\quad E_2=-\frac{13.6}{(2)^2}=-3.4$ eV

$n=1$ $\quad E_1=-13.6$ eV

$E_{1\to2}=-3.4-(-13.6)=+10.2$ eV

3. The radius of the Bohr's atom model, which is valued only for hydrogen or other ionised atoms with a single electron is given by

$$r_n=\left(\frac{n^2}{m}\right)\left(\frac{h}{2\pi}\right)^2\left(\frac{4\pi\varepsilon_0}{Ze^2}\right)$$

$\therefore$ For a given $Z=82$, $r\propto n^2$

$\therefore$ If the radius of the first orbit is R, the radius of the third orbit is n^2R *i.e.*, $9R$.

4. The size of the atom is of the order of 1 Å $=10^{-10}$ m.

5. Balmer series lies in the visible region.

7. According to Bohr's theory the wavelength of the radiation emitted from hydrogen atom is given by

$$\frac{1}{\lambda}=R\left[\frac{1}{n_1^2}-\frac{1}{n_2^2}\right]$$

Then, λ is minimum for minimum value of n_1 and n_2. Hence, $n=2$ to $n=1$

8. The frequencies of the emitted photon in the paschen series are given by, $\nu=Rc\left(\frac{1}{3^2}-\frac{1}{n^2}\right)$

where, $n=4, 5, 6, \ldots$

The highest frequency corresponds to $n=\infty$

$$\therefore\quad \nu_{\text{Highest}}=\frac{Rc}{9}=\frac{1.097\times10^7\text{ m}^{-1}\times3\times10^8\text{ m/s}}{9}$$
$$=0.37\times10^{15}\text{ s}^{-1}$$
$$=3.7\times10^{14}\text{ s}^{-1}$$
$$=3.7\times10^{14}\text{ Hz}$$

10. $r\propto n^2\Rightarrow\frac{r_{(n=2)}}{r_{(n=3)}}=\frac{4}{9}$

$$\Rightarrow\quad r_{(n=3)}=\frac{9}{4}R=2.25R$$

13. $R=\frac{2\pi^2k^2e^4m}{ch^3}=\left(\frac{1}{4\pi\varepsilon_0}\right)^2\frac{2\pi^2me^4}{ch^3}$

14. $\frac{1}{\lambda}=R\left[\frac{1}{4}-\frac{1}{9}\right]=\frac{5R}{36}$

$$\therefore\quad R=\frac{36}{5\lambda}$$
$$=\frac{36}{5\times6563\times10^{-10}}$$
$$=1.09\times10^7\text{ m}^{-1}$$

61

Nuclei and Radioactivity

Nucleons Protons and neutrons which are present in the nuclei of the atoms are collectively known as nucleons.

Atomic Number The number of protons present in the nucleus is called the atomic number. It is denoted by Z.

Mass Number The total number of protons and neutrons present in a nucleus is called the mass number of the element. It is denoted by A.

Number of protons in an atom = Z
Number of electrons in an atom = Z
Number of nucleons in an atom = A
Number of neutrons in an atom = $N = A - Z$

Nuclear Mass The total mass of the protons and neutrons present in a nucleus is called the nuclear mass.

Nuclide A nuclide is a specific nucleus of an atom characterised by its atomic number Z and mass number A. It is represented as ${}_Z^A X$

Where, X = Chemical symbol of the element

Z = Atomic number and

A = Mass number.

Isotopes The atoms of an element, which have the same atomic number but different mass number are called isotopes.

Isobars The atoms of different elements (different atomic number) but having the same mass number are called isobars.

Isotones The nuclides having the same number of neutrons are called isotones.

Isomers These are the nuclei with same atomic number and same mass number but in different energy states.

Atomic Mass Unit (amu) It is defined as $\frac{1}{12}$th of the mass of one ${}_6^{12}C$ atom. Its value is given by

$1 \text{ amu} = 1.660565 \times 10^{-27} \text{ kg} = 931 \text{ MeV}$.

Electron Volt It is defined as the energy acquired by an electron when it is accelerated through a potential difference of 1 volt and is denoted by eV.

$$1 \text{ eV} = 1.602 \times 10^{-19} \text{ J}$$

$$1 \text{ MeV} = 10^6 \text{ eV} = 1.602 \times 10^{-13} \text{ J}$$

Relation between Size of Nucleus and Mass Number It is found that the radius r of a nucleus is proportional to the cube root of its mass number.

$$r = r_0 A^{1/3}$$

Where, $r_0 = 1.2 \times 10^{-15}$ m

$= 1.2$ fermi for electrons as probes.

Nuclear Density The density of a nucleus is independent of the size of the nucleus and is given by

$$\rho_{nu} = \frac{\text{Nuclear mass}}{\text{Nuclear volume}} = \frac{m_{nu}}{\frac{4}{3}\pi R^3}$$

The nuclear density is of the order of 10^{17} kg m^{-3}.

Nuclear Forces These are the strong attractive forces which hold protons and neutrons together in a tiny nucleus. These are short range forces which operate over very short distances of about 2-3 fm from a nucleon. The nuclear force does not depend on the charge of the nucleus.

Mass Defect The difference between the rest mass of a nucleus and the sum of the rest masses of its constituent nucleons is called its mass defect. It is given by

$$\Delta m = Zm_p + (A - Z)m_n - m$$

Binding Energy It may be defined as the energy required to break up a nucleus into its constituent protons and neutrons and to separate them to such a large distance that they may not interact with each other.

It may also be defined as the surplus energy which the nucleons give up by virtue of their attractions when they become bound together to form a nucleus.

The binding energy of a nucleus ${}_Z^A X$ is given by

$\Delta E_b = [Zm_H + (A - Z)m_n - m] c^2$.

Binding Energy Per Nucleon It is the average energy required to extract one nucleon from the nucleus. It is obtained by dividing the binding energy of a nucleus by its mass number.

$$\Delta E_{bn} \text{ or } \overline{B} = \frac{\text{B.E.}}{A} = \frac{[Zm_H - (A - Z)m_n - m] c^2}{A}$$

In the mass number range $A = 30$ to 170, the binding energy per nucleon is nearly constant, about 8 MeV per nucleon.

Packing Fraction The packing fraction of a nucleus is its mass defect per nucleon.

$$\text{PF of a nucleus} = \frac{\text{Mass defect}}{\text{Mass number}} = \frac{\Delta m}{A}$$

It is directly related to the availability of nuclear energy and the stability of the nucleus.

Radioactivity

It is the phenomenon of spontaneous disintegration of the nucleus of an atom with the emission of one or more radiations like α-particles, β-particles or γ-rays. The substances which spontaneously emit these penetrating radiations are called radioactive substances.

Soddy-Rajan's Displacement Law *It states that*

(i) when a radioactive nucleus emits an α-particle, its atomic number decreases by 2 and mass number decreases by 4.

(ii) when a radioactive nucleus emits β-particle, its atomic number increases by 1 but mass number remains same.

(iii) the emission of a γ-particle does not change the mass number or the atomic number of the radioactive nucleus.

Alpha Decay It is the process of emission of an α-particle from a radioactive nucleus.

$$^{A}_{Z}X \longrightarrow {}^{A-4}_{Z-2}Y + {}^{4}_{2}\text{He} + Q$$

Beta Decay It is the process of emission of an electron or a positron from a radioactive nucleus.

$$^{A}_{Z}X \longrightarrow {}_{Z+1}^{A}Y + \beta^- + \bar{\nu}\ (\beta^-\text{-decay})$$

$$^{A}_{Z}X \longrightarrow {}_{Z-1}^{A}Y + \beta^+ + \bar{\nu}\ (\beta^+\text{-decay})$$

Gamma Decay It is the process of emission of a γ-ray during the radioactive disintegration of a nucleus.

This occurs when a nucleus in an excited state makes a transition to a state of lower energy

$$\underset{\text{(Excited state)}}{^{A}_{Z}X} \longrightarrow \underset{\text{(Ground state)}}{^{A}_{Z}X} + \gamma$$

Radioactive Decay Law The number of atoms of a radioactive sample disintegrating per second at any instant is directly proportional to the number of undecayed radioactive nuclei present at that instant.

$$\frac{dN}{dt} = -\lambda N$$

The law may also be expressed as, $N = N_0 e^{-\lambda t}$

Where, N_0 is the number of nuclei at $t = 0$ and λ is decay constant.

Decay Constant It may be defined as the reciprocal of the time interval in which the number of active nuclei in a given radioactive sample reduces to 36.8% (or $1/e$ times) of its initial value.

Half-life The half-life of a radioactive substance is the time in which one-half of the initial number of nuclei disintegrates.

$$T_{1/2} = \frac{0.693}{\lambda};\ N = N_0\left(\frac{1}{2}\right)^n$$

Where, n = Number of half-lives in time $t = \frac{t}{T_{1/2}}$.

Mean-life It may be defined as the ratio of the combined age of all the atoms to the total number of atoms present in the given sample.

$$\tau = \frac{1}{\lambda} = \frac{T_{1/2}}{0.693} = 1.44\, T_{1/2}$$

Decay Rate or Activity of a Sample It is the number of radioactive disintegrations taking place per second in a given sample.

$$R = \left|\frac{dN}{dt}\right| = \lambda N = \lambda N_0 e^{-\lambda t} \text{ or } R = R_0 e^{-\lambda t}$$

Practice Questions

Level I

1. Nucleon is a common name for
(a) proton and electron (b) electron and neutron
(c) only neutron (d) neutron and proton

2. The size of atomic nucleus is of the order of
(a) 10^{-15} m (b) 10^{-12} m (c) 10^{14} m (d) 10^{10} m

3. The size of atom is of the order of
(a) 10^{-14} m (b) 10^{-12} m (c) 10^{-10} m (d) 10^{10} m

4. The nucleus of an atom consists of
(a) electrons and protons
(b) Only neutron
(c) neutrons and protons
(d) protons, electrons and neutrons

5. The mass number of a nucleus is
(a) always less than its atomic number
(b) always more than its atomic number
(c) sometimes more than and sometimes equal to its atomic number
(d) None of the above

6. Particles which can be added to the nucleus of an atom without changing its chemical properties are
(a) electrons (b) protons
(c) neutrons (d) α-particles

7. The number of electrons in an atom of atomic number Z and mass number A is
(a) Z (b) A
(c) $A - Z$ (d) None of these

8. One atomic mass unit is equal to
(a) mass of one atom of hydrogen
(b) mass of one atom of $_6C^{12}$
(c) $\frac{1}{12}$ th of the mass of one atom of $_6C^{12}$
(d) None of the above

9. The nuclear $_6C^{13}$ and $_7N^{14}$ can be described as
(a) isobars (b) isotone
(c) isotopes of carbon (d) None of these

10. The mass density of a nucleus varies with the mass number A as
(a) A^2 (b) A
(c) $\frac{1}{A}$ (d) Å

11. The nuclear force
(a) obeys inverse square law of distance
(b) obeys inverse third power law of distance
(c) is a short range force
(d) is equal in strength to the electromagnetic force

12. If M is the atomic mass and A is its mass number. Then, $\frac{M-A}{A}$ is called
(a) binding fraction (b) fermi energy
(c) mass defect (d) packing fraction

13. Radioactivity was discovered by
(a) J J Thomson (b) W Roentgen
(c) H Becquerel (d) M Curie

14. In α-decay
(a) mass number A decreases by 4 and atomic number Z increases by 2
(b) A decreases by 4 and Z decreases by 2
(c) A increases by 4 and Z increases by 2
(d) None of the above

15. In β-decay
(a) A remains unaffected, Z increases by 1
(b) A is unaffected, Z decreases by 1
(c) A increases by 1 and Z is unaffected
(d) None of the above

16. In gamma (γ) decay
(a) both A and Z increase by 1
(b) both A and Z decrease by 1
(c) neither A nor Z changes
(d) A is always equal to Z

17. Alpha rays emitted from a radioactive substance are
(a) negatively charged particles
(b) hydrogen nuclear
(c) helium nuclear
(d) None of the above

18. Beta rays emitted by radioactive substance are
(a) electromagnetic radiations
(b) charged particles emitted by the nucleus
(c) electrons orbiting around the nucleus
(d) None of the above

19. A radioactive element ^A_ZX, on emitting and α-particle, changes into
(a) $^{A}_{Z-2}Y$ (b) $^{A-4}_{Z-2}Y$
(c) $^{A-4}_{Z}Y$ (d) None

20. The nucleus $^{115}_{48}$Cd, after two successive β-decays will give
(a) $^{115}_{50}$Sn (b) $^{113}_{50}$Sn
(c) $^{117}_{50}$Sn (d) None of these

21. Which of the following isotopes is normally fissionable?
(a) $^{238}_{92}$U (b) $^{235}_{92}$U
(c) $^{239}_{93}$Np (d) $^4_2$He

22. Isotopes have the same
(a) atomic number (b) mass number
(c) avogadro's number (d) None of these

23. The mass of a neutron is nearly same as that of
(a) a proton (b) a meson
(c) an epsilon (d) an electron

24. The mass defect per nucleon is called
(a) binding energy (b) packing fraction
(c) ionization energy (d) excitation energy

25. The strongest force in the nature is
(a) electric force (b) gravitational force
(c) nuclear force (d) magnetic force

26. Neutron was discovered by
(a) J J Thomson (b) James Chadwick
(c) Rutherford (d) None of these

27. The half-life (T) and the disintegration constant (λ) of the radioactive substance are related as
(a) $\lambda T = 1$ (b) $\lambda T = 0.693$
(c) $\frac{T}{\lambda} = 0.693$ (d) $\frac{\lambda}{T} = 0.693$

Level II

1. The energy equivalent of 1 kg of matter is about
(a) 10^{-15} J (b) 1 J (c) 10^{-12} J (d) 10^{17} J

2. The ratio between the radii of nuclei with mass numbers 27 and 125 is
(a) 5 : 3 (b) 3 : 5
(c) 27 : 125 (d) 125 : 27

3. Size of nucleus is of the order of
(a) 10^{-10} m (b) 10^{-15} m
(c) 10^{-12} m (d) 10^{-19} m

4. For effective nuclear forces, the distance should be
(a) 10^{-10} m (b) 10^{-13} m
(c) 10^{-15} m (d) 10^{-20} m

5. The masses of neutron and proton are 1.0087 amu and 1.0073 amu, respectively. If the neutrons and protons combine to form a helium nucleus (alpha particles) of mass 4.0015 amu the binding energy of the helium nucleus will be (1 amu = 931 MeV).
(a) 28.4 MeV (b) 20.8 MeV
(c) 27.3 MeV (d) 14.2 MeV

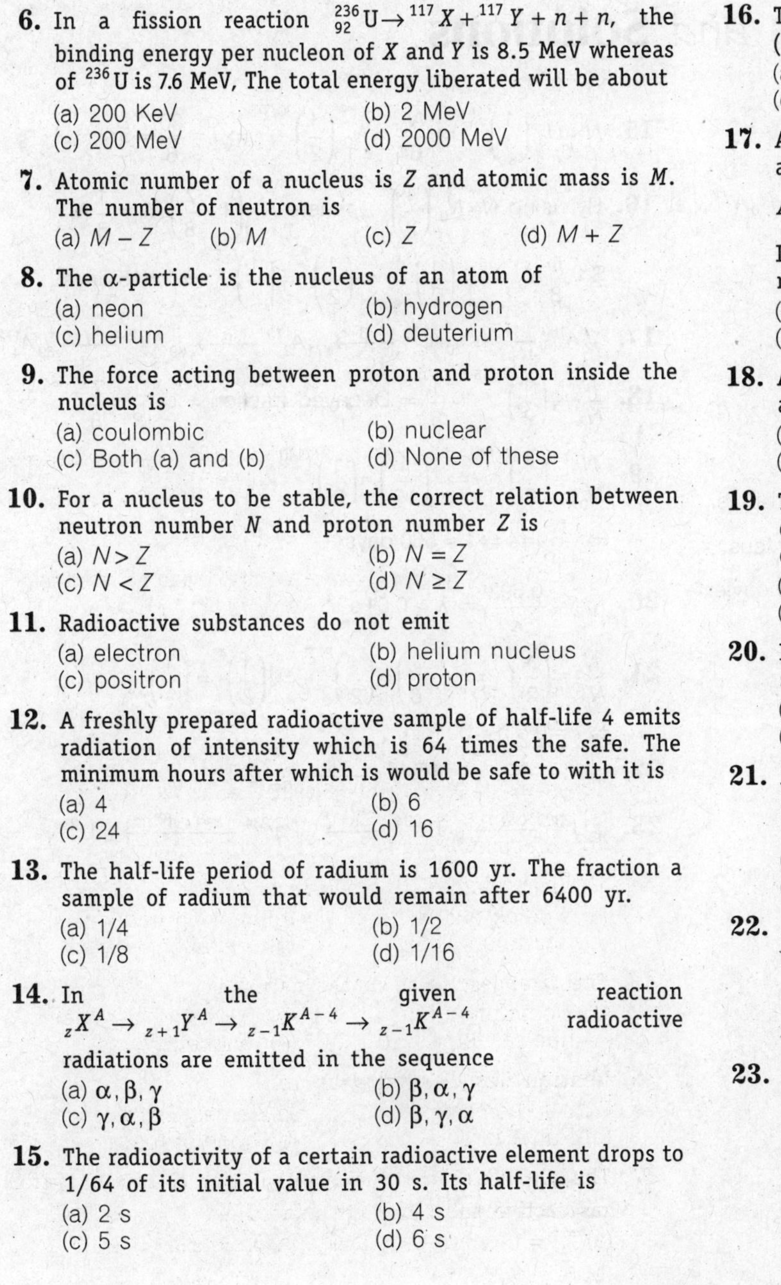

6. In a fission reaction $^{236}_{92}U \rightarrow {}^{117}X + {}^{117}Y + n + n$, the binding energy per nucleon of X and Y is 8.5 MeV whereas of ^{236}U is 7.6 MeV, The total energy liberated will be about

(a) 200 KeV (b) 2 MeV
(c) 200 MeV (d) 2000 MeV

7. Atomic number of a nucleus is Z and atomic mass is M. The number of neutron is

(a) $M - Z$ (b) M (c) Z (d) $M + Z$

8. The α-particle is the nucleus of an atom of

(a) neon (b) hydrogen
(c) helium (d) deuterium

9. The force acting between proton and proton inside the nucleus is

(a) coulombic (b) nuclear
(c) Both (a) and (b) (d) None of these

10. For a nucleus to be stable, the correct relation between neutron number N and proton number Z is

(a) $N > Z$ (b) $N = Z$
(c) $N < Z$ (d) $N \geq Z$

11. Radioactive substances do not emit

(a) electron (b) helium nucleus
(c) positron (d) proton

12. A freshly prepared radioactive sample of half-life 4 emits radiation of intensity which is 64 times the safe. The minimum hours after which is would be safe to with it is

(a) 4 (b) 6
(c) 24 (d) 16

13. The half-life period of radium is 1600 yr. The fraction a sample of radium that would remain after 6400 yr.

(a) 1/4 (b) 1/2
(c) 1/8 (d) 1/16

14. In the given reaction $_zX^A \rightarrow {}_{z+1}Y^A \rightarrow {}_{z-1}K^{A-4} \rightarrow {}_{z-1}K^{A-4}$ radioactive radiations are emitted in the sequence

(a) α, β, γ (b) β, α, γ
(c) γ, α, β (d) β, γ, α

15. The radioactivity of a certain radioactive element drops to 1/64 of its initial value in 30 s. Its half-life is

(a) 2 s (b) 4 s
(c) 5 s (d) 6 s

16. The half-life of Bi^{210} is 5 days. What time is taken by $(7/8)$th part of the sample to decay?

(a) 3.4 days (b) 10 days
(c) 15 days (d) 20 days

17. A radioactive nucleus undergoes a series of decay according to the scheme

$$A \xrightarrow{\alpha} A_1 \xrightarrow{\beta} A_2 \xrightarrow{\alpha} A \xrightarrow{\gamma} A$$

If the mass number and atomic number of A are 180 and 72 respectively, then what are these numbers of A_4?

(a) 172 and 69 (b) 174 and 70
(c) 176 and 69 (d) 176 and 70

18. A radio-isotope has a half-life of 5 yr. The fraction of the atoms of this material that would decay in 15 yr will be

(a) 1/8 (b) 2/3
(c) 7/8 (d) 5/8

19. The half-life of polonium is 140 days. After how many days, 16g polonium will be reduced to 1g (or 15g will decay)?

(a) 700 (b) 280
(c) 560 (d) 420

20. In a radioactive decay, the half-life of radioactive substance is $t_{1/2} = 69.3$ s. The decay constant is

(a) $0.01\ s^{-1}$ (b) $0.1\ s^{-1}$
(c) $10\ s^{-1}$ (d) $1\ s^{-1}$

21. After two hours, one-sixteenth of the starting amount of a certain radioactive isotope remained undecayed. The half-life of the isotope is

(a) 15 min (b) 30 min
(c) 45 min (d) 1 h

22. A nucleus $_nX^m$ emits one α and one β particles. The resulting nucleus is

(a) $_nX^{m-4}$ (b) $_{n-2}Y^{m-4}$
(c) $_{n-4}Z^{m-4}$ (d) $_{n-1}Z^{m-4}$

23. In the given nuclear reaction A, B, C, D, E represents

$$_{92}U^{238} \xrightarrow{\alpha} {}_BTh^A \xrightarrow{\beta} {}_DPa^C \xrightarrow{e} {}_{92}U^{234}$$

(a) $A = 234, B = 90, C = 234, D = 91, E = \beta$
(b) $A = 234, B = 90, C = 238, D = 94, E = \alpha$
(c) $A = 238, B = 93, C = 234, D = 91, E = \beta$
(d) $A = 234, B = 90, C = 234, D = 93, E = \alpha$

Answers

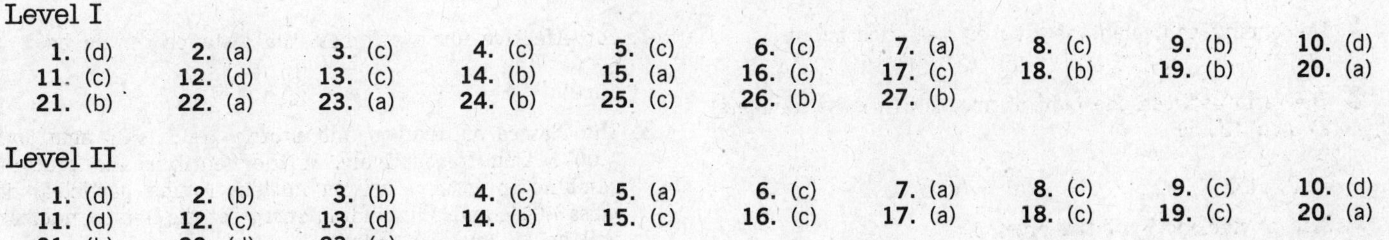

Level I

1. (d)	**2.** (a)	**3.** (c)	**4.** (c)	**5.** (c)	**6.** (c)	**7.** (a)	**8.** (c)	**9.** (b)	**10.** (d)
11. (c)	**12.** (d)	**13.** (c)	**14.** (b)	**15.** (a)	**16.** (c)	**17.** (c)	**18.** (b)	**19.** (b)	**20.** (a)
21. (b)	**22.** (a)	**23.** (a)	**24.** (b)	**25.** (c)	**26.** (b)	**27.** (b)			

Level II

1. (d)	**2.** (b)	**3.** (b)	**4.** (c)	**5.** (a)	**6.** (c)	**7.** (a)	**8.** (c)	**9.** (c)	**10.** (d)
11. (d)	**12.** (c)	**13.** (d)	**14.** (b)	**15.** (c)	**16.** (c)	**17.** (a)	**18.** (c)	**19.** (c)	**20.** (a)
21. (b)	**22.** (d)	**23.** (a)							

Hints and Solutions

Level II

1. $E = mc^2 = 1 \times (3 \times 10^8)^2 = 9 \times 10^{16} \approx 10^{17}$ J.

2. Nucleus of a mass number A has a radius, $R = R_0 A^{1/3}$, where $R_0 = 12 \times 10^{-15}$ m

$$\therefore \quad \frac{R_{27}}{R_{125}} = \left(\frac{27}{125}\right)^{1/3} = \left(\frac{3^3}{5^3}\right)^{1/3} = \frac{3}{5}.$$

5. B.E. $= \Delta mc^2 = \Delta \times 931$ MeV
$= [2\,(1.0087 + 1.0073) - 4.0015] \times 931 = 28$ MeV.

6. $\Delta E = 8.5 \times 234 - 7.6 \times 236 = 195.4$ MeV ≈ 200 MeV.

7. $N = M - Z$ = Total number of nucleons – number of protons.

8. Both coulomb and nuclear force act inside the nucleus.

9. For stability in case of lighter nuclei $= \frac{N}{Z} = 1$ and for heavier nuclei $\frac{N}{Z} > 1$.

12. $\frac{1}{64} = \left(\frac{1}{2}\right)^n$ or $\left(\frac{1}{2}\right)^6 = \left(\frac{1}{2}\right)^n$

$\therefore n = 6$,

Time to work safely $= 6 \times 4 = 24$ h

13. Fraction $= \frac{N}{N_0} = \left(\frac{1}{2}\right)^{\frac{6400}{1600}} = \left(\frac{1}{2}\right)^4 = \frac{1}{16}$

15. $N = N_0 \left(\frac{1}{2}\right)^{t/T} \Rightarrow \frac{N_0}{64} = N_0 \left(\frac{1}{2}\right)^{30/T} \Rightarrow T = \frac{30}{6} = 5$ s

16. By using $N = N_0 \left(\frac{1}{2}\right)^{t/T}$, where $N = \left(1 - \frac{7}{8}\right) N_0 = \frac{1}{8} N_0$.

So, $\frac{1}{8} N_0 = N_0 \left(\frac{1}{2}\right)^{t/T} \Rightarrow \left(\frac{1}{2}\right)^3 = \left(\frac{1}{2}\right)^{t/5} \Rightarrow t = 15$ days.

17. ${}_{72}A^{180} \xrightarrow{\alpha} {}_{70}A_1^{176} \xrightarrow{\beta} {}_{71}A_2^{176} \xrightarrow{\alpha} {}_{69}A_3^{172} \xrightarrow{\gamma} {}_{69}A_4^{172}$

18. $\frac{N}{N_0} = \left(\frac{1}{2}\right)^{15/5} = \frac{1}{8} \Rightarrow$ Decayed fraction $= 1 - \frac{1}{8} = \frac{7}{8}$

19. $\frac{N}{N_0} = \left(\frac{1}{2}\right)^{t/140} \Rightarrow \left(\frac{1}{16}\right) = \left(\frac{1}{2}\right)^{t/140}$

$\Rightarrow \frac{t}{140} = 4 \Rightarrow t = 560$ days

20. $T_{1/2} = \frac{0.693}{\lambda} \Rightarrow \lambda = 0.01\ \text{s}^{-1}$.

21. $\frac{N}{N_0} = \left(\frac{1}{2}\right)^{t/T} \Rightarrow \left(\frac{1}{16}\right) = \left(\frac{1}{2}\right)^{2/T} \Rightarrow \left(\frac{1}{2}\right)^4 = \left(\frac{1}{2}\right)^{2/T}$

$\Rightarrow T = 0.5$ h $= 30$ min

22. ${}_nX^m \xrightarrow{\alpha} {}_{n-2}X^{m-4} \xrightarrow{-\beta} {}_{n-1}Z^{m-4}$.

23. ${}_{92}\text{U}^{238} \xrightarrow{\alpha} {}_{90}\text{Th}^{234} \xrightarrow{\beta} {}_{91}\text{Pa}^{234} \xrightarrow{e(_{-1}\beta^0)} {}_{92}\text{U}^{234}$